Geography

&

Geographers

SIXTH EDITION

Geography

&

Geographers

SIXTH EDITION

Anglo-American
Human Geography
since 1945

R. J. JOHNSTON

J. D. SIDAWAY

A member of the Hodder Headline Group
LONDON

Distributed in the United States of America by
Oxford University Press Inc., New York

First published in Great Britain in 1979

This edition published in 2004 by
Arnold, a member of the Hodder Headline Group,
338 Euston Road, London NW1 3BH

http://www.arnoldpublishers.com

Distributed in the United States of America by
Oxford University Press Inc.,
198 Madison Avenue, New York, NY10016

British Library Cataloguing in Publication Data
A catalogue record for this book is available from the British Library

Library of Congress Cataloging-in-Publication Data
A catalog record for this book is available from the Library of Congress

ISBN 0 340 80860 8

1 2 3 4 5 6 7 8 9 10

Typeset in 10 on 13 pt Gill Sans Light by Phoenix Photosetting, Chatham, Kent
Printed and bound in Malta

What do you think about this book? Or any other Arnold title?
Please send your comments to feedback.arnold@hodder.co.uk

Contents

Preface

I remember being at a party in Minneapolis, sitting on the floor with other guests in a loose circle, taking turns saying what we did. There was a nurse, a medical researcher, a planner... When I said I was a graduate student in economic geography, one of them burst into uncontrollable laughter. 'So what do you do, find new places?'

(Barnes 2002, p. 9)

I do think that sometimes we have written the history of geography as though it were something quite exotic but harmless, consigned, at the very least, to the last century, if not to oblivion: from our lofty positions as postmoderns, postcolonials or whatever, we detach ourselves from our predecessors without so much as a backward glance. Isn't it about time we took a more modest view? Perhaps that history which we want to transcend is precisely what makes our own geographies possible? Now there's a thought.

(Driver 2002, p. 230)

Geographers themselves have been very bad at writing their own history.

(N. Smith 2003, p. xxii)

Human geography has been through many changes – in terms of its foci, methods and styles of presentation. Reflecting aspects of this, there have been five previous editions of this book (1979, 1983, 1987, 1991, 1997), all sole authored by Ron Johnston. A few words are in order by way of a preface to this new jointly-authored edition to explain some of the changes made and the rationales behind them.

We begin, however, with an extract from the Preface to the first edition which sets out something of the original rationale and limits (that full preface and all subsequent prefaces also appear in the fifth edition). Aside from the detail of individual personal involvement in the discipline (now both broader, by the addition of a co-author and protracted, by another twenty years of involvement on the part of the original author), these hold true for the present edition.

Most students reading for a degree or similar qualification are required to pay some attention to their chosen discipline's academic history. The history presented to them commonly ends some time before the present. This has advantages for the historian, because the past is often better interpreted from the detachment of a little distance and there is less chance of hurting scholars still alive. But there is a major disadvantage for the students. In virtually every other component of their courses they will be dealing with the discipline's current literature, and so if the history ends some decades ago, they are presented with the contemporary substance but not with the contemporary framework, except where this is very clearly derivative of the historical context.

This state of affairs is unfortunate. Students need a conspectus of the current practice in their chosen discipline and should encounter a relevant overview which describes, and perhaps explains too, what scholars believe the philosophy and methodology of the discipline presently are and should be. Such an overview will allow the substantive courses comprising the rest of the degree to be placed in context and appreciated as examples of the disciplinary belief system as well as ends in themselves.

As a discipline expands, so the need for a course in its 'contemporary history' will grow too. In the last few decades, for example, most disciplines, and certainly human geography, have expanded greatly, with expansion measured by the number of active participants and their volume of published work. And the more active members there are, almost certainly the greater the variety of work undertaken, making it difficult for individual students to provide their own conspectus of the discipline from their own reading. Hence the need for a 'contemporary history' course at the present time.

The present book is the outcome of teaching such a course for several years, and is offered as a guide for others, both teachers and students. As with all texts, it has many idiosyncrasies. The course on which it is based is taught to final-year students reading for honours degrees in geography, and is probably best used by people at that level since it assumes familiarity with the concepts and language of human geography. Further, my view is that students probably benefit most from a framework after experiencing some of its contents; this book provides the matrix for organizing the individual parts rather than a series of slots into which parts can be placed later, which would be the case if the course were taught early in the degree.

A series of constraints circumscribes the contents and approach of this contemporary history. First, it deals only with human geography, for several reasons. The most important is that I find the links between physical and human geography tenuous, as those disciplines are currently practised. The major link between them is a sharing of techniques and research procedures, but these are shared with other disciplines too, and are insufficient foundation for a unified discipline. (What price a department of factorial ecology?) Further, my own competence, work and interests lie wholly within human geography and although I have been trained with and by and have worked among physical geographers, and have obtained stimuli from this, I am incompetent to write about physical geography. And finally, much of the human geography discussed here is of North American origin, and many geographers there, especially in the United States, encounter no physical geography as it is understood in British universities. To a considerable extent, therefore, human and physical are separate, if not independent, disciplines. Throughout the book, I use the terms 'geography' and 'human geography' interchangeably.

The second constraint is cultural; the subject matter of the book is Anglo-American human geography. Most of the work discussed emanates from either the United States or the United Kingdom: there are some contributions from workers in Australia, Canada and New Zealand, but the efforts of geographers in the rest of the world are largely ignored. (A partial exception is Sweden, *which has major academic links with the Anglo-American tradition; much Swedish geographical work is published in English.) Such academic parochialism in part reflects personal linguistic deficiencies, but it is not entirely an idiosyncratic decision. Contacts between Anglo-American human geography, on the one hand and, say, that of France and of Germany, on the other, have been few in recent decades, so to concentrate on the former is not to commit a major error in separating a part from an integrated whole.*

The final constraint is temporal, for the book is concerned with Anglo-American human geography during the decades since the Second World War only. Again, this is in part a reflection of personal competence, for I have been personally involved in academic geography for the last twenty years. But the Second World War was a major watershed in so many aspects of history, not least academic practice, and much of the methodology and philosophy currently taught in human geography has been initiated since then (Johnston, 1979, pp. ix–xi).

Since 1979, the book has expanded considerably. In order to contain it within reasonable margins, in this sixth edition we have cut back some of the details on behavioural geography that appeared in the earlier editions (veteran readers will notice that this no longer has a chapter of its own) and shortened some other sections. These selective cuts have allowed us to accommodate more on poststructuralism, postmodernism, postcolonialism and feminist geographies (through two new chapters derived in part from what hitherto was a single chapter entitled 'The cultural turn'), as well as to rearrange the chapter on radical geography and update others. In all cases we have sought to strike a balance between length and scope. Nor are we trying to write-out episodes of the history of the discipline. More or less everything covered in past editions remains here. We have however – with the benefit of hindsight – shifted the emphases somewhat. As with previous editions, the specific trajectories of significant subdisciplines, such as population, development, medical/health, or political geography (to name but four) are neglected here – on account of our word limit; such reviews appear annually in the journal *Progress in Human Geography* and are a feature of Gaile and Willmott's (1989, 2004) collections. However, we are aware that from such subdisciplinary vantage points, the shifts that *Geography and Geographers* outlines would be illuminated in different ways. In part, this is because the respective subdisciplines have been influenced by changes in the subjects with which they (sometimes uneasily) share affilation; development geography with development studies and branches of area studies for example. In part it is because paradigmatic change in human geography has always been profoundly uneven, with individuals in some places, departments and fields of study setting agendas that only later came to have much wider influence across a heterodox discipline.

The addition of new material on recent trends in the discipline is complemented here by wider discussions of the contexts within which earlier disciplinary debates and developments occurred. The last decade has seen an increase in the amount of research and writing on the history of human geography since 1945 – especially on the decades prior to 1980. This has included not only retrospectives written by those involved and other biographical works but also by scholarly interpretations of some of the major events and personalities produced by those interested in applying the perspectives and methods of the history of science to geography. As in the previous editions, however, the book depends almost entirely for its source material on the published record, on 'the written statements of others' as it was decribed in the original Preface (on which approach see also Keylock, 2003, and Lorimer, 2003). But that published record now includes a substantial volume of historical and interpretative material, which means that this current edition is less a history created from the contemporary debates and substantive contributions and more reliant – particularly in the earlier chapters – on biographical and autobiographical recollections of the conditions of their production.

The growth of historiographical work on recent human geography is in itself indicative of the importance that many geographers give to an appreciation of their discipline's past. Some authors contend that this is unnecessary: Barnett (1995, p.417), for example, has 'doubts about the value of expending energy studying the history of geography as a means of throwing light on the state of the discipline today' (see also Thrift, 2002a). We are not so sure. Appreciation of a discipline's history – of where it has come from, and why it has its current contemporary form – is not only valuable when, as Barnett accepts, it is deployed in a 'political' context to sustain its professional identity, but also for an understanding of the discipline's present condition. To paraphrase Marx, 'geographers have made – and continue to make – geography, but not in conditions of their own choosing'. Geographers are socialized into intellectual communities with accepted bodies of knowledge and practices, and their orientations are constrained, though not determined, by the nature of the communities they join – as argued by one of the theories (of structuration – see p. 242) which a number of them have adopted to guide their work. Furthermore, the practice of geography itself illustrates one of the discipline's major contributions to the deployment of Marx's dictum: the 'conditions not of their own choosing' within which geographers operate are themselves spatially variable. Studying the history of geography – especially the recent history – is valuable not only for the light that it sheds on what geographers are and do today but also for the case study it provides of a wider concern – the geography of knowledge production and the importance of context therein.

Finally, what of the 'Anglo-American' in the subtitle? In recent years, the Anglo-American-ness of human geography has come under increased scrutiny. In the first place, several geographers have pointed to the continued (indeed in some ways increasing) relative dominance of English language geography *vis-à-vis* geography written in other languages (Desbiens, 2002; Garcia-Ramon, 2003; Gutiérrez and López-Nieva, 2001; Minca 2000; Short, Boniche, Kim, Li Li, 2001; see also Rodrígues-Pose, 2004). Thus Vaiou (2003, p. 136), writing from Greece, notes that:

> . . . the power-knowledge system, in which Anglophone scholarship can posit itself as international and even universal, has not (yet?) totally subsumed local initiatives.

Others have questioned what is excluded and included when the term Anglo-American is used (Samers and Sidaway, 2000; Minca, 2003). Not only are the United States and the United Kingdom (and geographers working in these countries) far from being exclusively 'Anglo', but geography produced there contains many 'foreign' influences – as will become clear in the chapters that follow. The way that other predominatly Anglophone contexts and geographers (for example, Australia, South Africa and New Zealand) are marginalized has also been critiqued (Berg and Kearns, 1998). The fact that one of the co-authors of this new edition is based in neither the United Kingdom nor North America, but in Singapore (although he was educated in the UK and has held academic posts there), and that some of his own geographical research has been conducted in Portuguese- and Spanish-speaking mileux has sharpened our sense of this (as Gregory, 1994, has also written regarding the impact of his move from the UK to Canada on his 'positionality'); the other author spent the first eleven years of his career in Australia and New Zealand, to which he has frequently returned. Nevertheless, we have retained the subtitle 'Anglo-American Human Geography since 1945'. But the book should be read with the caveat that it remains a survey of key debates within English language human geography in the past 60 years; with a primary focus on the UK and Anglophone North America. Even within this particular geographical tradition, we cannot adequately cover everything, however. More than twenty years ago, in a debate on the place of Marxism within radical geography (one of our concerns in Chapter 6), Walmsley and Sorenson (1980, p. 137) reminded readers of the UK-based journal Area that:

> To speak of a 'Marxist approach' [in geography] is therefore to distill a highest common factor from a variety of writings.

Our distillations here mean that this is not the story of Anglophone human geography (which is itself is certainly not the story of human geography tout court over the past 60-odd years). To pretend otherwise would take us into the realm of the mythological map described by the Argentinian Jose Luis Borges in one of his extraordinary fables. In Borges' story, the cartographers of an imaginary Empire 'draw up a map so detailed that it ends up exactly covering the territory' so that the 'real' territory underneath the map is obscured. The people of this Empire came to relate more closely to this map than they did to the original territory underneath (they live, work, and play on it, etc.) When, eventually, the map frays and disintegrates, the people are unnerved and nostalgic for the map they once knew and lived upon, feeling that they have lost something of their reality.

Our account of Geography and Geographers makes no such claims to be a replacement for an encounter with the original writings that are précised here. Moreover, readers should not be unnerved if they find – as they venture out into the broader fields of human geography – that some things are not quite as neat or clear as they might have been led to believe from this text alone.

We close this Preface with another extract from the one written twenty-five years ago. In acknowledgement of how supportive personal and professional 'contexts' had aided its production, the Preface of the first edition of Geography and Geographers had the following to say:

> I make it clear in Chapter 1 that the progress of any individual's academic career depends considerably on the actions (and sometimes inactions) of others. No academic is an island (Johnston 1979, p. xii).

To the very many who have assisted Ron Johnston over the years and who are named in previous editions (plus his – relatively – new colleagues at Bristol with whom he so enjoys interacting), James Sidaway would like to add thanks to his colleagues at the Department of Geography at the National University of Singapore; a stimulating and relatively diverse intellectual environment (see Olds, 2001) from which to reflect on the dynamics of *Anglo-American Human Geography since 1945*.

Ron Johnston and James Sidaway
Bristol and Singapore

Acknowledgements

The authors and publisher are grateful to the following for permission to reproduce figures included in this book:

Allan Pred and the Department of Social and Economic Geography, University of Lund, for Figure 4.5; Association of American Geographers for Figures 3.2 and 3.3; Barbara Kennedy and Prentice-Hall for Figures 4.2 and 4.3; David Harvey for Figures 3.1 and 7.1; Derek Gregory and the Royal Geographical Society for Figure 6.2; Derek Gregory for Figure 6.1; Geraldine Pratt for Figure 8.1; Olavi Gräno for Figure 10.1; Oxford University Press for Figure 4.6; Peter Haggett for Figure 4.1; Reg Golledge and Guilford Publications for Figure 4.7; Richard Peet for Figure 10.2; Royal Statistical Society for Figure 3.4.

Any omissions brought to our attention will be corrected in future printings.

1
The nature of an academic discipline

… most effective academic communities are not that much larger than most peasant villages and just about as ingrown …

(Geertz, 1983, p. 157)

… the distinctive cultures within academic communities … refer to sets of taken-for-granted values, attitudes and ways of behaving, which are articulated through and reinforced by recurrent practices among a group of people in a given context.

(Becher and Trowler, 2001, p. 23)

This book is a study of part of an academic discipline, particularly of changes in its approaches and content. Approaches and content cannot be appreciated fully without understanding context, however, which this chapter provides. To study an academic discipline is to study a miniature society, which has a stratification system, a set of rewards and sanctions, and a series of bureaucracies, not to mention occasional interpersonal conflicts (some academic, others not). An outsider may perceive academic work as objective, but many subjective decisions must be taken: what to study and how; whether to publish the results; where to publish them and in what form; what to teach; whether to question the work of others publicly; and so on. As with all human decisions, they are made within the constraints set by the wider society.

Studying an academic discipline involves studying a society within a society; both set the constraints to individual and group activity. Two questions are focused on here: 'How is academic life organized?'; and 'How does that academic work, basically its research, proceed?'. Use of the term 'society within a society' strongly implies that academic life does not proceed independently in its own closed system but rather is open to the influences and commands of the encompassing wider society. A third necessary question, therefore, is 'What is the nature of the society which provides the environment for the academic discipline being studied, and how do the two interact?'. Answering these three questions is set within a framework of studying the ways in which academic life is institutionalized.

Disciplines and institutionalization

By far the most important contemporary identifier for an academic discipline is that it is taught in universities – it has departments named for it, degrees are awarded that carry its name, and the teaching for those degrees is undertaken by individuals who have been trained in and identify with the discipline. (This identifier is related to what Morrell, 1990, associates with the 'professionalization of science': scholars in full-time paid positions; specialist qualifications; formal training programmes; specialized publications; disciplinary solidarity and self-consciousness; and professional reward systems. Golinski, 1998, added a firm boundary between amateurs and professionals. See also Barton, 2003.) Geography exists as an academic discipline because there are people who call themselves geographers, who have geography degrees, and who teach on geography degree programmes in university departments of geography.

A university presence is thus an indicator of a discipline's existence: it is the key element in its institutionalization. It indicates that the discipline meets a felt need, in particular that there are students who want a higher education in geography and scholars who wish to teach them. This, however, for geography as with many other disciplines, is a relatively recent phenomenon: it dates only from the late nineteenth century (as illustrated by the chapters in Dunbar, 2002). That doesn't mean that geography didn't exist before the first courses were launched in universities: as some of the work briefly discussed in Chapter 2 indicates, it has a long and sometimes distinguished tradition as a form of inquiry and practice. But it was only from the 1870s on that it was formalized as an academic discipline, separate from the science and humanities disciplines that characterized the traditional universities.

Most disciplines are established in universities to teach a body of knowledge: they are identified by their subject matter. Their existence indicates a demand for instruction in that material, by people who are expert in it. Being an expert almost invariably means playing some part in producing and reproducing that body of knowledge, which involved undertaking original research in some aspects of the discipline and publishing the findings to inform other researchers and their students. Academic disciplines in universities involve teacher-researchers, people interested not only in the propagation of knowledge but also its advancement: indeed, the production of new knowledge is considered an essential component of university teacher-researchers – usually known as academics.

Although the creation of departments for training students by experts is a necessary component of the institutionalization of a discipline, it is far from sufficient. In order to promote both their discipline and their own work, academics need to be able to interact with colleagues interested in similar issues, most of whom will work at other universities. Some organizational structure is needed to facilitate this. It is invariably done by academic or learned societies, bodies established to promote a discipline through a variety of means, of which the most important include the holding of meetings at which research issues and findings can be discussed and the publication of research results, through books, journals and other media. All academic disciplines have such bodies, most of which are nationally organized; in some countries there may be several. Some of those societies may pre-date the creation of the academic discipline, having been inaugurated to promote its study before it achieved a separate identity and a body of professional scholars associated with it. Indeed, in many cases those societies were involved in promoting the discipline and lobbying for its presence in universities – perhaps even paying for the creation of teaching posts. Others were established after the formal institutionalization of the discipline. Most are open for anybody to join if they are prepared to subscribe to the discipline's advancement, but in effect membership is very largely confined to university staff and (postgraduate) students – especially if there is no named profession linked to the academic discipline which retains the practitioners' affiliation (as with medicine and architecture, for example). Some societies have closed memberships, limited to those who meet certain criteria (such as a postgraduate degree in the discipline); others have several membership categories which separately distinguish the professional academics from those with a non-professional interest in the subject.

Those societies have been central to the development of disciplines as individual academics create their own research agenda. Their conferences and seminars, journals and other publications have been the main media until relatively recently (when commercial journal publication on a large scale took off) whereby knowledge has been disseminated and debates about its production and interpretation conducted. They also undertake other important functions, one of which is the promotion and defence of the discipline as a whole. Even when established in a country's universities a discipline is not necessarily secure. There are struggles for wider recognition, for greater resources, for expansion into institutions where the discipline has yet to be established, and so forth. The learned societies play crucial roles in these tasks, acting as lobby groups for their discipline and seeking to ensure its health by influencing public and private decision-makers concerning its utility and value. And above them are even broader societies, representing a range of cognate disciplines, such as the Royal Society and the British Academy in the United Kingdom and the National Academy of Sciences and the American Academy of Arts and Sciences in the United States; these play a wider role in advancing the interests of their subject groupings.

The institutionalization of an academic discipline involves creating an identity, a subject with its own niche within the academic division of labour with which individuals are affiliated. In some cases, the discipline – like geography and history – has a name whose interpretation extends beyond academia, its vernacular definition (Johnston, 1986b). This may create some difficulties in establishing an academic identity, because while the two definitions/interpretations (or understandings) almost certainly overlap they may not coincide. This is certainly the case with geography. Much popular interpretation of the term is associated with the acquisition of basic information about the earth – what is where (what has sometimes been referred to as 'capes and bays geography') – and not with the contemporary concerns of academic researchers. Such interpretation is sustained by magazines such as the widely-circulated *National Geographic* (Lutz and Collins, 1992; Schulten, 2001) which carries much informative material about the earth's environments and peoples, but little that reflects geographers' current research. Similarly, periodicals such as *New Zealand Geographic* are closer to natural history than to geography; its definition and coverage of the subject has very little in common with the academic discipline whose practices are represented in the *New Zealand Geographer*.

Despite these issues of representation and appreciation, however, geography is a substantial academic discipline in the countries that we focus on in this book. In the United

Kingdom, for example, by the end of the twentieth century there were about 1600 staff in University and College departments offering geography programmes, with some 7000 places available on undergraduate degree programmes in geography each year, plus over 170 taught postgraduate programmes with nearly 3000 places available; in addition there were more than 800 full-time students registered for postgraduate research degrees, and a further 640 registered as part-time students. In the United States, the majority of universities lacked a geography department and there was a graduate programme in only a small minority. Nevertheless, there is a large number of geographers active there: the Association of American Geographers (the AAG) has some 6700 members and its annual meeting regularly attracts several thousand participants. (The AAG was very much a small, closed, elite organisation with high barriers to entry before 1950, when it merged with the American Society for Professional Geographers: James and Martin, 1978; Miller, 1993.) This large number of practising academics is part of a buoyant discipline whose interests are wide-ranging and whose contributions to knowledge advancement are substantial (Thrift, 2002). The nature of those contributions over a period of some six decades is the core of this book's concerns.

The academic working environment: disciplines and the academic division of labour

The continuing goal of an academic discipline is the advancement of knowledge, pursued within its own particular areas of study. Its individual members contribute by conducting research and reporting their findings, by integrating material into the disciplinary corpus, and by pedagogical activities aimed at informing others, promoting and reproducing the discipline; they may also argue for the discipline's 'relevance' to society at large. But there is no fixed set of disciplines, nor any one correct division of academia according to subject matter. As Livingstone (1992, pp. 28–9) puts it:

> The idea that there is some eternal metaphysical core to geography independent of historical circumstances will simply have to go ... geography has meant different things to different people in different places and thus the 'nature' of geography is always negotiated. The task of geography's historians, at least in part, is thus to ascertain how and why particular practices and procedures come to be accounted geographically legitimate and hence normative at different moments in time and in different spatial settings.

Those disciplines currently in existence are contained within boundaries established by earlier communities of scholars. The boundaries are porous, so disciplines interact. Occasionally the boundaries are changed, usually through the establishment of a new discipline that occupies an enclave within the pre-existing division of academic space. Moreover, the boundaries are not necessarily the same in all comparable institutions.

Just as there is no immutable set of disciplinary boundaries, so there is also no right way of undertaking research nor, in many cases, any exact criteria for determining whether research findings, and even more their interpretations, are correct. The 'right' and 'wrong' ways of doing research, the 'correct' and 'incorrect' interpretations of research findings, and the 'proper' ways of presenting knowledge and training students are all the product of decisions by academics themselves. Thus, not surprisingly, there is considerable debate within disciplines over these issues. At any one time, there may be consensus within a disciplinary community regarding both its subject matter and its research methods. But controversy is just as likely, as academics discuss the relevance of particular research findings, the validity of certain research methodologies, and so on. Indeed, there is controversy over the nature and definition of knowledge itself.

The study of the controversies and consensuses that characterize academic disciplines is the function of historians of science. (Science is used here as a very broad term encompassing the entire range of academic disciplines in the natural and social sciences: the *Oxford English Dictionary* defines science as 'an organized body of knowledge on a subject'.) To the outsider, the workings of a science are generally mysterious – especially regarding disciplines that require a great degree of prior training before original research is undertaken and whose literature is virtually impenetrable to the untrained. It is generally believed, however, that science is an objective activity undertaken within very strict rules, involving the continuous excitement of the search for new discoveries. Indeed, scientists frequently present themselves in this light. Certain values are universally subscribed to within academia, it is argued, with the main five being (according to Mulkay, 1975, p. 510):

1. The norm of *originality*: academics strive to advance knowledge, and conduct original research designed to discover and account for aspects of the world as yet not fully understood;
2. The norm of *communality*: all information is shared within the academic community – it is transferred through accepted channels (notably the research journals) and its provenance is always recognized when it is being used;
3. The norm of *disinterestedness*: academics are devoted to their subject, and their main reward is the satisfaction of participating in the advancement of knowledge – a reward that may bring with it charisma and promotion;
4. The norm of *universalism*: judgements are made on entirely impartial criteria, which take into account the academic merits of work only and make no reference to the personalities of the researchers; and
5. The norm of *organized scepticism*: knowledge is furthered by a continuing process of constructive criticism, in which academics are always reconsidering both their own work and that of others.

According to these five norms, therefore, academic work is carried out neutrally; there is a complete lack of partiality, self-seeking, secrecy and intellectual prejudice. Objective assessment criteria are assumed, as are high levels of ability and humility on the part of members of the academic community.

Against this ideal view of science and scientists, which many of the latter promote, are the results of studies in the history of science (most of which refer to the physical sciences: Mulkay, 1975; Mulkay, Gilbert and Woolgar, 1975; Latour, 1987, 1999; Latour and Woolgar, 1979). These show that the procedures adopted are frequently neither objective nor neutral, and they present a picture of disciplines growing 'by gathering more detail in areas already investigated, and by stumbling across new sets of facts in areas of experience never previously investigated' (Barnes, 1974, p. 5). Science is a culture, with each discipline comprising one or more subculture(s). It has its own rules and procedures which are open to change and hence are the subject of debate, even conflict. Furthermore (as will be suggested in more detail below), scientific cultures are parts of wider cultures, and although to some extent scientists – because of their (self-imposed) expert status – can impose their own views of themselves on their host societies, they are also subject to external influences (see Barnes, 1974).

Each scientific discipline is a separate academic community, therefore; many are groupings of several related communities. Their goal is the advancement of knowledge, but the definitions of advancement and of knowledge itself are influenced, if not determined, by the community's members. Thus, study of a discipline's history is not simply a chronology of its successes. It is an investigation of the sociology of a community, of its debates, deliberations and decisions, as well as of its findings. (See Watson, 1968, for an example of this; for a fictional account, see Cooper, 1952; an excellent introductory history is in Gribbin, 2002. Livingstone, 1992, p. 30, suggests that 'it might be helpful if we were to think of geography as a tradition that evolves like a species over time'.) Most of those communities – including geography – are divided into a substantial number of sub-communities involving individuals working on a particular subject matter, and/or set of problems, and/or particular methodology. Indeed, Geertz (1983, p. 157) argues that:

> ... most effective academic communities are not that much larger than most peasant villages and just about as ingrown ... From such units, intellectual communities if you will, convergent data can be gathered, for the relations among the inhabitants are typically not merely intellectual, but political, moral, and broadly personal (these days, increasingly, marital) as well. Laboratories and research institutes, scholarly societies, axial university departments, literary and artistic cliques, intellectual factions, all fit the same pattern: communities of multiply connected individuals in which something you find out about A tells you something about B as well, because, having known each other too long and too well, they are characters in one another's biographies.

Untangling such biographies, individual and collective, is the key to understanding geography's institutionalization and contemporary practices: its history indicates where it has come from and why it currently takes the forms that it does. Furthermore, the history of most of those communities involves both conflict with others (within a university for example: Johnston, 1998) and within the communities (Johnston, 2000c) over the allocation of resources and rewards. Such communities are frequently territorial, in the defence of their portion of the academic division of labour, and sometimes aggressively so in strategies to expand their portion of the whole.

Most investigations of a discipline's history take one of two general forms. The empiricist (or positive) approach portrays history as it happened, with each community treated separately; most such histories are written from a present-day perspective, and tend to interpret evidence as indicative of progress towards the discovery of truth – what is widely known as a 'Whig approach to history'. The other approach seeks generalizations on how sciences progress, which involves either an inductive approach – studying individual histories and identifying their common themes – or a deductive framework that provides a model of scientific progress against which events in a particular discipline are compared (i.e. it applies a particular scientific approach to science itself!). Most of the models currently available have been developed for, and tested on, the physical sciences. Their relevance to human geography has been suggested, however (e.g. Haggett and Chorley, 1967; Harvey, 1973), and they are presented here as a backcloth for a later evaluation of the substantive material arranged in Chapters 2–9.

Kuhn, normal science and revolutions

A framework for studying the history of science that has received much attention (indeed, the book is one of the most frequently cited by social scientists) is provided by T. S. Kuhn's (1962, 1970a) *The Structure of Scientific Revolutions*. As Kuhn (1970b) and many commentators have pointed out, this is a study in the sociology of science: it is a positive interpretation – a presentation of what scientists *actually* do – rather than a normative programme – an argument for what scientists *ought* to do. It generalizes from its observations, identifying common elements in disciplinary histories: Kuhn's goal was to identify 'what science, scientific research as it is actually practised, is really like' (Barnes, 1982, p. 1). Following Kuhn's death in 1996 a number of books on his life and work have been published and provide valuable introductions to, and critiques of, his work (e.g. Bird, 2000; Conant and Haugeland, 2000; Fuller, 2000; Sharrock and Read, 2002; Nickles, 2003).

Kuhn argued that scientists work in communities of researchers and teachers who share a common approach. They operate within an agreed philosophy, concur on the theoretical focus of their work and use accepted methodological procedures. They deploy those procedures to solve problems identified within the theoretical framework, thereby adding to knowledge (the store of problems solved) and extending the range of their theory. The framework, its procedures and its empirical substance are codified in their textbooks. What they share is termed a *paradigm*: 'a scientific community consists of men who share a paradigm' (Kuhn, 1970a, p. 176). As Popper (1959) expresses it, this means that once scientists are socialized into a research field they can proceed directly to its unsolved problems. The existing framework defines these problems, providing both a context and a methodology for tackling them. The researcher does not set out to tackle a problem *de novo*, therefore, but on the basis of what is already known in the chosen field. A paradigm is thus 'an accepted problem-solution' (Barnes, 1982, p. xiv), which by its very nature poses the next problem. Progress in science is achieved by problem solving.

To undertake research within a paradigm requires understanding and acceptance of its philosophy and methodology. This involves a period of training, during which the potential new researcher is socialized into the paradigmatic culture, that is, its way of thinking about its scientific problems – its language, literature, and methods of research, result presentation and argumentation. The key is provided by the paradigm's textbooks, the summaries of its literature which set out what is known and how more knowledge can be obtained. The training prepares individuals for work within an accepted mould:

> Scientific training is dogmatic and authoritarian ... [it] does not generate or encourage traits such as creativity or logical rigour; rather it equips scientists so that it is possible for them to be creative, or rigorous, or whatever else, in the context of a specific form of culture (Barnes, 1982, pp. 1–17).

Having been integrated into the paradigm, the scientist joins a research community. Such communities, sometimes termed 'invisible colleges', operate through close interaction involving attendance at specialized conferences and the private circulation of research papers in pre-publication form: their existence is reflected in citations to each other's work (Crane, 1972). Increasingly, electronic communications media allow community members to be in frequent, almost constant, contact and collaborative work without regular meetings is now common (Johnston, 2004a). Individual members receive recognition for the value of their work and attract the patronage of leaders who may assist their career advancement; some communities have only a few patrons, perhaps even one, and may be identified as a particular school of thought – perhaps focused on a single leading individual.

Research within a paradigm involves filling in the gaps; the researcher 'has to make the unknown into an instance of the known, into another routine case' (Barnes, 1982, p. 49). The paradigm provides the needed resources – guidance but not direction. Success, which brings the rewards of recognition, patronage and status, involves conforming to the paradigmatic norms (Mulkay, 1975, p. 515):

> It is clear that the quality or significance of a scientist's work is judged in relation to the existing set of scientific assumptions and expectations. Thus, whereas radical departures from a well-defined framework are unlikely to be granted recognition early under normal circumstances, original contributions which conform to established preconceptions will be quickly rewarded.

Thus the dominant norm of academic life is not one of the five listed above (p. 5), but rather conformity or convergence. Science is not the constant search for novel discoveries but rather the careful application of agreed procedures to the solution of problems in order to extend existing well-structured bodies of knowledge. Judgements about relevance and importance are being made all of the time, but within an academic environment carefully structured by the training process. Science progresses through filling the gaps in a pre-defined framework.

This operation of a paradigm is known as *normal science* (Kuhn, 1962, pp. 35–6):

> Perhaps the most striking feature of the normal research problems ... is how little they aim to produce major novelties, conceptual or phenomenal. Sometimes ... everything but the most esoteric detail of the result is known in advance ... the range of anticipated, and thus assimilable, results is always small compared with the range that imaginations can conceive ... the aim of normal science is not major substantive novelties ... the results gained in normal research are significant because they add to the scope and precision with which the paradigm can be applied. ...Though its outcome can be anticipated, often in detail so great that what remains to be known is itself uninteresting, the way to achieve that outcome remains very much in doubt. ...The man who succeeds proves himself an expert problem solver.

Within normal science, therefore, the researcher has available:

1. An accepted body of knowledge, ordered and interpreted in a particular way;
2. An indication of the puzzles that remain to be solved; and
3. A set of procedures for puzzle-solving.

Training within a paradigm provides the tools for extending the paradigmatic body of knowledge. The result is 'conventional, routinised practice' (Barnes, 1982, p. 11). This does not imply that normal scientific activity is necessarily one of 'long periods of dreary conformity' (p. 13), however, because extending and developing knowledge are not simply 'a matter of following instructions or rules. Rather, normal science is a test of ingenuity and imagination, with paradigms figuring largely among the cultural resources of the scientist' (p. 13). Solving problems is rarely easy; Kuhn (1970c, pp. 36–9) uses chess-playing as an example, arguing that much ingenuity as well as existing knowledge (practice) must be brought to bear if the problems posed in individual games are to be solved successfully.

Scientists are not omniscient. They do not understand everything – even within a particular paradigm – so their predictions occasionally prove inaccurate. While the process of normal science continues, therefore, slowly accumulating extra knowledge as problems are solved, it sometimes throws up anomalies, findings that are not in accord with the paradigm's assumptions. These must be accounted for (Barnes, 1982, p. 53):

Puzzle-solving activity frequently attempts to show that what is prima facie anomalous is either the spurious product of bad equipment or technique, or a familiar phenomenon in disguise. And most anomalies are successfully assimilated in this way.

Either the work was badly done or the researcher interpreted the results wrongly. Minor adaptation of the paradigm may be needed, but the general process of normal science continues.

Some anomalies cannot readily be accounted for, however, and they may continue to worry a few scientists, whose persistence leads to work on alternative paradigms, potential new frameworks that structure knowledge so that there are no anomalies. This is *extraordinary research*, conducted outside the bounds of the accepted paradigm. When it is successful, a 'revolutionary episode' is in progress. Regarding such research, Kuhn (1962, pp. 89–90) notes that:

Almost always the men who achieve these fundamental inventions of a new paradigm have been either very young or very new to the field whose paradigm they change ... obviously these are the men who, being little committed by prior practice to the traditional rules of normal science, are particularly likely to see that those rules no longer define a playable game and to conceive another set that can replace them.

The result is an alternative paradigm. Adherents of the current normal science are then asked to choose between two competing views of their subject: either the accepted mode of working is to be maintained, despite the anomalies, or a new sub-culture is to be adopted. The invitation is to discard existing authorities and habits and to take up new ones, which are claimed to be superior, because they are better predictors of that aspect of the world being studied. If the need for change is accepted, then a revolution in scientific practice occurs; one paradigm is replaced by another.

That choice between competing paradigms is an extremely difficult one because of their incommensurability; there are no common standards against which both can be compared. As Kuhn (1970a, p.148) points out, 'the proponents of competing paradigms will often disagree about the list of problems that any candidate for paradigm must resolve. Their standards or their definitions of science are not the same'. The new paradigm will almost certainly use some of the language and procedures of the one it is seeking to replace, but in slightly different ways, giving rise to considerable misunderstanding in discussions between the rival paradigms' protagonists. More importantly, however, the two groups of scientists may be looking at the world in very different ways:

> Both are looking at the world, and what they look at has not changed. But in some areas they see different things, and they see them in different relations one to the other. That is why a law that cannot even be demonstrated to one group of scientists may occasionally seem intuitively obvious to another (p. 150).

Thus, any switch from one paradigm to another is not forced simply by logic. It is what Kuhn calls a 'gestalt switch', a decision to abandon one way of viewing the world and replace it by another on intuitive grounds, rather than through the application of strict scientific criteria; a subjective decision has to be made that one is better than the other. Not all scientists may come to the same intuitive decision, therefore, so that some continue to work in the context of a paradigm that others have discredited. One of the often-cited examples of such a paradigm shift – on which Kuhn, 1957, wrote his first book – was the Copernican revolution in astronomy, as promoted by Galileo. Likewise, within western geography, Columbus's 'discovery of America' forced a revolution in world cartography.

Kuhn represents scientific activity as researchers trained to employ a proven mode of looking at their subject matter using an accepted methodology for solving problems. They proceed in a steady, cumulative manner, adding to the store of knowledge: small modifications may be needed to accommodate minor anomalies encountered en route. Occasionally, however, anomalies are detected which cannot either be explained away or accommodated. Some researchers may focus on these, developing new paradigms to account for them, as well as everything else that was already known. When this is achieved, the new paradigm is presented for approval. A revolution is invited, for the alternative paradigms are incommensurable: the community is asked to redirect its work. Science proceeds in a steady fashion along well-trodden paths, therefore, with occasional major breaks in its continuity marked by important changes in the organization of its material, in the definition of its problems, and in its techniques for problem-solving.

Criticisms of Kuhn's approach, and his response

Kuhn's work has stimulated a great deal of debate among philosophers of science, because it challenged orthodox views of scientific progress and implied, especially in the concept of revolutions, that some scientific decision-making was 'irrational' (see Watkins, 1970, on Kuhn's analogy between scientific and religious communities). Indeed, the introduction and treatment of the concept of the revolutionary episode attracted much of the attention (see Stegmuller, 1976), because most of the views that Kuhn was challenging were normative rather than positive; they prescribed what science *should* be like whereas Kuhn described what it was *actually* like.

A major problem with Kuhn's original presentation for many commentators was the varying use of the term 'paradigm'. Masterman (1970, p. 61) identified no less than 21 different usages, which 'makes paradigm elucidation genuinely difficult for the superficial reader'. From these, she distilled three main groups of definitions:

1. The *metaparadigms* (or metaphysical paradigms), which can be equated with 'world views', or general organizing principles;
2. The *sociological paradigms*, which are the concrete scientific achievements of a community defining their working habits; and
3. The *artefact* or *construct paradigms*, the classic works that provide the tools for future work.

The second provides the structure within which individual scientists work, whereas the third presents their means for puzzle-solving; the first comprises their overall view of the nature of science and its objects of study.

Kuhn accepted Masterman's representation of his work, and later writings clarified his views, focusing almost entirely on the second and third of Masterman's definitions. He indicated that if he rewrote the original book he would give primacy not to paradigms but to scientific communities (Kuhn, 1970a). These operate at various scales: the global community of natural scientists, for example; the main professional disciplinary groups (physicists, chemists etc.); and intra-disciplinary groups working on particular empirical problems (such as nuclear physicists). He focused on the last: 'Communities of this sort are the units that this book has presented as the producers and validators of scientific knowledge. Paradigms are something shared by members of such groups' (p. 178). With regard to the use of the term 'paradigm' in this context, Kuhn (1977, p. 460) suggested a two-part definition, the second component fitting within the first:

> One sense of 'paradigm' is global, embracing all the shared commitments of a scientific group; the other isolates a particularly important sort of commitment and is thus a subset of the first.

The global, or sociological, definition is of a *disciplinary matrix*: 'what the members of a scientific community, and they alone, share' (p. 460). It comprises (Kuhn, 1970c, pp. 152 ff): the accepted generalizations; shared commitments to particular models, or guiding frameworks for the construction and validation of theories (elsewhere – Kuhn, 1977, p. 501 – he equates the disciplinary matrix with a theory); and shared values regarding procedures. It also contains a fourth element that provides the second, and subsidiary, definition of paradigms, and which he claimed (Kuhn, 1977, p. xx) was the originally intended meaning. This is the set of *exemplars* (the construct or artefact paradigms in Masterman's classification), which are:

> ... the concrete problem-solutions that students encounter from the start of their scientific education, whether in laboratories, in examinations, or at the ends of chapters in science texts. To these shared examples should be added at least some of the technical problem-solutions found in the periodical literature that scientists encounter during their post-educational research careers and that also show them by example how their job is to be done (p. 187).

Solving a problem involves recourse to these exemplars; scientists deploy analogies, classic works that suggest how the current problem should be approached. Students learn about the exemplars, and apply them in their own training, in order to appreciate the empirical content of their disciplinary matrix. This provides them with a way of working:

> One of the fundamental techniques by which the members of a group, whether an entire culture or a specialists' sub-community within it, learn to see the same things when confronted with the same stimuli is by being shown examples of situations that their predecessors in the group have already learned to see as like each other and as different from other sorts of situations (pp. 193–4).

Revolutions can therefore involve:

1. The replacement of one exemplar by another;
2. Modification of the existing set of exemplars to accommodate new material; or
3. The replacement of the disciplinary matrix.

The last, a revolution in the sociological paradigm, is likely to be a major event in the history of a science; the first and second can occur without affecting the fundamentals of the disciplinary matrix. (Bird, 2000, p. 50, suggests a continuum of changes.)

The usual interpretation of Kuhn's work is that scientific communities operate within one paradigm, according to the normal science model, whereas according to Masterman (1970) and others it is possible to have long periods of either non-paradigm, multi-paradigm, or dual-paradigm activity. This possibility is addressed in Lakatos' (1978a) alternative view of the history of sciences. With Kuhn, Lakatos accepts that no theory (or paradigm) is falsified until a better one is available, but he posits long debates between competing theories. Central to those debates are what he calls *research programmes* (which are similar to Kuhn's paradigms as disciplinary matrices). Each programme has a hard core, an irrefutable central set of beliefs. Its methodological rules include a negative heuristic which directs attention away from the hard core, and it also includes a positive heuristic, directing researchers towards problems in the 'protective belt' that surrounds the core. Anomalies are solved in this protective belt, by the development of auxiliary hypotheses which can account for the observed deviations and so protect the programme's core.

Progress within a research programme depends on the ingenuity of the scientists in devising hypotheses that are both consistent with the core and can account for anomalies. Success 'hardens' the core, and is measured by the number of 'verifications' or successful predictions, not by failures ('refutations'). The core's content is never in doubt. (According to Lakatos, 1978b, p. 110, it is conventionally accepted and 'irrefutable', defining the problems within a preconceived plan.) Research programmes may falter, however. Their positive heuristic may fail to produce successful predictions, so that the programme enters a degenerative phase, when it is ripe for replacement by a new programme still in the progressive phase of substantially expanding its content. A programme shift occurs because the superiority of the new over the old can be demonstrated, in much the same way as Kuhn's paradigm shifts, except that the programme shift usually takes a considerable time. Change is not instantaneous, Lakatos claims (despite its presentation as such in 'scientific folklore', p. 85). Nor are there crucial experiments, the results of which convince a community that one programme is right and the other wrong. (Crucial experiments may be identified with hindsight, but these may not be recognized as such at the time when they are reported. There is a danger, Lakatos and others claim, of rewriting history as a series of crucial experiments.) Thus, much of the history of a discipline may involve two or more competing research programmes coexisting (Lakatos, 1978a, p. 69):

> The history of science has been and should be a history of competing research programmes (or, if you wish, 'paradigms'), but it has not been and must not become a succession of periods of normal science: the sooner competition starts the better for progress.

Lakatos not only recognized but also required theoretical pluralism (which led to criticism from Barnes, 1982, that his is a normative view of science, not a positive one like Kuhn's). Within this pluralist situation, 'Criticism of a programme is a long and often frustrating process and one must treat budding programmes leniently' (Lakatos, 1978a, p. 92). Although Lakatos denies Kuhn's concept of normal science as one of paradigm dominance in a discipline, he accepts that progressive research programmes comprise relatively routine extensions to knowledge through the testing of new hypotheses derived from the positive heuristic. Refutations are rare; the aim is verification and progress.

Popper argued against this, claiming that 'science is essentially critical' (1970, p. 55) and characterized not by normal science but by extraordinary research. To him, the normal scientist is really an applied scientist (Popper, 1970, pp. 52–3):

> 'Normal' science ... is the activity of the non-revolutionary, or more precisely, the not-too-critical professional: of the science student who accepts the ruling dogma of the day; who does not wish to challenge it; and who accepts a new revolutionary theory only if almost everybody else is ready to accept it – if it becomes fashionable by a kind of bandwagon effect. To resist a new fashion needs perhaps as much courage as was needed to bring it about ... The success of the 'normal' scientist consists, entirely, in showing that the ruling theory can be properly and satisfactorily applied in order to reach a solution of the puzzle in question.

For Popper, science consists of bold conjectures and the conduct of experiments designed to refute them. In his view of science (Popper, 1970, p. 77) hypotheses can never be verified, only falsified, so that disciplines are in constant revolution as researchers seek to prove that each other's theories are wrong (see p. 87).

Popper's concept of a 'revolution in permanence' has been criticized by Barnes (1982) as normative and not descriptive of science as actually practised. Kuhn's (1970, p. 243) response is that, '[Popper] and his group argue that the scientist should try at all times to be a critic and a proliferator of alternate theories. I urge the desirability of an alternate strategy which reserves such behaviour for special occasions'. According to this alternative strategy, most scientists are 'normal scientists' working routinely rather than critically. This view is supported by Eilon (1975), who classified management scientists into:

1. *Chroniclers*, whose role is to describe reality within the constraints of a particular paradigm;

2. *Dialecticians*, who stimulate debate and progress – a dialectician 'believes it is necessary to debate and argue issues in order to elicit the facts ... challenging stated views or records, in order to uncover what otherwise may remain hidden from an innocent observer' (Eilon, 1975, p. 361);

3. *Puzzle-solvers*, who advance the empirical content of the accepted paradigm;

4. *Empiricists*, who are like chroniclers in their focus on description;

5. *Classifiers*, who take information generated by empiricists and chroniclers and order it within the paradigm framework;

6. *Iconoclasts*, who destroy cherished beliefs, the assumptions on which they are built, the deductions, conclusions and interpretations, and expose the incompatibilities between theory and practice, between predicted and observed worlds – such iconoclasts may be destructive only, or they may be constructive in their presentation of alternative theories, in which case they are the agents of paradigm change; and

7. *Change-agents*, who are the applied scientists concerned not so much with the establishment of theories and facts but rather with the use of existing knowledge to create a better world.

Individuals may be in more than one of these archetypes (not necessarily contemporaneously). If Kuhn and Lakatos are correct, however, most will be chroniclers, puzzle-solvers, empiricists and classifiers (Mercer, 1977). The change-agents are conformists too, since they apply the accepted normal science, not challenge it. Thus Popper's argument focuses on a few key scientists only, and seeks to characterize the whole of science as if they were typical. Note, however, that in defending this view, Magee (1975, p. 41) claims that normal scientists' work can be studied in Popperian terms. They may 'take for granted, in order to solve problems at a lower level, theories which only a few of their colleagues are questioning', but they should be seeking intra-paradigm progress by using the methodology of conjecture and refutation. Barnes (1982) also contends that much 'normal science' research involves refuting conjectures.

Popper's arguments were extended by Feyerabend (1975), who claimed that history is a series of accidents – which is how it should be. Science should be allowed to evolve in that way, since this is the best means of ensuring progress. Most discoveries have been made by individuals who either deliberately or unwittingly flouted the rules, but modern scientific education tries to prevent this by constraining its practitioners into myopic paradigms. Feyerabend (1975, p. 187) claims that the only rule in science should be 'anything goes', in a scientific anarchy whose hallmark, like a political anarchy's, is 'opposition to the established order of things: to the state; its institutions, the ideologies that support and glorify those institutions'. Like Popper, however, Feyerabend presents a normative model, concerned with major scientific developments and not with their everyday extensions. Regarding the latter, if Lakatos rather than Kuhn is correct, revolutions take a long time so a discipline will be characterized by dissensus rather than consensus over much of its history. Is it likely that a body of scholars (especially a large body) will agree on ends and means and will not differ at all on fundamental interpretations, except very occasionally and then only for short periods. From research on radio astronomy, Mulkay (1978, p. 11) concluded that 'Scientific consensus … in a given area of interest is seldom complete'. A discipline may contain several branches (Mulkay, 1975, p. 520):

> In science, new problem areas are regularly created and associated social networks formed … The onset of growth in a new area typically follows the perception, by scientists already at work in one or more existing areas, of unresolved problems, unexpected observations or unusual technical advances, the pursuit of which lies outside their present field. Thus the exploitation of a new area is usually set in motion by a process of scientific migration.

This does not involve a paradigm shift, nor even a degenerating research programme. Rather, it indicates the establishment of a new paradigm-exemplar (in Lakatos' terms, a shift to another area of the positive heuristic or protective aureole). A new branch may be identified either by its focus on methods and techniques, or by its attention to, as yet, relatively ignored subject matter.

The branching process suggested by Mulkay allows for debate and movement within a paradigm/research programme without substantial conflict, since the disciplinary matrix/hard core is not being attacked, let alone the 'world view' (see p. 11). Kuhn (1977, p. 462) accepts this, noting that: 'Individual scientists, particularly the ablest, will belong to several such [branches] … either simultaneously or in succession', and Suppe (1977b, p. 498) notes that inter-branch consensus is usual:

> … to account for normal science all [one] has to assume is that scientists in a particular scientific community are in sufficient agreement on what theory to employ, what counts as good and bad science, what the relevant questions are, what sort of work to take as exemplary, and so forth.

The disciplinary matrix/hard core is central to the paradigm/research programme, not the exemplars and the type of problem attacked.

Training in its disciplinary matrix, therefore, allows researchers to move among branches of a scientific community. Some branches may eventually break away, establishing new communities – by 'quiet revolutions' (Johnston, 1978c). Such breaks may not be favoured by the parent community on political grounds, for they are likely to be against the interests of the disciplinary bureaucracy; separate communities competing for students and research funds, yet covering similar subject-matter, are unpopular. Thus, communities may be prepared to accommodate dissenting groups, even potential revolutionaries, rather than risk breakaway success. Such dissent is often contained, however, and may even be repressed (see Lichtenberger, 1984, for an example from within geography). Toulmin (1970, p. 45) notes that the conflict is frequently intergenerational: 'perhaps every new generation of scientists having any original ideas or "slant" of its own finds itself, at certain points and in certain respects, at cross-purposes with the immediately preceding generation'. Its seniors may decide to accommodate the differences, 'for the good of the subject'. But according to Mulkay (1978, p. 116), 'there are now several well-documented studies of instances where demonstrably competent scientists have been excluded from a field of study as their ideas have come to diverge from those in the majority'. Thus the competition between paradigms/research programmes may be contained within a discipline. In others, it results in the establishment of separate disciplines, usually after a stage in which the nascent discipline operates as a separate community within the parent body.

Kuhn and the social sciences

These critiques of Kuhn's ideas cover most of the elements of his thesis. Lakatos questions whether revolutions are achieved in short periods; Popper doubts the existence of normal science and Mulkay suggests that several paradigms (as exemplars) can coexist within a discipline which is not characterized by consensus. None, however, questions the basic (if implicit) world view that science is the study of an empirical world, in which subject and object can be separated, and that scientific progress is measured by the volume of successful predictions. This assumes a certain philosophy of knowledge, as made clear below (p. 20).

The assumption regarding predictive success as a measure of scientific progress raises doubts about the validity of Kuhn's thesis – plus those of Lakatos, Popper and Mulkay – to the social sciences. It has not prevented social scientists trying to fit Kuhn's model to their disciplines, however, an exercise which Kuhn himself thought non-viable (because of the great variety of incommensurable writings: Kuhn, 1970a, p. 165) and which has drawn scathing criticism (Barnes, 1982, p. 120):

> The popularity of debates about whether sociology has a paradigm, or whether there have been scientific revolutions in economics or in psychology, attests more to the prevalence of intellectual laziness than to the significance of Kuhn's thinking. He himself ... has stressed that a case for their utility has only been made in the context of the history of the natural sciences.

Kuhn's model is not positivist, but his conception of science is, for he talks of paradigms (especially exemplars) being assessed according to their predictive ability (1970c, p. 185). This is not a valid approach according to some social scientists, as parts of this book will show. Particular paradigms/research programmes may be assessed on the criterion of predictive accuracy, with degenerative phases following poor predictions (as Blaug, 1975, suggests for economics), but how does one assess different world views which offer varying basic conceptions of the nature of science? (This is Masterman's, 1970, first definition of a paradigm, which Kuhn did not respond to. See also Gutting, 1980, and Hacking, 1983.) A switch from one world view to another, from one conception of science to another, should fit Kuhn's model in that the two conceptions are incommensurable and the decision must involve an 'act of faith' rather than one compelled by defined criteria logically applied. But Kuhn's work does not address such a switch within a social science, since all of his examples come from the natural sciences (as Kuhn, 1977, himself stressed). Indeed, Fuller (2000, p. 228, his emphasis) notes that:

> Kuhn observed that social scientists could never agree on what counted as an exemplary piece of research, and so could never establish a common frame of reference for anchoring their disputes ... Accordingly, Kuhn concluded that the history of the social sciences has not witnessed a clear succession of paradigms because social scientists have been unable to agree on research exemplars

to underwrite the activity of normal science. . . . the peculiar character of the social sciences can be traced historically to the social scientists' having been guided by larger, conceptually unwieldy social problems that cannot be reduced to well-defined puzzles. Consequently historians of each of the social sciences have portrayed their disciplines' trajectory as pulled in three distinct directions that can be characterized independently of any intrinsic concern for the nature of social reality:

1. *From above (in an administrative or managerial capacity, as the trustees of state or business);*
2. *From within (in an ethical capacity, as the secular successor of pastoral theology);*
3. *From below (in a rhetorical capacity, as the voice of politically disenfranchised groups).*

A potential framework for analysing a social science discipline outwith the particular world view of Kuhn and his critics is outlined in Foucault's (1972) *The Archaeology of Knowledge.* This offers an analysis of the 'pure description' of discourses, unified systems of statements (however expressed) that can only be understood within their context (Foucault, 1972, p. 97): 'One cannot say a sentence, one cannot transform it into a statement, unless a collateral space is brought into operation'. Anything said or written can only be understood by those privy to the context of the discourse; as with a language, one can only comprehend the words, and the sequence in which they are used, because one understands the rules governing their use.

According to this view, the history of ideas is the history of discourses, of systems (somewhat akin to languages) used for the discussion of subjects that are defined within the discourses. There is, for example, no fixed definition of madness; each discourse that discusses it has its own definition and any discussion of madness is particular to that definition and the discourse in which it is set. The nature of a discourse is deposited in an collection of texts and practices, and it is the function of archaeology to reconstitute the discourse from such 'archives'; to describe and understand what was being done in a particular configuration (Foucault, 1972, pp. 138–40, 157–65). It describes the nature of the discourse without imposing a prescribed framework. As Foucault (1972, pp. 33–4) describes nineteenth-century medical science:

. . . [it] was characterized not so much by its objects or concepts as by a certain style, a certain constant manner of statement . . . medicine no longer consisted of a group of traditions, observations and heterogeneous practices, but of a corpus of knowledge that presupposed the same way of looking at things . . . [in addition it was] a group of hypotheses about life and death, of ethical choices, of therapeutic decisions, of institutional regulations, of teaching models, as a group of descriptions . . . if there is a unity, its principle is not therefore a determined form of statements; is it not rather the group of rules, which, simultaneously or in turn, have made possible purely perceptual descriptions? What one must characterize and individualize is the coexistence of these dispersed and hetero-geneous statements; the system that governs their division, the degree to which they depend upon one another, the way in which they interlock or exclude one another, the transformation that they undergo, and the play of their location, arrangement, and replacement.

Discourses are therefore sets of mutually agreed rules that govern description and discussion among the members who agree those rules, and are similar to the scientific communities given central place in Kuhn's (1970a) later statements. They are not independent of wider conditions, however. Archaeology may identify separate discursive formations, but these must be related to what Foucault (1972, p. 19) calls the *episteme*:

> ...*something like a world-view, a slice of history common to all branches of knowledge, which imposes on each one the same norms and postulates, a general stage of reason, a certain structure of thought that the men of a particular period cannot escape.*

This sets out how a particular world view (meta-paradigm?) predominates during a period and influences the contents and determines the parameters of 'individual' discourses (the idea of an individual is itself the product of a particular discourse, for example). Presumably, too, there must be periods of competition between *epistemes* (which may involve a similar process to that outlined by Lakatos). Foucault does not outline how such change occurs, however.

Foucault's ideas set the study of scientific disciplines more firmly in the context of the wider environment in which (and for which) they are practised than is the case with the other approaches discussed here, all of which very largely abstract the study of science from its social milieu. (As Berdoulay, 1981, p. 9, expresses it, 'little interest is paid to historical contexts or intellectual climates since the focus is placed on the internal evolution of each science'.) Such abstraction is especially unfortunate for the social sciences, the disciplines that investigate and interact with their milieux and whose contents, in the broadest sense if not in detail, are likely to be strongly influenced by that context. Just how social science and society interact remains to be mapped out in detail (as, of course, does the interaction between natural science and society because the contents of the former, too, are clearly influenced by the environmental constraints), and whether Foucault's proposal of a single dominating *episteme* at any time is valid is open to doubt. That human geography should be studied in its social context appears an irrefutable claim, however. The remainder of this chapter outlines that context.

Geographers, Kuhn and discourses

Soon after the appearance of Kuhn's (1962) classic volume the concept of a paradigm was introduced to the geographic literature by Haggett and Chorley (1967). Since then it has been widely used in discussions of geography's history, not least in previous editions of this book (on which see Mair, 1986). Its notion of normal science punctuated by revolutions was soon discarded, however, as it was realized that several incommensurate paradigms were co-existing within the discipline, and more seemed to be added on a regular basis without others being dropped: the discipline was seen as what Bird (2000, p. 31), following Hoyningen-Huene (1993), terms an 'immature science': a 'mature science' is one wherein normal science is practised within a single paradigm, whereas an 'immature science' has 'several competing paradigm-like schools'. Maturity only comes when there is consensus, when:

> ... *one school scores a victory over its competitors by producing a signal achievement. That achievement wins defectors from other schools and attracts the favour of younger scientists. Support for the competitors dwindles and they eventually die out.*

This suggests 'political' decision-making, at least in part. It may be that all members of a community accept the 'achievement' (with those who do not perhaps defecting to other disciplines), or it may be that those with power within the discipline impose it, by declining to make any appointments of people who challenge it, and by stifling dissent from within. According to Bird (2000, p. 32):

Immature science is that initial period in the history of a science that occurs when for the first time sufficient interest in a phenomenon or set of related phenomena crystallizes distinct groups or schools around particular theories or approaches; the schools not only pursue research on the basis of their favoured ideas but also compete with one another for intellectual, social and professional supremacy.

This book clearly demonstrates that on those terms geography has been an immature science throughout the period surveyed. It also, at least implicitly, poses the question whether it will ever reach maturity – as defined by Bird.

Indeed, unless such 'maturity' is imposed on a discipline by preventing dissent and debate, it is doubtful whether any discipline can be termed a mature science in a strict sense. That certainly may be the case with the social sciences. As Bird (2000, p. 267) notes, Kuhn's book 'had little direct influence on the functioning of the natural sciences but its impact on social science was enormous'. That impact included the provision of 'a template whereby the histories of the social sciences, almost entirely ignored in the *Structure* itself, could be described'. Whether that was a valid template for human geography is discussed in this book's final chapter: at this stage we merely note that too much emphasis in geographers' discussions of Kuhn has focused on the concept of cycles of normal science punctuated by revolutions and less on that of communities, their struggle for dominance and their promotion of alternative discourses – which Gregory (1994, p. 11) identifies as 'all the ways in which we communicate with one another . . . that cast networks of signs, symbols and practices through which we make our world(s) meaningful to ourselves and to others' in local contexts, 'the contexts and casements that shape our local knowledge'.

Three types of science

Little has been said so far about various conceptions of the nature of scientific activity, except for the material on different paradigms as 'world views'. It has been implicit that geographers share a world view, and that any differences in what they have done, and still do, reflect adherence to either or both of separate sociological paradigms and different exemplars (see p. 11). Changes in the relative importance of such paradigms and exemplars reflect responses by geographers, both individually and collectively, to changes in their external environment. But is this the case? Has there been just one 'world view' which all human geographers have shared during the period under review, or are there different conceptions of the discipline?

For human geographers, as social scientists, the answer to that last question is only likely to be 'yes' if for some reason they have ignored some of the main strands of contemporary social science thinking. (The remainder of this book suggests that for some brief periods this may have been the case, at least in part, and that the changes which occurred in the discipline over the period studied came about only when some encountered the overlooked literature!) In this sense, as Bird (2000, p. 269) argues, the social sciences differ significantly from the natural sciences:

> *Social scientists in particular are apt to think of the natural scientist's confrontation with natural reality as essentially unproblematic in a way that does not hold for themselves. The social sciences are necessarily hermeneutic – they do not seek to describe the laws of nature but instead to understand or interpret human behaviour. It is the need for interpretation, the finding of meaning, that is absent from the natural sciences.*

Kuhn (1991) contested this, Bird claims, because the natural world is not unchanging; as it changes so it stimulates changes in how it is studied within an agreed paradigm. Nevertheless, puzzle-solving natural scientists' aims do not include interpretation, whereas 'social scientists are actively engaged in looking for new, deeper interpretations' (Bird, 2000, p. 269).

Such searches for interpretations involve a number of different conceptions of science – different macro-paradigms in Kuhnian terminology – in disciplines such as human geography. Each has its own world view, its beliefs regarding both the nature of knowledge – its epistemology, or definitions of valid knowledge, and ontology, its answers to such questions as 'What can be known?' and 'How can we know it?' – and the means of obtaining it (its methodologies), plus its beliefs on the uses to which knowledge can and/or should be put. The remainder of this book illustrates the relative importance of those three conceptions within Anglo-American human geography since 1945 and the debates among the protagonists of the various positions. The present section provides a brief introductory outline of the three world views. (The classification is drawn directly from Habermas, 1972; Johnston, 1986a and 1989a.)

The empirical (or analytic) sciences draw on an empiricist world view: knowledge comes from direct experience and is based on the senses, especially visual observation. Their methodology calls for accurate observation, recording and reportage. Some identify this as a neutral, value-free position, in which the 'facts speak for themselves', a view countered by those who argue that all observation is theoretically based – what is recorded as present in a place reflects what is being sought and what is deemed to be important, and its classification reflects a prior selection of categories. Thus, empiricist work is not the presentation of unordered material, but the recording of information within an agreed and approved conceptual framework. As illustrated later (p. 46), for geographers in the decades prior to 1945 this involved the collection and recording of material within a framework which identified the physical environment as the major determinant of the pattern of human activity on the earth's surface.

A particular form of empirical science generally known as *positivism* is the approach most frequently assumed to be characteristic of all science. Its goal is not only to describe (in a geographical context, to show what is where), but also to explain (to say why it is there). Such explanation is provided by presenting individual occurrences as examples of general laws (of the form 'if A then B': if B is present in a place, it is because A is there also). The goal of positivist science is to identify laws, statements with general – if not universal

– applicability. These provide not only an explanatory procedure (the distribution of B can be accounted for by the distribution of A in the above example) but also a predictive device – the presence of further occurrences of A can be used to predict future occurrences of B.

Empirical science involves the collection and reporting of information; positivist empirical science uses it to produce a particular form of explanation. The individual event is an example of the operation of one or more general laws. The predictive content of those laws can be used in processes of technical control; the presence of B in a place can be ensured (if it is desired) by putting A there, or B's absence (if wished) can be guaranteed by preventing the occurrence of A there. Successful positivist physical science can be used to manipulate and control the environment through the application of known physical laws; successful positivist social science can be used to manipulate and control society through the application of known laws of human behaviour.

The hermeneutic sciences deny the existence of a separate empirical world outside the individual observing it. No observation and description can be neutral, it is argued, but involves interpretation of the world as it is perceived through a system of meanings, which are human constructs developed by individuals through a continuous process of socialization and resocialization in contact with others. Thus, as a human I am more than a combination of living cells; I have both powers of reason and emotional traits. I share many characteristics with others, some (such as age and sex) based on biological criteria, but others (such as religious beliefs and class position) based on human constructs that are far from universal – my interpretation of my class position may differ from that of others, who may also disagree among themselves. All of these characteristics influence how I act, because I draw on them, and my interpretation of what they mean (what I think a person in 'my class' should do, for example), to guide my thinking and acting: thus the only way to understand what I do is to understand me. I observe the world and ascribe meanings to what I see from within the context of my understandings of phenomena and how they work. I then act in accordance with those meanings, which may differ from the meanings that an empirical scientist observing me may choose to use. According to a hermeneutic scientist, the meanings that matter are mine, since they are the foundations for my behaviour.

In the hermeneutic sciences, therefore, general laws of human behaviour are impossible, because humans, with their powers of memory and reason, cannot be treated as equivalent to machines that always respond in the same way to an identical stimulus (which is what the positivist sciences proclaim). Hermeneutic science does not offer explanations, but rather understandings. Its goal is to appreciate what people believe, how those beliefs develop within societies, and how they are drawn upon as the bases for actions. Such appreciation helps one to understand the past and the present, and may provide a guide to the future, but it is in no way predictive: it cannot say, 'if A, then B'.

Empirical sciences, especially positivist sciences, can be applied in strategies aiming at control of environments and societies. Hermeneutic sciences cannot. This does not mean that they cannot be applied within society, however; far from it. The understanding that is gained from hermeneutic appreciation can be used to promote self- and mutual appreciation, thereby enriching societies by making people better aware of both others and themselves.

Critical sciences differ from the other two, accepting neither the implicit determinism of the positivist nor the voluntarism of the hermeneutic: the former implies that people ultimately have no control over their lives, whereas the latter implies that they have complete control. According to critical sciences, people live within societies which are complex organizations created to ensure both individual, day-to-day and collective, inter-generational survival. Those organizations involve rules which must be operated if the society is to continue.

People are 'free' to interpret a society's rules in a variety of ways, as long as they do not transgress its boundaries between the acceptable and the unacceptable. In capitalist societies, for example, the rules require the production of food for sale at a profit but do not determine what foods will and will not be profitable – that is decided by individuals, both separately and collectively, and over time the types of food produced and consumed may change. Hermeneutic processes are involved, therefore, because the operation of a society depends on how people interpret its rules. Furthermore, conditions change (as a result of environmental variations, both temporary and secular, for example) and these changes must be interpreted and responded to. In the critical sciences, therefore, it is necessary to appreciate the basic rules by which a society operates in order to achieve a fundamental understanding; to appreciate what happens in particular circumstances, it is necessary to appreciate how the people operating the rules interpret them. This can be appreciated via an analogy with 'the rules of the game', thus, all sports have basic rules. Participants interpret those rules, and plan courses of action within them. To understand the sport, you must know the rules; to appreciate a particular game, you must understand how the participants have decided to operate within those rules.

Critical science is also applicable, but in a different way. Its goal is to ensure that people understand the rules by which a society operates (even though they may be hidden and unwritten, and can only be determined through abstraction from the many different interpretations of the rules that lead to the empirical world of appearances). Once people understand the rules, then they understand the society's fundamentals – they are emancipated. They are then freed from constraints to their understanding and can, if they wish, become involved in the transformation of society, changing the rules to a set which they find more acceptable.

These are three very different conceptions of science, of what it is, how it is done, and what its purpose is. If people disagree over the relative merits of the different views, then there will be debate between adherents of the various causes (and perhaps variants within each) promoting their own views. Any one discipline may therefore incorporate competition over the relative merits of each approach, as well as competition within each as to the proper way for that particular form of science to be practised. There can be a hierarchy of debates within a discipline such as human geography, therefore: at the most fundamental level, there is debate over the relevant world view; lower down, there can be debate within each world view over the conduct of research; and at the lowest there can be debate over procedural details, as set out by different exemplars. A revolution at the lowest level – adopting a new exemplar, a new way of observing/interpreting, or a new way of analysing data, for example – need not imply any change at the higher levels: the world view and disciplinary matrix remain constant, and the research community simply changes some aspect of its way of working. Major revolutions, on the other hand, involve a change in world view.

Human geography is not alone among the social sciences in having experienced all three levels of debate in recent decades. In general terms, the initial debates were within the empirical/analytic world view, and were followed by the introduction, in turn, of cases for each of the other world views, as well as debates within each regarding procedures and exemplars. Thus, the task of charting the history of Anglo-American human geography over the last five decades involves identifying the major features in these various debates. That is the role of the next eight chapters; they are followed by one which evaluates those debates, not by trying to reconcile the various positions, but rather by setting them in context and seeking to appreciate why and when they occurred and were settled (to the extent that they were).

The external environment

The discussion so far has suggested that scientific disciplines (and/or discourses) are communities, small societies which are microcosms of their containing social systems. As such, the proper study of how they operate is sociological, although philosophy may provide a normative framework.

Sociological studies of academic disciplines accept that such communities are not autonomous. Their members are not isolated, and they need the support of a wider society in order to exist: society employs academics to teach and research – either collectively, because universities receive public funding to teach and undertake research, or through market systems, whereby students pay for their education and sponsors pay for research. Whereas scientists may to some extent be able to impose their own priorities over what type of work is done, they are strongly influenced by external factors (Barnes, 1982, pp. 102–3):

> Social, technical and economic determinants routinely affect the rate and direction of scientific growth. . . . It is true that much scientific change occurs despite, rather than because of, external direction or financial control. . . . Progress in the disinterested study [of certain] . . . areas has probably occurred just that bit more rapidly because of their relevance to other matters.

The study of a discipline must be set in its societal context. It must not be assumed that members of academic communities fully accept that context and its directives and impulses. They may wish to counter them, and use their academic base as a focus for discontent and promotion of alternatives. But the (potential) limits to that discontent are substantial. Most university academic communities are dependent (indirectly if not directly) for their existence on public funds disbursed by governments which may use their financial power to influence, if not direct, what is taught and researched. Some universities (notably in the USA) are dependent on private sources of finance, so they must convince their sponsors and students that their work is relevant to current societal concerns (as Taylor, 1985c, suggests).

In that context, the Second World War is more than a convenient period from which to commence this chapter on the history of human geography; it marked a major watershed in the development of the societies which are the prime focus of the book – the United Kingdom and the United States. It cannot be considered in isolation, however. Just as important for the present discussion are the world-wide economic depression which preceded it and the Cold War, the economic boom, and then the recession and restructuring which followed. For the first time, a major international conflict was not determined solely by sacrifices in battles on land and sea, although there were many of them during the Second World War. And the extra dimensions of this war did not just involve the development of air space as a further arena for conflict – as well as restructuring views of spatial relationships (Schulten, 2001). The war was fought not only between military forces with guns and bombs but also between scientists, and victory was hastened, if not ensured, by the scientific superiority of the Allied Powers, most obviously at Hiroshima and Nagasaki. Science and technology had long been major elements in the developing industrialization of the western world, but their dominance was established between 1939 and 1945, and there was to be no retreat from the many technological advances made by the researchers involved in the military effort. Thus the war heralded the predominance of technology and 'science' in human affairs.

Associated with this growth in scientific activity, and its consequent prestige (with governments and with society at large), was a parallel development of social engineering. The major economic depression of the 1930s, inaugurated by the Wall Street crash of 1929, had a massive impact on governments and stimulated many measures aimed at relieving poverty and deprivation, simultaneously assuaging the liberal conscience. In the United States, this was represented by the New Deal legislation of President Roosevelt's governments, which aimed at relief and encouragement to industry and, through the Social Security Act, providing public support for those who, by no fault of their own, were indigent. Similar measures were introduced by the National Government in Britain; more were foreshadowed by plans formulated during the war, such as those promoted in the Beveridge Report on social security, and the Labour party's landslide election victory in 1945 heralded the introduction of many social democratic policies which gave government a much greater peacetime role in the organization of the economy and society than previously envisaged.

This development of social engineering was associated with a rising status for the social sciences, and a great expansion in their activities. Economics achieved prestige first, notably through the contributions of Keynes and others to solving problems of the depression, the organization of economies during wartime, and participation in the planning of a new world economic order after the war. Others followed. Social psychological research was widely used in the evaluation of personnel by the armed forces, and after the war opinion surveys proved valuable to governments and political parties while market research was increasingly used by industry and commerce (along with psychology in its advertising efforts). All of these fields adopted the 'scientific methods' of the more prestigious hard sciences, and their successes were envied by other disciplines, such as sociology, social administration and, later, geography. To be scientific was to be respectable and useful.

The war years saw the end of the extreme economic deprivations of the depression, as manufacturing output was boosted to provide the machinery of war. Afterwards, there were many years of doing without to be compensated for, and with full employment, government direction of, and increasing involvement in, economic affairs, plus the need to re-equip industries, the two decades following the war were characterized by an economic boom in the western world. Technological developments that had emerged in the 1920s–1930s, and which had been finessed in wartime, found wider applications in mass markets and continued to be fostered by Cold War research and development. Apart from the greater government involvement, this era in industrial development was marked by another major new characteristic, the advance of the giant firm, including the multi-national corporation. The concentration and centralization of capital proceeded rapidly; the average size of firms and factories increased and the economy of the world became dominated by a relatively small number of concerns. The decline and eclipse of the overseas Empires in the context of the rise of the American and Soviet super-powers and the birth of the 'Third World' out of the debris of war and imperialism, all reinforced the sense of a fast-changing 'new world'.

Rebuilding the ravaged war arenas placed new demands on societies, and the planning profession emerged from earlier obscurity to take on a major role in preparing the blueprint for a new social order. The need for such action was realized during the war in the United Kingdom with the preparation of a series of reports concerned with future land-use patterns, and with the spatial distribution of economic activity, at local and regional scales. Cities were to be rebuilt; New Towns were to be constructed; a more balanced inter-regional distribution of industry and employment was to be ensured; agricultural land was to be protected and residential environments were to be improved: all of this made great demands on social scientists, as well as engineers (an opportunity recognized by some geographers: Johnston, 2002a, 2003a, 2003b). The greater degree of commitment to the private ownership of land in the United States led to slower acceptance of the need for spatial planning there, but its heyday came with the rapid growth of problems involved in catering for the upsurge of automobile ownership and use: transport planning and engineering soon became major activities, allied with the automobile industry and the companies which constructed the major highways (many of which were designed for 'strategic' defence purposes in the Cold War).

All of these tasks – economic growth and planning; spatial planning; social administration; technological change; management; etc. – generated a need for educated personnel, and the universities received unprecedented demands for their graduates to serve the new needs of society. Education expanded rapidly: existing universities and colleges grew and many more were founded. Science and social science departments expanded to meet student demand. Their extra staff were involved in research, which became a salient component of academic life and so increased the tempo of paradigm development and questioning. Rather than places where a small elite was educated for the professions and a few privileged individuals followed their research interests, the universities became centres of society's development – the 'white-hot technological revolution' which Harold Wilson promised the British in the early 1960s. Research projects became bigger, supported by large grants from outside bodies (including government-established research councils) and carried out by specially employed graduates; the rate and volume of publication increased exponentially (Stoddart, 1967a; Johnston, 1995a, 1995b, 1996a).

The years from 1945 to about 1965 were a period of scientific and technological dominance, therefore. It was argued that the problems of production had been solved, because enough goods and services could be provided to satisfy all (and such benefits – it was argued – would soon accrue to the 'developing world' too). The problems of distribution were still being tackled, however, for as yet there was inequality of provision at all spatial scales. But these could be handled, it was argued, and the prospect of a prosperous and healthy life for all was widely canvassed. Academic disciplines were contributing substantially to this problem-solving by their own scientific progress. Advances in the natural sciences and technologies were solving the problems of production – of food, housing and consumer goods – as well as of ill-health. And advances in the social sciences were aiding in the management of success. Investment in education was thus investment in social progress (as well as an investment in the life chances of the individuals involved).

The deprivations of the 1920s and 1930s produced political responses two decades later, characterized by a determination not only to ensure no return to economic depression but also to provide permanent protection to those who suffered short- or long-term deprivation. The Beveridge Report in the UK identified five causes for concern: want, disease, ignorance, squalor and idleness. Policies aimed at their removal led to the creation of the major edifice of the Welfare State, which offered basic minimal standards of living for all, through such mechanisms as: a National Health Service that was free at the point of demand; a universal education service for all aged between 5 and 14 (later 15 and then 16), plus subsidized further and higher education systems; subsidized state housing; universal child allowances; unemployment benefits; benefits and care for the sick and disabled; and universal pensions. Other countries created different structures, but the overall pattern in the 'developed world' was of a major state role in sustaining its citizens (see Johnston, 1992).

Growth of the 'interventionist state' involved a major change to the nature of polity as well as society. A much wider range of activities came within government orbits, and the public bureaucracies grew accordingly – with consequent benefits in both employment opportunities for graduates and outlets for applying scientific and social scientific research. The decades after the Second World War saw the dominance of the welfare-corporate state in public affairs, with many professional groups (including scientists and social scientists) providing policy advisers and analysts.

Despite the successes of this initial post-war period, some doubted the desirability of such an all-embracing state. These concerns were growing during the 1960s, and by the early 1970s were having a major impact on the world scene. The seeds of doubt were many. Initially they focused, especially in the United States, on the problems of nuclear weapon development and of war, particularly the increasingly unpopular conflict in Vietnam and surrounding countries where technology was not carrying all before it against strong popular resistance and the casualty rates were increasingly deplored. Alongside were a number of major humanitarian concerns, including doubts about the inequalities that continued, both on a world scale and within the 'successful' capitalist societies. Poverty was not being alleviated; if anything the disparities between rich and poor were being extended, and absolute standards of living remained appallingly low in many parts of the world. The prospects for solving these problems were much less rosy than they had been a few years earlier, it seemed.

Furthermore, it was increasingly realized that success was being bought at considerable cost. Scientific and technological advancement required the dominance and discipline of the machine and the large factory. Work for large proportions of the labour force was being made more repetitive and boring as skilled tasks were taken over by automated production and assembly lines. Alienation of the individual from society was increasing. Particular groups suffered more than others, as the result of prejudice and discrimination. The status of black people and women became the foci of emerging civil and human rights movements which extended later to other oppressed groups within western society. Finally, interest was kindled in the growing degradation of the environment to fuel the production goals of advanced capitalist societies.

The problems of the dignity of the individual, the repression of minorities, the quality of life and the depletion of environmental resources were not new in the late 1960s. What was realized then, however, was that the form of social 'progress' advanced during the previous decades was in many cases exacerbating and not solving such problems. As the realization grew, so the proposed solutions varied. To some, the problems could be solved by greater state involvement, on international and national scales. Human and civil rights must be protected; greater equality must be achieved through the redistribution of wealth; the environment must be conserved, and where necessary preserved. In the language of the previous section, the research programme was maintained, but major efforts were made within its positive heuristic to solve the many anomalies. To others, this solution was insufficient. It would simply generate new anomalies because, according to the developing critique of capitalist systems, these are necessary to social 'progress'; capitalism, it was argued, necessarily survives on inequalities, on alienation and on the degradation of the environment.

Universities were the focus of much of this developing concern. There were major confrontations between students and the authorities in the late 1960s, for example, in particular at Berkeley, Chicago, London and Paris, and the student body was at the forefront of the anti-war movements. Some academics, notably in the social sciences, focused on the 'managerial' issues involved in producing a 'better, more equal' society, and these were considered more crucial than the 'production' issues covered by the natural sciences and technologies. A threefold division developed. In one, the need for social scientists to become more active in developing solutions to the problems of distribution and environmental depletion was advanced: social science must become more 'relevant', more 'policy-oriented', within the constraints of the proposed societal 'research programme'. A second argued for greater concentration on the problems of individual alienation; people should be released from the overbearing dominance of the machine and the big organization and encouraged to take a much greater part in creating their own lives. The individual needed protection against the increasingly distrusted expert. Finally, a third group developed a critique of capitalist society, seeking to show that while specific problems may be soluble, this would merely lead to others, while the general problems would remain because they are endemic to that mode of social organization. The call was for major social reform – from some, revolution (the vanguard of which was often identified with the Vietnam war and other Third World liberation struggles) – as the only long-term solution to the problems of human dignity and inequality. Feminist and civil rights movements in western societies emerged out of similar radical commitments.

The force of these arguments can be identified in a variety of ways, not least the declining popularity of scientific and technological subjects among students and the growing demand for places in the social sciences and humanities in the 1960s and 1970s. A further major problem then arose, because the capitalist world spent much of the 1970s in economic recession. The long boom was over.

The recession reflected the failure of state policies of demand management employing Keynesian principles, it was argued, and the search for an alternative saw a growing divergence between political parties. In Britain, for example, the relatively high degree of cross-party agreement over demand management broke down after 1974, with the Conservative party promoting a greater emphasis on free markets and a reduction in the direct role of the state. The post-war political consensus (in which Labour and Conservative policies had converged) was thus breaking down and the sense of crisis and change was reinforced by the revival of violent conflict over Northern Ireland and of nationalist claims in Scotland and Wales, all of which contested the established arrangements of the British state (Nairn, 1977). This growing polarization added to Britain's problems, some claim, because of the uncertainty it engendered about the future; a change of government would bring a major shift in policy. In the United States, similarly, there was a rise in support for 'new right' policies promoted within the Republican party, which countered the liberal policies of the Democrats in the 1960s.

To some social theorists, recession and its major impacts (notably unemployment) should accelerate the demands for reform and revolution. Both the United Kingdom and the United States at the end of the 1970s elected right-wing governments dedicated to programmes of economic regeneration by a reduction in public expenditure and a liberalization of those capitalist forces that produced the inequalities so widely condemned only a decade earlier. The role and size of the state were to be significantly reduced (Gamble, 1988); its task was to provide the infrastructure for a buoyant economy (particularly through sound management of public finances and the removal of restrictive practices – notably, though not only, by trades unions). 'Enterprise' was to be encouraged by a system which rewarded successful initiatives and risk-taking, and the result – it was claimed – would be a wealthier society from which all would benefit, while the state provided protection only for those in proven need – whose 'rights' for such assistance were balanced by state-created 'obligations' (Johnston, 1992).

The contemporary situation

Education has been subject to significant policy changes since the 1970s because of this shift. For the first time for more than two decades, expenditure on higher education in

Britain was cut in 1981, and the numbers of students undertaking undergraduate degrees and postgraduate training were reduced. The cuts were selective, with relative protection for science and technology – growth in which was seen as necessary for economic progress – alongside substantial reductions in the social sciences, believed by many politicians to be the homes of left-wing radicals and the fomenters of discontent. Research funds were similarly cut and redistributed. The reaction to these policies took the form, in part, of an attempt to defend academic freedom and independence and the need for a 'critical conscience' within society (which involves curricula designed to develop critical intellects as well as foster 'transferable skills' to be deployed by graduates in the labour market) but there was also a desire to reorient work within disciplines and make them more 'relevant' to current societal concerns.

The educational system within which the research components of academic disciplines are located has been closely involved in economic, social and political change during the last 40 years. It benefited from the boom years of the first two decades. Expansion was rapid and academic activity was considerable. It was then cut back, especially in the UK, as – to some decision-makers at least – expansion, especially expansion in the arts and social sciences (excluding business studies and management), was seen as an unaffordable luxury. Economic progress did not require large numbers of students and potential researchers being trained in disciplines with little relevance to perceived societal needs and working on topics that were critical of societal structure. Disciplines and scholars had to prove their relevance and sell their skills in the marketplace. Academic freedom was not entirely removed, but was to be curtailed, simply by denying it resources. The result is that after participating gleefully in the booms of the 1950s and 1960s, academia went into deep depression, suffering internal and external crises of confidence and subject to considerable political direction.

There was a reversal in political attitudes towards higher education at the end of the 1980s, if not also in the funding provided. In the United Kingdom, for example, there was a growing realization that national competition in the restructured global economy required developing human resources to their full potential, through a substantial increase in the participation rate of the 18–25-year-olds in further and higher education and an expansion of continuing education for older people. It was argued that the UK had a lower percentage of its population in higher education and obtaining relevant qualifications compared with competitor, more successful economies – such as the United States and much of continental Europe. More qualified students were needed, and universities should be allowed to expand – though in a more rigorous market system. (For an evaluation of these policies, see Wolf, 2002.)

Thus, despite a demographic downturn (which particularly affected the size of the teenage population in the socio-economic classes from which students traditionally moved into higher education), universities, polytechnics and colleges (most of them later elevated to university status) were expected to expand their provision and numbers. But, in line with the economic ideology of the governing party, they were expected to become more efficient in doing their teaching (i.e. to take more students without additional resources), and to obtain more income (especially for research and for continuing education) from sources other than the state. Further, there was an increased emphasis on the 'customer pays' principle (for long the norm in North America), with students meeting more of the costs of their education (in part, it was argued, because they would benefit from higher incomes as a consequence of their qualifications and expertise) and so being more concerned with getting 'value for money'; courses with a clear vocational orientation became more popular.

The UK government also became increasingly concerned over accountability for the funds provided to the universities for research. These were thought to be too widely spread and their use subject to insufficient evaluation. From the late 1980s on, therefore, funding for research in each discipline was to be concentrated on those institutions where work was evaluated as of high quality internationally, and a series of regular Research Assessment Exercises (RAEs) was instituted which grade all departments; the higher the grade achieved, the more money provided and the greater the amount of time and resources available for research. At the same time, the Research Councils, which provide funding for individual projects, were restructured to promote 'user interests' and were directed to focus their funding on areas of national economic importance identified through a regular Technology Foresight exercise. Financial pressure was thus used to promote a particular orientation to research (and teaching) within universities, one that was sympathetic to the ideology of the 'enterprise economy' (Johnston 1995a, 1995b). In addition, the ways in which universities were funded meant that whereas success in the RAEs brought substantial financial rewards, teaching activities did not; indeed, student numbers in universities were capped for some years, so that no extra income could be obtained and research – both income from external sponsors and the public money allocated according to RAE grade – was the main source for new income. Not surprisingly, research occupied an increasingly important place in academic life, putting pressures on individuals which many believed was to the detriment of their teaching roles (Sidaway, 1997).

There have now been five RAEs in the United Kingdom. After each, the distribution of the rewards has become increasingly concentrated on the highest graded departments (there are now eight grades, but almost all of the money goes to the top three). This has increased the pressure on departments and their members to be successful according to the criteria employed by the RAE panels. These are supposed to recognize research quality, both retrospective and prospective, but the main 'evidence' used in those judgements, especially in disciplines like geography, are publications. There are many claims that papers take precedence over books and that papers in certain journals are considered of higher quality than others (e.g. Short, 2002). Certainly some journals are cited much more than others among the four publications that staff members are required to submit as indicative of their best work (Johnston, 2003d). In addition, other 'indicators' are deployed to assist in the subjective judgements, such as research income and studentships gained, and citation indices.

In part as a response to the claims that the RAEs were over-emphasizing research at the expense of teaching, a parallel external evaluation of teaching quality was established in the mid-1990s, though those departments that were highly rated received no rewards other than the status of the perceived distinction, and very few indeed got the 'unsatisfactory' grades that threatened their ability to recruit students (Johnston, 1996f). Furthermore, although some of the evaluation involved external assessors observing and grading actual teaching sessions, much of it focused on other aspects of curriculum design, student success and so forth. The assessment procedure was as much a bureaucratic inspection of bureaucratic practices as it was an evaluation of the quality of the student learning experience. Its impact has been to further increase the pressures on staff, alongside the increased pressure to obtain research grants and contracts and publish high quality research to win high RAE grades. This has occurred during a period of very significant reductions in the resourcing of universities on a per capita (student) basis: research and teaching productivity has been increased, at substantial, if unmeasurable, costs (Johnston 1994c, 1995a, 1995b).

This audit and accountability culture in British universities (Johnston, 1994b) has spread to a number of other countries, but not the United States where the decentralization of responsibility for higher education, the existence of a large number of private universities and the market-orientation of education provision has precluded the introduction of centralized evaluations. Nevertheless, as Luke (2000) demonstrates with regard to political science there, there are similar pressures to win grants, produce high quality research papers in the 'right' journals, and gain high citation indices as universities compete for the best staff and graduate students, and the reputations that go with them. And although there aren't centralized bureaucratic evaluations as in the UK, there is a variety of reputational exercises that result in rankings of departments and institutions in 'league tables' which are widely used to promote institutional prestige. As he puts it, these exercises, and the inputs on which they are based, involve 'arithmetical economies of professional correctness [that] drive or stall careers' on the basis of which 'universities and disciplines . . . track their various cases of success and failure, growth and decline, winners and losers in this complex symbolic economy' every bit as much as do companies listed on the Stock Exchange (Luke, 2000, pp. 212–13). It is the outcome of his description of academic life as:

> . . . an existence pegged to perpetual examinations: seminar discussions, research papers, dissertation defenses, conference papers, journal submissions, book contracts, teaching evaluations, committee assignments, tenure hearings, academic promotions, annual reports . . . (p. 217).

These are now routine components of the academic profession. Its members are compelled to 'trade actively in the sign-value economies of professional correctness' and forced 'to adhere correctly to very clear disciplinary expectations in order to succeed' (p. 226). Academics research and publish in order to succeed in their chosen careers: the results of what they do – their publications – form the store of knowledge that represents their discipline's achievements. What they have chosen to write about, and why, determines the contemporary nature of their science.

Departments of geography and their individual members have had to respond to these political, institutional and potential market changes, therefore, and to restructure their course and research offerings accordingly. The nature of the science that they practised and taught was necessarily strongly influenced by the 'culture of the times' (which does not mean that all conformed to it). As Livingstone (1992, p. 347) expresses it, this is because, 'geography changes as society changes, and . . . the best way to understand the tradition to which geographers belong is to get a handle on the different social and intellectual environments within which geography has been practised'. As we seek to appreciate the history of geography over recent decades, we have to do this in the context of the constraints within which it has been practised.

Academic life: the occupational structure

Pursuit of an academic discipline in modern society is part of a career, undertaken for financial and other gains; most of its practitioners see their career as a profession, complete with entry rules and behavioural norms. In the initial development of almost all current academic disciplines, some of the innovators were amateurs, perhaps financing their activities from individual wealth. There are virtually no such amateurs now; very few of the research publications in human geography are by other than either a professional academic trained in the discipline or a member of a related discipline with interests in some aspects of geography. The profession is not geography, however. Rather, geography is the discipline professed by individuals who probably state their occupation as university teacher or some similar term. Indeed, the great majority of academic geographers are teachers in universities or comparable institutions of higher education; 'university' is used here as a generic term. Academic geographers are distinguished from other professional geographers (many of whom are also teachers) by their commitment to all three of the basic canons of a university: to propagate, preserve and advance knowledge. The advancement of knowledge – the conduct of fundamental research and the publication of its original findings – identifies an academic discipline; the nature of its teaching follows from the nature of its research.

The academic career structure

University staff members – hereafter termed academics – follow their chosen occupation within a well-defined career structure, of which two variants are relevant to this discussion: the *British model* and the *American model*. Entry to both is by the same route. With rare exceptions, the individual must have been a successful student as an undergraduate and, more especially, as a postgraduate. The latter involves pursuing original research, guided by one or more supervisors expert in the relevant specialized field. The research results are almost invariably presented as a thesis for a research degree (usually the PhD), which is examined by relevant experts; possession of a PhD is now an almost obligatory entrance ticket for both models.

While pursuing the research degree, most postgraduate students obtain experience in teaching undergraduates. Some universities, notably those operating the American model, finance many research students through such teaching activities. The individual may then proceed to further research experience, or may gain appointment to a limited-tenure university teaching post, offering an 'apprenticeship' in the teaching aspects of the profession while either the research degree is completed or the individual's research expertise is consolidated.

Beyond these limited-tenure positions lie the permanent teaching posts, which is where the two models deviate. In the *British model*, the first level of the career structure is the lectureship. For the first years of that appointment (usually three) the lecturer is on probation: training in teaching and related activities is provided, annual reports are made on progress as teacher, researcher and administrator, and advice is offered on adaptation to the demands of the profession. At the end of the probationary period, the appointment is either terminated or confirmed.

Appointment in this model is almost always to a department, which in many cases is named for the discipline which its staff members profess; others may be in a broader school or division — of social sciences, say. The prescribed duties involve undertaking research and such teaching and administration duties as directed by the head of the department. The lecturers are on a salary scale and receive an annual increment; accelerated promotion may be possible. In the United Kingdom there is an 'efficiency bar' after a certain number of years' service; 'crossing the bar' involves a promotion, and is determined by an assessment of the lecturer's research, teaching and administrative activities.

Beyond the lectureship are further grades into which the individual can be promoted. In the universities that were established before the 1990s, the first is the senior lectureship for which there is no allocation to departments but competition across the entire institution. Entry is based again on assessments of the lecturer's conduct in the three main areas of academic life, and in many universities these include evaluations of research performance and potential from outside experts. (The Universities of Oxford and Cambridge are exceptions to this: they do not have a senior lecturer grade, and their salary scale for lecturers is much longer.) The next level is the readership, a position generally reserved for scholars with established research records. The criteria for promotion to it require excellence in research (as demonstrated by their publications and influence) alongside satisfactory performance (at least) on the other criteria. In many universities it is now possible for promotion directly from lectureship to readership. In the post-1990 universities (most of them originally established as polytechnics) the promotional grades were principal and senior lecturer, with readerships only very rarely created.

The final grade (associated with academic departments as against administration of the university as a whole) is the professorship. Although superior in status to the others, this may not be a promotional category: until recently most professors were appointed from open competition preceded by public advertisements. Initially the posts of professor and of head of department were synonymous, so a professor was appointed (from a field of applicants after public advertisement) as an administrative head, to provide both managerial and academic leadership. With growing departmental size in recent decades, however, and the development of specialized sub-fields within disciplines, each requiring separate leadership, it has become common for departments to have several professors. In most, the headship is a position independent of the professoriat to which other grades may aspire, although many heads are also professors. (The post-1990 universities had very few professorships while they were polytechnics.)

Finally, in the British model promotion is possible to non-advertised, personal professorships. These positions are becoming increasingly common; in most cases, a personal professorship is awarded for excellence in research and scholarship.

The system under the *American model* is simpler. There are three permanent staff (or 'faculty' as they are known there) categories: assistant professor, associate professor and professor. The first contains two sub-categories – those staff on probation who do not have 'tenure' and those with security of tenure. Each category has its own salary range but no automatic annual increments. (In the United States, these scales vary from university to university; the United Kingdom has a national salary scale that applies in all universities with only slight local modifications.) Salary adjustments result from personal bargaining, on the basis of academic activity in the three areas already listed, and salaries for the three categories may overlap within a department. Movement from one category to another is promotional, as a recognition of academic excellence. Professorships are simply the highest promotional grade and do not carry obligatory major administrative tasks. Heads (more usually termed Chairs) of departments in the American model are separately appointed, usually for a limited period only, and they need not be professors (usually referred to as 'full professors').

Status, rewards and promotion prospects

The rewards for academics are the salary levels, the profession's general status, the particular standing of its individual promotional categories, the relative independence and flexibility of the working conditions, and the intrinsic benefits of being involved in teaching, learning and original research. The tangible rewards – the payments – are determined by the academic's position within the career structure. Promotion must be 'earned'.

Academic work has three main components – research, teaching, and administration. Entrants to the profession have little or no experience of academic administration and their only teaching has probably been as assistants to others. Thus it is very largely on proven and potential research ability that an aspirant's initial potential for an academic career is judged. Research ability can be partly equated with probable teaching and administrative competence, since all require some of the same personal qualities – enthusiasm, orderliness, incisive thinking, and ability to communicate orally and in writing: most universities provide appointees with training in teaching and administrative skills. To a considerable extent, however, academics gain their first position on faith in their potential (as demonstrated by their letters of application and curricula vitae, references, and their performance at formal and informal evaluation processes, such as interviews and seminars), hence the usual probationary periods before tenure is granted.

Once admitted to the profession, staff undertake all three types of work, so that promotional prospects can be more widely assessed. Teaching and administration have traditionally carried less weight with those responsible for promotions than research. This is partly because of perceived difficulties in assessing performance in the first two, and partly because of a general academic ethos which gives prime place to research activity in peer evaluation.

Although not necessarily progressive in terms of increasing level of difficulty, administrative tasks tend to be more complex and demanding of political and personal judgement and skills as the academic becomes more senior. A person's ability to undertake a certain task can often only be fully assessed after appointment or promotion to the relevant position (this has been called the 'Peter principle': Peter and Hull, 1969), so decisions must frequently be based on perceived potential; although it is possible to point to somebody whose administrative skills are insubstantial, it is not always easy to assess who will be able to cope with the more demanding tasks.

It has long been argued that assessment of teaching ability is difficult (although clear inability is often very apparent). Student and peer evaluations are possible and are increasingly used, as is external scrutiny of students' work. But criteria for judging teaching performance at university level are ill-defined, and expectations of a lecturer, tutor or seminar leader often vary quite considerably within even a small group of students, as well as among external assessors. Thus the majority of teachers are usually accepted as competent if undistinguished. (The 'inspections' of teaching sessions – most of them lectures – undertaken during the 1995 Quality Assessment of Teaching in English University Departments of Geography invariably rated the majority as 'satisfactory', with a substantial minority being deemed 'excellent' and very few – none in most cases – 'unsatisfactory': Johnston, 1996f.) In most universities now, promotion exercises require proven excellence in at least two of the three criteria generally considered – research, teaching and administration; some add a fourth criterion – service to the wider community.

Research performance is a major criterion for promotion, therefore, although a relatively undistinguished record in this area can be compensated by excellence elsewhere. (Some argue that teaching competence is not only undervalued, but that as a consequence of the increasing emphasis on research in most universities it is receiving less attention: Jenkins, 1995; Sidaway, 1997.) How is research ability judged? Details of how research is undertaken are considered in the next section; here the concern is with its assessment rather than with stimulus and substance.

Successful research involves making an original contribution to a field of knowledge. It may involve the collection, presentation and analysis of new information, within an accepted framework; it may be the development of new ways of collecting, analysing and presenting facts; it may comprise promoting a new way of ordering facts – a new theory or hypothesis; or it may be some combination of all three. Its originality is judged through its acceptance by those of proven expertise in the particular field. The generally accepted validation procedure is publication, hence adages such as 'unpublished research isn't research' and 'publish or perish'.

The main publishing outlets for research findings in most disciplines are their scholarly journals, which operate fairly standard procedures for scrutinizing submitted contributions. Some of the major journals are published by academic learned societies and others by commercial companies (Luke, 2000; Johnston, 2003d). Manuscripts are submitted to the editor, who seeks the advice of qualified academics on the merits of the contribution; these referees will recommend either publication, rejection, or revision and resubmission. When accepted, a manuscript will enter the publication queue, which may be up to two years long.

Although widely accepted, this procedure is subjective, because it is operated by human decision-makers. The opinions of both editor (on the manuscript and on the choice of referees) and referees may be biased or partial, so a paper can be rejected by one journal but accepted by another, even without alteration. (On the canons of editorship see, for example, Hart, 1990 and Taylor, 1990c; for a radical alternative, see Symanski and Picard, 1996.) Most disciplines have an informal prestige ranking of journals, and it is considered more desirable to publish in some rather than others, because of the stringency of their review procedures, their circulation, readership and hence visibility, and their generally-assumed status (Luke, 2000; Johnston, 2003f). In addition, over recent decades much effort has been put into the development of citation indices to rate journals, individual articles in journals (plus books), and authors. An American company (ISI) scans all the items referenced in a large selection of journals. Collation of this material allows it to provide data on: the number of times each author is cited by others – taken as evidence of the impact and importance of her/his work; the number of times each item is cited – taken as evidence of its importance in advancing knowledge; and the number of times each journal is cited – taken as evidence of the importance and impact of the items it publishes. (Yeung, 2002, details how these citation counts and impact factors are calculated. Several geographers have deployed them to identify the most influential geographers according to their citation frequency: e.g. Bodman, 1991, 1992; Whitehand, 1985.) Citation counts for individuals and the journals in which they publish are often taken into consideration by appointment and promotion committees. The issue of the standing of journals and the use of citation counts has become crucial in the UK since the mid-1980s because of the use of publication data as a performance indicator for the periodic RAEs, which not only rate every department but also determine its future funding (the better get more money; see Johnston, 1993b – see p. 30).

Some research results are published in book form, rather than as journal articles. Most academic books in geography are texts, however, published by commercial companies whose main interest is marketability among the large student population. The textbook may be innovative in the way that it orders and presents material, and can be beneficial to its author's reputation (and bank balance), but it is not usually a vehicle for demonstrating research ability. (On types of books published, see Johnston, 1986a, pp. 165–6.) Many companies, including university presses, publish research monographs, however, presenting the results of major research projects or theoretical elaborations to relatively small academic markets. Their decisions on whether to publish are made on academic as well as commercial grounds, usually with the aid of academic referees, and their output is validated through the journal book-review columns.

Processes of promotion and appointment: patronage

Whatever the weighting given by appointment and promotion committees to the three main academic activities (others are pursued by some, such as consulting for outside bodies and contributions to the work of learned societies), how they make assessments is frequently contentious. One of the main sets of 'objective' information that can be presented to them is lists of publications, most of which have been validated by academic journals. But how is such information evaluated?

Two modes of assessment are widely used and relied upon: the written opinion of a third party (either a referee, selected by the applicant, or an assessor, selected by the committee); and the interview, sometimes associated with presentation of a lecture or seminar. The British model places considerable weight on the former. Applicants must supply a list of referees who will provide opinions on their suitability for the post: applicants are likely to ask people, especially senior people they have worked with, and are believed to be favourably inclined towards them, to act in this capacity. As appointment committees tend to be influenced by such evaluations, especially when preparing a shortlist of candidates to be interviewed, the opinions of well-respected referees are often crucial. Thus, certain leaders in a subject often find it easier to get their candidates appointed to posts than do others: there is a considerable element of patronage involved in obtaining a university post, especially a first university post. Increasingly, too, it seems that appointment committees for junior posts are influenced by where candidates obtained their postgraduate training: attendance at a highly-rated graduate school is considered an advantage.

Promotions under the British model are frequently strongly influenced by the head of the candidate's department, although in most places now he or she is expected to consult senior colleagues before making a recommendation. Reports must be made on each lecturer: annually during the probation period; at the confirmation stage after probation; on reaching the 'efficiency bar'; and for either accelerated promotion within the lecturer scale (or beyond it, to 'discretionary points'), or promotion to senior lecturer. This also contains a strong element of patronage, although constraints are built into the committee system to promote fairness for all, including the right either to present one's own case or to appeal against a decision. Some universities use outside referees and assessors when considering promotions to senior lecturer; promotions to readerships and professorships almost invariably involve such consultation.

Referees, assessors and interviews are also used in the appointment of professors. Referees nominated by the candidates provide a confidential report on their potential for the job in question. Assessors nominated by the university evaluate the list of candidates, suggest other worthy candidates who might be approached, and in many cases attend the formal interviews: their potential patronage power is great.

Procedures are slightly different under the American model. More weight is usually given to an enlarged interview, with candidates giving seminars to the department and meeting with various groups of staff. (Such procedures are increasingly used in British universities.) The reference is still important, however, especially for aspirants to first teaching positions, and a letter from a respected leader in a field, especially one working in a prestigious graduate school, can be very influential in gaining an appointment for a former student. The individual candidate is more active in this system than in the British, however, perhaps canvassing for interviews during the annual conferences of scholarly societies, for example. For promotions and for salary rises there is considerable bargaining between individual, department chair and university administrators; external referees' opinions may be sought when tenure is being confirmed, or promotion to full professor proposed.

In all of these procedures the applicants depend to a considerable extent on the opinions of senior academic colleagues in evaluating their potential, performance and prospects. Some opinions carry more weight than others, and so it is important when developing a career to identify potentially influential individuals, to keep them informed of your work, and to enlist their support for your advancement. Because of the lack of truly objective criteria for measuring research, teaching and administrative ability, such patronage is crucial.

Other rewards and the sources of status

The tangible rewards of an academic career are the salary and the lifestyle, plus the occasional extra earnings that are possible – for examining, writing, lecturing, and consulting. In addition the hours are flexible, the possibilities for travel are considerable, and the constraints on when, where, and how work is done are relatively few compared with most other professions (on which see discussions of recent labour contracts: Rose and Prevalin, 2003). Other, less tangible, rewards include involvement with the intellectual development of students. There is also the charisma associated with recognized excellent teachers, and even more so for leading researchers, whose publications are widely read, whose invitations to give outside lectures are many, and whose opinions as examiners, referees and reviewers are widely canvassed. The conduct of research brings its own rewards, apart from the charisma; the satisfaction from having identified and solved a significant problem is often considerable, as is that from publishing a widely – and positively – cited article or book.

Academic life also offers a reward common to many social systems: power. Patronage is power, as is work as examiner, referee or reviewer. Others' careers are being affected, and exercise of this power can bring with it the loyalty and respect of those who benefit. Because the academic system is so dependent on individuals' opinions, because some individuals' opinions are more valued than others', and because power is a 'commodity' widely desired in most societies, many academics seek positions of influence.

Among the most influential positions in an academic discipline are the administrative headships of departments. Their holders can instruct other staff members (usually after consultation) in their teaching and administrative duties, they are frequently used by staff and students as referees for job and other (such as research grant) applications and their reports are crucial in the promotions procedure. The departmental organization of universities is a bureaucratic device which makes for relative ease in administering what may be a very large institution. (It also tends to fossilize disciplinary boundaries, as will be discussed later.) Departmental heads not only have power over members of their own discipline's staff, they also participate in their university's administration, and they treat within its committee system for departmental resources. As in all bureaucracies, there is a tendency for the status and power of the various departmental heads to be a function of the size of their 'empires' (Tullock, 1976; large departments in British universities certainly get the highest research ratings: Johnston, Jones and Gould, 1995). Heads of large departments, especially those which are also growing (growth being widely considered a 'good thing') and those attracting large numbers of students and research grants/contracts, are very often the most influential within a bureaucracy. Their heads have the incentive to build up their departments, which usually means increasing student numbers, since universities tend to allocate at least a major portion of their resources according to the numbers taught. This brings power and prestige, both within the university and beyond; it is an added reward for the academic bureaucrat, and the power over resources which it involves usually benefits the whole department. The successful department head may find that it leads to appointments to more senior positions within the university, such as a Deanship, overseeing the work of a group of departments.

Finally, the academic bureaucrat can gain power beyond the home university through, for example, positions on committees. These may be concerned with the subject through professional bodies, with the allocation of research moneys by public or private foundations, including government-funded Research Councils, or with a wide range of public duties. Again, the status and power obtained can spill over to others, since patronage is important in all of those roles.

Conclusions

The thesis of this chapter is that the history of an academic discipline must be set in a context comprising three elements: the occupational structure; the organizational framework for research; and the societal environment. These three interact in a variety of ways. The occupational structure is very much constrained by the societal environment, for example, as indicated by the negligible opportunities for promotion in British universities in the late 1970s and early 1980s because of the cuts in educational funding. Similarly, the framework for research, although established by and for academics, is subject to societal support. Some frameworks are much more acceptable than others, and so are more likely to receive the needed public finance.

In the following chapters, the content of human geography in Britain and North America since the Second World War is reviewed, within the context set by this discussion. The emphasis is on 'extraordinary research' rather than the cumulative achievements of 'normal science', stressing the debates over how research should be done in human geography. No attempt is made to test the models outlined in the section above on 'the academic working environment', although the ideas outlined there have clearly influenced the organization of the book. The main purpose is to present a reasoned summary of debates in human geography (the discipline being defined as comprising that which is claimed as human geography), based principally on the published record. The relationship between this summary and the models of scientific progress only resurfaces in the final chapter.

2
Foundations

*... **geographical imagination** A sensitivity towards the significance of PLACE and SPACE, LANDSCAPE and NATURE in the constitution and conduct of life on earth. As such, a geographical imagination is by no means the exclusive preserve of the academic discipline of geography ...*

(Gregory, 2000, p. 298)

Although this book is about human geography since 1945, any discussion of that period requires a brief outline of the nature of the discipline in preceding decades, for several reasons. The first is that although 1945 was a watershed year in many aspects of the social, economic and intellectual life of the countries being considered, it was not a significant divide in the views on geographical philosophy and methodology. Not surprisingly, the war years were not a major period of intra-disciplinary academic debate. Most academics spent the time either on active service or in associated intelligence activities: although some of those involved in the latter retained their teaching commitments, for most the everyday activities of teaching, pure research and administration were replaced by commitment to the war effort. (On UK geographers' war activities, see Balchin, 1987; on the US, see Stone, 1979.) It took a few years for academic life to return to something like normality, to assimilate the large numbers of new staff needed to replace the losses of the war years, to teach the backlog of students and to react to the new social and economic environments.

A second reason for retrospection relates to the processes of change in academic work. New paradigms are responses to the perceived failings of those currently in favour, not inventions produced in an intellectual vacuum. Thus post-1945 changes were reactions to the philosophies and methodologies developed and taught in the preceding decades; reactions to them cannot be studied without some knowledge of what went before.

Finally, change is not instantaneous in academic life. A new research programme may take years to mature, while experimentation with alternatives takes place, the programmatic statements are written, and converts are won over by prophets of the new approach. Meanwhile, the current paradigm prevails (or paradigms, if several have considerable support). Adherents continue in their accepted ways, researching, publishing and teaching generations of undergraduates according to the conventional wisdom. Even when a new paradigm has been crystallized, it may have to co-exist with its predecessors for several years, while competing for support among academics. This may be especially characteristic of the social sciences, in which interpretations of data are more evidently subjective than in the physical sciences; it is quite feasible for two or more separate world views to find adherents at the same time, quite possibly in the same academic department.

Geography in the modern period

The hallmark of an academic discipline, according to James (1972), is an educational organization which provides specialist training in the subject. James dates the beginning of such an organization for geography around 1874, when the first ten university geography departments were established in Germany (Wardenga, 1999; Schelhaas and Hönsch, 2002; see also Taylor, 1985c). Britain and the United States followed a little later, with the main developments there coming in the twentieth century. Thus, although the first modern geographical society was established in Paris, German universities took the lead in the establishment of geography as a distinctive field of modern study. Claval (1981, pp. 96–7, our translation) notes how:

> Towards the 1860s the economic development of Germany had been accompanied by the development of applied sciences, and the accompanying development of the universities itself demanded that they redefined their functions. ... it was the presence of geography in primary education that was the main stimulus to the growth in numbers of university teachers of geography after 1874. ... Certainly the new situation created by the unification of Germany between 1864 and 1871 imposed new demands in terms of texts and geography courses at the primary and secondary level. To this must be added the requirements of German imperialism ... the formation of the German empire in 1871 and the acquisition of colonies from 1884–85 (after the Congress of Berlin) gave birth to a new politics which was the impulse to the creation of new university posts in and departments of geography.

Before then, geography was investigated either by amateurs or by scientists trained in other fields. In the UK, for example, geography was a recognized area of scholarly work for several centuries, even though it had no separate disciplinary or departmental identity in the small number of universities then operating. Map-making, exploration and chorography (the description of the characteristics of different areas) were all taught at English and Scottish universities by the end of the sixteenth century, for example (Cormack, 1997; Withers and Mayhew, 2002). Geographical knowledge was important to traders who, along with bankers and private individuals, invested in expeditions in the expectation of benefiting commercially from the new knowledge obtained – about new lands and potential resources, for example, as well as new and quicker routes to known destinations. Increasingly, those involved in the exploitation of such resources called for state support and protection for their activities and contributions to the national wealth, which stimulated state-sponsored settlement, colonization and the growth of imperial naval power. The practice of geography was central to this imperial ethos of much of nineteenth century Europe.

Promotion of geography in this context involved the establishment of geographical societies in many national capitals and major trading cities. Among the first were those founded in Paris (1821), Berlin (1828), London (1830) and St. Petersburg (1845), with later creations in Manchester in 1884, Newcastle upon Tyne in 1887, Liverpool in 1891 and Southampton in 1897 (see Johnston 2003a, and, for a wider view, Heffernan, 2003). Many of these societies had royal patronage and were strongly supported by members of the mercantile, diplomatic and military classes. Their main roles were to collate and publish information, to sponsor expeditions, and to foster relevant scientific developments – as in navigational and mapping methods. A similar society – the American Geographical Society – was established in New York in 1851 as 'a merchant's information bureau' (Koelsch, 2002, p. 253).

Increasingly, these societies became involved in educational activities, promoting geography as a subject in their countries' schools and universities. In the UK, for example, the Royal Geographical Society (RGS) lobbied for geography's presence in the evolving school curricula (Keltie, 1886; Wise, 1986) and then, in the nineteenth century's last decades, turned its attention to the universities, realizing that to sustain the subject's presence in schools required trained teachers who had a university qualification in the discipline. The Society's attentions were focused on the Universities of Cambridge and Oxford, where posts were established, with RGS support for nearly 40 years, in the late 1880s, although chairs were not filled in either until the 1930s. (See Stoddart, 1975a, and Scargill, 1976.) Other universities took the lead in establishing full departments and degree programmes (Slater, 1988) – the first was at Liverpool in 1917 – as a result of varying pressures for geography teaching. Some of this pressure came from cognate disciplines, notably geology and economics, which required geography courses within their syllabuses: the first permanent chair was held by L. W. Lyde at University College London, for example, who was appointed to teach geography for economics students in 1903 (see Dickinson, 1976). By the Second World War, there was a geography department (albeit invariably small) in virtually every university and university college in the UK, and many of those in the British Empire too. (For more detail on this aspect of the discipline's history there, see Johnston 2003a. The essays in Steel, 1987, discuss British geography in the 1930s.)

There was no central pressure for geographical education in the United States to parallel that of the RGS, largely because of the decentralized nature of educational systems there. The establishment of geography teaching in some of the country's universities resulted from perceived needs in other degree programmes. One of these was geology, and some of geography's early protagonists – such as William Morris Davis (see p. 46) at Harvard – were trained geologists. Departments of economics and schools of business and commerce also identified the need for geography teaching (much of it in economic or commercial geography), and some of the earliest appointments of individuals to teach geography were in such institutions (Fellmann, 1986): indeed, the first fully-fledged department of geography – at the University of California Berkeley campus – emerged from such an origin, in 1898. Many of the courses had lapsed by 1920, but by then geography had been established elsewhere in a number of universities, although to nothing like the same relative extent as in the UK.

The geography degree programmes that were inaugurated involved individual teachers, many of whom were trained in other disciplines, but who were attracted to geography by its core interest in the relationships between people and their environments. Many of their stimuli came from early work in Germany and France, where a number went to study. By virtue of their primacy in establishing geography departments and the intellectual heritage of Humboldt and Ritter (see p. 48), French and especially German influences were strong in the original formulation of geographers' core agenda (Claval, 1981).

The late nineteenth and early twentieth centuries thus saw the transition from what James (1972) termed geography's classical age into its modern period. This lasted for about eighty years, being superseded after 1945 by what he calls its contemporary period.

James's modern period is virtually co-extensive with the decades surveyed in Freeman's (1961) *A Hundred Years of Geography*. He identified six inter-related trends in the geographical literature up to c.1960.

1. *The encyclopaedic trend* covered the collection of information about the world, particularly areas little known to Western Europeans and North Americans. Although the great age of discovery was over, and by the late nineteenth century much of the world had been visited by European explorers, vast tracts remained, notably in Africa, which if not *terra incognita* were almost empty on contemporary maps. Indeed, at the beginning of geography's modern period much of the North American continent itself remained to be settled by permanent farms.

2. *The educational trend*, in which the nascent academic discipline was establishing its role and relevance in educational systems, thereby ensuring its reproduction. (On the role of the RGS in this in the UK, see Freeman, 1980a, 1980b. On that of the Geographical Association, founded in 1893, see Balchin, 1993 and Walford, 2001.)

3. *The colonial trend* reflected a major preoccupation during the modern period's early decades, especially in Britain whose empire was being consolidated and developed into a spatial division of labour based on its metropolitan hub (see Driver, 1998, and the essays in Bell, Butlin and Heffernan, 1995). Organization of the commercial world required a great deal of information about the various countries concerned, the provision of which became a major task of geographical research while its propagation was the keystone of geographical education. Furthermore, part of the creation of an imperial national identity and ethos involved educational activities which gave children a sense of their identity in the world – and, by implication at least, of their superiority and that of their environment. (On school texts in the period, see Ploszajska, 1999, and Smith, 2001. Buttimer and Fahy, 1999, p. 179, argue that school geography in Ireland has been taught 'as an *instrumentum regni*, to transmit political, economic, and social attitudes of prevailing regimes . . . *transmitting* images rather than *evoking curiosity*'. More widely, on the role of geography as popularly understood in the creation of world views, see Schulten, 2001.) Geography was centrally involved in the creation of this imperial identity in the UK. In the USA, however, geographers were less involved, and a particular notion of American identity and destiny was created by historians such as Frederick Jackson Turner, who associated the American nation with its expanding frontiers: Kearns, 1984.

4. *The generalizing trend* describes the use to which data collected in the encyclopaedic and colonial traditions were increasingly employed. Academic study involved more than collecting and collating facts: these had to be interpreted, and the methods and aims of such interpretation defined the early paradigms of the discipline's development – as discussed below.

5. *The political trend* was reflected in the contemporary uses made of geographical expertise. Isaiah Bowman, trained at Harvard under Davis, became Director of the American Geographical Society in 1915, and was selected as an adviser to Woodrow Wilson at the conferences which re-drew the map of the world after the First World War (on which see Martin, 1980, and Smith, 1994), for example. He subsequently wrote one of the first books on political geography (Bowman, 1921. On Bowman's career, see Smith, 2003). In the UK, the first appointee to the School of Geography at the University of Oxford – H. J. (later Sir Halford) Mackinder – also wrote on political geography. His heartland model (Mackinder, 1890, 1904) presented the Eurasian continent as the fulcrum of world power, as encapsulated in the triplet:

    Who rules East Europe commands the Heartland;
    Who rules the Heartland commands the World-Island;
    Who rules the World-Island commands the World.

    Mackinder later became an MP and then a diplomat, but continued to write on geopolitical issues until the 1940s: his *Democratic Ideals and Reality* (Mackinder, 1919) summarized his views. (On Mackinder's career, see Blouet, 1987, and Parker, 1982.)

6. *The specialization trend* was a reaction to the growth of knowledge and the inability of any one individual to master it all, even within the single discipline of geography. Prior to the modern period, many scientists and other academics were extremely catholic in their interests and expertise. As the volume of research literature increased and the techniques of investigation demanded longer and more rigorous training so it became necessary to specialize first, in this context, as a geographer and then within geography.

From these trends three major paradigms (as disciplinary matrices) can be identified as characterizing the modern period in human geography. The development of each of these paradigms was strongly influenced by a small number of individuals, who left lasting impressions on the nature of geography as an academic discipline. Until after the Second World War there were very few geographers working in universities, and many of them had no training in the discipline. Their main role was as teachers, and many of them did relatively little research or publication of original work. A small number took up leadership roles, however, defining geography's academic agenda and strongly influencing what the discipline studied and its methods. Most of these occupied powerful positions within the discipline – as professors and departmental heads, for example – and were able, through combinations of the force of their personalities, the strength of their arguments and carefully-chosen appointments to their own and other departments, to play crucial roles in setting the discipline's academic directions. There were differences and debates, of course, but in small communities only a few ideas generally prevailed – a very different situation from the pluralism that developed in the second half of the twentieth century as geographers became much more numerous and key individuals, though still important, were less dominant.

Exploration

This first approach was carried over from the classical period; exploration was the major activity recognized as geography through most of the nineteenth century. The collection and classification of information about 'unknown' parts of the earth (unknown, that is, to Western Europeans and North Americans) was undertaken by explorers and navigators, with many of their expeditions sponsored by geographical societies. Information gained was used to enhance cartographic knowledge, and was disseminated widely through lectures and books. The map of the world was completed and filled in at an increasing pace.

The importance of exploration within geography declined in the late nineteenth century, although soon after his appointment at Oxford, Mackinder (who had been trained as a biologist) felt it necessary to establish his credentials as a geographer by becoming the first recorded person to climb Mt. Kenya. Much *terra incognita* remained, however, and the geographical societies maintained their interest in and sponsorship of expeditions: the RGS does so still. The work undertaken is very different from that of a century ago, reflecting developments in scientific technology and the available store of knowledge, but basic activities such as accurate map-making remain crucial to many successful expeditions – especially in more remote parts of the globe.

The American Geographical Society (AGS) also broadened from the exploration role on which it focused early in the modern period, but while promoting research in other areas of geography (see p. 73) it still supported investigations of relatively unstudied environments, such as the Arctic. The exploration tradition is maintained in the United States by the National Geographical Society (NGS) and its popular journal, the *National Geographic Magazine*. Like other magazines – such as *New Zealand Geographic* and the *Geographical* magazine (produced by the RGS, whose fellowship covers a wide range of interests beyond academic geography) – the *National Geographic* concentrates, though not exclusively, on material illustrating the relationships between people and their environments (with copious high quality photographic material and maps). In such media, the boundaries of geography and natural history are imprecise. (The NGS also has a TV channel devoted to similar material, and has given large sums of money in recent years to develop geographical programmes for US schools, after surveys revealed considerable ignorance about what is where in the world.)

Although most of it was not strictly exploration, the work summarized by Freeman under the colonial trend can be included here, since its aims were the collection, collation and dissemination of information. Much of the material was about commercial activities and infrastructure, as in volumes such as Chisholm's *Handbook of Commercial Geography* (first edition, 1899) and *Gazetteer of the World* (1895), which were aimed at the world of commerce, with companion volumes for schools (Wise, 1975). Their content comprised statistics and descriptions of production and trade, and a training in this type of geography was considered too limited (and indeed boring) by many because of its focus on the assimilation of large bodies of factual knowledge ('capes and bays' geography). Similar texts were produced in the USA (Barnes, 2001a; Fellmann, 1986; Lawton and Miller, 2001).

The value of such geographical information and expertise was widely recognized, and was called on during both World Wars when geographers were recruited into intelligence services. In the UK, for example, they were responsible for the preparation of reports about areas in which Allied troops were likely to be engaged, and their Second World War British Admiralty Handbooks (edited at Oxford and Cambridge under the leadership of Kenneth Mason and Clifford Darby, respectively: Clout, 2003a; Clout and Gosme, 2003) were put on sale afterwards. The comparable volumes produced in the United States by the Office of Strategic Services (of which Hartshorne was Deputy Head) – the Joint Army-Navy Intelligence Studies – remained classified documents, however.

Environmental determinism and possibilism

Environmental determinism and possibilism represented the first attempts at generalization by geographers during the modern period. Instead of merely presenting information in an organized manner, either topically or by area, geographers sought explanations for the patterns of human occupation of the earth's surface. Their major initial source for explanations was the physical environment, and a position was established around the belief that the nature of human activity was controlled by the parameters of the physical world within which it was set.

The origins of this environmental determinism lie in the work of Charles Darwin, whose seminal book *On the Origin of Species* (first published in 1859) influenced many scientists (see Livingstone, 1992; Armstrong, 1999, argues that Darwin was influenced by the pioneer geographer-naturalist Humboldt: see p. 48). Darwin's notions regarding evolution were taken up by an American geographer, William Morris Davis, in his cycle-of-erosion model of landform development (Vale, 2002). Ideas of natural selection and adaptation formed the basis of statements regarding environmental determinism, including Davis's (1906) programmatic paper identifying the core of geography as the relationship between the physical environment as the control, and human behaviour as the response (Stoddart, 1966; Martin, 1981; see also Campbell and Livingstone, 1983, and Livingstone, 1984 on the influence of Lamarckism in the development of geography, and Peet, 1985a, on a similar theme).

Chief among the late nineteenth-century environmental determinists was a German geographer, Freidrich Ratzel, who was trained in biology and anthropology. His *Anthropogeographie* (Ratzel, 1882–91) related the course of history to the earth's physical features (illustrating the survival of the fittest principle); and his *Politische Geographie* (Ratzel, 1897) adapted Darwinian arguments to states, which he treated as organisms that struggle for land (*Lebensraum*, or living space), with the strongest states able to expand territorially. This argument was later taken up by a Swedish conservative political scientist (Rudolf Kjellen) who coined the term geopolitics to signify the codification and study of this mode of political geography. Later, in the 1920s and 1930s, a German military officer and geographer (Karl Haushofer) elaborated such geopolitics to provide an element of the putatively 'scientific' underpinning for the 1930s–1940s Nazi policy policies of territorial expansion (Kost, 1989; Natter 2003; Parker, 1985). In turn, however, geopolitics soon acquired a life of its own with work in many European countries and Japan, as part of a wider conversation about sovereignty, space and power, in which geographers played a central (though not exclusive) role (see Dodds and Atkinson, 2000).

Ratzel's ideas were also promoted in the US by Ellen Churchill Semple, who opened her book *Influences of Geographic Environment* (1911) with the statement that 'Man is the product of the earth's surface'. Davis, as noted above, also adopted Ratzel's general approach, as did other productive and influential geographers – such as Davis's student, Ellsworth Huntington, who advanced theories relating the course of civilization to climate and climatic change (Huntington, 1915, 1945). In some hands, the environmental influences adduced were gross, and with hindsight it is hard to believe that they were taken seriously; Tatham (1953), for example, illustrates the extent to which authors were prepared to credit all aspects of human behaviour with an environmental cause.

Reaction to the extreme generalizations of the environmental determinists led to a counter-thesis, that of possibilism, which presented individuals as active rather than passive agents. Led by French geographers, followers of the *Annales*-school historian Lucien Febvre, the possibilist model had people perceiving the range of alternative uses to which they could put an environment and selecting that which best fitted their cultural dispositions. Taken to extremes, this approach could be as ludicrous as that which it opposed, but possibilists generally recognized the limits to action which environments set, and avoided the great generalizations which characterized their antagonists.

Debate over environmental determinism and possibilism continued into the 1960s (Lewthwaite, 1966; Spate, 1957, for example, proposed a middle ground with the concept of 'probabilism'). The doughtiest advocate of the determinist cause was the Australian Griffith Taylor, whose views so angered politicians interested in the white settlement of outback Australia that he was virtually hounded out of his homeland (Powell, 1980a). He argued that possibilists had developed their ideas in temperate environments which offer several viable alternative forms of human occupance. But such environments are rare: in most of the world – as in Australia – the environment is much more extreme and its control over human activity accordingly much greater. He coined the phrase 'stop-and-go' determinism to describe his views. In the short term, people might attempt whatever they wished with regard to their environment, but in the long term, nature's plan would ensure that the environment won the battle and forced a compromise out of its human occupants.

Many debates begin as two opposing, extreme views, and end with a compromise accepted by all but the most fervent devotees of each polar position. Thus, the lengthy discussion among geographers about whether people are free agents in their use of the earth or whether there is a 'nature's plan' slowly dissolved as the antagonists realized the merits in each case. (And some geographers studied human–environment interactions outside the confines of these debates: see Fleure, 1919.) While geographers strongly promoted environmental determinism, however, respect for their discipline was relatively low in the wider academic community, which rejected the approach. As a consequence, geography's next focus, which nevertheless had strong roots in environmental determinism, was very much an introspective and conservative one.

The region and regional geography

This third approach dominated British and American geography for much of the first half of the twentieth century. Like environmental determinism, it was an attempt at generalization, but it lacked structured explanation and so was of a very different type from the increasingly discredited law-making attempts of the previous writings (although much of it had strong implicit connections with environmental determinism).

More so than its predecessors, this third approach drew heavily on developments in Germany and France, where the roots of much contemporary geography can be found. Of great importance in Germany was the work of two individuals whom many identify as the founders of modern geography. Both died in 1859, one having established the modern roots of what became known as systematic geography and the other having performed a similar task for regional geography. And both accepted the definition of geography set out by the Enlightenment philosopher, Immanuel Kant (1724–1804), who lectured on physical geography at the University of Königsberg. He argued that knowledge can be organized and classified in two ways: because of similarities in origin wherever they occur (the logical classification, which is the basis of the various sciences); or because of similarities in when or where they occur – the discipline that looks at similarities in terms of time is history, whereas that which looks at similarities in terms of place of occurrence is geography (see May, 1970).

Alexander von Humboldt (1769–1859) was a naturalist with very broad scientific interests. He spent five years travelling in Central and South America, where he amassed a great deal of information about the environment and its exploitation by humans. He assembled this material (over a 20-year period in Paris) to show how environments varied, with differences in agricultural practices and patterns of human settlement reflecting interactions among altitude, temperature and vegetation. From this base, he developed an approach to the discipline which emphasized field collection of data and its synthesis through maps, leading to inductive generalizations regarding environmental characteristics and their links with human activity. The remainder of his career was spent assembling similar materials from a wide range of sources, which were then synthesized in his major published work – the five-volume *Kosmos* (Humboldt, 1845–62). In the first volume (1845), he provided an overview of the universe, which was followed by a volume (1847) on representations of the earth in art and literature and a history of scientific writing on the earth since Egyptian times; the third volume (1850) is largely concerned with astronomy. The fourth (1858) turned to human interactions with the earth, with a vast range of observational material described and used to derive generalizations about those inter-relationships; the final volume (published posthumously in 1862) dealt with geology and volcanology. (On Humboldt, see Martin and James, 1993; Bowen, 1970, 1981.)

Karl Ritter (1779–1859) was trained in a variety of disciplines – during which time he met, and was impressed by, Humboldt – and by 1811 had published a two-volume work on the geography of Germany. He was appointed to a chair of geography in Berlin in 1820 (a year after a similar appointment in history in Frankfurt). After early field work in Italy and Switzerland, as well as Germany, he travelled little and his teaching at Berlin and elsewhere was largely based on secondary sources. He focused on the connections between phenomena in places – of 'unity in diversity', which he believed represented 'God's plan'. This involved defining regions, separate areas of the earth's surface with distinct assemblages of phenomena. The material accumulated was used to produce his 19-volume (unfinished) *Erdkunde* (Ritter, 1817–59).

Regional geography was also the main focus of a third influential geographer – Paul Vidal de la Blache (1845–1918) who, unlike von Humboldt and Ritter, obtained a higher degree in geography after initial training in ancient history and literature. He was appointed to a post at the Sorbonne in 1898, where he maintained close links with the *Annales* school of historians. French geography had strong early connections to both mapping and history (Claval, 1999), and these were sustained by Vidal's concentration on defining and describing regions, relatively small homogeneous areas (*pays*) whose distinctive *genres de vie* resulted from the interactions of people with their physical milieux. Unlike some of his German contemporaries, however, he did not see those interactions as predominantly determined by the physical environment. He was attracted to possibilism (which he first encountered in Ratzel's *Anthropogeographie*). The environment offers people a range of options, and they choose how to modify nature according to their cultural and technological inheritances – as Lucien Febvre put it, 'nowhere necessities … everywhere possibilities'. Vidal's major contributions were his *Tableau de la Géographie de la France* (1903), an introduction to the multi-volume *Histoire de la France* (see Ozouf-Marignier and Robic, 1999), and the 15-volume *Géographie Universelle*, finished in 1948. Many of his students wrote dissertations on individual *pays*; they dominated French geography through the first half of the twentieth century (Buttimer, 1971) and fitted into the conservative and nationalist milieu of interwar France amidst territorial threats from Germany (see Gregory, 1994; Heffernan, 2001). French regional geography thus emphasized France's essential 'unity in diversity', blending climatic and cultural influences from the Mediterranean to the Atlantic into an essential *élan Francais*.

The early development of geography in Germany and France relative to the UK and the USA meant that as the academic discipline was being established in the latter countries some of those attracted to it sought inspiration and training from French and German sources. There was considerable interaction as well as reference to relevant literature, and it was the norm at both British and US universities during the first half of the twentieth century for would-be geographers to be fluent in one if not both of German and French. In these ways, ideas about the nature of geography infiltrated the English-speaking world from continental Europe. They were modified to fit local circumstances, but dominated contemporary thinking for several decades.

Hartshorne and the American view

The ideas and methods of regional geography were taken up in the United States after environmental determinism had been largely rejected, with several alternatives initially explored – such as geography as human ecology (the title of Barrows' 1923, Presidential address to the Association of American Geographers). In the late 1930s, two non-geographers published a major survey of American regionalism (Odum and Moore, 1938) and in 1939 the Association of American Geographers published a monograph – Richard Hartshorne's *The Nature of Geography: A Critical Survey of Current Thought in the Light of the Past* – which was rapidly established as the definitive statement of the current orthodoxy (see Stoddart, 1990). As Hartshorne (1948, 1979) later made clear, there was much debate among American geographers during the 1930s (most of it apparently unpublished, though see James and Mather, 1977) about the nature of their discipline. He was concerned about both the tone and the content of that debate (particularly in Leighley, 1937), and in 1938 he submitted a paper to the *Annals of the Association of American Geographers*, as a contribution to the philosophical discussions. He then proceeded to Europe for fieldwork on boundary problems, as part of his ongoing research into political geography. This was frustrated by the political situation, and he spent his time reading further European, mainly German, work on the nature of geography. He used this to extend his 1938 paper, adding the crucial sub-title; the result was a 'paper' of 491 pages (some 230,000 words) which became the major philosophical and methodological contribution to the literature of geography in English then available.

A synopsis of Hartshorne's book, and his interpretations of others' works, notably Hettner's, is not possible in a few paragraphs, and only the main conclusions can be highlighted here. It should be stressed that Hartshorne's statements were positive ones – of what geography is: they were only normative in the sense of him saying that geography should be what others (notably Hettner, whose approach to geography reflected a line of thinking through Kant and Humboldt to his own mentor, Richtofen) have said that it is. Thus, Livingstone (1992, p. 306) describes Hartshorne's project as seeking 'to determine the nature of geography from scrutinizing its history', and Lukermann (1990, p. 58) claimed that the *Nature* was, 'a search for authority to validate the conclusions drawn from selected premises – largely formulated by Hettner, who had philosophical associations and leanings rather than historical associates'. Butzer (1990) argued that Hartshorne was selective in his use of Hettner's material, and Gregory (1994, p. 51) claimed that, 'Hartshorne's views were developed through a highly selective exegesis of a German intellectual tradition. His approval of Hettner (in particular) was unrestrained, but the regional geography that he constructed was purged of both the physico-ecological and the cultural-historical implications that were indelibly present in Hettner'. In sum, Hartshorne transmitted to an American audience his interpretation of a particular German argument as to the nature of geography.

Hartshorne argued forcefully that the focus of geography is areal differentiation, the mosaic of separate landscapes on the earth's surface (see Agnew, 1990, on the representation of Hartshorne's focus as 'areal variation' rather than 'areal differentiation'). Thus, geography is defined as (Hartshorne, 1939, p. 462):

> ... a science that interprets the realities of areal differentiation of the world as they are found, not only in terms of the differences in certain things from place to place, but also in terms of the total combination of phenomena in each place, different from those at every other place.

Geography as a discipline 'is concerned to provide accurate, orderly and rational descriptions and interpretations of the variable character of the earth's surface' (p. 21) and:

> ... seeks to acquire a complete knowledge of the areal differentiation of the world, and therefore discriminates among the phenomena that vary in different parts of the world only in terms of their geographic significance – i.e. their relation to the total differentiation of areas. Phenomena significant to areal differentiation have areal expression – not necessarily in terms of physical extent over the ground, but as a characteristic of an area of more or less definite extent (p. 463).

The principal purpose of geographical scholarship is thus synthesis, the integration of material on relevant characteristics to provide a total description of a place – or region – which is identifiable by its peculiar combination of those characteristics. There is then, according to Hartshorne, a close (Kantian) analogy between geography and history; the latter provides a synthesis for 'temporal sections of reality' whereas the former performs a similar task for 'spatial sections of the earth's surface' (p. 460). From this separation of the roles of the two disciplines, Hartshorne concluded that there was no need for geographers to study change, since that was the province of historians.

To Hartshorne, regional definition and description lie at the heart of this integrating science – 'the ultimate purpose of geography, the study of areal differentiation of the world, is most clearly expressed in regional geography' – so that the discipline's research methods had to focus on regional definition and depiction. Regions are characterized by their homogeneity on prescribed characteristics, selected for their salience in highlighting areal differences. Identification of such regions 'depends first and fundamentally on the comparison of maps depicting the areal expression of individual phenomena, or of interrelated phenomena ... geography is represented in the world of knowledge primarily by its technique of map use' (pp. 462–4).

In this, Hartshorne emphasized map *use*. Although it is valuable for geographers to know something about map construction, the sciences of surveying and map projections are of only secondary interest to them; their prime task is map interpretation. Much of the information to be interpreted may have been placed on the maps by geographers during their fieldwork, and the role and nature of fieldwork were of considerable interest to American geographers during the period when Hartshorne was developing his ideas. Much work was done by American geographers at the time developing detailed methods for mapping land use as the bases for regional delimitation, including a series of intensive 'field camps' (see Whittlesey, 1954).

Preparation of a regional synthesis required materials both from other sciences specializing in certain phenomena (though usually not their areal patterning) and from the topical systematic specialisms within geography which complemented, but were eventually subsidiary to, regional geography. Physical, economic and political were the main systematic sub-divisions recognized within geography at the time Hartshorne wrote, although a later survey, set firmly within the regional paradigm, identified many other 'adjectival geographies' including population, settlement, urban, resources, marketing, recreation, agricultural, mineral production, manufacturing, transportation, soils, plant, animal, medical, and military, plus climatology and geomorphology (James and Jones, 1954). A number were of only minor importance, however, so that despite the apparent diversity of interests among geographers of the time, the 'classic' regional study usually followed a sequence comprising physical features, climate, vegetation, agriculture, industries, population and the like (Freeman, 1961, p. 142), and was summarized by a synthesis of the individual maps to produce a set of formal regions.

To most geographers of the period spanning the Second World War, including those who contributed to the survey edited by James and Jones (1954), which may have been why they were invited, regional geography was at the forefront of their discipline's scholarship and systematic studies were the providers of information for that enterprise. Thus to James, 'Regional geography in the traditional sense seeks to bring together in an areal setting various matters which are treated separately in topical geography' (1954, p. 9). Urban geographers studied towns because they 'constitute distinctive areas' (Mayer, 1954, p. 143), in line with the regional concept; political geographers studied the functions and structures of an area 'as a region homogeneous in political organization, heterogeneous in other respects' (Hartshorne, 1954a, p. 174); and in defining a 'new' field of social geography, Watson (1953, p. 482) saw it 'as the identification of different regions of the earth's surface according to associations of social phenomena related to the total environment' (see also Johnston, 1993a). Each topical specialism produced its own regionalization (as in agricultural geography, especially O. E. Baker's papers in *Economic Geography* during the 1920s and 1930s outlining the agricultural regions of various parts of the world), and each had links with the relevant systematic sciences. The key differentiating factor between geography and other, systematic, disciplines was the geographer's focus on the region. For Hartshorne, every geographer should have not only a substantive specialism (he considered himself a political geographer and wrote the chapter on that in *American Geography: Inventory and Prospect* – Hartshorne, 1954a) but also a regional specialism – and it was the latter that distinguished a geographer from scholars in other disciplines.

There was a tension within this promotion of regional geography, however. On the one hand, there was the presentation of regions – following Vidal's example – as small, homogeneous areas, with many countries comprising a patchwork mosaic of such separate districts, even though in many cases the boundaries between them were relatively indeterminate. In this view of the region, the geographer's field of study was inherently local – save in areas of little physical variation over large distances. On the other hand, the argument that geographers should be regional specialists was made at a much larger scale – an individual country, perhaps, but more commonly an entire continent or major sub-continental area. In this context, geographers would present themselves as specialists on, say, Latin America or the Indian sub-continent: their teaching would be at this scale, even if their research in and field knowledge of those areas was on specific parts only, and the textbooks written to support their teaching were structured at the larger scale. There was thus a hierarchy of regions: the large areas which were used to structure considerable sections of many degree programmes (courses on the regional geography of *x*), and the myriad small areas within those larger units which had their own unity and whose identification was the focus of much geographical inquiry and writing (some of it following Vidal's emphasis on small regional units with distinct physical characteristics, notably in soils and drainage, and associated agricultural specialisms: Buttimer, 1971, 1978a).

The British view

British geographers were less concerned with philosophical and methodological debate than their American counterparts during the 1920s, 1930s and 1940s (though see the exchange in the *Scottish Geographical Magazine* during the late 1930s, initiated by Crowe, 1938). They were apparently more pragmatic, less prone to contemplate the nature of their subject and more prepared, perhaps, to adopt the well-used adage that 'Geography is what geographers do'. But they too accepted that the *raison d'être* of geography was synthesis, the integration of the findings of various systematic studies, but with a strong emphasis on genesis distinguishing their approach from their American contemporaries', as in the studies of geomorphology and historical geography (Darby, 1953). According to Wooldridge and East (1958), 'geography … fuses the results, if not the methods, of a host of other subjects … [it] is not a science but merely an aggregate of sciences (p. 14).' '[I]ts *raison d'être* and intellectual attraction arise in large part from the shortcomings of the uncoordinated intellectual world bequeathed us by the specialists' (pp. 25–6) and 'in its simplest essence the geographical problem is how and why does one part of the earth's surface differ from another' (p. 28).

All of these statements indicate a strong trans-Atlantic common body of opinion (see Stoddart, 1990, regarding Hartshorne's influence on Woodridge) although, despite a statement that, 'The purpose of regional geography is simply the better understanding of a complex whole by the study of its constituent parts' (p. 159), the British writers did not elevate the regional doctrine as much as did their American counterparts. (Nor were they carried to excesses of environmental determinism in earlier decades.) Nevertheless, Wooldridge (1956, p. 53) wrote in 1951 that:

> the aim of regional geography … is to gather up the disparate strands of the systematic studies, the geographical aspects of other disciplines, into a coherent and focused unity, to see nature and nurture, physique and personality as closely related and interdependent elements in specific regions.

He argued that in any department of geography each staff member should be committed to the study of a major region (p. 64).

As in the United States, much early development in Britain involved work at two scales (Freeman, 1961, p. 84; Johnston, 1984d). On the large scale were efforts, such as Herbertson's (1905), to divide the earth into major natural regions, usually on the basis of climatic parameters and thus having some links with the earlier determinism. On the smaller scale, the aim was to identify individual areas with particular characteristics:

> The fundamental idea was that the small area would legitimately be expected to show some distinct individuality, if not necessarily entire homogeneity, through a study of all its geographical features – structure, climate, soils, vegetation, agriculture, mineral and industrial resources, communications, settlement and distribution of population. All these, it has often been said, are united in the visible

landscape, linked into one whole and dependent one on another. And more, every area, save those few never occupied by man, has been influenced, developed and altered by human activity, and therefore the landscape is an end-product, moulded to its present aspect by successive generations of people. The practice has therefore been to take an evolutionary view and . . . to attempt to reconstruct the landscape as it was a hundred, or a thousand years ago (Freeman, 1961, p. 85).

The delineation of regions at these two scales was the focus of much attention at this time, with attempts made to devise hierarchies (or 'orders') of regions, whereby smaller regions are grouped into larger units – with the various orders given separate names, such as 'tracts' and 'stows' (Unstead, 1933; Johnston, 1984d).

Although much of the work on regional definition and description was undertaken for pedagogical purposes, the practical value of appreciating regional divisions was also pressed. Notable in this respect was the work of L. D. (later Sir Dudley) Stamp. A geology graduate from the University of London, Stamp made the translation to geography when working as Professor of Geology and Geography at the University of Rangoon (his initial employment in Burma was as an oil geologist); he returned to the UK in 1926, to an appointment at the London School of Economics. Stamp developed wide interests, which included the role of regional geography in education, and he published a large number of school textbooks on all parts of the world during his career, as well as a much revised text on *The British Isles* (Stamp and Beaver, 1947) and several revisions of Chisholm's *Handbook of Commercial Geography*.

In 1930, Stamp launched what was then by far the largest research project undertaken by British geographers – the Land Utilization Survey of Britain. Over four years he mobilized some 250,000 students at c.10,000 schools to map land use over the entire country (a later survey was organized in Northern Ireland) at the scale of six inches to the mile. These were used as the raw information for the publication of maps of land use at the scale of one inch to the mile, for a series of county reports, many of them written by academic geographers and including regional summaries, and for his own summary volume on *The Land of Britain* (Stamp, 1946). (On the survey, see Rycroft and Cosgrove, 1999; Wise, 1968.) Stamp promoted the Survey in particular, and geographical skills in general, as valuable for planning land use (as in Stamp, 1934, 1946, 1949), and this was one of the main foundations for his later advocacy of applied geography (Stamp, 1948, 1960). His expertise on these matters led to him either serving on or advising a number of important government commissions regarding land use and related issues during the Second World War and after (such as the Royal Commission on Land Utilization in Rural areas – of which he was Vice-Chairman – and the Royal Commission for the Common Land: see Buchanan, 1968).

In addition to the definition of what are generally termed *formal (or uniform) regions* – areas of whatever scale that are relatively homogeneous on the phenomenon or phenomena involved in their definition, and different from neighbouring areas on those same criteria – there was also some interest in what became known as *functional regions*. These are also homogeneous areas on predetermined criteria, which apply to interactions between places: the unity to a functional region is provided by links to a common dominant node. Functional regions were introduced to British geography by Fawcett (1919), who suggested that the country's main functional regions – the tributary areas of its main cities – should be the territorial framework for a structure of regional government. These ideas were taken up by one of Fawcett's students, R. E. Dickinson, who prepared detailed definitions of the hinterlands of both large cities – Leeds and Bradford (Dickinson, 1930) – and market towns – in East Anglia (Dickinson, 1933). Dickinson travelled widely in France, Germany and the United States during the 1930s, assembling material on this aspect of urban geography and developing his argument – crystallized in his post-war text, *City Region and Regionalism* (Dickinson, 1947) – that functional regions should be the basis for dividing up a country for the purposes of public administration (on which, see Johnston, 2000b, 2002a). Dickinson was a strong proponent of the regional approach within geography and saw no tension between the formal and functional regional concepts. Indeed, in a 1939 paper he argued that the view of the region as developed by what he termed the 'landscape purists' (Dickinson, 1938, p. 12) was 'the "objective manifestations" of economic circulation . . . men and things in movement'.

A major difference between British and American geography by the 1950s was in attitudes to physical geography. Both countries had strong traditions of work in this field, and many geographers had academic roots in geology. But this tradition had slowly dissolved in North America (the United States much more than Canada) and interest in the physical environment, and particularly its understanding as against its description, waned (see Leighley, 1955). This may have been a consequence of the excesses of environmental determinism, with a subsequent desire to remove all traces of that connection and to see society as the formative agent of landscape patterns and change. Thus, with regard to geomorphology – the science of landform genesis – Peltier (1954, p. 375) wrote:

> . . . the geographer needs precise, factual information about particular places. What landforms actually exist in a given area? How do they differ? Where are they? What are their distribution patterns? The geomorphologist may concern himself with questions of structure, process, and stage, but the geographer wants specific answers to the questions: what? where? and how much?

What geographers were interested in, according to this view, was the geography of landforms: geomorphology, the genetic study of landforms, was a part of geology and was deemed outside the geographical enterprise.

Similar reactions saw the wholesale removal of climatology and biogeography from American geographical curricula, and their replacement by introductory courses in physical geography which described landforms, climates and plant assemblages – usually in a regional context – but paid little or no attention to their origins. There has been a substantial revival of physical geography in the USA in recent decades, however (see Marcus, 1979, and the essays in Gaile and Willmott, 1989), as a reaction to its perceived relevance to understanding and resolving environmental problems (see p. 346) and the technological advances in remote sensing and associated technologies.

This American trend was not repeated in Britain where, according to Wooldridge and East (1958, p. 47):

To treat geography too literally as an affair of the 'quasistatic present' is to make both it and its students seem foolish and superficial. It is true that our primary aim is to describe the present landscape; but it is also to interpret it. . . . Our study has therefore always to be evolutionary. . . . It is unscholarly to take either landforms or human societies as 'given' and static facts, though we must not let temporal sequences obscure spatial patterns.

Geography students at British universities in the 1950s rarely specialized in either physical or human geography, except perhaps in the final year of their course. Both were considered essential parts of a geographical education, as contributions to the genetic study of regional landscapes which was the integrating focus of geographical scholarship (see Johnston and Gregory, 1984; Cosgrove, 1989a). As researchers by mid-century, however, most British geographers specialized in either physical or human geography (though rarely exclusively so), but almost all had a regional specialism as well, in which they 'integrated' studies from 'both sides' of their subject, as widely illustrated in the regional textbooks of the period. The 'dogma of regional synthesis' (Darby, 1983b, p. 25) was being softened, however, and geographers were increasingly turning their attention from regions to systematic studies.

Historical geography and the study of change

One systematic specialism which stood slightly apart from the others was historical geography, whose study was based on the argument that investigations of the past were needed in order to comprehend the regional patterns of the present. Two separate approaches operated from the late 1920s on, though in very different ways: indeed one (the American) was not presented as historical geography.

The first approach was closely associated with the work of H. C. (later Sir Clifford) Darby in the UK (Perry, 1969; Darby, 2002). Darby was very much influenced by the work of Cambridge historians in the 1920s, and did his PhD (the first to be awarded in geography at Cambridge) on the medieval Fenland (Darby, 1940a, 1940b). He then turned his attention to the 1086 Domesday Book, editing a multi-authored set of regional volumes depicting the geography that it disclosed, county by county, to which he added a summary volume (Darby, 1977; Perry, 1979). At the same time, he was enunciating a broad approach to historical geography which combined detailed cross-sectional analyses of particular times – selected according to the availability of source materials – with linking narratives describing the intervening changes (as in his two edited volumes: Darby, 1936, 1973).

Darby's approach to historical geography was set out in several major essays (1953, 1962) and posthumously in a volume assembled from notes that he left from his lecture courses on the subject (Darby, 2002; he also left notes on his course on English landscape change – see Darby, 1951 – but without the illustrative material, which prevented these also being published in book form). During his career of some four decades at Cambridge, Liverpool, University College London, and again at Cambridge, Darby supervized a large number of research students, establishing a strong presence for historical geography within the discipline (Prince, 2000; indeed, he restructured the department at University College London after his appointment as head in 1949 to reflect the importance he gave to historical geography; Clout, 2003b). This lacked the dogmatism of the regional approach being promoted by others.

Largely contemporary with Darby's work in the UK was the second approach, centred on the works of Carl Sauer and his associates. Sauer was a Chicago geography graduate and strongly influenced by German work but, unlike Hartshorne, did not elevate the regional focus and concentrated on change rather than pattern. (On the differences between Hartshorne and Sauer, see Lukermann, 1990, and Butzer, 1990; for critical assessments of Sauer, see Stoddart, 1997b, and Symanski, 2002. Interestingly, some of Sauer's early work has strong environmental determinist tinges: see Sauer, 1918, pp. 421–2.) Sauer's focus was on the processes leading to landscape change up to the present and their reflection in artefacts found in the landscape, beginning at the prehuman stage of occupance (Mikesell, 1969); most of the work was conducted either outside the United States (particularly in Latin America) or in that country's less industrialized parts. Sauer's (1925) first methodological statement constrained geographical endeavour closely to the generic study of landscapes, emphasizing their cultural features (although work was also done on the borderlands between geography and botany his main external links were with anthropologists, especially Kroeber – see Kroeber, 1952); there was no glorification of the region, however. In his later 'sermons' – as he called his methodological and philosophical statements – Sauer (1941, 1956a) encouraged research over a much wider field, but emphasized the study of cultural landscapes, and the links which he had forged with anthropology, to produce a creative art-form whose hallmark was that it was not prescribed by pattern or method: the human geographer is obliged 'to make cultural processes the base of his thinking and observation' (Sauer, 1941, p. 24).

This genre of work involved neither detailed reconstruction of past geographies nor close consideration of regional boundaries. Instead, it led to a catholic historical geography whose rationale was that, 'through its study we may be able to find more complete and better answers to the problems of interpretation of the world both as it is now and as it has been at different times in the past' (Clark, 1954, p. 95). Not all American historical geographers followed this lead – Brown (1943), for example, worked on detailed reconstructions of past periods (Meinig, 1989) – but the 'Berkeley school', which Sauer founded and led for almost five decades, had many followers, and a particular point of view focused on a single iconoclast (Hooson, 1981). Sauer's influence was continued by his students, notably Leighley, Parsons and Clark (Bushong, 1981; Williams, 1983).

A major statement consistent with Sauer's approach was a symposium on 'Man's role in changing the face of the earth' (see Glacken, 1983) which resulted in a substantial publication (52 chapters plus discussions: 1193 pages in all) that had a very substantial impact (Thomas, 1956). The range of material included was vast. Its theme was identified by Sauer (1956b, p. 49) as:

. . . the capacity of man to alter his natural environment, the manner of his so doing, and the virtue of his actions. It is concerned with historically cumulative effects, with the physical and biologic processes that man sets in motion, inhibits, or deflects, and with the differences in cultural conduct that distinguish one human group from another.

It presented no grand methodology or set of general findings – indeed, in his closing statement Sauer (1956c) criticized the tendency of American authors who 'have an inclination to universalize ourselves' (p. 1133). The volume stressed both diversity in human response to environments and its impacts on them, with cultural differences providing the basis for that diversity. Mumford's (1956, p. 237) conclusion to the symposium has affinities with that advanced in the 1980s by adherents of structuration theory (see p. 244): 'the future is not a blank page; and neither is it an open book' (p. 1142). The symposium was updated some 30 years later (Turner *et al.*, 1990).

A contributor to Thomas's symposium, and also a member of the Berkeley school, was Glacken (1956), whose later *magnum opus* focused on the conceptions of nature that have been current in western thought at various times and places. *Traces on the Rhodian Shore* (Glacken, 1967) is a major survey of interpretations of nature, in which he demonstrates 'how all-pervading teleology has been in the history of Western interpretation of nature' (Glacken, 1983, p. 32). Like the Thomas symposium before it, this book is widely recognized as a classic on society–nature inter-relationships. But it was published at a time when that topic was receiving a rapidly diminishing amount of attention, and its impact was consequently less than might otherwise have occurred – as was also the case with Tuan's (1968) monograph on vernacular interpretations of *The Hydrological Cycle*.

This body of work stimulated by Sauer can be set in a wider frame of studies of human–environment interactions, whose concern is with anthropomorphically-generated change rather than the influence of the environment on people which characterized the early twentieth century (Turner, 2002). As Sack (2001) expressed it, geographers' basic concerns are with the environments that we encounter and the changes that we create in order to make them more comfortable for our desired lifestyles. Another stimulus for that strand of work – which became increasingly important in the late twentieth century – was *Man and Nature* by George Perkins Marsh (1864), widely recognized as the pioneer statement on environmental abuse by humans and the needs for conservation (Lowenthal, 2001).

Geography in the early 1950s

The early 1950s saw the appearance of two edited volumes whose contents characterize geographical practices at the time. *American Geography: Inventory and Prospect* (James and Jones, 1954) was a 'semi-official' compilation, produced to celebrate the fiftieth anniversary of the Association of American Geographers and presented as 'a progress report on the objectives and procedures of geographic research' (p. vii). Although each of the 16 chapters has a named author, all had been commented on in draft by a number of others, with some collaborating in their production. All but the first two chapters deal either with a systematic field within geography (urban, political etc.) or with geographical methods (field survey, air photo interpretation and cartography). But the first two – on 'The field of geography' and 'The regional concept and the regional method' (by Preston James and Derwent Whittlesey respectively) – dominate the book: Whittlesey's chapter is by far the longest.

Geography is defined by James (1954, p. 4) as '. . . concerned with the arrangement of things on the face of the earth, and with the association of things that give character to particular places'. He presents the region as 'the geographic generalization of phenomena associated in area' (p. 9) and the map as 'the fundamental implement of geographic research'. Whittlesey (1954) follows by claiming that 'Geographers are in general agreement that regional study is an essential part of their craft' (p. 21) and concludes that regional study 'underlies and is applicable to all aspects of geography' (p. 65). These views permeate the entire volume, with discussions of regions and the regional concept covering subject matter as diverse as political, agricultural, geomorphic, soil and zoogeographical regions, and regions in marketing geography. (On the dissolution of this core to geographical study provided by regions and maps, see Johnston, 2004b.)

The second book – *Geography in the Twentieth Century: A Study of Growth. Fields, Techniques, Aims and Trends* (Taylor, 1957 – this was an expanded version of a book originally published in 1951) – had a wider range of authors, with six from Canada (the editor, Griffith Taylor – see p. 47 – was a Professor at Toronto), seven from the USA, eight from England (including Darby, Stamp and Wooldridge), and one each from Czechoslovakia and Poland. Geography is defined in the editorial preface as 'the discussion of the *causes of patterns of distribution*' (p. v), and Taylor introduces the book as (p.3):

> . . . *an attempt to answer questions which are engaging the attention of all geographers. What are the salient features of modern geography? What are we trying to accomplish? How have our ideas as to what are the important fields of our discipline changed during the last fifty years? How do our studies touch the fields of allied disciplines? Have America, Britain, France, Germany, and the Slav nations and even Canada produced special contributions? . . . Broadly speaking, are there different schools of geographic thought which cut across national boundaries to some degree?*

The book is organized in three parts, with five further introductory chapters on the history of geography, ten on 'the environment as a factor', and thirteen on 'special fields of geography'. This structure – particularly the ordering of the last two sections – reflects Taylor's position as a 'stop-and-go determinist' (see above, p. 47), and although there are no chapters on regional geography or the regional concept (there is one on regionalism as regional administration) and the term 'region' does not appear in the book's index, Taylor states (without dissent) that 'Most geographers accept regional geography as the core of our discipline' (p. 8).

Together these two books clearly illustrate the transitional situation Anglo-American geography was in at the beginning of the post-1945 period. Systematic studies were coming to dominate its internal organization, but there was still a very strong tie to the regional concept and the belief in regional synthesis as the core of geographical knowledge and, for some at least as exemplified by Taylor's book, the remnants of environmental determinism in the primacy given to the 'environmental factor'.

Conclusions

This chapter has presented an extremely brief outline of geography during its 'modern period', since the focus of the book is on the ensuing 'contemporary period'. Three approaches have been identified, although deeper analysis may well indicate more co-existing during any one time (see Taylor, 1937) . All three lasted into the contemporary period, although one, the regional, dominated in the years before and just after the Second

World War. Its main focus was on areal differentiation, on the varying character of the earth's surface, and its picture of that variation was built up from parallel topical studies of different aspects of observed physical and human patterns. By the 1950s, initially in America and then in Britain too, there was growing disillusionment with the empiricist philosophy of regional geography. The topical specialisms slowly came to dominate disciplinary practice and regional synthesis was increasingly ignored.

In both countries, the developments set out here had been produced by a very small number of active geographers. In the United Kingdom, for example, there was no separate academic learned society organizing conferences for geographers alone until the mid-1930s, and by 1946 there were only about 120 employed in the country's universities — many of them lacking any formal training in the discipline (Darby, 1983b, p. 17): as he points out, citing an unsigned obituary in 1934, 'geography is far from having consolidated a definite position, British geography particularly so'. In the United States, the discipline was larger (in absolute terms) and better organized: the Association of American Geographers (which was small and difficult to join without an established research reputation) had been founded in 1904; in 1949 it merged with the Association of Professional Geographers and ended its restrictive practices. Nevertheless, the discipline was not strong in the country's universities with its academics, according to Schulten (2001, p. 125), finding 'little incentive to join the fight for their subject's independence even as they bemoaned its position within the social studies'. Thus, the changes discussed in the subsequent chapters were built on fairly shallow roots and coincided with a massive growth in the size (both absolute and, in the case of the UK, relative) of the academic geographic enterprise.

3
Growth of systematic studies and the adoption of 'scientific method'

Some carried the idea as far as to believe that the 'core of geography' lay in 'regional synthesis', in which the facts of geology, climate, agriculture, industry and so on could, by some artistry, be fused into a delineation of 'the personality of a region'... one must remember that much so-called regional geography was in no sense a synthesis, but simply a way of handling the facts of, say, agriculture or morphology.

(Darby, 1983b, p. 15)

Every beginning is difficult holds in all science.

(Marx, Preface to the First German Edition of *Das Capital*)

Dating the origin of a change in the orientation of a discipline, or even a part of it, is difficult. Several pieces which contain the kernel of the new ideas can usually be found in its literature, but often these are derivative of the earlier teachings of others, whose views may never have been published but only disseminated to their students; others may promote the ideas that are widely adopted later, but have no impact on those developments for a variety of reasons (see Johnston, 1993a, 1996b). Change can also emanate contemporaneously from several separate, though usually not entirely independent, nodes. An attempt to locate the first stirrings against the regional paradigm would be a futile exercise, therefore. Instead, the present chapter identifies the most influential statements published by geographers.

The critique of regional geography

Major change within a discipline involves both dissatisfaction with existing approaches and the promotion of an acceptable alternative disciplinary matrix (if not world view; see p. 11). The 1950s saw widespread dissatisfaction with the regional approach, as indicated by Freeman (1961, p. 141):'disappointment with the work of regional geographers has led many to wonder if the regional approach can ever be academically satisfying and to turn to specialization or some systematic branch of the subject'. He suggested three reasons for this. First, much regional classification was naive, particularly on the broader scale; generalizations such as Herbertson's (1905) world climatic regions were found on detailed investigation to contain too many discrepancies. The second, and perhaps most important to many people, was the 'weary succession' of physical and human activity 'facts' which characterized much regional writing: 'The trouble has perhaps been that many regional geographers have tried to include too much' (Freeman, 1961, p. 143). Third, one of the most influential models of regional writing, derived from work on the French *pays*, suggested that the whole of the earth's surface could be divided into clearly-identifiable regions, each with its own character: that this proved false was reflected by many pedestrian studies of areas lacking such 'personality'. A satirical essay highlighting the poverty of much regional geography was published anonymously in an early issue of the *IBG Newsletter* (Anon, 1968). The author's name was given as Llwynog Llwyd, 'an exiled Celt … [working in] an Antipodean University' – it was Keith Buchanan (see Johnston, 1999a). Buchanan's critique was first seen in two book reviews published in the late 1950s – Buchanan, 1958a, 1958b. On Harrison Church's 1957 work, *West Africa: A Study of the Environment and Man's Use of it*, for example, he concluded that it 'fails to capture anything of the quality of West African life or the vividness of the West African scene. These are lost, veiled in a grey harmattan haze of geological details and climatic statistics, of catalogues towns and production data' – 1958b, p. 278. (For examples of his own quest to portray the 'vividness of the scene' see Buchanan and Pugh 1958, and Buchanan, 1966.)

An earlier critique of regional geography as practised in the UK was Kimble's (1951) essay on 'The inadequacy of the regional concept'. He identified the regional concept as likely to occupy the core of most geographers' definition of their discipline, and claimed that they would 'contend that the highest form of geographical enquiry was a kind of "hunt-the-region" game, in which (provided we were offered enough clues) we were bound to discover that life in a given land or continent resolves itself into a neat pattern of cultural entities we call regions' (p. 151). But, he contended further, we have no agreed definition of a region (he had found no less than a hundred in the literature), which meant that geographers were unable to present a united front regarding their discipline to the wider academic world. Reviewing the literature on regions and their delimitation, he concluded that not only was there no agreement on how to define regions but also the concept was largely obsolete in the contemporary world:

> From the air it is the links in the landscapes, the rivers, roads, railways, canals, pipe-lines, electric cables, rather than the breaks that impress the aviator … regional geographers may be trying to put boundaries that do not exist around areas that do not matter (p. 159).

His later reference to the situation in Germany that, 'If the only type of regionalized unity possessed by modern … Germany was its circulation pattern, then the day of the region is nearly at the end, since mobility is the catalysts of regional diversity, and must sooner or later dissolve the whole compartmental structure of our civilization' (p. 168) makes clear that he was referring only to formal regions (see above, p. 54): functional regions may well exist. (The reference to Germany was based on Dickinson's work: see Johnston, 2000b.) Formal regions were of little contemporary interest, however, even in work on different parts of the globe:

> Whatever the pattern of the new age may be, we can be sure there will be no independent, discrete units within it – no 'worlds within worlds'. There will be no neatly demarcated 'regions' where geographers … can study a 'fossil' community. Man's 'region' is now the world. This does not render

superfluous the continued organization of geographical studies on a systematic areal basis. ... But it does mean that we should be well advised, when making these studies, to refrain from searching for 'unitary patterns of living', 'entities of distribution', and from assuming, in the manner of determinists, that 'regional unity' is the goal towards which civilized society is moving. ... At best a regional study can be only a personal work of art, not an impersonal work of science – a portrait rather than a blueprint. As such, it can have substantial value, but its value will lie in the realm of illumination and suggestion rather than of definitive analysis and synthesis. (p. 173)

Whereas Freeman, Kimble, Buchanan and others focused on the failings of regional geography as practised in the UK, Ackerman (1945) forcefully argued in the United States that insistence on the primacy of regional geography was undermining the associated systematic studies. Drawing on his experience of working in the wartime intelligence services, Ackerman identified two major failings of professional geographers there; their inability to handle foreign languages and the weakness of their topical specialisms. Regarding the latter, he categorized much geographical work as undertaken by scholars who were 'more or less amateurs in the subject on which they published' (p. 124), so that when called upon to provide intelligence material for wartime interpretation what they produced was extremely thin in its content. Regional geographers could provide only superficial analyses, and the division of labour within the discipline whereby people specialized in different areas of the earth was both inefficient and ineffective. (Gould, 1979, p. 140, called the geography of the 50 years prior to 1950 'shabby, parochial and unintelligent ... bumbling amateurism and antiquarianism'. On wartime work by geographers in the USA, see the report of the Hartshorne committee to the AAG – AAG, 1946; Harris, 1997b. For a comparable treatment of contributions by UK geographers, see Balchin, 1987, and Clout and Gosmé, 2003.)

Ackerman suggested that rectifying this major deficiency required much more research and training in the systematic specialisms. This need not necessarily be contrary to giving primacy to regional synthesis, he claimed, since more detailed systematic studies could lead to greater depth in regional interpretations. There is little evidence that his paper had an immediate impact, however, as illustrated by the abstracts of papers presented at the Association of American Geographers' annual meetings (published then in the *Annals* each year). These indicated no major shift in the orientation of academic work with the return to post-war 'normality', save in two cases – the abstracts presented by Garrison and McCarty for the Cleveland meeting in 1953, which were clearly based on a different methodology to that widely used (see below, p. 75 and Garrison, 2002, p. 108). The systematic fields had undoubtedly been gaining in importance prior to Ackerman's statement, and continued to do so, as indicated by their extensive treatment in the review volume edited by James and Jones (1954). But it was not until the mid-1950s that this was matched by widespread changes in disciplinary methodologies and philosophy.

Schaefer's paper and the response

A successful revolution against the regional paradigm got under way in the United States in the 1950s, initiated through debates over philosophy and methods. The first major contribution was a – posthumously published – paper by Schaefer (1953), which is often referred to by those seeking the origins of the 'quantitative and theoretical revolutions' (on its impact, see Cox, 1995, and Getis, 1993). Schaefer was originally an economist: he joined the group of geographers teaching in the economics department at the University of Iowa after his escape from Nazi Germany (Bunge, 1979).

Schaefer claimed that his paper was the first to challenge Hartshorne's interpretation of the works of Hettner and others. He criticized Hartshorne's exceptionalist claims for regional geography, and presented an alternative case for geography adopting the philosophy and methods of the positivist school of science (see Martin, 1990, p. 72). He first outlined the nature of a science and then defined the peculiar characteristics of geography as a social science. He argued that a claim for geography as the integrating science which put together the findings of the individual systematic sciences was arrogant, and that its products were somewhat lacking in 'startlingly new and deeper insights' (p. 227). A science is characterized by its explanations, and explanations require laws: 'To explain the phenomena one has described means always to recognize them as instances of laws'. Geography's major regularities refer to spatial patterns, 'Hence geography has to be conceived as the science concerned with the formulation of the laws governing the spatial distribution of certain features on the surface of the earth' (p. 227). These spatial arrangements of phenomena, not the phenomena themselves, should be the subject of geographers' search for law-like statements. Geographical procedures would be the same as those employed in other natural and social sciences: observation would lead to a hypothesis – about the inter-relationship between two spatial patterns, for example – which would then be tested against large numbers of cases, providing the basis for a law if it were verified.

Schaefer termed the argument against his definition of geography as the science of spatial arrangements *exceptionalist*. It claims that geography does not share the methodology of other sciences because of the peculiar nature of its subject matter – the study of unique places or regions – and puts geography in a similar situation as history, which studies unique periods of time. Using analogies from physics and economics, Schaefer argued that geography is not peculiar in focusing on unique phenomena. All sciences deal with unique events which can only be accounted for by integrating laws from various systematic sciences, but this does not prevent the development of laws – although undoubtedly making it more difficult: 'It is, therefore, absurd to maintain that the geographers are distinguished among the scientists through the integration of heterogeneous phenomena which they achieve. There is nothing extraordinary about geography in that respect' (p. 231).

In the second part of his paper, Schaefer traced the exceptionalist view in geography back to an analogy drawn by Kant between geography and history, an analogy repeated by Hettner and Hartshorne (see above, p. 50). Kant argued in his *Physische Geographie* (vol. I, p. 8) that, 'Geography and history together fill up the entire area of our perception: geography that of space and history that of time' (Schaefer, 1953, p. 233; on Kant more generally, see May, 1970). But when Kant was working, Schaefer claims, history and geography were cosmologies, not sciences, and a cosmology is 'not rational science but at best thoughtful contemplation of the universe' (p. 232). Hettner followed Kant's views and developed geography as a cosmology, arguing that both history and geography deal with the unique, and thus do not apply the methods of science. Schaefer argued that this is a false position, for in explaining what happened in a certain time period historians must employ the laws of the social sciences. Time periods, like places, are unique assemblages of phenomena, but this does not preclude the use of laws in unravelling and explaining them. History and geography can both be sciences, for 'What scientists do is … *They apply to each concrete situation jointly all the laws that involve the variables they have reason to believe are relevant*' (p. 239). Schaefer further argued that Hartshorne disregarded one aspect of Hettner's writing which was nomothetic in its orientation, and in doing this misled American geographers. (Müller-Wille, 1978, p. 55, claims that Hettner predated Christaller in the development of ideas regarding central place theory – see p. 79; Hartshorne made no reference to the paper by Hettner cited by Müller-Wille. On the same point, see Butzer, 1990, and Smith, 1990.)

The final part of Schaefer's paper reviewed some problems of applying a nomothetic (law-producing) philosophy to geography as a spatial, social science. He recognized difficulties of experimentation and quantification, for example, and suggested a methodology based on cartographic correlations. He argued that laws produced in geography are morphological (i.e. concerned with spatial forms), whereas those from other, 'maturer' social sciences are concerned with processes. In order fully to comprehend the phenomena assemblages described in geographers' morphological laws, therefore, it is necessary to deploy process laws from other social sciences, a procedure which requires team work (the last point was also made by Ackerman). Geography according to Schaefer, then, is the source of the laws on location, which may be used to differentiate the regions of the earth's surface.

Hartshorne's response

Schaefer's paper did not produce much direct reaction in print, despite later claims that it was a major stimulus to work in his proposed genre (Bunge, 1962). It drew considerable response from Hartshorne, however, first in a letter to the editor of the *Annals* (Hartshorne, 1954b) and later in three substantive pieces (Hartshorne, 1955, 1958, 1959): the last was another major book which, although probably not as influential as the 1939 volume, showed Hartshorne's continued importance to American geographers as an interpreter of their subject's methodology and philosophy.

The purpose of Hartshorne's first (1955) paper (which subsumed the earlier letter) was to indicate flaws in Schaefer's scholarship (see also Gregory, 1978a, p. 31). He begins with a discussion of the *mores* of methodological debate (Hartshorne, 1948). His main themes were that Schaefer was limited in his references, drew unsupportable conclusions, and misrepresented the views of others, so that, 'In every paragraph, in nearly every sentence of this third section, there is serious falsification, either by commission or by omission, of the views of the writer discussed' (p. 236: this statement refers to the third part of Schaefer's paper, which focused on Hartshorne's interpretations of Hettner). More generally, Hartshorne claimed that Schaefer's paper 'ignores the normal standards of critical scholarship and in effect offers nothing more than personal opinion, thinly disguised as literary and historical analysis' (p. 244). Since Hartshorne himself (1959, p. 8) strongly believed that 'geography is what geographers have made it', to him all methodological and philosophical statements should be based on a close and careful analysis of others' published works.

Although most of the 1955 paper examined Schaefer's 'evidence', in the final section Hartshorne turned to the anti-exceptionalist argument. He pointed out that in coming to the conclusion that geography should take process laws from the systematic sciences and use them to produce morphological laws, Schaefer came very close to preaching the sort of exceptionalist claim that he sought to destroy, so that his critique 'is a total fraud' (p. 237). Schaefer's position is summarized as: 'geography must be a science, science is the search for laws, and all phenomena of nature and human life are subject to such laws and completely determinable by them' (p. 242). Such scientific determinism is opposed to the summary of what geographers do set out in *The Nature of Geography,* which in any case was treated in a most cavalier way by Schaefer.

Hartshorne's second paper (1958) addressed Schaefer's claim that Kant was the source of the exceptionalist view. Literary analysis suggests that both Humboldt and Hettner reached the same position independently, being unaware of Kant's views when they were writing. May (1970, p. 9) suggests that both Hartshorne and Schaefer could have misunderstood Kant's conception of a science, however, and of geography's status as a science, although he confirms Hartshorne's dismissal of Schaefer's interpretation of the source of Kant's ideas (see the later exchange between Hartshorne, 1972, and May, 1972).

The third and most substantial piece in Hartshorne's rebuttal was a further monograph (*Perspective on the Nature of Geography*, Hartshorne, 1959). Its production was stimulated by Schaefer and also by requests from colleagues that he respond in detail to Schaefer's argument, but was also used to discuss other issues raised during the two decades since the publication of the original statement (Hartshorne, 1939). The discussion used a framework of ten separate questions/topics: the aim was to provide a methodology by which geography could meet its need for 'new conceptual approaches and more effective ways of measuring the interrelationships of phenomena' (p. 9), which could only develop out of an understanding and acceptance of the subject's 'essential character'.

The first set of questions concerned the meaning of areal differentiation, the definition of the earth's surface, the particular geographical interest in the integration of phenomena – 'the total reality [that] is there for study, and geography is the name of the section of empirical knowledge which has always been called upon to study that reality' (p. 33) – and the determination of what is significant for geographical study. His answers led Hartshorne to define geography as: 'that discipline that seeks *to describe and interpret the variable character from place to place of the earth as the world of man*' (p. 47). He considered that human and natural factors do not have to be identified separately – any prior insistence on this was a function of environmental determinist arguments – and that a division into human and physical geography is unfortunate, because it limits the range of possible integrations in the study of reality.

Turning to processes operating over time, Hartshorne argued that geographers need only study proximate genesis, since classification by form of appearance rather than by provenance is important for the geographical investigation of areal differentiation. As most landforms are stable, or virtually so, from the point of view of human occupance, for example, then study of their change is irrelevant to the aims of geography. According to this argument (see also p. 56 above), geomorphology, insofar as it is the study of landform genesis, is not part of geography, but the study of landforms is. With regard to cultural features in the landscape, Hartshorne made an important distinction between expository description and explanatory description: 'geography is primarily concerned to describe … the variable character of areas as formed by existing features in interrelationships … explanatory description of features in the past must be kept subordinate to the primary purpose' (p. 99). Thus, historical geography should be the expository description of the historical present, 'but the purpose of such dips into the past is not to trace developments or seek origins but to facilitate comprehension of the present' (p. 106); studies of causal development and genesis are the prerogative of the systematic sciences. By this statement, Hartshorne at least partly bridged the gap between his and Sauer's views of the discipline – perhaps reflecting that one of Sauer's students, Andrew Clark (whose PhD was on the European colonization of New Zealand, Clark, 1949) had joined Hartshorne on the staff at the University of Wisconsin-Madison.

In answering the question, 'Is geography divided between systematic and regional geography?', Hartshorne modified his position from that in *The Nature of Geography*. He accepted that studies of inter-relationships could be arranged along a continuum 'from those which analyse the most elementary complexes in areal variation over the world to those which analyse the most complex integrations in areal variation within small areas' (p. 121). The former are topical studies and the latter regional studies, but whereas 'every truly geographical study involves the use of both the topical and the regional approach' (p. 122), there is no argument that the latter is superior and that to which all geographers should aspire. Hartshorne thereby somewhat downgraded his earlier view regarding the centrality of regional synthesis in the geographical enterprise.

Regarding Schaefer's important question – 'Does geography seek to formulate scientific laws or to describe individual cases?' – Hartshorne argued for the latter, largely by pointing out the difficulties of establishing laws through geographical investigations. He did not argue against geographers seeking and using general laws for understanding individual cases, however: it is an 'erroneous presumption that to focus on studies of individual places and to focus on generic concepts are opposing alternatives mutually exclusive' (Hartshorne, 1984, p. 429). Scientific laws must be based on large numbers of cases, but geographers study complex integrations in unique places. Scientific laws can best be established in laboratory experiments which allow only a few potential influences to vary, but such work is rarely possible in geography. Interpretation of such experiments requires skills in the systematic sciences which are beyond the capability of geographers, and scientific laws suggest some kind of determinism, which is inappropriate to the human motivations that are in part the causes of landscape variations. For all these reasons, he argued, the search for laws is irrelevant to geography. Laws are not the only means to the scientific end of comprehending reality, however, instead:

Geography seeks (1) on the basis of empirical observation as independent as possible of the person of the observer, to describe phenomena with the maximum degree of accuracy and certainty; (2) on this basis, to classify the phenomena, as far as reality permits, in terms of generic concepts or universals; (3) through rational consideration of the facts thus secured and by logical processes of analysis and synthesis, including the construction and use wherever possible of general principles or laws of generic relationships, to attain the maximum comprehension of the scientific interrelationships of phenomena; and (4) to arrange these findings in orderly systems so that what is known leads directly to the margin of the unknown (pp. 169–70).

This, he says, is a perfectly respectable scientific goal. Its empiricist base is very similar to the overall goal of positivist work – p. 84 below – and is the reason why several commentators see very little difference in ends, if not means, between Hartshorne's work and that of spatial scientists.

Finally, in discussing geography's position within the classification of sciences, Hartshorne returned to the Hettnerian analogy of geography as a chorological science with history as a chronological science. This is valid, he argues, because it describes the way in which geographers have worked, on both topical and regional subjects. (This view was revived by Harris, 1971; see Earle, 1996.)

Reconciliations?

The major basis of their methodological and philosophical differences was that Hartshorne had a positive view of geography – geography is what geographers have made it – whereas Schaefer's was normative, of what geography should be, irrespective of what it had been. Over the decade after Hartshorne published his *Perspective*, the view associated with Schaefer prevailed with many geographers on both sides of the Atlantic, although his personal influence via the 1953 paper was probably very slight and the real iconoclasts of the 'revolution' were those discussed in the next section. (According to Smith, 1990, Hartshorne's view that geography should be what (he said) it had always been in effect 'turned the discourse of geography into a museum and [Hartshorne] appointed himself curator', Gregory, 1994, p. 285.) Indeed in Britain, although Hartshorne's two books were clearly widely read and referenced, Schaefer's paper was apparently not. It receives no mention in Freeman's (1961, 1980a) books, none in Chorley and Haggett's (1965b) trail-blazing *Frontiers in Geographical Teaching*, and only one in their major edited collection *Models in Geography* (Chorley and Haggett, 1967) – in the chapter by Stoddart (see, however, Stoddart, 1990). Thus it is not surprising that relatively little attention has been paid elsewhere in the geographical literature to the Schaefer/Hartshorne debate (Gregory, 1978a, p. 32. See also Martin, 1951 and Jones, 1956, for a separate, British, debate. Interestingly, Schaefer is not in the index of authors referred to in the encyclopaedic *Geography in America* either (Gaile and Willmott, 1989)). Schaefer and Hartshorne's importance to the discipline's history is not so much the influence of the two principals themselves as the clarification they brought to what became a major debate over disciplinary means and ends.

Guelke (1977a, 1978) argued that Hartshorne's and Schaefer's views were not so antagonistic as they themselves suggested (see also Gregory, 1978a, p. 31 and Entrikin,

1981, 1990). Hartshorne was generally very much a supporter of the scientific method as later defined by other geographers, but created problems for this method's application in geography by his view on uniqueness. Schaefer, on the other hand, not only accepted the full position of what geographers came to term 'scientific method', but also showed that uniqueness was a general problem of science, and not a peculiar characteristic of geography. Thus:

> In extending the idea of uniqueness to everything, Schaefer effectively removed a major logical objection to the possibility of a law-seeking geography and demonstrated that Hartshorne's view of uniqueness as a special problem was untenable for anyone who accepted the scientific model of explanation (Guelke, 1977a, p. 380).

Furthermore, Guelke argued, Hartshorne's distinction between idiographic and nomothetic approaches was misleading; both he and Schaefer ignored the possibility of geographers being major 'law-consumers'. To Hartshorne, the alternatives were either law-making or the description of unique places, while to Schaefer geographers had to develop morphological laws, and ignore the interest in process laws which characterizes the systematic sciences.

Guelke (1977a, p. 348) claimed that Schaefer's insistence on the need for geographers to develop laws had 'created a major crisis within the discipline'. Within a decade of Schaefer's paper being published, however, many human geographers, especially among the youngest recruits, had adopted at least part of his manifesto with their growing concern for quantification and law-making. Presented with a choice between such activity and the sort of contemplation of the unique advocated by Hartshorne then, as Guelke (1977a, p. 385) points out, 'Not surprisingly, most geographers opted for geography as a law-seeking science' because at that time (Guelke, 1978, p. 45):

> Universities were expected to produce problem-solvers or social-technologists to run increasingly complex economies, and geographers were not slow in adopting new positions appropriate to the new conditions. Statistics and models were ideal tools for monitoring and planning in complex industrial societies. The work of the new geographers, however, often lacked a truly intellectual dimension. Many geographers were asking: 'Are our methods rigorous?', 'What are the planning implications of this model?', and not 'How much insight does this study give us?', 'Is my understanding of this phenomenon enhanced?', 'Does this study contribute to geography?'. The last-mentioned question was considered of little consequence. Yet it should have been asked, because one of the weaknesses of the new geography was a lack of coherence.

Developments in systematic geography in the United States

Whether because of or independent from the statements by Ackerman (1945), Schaefer (1953) and Ullman (1953), systematic studies became much more important in the research and teaching of American geographers during the 1950s. (On Hartshorne's influence on systematic studies, see Butzer, 1990.) This did not mean a total departure from Hartshorne's contemporary views, since by 1959 he no longer gave primacy to regional studies, but the trend towards the scientific method proposed by Schaefer marked a clear break with the Hartshornian tradition.

The growing popularity of topical specialisms is illustrated in the review chapters in the collection edited by James and Jones (1954). Very few of the investigations reported there aimed at generating laws, however. Indeed, some could almost be categorized under the exploration paradigm, since their major purpose was the provision of new factual material: such work is best described as empiricist – it lets 'the facts' speak for themselves.

Fundamental to scientific progress in the approach espoused by Schaefer is the development of theory. Geographers were aware of the nature of theory pre-Schaefer, as shown by their references to theoretical work by non-geographers and a few – notably Harris and Ullman (1945; Ullman, 1941 – neither of these pieces was published in a geography journal) – wrote review papers summarizing that material. Subsequently, several of the reviews in the James and Jones (1954) volume refer to what is in one place termed location theory (Harris, 1954a, p. 299), but very few examples are cited of empirical investigations by geographers related to that body of theory. The chapter on urban geography, for example, cites seminal pieces on central place theory, such as Ullman's (1941) original paper, and devotes two pages to the three 'models' of intra-urban spatial patterns that had been reviewed a decade previously by Harris and Ullman (1945), but there is not a single reference to any work done by geographers since in the context of those models (Mayer, 1954, pp. 152–63). Thus, despite some precedents, very little work was done by geographers prior to the mid-1950s which followed the dictates of the 'scientific approach': they were aware of relevant work on spatial arrangements being undertaken by other scholars, but were not utilizing such approaches in their own research.

Once a new idea gains circulation through the professional journals it is available to be taken up by all. Initial development is usually concentrated in a few places only, however, where pioneer teachers encourage students to conduct research within the new framework and to publish their findings. Thus, most of the methodological changes in systematic studies in geography during the 1950s can be traced to a few centres in the United States. The changes were largely concerned with method, and their scientific underpinning was little stressed, although law-seeking was the clear goal. Certainly methods dominated the writings of both the pros and cons; many early contributions by the former group were in relatively fugitive, departmental publications, presumably because of difficulties in getting such 'new' material accepted by the journals (as described by Berry, 1993; see Barnes, 2001b; Johnston, 2004a).

The Iowa school

Although Schaefer was at Iowa until his death in 1953, he had little influence on changes promoted by geographers there, who for a number of years were members of the economics department and thus exposed to the approaches deployed in that more established social science. The group's leader was Harold McCarty, author of a major text on American economic geography (McCarty, 1940): associated with him were J. C. Hook, D. S. Knos, H. A. Stafford and, later, J. B. Lindberg, E. N. Thomas and L. J. King (McCarty, 1979; King, 1979a).

McCarty and his co-workers wanted to establish the degree of correspondence between two or more geographical patterns: they wanted to make map comparison more rigorous and generate laws of association akin to the morphological laws of accordance discussed by Schaefer. Interestingly, none of their publications refer to Schaefer's paper, although they do refer to works of, and assistance given by, Gustav Bergmann, a positivist philosopher of the Vienna school who also strongly influenced Schaefer and read the proofs of his 1953 paper (Davies, 1972a, p. 134; King, 1979a; Golledge, 1983. See also Martin, 1990). These laws were to be embedded in a theory, thus (McCarty, 1954, p. 96):

> If we are to accept the idea that economic geography is becoming the branch of human knowledge whose function is to account for the location of economic activities on the various portions of the earth's surface, it seems reasonable to expect the discipline to develop a body of theory to facilitate the performance of this task.

Such theory could be either topically or areally focused, and in its early stages of development would probably be restricted, both in its areal coverage and in the topics whose spatial inter-relationships it considered.

The purpose of theory is to provide explanations, of which McCarty recognized two types. The first involved searching for the causes of observed locational patterns, which 'can never produce an adequate body of theory for use in economic geography. . . . Variables became so numerous that they were not manageable, and, in consequence, solutions to locational problems were not obtainable' (p. 96). The second, and preferred, type focuses on associations:

> Its proponents take the pragmatic view that if one knew that two phenomena always appear together in space and never appear independently, the needs of geographic science would be satisfied, and there would be scant additional virtue in knowing that the location of one phenomenon caused the location of another (p. 97).

Such laws of association are built up in a series of stages: (1) a statement of the problem and the necessary operational definitions; (2) measurement of the phenomena (with consideration of attendant problems of sampling in time and space); and (3) a statement of the findings, in tabular or graphical form. These three descriptive stages precede analysis which seeks correlations between distributions:

> . . . the nub of the problem of research procedure seems to lie in finding the best techniques for discovering a, b and c in the 'where a, b, c, there x' hypothesis in order to give direction to the analysis. But where shall we search for its components? . . . One source of . . . clues lies in the findings of the systematic sciences. The other source lies in the observations of trained workers in the field or in the library (p. 100).

Geography, in seeking morphological laws, is thus to a considerable extent a consumer of the laws of other disciplines, which may be theoretically rather than empirically derived. According to the causal or process approach to explanation:

> Models may be created showing optimal locations for any type of economic activity for which adequate cost data may be obtained. These models may then be used (as hypotheses) for the comparison of hypothetical locations with actual locations. Divergences of pattern may then be noted

and the hypothesis altered to allow for them (often by inclusion of factors not ordinarily associated with monetary costs). Ultimately the hypothesis becomes generally applicable and thus takes on the status of a principle (McCarty, 1953, p. 184).

This statement, although not referenced as such, very faithfully reflects generally accepted views on how science progresses by the continual modification of its hypotheses, so as better to represent reality.

In their demonstration of this procedure, McCarty *et al.* (1956) discussed several statistical procedures for measuring spatial association and adopted the now well-known technique of múltiple regression and correlation – which had been used previously among geographers by Rose (1936) and Weaver (1943), both apparently after contacts with agricultural economists. McCarty's empirical context was the location patterns of manufacturing industries in the United States and Japan: other studies by the group included Hook's (1955) on rural population densities, Knos's (1968) on intra-urban land-value patterns, and King's (1961) on the spacing of urban settlements. Thomas (1960) had used similar procedures in his study of population growth in suburban Chicago, presented as a PhD. thesis to Northwestern University (where he was a contemporary of Garrison): he extended the methodology with a paper on the use of residuals from regression for identifying where the putative laws of association do not apply fully, thereby suggesting further hypotheses for areal associations. (This last paper developed on an earlier one by McCarty (1952) which was not widely circulated.) McCarty (1958) later expressed some doubts about the statistical validity of the procedure, but the method that he and his associates pioneered, with its focus on the testing of simple hypotheses derived either from observation or from theoretical deductions, became an exemplar for much research in the ensuing decades.

Wisconsin

The Department of Geography at the University of Wisconsin, Madison, has a long tradition of research with a quantitative bent: its early products included John Weaver's PhD. thesis on the geography of American barley production, which included a major section (published in his 1943 paper with no supporting methodological argument) using multiple correlation and regression to identify the influences of climatic variables on barley yields. Weaver later taught at the University of Minnesota, where he developed a widely adopted statistical procedure for defining agricultural regions (Weaver, 1954). Other work at Madison focused on the quantitative description of population patterns (e.g. Alexander and Zahorchak, 1943). A combination of these two interests was furthered by a group led by A. H. Robinson, whose main interests were in cartography; cartographic correlations were introduced to him by his research supervisor at Ohio State University, Guy-Harold Smith (Brown, 1978). Robinson also worked with R. A. Bryson, of the university's Department of Meteorology, who was a source of statistical ideas and expertise. (Cartographic work was for a long time called 'mathematical geography' by some.)

Robinson, like McCarty, wanted to develop statistical methods for map comparison, as indicated by the title of an early paper – 'A method for describing quantitatively the correspondence of geographical distributions' (Robinson and Bryson, 1957). Rose and Weaver's lead was followed with the adoption of correlation and regression procedures. Particular attention was paid to the problems of representing areal data by points (Robinson et al., 1961) and of using correlation methods in comparing isarithmic maps (Robinson, 1962). Two such map types began to appear more in geographic papers and books in the late 1950s and 1960s: isometric maps – based on a point-occurring data, such as precipitation and temperature; and isophletic maps – based on data occurring over space, especially within geographical areas called spatial units. The latter were normally represented by rate/ratio variables such as population density and crop yield per acre.

Like McCarty (1958), Robinson, too, was aware of difficulties in applying classical statistical procedures to areal data, and he proposed a procedure to circumvent one of these (Robinson, 1956). Thomas and Anderson (1965) later found this wanting, as it dealt with a special case only and not with the more general problems. Interestingly, however, the main early work on this topic was published by a group of Chicago sociologists, under the title *Statistical Geography* (Duncan, Cuzzort, and Duncan, 1961); perhaps even more interestingly, this work was virtually ignored by geographers, even though Brian Berry (1993, p. 439) developed a close working relationship with Dudley Duncan in the late 1950s and persuaded him to give the book that title.

The social physics school

This group's work was initiated and developed independently from the other three, and its early publications preceded Schaefer's paper by more than a decade. The leader was J. Q. Stewart, an astronomer at Princeton University who traced the origins of social physics in the work of a number of natural scientists who applied their methods to social data (Stewart, 1950). His investigations began when he noted certain regularities in various aspects of distributions that were akin to the laws of physics, such as a tendency for the number of students attending a university to decline with increasing distance of their home addresses from its campus. These observations led to his ideas on social physics, which he defined as:

> ... that the dimensions of society are analogous to the physical dimensions and include numbers of people, distance, and time. Social physics deals with observations, processes and relations in these terms. The distinction between it and mathematical statistics is no more difficult to draw than for certain other phases of physics. The distinction between social physics and sociology is the avoidance of subjective descriptions in the former (Stewart, 1956, p. 245).

Stewart established a laboratory at Princeton to investigate a wide range of such regularities.

Stewart introduced his ideas to geographers through a paper in *The Geographical Review* (Stewart, 1947). Four empirical rules were adduced:

1. The rank-size rule for cities showed that in the United States the population of a city multiplied by its rank (from 1 for the largest to n for the smallest) and standardized by a constant, equalled the population of the largest city, New York (Carroll, 1982);

2. At various dates the number of cities in the country with populations exceeding 2,500 was very closely related to the proportion of the population living in such places;

3. The distribution of a population could be described by the population potential at a series of points, in the same manner as the potential in a magnetic field is described in Newtonian physics; and

4. There was a close relationship between this population potential and the density of rural population in the United States.

From these regularities, Stewart claimed that (p. 485), 'There is no longer any excuse for anyone to ignore the fact that human beings, on the average and at least in certain circumstances, obey mathematical rules resembling in a general way some of the primitive "laws" of physics'. No reasons were given why this should be so (Curry, 1967, p. 285, called this a 'deliberate shunning of plausible argument'): the rules were presented as empirical regularities which had some similarity to the basic laws of physics. Causal hypotheses were not even postulated, let alone tested.

Stewart's main collaborator was William Warntz, a graduate of the University of Pennsylvania who was later employed by the American Geographical Society as a research associate, working on what he termed 'the investigation of distance as one of the basic dimensions of society' (Warntz, 1959b, p. 449; see also Warntz, 1984, where he remarks that he was introduced to Stewart's ideas via a book on *Coasts, Waves and Weather* – Stewart, 1945 – that he was reading when working as a weather observer during the Second World War. The book was 'prepared primarily to explain to marine and air navigators the physical environment ... [but] Stewart could not resist the temptation to include an exotic chapter describing potential of population and its sociological importance'.) The wide range of empirical regularities which they observed (see Stewart and Warntz, 1958, 1959) was used to develop their concept of *macrogeography* (Warntz, 1959b, 1959c). Warntz (1959b) claimed that geographical work was dominated by micro-studies: 'The tendency of American geographers to be preoccupied with the unique, the exceptional, the immediate, the microscopic, the demonstrably utilitarian, and often the obvious is at once a strength and a weakness' (p. 447) because 'the assembly of more and more area studies involving an increase in the quantity of detail does not mean *per se* a shift from the microscopic to the macroscopic' (p. 449). Geographers were in danger of being unable to perceive general patterns within their welter of local detail, and to counter this Stewart and Warntz suggested the search for 'regularities in the aggregate'.

As examples of that search, Stewart's concept of population potential was used to describe general distributions, and was related to a large number of other patterns in the economic and social geography of the United States. Although these findings were recognized as only empirical regularities, they could be used as the basis for theory development (Stewart and Warntz, 1958, p. 172): geography needed theory which, according to Warntz (1959b, p. 58), 'has as its aim the establishment and coordination of areal relations among observed phenomena. General laws are sought that will serve to unify the individual, apparently unique, isolated facts so laboriously collected'. Their approach to theory was inductive (see Figure 3.1) rather than deductive, although there was a clear underlying belief in the importance of distance and accessibility as influences on individual behaviour. The work of German geographer Walther Christaller was key for Warntz as well as Garrison, Ullman and others (see Bunge, 1968).

These macroscopic measures, particularly population potential, were used in a variety of contexts, as in Warntz's (1959a) *Toward a Geography of Price,* which established strong relationships between the prices of agricultural commodities in the USA and measures of supply and demand potential; Harris (1954b) had already used the potential measure in studies of industrial-location patterns, having been influenced by agricultural economist Colin Clark when he was studying at Oxford, noting that the measure he adopted from Clark's work was similar to J. Q. Stewart's (Harris also acknowledged help from Garrison and Isard): it was later taken up by a student there (Pred, 1965a). The 'macrogeographers' also did much work on various distance-decay functions (see Chapter 4, p. 119) and extended early Russian work on centrographic measures (Sviatlovsky and Eels, 1937; Neft, 1966); this was done both at the American Geographical Society (where its pioneering, mathematical nature ran contrary to the Society's general research interests) and later, under Warntz, at the Graduate School of Design's Laboratory for Computer Graphics and Spatial Analysis at Harvard University, where it was the forerunner of later developments in computerized cartography and GIS (see p. 176).

These lines of work contrasted markedly with that of the other three groups reviewed here, in a variety of ways. First was the issue of scale; Stewart and Warntz perhaps conformed more than any others to calls for a scientific approach which aimed at a high level of generality. Second there was their approach to theory: macrogeography was inductive in its search for regularity rather than testing deductive hypotheses. Finally, the analogies sought for human geography were in a natural science – physics – and not in the other social sciences.

W. L. Garrison and the Washington school

By far the largest volume of work in the spirit of Schaefer's and McCarty's proposals published during the 1950s came from the University of Washington, Seattle. The group of workers there was led by W. L. Garrison, whose PhD was from Northwestern University, where he was associated with Thomas (the two returned to Northwestern in the early 1960s; Taaffe, 1979). According to Bunge (1966, p. ix), Garrison had been influenced by Schaefer's paper, although his earliest publications indicate that he was applying the proposed methods to systematic studies in human geography before 1953: his 1950 PhD thesis was on the shopping centres of northern Chicago, following the exemplar set by Proudfoot's (1937) work, which identified a hierarchy of five shopping centre types in a comparative study of several cities (Garrison, 2002). Also involved was E. L. Ullman, who moved to Seattle from the closing department at Harvard in 1951 (he was previously at Chicago, as was Chauncy Harris: Harris, 1977, 1978, 1990, 1997a): Ullman had already done pioneering research on urban location patterns and transport geography (see Hay, 1979b; Morrill, 1984). Ullman was strongly critical of regional geography as traditionally practised and committed to a 'scientific approach', as illustrated by a commissioned paper published in 1953. He argued that spatial interaction should be the focus of work in economic geography rather than regional definition:

> Geographers conventionally spend much time mapping the characteristics and use of the land. This is important to many problems, but sometimes I feel that we do this simply because it is tangible and distinctive, in fact by now almost instinctive (p. 57)

and:

> ... areal differentiation [is] the current catholic definition ... I cannot accept areal differentiation as a short definition for outsiders because it implies that we are not seeking principles or generalizations or similarities, the goal of all science (p. 60).

Soon after Garrison and Ullman were recruited to Seattle a new chair of the department, G. Donald Hudson, was appointed from Northwestern: he shifted its emphasis from teaching to research, focused on four areas – cartography, economic geography, the Far East and the Soviet Union, and Anglo-America (Velikonja, 1994). He supported the work of Garrison and his students (Berry – 2002b – notes that although Ullman, as an established name, attracted many of the graduate students to Seattle, most of them chose to work with the more approachable Garrison), against some opposition from other colleagues. Hudson also worked hard to place them in other prestigious universities after graduation, thus aiding the spread of their pioneering ideas (80 MAs and 40 PhDs were completed during his headship – 1950–63). When Hudson retired, the Washington department was placed fourth in national rankings of graduate programs.

Garrison (2002, p. 105) records that a 'fork in the road' for him came in 1952 when he held a visiting post at the University of Pennsylvania. Encounters beyond geography introduced him to work on the spatial organization of markets and he decided to take some courses in statistics. He returned to Washington and recast his course in transportation geography. A large group of graduate students soon joined him, with several of them becoming leaders in the new methodology during the subsequent decade, including B. J. L. Berry, W. Bunge, M. F. Dacey, A. Getis, D. F. Marble, R. L. Morrill, J. D. Nystuen and W. R. Tobler (Garrison, 1979, 2002). The group also benefited from a 1959 visit by a Swedish geographer, Torsten Hägerstrand, who was developing methods for generalizing spatial patterns and processes (see below, p. 79), and from Garrison's contacts with university's business and engineering schools (Halvorson and Stave, 1978). Berry (1993) and Getis (1993) both provide accounts of the intellectual activity at Seattle during the mid-1950s: Getis stresses Hudson's role, and his 'inferiority complex that comes from being remote' (p. 530), which led him to place Washington graduates as faculty members in several of the main mid-western graduate schools (such as Chicago, Northwestern and Michigan Universities) in order to establish his department's intellectual reputation. This was also facilitated by their access to the department's reprographic facilities, which allowed them to circulate draft papers very widely (Velikonja, 1994; Morrill, 2002; Johnston, 2004a).

Garrison and his co-workers had catholic interests in urban and economic geography. Much of their research was grounded in theory gleaned from other disciplines, notably economics, although they were much attracted to Christaller's central place theory –

which Bunge (1968, p. 133) described as 'geography's finest intellectual product'. Their efforts were directed towards both testing those theories and applying them to planning problems. In the former activity they drew on a much stronger mathematical base than was the case at Iowa and Madison. They also searched widely for relevant statistical tests for analysing point and line patterns – the biological sciences provided several, such as nearest-neighbour analysis of point patterns (Dacey, 1962), whereas others, for grouping, classifying and regionalizing, were derived from psychology (Berry, 1968). Garrison (1956a, p. 429) argued that, 'there is ample evidence that present tools are adequate to our present state of development. No type of problem has been proposed that could not be treated with available tools', which contradicted a claim by Reynolds (1956), although he criticized some uses of standard techniques (Garrison, 1956b). The dominant thrust of the group's work therefore involved importing relevant normative theories plus mathematical methods and statistical procedures from other systematic sciences, with which to develop morphological laws.

The wealth of the work done at Seattle is illustrated by their major publications. Garrison (1959a, 1959b, 1960a), for example, contributed a three-part review article on the state of location theory. The first part reviewed six recent books – none by geographers – addressing the question 'What determines the spatial arrangement (structure, pattern, or location) of economic activity?' (Garrison, 1959a, p. 232). Each incorporated locational considerations into traditional economic analysis and offered valuable economic insights to traditional geographical problems.

Central place theory was the dominant location theory on which the group worked, however. This had several independent origins (Ullman, 1941; see also Harris, 1977, and Freeman, 1961, p. 201, who notes that findings akin to those in central place theory were reported by the 1851 Census Commissioners of Great Britain). Christaller's (1966) thesis attracted most attention, however (see Müller-Wille, 1978). Working in Germany in the 1930s, Christaller developed ideas regarding the ideal distribution of settlements of different sizes acting as the marketing centres of functional regions, within constraining assumptions relating to the physical environment and the goals of both entrepreneurs and customers: a translation became available in the late 1950s, and was published in 1966. Studies of functional regions were not novel, of course (see p. 54), and other geographers had tested Christaller's notions regarding a hierarchical organization of settlements distributed on a hexagonal lattice (e.g. the work of Brush, 1953, at Wisconsin); related, more inductive, work on 'principles of areal organization' was reported by Philbrick (1957: Philbrick's work was much influenced by that of a senior Chicago professor, Robert Platt. Platt, 1928, 1935 – in a discussion of the latter, R. E. Dodge concluded that there had been too much recent 'philosophising' in geography, and that only when there were plenty of 'good field studies of contrasted regions' would geographers have the background for 'becoming philosophical in our advancing years', p. 174). Dacey wanted to make the analysis of these spatial hierarchies more rigorous mathematically (Dacey, 1962), whereas Berry focused on empirical investigations of the settlement pattern north of Seattle and the retail centres in the city of Spokane (Berry and Garrison, 1958a, 1958b; Berry, 1959a), which work was facilitated by commercially-won contracts.

The second part of Garrison's (1959b) review article dealt with possible geographical applications of the mathematical procedures of linear programming, which identify optimal solutions to problems of resource allocation in constrained situations. He illustrated how neoclassical economic analytic procedures could be adapted for investigations of ideal spatial solutions to the problems of where to locate economic activities and how to organize flows of goods. Six problems which could be treated by linear programming were identified:

1. The *transportation problem*, which takes a set of points, some with a given supply of a good and some with a given demand for it, plus costs of movement, and determines the most efficient flow pattern of the good from supply to demand points which minimizes the expenditure on transport;
2. The *spatial price-equilibrium problem*, which takes the same information as the transportation problem, but determines prices as well as flows;
3. The *warehouse-location problem*, which determines the best location for a set of supply points, given a geography of demand;
4. The *industrial-location problem*, which determines the optimum location for factories from knowledge of the sources of their raw materials and the destinations for their products;
5. The *interdependencies problem*, which locates linked plants so as to maximize their joint profits; and
6. The *boundary-drawing problem*, which determines the most efficient set of boundaries (i.e. that which minimizes total expenditure on transport), for example, for school catchment areas.

If these are used to investigate actual patterns and not as the bases for future plans, the purpose, as Lösch (1954) put it, is to see whether reality is 'rational', whether decision-makers have acted in ways that would produce the most efficient solutions: efficiency is defined as cost-minimization, particularly transport-cost minimization. Relevant investigations by the Washington group included studies of inter-regional trade (Morrill and Garrison, 1960) and the optimal regional location of agricultural activities in the United States (Garrison and Marble, 1957).

In the final part of his review article, Garrison (1960a) dealt with four further books on locational analysis, which were empirical in orientation and shared a common interest in the agglomeration economies reaped by industrial clusters. Several topics and techniques were discussed, such as the use of input-output matrices to represent industrial systems, and Garrison concluded by stressing the need for geographers to investigate location patterns as systems of inter-related activities.

The empirical work with a planning orientation undertaken by the Seattle group is illustrated by their research on the impact of highway developments on land use and other patterns (Garrison et al., 1959). This book included four studies: Berry's on the spatial pattern of central places within urban areas; Marble's on the residential pattern of the city (as indexed by property values) and relationships between household characteristics – including location – and their movement patterns; Nystuen's on movements by customers to central places; and Morrill's on the locations of physicians' offices, both actual and the most efficient. In addition, Garrison worked on the impacts of highway improvements, and devised indices of accessibility based on graph theory (Garrison, 1960b: the work was continued by Kansky, 1963, after Garrison and Berry moved to the Chicago area). He also used the simulation procedures developed by Hägerstrand (1968) to investigate urban growth processes (Garrison, 1962), a topic extended by Morrill (1965).

Somewhat separate from the work of the others in the group, although aligned with their general purpose, was Bunge's thesis, *Theoretical Geography* (1962, reprinted in enlarged form in 1966). This displays a catholic view of geography, together with an acknowledged debt to Schaefer (Bunge worked at Iowa for a short period, and also at Madison, where he clashed with Hartshorne). Its basic theme is that geography is the science of spatial relations and inter-relations; geometry is the mathematics of space; hence geometry is the language of geography. The early chapters establish geography's scientific credentials, in a debate with Hartshorne's published statements, especially those concerning uniqueness and predictability. Bunge claimed that Hartshorne confused uniqueness and singularity (on which see Lewis, 1965): he opposed the claim that geography cannot formulate laws because of its paucity of cases by arguing for even more general laws, and countered the argument that geographical phenomena are not predictable with the claim that science 'does not strive for complete accuracy but compromises its accuracy for generality' (p. 12).

Having established geography's scientific credibility to his satisfaction, Bunge then investigated its language. An intriguing discussion of cartography led him to conclude that descriptive mathematics is preferable to cartography as a more precise language. The remainder of the book looked at aspects of the substantive content of the science of geography, beginning with 'a general theory of movement' and then a chapter on central place theory: 'If it were not for the existence of central place theory, it would not be possible to be so emphatic about the existence of a theoretical geography . . . central place theory is geography's finest intellectual product' (p. 133). Problems testing the theory suggested the need for map transformations (see also Getis, 1963), and the final chapter of the first edition clarified the links between geography and geometry: 'Now that the science of space is maturing so rapidly, the mathematics of space – geometry – should be utilized with an efficiency never achieved by other sciences' (p. 201). Bunge's *Theoretical Geography* is peppered with maps and geometrical visualizations of spatial relationships.

The richness of the work done by this group during the mid- and late 1950s continued in various locations after it broke up (only Ullman remained, although Morrill later joined the staff at Seattle). Berry was one of the most prolific and seminal, not only in his original field of central place theory (Berry, 1967) but also over a wide range of other topics in economic and social geography. His work always had a very strong empirical and utilitarian base (Yeates, 2001), whereas Dacey continued to work on the mathematical representation of spatial, especially point, patterns (e.g. Dacey, 1973) and Tobler (1995) moved into computer cartography. In total, the work of this significant group of scholars influenced the research and teaching of a whole generation of human geographers, throughout the world. In subsequent decades, the Washington department again provided a major lead in innovative work – this time on regional economic analysis: led by Morgan Thomas, a number of graduate students – some of whom were later appointed to the Washington faculty – produced innovative work on topics such as growth-pole theory, regional input-output analysis, and the spatial strategies of firms and corporations, and in turn several of them became leaders in this area of locational analysis (Velikonja, 1994).

From Seattle and elsewhere to Chicago and further

The developments outlined above marked the beginning of major changes in the field of human geography, which were rapidly taken up by others, within and beyond the United States. Although the focus was on theory and measurement, and the development of 'geographical laws' the work did not deviate too far from Hartshorne's expanded (1959) definition of the nature of geography (see p. 68); indeed, in a major programmatic statement, Berry (1964b) used the regional concept as the core for a revised framework of geographical research. The main difference between the new work, with its focus on systematic studies, and its regional predecessor was the greater faith of geographers in their ability to produce laws, to work within the canons of accepted scientific method, to master and apply relevant mathematical and statistical procedures, and to move out of their self-imposed academic isolation (Ackerman, 1945, 1963).

Diffusion of the new approach was rapid, involving a number of graduates from the four centres identified above, especially Seattle, plus other willing change-agents. Ned Taaffe, for example, trained in journalism and meteorology and, after experience teaching economics and statistics, was involved in the development of spatial analysis at Northwestern University (on which see also Hanson, 1993) and then moved to Ohio State University 'with a mandate to build a research department'. Taaffe had studied urban hinterlands using air traffic data for his Chicago PhD as exemplars of functional regions and following the stimulus of his mentor, Robert Platt (see above, p. 77): his supervisor was Harold Mayer. He then taught economic geography and statistics for four years in the economics department at Loyola University (Gauthier, 2002), before taking up a joint appointment with the Department of Geography and the Transportation Center at Northwestern in 1956 (Garrison was appointed to the latter in 1960). The graduate students that he worked with (and to whom he promoted the 'spatial view' which won converts to geography's role from other social sciences; Taaffe, 1974) included, almost contemporaneously with the Washington department, a number who were to become leaders in the field, such as Emilio Casetti, Ed Conkling, Larry Brown, Barry Garner, Howard Gauthier, Peter Gould, Frank Horton, David Reynolds and Maurice Yeates (Gauthier, 2002, p. 582).

At Ohio State, Taaffe appointed 'a group of geographers, each of whom influenced the development of spatial analysis in geography in a somewhat different way' (Taaffe, 1993, p. 423). He names Howard Gauthier, Les King, George Demko, Kevin Cox, John Rayner, Emilio Casetti, Larry Brown, Reg Golledge, John Arnfield and Harold Moellering. Golledge, King – Taaffe's 'most influential appointment' according to Getis (1993, p. 522) – Rayner and Bill Clark were all at the University of Canterbury, New Zealand when Harold McCarty was a visiting professor there in the late 1950s. Taaffe was also involved in several summer workshops conducted at Northwestern University with funding under the National

Defense Education Act, which introduced many other geographers to quantitative methods. (Taaffe, 1979, p.137, lists some of them.)

A further major centre to which the 'new geography' was initially transferred, and where a great deal was accomplished in the 1960s and 1970s, was the University of Chicago, which Brian Berry joined in 1958. (Indeed, there were several examples of early Chicago work – much of it inspired by Robert Platt, Charles Colby and, later, Chauncy Harris (Harris, 1990) – which foreshadowed the later developments.) Already on the staff when Berry arrived were Chauncy Harris, who had published pioneering papers on location theory and had used macrogeographic ideas in his research (see above, p. 70 and 75), and Harold Mayer, a leading urban geographer whose collection of essays (Mayer and Kohn, 1959) was a pioneering early urban text (including in New Zealand, which Mayer visited in 1961: Clark, 2002) and whose contents Berry lightly influenced (Berry, 2002b). The research that Berry stimulated (some of it involving staff and students at nearby Northwestern University) was carried forward by a large number of graduate students. It focused initially on central place studies, extending his Seattle work, but was soon expanded into a wide range of studies including the internal structure of cities, ethnic segregation and housing allocation, and the definition of urban built-up areas and their functional hinterlands. This work, much of which was undertaken for external sponsors – thus demonstrating the applied relevance of the 'new geography' – was widely cited, and the large numbers involved became nodes in what Yeates (2001, p. 524) has termed the 'continental and global network of professionals' associated with a further 'Chicago School' that very strongly influenced the development of human geography during that period. That influence spread beyond the fields of urban and economic geography on which Berry and his students specialized. Other research groups there were substantially impacted, such as Ginsburg's on patterns of economic development (Ginsburg, 1961), especially in Asia, and the work by Gilbert White and his associates (such as Ian Burton, Robert Kates, Thomas Saarinen) on issues of resource management (see below, p. 141).

Other centres were soon established. Two Washington graduates – John Nystuen and Waldo Tobler – were appointed to the University of Michigan at Ann Arbor, for example, and Bill Bunge to Wayne State University in Detroit. Together with others at Michigan State University, they established an informal inter-university seminar group which met at a tavern midway between the three centres at which they and invited visitors gave papers. Several of these were 'published' as the Michigan Inter-University Community of Mathematical Geographers (MICMOG) discussion papers, which were widely circulated – and which Tobler (2002, p. 309) reports were critical in attracting Gunnar Olsson to Michigan. Their publication was halted when *Geographical Analysis* was founded, but several of them (such as Gould's original paper on mental maps – see below, p. 148) had by then become influential 'mini-classics'.

The role of certain individuals and institutions in the promotion of change was thus crucial (on which see the exchange between Morrill and Johnston: Morrill, 1993, 1994; Johnston, 1994d). Their publications influenced geographers – especially young geographers – around the world (Adams, 2002; Clark, 2002). The work that they promoted succeeded, according to Berry (2002b, p. 561), because: (1) it was scientifically-conducted, and thus replicable; (2) theory was continually being improved, through the interplay of speculation and empirical analysis; (3) it was multidisciplinary; and (4) it was continually applied, creating a successful tension between theory and practice – to the benefit of both. They didn't 'take over' the discipline – as Wheeler's (2002a) analysis of articles published in major journals during the 1960s shows – but they were highly influential in setting the discipline's research and training agenda for several decades.

Scientific method in human geography

The changes just described heralded a potential major reorientation in the nature of much geographical research. This was not focused on any single blueprint, grand design or programmatic statement, however. No paper or book published in either the 1950s or the early to mid-1960s provided either a philosophy for the new approach or detailed how research should be conducted within that framework. Schaefer's paper said nothing about how geographical laws were to be derived, and although McCarty and his co-workers discussed methods in both general (McCarty, 1954) and specific (McCarty et al., 1956) contexts, they provided no programmatic statement for how the discipline should be practised. This exemplifies what Gregory (1978a, p. 47) notes, that 'geography has (with some notable exceptions) paid scant attention to its epistemological foundations': Livingstone (1992, p. 328) suggests that 'Geography's confrontation with the vocabulary of logical positivism [in the 1950s] … was a *post hoc* means of rationalizing its attempt to reconstitute itself as spatial science'. What was promoted was very largely a technical revolution which only later sought philosophical legitimation.

One piece that post-dated many of the early essays, but was then widely quoted in the 1960s as the new ideas spread, was Ackerman's (1958) essay on *Geography as a Fundamental Research Discipline*. This was mainly an analysis of research organization. He argued that the ultimate goal must be inter-disciplinary integration, and that, 'If any one theme may be used to characterize this period, that theme would be one of illuminating covariant relations among earth features' (p. 7). As a science, even one which is eventually an idiographic science since it deals with unique places, geography, according to Ackerman, needed to strive for 'an increasingly nomothetic component'. Its fundamental research:

> … need not necessarily be law-giving. … Much fundamental research in geography has not been law-giving in the strict sense but it has been concerned with a high level of generalization, and it has given meaning to other research efforts which succeeded it. In this sense it has a block-building characteristic (p. 17).

Such fundamental research 'is likely to rest on quantification … accurate study depends on quantification' (p. 30) and should 'furnish a theoretical framework with capacity to illuminate actually observed distributional patterns and space relations' (p. 28).

Ackerman issued a clarion call for theory development, the application of quantitative methods, and a focus on laws and generalizations to form the building-blocks for further nomothetic research. But his essay lacked any detailed discussion of how such research should be undertaken. Seven years later, a report of a National Academy of Sciences – National Research Council (1965, p.1) committee on *The Science of Geography* set out 'geography's problem and method' in the statement that:

Geographers believe that correlations of spatial distributions, considered both statistically and dynamically, may be the most ready keys to understanding existing or developing lifesystems, social systems, or environmental changes. In the past ... progress was gradual, however, because geographers were few, rigorous methods for analysing multivariate problems and systems concepts were developed only recently (p. 9).

This, too, was a general statement on research orientation with no accompanying detail on research procedures. And yet a paper published in 1963 had claimed that an intellectual revolution – the quantitative and theoretical revolution – had occurred in geography: 'The revolution is over, in that once-revolutionary ideas are now conventional' (Burton, 1963, p. 156). Something had become conventional, but nobody had written a full formulation for the discipline of what that something was!

Scientific method

The groups of researchers who proposed changes in the nature of human geography undoubtedly had a clear, if implicit, rationale for their arguments, but these were not discussed in detail in print. Nor, if their citations in the published works are any lead, did many research deeply into the philosophy that they were adopting (though a few, such as Peter Gould, regularly attended courses in philosophy throughout their subsequent careers: see Gould, 1999). The exceptions are the references to Bergmann in the Iowa group's papers (see Golledge, 1983) and in Bunge's (1962) thesis. Texts on statistical and mathematical procedures were widely quoted and, although many relied on those written for other disciplines (e.g. Blalock, 1960; Krumbein and Graybill, 1965; Garrison worked with Krumbein at Northwestern in the 1960s: Garrison, 2002, p. 110), several were produced by and for geographers (e.g. Gregory, 1963; King, 1969b). But there was very little discussion of either epistemology – the theory of what constitutes valid knowledge – or of ontology – the theory of what can be known: these were largely ignored (or considered 'common sense') and instead the emphasis was on methods. The first major work on the philosophy of the 'new geography' was not published until 1969, by a British geographer (who moved to the USA at about the time the book appeared), based on several years teaching the epistemology and ontology of science to geography undergraduates at the University of Bristol in order to give a philosophical foundation to the technical procedures (Harvey, 1969a; a parallel, but briefer statement is Moss, 1970).

Harvey identifies two routes to explanation (Figure 3.1). The first, the 'Baconian' or inductive route, derives generalizations from observations: a pattern is observed and an explanation developed from and for it. This involves a dangerous form of generalizing from the particular case, however, because acceptance of the interpretations depends too much on the unproven representativeness of the case(s) discussed and, perhaps, the charisma of the scholar involved (Moss, 1970). Thus the second route in Figure 3.1 is much preferred (though see Bennett, 1985b and Barnes, 1996). This also begins with observers perceiving patterns in the world; they then formulate experiments, or some other kind of test, to test the veracity of the explanations offered for those patterns. Only when ideas have been tested successfully against data other than those from which they were derived can a generalization be produced.

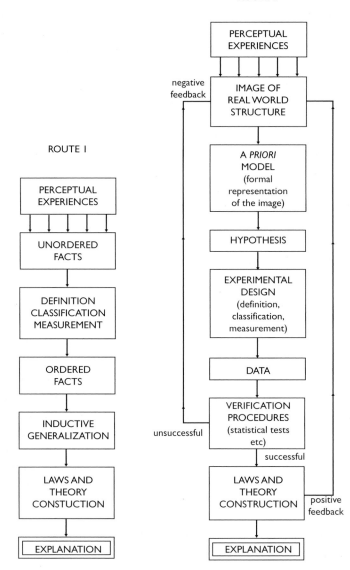

Figure 3.1 *Two routes to scientific explanation (Source: Harvey, 1969a, p. 34)*

Scientific knowledge obtained via the second route is 'a kind of controlled speculation' (Harvey, 1969a, p. 85). Its philosophy, known as positivism, was developed by a group of philosophers working in Vienna during the 1920s and 1930s based on procedures developed a century earlier in France (Gregory, 1978a; Guelke, 1978). It is based on a conception of an objective world in which there is order waiting to be discovered. Because that order exists – spatial patterns of variation and co-variation in the case of geography – it cannot be contaminated by the observer (a position known as empiricist). A neutral observer, acting on either personal observations or reading others' research reports, will derive a hypothesis (a speculative law) about some aspect of reality and then test it: verification of the hypothesis translates the speculative law into an accepted one. (For a more nuanced discussion of the search for order, see Symanski and Agnew, 1981.)

A key tenet of this philosophy is that laws must be proven through objective and replicable procedures: 'the plausibility or intuitive reality of a theory is *not* a valid basis for judging a theory' (Bunge, 1962, p. 3). A valid law must predict successfully, so that having developed an idea about certain patterns the researcher must formulate it into a testable *hypothesis* – 'a proposition whose truth or falsity is capable of being asserted' (Harvey, 1969a, p. 100) – for which an experiment can be designed. Data are then collected, and the hypothesis's validity evaluated. If the test results do not match the predictions, then either the observations on which the hypothesis was derived or the deductions on which it was based are thrown into doubt. There is thus negative feedback (Figure 3.1) and the image of the world has to be revised, creating a new hypothesis.

According to Harvey (1969a, p. 105):

> A scientific law may be interpreted as a generalization which is empirically universally true, and one which is also an integral part of a theoretical system in which we have supreme confidence. Such a rigid interpretation would probably mean that scientific laws would be non-existent in all of the sciences. Scientists therefore relax their criteria to some degree in their practical application of the term.

After sufficient (undefined) successful tests, therefore, a hypothesis may be accorded law-like status, and fed into a body of *theory*, which comprises a series of related laws. There are two types of statement within a full theory: the *axioms*, or givens – statements that are taken to be true, such as laws; and the deductions, or *theorems*, from those initial conditions, which are derived consequences from agreed facts – the next round of hypotheses. There is a positive feedback from the theory stage to the world view, therefore (Figure 3.1), so that the whole scientific enterprise is a cyclical procedure whereby the successes of one set of experiments become the building blocks for thinking about the next.

One stage in Figure 3.1 so far ignored is the *model*, a widely used term with a variety of meanings (Chorley, 1964). Models have two basic functions: as *representations of the real world*, such as a scale model, a map, a series of equations and some other analogue (Morgan, 1967); and as *ideal types*, representations of the world under certain constrained conditions. Both are used in the positivist method to operationalize a theory, as a guide to the derivation of testable hypotheses.

Quantification is central to this scientific method. Mathematics is particularly useful in developing models, as in the linear programming procedures discussed by Garrison. Relatively few geographers have strong backgrounds in mathematics, however (this was especially true in the 1950s), and so little work involved representing the real world as sets of equations. Instead the central role was given to statistics. Two types of statistics are available: *descriptive statistics* represent a pattern or relationship; *inductive statistics* are used for making generalizations about a carefully defined population from a properly selected random sample. They use the same procedures; the difference lies in how they are deployed. Many geographical researchers confused the two. Inductive statistics employ significance tests to show whether what has been observed in the sample probably also occurs in the parent population, so that if the data analysed are not a sample, such tests are irrelevant (some disagreement was expressed over 'what is a sample?': see Meyer, 1972 and Court, 1972). Many geographers use inductive methods in a descriptive manner only, however, using the significance tests as measures of the validity of their findings, asking what is the likelihood of a relationship that they have discovered arising by chance given data set's contents (as argued in Hay, 1985b).

The main attraction of statistics to many early adherents of the 'new geography' was their precision and lack of ambiguity – compared to the English language – in description. This was expressed by Cole (1969), who annotated a quotation from a well-known textbook (Stamp and Beaver, 1947, pp. 164–5), in which the text is Stamp and Beaver's and the annotations in parentheses, to show the ambiguities, are Cole's:

> The present distribution of wheat cultivation in the British Isles (space) raises the conception of two different types of limit. Broadly speaking (vague), it may be said that the possible (vague) limits (limit) of cultivation of any crop are determined by geographical (vague), primarily by climatic conditions. The limits so determined (how?) may be described (definition) as the ultimate (vague) or the geographical (vague) limits (Cole, 1969, p. 160).

Cole argued that the full quotation (only part is reproduced here) is so full of ambiguities that it could refer to about one million possible combinations of some forty counties and it is impossible to reconstruct a map from that description:

> ... the correlations suggested are so tentative and imprecise that they leave the reader still wondering why wheat is grown where it is. The application of a standard correlation procedure ... in itself would give a more precise appreciation of the relationship (p. 162).

Similar views became widely held during the 1960s, and quantification became the *sine qua non* of training in research methods (LaValle, McConnell and Brown, 1967). But they were only means to the end, as Gould (1979, p. 140) expressed in it a later retrospective:

> It was not the numbers that were important, but a whole new way of looking at things geographic that can be summed up in Whitehead's definition of scientific thought, 'To see what is general in what is particular and what is permanent in what is transitory'.

The scientific method increasingly adopted by geographers was a procedure for testing ideas, therefore, but a highly formalized one, about which there has been a great deal of debate among philosophers of science and others (Harvey, 1969a). Although many aspects of the method were used by geographers, their citations indicate relatively little training or exploration in depth into the full philosophy of positivism. Positivism, as used here, refers to what is often known as 'scientific method'. It is embraced by the philosophy of logical positivism, which claims that only scientifically obtained knowledge is valid knowledge (Johnston, 1986a, 1986b).

An alternative to positivism is critical rationalism, a view of science associated with the philosopher Karl Popper. He argued that any hypothesis can be found wanting by a single falsification. Harvey (1969a, p. 39) gave only eight lines to this approach, however, preferring to argue that only 'severe failure' – which he does not define – discredits a hypothesis totally (see, however, Moss, 1977; Bird, 1975; Petch and Haines-Young, 1980; Haines-Young and Petch, 1985). Hay (1985a), Marshall (1985) and Bird (1989) all present cases for adopting Popper's critical rationalism in human geography. The goal is the same as in positivism – to develop comprehensive theories which allow predictions with high degrees of certainty. The two differ on means, not ends. Critical rationalists believe that hypotheses can never be comprehensively verified, only falsified. If the researcher is a good observer and a logical thinker, falsification of hypotheses should be rare. If the test is successful, then the speculation in the hypothesis becomes an acceptable generalization. One successful test will not turn it into a universal law, however, since, according to Popper, all knowledge is provisional, subject to continued testing through critical experiments (Symanski and Agnew, 1981). Knowledge accumulates through the falsification of invalid hypotheses.

Reactions to scientific method

Despite (or perhaps because of) the lack of a clear programmatic statement of the 'new Theology' (Stamp, 1966, p. 18), at least until the appearance of Harvey's (1969a) book, reactions to the developments were many and varied. (James, 1965, p. 35, called the debate 'continued, bitter and uncompromising warfare'.) Two related issues were the main foci of contention: whether quantification was sensible in geographical research, and whether law-making was possible. As Taylor (1976) points out, to some extent the debate was inter-generational: some of the 'old guard' thought the proposals were just not geography and should be banished to another corner of academia.

The quantification issue was the less important, and few spoke out against it entirely, although its extent was criticized. Spate (1960a, p. 387) recognized quantification as 'an essential element':

This is, like it or not, the Quantified Age. The stance of King Canute is not very helpful or realistic; better to ride the waves, if one has sufficient finesse, than to stake attitudes of humanistic defiance and end, in Toynbee's phrase, in the dustbin of history (p. 391).

He identified three dangers, however. The first was a confusion of ends and means; some protagonists wanted to quantify everything (after Lord Kelvin, 'when you cannot express it in numbers, your knowledge is of a meagre and unsatisfactory kind', Spate, 1960b), but some things, like the positions of Madrid and Barcelona in Spanish thought, cannot be treated in that way. Secondly, there was the dogged analysis of trivia, producing platitudinous findings, a fault which Spate recognized as part of all academia, and especially its revolutions: 'Quantified or not, the trivial we will always have with us' (Spate, 1960a, p. 389), and the problem is usually the extreme positions taken up – Robinson's (1961) perks (the hyperquantifiers) and pokes (the hypoquantifiers). Finally, there was the quantifiers' vaunting ambition and belief that solution of the world's problems lay just around the corner.

Spate was more generous than many critics. Burton (1963) identified five types of criticism:

1. Geography was being led in the wrong direction;
2. Geographers should stick with their proven tool – the map;
3. Quantification was suitable for certain tasks only;
4. Means were being elevated over ends, with too much research on methods for methods' sake; and
5. Objections were not to quantification *per se* but to the quantifiers' attitudes.

He believed that quantification had already proved more than a fad or fashion, however. Geography would soon proceed beyond a stage of testing relatively trivial hypotheses with its new tools so that, 'The development of theoretical, model-building geography is likely to be the major consequence of the quantitative revolution' (p. 156).

One episode regarding the reaction to quantification concerns Stamp's reaction to Haggett's (1964) early paper on land use change in Brazil: Stamp suggested that Haggett's quantitative analysis could be likened to using 'an enormous steam hammer ... in the cracking of nuts'. These comments are included in the published record of the discussion of Haggett's paper (Haggett, 1964, p. 380) and end with an exclamation mark, with the implication that these may not have been Stamp's own views, though his call for those using quantitative techniques to 'tear up some of their results' suggests a negative attitude to at least some of the 'new lines of thought'. Haggett had defended his approach – prior to Stamp's summing-up – by noting that, 'While method has loomed large in this paper I hope that it has not blotted out the fact that ... traditional problems of forest depletion are reaching critical levels. Statistical analysis can help to clarify some of the problems and provide some checks on intuitive solutions' (p. 380). It is also recorded that a few days after the paper was given, Haggett was told by his Head of Department at Cambridge that he was 'bringing the subject of geography into disrepute by applying such mathematical methods' (Chorley, 1995, p. 360).

More critical to many geographers than quantification was the issue of theory, and in particular the role of laws in geography. For some, this continued the debate over environmental determinism, which was still active in Britain (Clark, 1950; Martin, 1951; Montefiore and Williams, 1955; Jones, 1956). Jones, for example, extended the debate to cover scientific determinism and its implications for human free will. Martin (1951, p. 6) had argued that possibilism is 'not merely wrong but is mischievous' because all human actions are determined in some way, so that in human geography:

Unless we can assume the existence of laws or necessary conditions similar in stringency to those of physical science, there can be no human geography nor social sciences worth the name, but only a series of unexplainable statements of bare events ... such laws cannot differ, except in respect of ... far greater complication, from those of physical science (pp. 9–10).

Jones (1956) indicated the impossibility of discovering universal laws about human behaviour and pointed to the use of two types of law in physics: the determinate laws of classical physics, which apply macroscopically; and the probabilistic quantum laws, which refer to the behaviour of individual particles. The latter allow for the exercise of free will within prescribed constraints, and their application in human geography would at least allow answers to be offered to the question 'how?' if not to 'why?'. But the question of causality clearly worried many, as indicated by Lewis's (1965) counter-argument that, 'it is erroneously assumed that causes compel their effects in some way in which effects do not compel their causes' (p. 26).

Golledge and Amedeo (1968, p. 760) addressed this same problem, pointing out that critics of law-seeking in human geography defined a law as a universal postulate which brooked of no exception: 'not all are aware [even among those who accept the nomothetic goal] of the nature, types, and relationships of scientific laws developed by philosophers of science'. Scientists use several types of law, however, and the veracity of a law-like statement can never be finally proven, since it cannot be tested against all instances, at all times and in all places. Four types were identified with relevance for human geographers:

1. *Cross-sectional laws* describe functional relationships (as between two maps) but show no causal connection, although they may suggest one;
2. *Equilibrium laws* state what will be observed if certain criteria are met;
3. *Dynamic laws* incorporate notions of change, with the alteration in one variable being followed by (and perhaps causing) an alteration in another. They may be either *historical,* for example showing that B would have been preceded by A and followed by C, or *developmental,* in which B would be followed by C, D, E, etc.; and
4. *Statistical laws* are probabilistic statements of the likelihood of B happening, given that A exists: all laws of the other three categories may be either deterministic or statistical, with the latter almost certainly the case with phenomena studied by geographers.

Having illustrated all four types, they concluded with regard to the existence of situations where laws seem not to fit that '… the idea of laws being strict universals no longer dominates in the interpretation of the concept' (p. 774): the goal is to advance knowledge by continually reassessing the validity of assumed laws.

This discussion was not part of an ongoing, published, debate on quantification and theory-building; it was a reaction to widely-held and discussed attitudes rather than to published critiques. There were none for several years in Britain, for example (Taylor, 1976), but there was one debate in the American literature, initiated by Lukermann's (1958) reaction to Warntz's views on macrogeography (see above, p. 76) and a paper by Ballabon (1957). The latter claimed that economic geography lacked general principles; it was 'short on theory and long on facts' (p. 218). Ballabon stressed the utility of location theory being developed by economists as a source for hypotheses. Lukermann responded that the main problem in Ballabon's and Warntz's arguments lay in the assumptions behind their hypotheses (Warntz's analogies with physics and Ballabon's with economics) which did not conform to his view of geography as an empirical science. Statistical regularities and isomorphisms with other subject matter do not provide explanations, so that hypotheses derived from such models test only the models themselves and (Lukermann, 1958, p. 9; see also Moss, 1970): 'the hypotheses to be tested are neither statistically nor rationally derived; that is, they are derived neither from empirical observation nor from deductions of previous knowledge in the social, economic or geographic fields'.

Berry (1959b) countered with the contention that models, for all their simplifications and unreal assumptions, offer insights towards understanding the real world: 'A theory or model, when tested and validated, provides a miniature of reality and therefore a key to many descriptions. There is a single master-key instead of the loaded key ring' (p. 12). Lukermann (1960a) was not convinced that models based on assumptions of perfect knowledge and competition, for example, could help towards understanding if they were not empirically derived: 'the crucial problem is the construction of hypotheses from the empirical realities of economic geography . . . more light is shed and less truth is sophisticated through inventory than through hunches' (p. 2). King (1960) claimed that all laws are really only hypotheses, and that deviations of observed from expected values in their testing indicate where the assumptions are invalid. Lukermann responded three times. The first paper showed the lack of consensus in 'explanations' of the geography of cement production in the United States (Lukermann, 1960b) because economic analyses ignored 'Historical inertia, geographical momentum, and the human condition' (p. 5). Secondly, in response to King, he presaged some of the arguments developed later by Sack, who worked with him at Minnesota (see p. 135), and pointed out that much of the theory being introduced to economic geography (such as Lösch's) was not based on providing understanding of, and explanation for, reality (Lukermann, 1961). Finally, a discussion of several aspects of the debate concluded with the statement that (Lukermann, 1965, p. 194):

> *Thus, we see scientific explanation as far removed from the context within which the macroscopic geographers would have us put it – the end product of geographic research. Science does not explain reality, it explains the consequences of its hypotheses.*

He called for explanations in geography to be based on observations and not on imported analogies which cannot offer explanations, only unreal assumptions. Lukermann's basic point, never fully tackled by his critics, was that tests showing conformity between empirical reality and a model were tests of the model only, and could not indicate how empirical reality was created if the assumptions on which the model was constructed were not themselves grounded in reality. (See Barnes, 1996, Chapter 9, for a full evaluation of Lukermann's work.)

This difference of opinion was over the way in which geographers should seek explanations and not about the positivist scientific method itself; it was concerned with the inputs to the images of the real-world structure (Figure 3.1). It is doubtful whether papers such as those of Jones, Lewis, and Golledge and Amedeo quieted the fears of others unconvinced by the quantifiers' arguments, any more than Berry and King convinced Lukermann. But the differences soon became a non-issue, at least in the published papers resulting from the research activities of geographers in many topical specialisms. As Burton claimed, by the mid-1960s the changes seem to have been widely accepted, and the regional approach had certainly been ousted from its prime position in the publications of

American human geographers (see Wheeler, 2002a). Increasingly, quantitative and theoretical material came to dominate not only the more obvious journals, such as *Geographical Analysis* (a 'journal of theoretical geography' founded in 1969, to a considerable extent because those adopting the new approach found difficulty in getting their work accepted by the established journals: Berry, 1993; Barnes, 2001b), but also the prestigious general journals, notably *Economic Geography* (especially after a change of editor), and the *Annals of the Association of American Geographers*. (*The Geographical Review* was an early partial 'convert' through the American Geographical Society's sponsorship of the macrogeographers, although Berry states that it rejected his early papers with Garrison as 'not geography': Halvorson and Stave, 1978; Berry, 1993; Barnes, 2001b.) Most of the work contributed little to theory, however. It was quantitative testing of theory- or model-derived hypotheses in some cases, but with little indication of how good the results were. In others, it was quantitative description that could inform theory and model development, but in itself was merely a series of 'factual reports'. By the 1970s, textbooks were being published which began with discussions of scientific method and quantification before proceeding to the substantive content of the 'empirical science' (Abler, Adams and Gould, 1971; Amedeo and Golledge, 1975); the 'revolution' was apparently becoming the orthodoxy.

Spread of scientific method

The initial development of systematic studies using the positivist scientific method in the USA was very largely focused on economic geography and associated economic aspects of urban geography. This reflects the relative sophistication of economics within the social sciences at that time and the existence of several approaches to 'location theory' (see p. 77), providing models for geographers to emulate, not only to advance their discipline but also to promote its cause in the search for utility to the worlds of business and government. The long tradition of empirical work in human geography meant, however, that with few exceptions research in the systematic areas mainly comprised the statistical testing of relatively simple hypotheses, with little mathematical modelling or writing of formal theory.

Contemporaneous with, and an important stimulus to, these developments in human geography was the emergence of a new discipline in the United States – *regional science*. (On regional science as stimulus, see Berry, 1995.) This was very much the product of one iconoclast scholar – Walter Isard, an economist who built spatial components into his models to provide a stronger theoretical basis for urban and regional planning than had existed previously. In general terms, regional science is economics with a spatial emphasis, as illustrated by Isard's (1956a, 1960) two early texts, but the Regional Science Association attracted relatively more practising geographers than economists. To some, regional science and economic geography are hard to distinguish: the former can be separately characterized by its greater focus on mathematical modelling and economic theorizing, however, whereas geographical work has remained more empirical and less dependent on formal languages. (Initially Isard, 1956b, saw geographers as doing the empirical tests of the regional scientists' models.) Over time, the interests of regional scientists broadened (Isard, 1975), but the strong theoretical base has remained. (The history of regional science, 40 years after the foundation of the Regional Science Association, is discussed in two issues – volume 17, numbers 2 and 3, 1995 – of the *International Regional Science Review*: see, in particular, Isserman, 1995.)

The nascent discipline did not create a substantial niche within American academia, however. (Garrison, 1995, likened it to Moses' 40 years wandering in the wilderness!) Nor did it have a lasting, substantial impact on geography and geographers, although the latter remain a considerable proportion of the Association's membership. Berry (1995) argues that, for him, relative disillusion with regional science was engendered by Isard's categorization of geographers as the empirical workers who tested the regional scientists' theories, which implied a subservient position for geographers in a two-class academic society and would hinder the reformation of economic geography that Berry sought. (This has an interesting parallel to the debates within geography on the division of labour between 'theorizers' and 'empirical testers'; see p. 94.)

The Regional Science Association has flourished internationally, however, and Isserman (1995, p. 261) claims that, 'Regional science has become a mainstream group within geography and geography departments . . . [and] . . . so successful within geography that it became worthy of caricature'. He then notes major tensions between those geographers who remain committed to the goals of regional science (almost certainly a relatively small number within the profession) and those whose interests lie elsewhere. Warf (1995, p. 192) points to these – 'Class and gender, historical sensitivity, the politics of the state, the recovery of the living subject and everyday life, the unintended reproduction of social worlds' – and invites a *rapprochement* between regional science and a geography inspired by what is now known as social theory. (Interestingly, the 1990s saw the recreation of a form of spatial economics – termed 'new economic geography' by its adherents – that has many parallels to regional science: on its relationships with geography, see Martin, 1999; Schoenberger, 2001; and Clark *et al.*, 2000b.)

The emphasis on statistical methods in so much of the new work in American human geography led to its partial *rapprochement* with physical geography. (One of the leading 'quantitative geographers' of the 1960s, Leslie Curry, trained as a climatologist but switched his interests to economic geography in the late 1960s. Others had similar wartime training – as essays in Gould and Pitts, 2002, illustrate.) More physical geography papers were published in the leading journals, more physical geographers were appointed to university departments, geologists such as Krumbein, Leopold, Schumm and Wolman were major sources of quantitative ideas, and there was a common interest in the training of graduate students (LaValle *et al.*, 1967). This shared concern over procedures was illustrated at a 1960 conference on quantitative geography, which resulted in two volumes on methodological developments, one for human geography and the other for physical geography (Garrison and Marble, 1967a, 1967b). Other conferences and summer schools to train geographers in quantitative techniques were held at this time (on their impact, see Gould, 1969; Taaffe, 1979), and American geographers were to the forefront in launching an International Geographical Union Commission on Quantitative Methods. Nevertheless, the rapprochement was far from full, as Marcus (1979, p. 522), himself a physical geographer, complained in his Presidential address to the AAG which was given just after the appearance of a special issue of the *Annals* to commemorate 75 years of American geography: 'not one article [of 30 in the issue] focused on physical geography, its roots, its evolution, its practitioners' (even though 42 per cent of all students enrolled in geography courses at US universities were studying physical geography and 35 of the AAG's Presidents had been practising physical geographers at the time that they held the post). There was a need for greater awareness and cooperation, with much hard work in order to generate a 'rational geography that fulfils the promise we hold for the study of earth and humankind together' (p. 532).

Expansion within American geography

Geography within the academic division of labour

The launch of the 'quantitative and theoretical revolutions' identified by Burton (1963) was concentrated on a few topical specialisms within American human geography only, so an early task for the 'revolutionaries' was to spread their ideas through the discipline, convincing others of the benefits which quantification and the associated scientific method could bring to their special interests. A major piece of advocacy was an NAS/NRC report (1965) on *The Science of Geography* which was prepared in order to chart research priorities within the discipline and establish a place for geography as a social science within the United States' National Academy (Johnston, 2000a). The case was presented for more 'theoretical-deductive' work to balance the earlier emphasis on 'empirical inductive analysis', the detailed argument being based on four premises:

> (a) Scientific progress and social progress are closely correlated, if not equated. (b) Full understanding of the world-wide system comprising man and his natural environment is one of the four or five great overriding problems in all science. (c) The social need for knowledge of space relations of man and natural environment rises, not declines, as the world becomes more settled and more complex, and may reach a crisis stage in the near future. Last, (d) progress in any branch of science concerns all branches, because science as a whole is epigenetic.
>
> The social need for knowledge of space relations means an imminent practical need. As the population density rises and the land-use intensity increases, the need for efficient management of space will become even more urgent (p. 10).

The committee members (E. A. Ackerman, B. J. L. Berry, R. A. Bryson, S. B. Cohen, E. J. Taaffe, W. L. Thomas Jr and M. G. Wolman) defined geography as 'the study of spatial distributions on the earth's surface' (p. 8) so it followed for them that, 'Geographic studies will be irreplaceable components of the scientific support for efficient space management' (p. 10). The positivist scientific method was being sold to geographers and at the same time geography was being sold to the scientific establishment as a positivist science, from whom financial research support could then be sought. (Until that time, geography had little access to major funding sources for large research programmes, though the Office of Naval Research – surprisingly, given its title – did provide some: Pruitt, 1979.)

The committee chose four problem areas to illustrate geography's potentials as a 'useful science'. The first was physical geography. The second was cultural geography, which studies 'differences from place to place in the ways of life of human communities and their creation of man-made or modified features' (p. 23), with a major focus on landscape development and the diffusion of specific cultural features over space and time: 'applying modern techniques to studying the nature and rate of diffusion of key cultural elements and establishing the evolving spatial patterns of culture complexes' (p. 24) was identified as a profitable avenue for development. The third was political geography, with proposed work on boundaries and resource management. Finally, the committee recognized location theory studies, an amalgam of work in economic, urban and transport geography in which the 'dialogue' between the empirical and the theoretical had gone furthest, 'revealing the potential power of a balanced approach when applied to other geographical problem areas' (p. 44). Location theory involved work on spatial patterns, the links and flows between places in such patterns, the dynamics of the patterns, and the preparation of alternative patterns through model-building exercises which identify efficient solutions.

In the development of the science of geography:

> A major opportunity seen by workers in the location theory problem area is that of integrating their work more closely with other geographers as they begin to deal with spatial systems of political, cultural, and physical phenomena. ... This could be achieved ... by the accelerated diffusion of techniques and concepts to other geographers, and communication on the definition of research problems. The result would be to hasten the confrontation of empirical-inductive studies by theoretical-deductive approaches throughout geography. ... Testing the theory in a variety of empirical contexts should aid in the overall development and refinement of viable theories. It should also serve to connect geographic progress to local problems more rapidly and more effectively (pp. 50–1).

The deductive-theoretical scientific methodology was central to the committee's blueprint for the advancement of geographical research, therefore. All geographers would have a role to play in this movement forward, for:

> Geographers have one other asset that should be capitalized on. Those who have been interested in the study of a specific part of the earth (regional geography) develop competences for interpreting the physical-cultural complexes of the regions that they study. Students of the way a particular part of the earth has evolved (historical geography) have other competences for interpreting the historical development and modification of a region. These two groups have students that are particularly qualified to undertake the field observation and field study of problems recognized in a more systematic way and to conduct field tests of generalizations arrived at through systematic study. ... The regional or historical geography specialist who has mastered the technique of field observation and historical study thoroughly ... can make himself indispensable if he understands the direction in which the generalizing clusters are headed and relates his work closely to their growing edges (p. 61).

A clear division of labour was being suggested, comprising theoretical-deductive 'thinkers' and empirical-inductive 'workers', a division which was apparently unequal in status and was resented by some as such (James, 1965; Thoman, 1965). Berry (1995 – and p. 92) reports a similar reaction to a proposed division of labour between regional scientists and geographers (all of which suggests parallels with a nineteenth-century division of scientists – reported in Russell, 1977 – into: the *original*, whose time is taken up with their own ideas; the *deputed* – 'men of little or no originality of mind but who are well trained and competent to work out problems suggested by others'; and the *drudges* – 'men who can make analyses, calculate constants, collect data, etc.' – the quotes are from Barton, 2003, p. 105). Although not all of the committee's recommendations were taken up, it did win institutional recognition for geography within the NRC with the establishment of a geography and regional science program: one of its main achievements, when under the direction of Ron Abler, was the establishment of a national centre for GIS in the 1980s (see p. 177).

A somewhat similar report was prepared a few years later for the Committee on Science and Public Policy of the National Academy of Sciences and the Problems and Policy Committee of the Social Science Research Council (Taaffe, 1970). Also the product of a committee (E. J. Taaffe, I. Burton, N. Ginsburg, P. R. Gould, F. Lukermann and P. L. Wagner), this was a difficult task because (as pointed out by Gauthier, 2002, p. 577) there had been considerable debate over the inclusion of geography because members of the other panels (for economics, sociology, psychology, anthropology and political science) did not consider geography as a social science. The report had to convince them otherwise: it did, and the committee members 'changed people's minds by making a strong argument for geography as a social science that made contributions to society and the development of public policy'. That strong case stressed human geography as 'the study of spatial organization expressed as patterns and processes' (pp. 5–6), incorporating people–environment relationships and cultural landscapes and stressing relevance to planning and other policy issues. Much of the report promoted human geography's cause that:

> ... there are many opportunities for the expansion and improvement of geographic research. If geography is to have a strong and beneficial impact on the constantly changing patterns of spatial organization of American society, it will be necessary to continue this development (p. 131).

This led to six conclusions regarding the discipline's needs: (1) greater collaboration among the social sciences; (2) alleviation of geography's manpower shortage; (3) establishment of centres for cartographic training and research; (4) development of remote sensing and related data bases; (5) greater support for foreign area study; and (6) programmes established 'to strengthen the mathematical training of geographers'. Human geography was presented as an integral component of the social sciences, increasingly sophisticated in its analytical tools, focusing on spatial organization, and offering particular skills in mapping and data acquisition.

There is little evidence that these two volumes, plus the efforts of successive directors of the NRC's geography and regional science programme and the growing volume of work on the geographical-regional science interface, had a major impact, however, and geography's hold on its place in the US scientific academy was tenuous. Thus, in 1997 a further report was published by a committee of sixteen. It was commissioned because of a 'well-documented growing perception (external to geography as a discipline) that geography is useful, perhaps even necessary, in meeting certain societal needs' (NAS-NRC, 1997, p. ix). To provide a showcase for geography's strengths as 'good science and socially relevant science' (p. vii), the committee was asked to (p. 2):

1. Identify critical issues and constraints for the discipline;
2. Clarify teaching and research priorities;
3. Link developments in geography to national educational needs;
4. Increase the appreciation of geography within the country's scientific community; and
5. Communicate with that community about the discipline's future directions.

In doing that, it focused almost entirely on a role for geography, and of types of geographical research, that was very similar to that laid out in the reports of thirty years previously (on which, see Johnston, 1997a, 2000a). The message was having to be repeated since the scientific credentials of geography (both human and physical) were still not widely appreciated within the American academic community: one result of its impact within the NRC was its establishment of a Committee on Geography (Turner, 2002, p. 66).

Geography's subdisciplinary fields

The argument advanced by proponents of the new methodology focused on a common set of procedures to tackle geographical problems. Berry (1964b) argued that the geographer's viewpoint emphasizes space, with regard to distributions, integration, interactions, organization and processes. Its data can be categorized in a single matrix (Figure 3.2) in which places form the rows and characteristics the columns: each cell defines a 'geographic fact'. Berry recognized five types of geographical study which focused on different elements of this matrix: study of either a single row (a place) or column (a characteristic); comparison of two or more rows (places) or columns (characteristics); or study of rows and columns together (regions). Adding further matrices, one for each time-

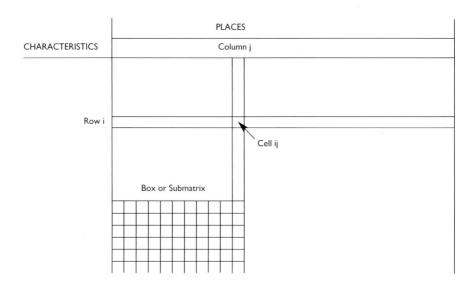

Figure 3.2 *The geographic matrix: each cell – ij – contains a 'geographic fact', the value of characteristic i at location j (Source: Berry, 1964b, p. 6)*

period (Figure 3.3), allows five further types of study, based on the earlier five but concentrating on changes over time. Thus, he concluded, systematic and regional geography are part of the same enterprise – a repetition of Hartshorne's (1959) arguments – with neither sufficient in itself.

Berry's matrices referred only to the characteristics of places; further matrices (Figure 3.4) show flows between places, with one matrix for each flow category in each time-period (Clark, Davies, and Johnston, 1974). Berry used this extension, though he did not formalize it, in a fusion of the procedures for formal and functional regionalization (see above, p. 54) to produce a general theory of spatial behaviour – a field theory, which he applied in a large study of the spatial organization of India (Berry, 1966, 1968). The techniques employed became widely used in the 1960s, as access to high-speed computers became easier. They were given the umbrella term 'factorial ecology' (Berry, 1971), and were widely applied in several geographic subfields, resulting in a methodological unity which was previously unknown across the various systematic specialisms.

One systematic area of geography colonized early by such new methods was that part of urban geography which dealt with the internal spatial structure of cities. Until the 1960s, little work had been done on this topic except with regard to commercial land uses (particularly the Central Business District and the relationship of the pattern of suburban shopping centres to the postulates of central place theory); almost no attention was paid to the human content of residential areas, perhaps because geography was seen as the science of places, not of people. Recognition that 'people live in cities' (Johnston, 1969) generated interest in residential areas, which gained much stimulus from the work of the urban ecology school of sociologists at Chicago (some of their works had been introduced to geographers earlier – Harris and Ullman, 1945; Dickinson, 1947 – but with little impact

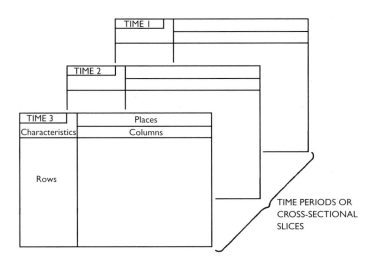

Figure 3.3 *A third dimension to the geographic matrix: each cell – ijt – contains a 'geographic fact', the value of characteristic i at location j at time t (Source: Berry, 1964b, p. 7)*

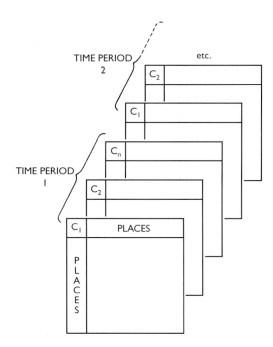

Figure 3.4 *Geographic flow matrices – one per commodity ($C_1 - C_n$) per time period (Source: after Clark, Davies and Johnston, 1974)*

for a decade or so: Agnew, 1997; Lichtenberger, 1997; Harris, 1990, 1992, 1997a). Social area analysis, and then factorial ecology, gained in popularity as a methodology (Berry, 1964a), with the allocation of land among competing groups being modelled, mapped and statistically analysed (Johnston, 1971; Timms, 1971).

By the mid-1960s use of statistical methods to test hypotheses was common across many of human geography's specialisms. They were united by their methods, remaining very separate identifiable branches within the geographical enterprise in terms of their substantive interests. The decline of interest in regional syntheses (see Taaffe, 1974), meant that human geography experienced a centrifugal trend with regard to substance, contemporaneous with a centripetal one with regard to procedures. Since positivist scientific method, and the statistical techniques with which it was associated by many geographers, was used much more widely than in human geography alone, the former trend was probably the most important.

Trans-Atlantic translation

By the early 1960s the quantitative and theoretical revolutions were having considerable impact beyond the United States, as the result of two agencies. The first was the publication of work by the American iconoclasts in the major journals. Secondly, and probably more importantly, during the 1950s and 1960s a number of British geographers went to the United States, either as postgraduate students or as visiting staff members (see Haggett, 1990); during the 1960s and 1970s many British academics were recruited to teach on the intensive summer-school courses for part-time students. Some of those visitors encountered the new ideas and disseminated them 'back home', in part via the newly-established (1962) Study Group in Quantitative Methods of the Institute of British Geographers (Gregory, S., 1976). Several, including Brian Berry, stayed in North America after completing their postgraduate training, and others were attracted to move there. (On why, see Berry, 1993, 2002a.)

Some UK geographers attracted to the 'new approach' had a local base on which to build. For most, this was in physical geography, arising out of the early use of statistics by climatologists (e.g. Crowe, 1936): as a result, perhaps surprisingly, the first undergraduate text in statistics for geographers was written by an English academic (Gregory, 1963), in which the positivist methodology is only implicit, however. His Preface speaks of the geographer's raw material 'becoming progressively more of a quantitative nature' and 'the need to present both data and conclusions in sound quantitative terms' (pp. xiii–xiv); statistical techniques are needed, but their use in hypothesis testing is not set out. In addition, there was some interest in location theory – it was taught at University College London in the early 1950s, for example (Halvorson and Stave, 1978; Berry, 1993; Barnes, 2001a, 2001b), and at the London School of Economics (Johnston, 2003b). Some work on industrial location (Smith, 1949; Rawstron, 1958; though see Rawstron, 2002) and settlement patterns was influenced by theoretical work, too (Dickinson, 1933; Smailes, 1946; note, however, the unwelcoming anonymous review of Christaller's thesis on central place theory in the *Scottish Geographical Magazine,* 1934; on Dickinson and Christaller, see Johnston, 2002a), but this was far from normal.

Although statistics courses were introduced to several British university departments of geography by the mid-1960s, and aspects of the scientific methodology were taught in at least a few (Whitehand, 1970), the main focus for the introduction of the 'new geography' to Britain during the early years of the decade was the University of Cambridge. The leaders were R. J. Chorley (an Oxford graduate and geomorphologist, who had studied geology in the United States: Beckinsale, 1997; Stoddart, 1997a) and P. Haggett (a Cambridge-trained human geographer, although his early published work was in biogeography; he had also visited the United States and experienced the developments there (Haggett, 1965c, p. vi, 1990; see also Haggett and Chorley, 1989). Their impact on British geography was considerable, through innovative research and teaching (Gregory, S., 1976); they supervized a substantial number of graduate students who proceeded to academic posts elsewhere and 'spread the message' in the same way that the 'space cadets' did in the USA (Hanson, 1993).

Chorley and Haggett worked on the adaptation of certain statistical techniques to geographical (both physical and human) problems (Chorley and Haggett, 1965a; Haggett, 1964; Haggett and Chorley, 1969), but their most lasting initial contribution was probably editing two collections of essays which emerged from extra-mural courses that they directed, aimed at introducing the 'new geography' to teachers. (Note that Barnes, 1996, emphasizes Haggett's role as a change-agent within British geography, but in so doing overlooks the substantial behind-the-scenes impacts of others, notably Stan Gregory who was very influential not only in establishing the Study Group on Quantitative Methods within the IBG, but also within the Geographical Association and the Joint Matriculation Board, whose examinations were used for entrance to most British universities.)

The first of these books – *Frontiers in Geographical Teaching* (Chorley and Haggett, 1965b) – was based on a 1963 course designed 'to bring teachers and like persons into the University, there to encounter and discuss recent developments and advances in their subjects' (p. xi). In it Wrigley (1965) discussed the changing philosophy of geography, identifying the increasing use of statistical techniques as the contemporary development 'of singular importance' (p. 15). He pointed out that techniques of themselves do not form a methodology and that, 'Geography writing and research work have in recent years lacked any general accepted, overall view of the subject even though techniques have proliferated' (p. 17). He offered no outline of such a view, however, arguing that eclecticism in mode of analysis was likely to be most productive: 'the best sign of health is the production of good research work rather than the manufacture of general methodologies' (p. 17) and 'The final test of the value of any intellectual labour is its ability to help men to understand questions in which they are interested' (p. 19).

Many of the other chapters interpret geography as if the 'revolutions' had not occurred in the United States, however: Smith's (1965) chapter on historical geography, for example, is an excellent British companion to the American statement published a decade earlier (Clark, 1954). Elsewhere, Pahl (1965) introduced the models of the Chicago school of urban sociologists and suggested a social geography in which the prime factor is distance (p. 95), but only the chapters by Haggett and Timms introduced much of the trans-Atlantic turmoil. Haggett (1965a) wrote on models in economic geography, both those based on simple views of the world, such as developments on von Thünen's (Chisholm, 1962), and those derived from observations of particular cases (e.g. Taaffe, Morrill and Gould, 1963). He noted that:

> Perhaps the biggest barrier that model builders in economic geography will have to face in the immediate future is an emotional one. It is difficult to accept without some justifiable scepticism that the complexities of a mobile, infinitely variable landscape system will ever be reduced to the most sophisticated model, but still more difficult to accept that as individuals we suffer the indignity of following mathematical patterns in our behaviour (Haggett, 1965a, p. 109).

He introduced the notion of indeterminacy at the individual level (see also Jones, 1956 and p. 68 above) and showed how random variables must be introduced to make models operational; his chapter on scale problems (Haggett, 1965b) illustrated methods of sampling and of map generalization from samples.

Timms (1965) demonstrated the use of statistical techniques for analyses of social patterns within cities (based on Shevky and Bell's social area analysis, and developed independently of Berry's work on this topic – see above, p. 97. Later work in this mould by Robson, 1969, followed a period spent working with Berry at Chicago, but earlier developments at Keele, also based on Shevky-Bell – Williams and Herbert, 1962 – illustrated that some at least of the changes in UK geography were largely independent of those occurring in US geography, depending instead on accessing the relevant literature in other disciplines). Timms (1965, p. 262) pointed out that:

> The sciences concerned with the study of social variation have as yet produced few models which can stand comparison with the observed patterns or which can be used to predict those patterns. ... Prediction rests on accurate knowledge of the degree and direction of the interrelationships between phenomena. This can only be attained by the use of techniques of description and analysis which are amenable to statistical comparison and manipulation. If the goal of geographical studies be accepted as the formulation of laws of areal arrangement and of prediction based on those laws, then it is inevitable that their techniques must become considerably more objective and more quantitative than heretofore.

The majority of the contributors to *Frontiers in Geographical Teaching*, almost all of whom were associated with the Department of Geography at the University of Cambridge, were not as committed to the 'new geography' as Timms (who later, like Pahl, became a professor of sociology; Wrigley became an economic historian/demographer, and President of the British Academy). This cannot be levelled at the editors, whose epilogue (Haggett and Chorley, 1965, pp. 360–1) presented a strong case for the 'theoretical revolution':

> We cannot but recognize the importance of the construction of theoretical models, wherein aspects of 'geographic reality' are presented together in some organic structural relationship, the juxtaposition of which leads one to comprehend, at least, more than might appear from the information presented piecemeal and, at most, to apprehend general principles which may have much wider application than merely to the information from which they were derived. Geographical teaching has been remarkably barren of such models. ... This reticence stems largely, one suspects, from a misconception of the nature of model thinking. ... Models are subjective frameworks ... like discardable cartons, very important and productive receptacles for advantageously presenting selected aspects of reality.

This view dominated their next, and substantially more influential, volume (Chorley and Haggett, 1967).

Models in Geography, most of whose contributors were also linked with the Cambridge department, was a major synthesis of most of the work completed before the mid-1960s by adherents to the 'quantitative and theoretical revolutions'. Individual authors were asked 'to discuss the role of model-building within their own special fields of research' (Haggett and Chorley, 1967, p. 19), which resulted in a series of substantive review essays, some dealing with topical specialisms (urban geography and settlement location; industrial location; agricultural activity – there were similar reviews for physical geography), some with particular themes ranging across several specialisms (economic development; regions; maps; organisms and ecosystems; the evolution of spatial patterns), and some with methods and approaches (demographic models; sociological models; network models). A catholic use of the term 'model' was deployed, allowing it as a synonym for a theory, a law, a hypothesis, or any other form of structured idea (see Moss, 1970). The approach was strongly nomothetic, however:

. . . the student of history and geography is faced with two alternatives. He can either bury his head, ostrich-like, in the sand grains of an idiographic human history, conducted over unique geographic space, scowl upon broad generalization, and produce a masterly descriptive thesis on what happened when, where. Or he can become a scientist and attempt, by the normal procedures of scientific investigation, to verify, reject, or modify, the stimulating and exciting ideas which his predecessors presented him with. (Harvey, 1967a, p. 551)

All the contributors had chosen the latter course: their focus was on models – on generalizations of reality – and methods were very much secondary.

The orientation of this significant volume is given by the editors' introduction. (Its significance lay in its two uses: first, as a synthesis and argument, the volume was widely read and used by researchers and teachers as a guide; second, as a series of major reviews, when republished in separate paperback volumes, the book was extensively employed as an undergraduate text.) Haggett and Chorley (1967, p. 24) presented the model as, 'a bridge between the observational and theoretical levels . . . concerned with simplification, reduction, concretization, experimentation, action, extension, globalization, theory formation and explanation'. It can be descriptive or normative, static or dynamic, experimental or theoretical (see also Chorley, 1964). It forms the basis for their proposed new paradigm, which made no attempt 'to alter the basic Hartshorne definition of Geography's prime task' (p. 38) but offered hope for much greater progress:

. . . the new paradigm . . . is based on faith in the new rather than its proven ability. . . . There is good reason to think that those subjects which have modelled their forms on mathematics and physics . . . have climbed considerably more rapidly than those which have attempted to build internal or idiographic structures (p. 38).

Models in Geography stands as a statement of that faith.

Although the editors and contributors to *Models in Geography* comprised many of the early active participants in the move to change British geography towards a 'more scientific' approach, others involved are not directly represented. Notable among them was a group who graduated at the University of Cambridge in the 1950s, having been tutored by A. A. L. Caesar. (Chisholm and Manners, 1973, p. xi, credit his role, one which continued until the end of the 1970s, with a steady stream of productive research workers from St Catherine's College.) It included Michael Chisholm, Peter Hall and Gerald Manners as well as Haggett, the only one who worked within the 'quantitative revolution'. Chisholm, for example, focused on theoretical developments in economic geography (e.g. Chisholm, 1962, 1966, 1971a) but with relatively little quantitative analysis (though see Chisholm and O'Sullivan, 1973), and both Hall and Manners were more concerned, as was Caesar, with geographical analyses of contemporary policy issues, although in some cases the analyses led to theory-derivation (Hall, 1981a, 1998).

Chorley and Haggett's editing, and their joint work on technical developments – such as trend surface analysis (Chorley and Haggett, 1965a) and network analysis (Haggett and Chorley, 1969) – reflected a belief in the unity of physical and human geography (further demonstrated in Haggett's – 1972, 2001 – major undergraduate text). This assumed that a shared interest in methods and techniques could unite the two – Haggett (1967, p. 664) writes on 'the basic proposition that a wide range of different geographical networks may be usefully analysed in terms of their common geometrical characteristics'. As in North America, if geometry (i.e. spatial form) was the focus of geographical analysis then physical and human geographers could find common cause (Woldenberg and Berry, 1967). Explanation of the geometry required the study of very different processes, however, and the two soon separated again.

The two edited books by Chorley and Haggett were the first major indication of change within British geography – and they appeared too late to assist geography's cause during the first stages of a major expansion of universities there. By the end of the 1950s, there were geography departments in just about every UK university, and many of them were expanding to meet growing demand from students. But as a discipline geography did not appear to have a high standing within British academia, and when a series of seven universities was founded in England in the late 1950s and early 1960s, only one (the University of Sussex) included geography within its course offerings from the outset (as a social science though including physical geography: there was no separate geography department, however, only a 'Geography Laboratory'). Two others included geographers within schools of environmental studies, as did two further universities established a little later in Scotland and Northern Ireland, but only one – the University of Lancaster – eventually established a Department of Geography, because it was having difficulties recruiting students for other disciplines. Thus geography, because of its image as not being closely linked with the burgeoning social sciences and the lack of an influential pressure group, failed to gain a place in a new group of universities, many of which soon became major research centres in the social and environmental sciences. (On this episode, see Johnston 2003a, 2004e.)

This marginalization of geography within the UK was exacerbated in the mid-1960s when a Social Science Research Council (SSRC; it was later renamed the Economic and Social Research Council – ESRC) was established to fund postgraduate and research work, and from which geography was initially excluded. In response to this, a number of geographers (led by Robert Steel, an Oxford graduate then professor of geography at the University of Liverpool and later to be Principal of University College Swansea) took the initiative of approaching the SSRC Chairman to promote their discipline's cause. He invited them to make a detailed case, a task undertaken for the group by Michael Chisholm (then a lecturer in the department of geography at the University of Bristol). His detailed document and case – not accepted by all departmental heads – was successful, and a Human Geography and Planning Committee was established within the SSRC (Chisholm 2001; Johnston, 2003e). Chisholm later developed his case for geography as a social science into two books (Chisholm, 1971c, 1975a) and edited a third which illustrated it with a series of major case studies (Chisholm and Rodgers, 1973). The first of these (written specifically as a review conducted for the SSRC) argued in its introduction that the real change in geography associated with quantification was 'a substantial tightening up in logical rigour' (Chisholm, 1971c, p. 2) involving three main themes (pp. 5–6):

1. All phenomena occur in a spatial context;
2. Economic and social processes require a built infrastructure (buildings and transport media); and
3. Human activity takes place within environmental contexts.

There were only five chapters: one considered static patterns (points, surfaces, regions and their correlation), another dynamic patterns (processes such as urbanization and economic development) and a third theories of spatial organization. The other two were concerned with research organization and priorities with seven of the latter identified (by the SSRC's Human Geography Committee and not just Chisholm): perception studies; simulation models; forecasting; regional taxonomy; environmental standards; population and migration; and processes of regional economic and social development. (These brief chapters were the core of the later, more extended treatment: Chisholm, 1975a.)

The relatively untouched

The NAS/NRC (1965) report (see above, p. 95) identified two main systematic specialisms within human geography that had been largely untouched by the developments outlined here: cultural and historical geography (see also Darby, 1983a). In addition, despite Berry's (1964b) attempt to reframe it, regional geography remained largely apart from the changes in methodological emphasis. Furthermore, political geography was described by Berry, 1969, as a 'moribund backwater' (though Muir, 1975 sought to apply quantitative methods to the field). Not all cultural, historical and regional geographers ignored the changes occurring elsewhere, and some were in the 'revolutionary' vanguard: two of the chapters in *Models in Geography*, for example, were written by David Grigg and David Harvey, whose empirical research for their PhDs was on historical topics (e.g. Harvey, 1985c). But in general terms the NAS/NRC report was correct; there is little evidence of early success in winning cultural, historical and regional geographers over to the new methodology.

Of the three groups, *historical geographers* were probably most concerned about their apparent isolation within the discipline. This was summarized by Baker (1972, p. 13) in terms of the approaches which historical geographers need to consider in greater detail:

An assumption is necessary here: that methodologically the main advances can be expected from an increased awareness of developments in other disciplines, from a greater use of statistical methods, from the development, application and testing of theory, and from exploitation of behavioural approaches and sources. . . . Rethinking becomes necessary because orthodox doctrines have ceased to carry conviction. As far as historical geography is concerned, this involves a questioning of the adequacy of its traditional methods and techniques.

All of these would have to be followed with care, and the potentials of the methodological developments assessed cautiously, but Baker clearly believed there was considerable scope for change, as had already been shown in economic and in social history, and perhaps even more so in archaeology (see Hodder and Orton, 1976; Renfrew, 1981). Particular areas of historical geography, including those relating to urban settlements (e.g. Ward, 1971), were more open to such changes, if for no other reason than the better quality and quantity of available data (e.g. Whitehand and Patten, 1977; Johnson and Pooley, 1982; Dennis, 1984). There were possible implications in such work, however, as Baker (1972, p. 28) noted:

> Studies in, for example, 'historical agricultural geography', 'historical urban geography' and 'historical economic geography' seem to offer possibilities of fundamental development, particularly in terms of a better understanding of the processes by which geographical change through time may take place. Such an organization of the subject would view historical geography as a means towards an end rather than as an end in itself.

In the early discussions of the relationships between historical geography and the 'theoretical and quantitative revolutions' most attention focused on quantification rather than theory. Vance (1978) pointed out that the development of theory does not have to involve 'quantitative abstraction', as his own work showed (Vance, 1970; see also Pred, 1977b, and Conzen, 1981). Available data can be manipulated to test theories regarding past spatial patterns (e.g. Goheen, 1970), but Radford (1981, p. 257) argued that theory is the more important: 'In the cities of the nineteenth-century United States, a set of principles ... was taken to something approaching a logical conclusion'. This assumes that theory is possible in historical geography. As illustrated in Chapter 5, some dispute this – for geography as a whole and not just for historical geography. The positivist method implies objectivity, but the geographer in describing a landscape is subjective:

> In describing a landscape, is he not committed by his past training and his past experiences – by his prejudices, if you will? Just as the portrait an artist paints will tell you much about the artist as well as his sitter, so the description of a countryside will tell you a great deal about the writer (Darby, 1962, p. 4).

Darby portrayed geography as both a science and an art:

> [It] is a science in the sense that what facts we perceive must be examined, and perhaps measured, with care and accuracy. It is an art in that any presentation (let alone any perception) of those facts must be selective, and so involve choice, and taste, and judgement (p. 6).

Such a position clearly separated those wedded to an implicitly idealist view of historical geography (see p. 196) from those advancing the cause of a more scientific approach, whether or not it was quantitative, though some would argue that the first quote from Darby could equally well apply to positivist work. (Positivistic training introduces subjectivity in choice of subject matter and approach too.) In any case, S. Gregory (1976) deployed statistical procedures to test hypotheses derived from Darby's (1977) classic work on the Domesday Book. Models were increasingly common in historical analyses, however, not only in studies by quantifiers (such as Taaffe, Morrill and Gould, 1963, on transport system evolution) but also in Vance's (1970) work on the role of wholesaling in the evolution of urban systems and, most especially, Meinig's studies of new world settlement, notably his four-volume work on the United States (e.g. Meinig, 1986, 1993).

Cultural geographers were less concerned about their apparent drift away from the mainstream of geographical activity than historical geographers, perhaps because of the lack of any parallel developments to those affecting geography in anthropology, the discipline with which many contemporary cultural geographers had most contact. (See Mikesell, 1967, for a general comparison of the two disciplines. Some anthropological work experienced major paradigmatic threats, if not changes, notably in the structural work of Claude Lévi-Strauss – see E. R. Leach, 1974 – but these were not discussed by geographers in the 1960s.) Increased geographical interest in diffusion, stimulated by Hägerstrand's (1968) work, led to contact between the spatial analysis and cultural analysis schools of thought, however (Clarkson, 1970). Nevertheless, as Mikesell (1978, p. 1) expressed it, 'Stubborn individualism and a seeming indifference to academic fashion are well-known characteristics' of cultural geographers, whose preferences are for: a historical orientation; a focus on the role of human agency in environmental change, on material culture, and on rural areas; links with anthropology; an individualistic perspective; and field work. (These are all illustrated in a book of essays on *Geography as Human Ecology*: Eyre and Jones, 1966; see also Turner, 1989.) Similarly, Porter (1978, pp. 30–1) concluded his review of 'geography as human ecology' with:

> . . . in the past 25 years those interested in the mutual relations of people and environment have taken an interesting journey in search of a satisfactory replacement for environmental determinism. Along the way they have been offered, but generally have declined to use, the shiny wares of gravity and . . . [other] models. . . . They have been impressed by, and at times been perhaps a bit envious of, the accomplishments of their colleagues in the analysis of spatial organization. . . . [But as the] impulse [in human ecology] is cosmographical, holistic and synthetic, it tends to reject the analytical methods of normal science.

Cultural geography was very largely a preoccupation within North American human geography at that time. The Berkeley 'school', founded and led for several decades by Carl Sauer, was the main focus and training centre, stressing the morphology of landscape (Sauer, 1925) and human intervention in landscape evolution through plant and animal domestication, the use of fire, the diffusion of ideas and artefacts, and the creation of settlements, for example (all themes reviewed in Thomas, 1956, and maintained by Sauer's disciples, such as Kniffen: see Matthewson, 1993). Sauer's approach was ecological and clearly opposed the perceived determinism of other workers; Duncan (1980) argued that members of the school tended to reify culture, however, promoting a form of 'cultural determinism' rather than seeing culture as a human creation that enables and constrains human agency and is itself constantly being reworked through that agency.

Another criticism of this dominant view of cultural geography was that it very largely ignored those elements of culture which are directly related to the production of goods and services, so that cultural geographers had little to offer either the growing number of spatial scientists interested in economic and urban geography or those promoting social geography, with interests in the concept of social class. Spencer and Thomas's introductory textbook (1973, p. 6) provided the following definitions:

Culture is the sum total of human learned behavior and ways of doing things. Culture is invented, carried on, and slowly modified by people living and working in groups as each group occupies a particular region of the earth and develops its own special and distinctive system of culture. Related single culture traits *that go together in practice form a* culture complex: *a large assemblage of* culture complexes *fit together into a* culture system. *A culture system followed by a population inhabiting a specific area of the earth forms a* culture region. *A group of related culture regions is termed a* culture world.

But their book concentrated on artefacts and certain aspects of social organization (religion and language) only, saying nothing about many of the salient aspects of 'the sum total of human learned behavior'. Zelinsky's (1973b) *The Cultural Geography of the United States* is similarly partial, though it introduces more material on the political content of societal organization.

This subdiscipline has been criticized on a number of grounds. Cosgrove (1983, p. 3) claimed that because it ignored the dialectic between nature and culture, 'it dissolved into either the idealist reification of culture as an agent of change or a semi-determinism dignified by the name "possibilism" ... This has left cultural geography theoretically impoverished, many of its studies existing in a theoretical vacuum' (p. 3), and he identified it as: 'so diffuse that one is tempted to characterize cultural geography more by its refusal to adopt economic or social theory as its guiding principle than by any unity of aim or method'. The economic and social theories that he promoted (discussed in Chapters 6 and 7 of this book) are not those of spatial science, however. But spatial scientists, too, found cultural geography atheoretical and empiricist in explicit orientation, yet often, as Duncan (1980) indicates, implicitly determinist. Few links developed between the two, however, and in addition there emerged what Duncan (1994, p. 401) identified as 'a civil war' within cultural geography since the early 1980s, during which:

... the older generation has been content to remain in their well-entrenched positions within the academy as the younger generation fired the occasional salvo at them to little apparent effect. The younger generation launched its attacks using an arsenal of theory-seeking weapons provided by suppliers in the humanities and social sciences.

The older generation was almost entirely North American; the younger had substantial membership from the UK. (We return to these transformations in Chapter 7's consideration of wider 'cultural turns'.)

Finally, the situation in *regional geography* was surveyed by Paterson (1974), whose essay had two main sections – 'On the problems of writing regional geography' and 'Is progress possible in regional geography?'. The first investigated six problems, including the growing shortage of subordinate materials (micro-regional studies), and the increasing submergence of regional distinctiveness, though:

... only a certain amount of innovation is possible if the regional geographer is to perform his appointed task, which is to convey to his reader the essentials of his region; to illuminate the landscape with analytical light. Landforms and climate are common to all terrestrial landscapes ... and human activities to most of them: how shall repetition be avoided? (p. 8).

So long as contrasts between region and region [remain], and no matter to what they are attributable, there is work for the geographer to do (p. 16).

He did not conclude that there is no possibility of progress, however, despite the constraints: regional geography can advance on two criteria – content and insight.

Reference to Zelinsky's (1973b) book illustrated the increased range of content currently being introduced; discussion of Meinig's work (e.g. Meinig, 1972) showed the ability of regional geographers to produce fresh spatial insights, although Paterson concludes that 'Adventurousness is not a quality that most of us associate with regional geography' (p. 9). Thus:

The way is open for regional studies which are less bound by old formulae; less obliged to tell all about the region; more experimental and, in a proper sense of the word, more imaginative than in the past, and covering a broader range of perceptions, either popular or specialist (p. 23).

Regional Geography['s] ... goals are general rather than specific; it is not primarily problem-orientated but concerned to provide balanced coverage, and its aims are popular and educational rather than practical or narrowly professional. Such relevance as it possesses it gains by its appeal ... to the two universal human responses of wonder and concern. ... One may recall Medawar's assertion that in science we are being progressively relieved of the burden of singular instances, the tyranny of the particular, and in turn assert that there is a frame of mind on which the particular exercises no tyranny, but a strong fascination (p. 21).

Elsewhere, Mead (1980, p. 297) strongly defended geographers who 'adopt other lands ... share other cultures ... [and] make a contribution to the store of knowledge about them'. Similarly, though with greater intensity, Hart (1982a, p. 1) claimed in his Presidential address to the AAG that:

Society has allocated responsibility for the study of areas to geography: this responsibility is the justification for our existence as a scholarly discipline.

This role involves responding to people's curiosity about places, promoting an 'understanding the meaning of an area [which] cannot be reduced to a formal process' (p. 2). Unfortunately, geographers were very insecure with that mission and so had retreated into 'scientism' which involved studying 'people abstracted from their real world contexts' (p. 16). The quantitative revolution was giving priority to 'techniques and procedures rather than places and people' (p. 17) and diverting attention from geographers' obligation to answer the key questions of 'how much of what is where and why it's there, about the where and why of places and people, about the land and how people have used and abused it' (p. 19) – about which there is so much 'woeful ignorance'. Thus to Hart (p. 29), an important element in the 'highest form of the geographers' art' (his term for regional geography) requires individuals to 'adopt a region, to immerse themselves in its culture, to acquire a specialist understanding of it'. Ten geographers from the University of California at Santa Barbara responded by arguing that just as Hart claimed that, 'We cannot allow ourselves to be intimidated by those who flaunt the banner of science' (Hart, 1982a, p. 5) so, 'We equally cannot allow ourselves to be intimidated by those who flaunt the banner of anti-science, those who would reject all that is scientific about the discipline, and those who would urge a return to the descriptive morass from which we have recently emerged' (Golledge *et al.*, 1982, p. 558) – especially at a time when geography was under threat in some American universities. Hart's (1982b, p. 559) response was that he was critical of shoddy work of any type, did not want geography to be forced into any particular mould, and that, 'we should be unwise to jettison so blithely one of our grand traditions merely because some of our colleagues do not understand, appreciate, or know how to practise it'. (See also Clout, 2003a.)

*   *   *

The implication is that there was a strongly perceived difference between, on the one hand, many historical geographers and, on the other, most cultural and regional geographers with regard to the degree to which they felt 'left behind' or 'relatively untouched' by the changes that occurred during the 1950s and 1960s in other branches of human geography. Historical geographers, at least, seem to have been impelled to consider the possibility of making methodological changes, whereas the other two groups continued to work within their established tradition (see also Mikesell, 1973). Not all historical geographers would agree with Baker's analogy from systems theory that simply 'Historical geography has a long relaxation time' (p. 11), however, and Chapter 5 illustrates the degree to which they mounted attacks against the positivist approach.

Conclusions

Negative reactions to the regional approach began to crystallize in the United States during the mid-1950s. The aims of research in human geography were not debated until then, and relatively traditional definitions of the field were still observed: the main issues concerned means and methods. The innovations of the period involved the strengthening of the systematic and topical geographies, and their release from a largely subservient relationship to regional geography, by attempts to develop laws and theories of spatial patterns, using models of various kinds for illumination, and applying mathematical and, especially, statistical procedures to facilitate the search for generalizations. Whereas regional geographers saw their discipline as, at most, law-consuming, those of the new persuasion aimed at producing their own laws, which could be used to explain particular regional outcomes.

These changed means to the geographic end were rapidly accepted in many branches of human geography, particularly in those topical specialisms dealing with economic aspects of contemporary life. They were soon accepted in the growing field of contemporary social geography, but were relatively ignored in historical geography and almost completely shunned in cultural and regional investigations, which, it was claimed, focus on unique characteristics of unique places. They also spread into the corresponding fields of study across the Atlantic (and across the Pacific, too), and within little more than a decade British geographers produced a major review volume (*Models in Geography*) containing 816 pages of testimony to the innovators' enthusiasm and their links (largely one-way) with other social sciences. But methods are insufficient to sustain an academic revolution unless they can be applied to a coherent substantive core, and the search for such a core is the subject of the next chapter.

4
Human geography as spatial science

By our theories you shall know us

(Harvey, 1969a, p. 486)

The changes in human geography that emanated from several centres in the United States during the 1950s were very much concerned with methods of investigation. The ultimate aim of geographical study – as set out in Hartshorne's revised definition (p. 66) – remained the same, or so it was argued: indeed, the definitions offered by Ackerman (1963) and the NAS/NRC committee (1965: see above, p. 93) suggest that human geographers had become even more ambitious in their goal of explaining 'the world-wide system comprising man and his natural environment'. Systematic studies were in the ascendant, however, and the implicit intention was to develop laws and theories within an, often unstated, positivist framework.

In this context, human geographers promoting the changes increasingly sought a clear identity for their discipline within the social sciences, alongside economics, sociology and political science. Adoption of the positivist philosophy required that disciplines be identified by their content rather than their methods, however, since many of the latter (especially those involving statistics) were common to all – or so it was believed. Geographers argued that their discipline provided a particular viewpoint and contribution to the overall social science goal of understanding society. Their focus was on spatial variables and the study of spatial systems – so that within their own discipline they elevated the concept of space over that of place, while also redirecting its focus away from the idiographic and towards the nomothetic.

Spatial variables and spatial systems

Geography is a discipline in distance, according to a Scottish professor's inaugural lecture (Watson, 1955; Johnston, 1993a), with the relative location of people and places as its central theme. Cox (1976) later argued that the contemporary importance of relative location within society stemmed from alterations in societal structure consequent upon technical change. The main interactions in less-developed societies are between relatively isolated groups of individuals and their physical environments, creating vertical relationships between societies and 'a spatially differentiated nature' (p. 192) as an obvious focus for geographical scholarship. With technological advancement, however, the main links are among individuals. Interdependence within and between societies increases with the more complex division of labour, so that the most important aspects of modern human existence relate to spatially differentiated societies, not to a spatially differentiated nature. This 'horizontal' inter-dependence between groups living in different places creates the patterns of human occupance on the surface of the earth, and provides the basic subject matter for human geographers.

The approach clarified: three pioneering textbooks

According to Kuhn, textbooks play a significant role in the transmission of paradigms within disciplines so that a clear statement of a major shift occurring should be provided when new sets of textbooks appear which codify a 'new approach'. For human geography, this occurred in the mid- and late-1960s. Three texts promoted the new approach, focusing on spatial arrangements (the areal differentiation in human activities and the spatial interactions which this produces) and on the role of distance as a crucial variable influencing the nature of those arrangements.

The pioneer among such texts was Haggett's (1965c) *Locational Analysis in Human Geography*. It presented material that he had been teaching to undergraduates for several years at the University of Cambridge. (On the stimuli to Haggett's work, see Haggett, 1990, and Chorley, 1995; on Chorley, see Stoddart, 1997a.) Its depiction of pattern and order in spatial structures was placed within a decomposition of nodal regions into five geometrical elements; a sixth was added in the second edition (Haggett, Cliff, and Frey, 1977). The book contained little programmatic material either 'selling' or 'justifying' the new approach: he noted at the outset that any book reflects its author's biases and made clear that his were a preference for quantitative over qualitative analysis and a search for 'order, locational order, shown by the phenomena studied traditionally as *human geography*' (p. 2, his emphasis).

Haggett's presentation of spatial systems was based on a simple schema comprising its major elements (Figure 4.1). This assumed a spatially differentiated society within which there is a desire for interaction within regional systems, and which results in patterns of *movement* – of goods, people, money, ideas, and so on – between places. The first stage in analysing nodal regions involves their representation. Most movement is channelled along routes, so the second stage involves characterization of those *channels* as networks comprising edges and vertices; in a transport system, many of the latter are the *nodes*, the organizational nexus. Their spatial arrangement forms the schema's third element, and the fourth investigates their organization into *hierarchies*, which define the importance of places within the settlement framework. Finally in the original scheme, there are the *surfaces*, the areas of land within the skeleton of nodes (settlements) and networks (routes) that are occupied by land uses of various types and intensities.

Patterns of human occupation of the earth change frequently, and the spatial order to such changes forms the sixth element in Haggett's revised schema. Change does not occur uniformly over space in most circumstances, however; it usually originates at one or a few nodes and spreads to others (as with the 'new' geography in the United States discussed

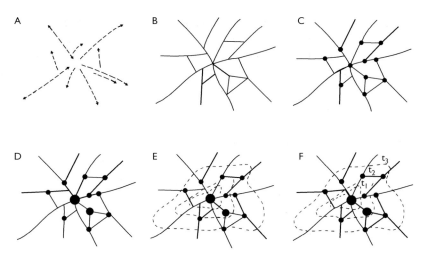

Figure 4.1 *The elements in Haggett's schema for studying spatial systems: A movement; B channels; C nodes; D hierarchies; E surfaces; and F diffusion (Source: Haggett, Cliff and Frey, 1977, p. 7)*

in the previous chapter), along the movement channels, through the nodes, across the surfaces and down the hierarchies. The processes of change over space and time thus involve spatial *diffusion*.

Haggett stressed his conception of geography as a science of distributions, emphasizing the regularities in various elements of these distributions: the first half of his book – titled 'Models of locational structure' – allocated a chapter to each of the schema's elements. The first edition (1965) was very reliant on work in other disciplines; the second (1977) illustrated the substantial amount of work done by geographers in the intervening decade. In his collection of semi-autobiographical essays, Haggett (1990) frequently reiterated his view of geography's 'emphasis on space and on geometry' (p. 5), which he expressed as personal, 'though I hope not wholly ... quirky'. Maps, as demonstrations of spatial structure, form the foundation of his geography, as illustrated by essays on 'Levels of resolution', 'The art of the mappable', 'Regional synthesis', and 'The arrows of space'. Thus, although he recognized that 'there are other delights in geography' (p. 184), he retained a 'simple delight in the beauty of geographical structures and the challenges posed in finding them and mapping them' (see also Gould, 1993, and Gregory, 1994, for more reflections on the aesthetics of spatial science). Although *Locational Analysis* ... covered human geography only, Haggett believed in the indissolubility of physical and human geography, as argued in his biographical essays (Haggett, 1990) and introductory texts (Haggett, 1972, 2001). In 1991 he wrote that, 'Geography is now too large, too multicultural and, hopefully, too mature, to be tempted by any single orthodoxy. Yet even a braiding stream may sometimes converge on a few major channels and I hope geography may ever delight in rediscovering how much it has to gain from allowing environmental and societal themes to merge together' (Haggett, 1991, p. 302).

Other texts produced in that period took a similar approach, although differing in emphases. Morrill's (1970a) title – *The Spatial Organization of Society* – clearly emphasized his view of the role of geographical analysis in the larger task of the social sciences: human geography's core elements are 'Space, space relations, and change in space – how physical space is structured, how men relate through space, how man has organized his society in space, and how our conception and use of space change' (p. 3). Space has five qualities relevant to the understanding of human behaviour – (1) distance, the spatial dimension of separation; (2) accessibility; (3) agglomeration; (4) size; and (5) relative location – which can be put together to build theories:

> *Virtually all theory of spatial organization assumes that the structure of space is based on the principles of minimizing distance and maximizing the utility of points and areas within the structure, without taking the environment, or variable content of space, into account. Although the differential quality of area is interesting and its effect on location and interaction is great, most of the observable regularity of structure in space results from the principles of efficiently using territory of uniform character. The theoretical structures for agricultural location, location of urban centres, and the internal patterns of the city are all derived from the principle of minimizing distance on a uniform plane* (Morrill, 1970a, p. 15).

Thus, all land use and location decisions are taken to minimize movement costs. The spatial approach (i.e. geography) claims that one particular variable on which it concentrates – distance – is a significant influence on human behaviour and seeks accounts for observed spatial patterns within this framework. And so in Morrill's book:

> *... the explanation of spatial structure proceeds from the deductive – what would occur under the simplest conditions – to the inductive – how local factors distort this 'pure' structure. To begin with, all the local variation may introduce is a risk of missing the underlying structure. Modern theory of location therefore stresses the spatial factors – above all, distance – which interact to bring about the regular and repetitive patterns* (p. 20).

Morrill's summarizing 'theory' of spatial structures proceeds as follows:

1. Societies operate to achieve two spatial efficiency goals:
   (a) to use every piece of land to the greatest profit and utility; and
   (b) to achieve the greatest possible volume of interaction at the least possible cost.
2. Pursuit of these goals involves four types of location decisions:
   (a) the substitution of land for transport costs when seeking accessibility;
   (b) substituting production costs at sites for transport costs when seeking markets;
   (c) substituting agglomeration benefits for transport costs; and
   (d) substituting self-sufficiency (higher production costs) and trade (higher transport costs).
3. The spatial structures resulting from these decisions include:
   (a) spatial land-use gradients; and
   (b) a spatial hierarchy of regions.
   These are somewhat distorted by environmental variations to produce:
   (c) more irregular but predictable patterns of location.

Whereas over time distortion may result from:
(d) non-optimal location decisions; and
(e) change through processes of spatial diffusion.

Like Haggett, therefore, Morrill focused on the geometry of human organization of activities on the earth's surface. Whereas Haggett emphasized pattern, however, Morrill paid more attention to decision-making processes which would produce the most 'efficient' patterns, as foundations for appreciating the imperfect examples of such patterns which are observed in the 'real world'. The importance of economic and spatial variables is less dominant in the third edition of the book, however (Morrill and Dormitzer, 1979, p.7). Location theory is presented as providing:

> ... fairly simple models that permit us to highlight some essential principles and factors of human location. The real world, of course, does not correspond very closely to the patterns projected by location theory because the human landscape is the complex product of many different forces – historical, physical, cultural, political, and behavioral, as well as economic (spatial).

Nevertheless, location theory is presented as revealing, 'the basic spatial order that underlies our often confusing world ... the landscape around us makes sense when viewed as the outcome of human decisions to use land rationally in the context of a particular culture, level of technology, and physical environment' (p. xix). Later, however, in a paper on 'Some important geographic questions', Morrill (1985) returned to a strong focus on spatial variables.

A third, highly influential text in this mould was produced by Abler, Adams and Gould (1971; see Palm, 2003; interestingly, whereas Haggett's book was written for UK undergraduate audiences, based on a course he had developed at Cambridge over the previous eight years, the Abler *et al.* book was based on an introductory graduate-level course at Penn State University: Abler, 1993, p. 66). *Spatial Organization* has a stronger focus on positivist methodology (see also Gould, 1977, 1978). Like Haggett, its authors emphasized the search for order, noting that this was the prime goal of sciences, that in their view human geography is a social and behavioural science, and all societies 'impose order on our experience continua ... order ... is a fundamental requirement of human welfare. The need for order must be fulfilled, even if the order must be created where none can be discovered' (Abler, Adams and Gould, 1971, pp. 6–7). Order can be produced in a variety of ways. They identify four – theological, aesthetic and emotional, common sense, and scientific: for them, the scientific is the most important because it is 'adaptable whereas the others are rigid. Its verification and replication procedures enable [it] to remain viable in the rapidly changing world it creates. Far more than the others, it is a supra-individual, empirical ordering system' (p. 19: i.e. it is 'objective').

For Abler, Adams and Gould (1971, p. 20) geography's 'one basic question [is] "Why are spatial distributions structured the way they are?"' (p. 20). Like Haggett, tackling that question needs a textbook that not only synthesizes the relevant available knowledge but also sets out the methodology for such a task. Haggett has 'Methods in locational analysis' as the second part of his book, introduced by the statement that, 'Further development of the locational models ... depends largely on our ability to test them against existing geographical patterns' (Haggett, 1965b, p. 185): that ability is set out in four chapters covering data collection and description, region building and hypothesis testing. For Abler, Adams and Gould, however, methods take precedence. The first two sections of their book are on 'Order, science and geography' and 'Measurement, relationship and classification': only then do they turn to the substantive material, with sections on 'Location and spatial interaction', 'Spatial diffusion', and 'Spatial organization and the decision process'. (Palm, 2003, notes that this emphasis on the nature of geography as a science reflects both Abler's and Adams' experiences as graduate students at the University of Minnesota, where their advisor was Fred Lukermann, who wrote on that issue at the time (Lukermann, 1964a, 1964b). To Lukermann – 1964b, p. 167 – geographers should focus on interactions within spatial systems, with their discipline presented as 'a catalogue of questions, and the questions – not the phenomena, not the facts, not the method – are geographic'.) Morrill focused on the substantive material alone, and in a slightly later book Amedeo and Golledge (1975) used a similar organization to Abler *et al.* to introduce geographers to scientific reasoning, especially theory construction.

These textbooks illustrate the centrality of space and distance as the major focus of geographical interest in the 1960s. An emphasis on observed patterns rather than abstract theoretical arrangements was noted in King's (1969b, p. 574) review of 'The geographer's approach to the analysis of spatial form ... the mathematics which are used and the geometrical frameworks which are favored'. He focused on descriptive mathematics, which represent 'what is' rather than 'what should be', realizing that, 'when they are pursued to their extremes in very formal terms these studies [of 'what should be'] run the risk of appearing as seemingly sterile exercises in pure geometry' (p. 593; see also King, 1976, 1979b). Geographers had by then not proceeded very far in providing process theories which would account for observed spatial patterns, however: they were working backwards, identifying order that called for explanation rather than deducing what the world should be like from knowledge of human behaviour.

In almost all of this work, space was treated as a continuous variable; there was very little on its discontinuous nature in some aspects of human organization. Bounded spaces, at a great variety of scales, from the largest nation-state through to the 'bubble of personal space' around each individual, were largely ignored by geographers promoting their discipline as spatial science, perhaps because they found generalizations more difficult to identify than in work on continuous space. The study of territories had been advanced by a French political geographer (Gottmann, 1951, 1952), whose work had little impact on his American contemporaries (Johnston, 1996b, 2004d): despite his periods of working there, he was 'outside the project'. Interestingly, some 40 years later, Cutter *et al.* (2002, p. 307) had, 'Is there a deeply held human need to organize space by creating arbitrary borders, boundaries and districts?' as the second of their 'big questions in geography'.

Spatial theory

Just as the methodological developments reviewed in the previous chapter lacked clear guidelines from programmatic statements, the growth of the spatial viewpoint similarly lacked any manifesto. (Watson's 1955 paper was not widely referenced: Johnston, 1993a.)

The only attempt to provide a lead – apart from general statements about geography and geometry, such as Bunge's (1962) – was a paper by Nystuen (1963) which reached a wider audience when reprinted in 1968. His objective was, 'to consider how many independent concepts constitute a basis for the spatial point of view, that is, the geographical point of view' (p. 35: page references are to the 1968 reprint). Rather than analyse the 'real world', with its many distorting tendencies, he sought clarity in considering abstract geographies.

To illustrate his basic concepts, Nystuen used the analogy of a mosque completely lacking furniture (i.e. an isotropic plain) in which a teacher chooses a location at random. The students then distribute themselves so that they can see and hear the teacher; their likely arrangement is in semicircular, staggered rows facing and as close as possible to the teacher's position. This arrangement has three characteristic features:

1. *Directional orientation* – all students face the teacher, to perceive expressions and to hear better;
2. *Distance* – the students cluster around the teacher, because audibility diminishes with distance; and
3. *Connectiveness* – they arrange themselves in rows, organized so that each has a direct line of sight to the teacher.

The third is in part a function of distance and direction, but not entirely so:

A map of the United States may be stretched and twisted, but so long as each state remains connected with its neighbors, relative position does not change. Connectiveness is independent of distance and direction – all these properties are needed to establish a complete geographical point of view (Nystuen, 1968, p. 39).

In addition:

Connections need not be adjacent boundaries or physical links. They may be defined as functional associations. Functional associations of spatially separate elements are best revealed by the exchanges which take place between the elements. The exchanges may often be measured by the flows of people, goods, or communications.

Within the mosque, therefore, the connectivity between teacher and student involves not only a direct line of sight between them but also a direct flow from one to the other, in this case of ideas.

Nystuen presented these three concepts as both necessary and (probably) sufficient for the construction of an abstract geography, grounded in the study of sites (abstract places) rather than of locations (real places).

The terms which seem to me to contain the concepts of a geographical point of view are direction *or* orientation, distance, *and* connection *or* relative position. *Operational definitions of these words are the axioms of the spatial point of view. Other words, such as pattern, accessibility, neighborhood, circulation, etc., are compounds of the basic terms. For abstract models, the existence of these elements and their properties must be specified* (p. 41).

Nystuen was unsure, however, whether these three comprised the full set of necessary and sufficient concepts for a geographical argument (see also Papageorgiou, 1969): boundary might be a primitive concept too rather than derivative of the basic three, but bounded space was of much less interest to spatial theorists than continuous space (albeit often transformed: Haggett, 1990; Cliff and Haggett, 1998).

Nystuen's general case, that arguments in human geography could be based on a small number of foundational concepts, was implicitly accepted by much of the work in 'the spatial tradition', although rarely explicitly referred to. Haynes (1975) suggested an alternative approach to writing theory in human geography, based on the mathematical procedures of dimensional analysis. Five basic dimensions – mass, length, time, population size, and value – were defined and manipulated to indicate the validity of functional relationships, such as distance-decay equations (see p. 119), by checking their internal consistency. His defence of this approach is that:

> Although most quantitative geographers would probably claim to be engaged in the discovery of relationships, it appears that geography has not passed the first stage [in the development of a science] with any degree of rigor. ... With no clear idea of which variables are relevant and which particular characteristics in a system should be isolated, it is pragmatic to define our measurement scales with regard to a particular set of observations rather than the other way round. The method of physical science ... is a superior system, as measurements can be interpreted exactly, different results compared, and experiments replicated (p. 66).

This deductive approach is not as closely tied to a 'spatial view' as Nystuen's but has the same goal – the derivation of a set of fundamental concepts which can form the basis for writing geographical theory to be tested in the 'real world' (see also Haynes, 1978, 1982).

These attempts at isolating human geography's primary concepts differed from most contemporary efforts at producing geographic theory which, according to Harvey (1967b, p. 212), were 'either very poorly formulated or else derivative'. Central place theory, for example, was based entirely on economic postulates about how people behave as 'rational economic actors' with regard to the costs of travel, producing a theory about the size and spacing of settlements. Its attraction to many was that geographers could contribute their own basic concept to theory development, and need not be totally dependent on other disciplines. Harvey (1970) identified a group of concepts which could comprise geographical elements in building integrated social science theories – location, nearness, distance, pattern, morphology; most are compounds of Nystuen's basic terms.

An example of theory development involving both derivative (from other disciplines) and indigenous (geographical) concepts was research on spatial diffusion, which received considerable attention in the late 1960s (Brown, 1968). The basic behavioural postulate, taken from sociological research, was that word of mouth is the most effective form of communication about innovations. Geographers introduced the effect of distance on this contact: much interpersonal communication is between neighbours, so information about innovations should spread outwards in an orderly fashion from the initial adopters' locations. Pioneer work on this hypothesis was conducted in Sweden by Hägerstrand, who introduced it to the Washington school in the 1950s, where it was taken up by Morrill

(1965, 1968, 2002) whose doctoral research was undertaken in Sweden. Hägerstrand's major work was made available in an English translation in 1968. Much subsequent research has been done on diffusion processes and, even more, on patterns of spatial spread which are assumed to result from diffusion processes (see Abler, Adams and Gould, 1971, Chapter 11; Brown, 1981; see also p. 170).

Work on spatial diffusion was increasingly concentrated on topics in medical geography, in which the notions of spatial spread across space and down settlement hierarchies is valid because of the role of direct human contact in the transmission of many diseases (see Thomas, 1992). The lead in much of this work was provided by Haggett and Cliff and included classic spatial epidemiological investigations of influenza, measles and AIDS as well as more general studies (e.g. Cliff and Haggett, 1988; Haggett, 1994, 2000). Changes in communications technology, among others, have had substantial impacts on these flows, introducing new technical issues (Cliff and Haggett, 1995).

Social physics and spatial science

Two of Nystuen's three basic concepts – distance and connectivity – have received much more attention from those advocating geography as a spatial science than the other. Direction has been relatively ignored, except for some work on migration patterns (Wolpert, 1967; Adams, 1969). A substantial volume of work on spatial science followed the agenda established by the social physics school (p. 75). The relationship between distance and various types of interaction – migrations, information flows, movements of goods, etc. – had been identified by several nineteenth-century workers, such as Carey (1858), Ravenstein (1885; Grigg, 1977; Tobler, 1995), and Spencer (1892). Their impact is unclear: McKinney (1968) suggested that Stewart and others were unaware of the seeds of the 'gravity model' and 'population potential' ideas in Carey and Spencer's writings, and claimed that 'current geographers could learn much' (p. 105) from their publications; Warntz (1968) retorted that Stewart was well aware, although McKinney's rebuttal pointed out that Stewart did not refer to them in his 1940s' papers, only in the 1950s. Ravenstein's papers, on the other hand, were very influential on later research into migration patterns. Interestingly, the pioneering work on distance-decay and the gravity model, as with much of the rest of spatial science, was done outside geography: as Tocalis (1978, p. 124) expressed it, 'geographers' contributions to the theoretical evolution of the gravity concept were minor', although one major contributor – Alan Wilson – later 'became a geographer' (Wilson, 1984b).

Apart from Stewart's work, one of the major social physics' influences on geographers was Zipf's (1949) 'principle of least effort'. If individuals organize their lives to minimize the amount of work undertaken and movement involves work, then movement-minimization is part of the general principle of least effort. To explain this, Zipf expanded Stewart's finding that with increasing distance from Princeton, fewer students from each state attended that university. Two aspects of work are involved: (1) that needed in acquiring information about the university; and (2) that needed in travelling there. Thus, the greater the distance between potential students' homes and Princeton, the less they are likely to know about the university and the less prepared they will be to travel there. The validity of this argument was tested against many data sets: material on the contents of newspapers and on their circulation illustrated the expected distance-decay trend in information flows, for example, and data on movements between places showed that the greater the distance separating them, the smaller the volume of inter-place contact.

Zipf called this regularity the P_1P_2/D relationship, and Stewart noted the analogy between it and the Newtonian gravity formula, hence its popularization as the 'gravity model'. It was fitted to flow data in many research projects, as shown in Carrothers' (1956) and Olsson's (1965) reviews. To achieve reasonable statistical fits, the various elements of the equation had to be weighted (P_1P_2 – the measures of mass at the origin and destination respectively, indicators of interaction-generation potential; and D – the distance between the two places). Because different weights were determined empirically in almost all studies, Olsson (1965, p. 48) claimed that the gravity model of interaction was, 'an empirical regularity to which it has not yet been possible to furnish any theoretical explanation'. (Wilson, 1967, 1970, later offered a statistical explanation and developed a whole family of interaction models based on statistical mechanics.) Empirical studies showed that the strength of the influence of distance varied from place to place, from population to population, and from context to context, but it was invariably related to the volume of interaction to some extent: the influence of distance on flow volumes seemed virtually universal, but no available theory could account for the variability in the strength of its impact.

It was not only in social physics that distance was receiving attention at this time. Economists and sociologists were becoming increasingly aware of its influence on behaviour (Pooler, 1977), the former in location theories and Isard's development of regional science, and the latter in studies by the Chicago school on urban residential patterns (Johnston, 1971, 1980b). Thus (Pooler, 1977, p. 69):

> . . . a number of geographers became aware of the spatial enquiries that were being undertaken in a social science context outside their own discipline and, upon realizing their relevance to geography, proceeded to emulate them. The appearance of the spatial tradition was prompted, not by discoveries from within geography, but by an awareness and acceptance of investigations external to the discipline. The space-centred scientific enquiries of other social sciences became paradigms for geographers, simply because those enquiries, being spatial, were seen to be of relevance by some practitioners.

This fitted both the philosophical framework outlined by Schaefer (1953) and the 'quantitative revolution'. In adopting spatial viewpoints pioneered in other disciplines, however, human geographers were frequently selective in what they imported. Work on urban residential patterns concentrated on certain aspects of the urban sociology of the Chicago school, for example. Robert Park's dictum relating social distance to spatial distance stimulated much work on residential segregation (Peach and Smith, 1981), but the social Darwinism and ecological theory underlying this dictum was largely ignored (though see Robson, 1969; Entrikin, 1980) and the humanistic concerns in Park's work were only identified later when spatial science was losing popularity (Jackson and Smith, 1981, 1984).

In their spatial analyses some social scientists looked not only at the influence of distance, but also at its meaning and measurement. Stouffer (1940), for example, established a relationship in which migration between places X and Y was accounted for not so much by the distance between them, but rather by the number of intervening opportunities. He measured distance in terms of opportunities; the greater the number of opportunities available locally, the less work that has to be expended in moving to one. (Berry, 1993, refers to contacts with Stouffer when he was a student at the University of Washington.) Others followed this flexible approach to measurement of the basic variable. Ullman (1956), for example, developed a schema for analysing commodity flows in which the amount of movement between two places was related to three factors:

1. *Complementarity* – the degree to which there is a supply of a commodity at one place and a demand for it at the other;
2. *Intervening opportunity* – the degree to which either the potential destination can obtain similar commodities from a nearer, and presumably cheaper, source or the potential source can sell its commodities to a nearer market; and
3. *Transferability* – for complementarity to be capitalized on, movement between the two places must be feasible, given channel, time and cost constraints.

This was not as easily tested statistically as the 'gravity model' (Hay, 1979b). Fitting such models also requires accepting that the influence of distance, measured as either time or cost, varies from place to place and from time to time, producing time – and cost – distance maps that are transformations of the traditional grid (Abler, 1971; Forer, 1974; Janelle, 1968, 1969). This issue was taken up by later work on 'local statistics' (Fotheringham, Brunsdon and Charlton, 2001; see also p. 172 below).

Analyses of movement patterns were stimulated not only by their obvious relevance to geography's growing spatial science focus and its development of location theories, but also by their applicability in forecasting contexts. Planning land-use patterns and transport (especially road) systems became increasingly sophisticated technically during the 1950s and 1960s. Data analyses showed both the traffic-generating power of various land uses and the patterns of interaction between different parts of an urban area, with the gravity model being used to describe the latter. Future land-use configurations were then designed, their traffic-generating potential derived, and the gravity model used to predict flow patterns and identify needed road systems. Later models, most based on Ira Lowry's, assessed different land-use configurations in terms of traffic flows, thereby suggesting the 'best' directions for future urban growth (see Batty, 1978; on the extent of their application, see Batty, 1989).

The demands for sophisticated planning devices stimulated much research using gravity and Lowry models. American economists initiated this but it was later taken up by British workers, including Alan Wilson, who was appointed to a professorship of geography at the University of Leeds in 1970. (He was trained as a physicist and became interested in traffic forecasting when a city councillor in Oxford: Wilson, 1984b.) Wilson (1967) derived the gravity model mathematically, thereby giving it a stronger theoretical base, and extended Lowry's model into a more general suite concerned with location, allocation and movement in space (Birkin *et al.*, 1990: see below, p. 351; these later became the foundation of a major commercial operation at the University of Leeds – GMap Ltd.)

Collaboration between academic geographers and practising planners on these modelling exercises led to developments which paralleled those in regional science in the United States. Two new British journals catered for these research areas – *Regional Studies* and *Environment and Planning* (now *Environment and Planning A*): both attracted contributions and readers from other social sciences (Johnston and Thrift, 1993; Johnston, 2003d). The new geographical methodology was proving of considerable applied value, therefore. Careers as planners became extremely popular among geography graduates in the 1960s and 1970s, and academic geographers' growing desire for their discipline to equal that of other social sciences in its policy-making relevance seemed well on the way to fulfilment. Geographers' analyses of spatial patterns and interactions were resulting in applicable models which could be used to identify feasible future locational and flow patterns.

Systems

The study of systems was introduced to the geographical literature by Garrison (1960a) and Chorley (1962), although Foote and Greer-Wootten (1968) claimed that systems analysis was promoted in Sauer's (1925) programmatic statement *The Morphology of Landscape* with the words 'objects which exist together in the landscape exist in interrelation'. More generally, the notion of a system has a long history, as Bennett and Chorley (1978, pp. 11–14) point out: teleological traditions, for example, postulate the world as 'a vast system of signs through which God teaches man how to behave' (p. 12), whereas functionalism links observed phenomena together as 'instances of repeatable and predictable regularities' of form.

However, the field of modern systems analysis as applied to geography in the 1960s was a derivation from a Cold War project of managing complex military systems. Developed first at the US Air Force Research and Development (RAND) 'think tank' in Santa Monica, California, systems analysis embodied postwar American scientific application across a spectrum of science, engineering, economics, political science and sociology (Collins, 2002; Hughes, 2000). Its impacts in the late 1950s and early 1960s on both military thinking (warfare strategies and nuclear weapons systems) and public policy (the growth of centralized top-down decision making and technocratic 'expertise') were profound. Its appeal lay in the bold claims it made to predict trends and outcomes and the sense of rational order that it claimed to bring to bear on complex problems (at the same time as moving them out of the arenas of political and public debate). The keystones of such study of systems were *connectivity* and *prediction*. Although geographers made little or no contribution to developments at RAND or to the status of general systems theory, geography would inevitably be influenced. Thus, Harvey's (1969a) *Explanation in Geography* adopts key aspects of the logic of systems analysis. He points out that reality is infinitely complex in its links between variables, but systems analysis provides a convenient abstraction of that complexity in a form which maintains the major connections (p. 448).

A system comprises three components:

1. A set of elements;
2. A set of links (relationships) between those elements; and
3. A set of links between the system and its environment.

The last component may be absent, creating closed systems. These are extremely rare in reality ('everything is related to everything else'), but are frequently created for analytical purposes either experimentally or, more usually in human geography, by imposing artificial boundaries in order to isolate a system's salient features. Thus, just as an internal-combustion engine comprises a set of linked elements which receives energy from, and returns spent fuel to, its environment, so a set of settlements linked by communications networks forms a spatial system, with links to other settlements outside the defined area of the system providing the contacts with the environment. A system's elements have volumetric quantities and material flows along the links; as the system operates, the various quantities may change.

Systems terminology was widely adopted by human geographers in the 1960s, but much of the early literature on systems analysis was programmatic rather than applied; it suggested how the terminology might be applied, often reinterpreting old material (McDaniel and Eliot Hurst, 1968). Relatively few applications were reported, and more than a decade later much of the literature assessed in a major review was written by other scientists (Bennett and Chorley, 1978). Nevertheless, Harvey (1969a, p. 479) wrote that:

> If we abandon the concept of the system we abandon one of the most powerful devices yet invented for deriving satisfactory answers to questions that we pose regarding the complex world that surrounds us. The question is not, therefore, whether or not we should use systems analysis or systems concepts in geography, but rather one of examining how we can use such concepts and such modes of analysis to our maximum advantage.

In seeking answers to this question, two variants on the systems theme have been employed. The first is *systems analysis*; the second is *general systems theory*, which was an attempt (no longer considered relevant) to provide a more unified science than current disciplinary boundaries allow.

Systems analysis

Several typologies have been suggested for studying geographical systems (Harvey, 1969a, pp. 445–9). Chorley and Kennedy (1971) identified four types (Figure 4.2):

1. *Morphological systems* are statements of static relationships – of links between elements: they may be maps showing places joined by roads, or equations describing the functional relationships between variables. Much of the spatial analysis outlined earlier in this chapter described such morphological systems.
2. *Cascading systems* contain links along which energy passes between elements: factories are cascading systems, for example, with the output from one part forming the input for another. Each element may be a system itself, producing a nesting hierarchy of cascading systems, as with Haggett's (1965c) nodal regions and the input–output matrix representation of an economy (Isard, 1960). Berry (1966) linked these two examples of cascading systems in his inter-regional input–output study of the Indian economy. Within each element, the material

flowing through is manipulated in some way (the industrial process in a factory, for example). The nature of the manipulative process may be ignored entirely in the investigation, with focus on the inputs and outputs only: such a representation of the element is termed a black box. White-box studies investigate the transformation process, whereas grey-box analyses make a partial attempt at their description.

3. *Process-response systems* are characterized by studies of the effects of linked elements on each other. Instead of focusing on form, as in the first two types, these are studies of processes, of causal inter-relationships. In systems terms these may involve, for example, the effects of one variable, X, on another, Y; in the analysis of spatial systems they could involve the effect of variable X in place *a* on variable Y in place *b*, as with the transmission of a disease from one area of a country to another.

4. *Control systems* are special cases of process-response systems, having the additional characteristic of one or more key elements (valves) which regulate the system's operation and may be used to control it.

Attention focused on process-response and control systems. Langton (1972), for example, suggested that the former provide an excellent framework for studying change in human geography. He identified two sub-types. *Simple-action systems* are unidirectional in their nature: a stimulus in X produces a response in Y, which in turn may act as a stimulus to a further variable, Z. Such a causal chain merely reformulates 'the characteristic cause-and-effect relation with which traditional science has dealt' (Harvey, 1969a, p. 455); in another language it is a process law. More important is the second sub-type, *feedback systems*. According to Chorley and Kennedy (1971, pp. 13–14), 'Feedback is the property of a

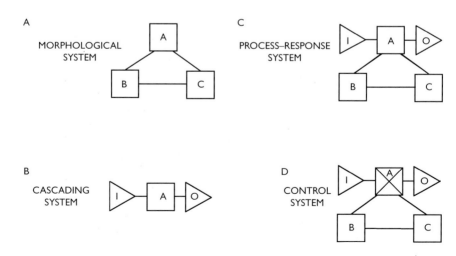

Figure 4.2 *Types of system: A, B and C indicate system elements, I represents input, O represents output, and in the control system A is a valve (Source: Chorley and Kennedy, 1971, p. 4)*

system or sub-system such that, when change is introduced via one of the system variables, its transmission through the structure leads the effect of the change back to the initial variable, to give a circularity of action'. Feedback may be either direct – A influences B which in turn influences A (Figure 4.3A) – or it may be indirect, with the impulse from A returning to it via a chain of other variables (Figure 4.3B). With *negative feedback* the system is maintained in a steady state by self-regulation processes termed homeostatic or morphostatic: 'A classic example is provided by the process of competition in space which leads to a progressive reduction in excess profits until the spatial system is in equilibrium' (Harvey, 1969a, p. 460). But with *positive feedback* the system is characterized as morphogenetic, changing its characteristics as the effect of B on C leads to further changes in B, via D (Figure 4.3D).

The concept of feedback, with the associated notions of homeostasis and morphogenesis, provides 'the nuclei of the systems theory of change' (Langton, 1972, p. 145). In many spatial systems, feedback may be uncontrolled; others may include a regulator, such as a planning policy (Bennett and Chorley, 1978). There were few geographical studies of such feedback processes, however. For homeostatic systems, Langton cited investigations of central place dynamics in which the pattern of service centres is adjusted as the population distribution changes, to reproduce the previous balance between supply and demand factors (Badcock, 1970). Morphogenetic systems are illustrated by Pred's (1965b) model of the process of urban growth, in which expansion in a sector generates further growth there, as in Myrdal's (1957) more general theory of cumulative causation. Such systems modelling has been used to predict urban futures (Forrester, 1969). In most of these studies the input from systems theory was relatively slight, however, leading Langton (1972, pp. 159–60) to the paradoxical conclusions that:

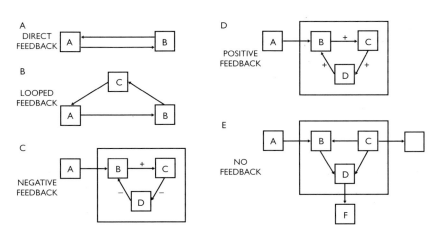

Figure 4.3 *Various types of feedback relationships in systems (Source: Chorley and Kennedy, 1971, p. 14)*

First, there is little correlation between the extent of the penetration of the terminology of systems theory and the rigorous application of its concepts. The empty use of terminology, which is typified by the use of the term feedback as an explanatory device rather than as a description of a fundamental research problem, must be counter-productive in a situation in which the terms themselves may be given many subtle different shades of meaning. . . . Second, somewhat paradoxically, many of the concepts of systems theory are already used in geography without the attendant jargon and without apparently drawing direct inspiration from the literature of systems theory.

One of the most substantial attempts to apply systems theory to a problem in human geography was Bennett's (1975) study of the dynamics of location and growth in northwest England. Having represented the system – its elements, links and feedback relationships – he estimated the influence of various external (i.e. national) events on the regional system's parameters, isolated the effects of a government policy on the system's structure, and forecast the region's future spatio-temporal morphology. He developed the forecasting aspects of this methodology in later papers (Bennett, 1978a, 1979), suggested how an optimal distribution of government grants could be achieved (Bennett, 1981b) and outlined the likely spatial variation in the impact of a new tax (the 'poll tax': Bennett, 1989b).

One area of investigation which firmly adopted the systems approach covers the intersection of human and physical geography. The *ecosystem* is a process-response system involving energy flows through biological environments, most of which include, or are affected by, people. It is also a control system whose living components regulate the energy flows: 'they further represent a major point at which human control systems must intersect with the natural world' (Chorley and Kennedy, 1971, p. 330). Most naturally occurring ecosystems are homeostatic for much of the time (see Chapman, 1977, Chapter 7), but human 'interference' often transforms them into morphogenetic systems, with potentially catastrophic effects (Johnston, 1989b).

Stoddart (1965, 1967b) argued that the ecosystem should be employed as a basic geographical principle, as did other programmatic statements (e.g. Clarkson, 1970), including two based on the associated concept of community (Morgan and Moss, 1965; Moss and Morgan, 1967). But Langton's conclusion about relatively little substantive research in human geography based on systems' thinking remained valid (see Grossman, 1977). Similar attempts, but involving less consideration of the biotic environment, were made in allied disciplines, and were occasionally been imported into the geographical literature. Sociologists' human ecosystem models (e.g. Duncan, 1959; Duncan and Schnore, 1959) were used as frameworks for investigating migration (Urlich, 1972) and urbanization (Urlich Cloher, 1975), for example, and the operational research techniques of economists, with their important feedback mechanisms, have stimulated work in transport geography (e.g. Sinclair and Kissling, 1971).

The most comprehensive early attempt to forge a systems approach to geographical study was Bennett and Chorley's book (1978), written to provide 'a unified multi-disciplinary approach to the interfacing of "man" with "nature"' (p. 21), with three major aims:

First, it is desired to explore the capacity of the systems approach to provide an inter-disciplinary focus on environmental structures and techniques. Secondly, we wish to examine the manner in which a systems approach aids in developing the interfacing of social and economic theory, on the one hand, with physical and biological theory, on the other. A third aim is to explore the implications of this interfacing in relation to the response of man to his current environmental dilemmas. . . . It is hoped to show that the systems approach provides a powerful vehicle for the statement of environmental situations of ever-growing temporal and spatial magnitude, and for reducing the areas of uncertainty in our increasingly complex decision-making arenas.

This task involved elucidating not only the 'hard systems' of physical and biological sciences but also the 'soft systems' characteristic of the social sciences. The latter cover a large and fertile literature concerned with, first, the cognitive systems describing people as thinking beings and their decision-making systems (as individuals and in groups) and, second, with the socio-economic systems made up of very many of these interacting individuals and groups. They then attempt to interface the two types, because:

. . . in large-scale man-environment systems the symbiosis of man as part of the environment of the system he wishes to control introduces all the indeterminacies of socio-economic control objectives. . . . In particular, we need to ask what are the political and social implications of control, and for whom and by whom is control intended? (p. 539).

Their essay ends with a discussion of the substantial problems involved in such interfacing, many of which are firmly tackled in the text.

Use of systems analysis in human geography assumes (usually implicitly) that valid analogies can be drawn between human societies on the one hand and both natural phenomena-complexes and machines on the other. Individual system elements have predetermined roles, and can only act and change in set ways – depending on the system's structure and its inter-relationships with the environment. As a descriptive device, this analogy allows the structure and operation of society and its components to be portrayed and analysed, providing a source of ideas from which hypotheses can be generated (see Coffey, 1981). And once a system has been defined and modelled, systems analysis can predict the likely nature of the elements and links following certain environmental changes (such as the introduction of new elements and/or links, as in the classic Lowry model used to predict the impact of new land-use configurations on traffic flows: Batty, 1978).

The potential fertility of this analogy was examined in Wilson's (1981b) discussion of methods for analysing environmental systems. He defined environment as 'natural, man-nature, and manufactured "systems of interest" ' (p. xi), in all of which, 'the main concern is with *complicated* systems whose components exhibit high degrees of interdependence. The behaviour of the "whole" system is then usually something very much more than the sum of the parts' (p. 3). He argued that moorland ecosystems, water resource systems and cities (his three initial examples) can all be studied in the same way, and set out available methods for that; a further book (Wilson, 1981a) presented the mathematics for studying systems in which the rates and directions of change suddenly alter, and he returned to the topic in a later summary volume (Wilson, 2000). Huggett (1980) similarly argued that systems analysis has wide applications in both human and physical geography, plus the interface where people and environment interact (see also Huggett and Thomas, 1980). Once a system has been successfully modelled, it can be manipulated using control theory: 'a *dynamic* optimization technique ... [that] permits optimal allocation over long time horizons ... [and] shifts emphasis from mere model construction to model use' (Chorley and Bennett, 1981, p. 219). Such a combination of models describing systems with a theory of system control has a wide range of potential applications, according to Chorley and Bennett, in such fields as pollution control, catchment management, inter-area resource allocation and urban planning. It suggests a commonality of interest, focused on methods, between applied physical and applied human geography.

Systems theory, information and entropy
A system has been defined so far here as a series of linked elements interacting to form an operational whole. This was challenged by Chapman (1977, p. 6) who opened his book with:

> I do not think that the concept of a system will have any great operational consequences in geography for a long time yet. It represents an ideal that the real world does not fully approach. On the other hand, in conceptual terms I think the concept is extremely important and useful, and that it has a great and immediate role to play for those who are about to plan the strategy of their research. As a framework for analysis, it has no current peers.

For him, a system comprises a series of elements which can take alternative states, and his definition – following Rothstein (1958) – is:

> A system is a set of objects where each object is associated with a set of feasible alternative states: and where the actual state of any object selected from this set is dependent in part or completely upon its membership of the system. An object that has no alternative states is not a functioning part but a static cog (p. 80).

An example is a number of farms, each comprising a series of fields: every farmer has to decide how to use those fields. Each decision will in part reflect the farm's general operations and the uses to which all other fields are put; in part, too, it will be a function of the external market and the decisions made by other farmers regarding use of their own fields. Thus, there is a large number of possible states for the system of fields – different configurations of land uses. According to Chapman, systems analysis should involve investigating those configurations and placing the observed pattern within the context of the alternatives:

> ... to theorize merely about what does exist is not very useful. If we restrict ourselves to that alone, all explanation will be merely historical accidental. At all stages it is most important to include consideration of what else could have been. The definition of organization in a system even explicitly requires the assessment of what else could have been (pp. 120–1).

Taylor and Gudgin (1976) argued similarly in a different context: instead of simply asking 'is there a bias [towards one political party] in the electoral districting of a borough?', they ask 'what is the likelihood of a bias occurring, given the system constraints?' (the number of different ways that the districts could be constructed). This allowed them to they set the study of electoral districting, the aggregation of spatial units into constituencies and its consequences, on a strong statistical footing (Gudgin and Taylor, 1979; Johnston et al., 2001).

Such analyses focus on one configuration of the system as a sample from a set of possible configurations, and among their key concepts is *entropy*. In the second law of thermodynamics an increase in system entropy involves an increase in uncertainty, as with the introduction of a layer of hot water to a body of cold water. Initially, the two are separate, and one can be completely certain about the location of the hot molecules, for example. But with no external influence the two slowly mix, until all are at the same temperature. As the mixing proceeds, so the entropy increases.

Social scientists have drawn their usage of entropy from two separate, though linked, definitions. *Thermodynamic entropy* relates to the most probable configuration of the elements within the system constraints, as just illustrated. In *information theory*, entropy refers to the distribution of the elements across a set of possible states, and is an index of element dispersion. One can be completely certain about a distribution, in terms of predicting where one element will be, if all elements are in the same state; conversely, one will be most uncertain when elements are equally distributed through all possible states, so that prediction of the location of any one element is most difficult. (See Webber, 1977, and Thomas, 1982 on the relationship between entropy and uncertainty.)

In its simplest form, the information-theory measure of entropy is another descriptive index, but it can be developed in a variety of ways. Chapman (1977) illustrates three uses:

1. As a series of indices of variations in population distributions;
2. As an index of redundancy in a landscape, where redundancy is defined as relating to a regular sequence so that it is possible to predict the land use at place *a*, for example, from knowledge of the land uses at neighbouring places; and
3. As a series of measures of reactions to situations in states of uncertainty.

In general terms these continue the tradition of Stewart and Warntz's macrogeography (p. 75): the aim is to describe a pattern rather than to explain it, although the nature of the constraints used to derive the entropy measures provides an input to explanatory modes of analysis (Webber, 1977).

The use of entropy as developed in statistical mechanics was introduced to the geographical literature by Wilson's (1970) extensions to the gravity model. His initial example was a flow matrix. The number of trips originating in each of a series of residential areas is known, as is the number ending in each of a series of workplace areas, but the entries in the cells of the matrix – which people move from which residential area to which workplace area (the flow pattern) – are unknown. What is the most likely flow pattern? Even with only a few areas and relatively small numbers of commuters, the number of possibilities is very large. Wilson defines three system states.

1. The *macro-state* comprises the number of commuters at each origin and the number of jobs at each destination;

2. The *meso-state* consists of a particular flow pattern: five people may go from zone A to zone X, for example, and three from the same origin to zone Y, but it is not known which five are in the first category and which three in the second.
3. Finally, a *micro-state* is a particular example of a flow pattern – one of the many possible configurations of eight people moving from zone A, five to X and three to Y. Entropy-maximizing procedures find that meso-state associated with the largest number of micro-states: the most probable distribution is that with the greatest number of micro-states giving rise to it. (For illustrations, see Johnston and Pattie, 2000, 2003.)

The most-likely (maximum likelihood) distribution corresponds to the position where we are most uncertain about the micro-state of the system, as this has the largest possible number of such states and we have no grounds for choosing between them. This approach, too, follows the macrogeography tradition. It is not an attempt at explanation and Wilson sees his work illustrating:

> ... the application of the concept of entropy in urban and regional modelling; that is, in hypothesis development, or theory building. ['Model' and 'hypothesis' are used synonymously, and a theory is a well tested hypothesis.] ... the entropy-maximizing procedure enables us to handle extremely complex situations in a consistent way (pp. 10–11).

In reviewing Wilson's presentation, Gould (1972, p. 689) termed it 'the most difficult I have ever read in geography' but continued, 'he has planted a number of those rare and deep concepts whose understanding provides a fresh and sharply different view of the world'.

The hypothesis that the entries in the flow matrix conform to the most likely distribution can be tested against 'real' data. If it is falsified, either entirely or in part, it can be refined by building in more constraints. Wilson does this with intra-urban transport models, for example, by introducing travel-cost constraints, different types of commuters (class, age, etc.), different types of jobs, and so on. The aim is to describe the most likely system structure from a given amount of information, which is incomplete. He subsequently developed both the theory of his modelling and the substantive applications (see Wilson, 1981b). A general text (Wilson, 1974) introduced a whole family of models that can be used to represent, and then forecast, the various components of a complex spatial system such as an urban region. Some of these models were expanded (e.g. Rees and Wilson, 1977, on demographic accounts) and applied, with varying success, to the West Yorkshire region (Wilson, Rees and Leigh, 1977).

Wilson's work has been applied and developed by others (see Batty, 1976, 1978, for example), though rarely in other contexts. Webber (1977) extended Wilson's argument that the purpose of entropy-maximizing models is to draw conclusions from a data set that are 'natural' in that they are functions of that data set alone and contain no interpreter bias. For him, they provide a convenient way of organizing thinking about a complex world, and he identifies an 'entropy-maximizing paradigm' (p. 262). At Leeds, Wilson's work on the entropy-maximizing approach was extended into the field of micro-simulation (Ballas *et al.*, 2002; Birkin and Clarke, 1988, 1989; Clarke and Holm, 1988; Clarke, 1996; Williamson *et al.*, 1998) which produces statistically reliable estimates of micro-level characteristics of a population from macro-data. Given the number of people in each age group in each of a number of small areas, for example, and, separately, the number with cancer and the cross-tabulation of age by cancer for a larger area comprising those small areas, it lists the individuals in each area in each age group who are estimated to have cancer: as with entropy-maximizing, these are the maximum-likelihood estimates given the constraints (the number of people in an age group with cancer in all of the small areas must equal the sum for the larger area).

One of the few examples of the application of entropy-maximizing models to other research contexts is in electoral geography. It may be, for example, that information on the number of votes for each party in each district at each of two elections suggests that the number of voters who changed their choice between the elections varied across districts, but no district-by-district data are available to see if this is the case. Johnston (1985b) adapted Wilson's method to address this issue using national survey data on party-switching as a constraint to enable estimates of the volume and direction of switching in each district. Tests using available data have shown that the estimates are generally very accurate representations of the actual patterns (Johnston and Pattie, 2000, 2003), and the method has been employed in a large number of applications to demonstrate that there are significant spatial variations in various form of electoral behaviour (Johnston and Pattie, 2001). They also linked it to other attempts to tackle one of the major statistical issues in quantitative social science – the solution of the ecological inference problem. This relates to how individual relationships and behaviour can be inferred from aggregate data, such as differences between ethnic groups in their turnout at elections and spatial variations in those differences, when there are no data on turnout by ethnic group only on the ethnic composition and turnout rates of different areas (King, 1997; Johnston and Pattie, 2001).

In emphasizing aggregate patterns, this work is macrogeographic; according to Webber (1977. p. 265), 'The entropy-maximizing paradigm asserts ... that, though the study of individual behavior may be of interest, it is not necessary for the study of aggregate social relations'. The patterns predicted by the models are functions of the constraints (the information provided at the meso-state), so that knowledge of them means that 'the entropy-maximizing paradigm is capable of yielding meaningful answers to short-run operational problems' (p. 266) of immense value for immediate planning purposes. But:

> ... in the longer run, much of the economic system is variable: the constraints and the spatial form of the urban region may change ... the research task facing entropists is (1) to identify the constraints which operate upon urban systems, which is partly an economic problem; (2) to deduce some facets of the economic relations among the individuals within the system from the use of the formalism; and (3) to construct a theory which explains the origins of the constraints. Only when the third task has been attempted may the paradigm be adequately judged (p. 266).

The entropy-maximizing model acts not only as a 'black-box' forecasting device (see p. 124), therefore, but also as a hypothesis: if a system's operation is to be understood, the axioms – the constraints – must themselves be explained. Given the nature of the constraints (in Wilson's initial example, why people live where they do, why people work where they do, and why they spend a certain amount of time, money and energy on transport), the task is a major one: entropy-maximizing models aim to clarify it and indicate the most fruitful avenues for investigation.

Dynamic processes

The study of systems allows dynamic processes to be incorporated within geographical analyses, instead of focusing on static patterns that are the outcomes of such processes. Thus, much of the mathematical development reviewed above has been concerned with such processes, to advance understanding of change and the ability to forecast it. (On the use of the term 'process' in this context, see the critique by Hay and Johnston, 1983.) Dynamical systems theory and analysis were the focus of a major research programme conducted at the University of Leeds by Alan Wilson and his associates from the mid-1970s, for example, during which a number of major advances were made; in particular, attention was directed away from relatively straightforward linear modelling to complex representations in which change is presented as discontinuous and not necessarily unidirectional – often termed chaotic (see Wilson, 1981a).

Many geographical analyses of dynamical systems have focused on static spatial patterns or structures, representing these as equilibrium or steady-state situations within the ongoing dynamic processes. Change is then handled, as Clarke and Wilson (1985b, p. 429) describe it, 'by forecasting (in some other theory or model) the independent variables associated with a system and then calculating the new equilibrium or steady state'. (There are parallels here with Darby's approach to historical geography, linking cross-sections through narratives of change, see p. 56) Their applications of dynamical systems analysis suggest that this approach is not tenable, however, because in complex systems 'There are too many possibilities of transition to different kinds of equilibrium or non-equilibrium states' (Clarke and Wilson, 1985b, 431), which casts doubts on the validity of the traditional approach to forecasting and hence the contribution of geographical modelling to planning. The nature of that contribution must be rethought, therefore, because conditional forecasting is of little value – 'there are simply too many possible futures for this to be useful' (p. 446). The new contributions, they argue, could involve the following:

> First, it may often be possible to recognize the 'nearness' of some instability or structural shift to an undesirable state. Policy can then be focused on conservation. Secondly, it may be possible to see how to bring about a shift to a new desired state by changing policy in order to move a parameter through some critical value. Thirdly, both the ideas of dynamical analysis and the capabilities of modern computer technology lend themselves to the construction of planning systems focused on information retrieval ... and monitoring; so that at least planners, and policy makers are in a position to respond more rapidly when difficulties are identified (p. 446).

Geographers thereby come more to terms with the inherent complexity, and hence unpredictability, of the world.

The theory of systems and general systems theory

Like regional science and the impact of Walter Isard, the development of General Systems Theory (GST) was very much tied up with one man – Ludwig von Bertalanffy (see von

Bertalanffy, 1950). He focused on isomorphisms, the common features among the systems studied in different disciplines: GST's 'subject matter is the formulation and derivation of those principles which are common for systems in general' (Walmsley, 1972, p. 23). The goal was to write meta-theories with rules that apply in a variety of contexts; application was usually by analogy from one discipline to another (as in Chappell and Webber's, 1970, use of an electrical analogue of spatial diffusion processes and in work on artificial intelligence using computer modelling: Couclelis, 1986a). GST was presented as offering geographers an organizing framework, an empirical exercise using inductive procedures to fashion general theories out of the findings of particular disciplines (Coffey, 1981).

Although it was claimed that there have been no advances in either the theoretical base or the empirical application of GST (Greer-Wootten, 1972), some advances were made using models of one system as metaphors for understanding another. Woldenberg and Berry (1967) drew analogies between the hierarchical organizations of rivers and central-place systems, for example; Berry (1964a) argued that cities are open systems in a steady state, as exemplified by the stability of their behaviour-describing equations; several authors (e.g. Ray, Villeneuve and Roberge, 1974) applied the concept of allometry – that the growth rate of a component of an organism is proportional to the growth of the whole; and Haggett (1965c, p. 22) was attracted to Thompson's (1917) work *On Growth and Form*, which 'illustrates how many subjects find common ground in the study of morphology; there is inspiration still to be found in his treatment of crystal structures or honeycomb formations'.

More recently, some analysts have been attracted to the concept of fractals (Goodchild and Mark, 1987, p. 265). If a line is measured at two scales, the second larger than the first, then we might expect its length to increase as a ratio of the two scales. In many areas of geography, however, this is unlikely to be the case: as the scale of a map increases (i.e. the representative fraction falls and more detail is shown) the length of a line – such as a stretch of coast – will probably increase by more than the ratio of the scales, because extra detail is added. Fractals are the geometrical objects that operate in this manner: even though the two lines may be generated by the same process (i.e. they are technically self-similar so that, for example, any part has the characteristic features of the whole), at different scales more detail can be shown. The concept was extensively used by Batty and Longley (1994) in analyses of urban form – both the shapes of entire built-up areas and those of their component parts; identification of fractal regularities allowed them to simulate urban growth and change.

According to its proponents, GST's advantages for human geography lie in its inter-disciplinary approach, its high level of generalization, and its concept of the steady state of an open system (Greer-Wootten, 1972; Walmsley, 1972), but they also contended that geography's strong empirical tradition means that it has more to contribute than to take from GST. One critic, however, claimed that, 'General systems theory seems to be an irrelevant distraction' (Chisholm, 1967, p. 51). Chisholm summarized the case for GST as follows:

1. There is a need to study systems rather than isolated phenomena;
2. There is a need to identify the basic principles governing systems;

3. There is value in arguing from analogies with other subject matter; and

4. There is a need for general principles to cover various systems.

He argued that something as grand as a meta-theory is unnecessary in order to convince people of the need to understand what they study, of the value of inter-disciplinary contact, and of the potential fertility of arguing by analogy. His case was generally accepted, and references to general systems theory have disappeared from the discipline's literature.

Systems and human geography

Although a considerable number of programmatic statements were written about the benefits of adopting a system approach in human geography, relatively few applications were reported outside a few topical areas: the study of land use and transport patterns, as in the many analyses by Wilson and his co-workers discussed above; the study of input-output matrices (for examples, see Isard, 1975); and the study of population changes. With the last of these, for example, Woods (1982) promoted a more theoretical approach to population geography than had previously characterized the sub-discipline, with an emphasis on systems, and with Rees he edited a pioneering collection of essays launching an approach termed 'spatial demography' (Woods and Rees, 1986). Many of the essays in the latter treated the three main components of a population system – birth, death, and migration – in a multi-regional spatial systems framework, which addressed the issue (Rees, 1986, p. 97):

> Given that the characteristics of the population vary in interesting ways across space and that their time paths of development may be very different … how do we represent the processes of demographic change in formal models which will make the predictions about the future path of development possible?

The nature of the proposed accounting systems for inter-regional population changes was set out in detail in Rees and Wilson (1977).

A further area in which systems thinking was suggested concerns the inter-relationships between society and nature, including ecology. There were some attempts to integrate the two through input–output and related models (as in Bennett and Chorley, 1978) and a number of authors presented flow diagrams of human-nature inter-relationships that portrayed them as systems (as in Blaikie, 1985; Cooke and Reeves, 1976; Goudie, 1986a; Huggett, 1980; and Wilson, 1981b). In general, however, the concept of a system has been applied much more by physical than by human geographers. A small group of the latter has continued to work on the formal representation of spatial systems. Wilson (2000, p. vii) claimed some 30 years after his first essays into the area that such modeling of urban and regional systems remained under-developed yet had enormous potential for policy-making and planning: for him, geography's 'classical theorists' remained von Thünen, Weber, Palander, Hoover, Hotelling, Christaller and Lösch, Burgess, Hoyt, Harris and Ullman, plus the original formulators of the gravity model.

Spatial separatism

Opposition to arguments for human geography as a spatial science developed largely as counters to claims for its separate status within the social sciences, with distance as the key variable. Crowe (1970), for example, portrayed using the spatial variable in nomothetic studies as naive spatial determinism.

The most sustained argument against geography as a spatial science – what he called the 'spatial separatist' theme – came in a series of papers by Sack, a former associate of Lukermann at the University of Minnesota (see p. 90). Reality has three dimensions – space, time and matter – and geography, according to the spatial separatist view, is the science of the first. Sack contended that space, time and matter cannot be separated analytically in an empirical science, however, and that geometry is not an acceptable language for such a science (Sack, 1972). Geometry is a branch of pure mathematics that is not concerned with empirical facts; its laws are static, with no reference to time, and they are not derivable from any dynamic or process laws.

Geographic facts have geometric properties (e.g. locations) but if, as Schaefer proposed, geographical laws are just concerned with the geometries of facts, they will provide only incomplete explanations for them. To illustrate this contention, Sack used an analogy of chopping wood. If the answer to the question 'Why are you chopping wood?' is 'because the force of the axe on impact splits the wood', then it is a static, geometric law; but if the answer is 'to provide fuel to produce heat', then it is an instance of a process law, which incorporates the geometric law. In this analogy, a process law is equated with the intention behind an action. The static laws of geometry are sufficient to explain and predict spatial patterns, so that if geography aimed only to analyse points, lines and shapes on maps it could be an independent science using geometry as its language. But, 'We do not accept the description of the changes of its shape as an explanation of the growth of a city' (p. 72), so that 'Geometry alone, then, cannot answer geographic questions' (p. 72), leading to the conclusion that:

> To explain requires laws and laws (if they are valid) explain events. Since the definition of an event implies the delimitation of some geometric properties (all events occur in space), the explanation of any event is in principle an explanation of some geometric properties of events (p. 77).

Thus geography will be closely allied with geometry in its emphasis on the spatial aspects of events (the instances of laws), but geometry alone is insufficient as a basis for explanation and prediction since no processes are involved in the derivation of geometries.

Bunge's (1973a) response claimed that spatial prediction was quite possible with reference to the geometry alone, as instanced by central place theory and Thünian analysis of land use patterns. Such geometries provide 'classic beauty', and 'purging geometry from geography reduces our trade to no apparent gain' (p. 568). Sack (1973a) replied that the static laws espoused by Bunge are only special cases of dynamic laws having antecedent and consequent conditions, and that:

> Although the laws of geometry are unequivocally static, purely spatial, non-deducible from dynamic laws, and explain and predict physical geometric properties of events, they do not answer the

questions about the geometric properties of events that geographers raise and they do not make statements about process (p. 569).

Sack did not argue, as Bunge supposed, that geometry should be purged from geography, only that space should not be considered independently from time and matter. He further contended that (Sack, 1973b, p. 17):

... for a concept of physical space to conform to the rules of concept formation and be useful in a science of geography every instance of the geometric or spatial terms must be connected or related to one or more instances of non-geometric terms (to be called substance terms).

Thus, physical distance is not a concept in itself: it is necessary to know the terrain that a road crosses, for example, in order to assess the significance of its length in a gravity model – geometry alone is not enough. Since there is no such thing as empty physical space, there are no frictions of distance *per se*. There are frictions which demand work in crossing a substance, but the substance itself and the context in which it is being crossed create the frictions (such as transport costs), not simply the distance: 'There are frictions and there are distances, but there is no friction of distance' (Sack, 1973b, p. 22). Geography, according to Sack, is concerned to explain events and so requires substantive laws: such laws may contain geometric terms, such as the frictions of crossing a substance, but these terms alone are insufficient to provide explanations.

The spatial separatist approach proposes an independent position for geography within the social sciences using geometry as its language, but Sack (1974b, p. 446) contended that, 'The spatial position's aim of prying apart a subject matter from the systematic sciences by arguing for spatial questions and spatial laws does not seem viable'. Instead, two types of law relevant to geographical work must be identified (Sack, 1974a).

1. *Congruent substance laws* are independent of location: statements of 'if A then B' are universals which require no spatial referent; and
2. *Overlapping substance laws*, on the other hand, involve spatial terms: 'if A then B at C' in such cases contains a specific reference to location.

Both are relevant and necessary in answering geographical questions, so no case can be made for a necessary 'spatialness' to human geography's substance laws.

Extending his argument, Sack (1981, pp. 3–4) contended that, 'Space is an essential framework of all modes of thought' but 'geographic space is seen and evaluated in different ways at different times and in different cultures'. His book illustrated this by examining several approaches to the study of space: that of the social scientist concerned with objective meanings of space; that of the social scientist concerned with subjective meanings; the practical view of people who live in and learn about space (he used children as his example); the mythical and magical views of space; and the societal conceptions within which organizations and institutions structure and use space. Only the first of these is the concern of 'spatial separatists', whose approach takes space out of its relational context, with the consequence that, 'Ignoring spatial relations or conceiving them non-relationally will hinder the discovery and confirmation of social science generalizations' (p. 85).

May (1970, p. 188) also argued against Schaefer's claim that geography is the study of spatial relations:

> If we extend Schaefer's argument to include time, and assign the study of temporal sequences or relations to the historian, then the only conclusion respecting this matter that can be drawn is that economic, social, political, and other relations must be non-spatial and non-temporal. Hence economics, sociology, political science, etc. are non-spatial, non-temporal sciences. But this is absurd ... insofar as economics qualifies as a science possessing empirical warranty, then its generalizations must apply to given spatio-temporal situations.

If all sciences have a spatial content, what defines a separate discipline of geography? May lists five possibilities:

1. *Geography is a 'super-science' of spatial relations*, 'a generalizing science of spatial relations, interactions and distributions' (p. 194) drawing on the findings of other sciences. This would leave the latter truncated and their studies unfinished. Such an approach had already proved unsuccessful; 'the issue of the conception of geography as a generalizing or law-finding science that somehow stands above the social sciences and history is not even appropriately debatable' (p. 195).
2. *Geography is a lower-level science of spatial relations*, applying in empirical contexts the laws of higher-level, generally more abstract sciences. (This may be a valid description of much of the geography produced in the 1960s.) This again truncates the latter sciences and raises the question, 'What differentiates economic geography from economics, and vice versa?'.
3. *Geography is the study of geographical spatial relations.* This implies that there are spatial phenomena not studied in other social science disciplines and which can therefore be claimed as geography's; May could conceive of no objects which are purely geographical (or, in the parallel argument, purely historical either).
4. *Geography is the study of 'things in reality' spatially.* Yet again, this abstracts from other sciences; May admits that certain 'bits and pieces' are not studied elsewhere, but argues that they do not offer a satisfactory empirical foundation for a separate discipline.
5. *'Geography is not a generalizing or law-finding science of spatial relations'* (p. 203).

The first four indicate that, because of the analytical indissolubility of time, space and matter, all social sciences are concerned with spatial relations, so that May, like Sack, argued that geography cannot claim an independent status on the basis of the spatial variable and the geometrical aspects of space alone.

Moss (1970, p. 27) reached a similar conclusion:

> ... geometrical relationships must be assigned economic, social, physical, or biological meaning before they can in any sense become explanatory ... though geometries may be important tools in geographical study and research, they cannot be a source of theory since their analogy with geographical phenomena is simply through particular logical structures, and not through explanatory deduction ... such an application implies that space, area, distance, etc., are important in and of

themselves, quite independently of any implications they may have in terms of diffusion, of cost, of time, or of process. This is manifestly false (p. 27).

Gregory (1978b, 1980) also criticized the extremely narrow, even superficial, view of spatial processes identified in many spatial scientists' work. Their claims are instrumentalist, involving theories which cannot be validated conclusively but can only be evaluated pragmatically against the real world. He argued that Bennett (1974), for example, accepted that his models did not mirror actual processes but assumed that they did in order to allow policy formulation (and therefore produced self-fulfilling prophecies – as Lukermann had argued: see p. 92): because they can postdict the world as it presently is, it is assumed that they explain it and can be used to predict the future.

Bounded spaces and territoriality

Sack's arguments against the 'spatial separatist' theme did not involve him rejecting a 'spatial viewpoint' at the core of human geography, and later works (Sack, 1983, 1986) promoted a theory of territoriality as a basis for understanding certain aspects of human behaviour. Territoriality was defined as 'a human [spatial] strategy to affect, influence and control' (1986, p. 2) and he showed how:

> . . . under certain conditions territoriality is a more effective means of establishing differential access to people, or resources, than is non-territoriality. It can be bounded thus readily communicated; and it can be used to displace personal relationships, between controlled and controller, by relationships between people and 'the law of the place'. (Sack, 1983, p. 57)

He exemplified this with case studies, concluding that (1986, p. 215):

> . . . it is clear that territoriality alone cannot alter social relations to the point of changing the complexion of an entire society, but it can, through its own internal dynamics, set in motion heretofore unforeseen, and often undesirable, social consequences. This was true with ancient civilizations. It was true with the Catholic Church. It was the case with the American territorial system and the work place. By all accounts it is true in socialist countries and one can expect it will be true in attempts at establishing more utopian communal organizations. Territoriality's effects are multiple, important, and must be reckoned with.

Sack's replacement for the 'spatial separatist' theme involved a theory in which space is used by people, individually and collectively, to promote social goals, an argument taken up by others. (See Johnston, 1991, for an extension of Sack's work.) Wolch and Dear's (1989) book *The Power of Geography* is subtitled *How Territory Shapes Social Life*, but they do not deploy territoriality as defined here, and their focus is largely on what is discussed later – p. 233 – as locality research. Cox's (1989) chapter was relevant to the territoriality theme, however, emphasizing what he terms 'the politics of turf'.

As noted above (p. 116), territoriality had been promoted earlier by Gottmann (Johnston, 1996b); Taylor (1994) characterized its use as arguing for a 'world of containers' (see also Adams, 1995; Agnew, 1994; Mann, 1996; Storey, 2001; and Taylor, 1995). It has received comparatively little attention from human geographers in general, however (one exception in the textbook literature is Storey, 2001), although Cutter, Golledge, and Graf (2002, p. 308) claimed that 'humans, by their very nature, are territorial'.

*   *   *   *   *

The arguments reviewed in the present section are critical of much of the work undertaken by geographers in the paradigm which dominated the 1960s, impelled by the 'Victorian myth of the supremacy of the natural sciences' (Gregory, 1978a, p. 21). The case for spatial analysis continued to be argued, however. Gatrell (1983), for example, countered Sack's critique of spatial science – while accepting his case that the separation of space from substance is untenable. He did not confine spatial analysis to a positivist philosophy, however, stating that:

> My response to both structuralists and humanists [see below] is that, since they too deal with relations (among individuals or social groups, or between man and his environment), they cannot avoid the notion of space, since any relation defines a space. Moreover, because every relation has a geometry associated with it . . . they cannot avoid the fact that geometry underlies much of what they deal with. Structures . . . are intrinsically spatial, but not in any simple geographical sense (p. 5).

His definition of space is much broader than simply distance, therefore, and he promoted spatial analysis not as a separate paradigm of geography, but as an arsenal of tools to be used in all empirical research. Much of that research, he argued elsewhere (Gatrell, 1985, p. 191), involves portraying objects arranged in space, investigating the role of distance as a constraint on human spatial organization, and achieving efficiency in locational arrangements.

Behavioural geography

Although not apparently directly influenced by the arguments of Sack and others regarding geography and geometry, by the end of the 1960s some critiques of 'quantitative and theoretical geography' were being articulated on the grounds that testing of models of spatial organization and behaviour based on rational decision-making dominated by monetary criteria (and hence, in geography, minimizing transport costs) were not substantially aiding understanding. They were too simplistic in their assumptions about how people make decisions and behave. Instead, there were calls for more 'realistic' modelling based on observed rather than assumed decision-making processes.

These proposed modifications to the spatial-science approach stimulated work that became known as 'behavioural geography', whose birth was announced in a seminal book of essays (Cox and Golledge, 1969), whose maturity was reviewed twelve years later in a companion volume (Cox and Golledge, 1981) and which was further synthesized in two editions of a major textbook (Golledge and Stimson, 1987, 1997). Its essential ingredients, as set out by Golledge and Timmermans (1988), were:

1. A search for models which were alternatives to those of normative location theory based on economically and spatially rational beings;

2. A search to define environments other than objective physical reality as the milieux in which human decision-making and action took place;
3. An emphasis on process rather than structural explanations of human activity and the physical environment;
4. An interest in unpacking the spatial dimensions of psychological, social, and other theories of human decision-making and behaviour;
5. A change in emphasis from aggregate populations to the disaggregate scale of individuals and small groups;
6. A need to develop new data sources other than the generalized mass-produced aggregate statistics of government agencies which obscured and over-generalized decision-making processes and consequent behaviour;
7. A search for methods other than those of traditional mathematics and inferential statistics that could aid in uncovering latent structures in data, and which could handle data sets that were less powerful than the traditionally used interval and ratio data; and
8. A desire to merge geographic research into the ever broadening stream of cross-disciplinary investigation into theory-building and problem-solving.

Towards a behaviouristic spatial science

The main ground for disillusion with 'spatial science' was thus a growing realization that many of the models being propounded and tested provided poor descriptions of reality; progress towards the development of geographical theory was painfully slow and its predictive powers consequently weak. The large body of work based on central place theory, for example, was built on axioms regarding human behaviour regarding choice between spatial alternatives, from which a settlement pattern was deduced. But the deductions were often only weakly reflected in settlement morphologies. The theory suggested how the world would look under certain circumstances of economic rationality in decision-making; that those circumstances did not prevail suggested that the world should be looked at in other ways in order to understand how people structure spatial organization. As Brookfield (1964, p. 285) put it with regard to the models then popular:

> We may thus feel that we have proceeded far enough in answering our questions when, by examination of a sufficient number of cases, we can make assertions such as the following: population density diminishes regularly away from metropolitan centres in all directions; crop yields diminish beyond a certain walking distance from the centres of habitation; air-traffic centres lying in the shadow of major centres do not command the traffic that their populations would lead us to expect. . . . Such answers, which represent the mean result of large numbers of observations, whether statistically controlled or otherwise, are valuable in themselves, and sufficient for many purposes. But each is also an observation demanding explanations which may seem self-evident, or which may in fact be very elusive. Furthermore, there will be exceptions to each generalization, and in many cases, there are also limits to the range of territory over which they hold true. Both the exceptions and the limits demand explanation.

The concern was therefore not with the basic goal of establishing generalizations and theories, but rather the route being taken to that goal. Better models than those of 'rational economic man' were needed, and their search took a more inductive route than previously followed. Rather than base hypotheses on assumptions about behaviour, models were to be constructed that replicated observed behaviour.

Rationality in land-use decisions

Some of the earliest attempts by geographers to explore behaviour inductively, as a prelude to later modelling, were investigations of human responses to floods and other environmental hazards initiated at the University of Chicago during the late 1950s and early 1960s. Their director was Gilbert White, whose own thesis on human adjustment to floods was published in 1945, and who has been described as, 'the outstanding geographer in the man-land tradition, in the study of natural resources and hazards, and the study of the human environment' (Kates and Burton, 1986b, p. xi. White is one of the most honoured of geographers, having been awarded both the Public Welfare Medal of the National Academy of Sciences in 2000 – its highest award – and the National Medal of Science in 2001: Turner, 2002, p. 68 – they aren't mentioned in White, 2002). Water resources were his main focus, in which 'he found himself a leader in the newly developing geography of perception, the world inside people's minds'. (A collection of his writings and of valedictory essays is provided by Kates and Burton, 1986a; White, 2002, is an autobiographical essay.)

White's associates developed a behaviourist approach for studying reactions to the hazards, based on Herbert Simon's (1957) theories of decision-making. Roder (1961), for example, categorized Topeka residents according to their attitudes to the probability of future floods there, concluding that:

> *Flood danger is only one of the variables affecting the choices of the flood-plain dweller, and many considerations operate to discourage a resident from leaving the flood plain, even when he is aware of the exact hazard of remaining* (p. 83).

Such behaviour did not fit easily into notions of profit-maximizing decision-making. Alternative theories were needed.

A major exponent of this behaviouristic approach was Kates (1962, p. 1), whose study of flood-plain management began: 'The way men view the risks and opportunities of their uncertain environments plays a significant role in their decisions as to resource management'. Kates developed a schema for studying such decision-making based on four assumptions:

1. *People are rational when making decisions.* Such an assumption may be either normative/prescriptive – describing how people should behave – or descriptive of actual behaviour. The latter seemed most fruitful, both for understanding past decisions and for predicting those yet to be made. Kates suggested adoption of Simon's (1957) concept of bounded rationality. Decisions are made on a rational basis, but in relation to the environment as it is perceived by the decision-maker, which may be quite different from either 'objective reality' or the world as seen by the researcher. Rational decision-making is constrained, therefore, and is not

necessarily the same as the maximum rationality assumed in the neo-classical normative models discussed earlier; people make decisions in the context of the world as they observe and interpret it, which may differ from others' perceptions (including those of geographers studying them).

2. *People make choices.* Many decisions are either trivial or habitual and accorded little or no thought immediately before they are made. Some major decisions regarding environmental use may also be habitual, but such behaviour usually develops only after a series of conscious choices has been made, which may generate a stereotyped response to future similar situations.

3. *Choices are made on the basis of knowledge, which is usually only partial.* Only very rarely can decision-makers bring together all of the information relevant to their task, and they are frequently unable to assimilate and use all that is available.

4. *Information is evaluated according to predetermined criteria.* In habitual choice the dominant criterion is what was done before, but in conscious choice the information must be weighed according to certain rules (individually-determined, though usually in a social context). Some normative theory prescribes maximizing criteria (of profits, for example); descriptive theory may use Simon's notion of satisficing behaviour, involving decision-makers who seek a satisfactory outcome only (a given level of profit, perhaps – as in Rawstron's, 1958, industrial location theory: see Smith, 1981).

Models based on such behavioural axioms are likely to differ very substantially from those which assume not only rationality but also complete information, perfect decision-making ability and common goals. As Kates (1962, p. 16) describes his model, 'men bounded by inherent computational disabilities, products of their time and place, seek to wrest from their environments those elements that might make a more satisfactory life for themselves and their fellows'. As a consequence (p.19):

> *Thus, a descriptive theory of choice must deal with the well informed and the poorly informed and the choices that men make under certainty, risk or uncertainty ... such a theory must deal with the eventuality that not only do the conditions of knowledge vary, but the personal perception of the same information differs.*

People behave rationally, but within constraints, many imposed by their contexts – the local cultures in which they have been socialized to make decisions.

The results of decision-making that do not match the predictions from the theories employed by normatively-inclined spatial scientists do not imply irrational behaviour, therefore. Most decisions are made rationally on the basis of, probably non-random, selections of information, are intended to satisfy a goal which does not imply making a perfect decision, and are based on criteria which vary somewhat from individual to individual. Having learned a satisfactory solution to a given class of problems, decision-makers apply it every time such a problem occurs, unless changed circumstances require a re-evaluation.

Kates wanted to understand why people chose to live in areas that are prone to flooding. Their information was based on their knowledge and experience, and they varied in the certainty of their perceptions regarding further floods. In justifying their decisions, most were boundedly rational; they made conscious choices to satisfy certain objectives. Similar findings were reported by others of White's co-workers and had impacts on public policy formulation internationally (White, 1973, 2002), covering a wide range of environmental hazards such as floods, water management, and desertification (Burton, Kates and White, 1978). Their initial impact on the wider geographical enterprise was not great, however, especially in the early years of their work, perhaps because they were operating close to the boundaries between human and physical geography. Later work in other fields brought Simon's ideas more forcefully before the geographical audience, however.

This area of research, more than any other in recent years, has seen the sub-disciplines of human and physical geography come closest together. This is desirable, according to Cooke (1985a, 1992), not only because of the importance of topics such as human response to hazards (as in Hewitt, 1983) and society-induced modifications of the physical environment (Goudie, 1986a; Cooke, 1985b), but also because of the integrating role that geographers could play between the physical and the social sciences. Little of the work on these important topics does integrate the two types of science, however (Johnston, 1983a, 1986a), though Cooke (1985a, p. 146) argues that:

> ... some extremists ... in writing the post-war history of geography ... will be tempted to ignore or underplay, for example, those geographers who have contributed most influentially to studies of the relations between communities, cultures and the physical environment. The names of Carl Sauer and Gilbert White, and their numerous students, will not figure prominently in their reviews.

It is difficult to find anything in the writings of Sauer and White that could be categorized as physical geography and reviewed as such, however (e.g. in K. Gregory, 1985, 2000; see, however, Stoddart, 1997b and Symanski, 2002, on Sauer as a geomorphologist and fieldworker). In a programmatic statement arguing for the centrality of human-environment interactions in the contemporary definition of geography (particularly in the United States), most of Turner's (2002) references were to work by human geographers. He noted (p. 69) that his argument paid little attention to geography's bridging function between the humanities and sciences, which he also associated with geographers in general: his goal was to shift geography away from its strong linkage – at least in many external views of the discipline – with the humanities to a human-environment science, which he claimed is now a major area of work within American geography. (Kates, 1987, had earlier identified this as a 'road not taken' and thus an opportunity missed by geographers given the growing importance of global environmental concerns.) But physical and human geographers apparently have different agendas (Clifford, 2002; Johnston, 2003d; Ferguson, 2003).

Research by Sauer, White (see Kates and Burton, 1986a), and Cooke (1985b), among many others, throws considerable light on how individuals interpret and use the natural environment (Blaikie, 1985, sets it in a realist framework – see p. 240), while others have explored their impact on the environment (e.g. Goudie, 1986a; Huggett, 1994). Such interactions have long been of interest to geographers, and a strong case has been made for retaining them as a major focus of geographical teaching (Pepper, 1987); Douglas (1983) illustrated their importance in the urban context. But study of the interactions does not necessarily integrate the scientific studies of physical and human processes (for an exploration of the semantics of this argument, see Johnston, 1986b; see also Graham, 1986). Nor is such integration needed for, according to Sayer (1983, pp. 55–6):

> ... in human geography ... we may be interested in the causes of flooding and this will often include 'social' as well as 'natural' events. But although floods may be the effects of social actions this does not make the floods social ... Understanding the social character of the actions which caused the floods ... would not be essential for understanding the latter.

Many pieces of research demonstrate that people act according to 'manufactured' views of environmental resources in their conflict 'over who should benefit from the exploitation of the natural resource base' (Rees, 1985, p. xv) and geographers may well, as Pepper (1987) argues, seek to alter those views. This may eventually produce an interesting outcome in terms of future behaviour, but little contemporary research perceives the need to deploy understanding of physical processes in order to advance an appreciation of human behaviour, or vice versa. Flowerdew (1986, p. 263) contends that 'basically ... most human geography is essentially irrelevant to physical geography and vice versa', and one of the major attempts to synthesize contemporary physical and human geography around environmental issues (Simmons, 1997) fails, despite many other strengths (Johnston, 1999b).

The decision process in a spatial context

In the 1960s many human geographers were probably introduced to the behaviourist approach by Julian Wolpert's (1964) paper, based on his Wisconsin PhD thesis with field data from Sweden. The normative theory then espoused by many geographers assumed a rational economic decision-maker who:

> ... is free from the multiplicity of goals and imperfect knowledge which introduce complexity into our own decision behavior. Economic Man has a single profit-maximizing goal, omniscient powers of perception, reasoning, and computation, and is blessed with perfect predictive abilities ... the outcome of his actions can be known with perfect surety (p. 537).

In the study of spatial patterns, however, 'Allowance must be made for man's finite abilities to perceive and store information, to compute optimal solutions, and to predict the outcome and future events, even if profit were his only goal' (p. 537). Farmers face an uncertain environment – both physical and economic – when making the decisions that in aggregate result in a land-use map. Wolpert suggested that differences between these decisions and those that would be made by 'economic man' reflect aspects of the farmers' economic and social environments.

Comparing the observed labour productivity of farms in an area of Sweden with what could have been achieved under optimizing decision-making, Wolpert decided that the farmers were probably satisficers, although such a conclusion is difficult to verify without detailed knowledge of aspiration levels. How they acted was undoubtedly contingent upon their available information, and he argued that spatial variations in the levels of potential productivity achieved were the consequences of parallel spatial variations in knowledge. Only conspicuous alternatives are considered, it was suggested, and the result is rational behaviour, adapted to an uncertain environment. Gould (1963, 1965) approached a similar subject – land use decisions in Tanganyika – using a different approach based on the mathematical theory of games. (See also Chapman, 1982, who uses games to illustrate decision-making in uncertain situations.)

Wolpert (1965) continued his theme regarding the role of information with studies modelling the decision-making behind observed aggregate patterns of migration. He contended that the gravity model is inadequate to represent such flow patterns; indeed, 'Plots of migration distances defy the persistence of the most tenacious of curve fitters' (p. 159; see also Taylor, 1971a). Boundedly rational individuals make sequential decisions: first, whether to move, and second, where to, doing both on the basis of place utilities – their evaluations of the degree to which each potential location, including that currently occupied, meets defined needs. The information on which these utilities are computed is invariably far from complete; indeed for many places people have none. Each individual has an action space – 'the set of place utilities which the individual perceives and to which he responds' (Wolpert, 1965, p. 163) – whose contents may deviate considerably from that portion of the 'real world' which it purports to represent. Once the first decision – to migrate – has been made, then the action space may be changed as the would-be mover searches for potential satisfactory destinations and, if necessary, extends the space if no suitable solution to the search can be found (see Brown and Moore, 1970).

Wolpert's papers heralded the development of behavioural geography (Cox and Golledge, 1969, pp. 1–3), an approach 'united by a concern for the building of geographic theory on the basis of postulates regarding human behaviour … upon social and psychological mechanisms which have explicit spatial correlates and/or spatial structural implications'. Early work focused on topics related to decision-making in spatial contexts, much of it involving researchers associated with the Ohio State University. Golledge (1969, 1970), for example, looked at models of learning about space and of habitual behaviour therein, and with Brown investigated methods of spatial search (Golledge and Brown, 1967). Others researched the information flows on which decisions are based, indicating the influence of local context on behaviour (Cox, 1969), and Brown and Moore (1970) extended Wolpert's place utility and action space concepts for the study of intra-urban migration.

The fundamental aim of behavioural geography, according to a review by Golledge, Brown and Williamson (1972, p. 59), is to derive alternative theories to those based on 'economic man', 'more concerned with understanding why certain activities take place rather than what patterns they produce in space'. This involves 'the researcher using the real world from a perspective of those individuals whose decisions affect locational or distributional patterns, and … trying to derive sets of empirically and theoretically sound statements about individual, small group, or mass behaviors'. Individuals are active decision-makers, not passive reactors to institutionally-created stimuli (Cox and Golledge, 1981).

In evaluating such behaviouristic endeavours, Golledge, Brown and Williamson indicated the seminal influence of Hägerstrand's (1968) use of the concept of a mean information field (analogous to the action space of a place's residents) to model migration flows and the adoption of innovations. Further developments included a series of pioneering papers by Wolpert and his associates on political decision-making. Regarding the distribution of certain artefacts in the landscape, Wolpert (1970, p. 220) pointed out that the location of, for example, a public facility in an urban area is frequently the product of policy compromise:

> Sometimes the location finally chosen for a new development, or the site chosen for a relocation of an existing facility, comes out to be the site around which the least protest can be generated by those displaced. Rather than being an optimal, a rational, or even a satisfactory locational decision produced by the resolution of conflicting judgements, the decision is perhaps merely the expression of rejection by elements powerful enough to enforce their decision that another location must not be used ... These artefacts are rarely 'the most efficient solutions', and frequently not even satisfactory neither for those responsible for their creation nor for their users.

(This argument avoids considering any definition of optimal, in either economic or political terms.) Such decisions involve what Wolpert terms maladaptive behaviour. Kates and others had suggested that decisions are adaptively rational, within the constraints of uncertainty, utility and problem-solving ability. Coping strategies under the mutual exchange of threats between interested parties can involve decision-making which does not involve the careful and methodical investigation of alternatives until a satisfactory solution is found, however. Instead, decisions are the consequences of conflict between groups with different attitudes and motivations, and are not the result of joint application of criteria on whose relevance there is a consensus.

> This formulation lays the framework for the interpretation of locational decisions which appear to be more the product of pressurised responses than the end result of a dispassionate and considered selection of alternatives posited by the classical normative approaches or even the Simon scheme of bounded rationality (Wolpert, 1970, p. 224).

The approach was applied in a variety of contexts, such as the routes for intra-urban freeways and the siting of community mental-health facilities (Wolpert, Dear and Crawford, 1975). Many of the outcomes of such decision-making processes reflected the uneven distribution of power among the various groups of participants.

Mental maps

One concept enthusiastically adopted by a number of workers was that of a mental map of the environment which guides a decision-maker's deliberations. The term was not new to the geographical literature, having been used in Wooldridge's (1956) descriptions of the perceived environments within which farmers make land-use decisions. Gould (1966) revived it in a seminal, widely-circulated discussion paper, which included his guiding belief that:

> If we grant that spatial behavior is our concern, then the mental images that men hold of the space around them may provide a key to some of the structures, patterns and processes of Man's work on the face of the earth (p. 182; reference to 1973 reprint).

Increasingly, he argued, location decisions involve perceived environmental quality, so it is necessary to know how people evaluate environments and whether their views are shared by their contemporaries. To investigate such questions, Gould asked respondents in various countries to rank-order locations according to their preferences for them as places in which to live, and these rankings were analysed to identify their common elements – the group mental maps (Gould and White, 1974, 1986). Such maps, he argued, are useful not only in the analysis of spatial behaviour but also in planning social investments – such as offering differential salaries to attract people to less desirable areas (Gould and Ola, 1970).

Those who followed Gould's lead investigated a range of methods for identifying and analysing spatial preferences (Pocock and Hudson, 1978). Their results made little impact on theoretical development, however, and Downs (1970, p. 67) wrote that:

> Even the most fervent proponent of the current view (that human spatial behaviour patterns can partially be explained by a study of perception) would admit that the resultant investigations have not yet made a significant contribution to the development of geographic theory.

Apart from Gould's rank-ordering procedures, Downs identified two other major approaches to the study of environmental images. The *structural approach* inquires into the nature of the spatial information stored in people's minds and which they use in their everyday lives – Lynch's (1960) book was a model for such work: his five-element categorization of urban environments based on map-drawing exercises comprised paths, boundaries, districts, nodes and landmarks as the main components of the urban scene identified by users. The *evaluative approach* addresses the question: 'What factors do people consider important about their environment, and how, having estimated the relative importance of these factors, do they employ them in their decision-making activities?' (Downs, 1970, p. 80).

With this latter approach geographers moved into the wider field of cognitive mapping – 'a construct which encompasses those cognitive processes which enable people to acquire, code, store, recall and manipulate information about the nature of their spatial environment' (Downs and Stea, 1973, p. xiv). They worked alongside both psychologists, who were becoming increasingly interested in the individual's relationship to a wider area than the proximate environment and the development of relevant non-experimental research techniques, and designers concerned with creating more 'liveable' environments. The journal *Environment and Behavior* was launched in 1969 to cater for this inter-disciplinary market, but despite some interest (e.g. Tuan, 1975a; Downs and Stea, 1977; Pocock and Hudson, 1978; Porteous, 1977) the general field has not made a major impact within human geography. Gold (1992) argued that although a small number of scholars have continued working in this area, the challenges from other types of work (see Chapters 5–7 below) meant not only that it failed to develop into a large component of the discipline, but also that it was marginalized, as both passé and tainted with the generally perceived problems of positivism. Gold quotes Cloke, Philo and Sadler (1991) as presenting cognitive-behavioural geography as forming: 'something of a "bridge" leading from the "peopleless" landscapes of spatial science through to the "peopled" landscapes of humanistic geography' (Gold, 1992, p. 242). The impression he gives is of a small specialism 'retaining a precarious autonomy on the fringes of human geography' (p. 246).

The concept of 'mental map' and the associated process of 'cognitive mapping' – which 'seems to imply the evocation of visual images which possess the kinds of structural properties that we are familiar with in "real" cartographic maps' (Boyle and Robinson, 1979, p. 60) – became the centre of considerable debate both among behavioural geographers and between them and outside critics. Gould's initial work, and that which it stimulated, was criticized as the study of space preferences only (Golledge, 1981a; see also Golledge, 1980, 1981b; Guelke, 1981a; Robinson, 1982). But, as Downs and Meyer (1978, p. 60) made clear, 'perceptual geography' – 'the belief that human behaviour is, in large part, a function of the perceived world' – extends much further than the elicitation and mapping of space preferences.

The basic arguments of behavioural geography are that:

1. People have environmental images;
2. Those images can be identified accurately (i.e. quantitatively) by researchers (as in landscape evaluation: Penning-Rowsell, 1981); and
3. 'There is a strong relationship between environmental images and actual behaviour' (Saarinen, 1979, p. 465).

The nature of those images – whether they are maps in the generally understood sense of that word and whether they can be apprehended by researchers – remained a problem: the concept of a 'mental map' may be a red herring but, to behavioural geographers, the argument on which it is based is not. (For an early review of research into cognitive mapping, see Golledge and Rushton, 1984.) Similarly, the concepts of cognitive mapping were increasingly used in work on the history of cartography (on which see Lewis, 1998).

Time-geography

One area of work sometimes identified as behavioural, but which extends into the humanistic and realist philosophies discussed in later chapters, was developed by Hägerstrand from the late 1960s on and introduced to a wider audience by Pred (1973, 1977a). As interpreted by Carlstein et al. (1978), time and space are resources that constrain activity. Any behaviour requiring movement involves individuals tracing a path simultaneously through space and time, as depicted in Figure 4.4, where movements along the horizontal axis indicate spatial traverses and those along the vertical signify the passage of time. All journeys, or lifelines, involve movement along both and are displayed by lines that are neither vertical nor horizontal: vertical lines indicate remaining in one place; horizontal lines are not possible for people, though they are (or virtually so) for the transmission of messages (see Adams, 1995).

Movement in space and time is constrained in three ways, according to Hägerstrand:

1. *Capability constraints* include the biological need for about 8 hours sleep in every 24, and movement across space is constrained by the available means of transport;

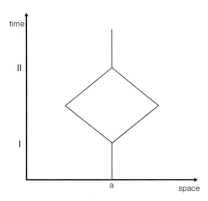

Figure 4.4 *The time-space prism. In this simple example, a person cannot leave place a until time I and must return there by time II; the prism between those two times indicates the maximum available spatial range of travel*

2. *Coupling constraints* require certain individuals and groups to be in particular places at stated times (teachers and pupils in schools, for example) and thus limit the range of mobility during 'free time'; and
3. *Authority constraints* may preclude individuals from being in stated places at defined times.

Together, these three define the time–space prism (Figure 4.4) which contains all of the possible lifelines available to an individual who starts at a particular location and has to return there by a given time.

Pred (1977a, p. 207) claimed that time-geography 'has the potential for shedding new light on some of the very different kinds of questions customarily posed by "old-fashioned" regional and historical geographers, as well as "modern" human geographers' because:

> It is ... a great challenge ... to cease taking distance itself so seriously ... to accept that space and time are universally and inseparably wed to one another; to realize that questions pertaining to human organisation of the earth's surface, human ecology, and landscape evolution cannot divorce the finitudes of space and time ... it is a challenge to turn to the 'choreography' of individual and collective existence – to reject the excesses of inter- and intradisciplinary specialization for a concern with collateral processes (p. 218).

Thus time-geography was in part a critique of spatial analysis as currently practised by human geographers. For Hägerstrand it was much more, however, because he was addressing problems concerned with the quality-of-life implications of packing people together in space and time: for example (Hägerstrand, 1984, p. 375), we are enabled to:

> ... see existing together what we otherwise have chosen to see apart. Neighbour meets neighbour in some sort of association. My concern now will be with how their presence together has come about, how they go along together and what is going to happen ahead in time.

(For biographical details on Hägerstrand, whose own lifeline strongly influenced his academic work, see the chapter on him in Buttimer, 1983.)

To explore what Pred (1977a, p. 213) calls the 'principle of togetherness', Hägerstrand employed three concepts:

1. *Paths* (or lifelines in the earlier terminology) are 'successions of situations' (Hägerstrand, 1982, p. 323) traced by individuals. To study paths alone is just to map outcomes (in the same way that geographers map migrations or shopping trips); investigation of the path alone may reveal very little about the purpose and meaning behind the events that it incorporates, because it tells nothing about the 'living body subject, endowed with memories, feelings, knowledge, imagination and goals – in other words capabilities too rich for any conceivable kind of symbolic representation but decisive for the direction of paths' (p. 324).

2. *Projects*, goals and strategies for project fulfilment are the activities which generate paths, whose intersections produce situations, particular moments in the flow of history in particular places.

3. *Dioramas*. Geographical study of paths and projects has traditionally involved the concept of landscape, devised to represent 'the momentary thereness and relative location of all continuants' (p. 325). Hägerstrand claimed that this concept insufficiently incorporates 'the human body subjects, the keepers of memories, feelings, thoughts and intentions and initiators of projects' (p. 320) and preferred the concept of *diorama*, normally used to denote static museum displays which depict people and animals in their usual environments. The concept implied to Hägerstrand that, 'All sorts of entities are in touch with each other in a mixture produced by history, whether visible or not … [we] appreciate how situations evolve as an aggregate outcome quite apart from the specific intentions actors might have had when they conceived and launched projects out of their different positions' (p. 320).

Hägerstrand illustrated his concepts with a description of his childhood home, demonstrating the importance of coupling, authority and capability constraints on the flow of daily life and the dioramas (particular situations) that resulted. (See also Pred's, 1979, application of the concepts to his academic career.) The study of paths alone is insufficient if time-geography is adequately to portray the 'real life of real people' (Hägerstrand, 1982, p. 338); thus autobiographical material (as in Buttimer, 1983; Billinge, Gregory and Martin, 1984) provides an important source on projects and dioramas because, 'Only one's own experience is able to provide the kind of intimate detail which can bring the study of project and situation into any real depth. He is after all an expert on his own networks of meanings'(Hägerstrand, 1982, p. 338).

Most interpretations and applications of Hägerstrand's initial work focused on the study of paths, and were set in the positivist mould of other behavioural geography enterprises. Indeed, this aspect of time-geography was the only one presented in an introductory review by Thrift (1977), who emphasized that a '"physicalist" approach is the backbone' (p. 4). With it, for example, Parkes and Thrift (1980) sought 'to place time firmly in the minds of human geographers' (p. xi) in an approach they termed chronogeographical, arguing that, 'Together, territories, societies and times are the principal components of urban and social geography' (p. 34).

The concept of diorama, and the 'togetherness' of a situation that it denotes, were absent from these early presentations, apart from passing references such as Thrift's (1977, p. 7), quoting Hägerstrand (1975), that 'every situation is inevitably rooted in past situations'. Projects were also mentioned, as in Thrift's (1977, p.7) statement that, 'All human beings have goals. To attain these they must have projects, series of tasks which act as a vehicle for goal attainment and which, when added up, form a project', but it was implicit that those projects can be treated in the same sort of aggregate data analysis and policy prescription mould that characterize most behavioural geography (see Palm and Pred, 1978). Van Paassen (1981) argued that Hägerstrand's work is essentially humanistic, however, aiming 'to provide insight into what is specifically human in man's nature and ... [to] elucidate the specific human situation' (p. 18), a case accepted by Hägerstrand (1982) in his reference to human intentions.

The concept of diorama later led authors to associate Hägerstrand's work not so much with the humanistic approaches outlined in the next chapter, but rather with the realist proposals discussed in Chapter 6. The social theorist Giddens (1984), for example, drew heavily on Hägerstrand in his arguments for a structurationist approach (see p. 242), (Note, however, Gregson's, 1986, critique of Giddens' attempts to incorporate time-geography into structuration theory, but also Gregory's, 1985a, p. 329, contention that time-geography 'must draw on substantive theories of structuration for its explications of contingency and necessity'.) In all of these applications, however, authority constraints and their associations with bounded spaces have been largely ignored, with continuous time–space the dominant concern.

Most criticisms of time-geography focused on the physicalist description of paths. Thus Baker (1979, p. 563) argued that:

> While space and time may usefully be considered as resources whose competitive allocation gives rise to patterns of use which may be observed empirically and modelled theoretically, the nature of that human struggle to control and structure time and space – the process underlying the form – should be of paramount concern rather than descriptions of temporal or spatial organisation.

As with other aspects of spatial science, description of outcomes, however sophisticated, cannot elucidate the processes involved in their production. (Processes here are defined as mechanisms, the products of human agency, and not just sequences: see Boots and Getis, 1978; Haining, 1981; Hay and Johnston, 1983.) Thrift and Pred (1981, p. 277) responded to Baker by denying his physicalist interpretation; to them:

> ... time-geography is much more than that. It is a discipline-transcending and still evolving perspective on the everyday workings of society and the biographies of individuals. It is a highly flexible and growing language, a way of thinking about the world at large as well as the events and experiences, or content, of one's own life.

They argued that 'time-geographers' are necessarily concerned with underlying processes, with the ideological uses of time and space as devices to channel individual paths, and with the crucial role of human agency in the production of particular situations. They tied time-geography into Giddens' ideas on structuration and also with developing Marxist humanism, concluding that:

> Some see the graphs used in time-geography as just neat pieces of art but others, in turn, are able to internalize the perspective represented by the graphs and use the path and project language as a way of thinking about themselves and the world. This will we believe be the lasting legacy of time-geography (p. 284).

Baker's (1981, p. 440) response was largely positive, accepting that time-geography could be of value in a reorientation of geographical work: 'we should be examining the social organisation of space and time, not the spatial and temporal organisation of society for this is to put the cart before the horse'. Gregory (1985a) was more cautious, however, arguing that Hägerstrand too readily focused on paths rather than on the people whose projects fashion those paths, thereby failing to explore the meanings that are hidden beneath the tasks that produce the biographies. (Elsewhere, Gregory – 1994 – implied that the fault is more with those applying Hägerstrand's ideas than with Hägerstrand himself.)

Hägerstrand's papers were written before the 'information technology revolution' which enabled the almost instantaneous transmission of information to multiple sites around the globe and promised virtual reality, whereby people in one place could operate as if in another. This led Adams (1995) to promote a reconsideration of what he termed 'personal boundaries in space-time', using Janelle's (1973) concept of 'personal extensibility', which he defines as 'the ability of a person (or group) to overcome the friction of distance through transportation or communication' (Adams, 1995, p. 267). As that ability increases and 'distant connections become easier to maintain' (p. 268), so interaction patterns alter, to the extent that 'Some believe that time-space and cost-space convergence have reached the point that one's location is of little or no significance for an increasing variety of interactions'. Extensibility promotes the transcendence of place, breaking down the crucial role of spatially bounded locales (see p. 235) as interaction containers. Thus people are both point-entities and extensible persons. They comprise (p. 269):

> A) a body rooted in a particular place at any given time, bounded in knowledge gathering by the range of unaided sensory perception and, in action, by the range of the unaided voice and grasp; and
> B) any number of fluctuating, dendritic, extensions which actively engage with social and natural phenomena at varying distances. This dynamic entity depends on media.

Acceptance of this argument requires a reworking of the importance of the presence/absence distinction in much analysis of human behaviour, and a new form of social geography (heralded, Adams argues, by Webber in 1964). It implies the need to distinguish between the geography of the body from that of the person: the former is grounded in space–time, but technology removes that constraint for the latter, with many implications for the exercise of power and responsibility.

Methods in behavioural geography

Whereas early theory- and model-builders of the spatial-science school of human geographers derived much of their stimulus from neo-classical economics, in some cases via regional science, the alliance for behavioural geography was mainly with other social sciences, notably psychology and sociology. The behaviouristic approach is largely inductive, aiming to build general statements out of observations of ongoing processes. The areas studied were very much determined by the work in the spatial-science school, however. As Brookfield's statement quoted earlier suggests (p. 140), the spatial scientists' models and theories, such as central place theory, raised many of the queries which the behaviourists followed up, stimulated by observations of the theories' failings when matched against the 'real world'. In terms of the accepted route to scientific explanation (Figure 3.1), therefore, behavioural geography involved moving outside the accepted cyclic procedure to input new sets of observations on which superior theories might be based. In doing this, it did not move far from the spatial-science ethos – and many of the methods were those used in that work.

Somewhat away from this general orientation of behavioural work, Pred (1967, 1969) presented an ambitious alternative to theory-building based on 'economic men' in a two-volume work *Behavior and Location*. His critique of location theory was based on three groups of objections concerned with:

1. *Logical inconsistency* – it is impossible for competing decision-makers to arrive at optimal location decisions simultaneously;
2. *Motives* – maximizing versus satisficing behaviour; and
3. *Capacity* – human ability to collect, assimilate, manipulate and use all possible information.

To him (Pred, 1967, p. 17):

> Bunge's theoretical geography is easily distinguished from geographical location theory because its optimal final goals are disassociated from the interpretation of real-world economic phenomena … and because these same goals can only yield a body of theory that for all intents and purposes is totally abehavioral and static rather than dynamic.

Location and land-use decisions are made with imperfect knowledge by fallible individuals and as a consequence there is bound to be disorder in the ensuing spatial patterns. (For another critique, see Barnes, 1988.)

As an alternative, Pred proposed a behavioural matrix (Figure 4.5), whose axes are quantity and quality of available information and ability to use that information: completely informed rational decision-makers occupy the bottom right-hand corner. Because of the nature and importance of information flows, decision-makers' positions on the first axis partly depend on their spatial locations; positions on the second reflect aspiration levels, experience, and the norms of any groups to which the individuals belong (many of which are spatially bounded). Different people in the same matrix position could vary in their decisions, therefore, if they acted on different information and in the pursuit of different

ABILITY TO USE INFORMATION

QUANTITY AND QUALITY OF INFORMATION

towards optimal solution

towards perfect knowledge

Figure 4.5 *The behavioural matrix (Source: Pred, 1967, p. 25)*

goals, even if their stores of knowledge and ability to use them were volumetrically commensurate. Similarly, people occupying different positions could make the same decision, based on different information and/or different ways of using it.

Individuals do not stay at the same position in the matrix; as they learn and react, so their positions change. Pred's (1969) second volume introduced a dynamic element, by shifting individuals through the matrix; as they make decisions, they change the environment in which they and others operate. As people learn, they may both acquire more and better information and become more skilled in its use; they shift towards the bottom right-hand corner of the matrix, some of them in advance of others who benefit from the decision-leaders' experience. The unsuccessful are gradually eliminated, so that a concentration of 'good' decision-makers close to the optimum position evolves, although new entrants to the matrix will probably not be located there. Changes in the external environment (such as market prices for farmers or the closure of some outlets for shoppers) generate parametric shocks, however, which result in decision-makers becoming less informed and less certain; as a consequence they are shifted back towards the upper left-hand corner and another learning cycle begins. As long as parametric shocks occur relatively frequently then optimal location patterns will never emerge, except perhaps by chance: the environment will have changed before all people reach the bottom right-hand corner of the matrix.

Pred (1969) presented the behavioural matrix as a 'gross first approximation' (p. 91), arguing that any theory is better than none (p. 139), even if the model itself is literally untestable (p. 141; see also Pred and Kibel, 1970). Harvey (1969b) treated it to a scathing review, however, calling the two dimensions vaguely defined, ambiguous, unoperational, and an over-simplification of the complex nature of the factors influencing behaviour. Indeed, Harvey (1969c) was generally sceptical about the potential of any behavioural location theory, a view shared by Olsson (1969) who pointed out the difficulties of studying processes and demonstrated that much behavioural geography involved only inferring processes from aggregated data on individual behaviour.

Others argued that such inference could be very strong, however. Rushton (1969), for example, accepted that any one pattern of behaviour – what he termed *behaviour in space* – was largely a function of the spatial structure within which it occurred (the choice of shopping centre to patronize, for example), but general *rules of spatial behaviour* could be deduced from examining the types of preferences displayed within particular patterns: 'To say that these preferences do not exist independently of the environment where the decision is made is to argue that environments could exist about which the person would be unable to reach a decision' (p. 393). Thus a distance-decay pattern reflects the details of the environment in which it is observed, and its production involves decision-making based on certain rules, which Rushton claimed his analytical procedure could isolate. Its validity was queried, however (Pirie, 1976), and, like Pred's behavioural matrix, it did not attract many disciples. (Rushton's arguments suggest activity in a 'taken-for-granted world', see p. 208.) Few others took up the explicit notion of the behavioural matrix, but many of the ideas that it was founded on were explicit in other studies, such as those of industrial geographers who studied the spread of 'best practice' methods (see p. 80).

Harvey (1969c) suggested two alternatives to behavioural location theory – further development of normative theory and the construction of a stochastic location theory: he claimed that both offered more immediate pay-offs for understanding spatial patterns than behavioural theory, because of the latter's conceptual and measurement problems. A stochastic approach was also favoured by Curry (1967), who argued that large-scale patterns are the outcomes of small-scale indeterminacy; individual choices may be random within certain constraints, but when very many of them are aggregated they may display considerable order. Similarly, Webber (1972) attempted to model locational decision-making processes in states of uncertainty using normative approaches, concluding that 'uncertainty increases agglomeration economies' (p. 279), thereby leading to greater concentration of economic activities and people into cities than predicted by models based on 'economic men' (see also Richardson, 1973; Johnston, 1976c; Scott, 1988). Game theory is a mathematical procedure developed to handle decision-making in uncertainty that has received little attention from human geographers (Gould, 1963); the most ambitious attempt to use it, which had very little impact, is in Isard *et al.* (1969).

For some critics, therefore, micro-analysis at the level of the individual is one or more of impossible, unnecessary or misleading: macro-analysis, and the morphological laws that it produces, provides sufficient insight to the behaviour that generates aggregate patterns. Both are needed according to Watson (1978), however: macro-analysis provides an initial overview, posing questions which can only be answered by behavioural study. (See also Sayer, 1984, 1992a, on extensive and intensive research: p. 242.)

The behavioural approach did not stimulate a major revolution away from the spatial-science focus within human geography, therefore, but rather generated an extension to it – which over time became increasingly the norm as the assumptions underlying the original models were rejected as unrealistic. Whereas those normative approaches started with simplifying assumptions about human behaviour and deduced what spatial patterns follow from the axioms, behaviourists employed inductive procedures to identify the rules of behaviour, using these to predict (and therefore 'explain') spatial patterns (Gale and Golledge, 1982). Their approach involved a sequence of inter-related investigations. An individual is faced with a decision, with either a direct spatial input or spatial consequences. To make it, criteria are established and information is collected to be evaluated against the criteria. That may lead to a decision; alternatively, no satisfactory outcome could be identified so the individual may then alter the criteria, collect more information, or both. (This pragmatic approach to problem-solving is similar to the procedures of the scientific method outlined in Figure 3.1.)

Whereas much of the initial work done in the spatial-science mould could be conducted using either published data sources (such as censuses) or relatively small field-collection exercises, the behavioural approach generally requires specific data collection from the individual decision-makers. The need for social surveys of various kinds furthered the growing links between geographers and sociologists, psychologists and, to a lesser extent, political scientists, and led to an expansion in the data-handling procedures necessary for the training of geographers. One of the problems in their use is that many of the topics studied in human geography involve very large numbers of individual decisions – as in migrations, journeys to work and to shop, voting decisions, and so on. Very large sample surveys may be necessary to produce valid generalizations about such behaviour, especially across a range of places, but resource limitations have meant concentration on both small selections and only limited segments of the full behavioural sequence.

The behavioural sequence has also been applied in branches of human geography that deal with topics involving relatively few decision-makers. In the study of diffusion, for example, Brown (1975) attempted to divert attention away from overall patterns of spatial spread and the reasons for adoption (or not) to the decision-making which brings certain innovations to places; most of these innovations involve selling products, which he terms 'consumer innovations' (see also Brown, 1981). Similarly, a number of industrial geographers have moved away from investigations of aggregate patterns, which could be compared to those predicted by application of neo-classical economic analysis (Smith, 1971), to the study of decision-making behaviour within firms (e.g. Hamilton, 1974; Carr, 1983; Hayter and Watts, 1983; Schoenberger, 1993). Not all of this work involved large data sets whose analysis called for sophisticated quantitative analysis, but the overall approach was similar – seeking to establish general patterns of behaviour as revealed by available data, as in Dicken's (2003) classic work on globalization.

The analytical procedures employed within behavioural geography became increasingly sophisticated during the 1980s, paralleling developments in statistical procedures for analysing categorical data. Most of the research involved analysing behaviour within the framework of the spatial-science approach and its general positivist orientation. The goal was to explain, using mathematical modelling and statistical analysis, variations in aspects of behaviour (choice of travel mode for the journey to work, for example) in terms of variations in a number of independent variables (such as the characteristics of the decision-makers and the milieux in which their decisions were made: see Kitchin, 1996). Data for such studies are usually categorical in form, involving classifications (which travel mode was used, for example, and the gender of the person concerned) rather than variables measured on interval or ratio scales. Wrigley (1985) provided a major overview of the relevant statistical procedures for analysing such data; Davies and Pickles (1985) explored the important issue of inferring secular trends from cross-sectional data, while others promoted the analysis of longitudinal data comprising repeated interviews with the same individuals (Dale, 1993). Methods for quantifying attitudes and other aspects of human characteristics and behaviour have been explored, involving both increasingly sophisticated survey instruments for investigating how people cognize and learn about their spatial environments (Golledge and Timmermans, 1990; Timmermans et al., 2001) and technical procedures for representing those cognitions quantitatively (see Aitken et al., 1989).

Many of the choice models underpinning work in behavioural geography are based on theories of utility maximization. This approach was heralded by Cadwallader (1975), exemplified in fuller detail by Wrigley and Longley (1984), and became the basis for a burgeoning literature (as displayed in great detail in Golledge and Timmermans, 1988, and reviewed in Timmermans and Golledge, 1990; Timmermans et al., 2001). Such theories propose that decision-makers select from within the choice sets presented to (and perceived by) them, according to the utility which they allocate to each of the alternatives evaluated: as Timmermans and Golledge (1990, p. 312) express it, all 'are based on (variants of) a conceptual model that explicitly relates choice behaviour to the environment through consideration of perceptions, preference formation and decision-making' (utility being a measure of preference). A full analysis of discrete choices thus involves knowing:

1. The available choice set;
2. The elements of the choice set considered by each individual;
3. The criteria on which each member of the choice set was evaluated by individual decision-makers; and
4. The relative importance they attached to each criterion.

Bird (1989), following Desbarats (1983), illustrated this (Figure 4.6). The process starts with a listing of all possible opportunities. Some are discarded to form an 'objective choice set'; evaluation of its elements results in some being discarded as unacceptable, producing an 'effective choice set'; and further evaluation leads to its reduction to a 'target choice set' from which the final selection is made. A potential house-buyer in a town 'discards' many of the available homes through ignorance, for example, and then whittles down those perceived as viable purchases to a final list from which the selection is made (with, in some cases, a recursive loop to identify further viable buys if none in the final choice set either proves acceptable or can be bought).

Other work within this general framework combines categorical data with other forms, such as indicators of the local context within which decision-makers operate. Studies of

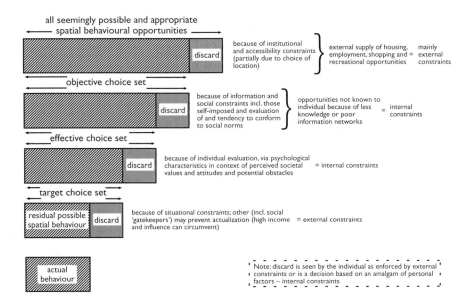

all seemingly possible and appropriate
spatial behavioural opportunities

discard — because of institutional and accessibility constraints (partially due to choice of location) } external supply of housing, employment, shopping and recreational opportunities = mainly external constraints

objective choice set

discard — because of information and social constraints incl. those self-imposed and evaluation of and tendency to conform to social norms } opportunities not known to individual because of less knowledge or poor information networks = internal constraints

effective choice set

discard — because of individual evaluation, via psychological characteristics in context of perceived societal values and attitudes and potential obstacles = internal constraints

target choice set

residual possible spatial behaviour discard — because of situational constraints; other (incl. social 'gatekeepers') may prevent actualization (high income and influence can circumvent) = external constraints

actual behaviour

Note: discard is seen by the individual as enforced by external constraints or is a decision based on an amalgam of personal factors – internal constraints

Figure 4.6 *Choice sets in the spatial decision-making process (Source: Bird, 1989, p. 145, after Desbarats)*

voting behaviour, for example, have investigated the decision of which party to support according to both the characteristics of the individuals concerned and various perceived and objective indicators of their local milieux. (See, for example, Pattie and Johnston, 1995; Fieldhouse, Pattie and Johnston, 1996; MacAllister *et al.*, 2001.)

Behavioural geography, understanding and explanation

Behavioural geography is now widely accepted within the positivist orientation. Some of it seeks to account for spatial patterns by establishing generalizations about people–environment inter-relationships, which may then be used to stimulate change through environmental planning activities that 'modify the stimuli which affect the spatial behavior of ourselves and others' (Porteous, 1977, p. 12). Initially, it was hoped, a 'powerful new theory' (Cox and Golledge, 1969) would emerge and a decade later Golledge (1981a, p. 1338–9) claimed that substantial advances had already been made through studying what he called process variables – 'individual preferences, opinions, attitudes, cognitions, cognitive maps, perceptions, and so on'.

Apart from technical issues, the positivist foundation of most behavioural geography has been subject to considerable debate, as part of a wider consideration of the relevance of that philosophy to human geography. Golledge has made major contributions, arguing that positivism is a constraining philosophy, and that (Couclelis and Golledge, 1983, pp. 333–4), 'behavioural geography has evolved by gradually shedding the tenets of the philosophy out of which it was born, as these have come to be seen as barriers to further progress and understanding'. He prefers 'analytical research' to describe his preferred approach, which is 'not so much a philosophy as a distinct mode of discourse, a space of possibilities for theoretical languages that meet the criteria of clarity, coherence, intersubjective validity, and a concern never to lose sight of experience' (p. 334). Nevertheless, he retains one of the central tenets of the positivist programme, as illustrated by references to 'a search for generalizations' (Golledge and Couclelis, 1984, p. 181), 'significant generalizations ... about particular sub-groups' (Golledge, 1980, p. 16) and the need to shift research away from 'the more narrow perspective of behaviour in space' towards 'a general understanding of spatial behaviour' (Golledge and Rushton, 1984, p. 30; see also p. 155 above). In his AAG presidential address, Golledge (2002, p. 12) argues that geographers have a 'common set of primitives and concepts' which define the discipline, that from these they have developed a 'huge array of empirically verified factual data, spatial theories and models, innovative methods of spatial analysis, unique modes of representation, and practical usefulness for decision-making and policy formulation'. Those primitives include 'place-specific identity, location, magnitude, time, boundary and distance' (p. 7), with which geographical information is both informally and formally acquired: behavioural geographers study the informal processes through their own formal procedures.

Golledge and Stimson claimed that *analytical behavioural geography* is based on 'what is truly positive in positivist thought' (Golledge and Stimson, 1987, p. 9). They rejected the 'classic positivist separation of value and fact' and argued for a positivist position which can 'interpret values and beliefs in a scientific manner'. This they term a transactional or interactionist position, characterized by:

(a) the importance of logical and mathematical thinking; (b) the need for public verifiability of results; (c) the search for generalization; (d) the emphasis on analytic languages for researching and expressing knowledge structures; and (e) the importance of hypotheses testing and the importance of selecting the most appropriate bases for generalization or theorizing.

The goal is to develop quantitatively verified theory (Macmillan, 1989b).

This continued emphasis on key elements of the positivist philosophy links to a second, much less substantial, area of work. Pipkin (1981) noted that much effort had been expended on identifying behaviour patterns but little on exploring the underpinning mental constructs. Understanding why people behave as they do has not been advanced very far, therefore; as Greenberg (1984, p. 193) expressed it, 'For the most part, the intention of behavioural-perceptual geographers has not been to explain the spatial organisation of society, but to illuminate the spatial behavior of individuals'.

Artificial Intelligence (AI) was presented as offering much to the study of cognitive processes (T. Smith, 1984), using computer-modelling procedures to represent the decision-making processes and thereby gaining insights (by analogy) to the nature of the human brain. Couclelis (1986a, p. 2) indicates that this involves the 'human computer' metaphor according to which, 'cognitive functions such as problem-solving, pattern-recognition, decision-making, learning, and natural language understanding are investigated by means of computer programs that purport to replicate the corresponding mental processes'. The ability to replicate processes by predicting their outcomes (as in Smith, Clark and Cotton, 1984) cannot be equated with understanding them, however. Couclelis (1986a, p.111) concluded a detailed discussion of AI's utility in the study of human behaviour by noting that 'reliable predictions can be made about intentional systems even by theories which . . . are totally vacuous psychologically'. Whether one wants to know how or why people behave is crucial: AI can reproduce the former, it is claimed, but can it assist in the latter? Nystuen (1984, p. 358) doubts even the former claim, however, arguing that:

> I see little potential in AI methods available today in addressing problems considered important in the spatial decision-making literature, such as the decision to migrate . . . These processes would require elaborate models of spatial cognition and tradeoff behavior whereas even the simplest model of a child's wayfinding is complex and contains major unresolved methodological problems.

If the claim were sustained, however, it would only provide a constructed explanation (see the discussion of Lukermann's arguments above, p. 92), but:

> I am struck by the fact that careful empirical analysis by biologists describing the anatomy and behavior of bats did not lead to the discovery of how bats navigated in the dark. The explanation was beyond imagination until a purely human system (radar, followed by sonar) was invented and by analogy applied to the behavior and anatomy of the bat. Then all the things fell into place (p. 359).

In other words, if you can reproduce a process then you may well gain some appreciation of it or, as Nystuen put it:

> If a constructed computer program can repeatedly resolve an issue under varying spatial conditions in a way that is considered useful to geographers, then one might say that we understand the issue. This is a sufficient claim: the problem has been solved by whatever logic or capacities the program has at hand. There is no need to claim that this is necessarily the way human spatial decision-making works (p. 359).

Others reject such an instrumentalist argument, however (e.g. Gregory, 1980: see the discussion of automated geography, p. 179.) Openshaw (1995), on the other hand, argued for the power of artificial intelligence software for understanding and simulating human behaviour (see also Openshaw and Openshaw, 1997).

Thrift (1981, p. 359) argued that by the end of the 1970s:

> The halcyon days of behavioural geography are long gone. With them have passed the days when behavioural geographers made inflated claims for the explanatory power of their subject area. But the subject area still has its place in human geography.

He recognized two criticisms of behavioural work: those which perceived it presenting the individual decision-maker as little more than an automaton responding to stimuli in a programmed way; and those which claimed that it ignored the characteristics of society as a whole which are greater than the sum of its individual parts. He argued that behavioural geography might be presented as 'half-blind': 'But to say that behavioural geography is therefore half-blind is not to say that it can see nothing at all. Its explanations may be limited. That does not mean that they are therefore non-existent' (p. 359).

If Thrift's conclusion were valid, one would anticipate a slowing-down in the pace of work within behavioural geography. It could be argued that the opposite has occurred; a substantial volume of work was conducted and reported during the 1980s (and summarized in reviews such as Golledge and Rushton, 1984; Golledge and Timmermans, 1990; Timmermans and Golledge, 1990; Timmermans *et al.*, 2001) which, in the context of the normal science model outlined above (p. 7), has achieved substantial progress. It could also be claimed, however, that behavioural geography has not only become a minority interest but has also become increasingly isolated within human geography (Gold, 1992), because of both the theoretical position and analytical sophistication achieved by its leading practitioners and what Cloke, Philo and Sadler (1991, p. 67) call its 'partial treatment of people' (which they contrast with their 'complete neglect in spatial science'). Many human geographers have accepted the need to collect and analyse individual data through questionnaires and similar methods, to portray how people learn about, represent and behave in space. Others have rejected that approach entirely, because it cannot provide telling insights into individuals – thus making it 'somewhat limiting', 'dehumanising', 'pallid' and 'horribly reductionist' according to Cloke, Philo and Sadler. Behavioural geography is just one of many components of an increasingly diverse discipline: it made a considerable general impact upon geographical practice in its early years and has since been advanced by a small group of specialists somewhat apart from the mainstream (as discussed in Gold, 1992).

Against those claims are arguments – closely aligned to Golledge's distinction between 'positivist law-seeking' and 'analytical research' – which see the methods and approaches developed within behavioural geography as necessary components of understanding central areas of geography's research agenda (Johnston, 2000c). Many millions of people migrate every year; many millions vote in national elections; very many millions commute daily – and so forth. Although full understanding of these events requires appreciation of why individuals acted as they did, that is virtually impossible because of the scale of the task. General patterns of behaviour can only be uncovered through combinations of:

1. Analyses of the aggregate situation – the number of migrations between given origins and destinations, for example;
2. Analyses of general relationships within such situations – the proportion of migrants in different age and educational groups, for example; and
3. Analyses of the reasons for individual decisions.

The first two can only be achieved through work – usually quantitative – on large data sets, which indicate the size and nature of the issue, give an overall picture of general patterns that call for further investigation, and identify some of the relationships that might assist in developing explanations for the observed patterns. Such explanations need not, in the strict positivist mould, imply general laws of cause and effect: they may be simply accounts of a particular situation which can be assessed against theoretical models of the behaviour patterns involved and generate ideas to be tested in new situations. In mass societies, behavioural geography provides insights to mass behaviour. Further, some of the methods developed for studying behaviour have been adapted for particular purposes – such as wayfinding by visually-impaired individuals – and applied in a number of contexts (Golledge, 1993: Golledge's work – he is himself visually-impaired

– was strongly critiqued for its interpretations of disablement; see Imrie, 1996; Gleeson, 1996; and Golledge, 1996).

The continued vitality of the group of specialists working on cognitive-behavioural topics is illustrated by Golledge and Stimson's (1987) text on *Analytical Behavioural Geography* and its 1997 successor *Spatial Behavior: A Geographic Perspective*. They introduced the approach, and its origins in the 1960s, as a recognition that (Golledge and Stimson, 1987, p. 1):

> ... in order to exist in and to comprehend any given environment, people had to learn to organise critical subsets of information from the mass of experiences open to them. They sense, store, record, organise and use bits of information for the ultimate purpose of coping with the everyday task of living. In doing this, they create knowledge structures based on information selected from the mass of 'to whom it may concern' messages emanating from the world in which we live. Different elements from these various environments are given different meanings and have different values attached to them. It was the explicit recognition of the relationship between cognition, environment and behaviour that initially helped to develop behavioural research in geography.

They illustrated how the work developed, and structured the sub-discipline's approach through a diagram which places individual decision-makers at the interface between environment and behaviour, learning and acting within the environment and changing it as they act (Figure 4.7). The organization of their book, covering both the methods used by behavioural geographers and their substantive achievements in various topical areas, provides a clear view of a vital sub-discipline; as does the size of their bibliography, along with the large number of other pieces listed in the review papers on which parts of this chapter have drawn.

A later, much-revised, edition extended the coverage of material that illustrated not only the continued volume of geographic work but also the strong links that were being forged

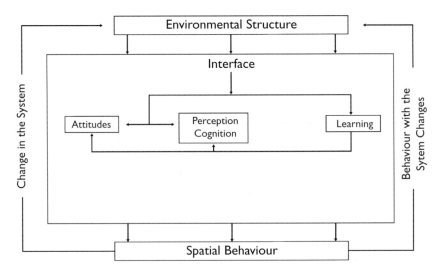

Figure 4.7 *The society-environment interface (Source: Golledge and Stimson, 1987, p. 11)*

with psychology. Behavioural geography was defined as (Golledge and Stimson, 1997, p. 29 – their emphasis):

> ... *characterized by a concern both for* scientific rigor *or* experimental realism *and for* phenomenological and anthropomorphic understanding of human-environment systems *and relationships.*

Its concerns covered 'philosophical' topics such as: experimental design; data collection procedures; the search for validity and reliability; the selection of appropriate analytical methods; the choice of a 'modern, analytical, epistemological basis'; innovative models of behaviour and environments; recognition of socially-constraining dimensions; and differing viewpoints based on 'bottom-up' or 'top-down' approaches. Six main subject areas were identified – cognitive mapping and spatial behaviour; attitudes, utility, choice, preference, search and learning; consumer behaviour; location decision-making; wayfinding, mode choice and travel behaviour; and mobility and migration – on the grounds these, 'lend themselves more to the process of measurement, model building, abstraction, generalization, and theory building than do other areas of human geography' (p. 30). The result – as stressed by Golledge (2002, p. 126) in a recent review – is 'an extra explanatory dimension to more traditional geographic research' examining cognitive processes in a wide range of settings.

One of the intriguing aspects of this subfield and its recent development is that those who write about behavioural geography, such as Golledge and Stimson (1997), restrict it to the study of certain types of behaviour. The substantive chapters of their book deal with choice of transport mode, choice of shopping centre to patronize, migration, residential mobility within cities, and the problems of specific groups within the population. Other forms of decision-making, such as those related to the location of production and service facilities, are apparently outside the remit of behavioural geographers. And yet a great amount of work is being done on such decision-making processes and their outcomes, which involves collecting data from the individuals making the location decisions at a great range of scales from the global, through the national and regional to the local – albeit in many cases within theoretical frameworks that have few links to the models that stimulated much of human geography's urban and quantitative revolution. The theoretical frameworks within which such authors deal (as with Dicken's 2003 work on globalization, and Schoenberger's 1997 work on corporate behaviour) come from political economy and concepts of explanation that are discussed in the next chapter. (The journal *Regional Studies* carries a great deal of this work.) But many of the data collection methods are behavioural – even if there is little complex statistical analysis – and the goals are, as in so much else discussed in this chapter, to identify and account for general patterns of behaviour in space. (According to Scott, 2000, p. 24, this separation was because behavioural geography 'became more or less the preserve of a few highly specialized researchers who turned increasingly to experimental psychology for their inspiration'. Indeed, as long ago as 1976, Cullen – 1976, p. 400 – had argued that although behavioural geography should have a great deal to offer for those interested in macro-patterns, it was failing to do so, and was instead an 'intellectual backwater', 'every bit as mechanistic as the neoclassical economic geography it was supposed to replace': Scott, 2000, p. 24.) As with so much in contemporary geography, it is difficult to draw boundaries between different sections of the subject.

Spatial (or geo-)statistics

The application of various approaches to 'geography as spatial science' over the last half-century has involved much attention being given to quantitative data analysis. Initially, most of the researchers involved followed Garrison (1956a) in accepting that statistical procedures developed for other fields of enquiry could be adopted for geographical investigations without difficulty. Some suggested necessary modifications – as in spatial sampling (Berry and Baker, 1968) – but, despite Robinson's (1956; see p. 72) early work, it was generally assumed that no technical problems prevented the application of standard procedures to spatial data sets. A number of textbooks appeared, especially in the late 1960s, which made little reference to any peculiarities of geographical data; they differed from the texts produced by other social scientists only in the nature of their examples. And even in the 1980s, few contributors to a book on *Recent Developments in Spatial Data Analysis* – Bahrenberg et al., 1984 – discussed spatial data *per se*; most of their work referred to the use of standard statistical procedures in geographical applications. (This was also the case in a major review of quantitative geography in the UK – Wrigley and Bennett, 1981 – and an earlier special issue of *The Statistician* – Taylor and Goddard, 1974 – in which geographers introduced statisticians to their quantitative applications, with only one paper – Unwin and Hepple, 1974 – dealing with the particular problems of spatial data, what Taylor and Goddard – 1974, p. 151 – refer to as 'the peculiar nature of geographical data, particularly the lack of spatial independence'.) Others simply adapted standard procedures to geographical problems, as with Chorley and Haggett's (1965a) application of polynomial regression to the analysis of spatial patterns – what they termed trend surface analysis.

Indeed, relatively few texts have since focused on techniques for spatial (or map) analysis, although some general texts on statistical analysis for geographers (such as Taylor, 1977) have included such material. Unwin (1981), for example, dealt with point, line, area and surface patterns, along with map comparison, providing a clear emphasis on spatial statistical analysis (see also O'Sullivan and Unwin, 2003); Lewis (1977) covered point and line patterns for a more advanced audience; Upton (a statistician) combined with Fingleton (a geographer) in an advanced two-volume treatment of aspects of spatial data analysis (Upton and Fingleton, 1985, 1989); Gatrell, also in collaboration with a statistician, published a text with worked examples on a CD-ROM (Bailey and Gatrell, 1995); and Fotheringham, Brunsdon and Charlton (2000) brought out a book as 'a statement on the vitality of modern quantitative geography . . . where the [recent] emphasis has been on the development of techniques explicitly for *spatial* data analysis' (pp. xi–xii). Similarly, relatively few followed the paths set out in two editions of a book on mathematical models (Wilson and Kirkby, 1975; Wilson and Bennett, 1985). To some extent, spatial statistical analysis – as against statistical analysis in geography – was a minority activity.

In this context, there has been infiltration of human geography by technical developments elsewhere. One such was work on classification (a procedure common to the life sciences) and its links to *regionalization*. Berry used these widely in his ideas on regional analysis (Berry, 1964b: see above, p. 97) in studies of, for example, urban residential areas (or factorial ecology: Berry, 1971) and others have deployed variants on them for the task of defining electoral areas such as Parliamentary constituencies and congressional districts (Johnston, 2003c): methods of classification have been substantially advanced in recent years using high-speed computers for the large dataset manipulations involved in the analysis of remotely-sensed imagery (Mather, 1999; Tso and Mather, 2001). Elsewhere, Wrigley (1973) pointed out the problems involved in the use of percentage and proportional data in linear regression and related methods and in a series of publications (Wrigley, 1976, 1985) introduced the use of logit and other forms of *categorical data modelling*. These are now widely used in work with such data – for example, voting studies in which the values are binary (either yes, the individual voted for a given party, or no, he/she did not: Pattie and Johnston, 2000).

Jones (1991) introduced methods for exploring varying relationships from work in education. It may be hypothesized, for example, that a student's performance reflects not only her/his innate ability but also home background, school type, the quality of teaching provided, and so forth. Thus, for example, a student from a supportive home background may perform better in a set of tests than one with the same innate ability but from a less supportive background, but the better the teaching provided to the two, the smaller the gap between their performance. This suggests an interaction effect between the independent variables – when operating together they have a greater impact than when operating separately. Such interaction effects can be modelled within standard general linear models (e.g. Russell, 1997) but Jones has demonstrated that *multi-level models* developed by educational researchers are more efficient ways of estimating those interactions in complex data sets and has applied them to a range of geographical problems such as differing voting patterns across regions (Jones, Johnston and Pattie, 1992) and disease patterns (Jones and Duncan 1996, 2002): they also have the advantage that they explicitly take into account and correct for the influence of any spatial autocorrelation (see below) that may be inherent in data, such as those collected using cluster sampling which have autocorrelation effects in-built.

Various aspects of spatial interaction have continued to be a focus of formal modelling work, as in major studies of the spatial diffusion of diseases (much of it summarized in Haggett, 2000). Bennett and Haining (1985; Bennett, Haining and Wilson, 1985) placed such work at the forefront of methodological developments in the discipline. Much of it was summarized by Wilson and Bennett's (1985) volume on *Mathematical Methods in Human Geography and Planning* in a *Handbook of Applicable Mathematics* series.

Others sought to ensure proper use of the standard statistical procedures (e.g. Jones, 1984; Wrigley, 1984), with the use of statistical significance tests forming the basis of further debate (Summerfield, 1983; Hay, 1985b). Better ways of testing hypotheses were also expounded, not only with regard to the use of categorical (or nominal) data (e.g. Fingleton, 1984; Wrigley, 1984), but also in terms of pattern analysis (Upton and Fingleton, 1985) and representing relationships through structural models (e.g. Cadwallader, 1986).

Much of this work has been criticized for its reliance on methods that impose structures on data rather than 'letting the data speak for themselves' (Gould, 1981a); the mathematics of q-analysis was proposed to meet the latter criterion (Gould, 1980; Beaumont and Gatrell, 1982; Gatrell, 1983; see also the essays edited by Macgill, 1983) but was not taken up. More interest was shown in exploratory data analysis – the inductive interrogation of data sets unconstrained by prior hypotheses and assumptions such as those underpinning the general linear model (Cox and Jones, 1981; Wrigley, 1983). By assuming less, it was argued, you may discover more.

Increasingly, however, the assumption that all geographers needed was an appreciation of standard procedures was considered invalid. Instead, it was contended that geographical data of various forms required specific procedures because of their particular nature. Geographers thus became involved – in some cases in collaboration with statisticians – in the development of those procedures, as illustrated in the next sub-sections. Interestingly, some of the earliest work on these issues was done by non-geographers (e.g. Duncan et al., 1961).

Spatial autocorrelation

During the late 1960s a group of researchers at the University of Bristol began to question the widespread assumption about the relevance of standard statistical procedures for analyses of spatial data. Statisticians had for long recognized difficulties in applying the general linear model – notably in its regression and correlation form – to the time-series data used in economic analysis and forecasting because of what was termed autocorrelation. One of the model's assumptions is that all observations are conditionally independent of each other; the magnitude of one reading on a variable should in no way influence that of any other. Such autocorrelation clearly exists in most time series: the value of the retail price index at one date, for example, strongly influences its value at nearby later dates, and is itself influenced by preceding values. (An early example of this being brought to geographers' attention was in the discussion in Chisholm, Frey and Haggett, 1971, p. 465.) Because of such inter-dependence between adjacent observations, conventional regression methods could not be used: autocorrelation leads to inefficient regression coefficients because of under-estimated standard errors and casts doubt on the validity of any forecasts using those models, as well as over-estimating the goodness-of-fit measure (usually the correlation coefficient). The estimated impact of the independent variable on the dependent was reliable, but because the standard error of that estimate was overstated with autocorrelated data the strength of the relationship appears statistically less significant than would have been the case without autocorrelation.

The Bristol group (led by Peter Haggett, Andrew Cliff and Keith Ord – the last-named is a statistician) argued not only that this autocorrelation problem applied to spatial data sets too, but also that it was much less tractable than with temporal series. Time proceeds in one direction only, but space is two-dimensional, and the independence requirement can be violated in all directions around a single point. Spatial autocorrelation can therefore involve all neighbours influencing all others with regard to the values of a particular variable, as recognized by some statisticians (e.g. Geary, 1954) and hinted at by geographers such as Dacey (1968), whose work stimulated the Bristol investigations. (Andrew Cliff worked as a graduate student with Dacey at Northwestern University in the early 1960s.) Considerable effort was expended on this problem over a number of years (Cliff and Ord et al., 1973, 1981), covering a wide range of spatial applications, including the well-known gravity model (Curry, 1972; Johnston, 1976a; Sheppard, 1979; Fotheringham, 1981; Tiefelsdorf, 2003).

The spatial autocorrelation problem severely constrains the application of conventional statistical procedures in geographical analyses if the statistical significant of regression estimates is a focus of attention. Several people thus argued that application of regression methods, and others based on the general linear model such as principal components and factor analyses, was invalid with spatial data sets (Haining, 1980, p. 24). As Harvey (1969a, p. 347) put it:

> The choice of the product-moment correlation coefficient for regionalization problems appears singularly inappropriate, since one of the technical requirements of this statistic is independence in the observations. Since the aim of such regionalization is to produce contiguous regions which are internally relatively homogeneous, it seems almost certain that this condition of independence in the observations will be violated.

Gould (1970a) noted that spatial autocorrelation reflects the order that geographers were seeking to establish with their laws and theories, and it was somewhat paradoxical that its presence prevented its identification through accepted technical procedures. As Tobler (1970, p. 236) expressed it more prosaically, the 'First Law of Geography . . . [is that] . . . Everything is related to everything else, but near things are more related than distant things' – or, in other words, spatial autocorrelation is the core of geography.

On realizing the force of the case, however, some accepted that conventional statistical procedures could not be applied in their work (e.g. Berry, 1973b) and the Bristol group omitted them from their rewrite of Haggett's major text (Haggett, Cliff and Frey, 1977). The second part of the book – Locational Models – was much expanded and rewritten. In the first edition (Haggett, 1965c), the chapter on 'Testing' included a section on 'Testing via statistical methods' which included standard linear regression analysis. The comparable chapter in the second edition omitted that material, however, on the grounds not only that (Haggett, Cliff and Frey, 1977, p. 329):

> Since the first edition of this book appeared, the use of conventional statistical methods and tests of significance . . . has become commonplace in human geography. It is not the purpose of this chapter to outline the procedures for carrying out such analyses.

but also:

> . . . the aim of this chapter is to examine those properties of geographical data which make their analysis using statistical methods of the sort cited more difficult than might at first appear.

For them, the lesson to be learned from appreciation of the problems of spatial dependence and autocorrelation in geographical data was that, 'If geographers continue to apply the usual forms of many of the basic statistical models to spatially autocorrelated data, then a very severe risk is run of reaching misleading conclusions' (Haggett, Cliff and Frey, 1977, p. 336). Others have carried the argument forward, developing methods – termed spatial econometrics by Anselin (1988: Anselin studied regional science with Isard – see p. 91) – for modelling with spatially interdependent data sets. (Such software is now generally available through the world wide web.)

Many continued to apply the methods, however, either in ignorance of the autocorrelation case or on the grounds that the biased-coefficients problem refers only to the use of the general linear model in forecasting and prediction, and does not affect use of the procedures for either description (see Johnston, 1978a) or certain types of ecological analysis (Johnston, 1982c, 1984f).

Spatial forecasting

One of the Bristol group's substantive interests was in spatial forecasting, involving the development of procedures for estimating how trends – in the spread of a disease, for example, and of prices and unemployment – would proceed through time and over space (Haggett, 1973; Cliff et al., 1975). They organized a major symposium on this (Chisholm, Frey and Haggett, 1971) and stimulated a considerable volume of work, much of it technical, on the problems of identifying and forecasting spatio-temporal trends (e.g. Bennett, 1978b). Hägerstrand's work on diffusion patterns provided the foundation for much of this research, which focused on the patterns of spread rather than on their generating processes, and spawned a literature on technical aspects of forecasting (e.g. Bennett, 1979) and deducing 'spatial processes' from mapped patterns (Haining, 1981, 1990). Haggett (1994, p. 6) continued to maintain that 'prediction plays an essential part in the building of models of geographical systems', although he invariably illustrated this with reference only to epidemiology. Gregory (1994, p. 59) argues that Haggett's 'main concerns have always been descriptive-predictive', and that he has little interest in 'theoretical questions' and explanation. Haggett himself agreed with this in a published interview (Browning, 1982, p. 54): in response to a statement that 'It seems to me that you are naturally inclined towards models but not necessarily theory' he replied, 'Yes ... I think that the broader theories of the subject are not something I can cope with easily'.

Hay's (1978) review of this work challenged what he saw as its fundamental assumption, that phenomena behave coherently in both time and space. He questioned the assumed stability of inter-place inter-relationships over time in analyses such as Martin and Oeppen's (1975) work on market-price variations, and argued instead for consideration of the value of catastrophe theory, wherein small changes in the control variable(s) can stimulate major changes in the dependent variable being studied (such major changes are the catastrophes). If catastrophes occur, then the linear extrapolations typical of the Bristol group's work have clear limitations as forecasting procedures. There have been relatively few geographical applications of this relatively new area of mathematics, however (Wilson, 1976a, 1981a: it has received more attention among physical geographers – Thornes, 1989a, 1989b).

The modifiable areal unit problem and ecological inference

A further problem characteristic of much geographical data is what became termed the modifiable areal unit problem (*maup*). There are many ways in which a large area can be subdivided into smaller units for data collection, reporting and analysis, and geographers showed that different divisions of the same area could result in different analytical outcomes: the relationship between old age and long-term illness may differ in its strength (and even direction) depending on which particular set of areas was used in the analysis. The importance of this issue became apparent in studies of electoral redistricting (Gudgin and Taylor, 1979), as in the re-apportionment exercises undertaken after every decennial census in the United States when the goal is to produce Congressional (and other) districts as equal in their populations as possible. Each State is allocated a number of districts. Maps of proposed districts – subdivisions of the State – are created using population data for much smaller areas than the districts, so that each district is an amalgamation of many of those small areas, which should be contiguous. Analysts using computers could identify a very large number of possible ways of producing a set of districts in any State, each of which would have its own electoral impact: it could be possible, for example, for a State that has been allocated 12 districts to have a majority of its seats won by either the Democratic or the Republican party, depending on how the map is drawn. The implications of the *maup*, therefore, are that one's findings apply only to the particular map configuration used; they may not be more generally applicable. Different maps may result in different geographical conclusions. (The original examples of this were given by Morrill's – 1973, 1981 – work on redistricting in Washington state, and Openshaw and Taylor's – 1979 – on the impact of different redistrictings in Iowa. Rossiter and Johnston – 1981 – extended Gudgin and Taylor's – 1979 – classic work on the statistical underpinnings of the geography of redistricting to develop a computer program which identifies all of the possible outcomes; see also Cirincione et al., 2000.)

The *maup* issue was first noted by Gehlke and Biehl (1934) and further generalized by Yule and Kendall (1950). Gehlke and Biehl had data on numbers of juvenile delinquents and median household incomes in the 252 census tracts in the Cleveland metropolitan area: the correlation between those two variables was −0.502. But as the tracts were aggregated into larger units (of approximately similar size), so the correlation increased: with 175 units, it was −0.580; with 125, −0.662; with 100, −0.667; and with just 25 it was −0.763. Using data on wheat and potato yields in English counties, Yule and Kendall (1950) found even greater variation according to the number of units: using all 48 English counties, the correlation was only 0.22; with 24 groups of counties, 0.30; with 12 counties, 0.58; 6 counties, 0.76; and with just 3 counties, 0.99. In these studies, just one example of each aggregation (e.g. into 6 groups of English counties) was employed, but in almost all cases there are many different ways in which n units can be aggregated into k regions, where k is smaller than n. Each regionalization might produce a different correlation coefficient, as demonstrated by Openshaw and Taylor (1979). They had data on the percentage of the population aged over 60 and the percentage of the votes cast in the 1968 Presidential election obtained by the Republican candidate for Iowa's 99 counties. The correlation between these two was 0.346. With 30 zones (i.e. aggregations of contiguous counties), the average correlation was 0.33, but with a standard deviation 0.11; as the number of zones decreased, the standard deviation increased. And even this figure concealed the extent of the variation: with 30 zones, for example, it was possible to get a correlation of 0.98 between the two variables at one extreme, and of −0.73 at the other. In effect, as Openshaw (1984a) later demonstrated, it is virtually possible to produce a regionalization of the 99 Iowa counties to produce any desired OLS relationship between the two variables – both the correlation and the slope coefficient.

Openshaw (1984a, 1984b) showed how different spatial aggregations of the same data set (counties into regions, perhaps, or census enumeration districts into social areas) can produce very different correlations between two variables as a result of the interaction of two influences – scale and aggregation; indeed, his simulations suggest that with many data sets any correlation between +1.0 and −1.0 might be obtained, so that the particular aggregation employed needs careful justification (see Wrigley, 1995). Openshaw and Taylor (1981) explored three responses to such findings:

1. It is an *insoluble problem*, and so can only be ignored;
2. It is a *problem that can be assumed away*, with the results obtained from the particular available data set being accepted as 'the real ones'; or
3. It is a *very powerful analytical device* for exploring various aspects of geography and spatial variations, since alternative regionalizations can be produced – this allows the creation of frequency distributions with which one regionalization can be compared (as with the example from Cirincione *et al.*, 2000, cited above), and of optimal regionalizations for particular purposes.

Most geographers and other spatial analysts have at least implicitly adopted the first of these (and perhaps even the second) – in part because they lack the available data which would allow the third response to be adopted.

Associated with this work on ecological inference and the *maup* has been the development of inductive procedures for classification and regionalization, using Artificial Intelligence (AI: Openshaw and Openshaw, 1997). For example, a region-building exercise may begin with a 'representative sample' of the *n* building blocks being selected as the *k* 'cores' for the regions and then a genetic algorithm allocates the remaining $(n - k)$ building blocks to those cores through a 'learning process' until homogeneous regions are created. The algorithm is re-run a large number of times, and the 'best' available regionalization then selected on a predetermined criterion. Such procedures are often termed 'unsupervised' because the cores are randomly selected. An alternative – 'supervised' – procedure involves creating 'ideal type' cores as the nodes for the regions, rather than using samples of the building blocks; there must therefore be a predetermined number of regions. The cores have a given 'population mix', which may be derived either a priori or empirically, from that or another data set. Having created those cores, the building blocks are then regionalized using neural net methods, with the nature of the cores changing during the learning process. (For an example, see Mitchell *et al.*, 1998.) Openshaw *et al.* (1995) used such a procedure to classify residential areas in England. Using census data (85 variables),

145,716 census enumeration districts (EDs, population average c.500), were the building blocks for a clustering into 60 types, themselves aggregated into 17 super-clusters.

These analytical advances have been used to develop regionalizations for practical applications, as in the design of reporting (or output) areas for censuses. Early work on functional regions around cities using flow data (notably for commuting) was used to define metropolitan regions in the United States and travel-to-work areas in the UK (e.g. Berry et al., 1969; Coombes et al., 1982). At smaller scales, in the UK census from 1951–91, for example, the smallest data-reporting units were the enumeration districts (EDs) – small areas used for the administration of the census collection and tabulation procedures. They were defined for administrative convenience only, and bore no necessary relationship to the underlying geography they were portraying. Many users – private and public sector as well as academic researchers – argued the desirability of these being defined so that they were relatively homogeneous on defined characteristics, within prescribed constraints, notably relating to their size (e.g. population or household minima or maxima). Using data for even smaller areas than EDs (postcode sectors), Martin et al. (2001) used one of Openshaw's classification algorithms (AZP: Openshaw and Rao, 1995) to produce a set of Output Areas (OAs) after the census data had been collected, which met certain criteria – a target population (i.e. average population) with given population minima and homogeneity on specified other variables (such as housing tenure) plus a shape constraint. The result is a geography for publishing data from the 2001 UK census with reporting units that are much more homogeneous than heretofore (Martin et al., 2001).

Ecological fallacies and inference

Linked to this work on the *maup* was an increasing appreciation of the problem of ecological inference. Much statistical work involves the analysis of data about population aggregates taken from censuses, such as the relationships between a population's age and its health status, from which inferences about individual behaviour are then drawn: if there is a positive relationship between the average age of an area's population and the proportion of its members suffering long-term illnesses, it may be inferred that older people are more likely to suffer in that way. But, as classic works in sociology and statistics had shown (and as reviewed in King, 1997), such an inference may be unsustainable when data on individuals are available.

The response to that case was twofold: care in the interpretation of what became known as 'ecological correlations' (i.e. analyses based on aggregate data, such as those derived from censuses for administrative areas, but interpreted as showing a relationship at the individual level); and attempts to resolve the problem. Regarding the former, given the available data for tackling many spatial problems, geographers had little alternative but to continue making such inferences – all the while being aware of both the nature of various inferential problems involved (Alker, 1969), and the extra issues raised by Openshaw's work on the *maup*. Only in the late 1990s was a procedure developed which its author claimed resolved the ecological inference problem, providing a method of accurately estimating individual behaviour from aggregate data (King, 1997). Its relevance to geographical work was assessed a few years later (Sui et al., 2000), and a few applications have been undertaken. At the same time, other ways of solving the problem have been advanced, such as the entropy-maximizing and micro-simulation approaches discussed above (Johnston and Pattie, 2001). In all of these, the goal is to derive valid statements about individual behaviour from aggregate data.

Point pattern analysis

The analysis of point patterns was one of the earliest focuses of quantitative interest among geographers, in large part because central place theory and similar models suggested regular patterns for punctiform data: nearest neighbour analysis was adapted from ecology for their analysis (e.g. Dacey, 1962; King, 1962). As such models attracted less attention, so point pattern analysis declined in its importance in human geography. It was revived and much extended, however, in a series of publications by Openshaw.

In studies of the nuclear industry, for example, he evaluated the potential impact of bombing different targets and of selecting different locations for nuclear power stations and hazardous waste disposal by analysing the distribution of population relative to selected points (Openshaw et al., 1983; Openshaw, 1986; Openshaw, Carver and Fernie, 1989). The latter work linked with his later studies of the clustering of rare events round certain points – such as particular cancers linked to possible radiation sources – inductively suggesting cause-and-effect relationships: if significant clusters are identified, this provides strong circumstantial evidence that there is a local cause of the disease, worthy of closer investigation. He began this work by building a *Geographical Analysis Machine (GAM)* which inductively sought all possible clusters in a point pattern, such as one for cases of childhood leukaemia (Openshaw et al., 1997). This involved using massive computing power to identify those clusters – groups of points which were unlikely to occur by chance.

Critiques of Openshaw's approach focused on details rather than the core argument – that inductive searches for patterns can stimulate hypothesis development. With spatial autocorrelation, however, and the problems of under-estimated error terms, the significance of clusters may be over-emphasized, leading to developments of tests which allow for that autocorrelation – as in Markov Chain Monte Carlo methods (Ward and Gleditsch, 2002). Alternative approaches are set out in Elliott et al. (1996, 2001) and Wakefield et al. (2001).

Local statistics

As stressed repeatedly in this book, one of the basic tenets of geographical work is that places differ. If that is the case, then the nature of statistical relationships may vary across space – as suggested by varying gravity model exponents (p. 120) and the application of multi-level models in geographical research. Furthermore, following from that observation, if the nature of a relationship varies across space, why is that the case: what other variables are related to such variation? To answer such questions, geographers have been involved in the development of what are known as *local statistics*, as applied to point patterns, univariate and multivariate relationships, and flow patterns (Fotheringham, 1997; Unwin, 1996). The issue was raised early by King (1976, p. 304):

There are no general laws in social science that are consistent over time and independent of the context in which they are imbedded. The search for law-like generalization of cause and effect relationship is an illusion. Any particular patterning of events will not remain stable for very long, and generalization about them cannot provide a firm theoretical basis for intervention.

Jones and Hanham (1995) suggested that the reference to context means that relationships vary over space as well as time (and thereby linked their work on local statistics to the realist critique of positivism discussed on p. 240).

A substantial component of the literature on certain types of local statistics has been reviewed by Fotheringham *et al.* (2002, p. 241: their emphasis), whose book 'is based on the premise that relationships between variables at different points in space *might* not be constant over space'. Because of that, an analysis which does not allow for such spatial variation commits what is known as Simpson's paradox, which is the 'reversal of results when groups of data are analysed separately and then combined' (Fotheringham *et al.*, 2002, p. 7). In the former case, as they illustrate, spatial disaggregation may show two negative relationships between a pair of variables, but when they are aggregated into a single data set the relationship is positive.

A number of procedures have been explored to test for the existence of this paradox and, where necessary, identify the separate relationships between different sets of observations within a population. One, as discussed above (p. 165), is *multi-level modelling*, which takes a linear relationship between two variables and inquires whether its parameters (the intercept and slope coefficients) vary according to subsets of the population, which might be spatially defined: 'Is the relationship between economic deprivation and the propensity to vote for left-wing political parties the same across all regions of a country?' for example (Jones *et al.*, 1992). Another, developed by geographers – the *Spatial Expansion Method* (Jones and Casetti, 1992) – related the parameters of a regression equation to other variables. Most of the applications were aspatial – they simply tested for differences between subsets of the population, however defined: it was possible to produce a spatial model so that, for example, the strength of a relationship (between distance from the CBD and population density, say) varied by sector of the city. This is a rather limited approach, however, and, as with multi-level modelling, operates with pre-determined subsets of the population rather than inductively, searching for variations in relationships – as with Openshaw's searches for clusters of points. (Jones and Bullen, 1994, report on a comparison of the two methods.)

To extend the search process, Fotheringham *et al.* (2002) developed a technique which they term *Geographically Weighted Regression (GWR)*. It tests whether there is spatial variation in the strength, intensity, and direction of a relationship inductively through analysing separate subsets of the population of data points, defined by their proximity to a randomly-selected core at different scales. This GWR procedure is similar to Openshaw's GAM just discussed, and Openshaw (1998) himself produced a similar *Geographical Explanations Machine* to undertake similar inductive explorations. With such methods it is possible to explore whether relationships – such as that between school performance and the characteristics of its catchment area varies spatially.

One aspect of the study of local statistics is related to the issue of spatial autocorrelation (see p. 166). For example, one of the standard spatial autocorrelation statistics may indicate spatial clustering of a variable across a map of areas for which a variable has been measured, but not whether this involves a single core of high values for the relevant variable or a series of local clusters, or 'hot spots'. Geographers, such as Anselin (1995) and Getis (Ord and Getis, 1995), have developed measures which can identify such clusters – such as a G^* measure which identifies the degree of clustering of similar values around each area and bearing correlograms indicate whether trends in a variable are stronger in some directions than others; wombling methods identify whether certain boundaries (e.g. between two adjacent areas) act as barriers to such a trend, blocking their development. (For examples of an application of these methods, see O'Loughlin, 2002.)

* * * * *

The discussion in this section indicates that the half-century or more since the launch of geography's 'theoretical and quantitative revolutions' has witnessed a great deal of work using mathematical and statistical procedures and involving increased sophistication in the nature of the applications. There have been two main strands to this. The first has involved adopting – and, where necessary, adapting – procedures developed elsewhere that are relevant to the analysis of geographical data. The second has involved the development of procedures within geography – linked to adjacent disciplines – that allow the proper analysis of spatial data. Together, these have been, and remain, substantial strands within human geography. They may no longer occupy a central place within the discipline's literature, as was the case in the 1960s and 1970s, but they are still the foundation of much geographical analysis. Furthermore, according to Golledge (2002, p. 12):

> Today we have all the components deemed necessary to define and justify the existence of a scientific discipline – a huge array of empirically-verified factual data, spatial theories and models, innovative methods of spatial analysis, unique modes of representation, and practical usefulness for decision-making and policy formulation.

Computers and GIS

Very few of the statistical and mathematical developments discussed above could have occurred without rapid cumulative changes in technology which allowed the massive volume of required computation to be undertaken increasingly easily and quickly, at decreasing relative prices (Rhind, 1989; Longley et al., 2001, pp. 445–6). As the technology advances ever-more rapidly, many different 'geofutures' can be visualized (Clarke, 1998; Armstrong, 2000).

Computers became generally available for research in Universities in the 1960s, and geographers were soon using them. There was much initial collaboration in writing, developing and operating programs, as illustrated by an early catalogue (Tarrant, 1968), with texts on computer use by and for geographers (Dawson and Unwin, 1976; Unwin and Dawson, 1985). There were two major areas of use from the outset – multivariate statistical analyses and computer mapping (Hägerstrand, 1967; Haggett, 1969). With the former, most geographers increasingly relied on packages developed for wide use – such as SPSS, MICROTAB and MINITAB – although developments in specialized fields of spatial analysis (such as spatial autocorrelation) required custom-built programs. For most human geographers, programming was no longer a required skill by the 1980s, since almost all of their requirements could be met by standard packages.

This increasing reliance on large computers led to the creation of an approach termed *geocomputation*, which incorporates such topics as data visualization and transformation, representing and modelling spatial interactions, and generalization regarding spatial processes (Longley, 1998). Furthermore, according to Macmillan (1998, p. 257), such is the computing power now available that it allows more than just a step change in the geographer's ability to manipulate information to answer traditional questions:

Technical advances have been so advanced that the problems we can think about have changed. Moreover, there has been a transformation in the kinds of thoughts we can have [by analogy with computing power expansion and mathematics]. As it became possible to find solutions to mathematical problems computationally, so it became possible to think about new classes of problems that could be solved.

Geocomputation is but one part of a wider area of technical development, which has been termed *geoinformatics* and incorporates not only geocomputation but also geodesy, cartography, photogrammetry, global positioning systems, remote sensing, geostatistics and geographical information systems (Curran, 2001b). A number of these – notably remote sensing – have received considerable attention within physical geography. The analysis of remotely-sensed images – initially from planes; increasingly from spacecraft – assumed considerable importance because the images provided immediate, regular and frequent information on parts of the world which were difficult to access physically, allowing not only detailed mapping but also estimations of environmental conditions (such as biomass volume, soil wetness and river sediment loads) and assessment of changes, especially short-term. Furthermore, such images are the only source which provide data at the global scale, increasingly important for modeling environmental changes. They have attracted relatively little use in human geography, however, except in work on land use and defining boundaries of different types of built-up area (Longley and Mesev, 2000; Longley, 2002; Mesev, 2003) .

Openshaw (1994, 1995) has argued that the computational power now available can transform the practice of human geography, providing that (1994, p. 504) 'you are neither blinded by past prejudices about science, not scared of the words computational human geography, nor too hyped up by an overenthusiasm for AI or infected by the neural net virus' (on which see Fischer and Gopal, 1993). His approach was empiricist and inductive, calling for, 'greater intelligence by first becoming less sophisticated in our analysing and modelling technology and then more than compensating by computational intensity' (p. 503). He rejected (1995, p. 161) 'a qualitative, linguistically defined understanding of how a whole system works in vague and general terms' and promoted 'a detailed and precise computer model of one small part of it', using fuzzy set logic as 'a new scientific paradigm for doing geography' (Openshaw, 1996). He called for a HPC (high performance computing) culture within geography focusing on HSM (human system modelling), and the University of Leeds established a Centre for Geographical Computation to advance this work (as illustrated in Openshaw and Rao, 1995): the book by Openshaw and Openshaw (1997) illustrates some of the potential uses of AI within this strategy.

Whereas massive computing power has enabled major advances in modelling and data analysis, it has also stimulated improvements in basic analytical procedures. In particular, the development of visualization methodologies – such as the ability to graph relationships on computer screens and to explore maps (Unwin, 1994) – has aided exploratory data analyses, such as inquiring whether there is a linear relationship between two variables (something that was often assumed because of the time-consuming procedures involved in graphical procedures: Jones and Almond, 1992; Jones and Wrigley, 1995), as well as allowing spatial exploratory data analyses (Anselin, 1998). Thus, computing power has enabled not only massive advances in spatial analysis but also improvements in standard applications. These include mapping. The availability of computer software mapping packages has made much pen-and-ink cartography obsolescent, and allows exploratory maps to be drawn and rapidly displayed on screen. As Dorling and Fairbairn (1997, p. 4) express it, 'the craft skills required to undertake map-making are diminishing in importance'; map-making has moved from the field and the drawing board to the laboratory and the keyboard (Rhind, 2003).

Geographical Information Systems

Spatial data capture, storage, integration, display and analysis have been advanced since the early 1980s by the development of *Geographical Information Systems* (GIS: Curran, 1984; Green *et al.*, 1985; Chrisman *et al*, 1989; Foresman, 1998; Longley *et al.*, 1999a), which bring together rapid advances in computer cartography and data collection in dedicated machines (comprising both hardware and customized software) for the analysis of the three main types of spatial data: those referring to points (such as mapped locations), to areas (such as towns and fields), and to lines (transport routes, for example). Increasingly, data produced by a wide variety of agencies are geocoded (i.e. given unique spatial references which facilitate spatial analysis), and technological advances are leading to the introduction of computers with which it is possible to gather, store, display and analyse spatial data. Different geocoded data sets (i.e. different maps) can be integrated within a GIS, which performs the technically-demanding tasks of transforming different coordinate systems to a common structure and interpolates unknown values from various point and line three-dimensional data (Longley *et al.*, 2001, is an example of the many textbooks in this area). GIS are, according to Longley (2000, p.157), 'fundamentally a facilitating and applications-led technology, which transparently assesses the importance of space, and as such should be central to our geographical understanding of the world'. Advances in GIS, as he notes (Longley, 2004), have been such in recent years as to blur the distinction between iconic and symbolic modelling: whereas initially GIS stored maps in their iconic form, increasingly they are able to store symbolic (e.g. formulaic) representations of environments and their process systems, in four dimensions.

Development of this technology in the United Kingdom was heralded and promoted by a major project initiated to mark the 900th anniversary of the 1086 Domesday Book census. A GIS to provide a modern equivalent was developed and marketed as a teaching aid for schools and other educational institutions (Goddard and Armstrong, 1986). Its massive data base could be used to display a wide range of maps (including the Ordnance Survey 1:50000 series for the whole of Great Britain) and pictures, and could also be analysed interactively (Openshaw et al., 1986): the technology on which it was based is now obsolete. Other major stimuli included early work on computer cartography at the Experimental Cartography Unit in London, the Departments of Geography at the Universities of Durham and Edinburgh, and the Laboratory for Computer Graphics and Spatial Analysis in the Graduate School of Design at Harvard University (for histories of GIS, see Foresman, 1998, and Mark et al., 1996).

GIS allow many problems to be addressed that previously could not be afforded in terms of the time and resources necessary for data collection, analysis and display: as such, they are the basis for much applied research work (see p. 334). The British Economic and Social Research Council established a network of Regional Research Laboratories to explore their potential as research tools in the late 1980s, most of them located in university departments of geography (the October 1988 issue of the *ESRC Newsletter*, was devoted to the topic 'Working with geographical information systems') and the United States National Science Foundation invested US$5.5 million in a National Center for Geographic Information and Analysis, based at three sites (see the announcements in the Association of American Geographers' *Newsletter* for August 1987 and October 1988 and Fotheringham and MacKinnon, 1989): a key individual in winning funding for the latter was Ron Abler, then responsible for geography in the NSF and later Executive Director of the Association of American Geographers (see also p. 95). Their use was promoted in teaching (Maguire, 1989; Fisher, 1989a); an Association for Geographic Information was established in the United Kingdom, following a major report by a House of Lords Select Committee for which a geographer (Rhind) acted as scientific advisor (Rhind, 1986; Rhind and Mounsey, 1989); several specialist journals have been launched (such as the *International Journal of Geographical Information Systems*: in 1997 *Systems* was replaced by *Science*); a bibliography of over 1,000 items was published in early 1990 (Bracken et al., 1990); and a major encyclopaedic survey was published in the following year (Maguire et al., 1991: a second, much revised and rewritten edition, appeared eight years later; Longley et al., 1999; for a review of work in urban geography alone, see Sui, 1994). There has also been a large number of textbooks published to cater for teaching GIS, alongside specialist technical volumes, and others have made explicit the role of GIS in spatial data analysis (O'Sullivan and Unwin, 2003).

In his 1989 presidential address to the Canadian Association of Geographers, Roger Tomlinson (1989, p. 298), a pioneer in the development of GIS from the 1960s on, referred to their growing use in the following terms:

> Geographers have a crucial role to play in integrating a wide variety of technologies into new forms of 'earth description' which will act as a foundation for geographical methodology and open the way to richer forms of spatial analysis and geographical understanding.

Spatial problems will multiply and become more complex in the future, and geographers' ability to handle and analyse large bodies of data in the search for solutions using GIS should demonstrate the strength of their 'integrating science', as part of a 'data are good ethic' (p. 292; see also p. 185 below). Whereas many of those involved in the development of GIS have largely focused on the resolution of the technical issues involved with integrating data bases and their statistical manipulation, and cautioned against over-optimism regarding their potential (see Goodchild, 1995), some of its promoters have made grand claims, as illustrated by Openshaw's (1991) reaction to Taylor's (1990a) separation of geographical information systems from 'geographical knowledge systems' (see the discussion on p. 354). At its core, however, the use of GIS is characterized, according to one of its leading practitioners – Michael Goodchild – as using 'geographic location as a common key to link data' (Schuurman, 1999, p. 10): the more that is done using such data, the more central 'geography' becomes to a wide range of practices.

Others have expressed concerns regarding the potential power being sought for applications using these information systems (see Curry, 1994, and several of the essays in Pickles, 1995a). Pickles (1995b, p. 2), for example, argues that GIS are much more than 'merely more efficient counting machines' providing more accurate descriptions and visual images: their 'virtual representations will produce illusions that will be so powerful it will not be possible to tell what is real and what is not real' (p. 10). For others, their use, whether in sophisticated marketing procedures (i.e. geodemographics: see Batey and Brown, 1995; Birkin, 1995; for a critique see Goss, 1995) or military applications (Smith, N., 1992), raises moral and ethical issues (none of which are specific to GIS but apply to any application of 'knowledge'). To Curry (1995), GIS involve ethical inconsistencies which are necessarily built into systems and can be used to advance surveillance (whether by the state or by other bodies) very substantially. (These issues are discussed in Pickles, 1995a; Longley et al., 1999a; on the wider issue of representation, see Cosgrove, 2001.)

In responding to some of these critiques, Sui (1994) has categorized them into those which stress one or more of the following:

1. *Ontological inadequacy* – GIS present a limited, Cartesian representation of reality, ignoring social and cultural representations;
2. *Epistemological insufficiency* – GIS are deeply rooted in positivist modes of thinking;
3. *Methodological insufficiency* – GIS applications lack coherent theory and are biased by their use of secondary data; and
4. *Ethical inconsistency* – the values embedded in GIS are ignored, along with any recognition of subjective differences in representations of reality.

He claimed that the critiques have 'at best, been refuted by the GIS community or, at worst, have been totally dismissed as anti-progress and anti-science nuisances' (Sui, 1994, p. 268). Examples are presented of GIS researchers who have addressed each of the four issues, showing that (p. 271):

... the GIS community has realized that the implementation of GIS should go beyond mere technical decisions justified by matters of efficiency and give the ethical use of this information a serious consideration. ... GIS, if not a fertile ground for common search, at least has initiated a search for common ground.

(The last sentence draws on the title of Golledge, Couclelis and Gould's, 1988, collection.) Nevertheless, he concluded by noting that, 'so far, GIS enthusiasts and GIS opponents have been mutually hostile or at least dismissive of each other's views' (p. 272) and suggested that closer cooperation is needed in which, 'GIS enthusiasts must avoid the imperialistic claim that science is the only guarantor of objective truth. Post-modernists must relinquish the playful cynicism in their critiques on the scientific chauvinism of GIS'. Schuurman (2000) has argued that such cooperation is now developing. She suggests that critiques published during the 1990s drew responses from GIS specialists, which led to the establishment of an NCGIA initiative on the social impacts of GIS. Nevertheless, she feared that the lack of a common vocabulary could reduce the impact of any cooperation, with the critics using approaches based in the sociology of science that have little in common with the scientific and technological languages employed in GIS. For Goodchild, many of the critiques – which focused on GIS use in a range of non-academic contexts – had considerable validity. To him, a 'GIS is a machine that is capable of a wide range of operations and these in turn are compatible with a wide range of philosophical positions' (Schuurman, 1999, p. 5): it can be used both to identify unique features in a data set and to search for 'the general processes that operate on those unique conditions' (p. 6).

The advances in computer technology, including GIS, have had very substantial impacts on the practice of cartography and other forms of graphic information display. Only a small number of geographers are involved in research on cartographic methods (see MacEachren, 1995), but their work on visualization has allowed major advances in the computerized presentation of large and complex data sets (see Dorling, 1995).

Dobson (1983a) argued that dealing with these massive data sets will require the development of *automated geography,* an 'integrated systems approach to geographic problem solving in which the problem is defined, the appropriate methods are chosen, and the tools are selected from a broad repertoire of automated and manual techniques' (p. 136). This would be highly dependent on computer hardware and software developments (sufficient of which were already available; though see Cowen, 1983) and would facilitate participation in public policy research on a large scale. Most commentators on Dobson's paper (in the August 1983 issue of *The Professional Geographer*) argued that automated geography was a misnomer, since the main benefits of the hardware and software that he described related to the scale and speed of data manipulation only. They preferred less emotive terms such as 'computer-assisted geography' or 'computer-assisted geographic systems', and some, like Poiker (1983), argued that the case was no more than one for another set of tools, just as the case for quantification turned out to be decades earlier: 'our tool seems to attract an inappropriate number of prophets' (p. 349). Dobson (1983b) disagreed, however, arguing that, 'what I am talking about is not a system or collection of systems. It is a *discipline* which uses human and electronic cybernetic systems to further understanding of physical and social systems' (p. 351), with some decisions (e.g. with regard to how data are displayed) taken by the computers, not by people. Thus, computers should be programmed so that they incorporate 'the character of our discipline', presenting the results of geographical analysis without the detailed intervention of geographers (see Couclelis, 1986b; Fisher, 1989b; Haines-Young, 1989).

Dobson's arguments were revisited a decade later. He claimed that (Dobson, 1993, p. 431):

> GIS has become a sine qua non for geographic analysis and research in government, business and academia. This advance has been hailed widely as a technological revolution, but I proposed a more exciting prospect beyond technology. The strength of GIS innovation and diffusion suggests that science and society are in the beginning stage of a technological, scientific and intellectual revolution as profound as earlier revolutions brought on by the printing press or the computer.

Nevertheless, he expressed concerns over the amount of geographical research done using GIS, other than in mapping and survey (p. 432), suggesting that 'the GIS community is still searching for a greater sense of purpose' (p. 433), and claiming that, 'the current state of GIS is woefully deficient when compared to our predecessors' ultimate goal of representing landscapes as three-dimensional geographic units with interactions of multiple phenomena in space and time, with order' (p. 434). He ended with a call for geographers to become more involved in what was clearly, to him, an unfulfilled revolution (p. 438):

> The technological revolution, understandably, may be led by private companies and government laboratories, and technical leadership may come from many fields. But academic geographers are essential to the scientific and intellectual revolutions. Geographers are needed as consummate leaders in conceptual design and in geographic analysis employing GIS.

Others agreed, while noting that hardware and software developments, although substantial, were still far from those needed for completing Dobson's revolution (Armstrong, 1993; Cromley, 1993). But whereas some were optimistic about the growing use of computers in all aspects of geography (and not just those involving numerical applications: Monmonier, 1993), others were pessimistic. Marble and Peuquet (1993, p. 446), for example, argued that since 1983, 'the impact of the computer upon geographic research appears to have been even less than our most pessimistic estimates', in part because of 'a substantial turning away from those activities that GIS can do best' (p. 447). Goodchild (1993, p. 445) appeared to agree: 'Whether or not GIS and automated geography have anything to offer to geographic research, we cannot escape the fact that GIS has had a significant impact on many kinds of human activity'. This was reflected in the subtitle of Sheppard's (1993) contribution – 'What kind of geography for what kind of society?' – and in Pickles' (1993) rehearsal of arguments regarding the impact of technology on geographical and other practices (see p. 178).

The technical advances have not been associated with parallel developments in substantive geographic theories it is argued, therefore, in large part because (as discussed in later chapters) spatial analysis has been somewhat marginalized within the discipline. In some of the continuing work, the 'traditional' models associated with the developments of the 1950s/1960s have provided the basic underpinning, focusing on optimum distributions of points and lines and on flows between those points along the lines. Wilson (1984a) claimed that mathematical development enables us to build new models by combining old problems (for example von Thünen's and Weber's) with new methods, claiming that comprehensive models can now be built combining macro-population backcloth, macro-economic backcloth, spatial interaction, the location of population activities, the location of economic activities, and the development of economic infrastructure into representations of spatial pattern or settlement structure. Two papers 'demonstrate the ability of models of spatial interaction and structure to reproduce the results of classical industrial location theory' (Birkin and Wilson, 1986, p. 305) and they are the foundation for the applied work undertaken at Leeds (Birkin, Clarke and George, 1995: see p. 351), but relatively few workers now concentrate on such modelling, preferring the behavioural approaches detailed above. Even more prefer non-positivistic approaches, leaving the substantial GIS community somewhat isolated within geography as a whole, with its focus largely external rather than internal: indeed, Obermeyer (1994) claimed that GIS now meets all of the criteria for identification as a separate profession.

Indeed, to some the last term in GIS should be changed to Science. Goodchild (1992, p. 31) made such a case, arguing that while 'spatial data handling may describe what we do' and that many of the advances in GIS have been technology-driven, there were two questions that suggested the change of name. The first concerned *GIS as science*, addressing a particular set of scientific questions that are generic rather than restricted to particular applications; the second concerned *GIS for science*, as a toolbox with wide applications across many sciences. Regarding the first set, he argued that because geographical (or spatial) data have unique properties, then this leads to a set of generic issues that such a science would cover: these relate to data collection, measurement and capture, spatial statistics, data modelling and theories of spatial data, algorithms for representing data, data display, and analytical tools. In each, he claims, there are 'clearly challenging scientific questions [in which] . . . the spatial context appears to be distinctive' (p. 40). Addressing such key questions is the core of his nascent geographic information science, which focuses on technological solutions to the many issues relating to spatial data handling, whose relevance is widespread across other sciences and in myriad public and private sector applications.

GIS have transformed a substantial proportion of geographic research in recent decades (in physical as well as human geography, as illustrated by papers in the relevant specialized journals). In addition, they have become widely used commercially and by public agencies for the storage, display and analysis of myriad types of spatial data. As such, skills with GIS are seen as important for future generations of graduates and geographers have argued that GIS should form a central component of degree programs, providing graduates with 'transferable skills' that they can apply in a range of careers. Indeed, GIS has been presented by some as a 'saviour' for the discipline, providing it with a *raison d'être* within the educational structure and a component of the discipline which should enable it to attract students. In surveys of graduate employment and academic job opportunities in the mid-1990s, for example, the Association of American Geographers found that more programs were preparing graduates for careers in GIS and remote sensing than any other specialism, that GIS was the modal employment category for new graduates, and that GIS specialists were in most demand for posts in United States geography departments – with many more to be hired over the next decade than were expected to retire, resulting in a rebalancing of the profession. (The reports are reproduced in NAS-NRC, 1997: see also p. 382.)

In reporting on a 'renaissance' in geography during the 1990s, the NAS-NRC (1997) volume *Rediscovering Geography* paid particular attention to spatial analysis and GIS as indicative of the discipline's relevance to contemporary social problems. GIS, geographic visualization and spatial statistics get much of the coverage in the chapter on 'Geography's techniques' – indeed, that chapter makes no reference to the methodologies deployed in other areas of geography (such as those discussed in the next chapters). The case for promoting geography in this way is clarified in the chapter's conclusion (p. 69):

> *Current trends in geography's techniques suggest a future in which researchers, students, business people and public policy makers will explore a world of shared spatial data from their desktops ... The users of the future will also bring different world views and theoretical perspectives to these tools. They will challenge the adequacy of current techniques for analysing and understanding geographic phenomena, posing challenges that must be taken up by developers when designing next-generation tools and theories.*

Indeed, the UK Office of National Statistics has made some of its data available through an online GIS.

Similarly, chapters on 'Geography's contributions to scientific understanding' and 'Geography's contributions to decision making' focus substantially on spatial analysis and GIS applications – including a 'national spatial data infrastructure'. Not surprisingly, therefore, when it comes to the report's recommendations for 'Strengthening geography's foundations' with regard to research and teaching priorities, the section on 'Geographic competency among college and university students' calls for (pp. 150–1):

> *... efforts to ensure that ... [they] have access to geography courses and perspectives that go beyond a concern with "where things are" to provide a basic conceptual and analytic grounding in the spatial and environmental dimensions of human and physical processes.*

Furthermore (p. 160):

> *The discipline of geography is in a period of transition from a past where most geographic information was transmitted in the form of paper maps to a future in which most geographic information will be transmitted through digital information systems. ... Geographers need to learn about these spatial information sources and understand how to use them appropriately in their work. Academic geographers also need to consider how new technologies and data sources will create new opportunities for collaborations with the private sector.*

> *If geography is to meet the challenges of rapid technological change, steps must be taken to familiarize students with new technologies for data analysis and display. ... Technology now plays a pre-eminent role in a wide range of geographic research ... Continued advances of this sort will require a substantial coterie of geographers who understand new technologies and can use them effectively.*

As far as the report is concerned, the future of American geography lies very much with spatial analysis and its enabling technologies, such as GIS. Certainly, GIS is rapidly expanding as a technology, enabling not only the relatively easy resolution of previous difficulties regarding the integration of spatially-coded data sets, but also both a wide range of commercial/public sector applications and the ability to pose questions previously unconsidered. For Longley *et al.* (1999b, p. 1) GIS is a 'generic term denoting the use of computers to create and depict digital representations of the Earth's surface', thereby enabling a wide range of geographical questions to be addressed. By 1997 it was being taught in over 1,500 universities and there were some 500,000 regular users in an industry worth US$12 billion annually. GIS has its own learned societies and literature, and a number of major annual conferences – but the adjective in its title is more than symbolic: geography is the academic discipline most closely connected with developments in the application and teaching of GIS, if not in the enabling hardware developments, with potentials that extend well beyond the narrowly technical (Gilbert, 1995).

GIS has also proved a vehicle for reintroducing maps to geography – albeit in a very different form from previous situations (Kain and Delano-Smith, 2003; Rhind, 2003). In the 1950s, the map was still being promoted as *the* foundational geographical tool (James, 1954, p. 9). Fifty years later, editors were bemoaning their absence from many geographical papers (Martin, 1998; Wheeler, 1998; see also Johnston, 2004b). Dorling (1998), however, argued that mapping is becoming much more common outwith the discipline, in a wide range of contexts:

> Maps have become a very common currency. People in western societies now consult maps so often that they often do not remember using them. These images have become commonplace, from bus maps to maps of offices, to maps in newspapers, in books, and on the news. They are so common that we often fail to question their authority, fail to ask why they are drawn as they are (p. 279).

Many of those maps are used to change the way in which people think about the world (as happened in the Second World War when new projections were used to demonstrate America's proximity to Europe with regard to potential aerial attack: Schulten, 2001). 'Not all maps simplify, subvert, collude or conceal' (Dorling, 1998, p. 287), but their use as a means of informing and educating should remain a focus of geographers' concerns.

Moving forward

Much of the remainder of this book is concerned with alternative approaches to human geography from those outlined in this chapter; many were initially based on critiques of 'positivist spatial science', and some have attracted large numbers of adherents. If the paradigm model of revolutions and normal science discussed in Chapter 1 is relevant to human geography, then as a consequence – given the later developments discussed in the following chapters – interest in the approaches set out here should have waned in the 1970s and 1980s, if not disappeared totally. In relative terms there has undoubtedly been some decline, as the alternative world views on offer (discussed later in this book) have attracted substantial attention. But a considerable amount of work is still being done which is firmly based within the world view described here, and there continue to be substantial advances in the methods and applications of spatial analysis (as illustrated in O'Kelly's, 1999, listing of some of the most influential papers in *Geographical Analysis* over its first 30 years of publication). Some of its adherents have sought to accommodate the critiques, while others have counter-attacked and argued for the validity and vitality of their point of view. There is a general consensus among the counter-attackers that modelling, with associated quantitative analysis, is a viable approach to human geography, though there is considerable variability in emphasis as to the way forwards.

According to Wilson (1989b, p. 29), modelling within human geography has led to 'dramatic advances' and has 'a substantial contribution to make in the long term' (Clarke and Wilson, 1989, p. 30). Wilson (1989b, p. 30) accepts the limitations of the approach – models 'have relatively little to offer in relation to individual behaviour directly', but are important tools which can 'help to handle complexity in a variety of situations'. His review focuses on work (much of it his own) which has sought to extend the 'classics' of location theory (von Thünen, Weber, Burgess and Hoyt, and Reilly; see also Clarke and Wilson, 1985b; Wilson, 2000), and which he considers has provided, through its mathematical sophistication, substantial advances in understanding. (Wilson, 1989b, claims that the use of mathematics to model complexity distances his work from positivism: statistics are needed to calibrate and test models, but 'a purely statistical approach to theory and model-building is limited in scope and is also more directly connected to positivism', p. 41.)

The modellers' achievements are similarly lauded by Macmillan (1989a, 1989b), who equates their activity with 'quantitative theory construction'; to him theories are empirically testable statements of 'universal empirical propositions, law-like generalizations' (1989a, p. 93), so that modelling involves the development of theories which contain 'quantifiable propositions' that can be tested. It has already 'helped geography to achieve widespread and significant advances' (1989b, p. 292), and the feelings within the modelling community are of 'frustrated optimism rather than pessimism' (p. 291). He resists a return to focusing on the uniqueness of places (see Chapter 6), arguing that (p. 305), 'if we want to understand famines, we must look at famine processes wherever they occur and test our theories about them accordingly'.

For some authors, spatial analysis retains – or should retain – a central position within geography. Casetti (1999, p. 339), for example, identified three modes of inquiry – literary, academic and mathematical. His preference is clearly for the last of these, arguing that, 'In geography in general, and in human geography in particular, the mathematical mode of inquiry is progressing much too slowly ... [to have the required] positive influence on ... the evolution of the social *SCIENCE* called geography' (his emphasis). Like others involved with the quantitative revolution (e.g. Getis, 1993), he feared that the spatial analytic viewpoint was being marginalized within geography. It had 'saved geography from extinction as a serious university discipline, by attracting and training good students, by writing articles and books that developed theory and method, by gaining a foothold in science at large, and by applying these methods and theories to contemporary social problems' (Morrill, 1993, p. 442) – but these gains were at risk as geography becomes increasingly 'anti-science' (p. 446).

Several authors have argued for a shift in emphasis within the approach, however, as a consequence of recent developments in information technology and data availability. Macmillan (1989b) identifies three separate areas of modelling activity: statistical, mathematical and data-based, which is largely inductive in orientation. The case for the last was forcefully put by Openshaw (1989, p. 71) who terms 'the application of a mathematical tool kit to urban and regional systems modelling within a hypothetico-deductive framework ... [as in Wilson's work] ... noble objectives'. He claims that the available models have not been much used, however (see also Batty, 1989), leading to the situation whereby 'so much of the intellectual capital of quantitative human geography [is] encapsulated in theoretical models that seemingly serve no useful purpose outside of geography itself' (p. 72). The deductive route to understanding, and eventually to applied work, 'has been taken too far and has not been particularly successful' (p. 73):

> There is no doubt about either the quality of the work or of the utility of the mathematical methods; rather, criticism is focused on the lack of applied relevancy, the lack of attention to empirical study, and the absence of explicit geography.

The recent explosion in data collection, and of data provision in machine-readable form, offers many new research opportunities. Openshaw proposes that geographers capitalize on that wealth of data with inductive work which he defines as 'Data-driven computer modelling in an information economy'. The prime concern of data owners, he argues, including those in the public sector who are increasingly required to justify the costs of data collection by their sale to users, is to 'add value' to their information, by analyses which make it more readily usable, and hence saleable. Theory is much less relevant than the ability to conduct spatial analysis of data, which relies much more on inductive approaches than deductive, a situation which he accepts is pragmatic but which he proposes as a means of ensuring the short-term survival of geography as an academic discipline (p. 81):

> ... never before in human history has so much information about so many people and their spatial behaviour patterns been stored in computers and therefore, theoretically speaking, accessible for analysis. Yet it appears that if geographers want access to such rich data sources as now exist they will in future either have to pay or join the data-keepers in providing information services (pp. 81–2).

He chose the latter way forward, using the analytical skills of geographers, including GIS, not to advance theoretical understanding but rather to improve business and predictive efficiency by inductively seeking methods that work – as with answers to questions such as 'Given the population profile of an area, what pattern of spending can be expected there?' and 'Can house prices in that area be predicted with accuracy?'. Databases should be explored to identify patterns that provide useful, and hence saleable, information.

Openshaw's call for a return to inductive methods as a way of adding value to data, and thereby to prove the utility of geography within modern society, is backed by others who identify technical ability with quantitative methods as one of the geographers' strongest selling points (e.g. Beaumont, 1987). Thus Rhind (1989, p. 189), who later became director-general of the British Ordnance Survey when it was being 'commercialized', argued that geographers should develop as 'gatekeepers' to usable information, as a way of staying 'central to the action'. These are clearly calls for more applied geography (discussed in more detail below, Chapter 9).

The apparent division between inductive 'number-crunchers' and 'deductive modellers' suggests a growing split within the body of human geographers concerned with quantitative analysis. On the one hand, there are those who promote widespread application of well-known, usually relatively straightforward and easily applied methods – though not necessarily to meet commercial objectives. On the other hand, there are those who advance the development of sophisticated procedures, whose use demands considerable technical expertise. Cox (1989) argued that the latter have had a very limited impact on geography as a whole, because: first, they have shown that spatial data are 'messy', requiring special analytical procedures which are not generally available, and so set 'intellectual and practical difficulties [which] have limited widespread understanding and application of the more correct procedures that have been produced' (p. 206); and second, with few exceptions the procedures have not been applied to problems that are in the mainstream of attempts at geographical understanding, have little basis in known 'human processes or behaviour', and so are peripheral to most geographers' interests. Thus, much quantitative analysis has been marginalized within geography, while supporters of Openshaw's approach and the use of GIS have promoted their saleable expertise (Cox, 1989, p. 207):

> It is clear that geographers specializing in geographical information systems will survive only by combining considerable technical expertise with a taste and talent for the Realpolitik of grants, contracts, committees, administrators, and entrepreneurs. A canny awareness of commercial and political realities will be as necessary as any particular intellectual qualities.

For Cox, this carries the danger that 'preoccupation with data will omit imagination and creativity' (p. 208) but, as the later chapter on applied geography shows, many see it as a major way to protect the discipline in a context where utility and saleability are the crucial indicators of the worth of its work.

While some geographers continue to promote the development of analytical methods within their discipline, and some at least link this to better explanatory procedures and predictive methods that will lead to a wider applicability and application of geographers' skills, many more are relatively unconcerned with either the sophistication of method or the search for grand generalizations. As Flowerdew (1986) forcefully pointed out, their work is very largely empiricist in orientation, having as its goal the portrayal of the 'objective' world as they perceive it, and of the salient elements which they identify as needing (or offering interesting) research. A great deal of it describes the changing geography of the world, and the amount and rapidity of change have called forth a great volume of published work.

This work is not entirely atheoretical – as critics of the empiricist and positivist positions on value-freedom and neutrality point out, the choice of what to study (i.e. what is significant) and how to study it must be theoretically informed, however implicitly. Nor is it undertaken in isolation from the theoretical and methodological debates and developments taking place elsewhere in the discipline. A large number of geographers prefer not to get embroiled in those, however, but rather to draw on them, as they see fit, to inform work whose orientation is close to Hartshorne's well-known call 'to describe and interpret the variable character from place to place of the earth as the world of man'.

Conclusions

As stressed in the previous chapter, much of the force of the developments in human geography during the 1950s and 1960s concerned methodology and the approach to traditional geographical questions. In addition, however, attempts were made to inaugurate and press a particular geographical point of view, with two main themes. The first – the spatial-science viewpoint – was fairly widely and rapidly accepted, and many geographers placed spatial variables at the centre of their research efforts: as will be indicated later, their work came under increasing attack from the late 1960s. The second – the systems approach – has received much less detailed attention, despite frequent approving gestures, except in studies of environmental and demographic systems. Compared with the spatial-science view, which could be rapidly assimilated within the developing statistical methodology, the systems approach was technically much more demanding, and perhaps for that reason attracted fewer active researchers (though see Coffey's, 1981, defence).

Human geography as spatial science was inaugurated in North America in the 1950s. By the end of the 1960s it was providing much of the material for many of the journals published throughout the English-speaking world (Wheeler, 2002a). Much research was positivist in its tone, if not its detail, seeking not only to describe patterns of spatial organization but also to account for (explain) these as consequences of the influence of distance on human behaviour. A great deal of it used quantitative methods, and it contributed to bodies of theory, either about spatial organization in general or certain aspects of it in particular. It has influenced other academic disciplines (even though, as Laponce, 1980, expressed it, geography had less impact on the other social sciences than vice versa) and the planning profession.

Since the 1970s, positivist spatial science has been under considerable attack among Anglo-American human geographers. This attack had little initial effect on the volume of work done in this paradigm, as illustrated by a major review of *Quantitative Geography* by British workers (Wrigley and Bennett, 1981); this work has been stimulated and aided by advances in data-handling technology and display. The approach was also fostered outside the Anglo-American realm, especially in Western Europe where the reaction to quantification has been stronger than in Britain and North America (see Bennett, 1981c). Many of the models and theories that acted as the foundations to the pioneering work – such as central place theory – are now largely consigned to disciplinary history, as stimuli to work that eventually proved relatively unproductive but generated interest in a wider range of issues that remain central to a geographical agenda, along with the methods needed to address that agenda.

The partial disappearance of work in the spatial-science mould from many of the discipline's mainstream journals has suggested to some that it is no longer a viable and vibrant area of work. The field of GIS, for example, has spawned its own suite of outlets and professional societies, much like remote sensing before it, and other specialist journals, such as *Location Studies, Computers and Environmental Modelling* and *International Journal of Geographical Information Science* have been launched for those who continue to apply mathematical and statistical procedures to large spatial data sets. This is part of the specialization and fragmentation that now characterize human geography (Johnston, 1996a, 2004b) and, given the large volume of work done in other parts of the discipline, means that much of what is being reported can readily go unnoticed.

This great volume of work suggests that there has been 'progress' within the positivist approach. There have been substantial advances in the development and adaptation of sophisticated modelling and analytical techniques: some, however, thought these advances, although 'scholarship of the highest order', may reflect 'a misdirection of effort' (King, 1979b, p. 157) because they have not illuminated spatial organization as much as they might. New techniques continue to be advanced, assisted by massive technological advances in data handling. Empirical work in the spatial-science context has very much taken the form of case studies set in a general theoretical context, however, and – despite the efforts of some general surveys (e.g. Haggett, Cliff and Frey, 1977) – it is not clear whether such case studies have provided much general understanding. What is without doubt, however, is the volumetric impact of spatial science on human geography. A 'paradigm' in the sense of a community with a clear world-view was established within geography in the 1950s and 1960s, and has remained strong and vibrant within the discipline ever since. Its nature has changed considerably since then, with the formal models of spatial structures being largely forgotten and replaced by new approaches. The methods applied have changed too, with greater technological power and sophistication. Thus the macro-paradigm has remained intact, but the meso- and micro-paradigms have been subject to revolutions – the latter more frequently than the former.

Meanwhile, other approaches to geographical study have been introduced and debated, many of which have few links with those introduced here: in many cases, the subject matter addressed does not call for the forms of analysis discussed in this chapter. They are discussed in the following chapters, exemplifying the rich variety in geographical scholarship which emerged, in various ways, from the 'revolutions' inaugurated in the decades after the Second World War.

5
Humanistic geography

Abstraction and fragmentation in human geography are related facets of a broader cultural condition, and as such they should not be confused with a law of nature.

(Ley, 1989, p. 244)

Although behavioural geography involved a reorientation of the work undertaken within the spatial-science approach, it maintained the generally positivist framework of that genre of work. Alongside it from the early 1970s, though with roots extending much further back, emerged a fundamental critique of the entire positivist approach, including behavioural geography. It also argued for a focus on the individual as decision-maker, but denied the goal of explanation and prediction that was inherent to the behavioural approach; its goal was appreciation and understanding of the particular.

There was no coherent body of support for any of the alternatives to positivism proposed, but the critics were united in their opposition to what was being promoted as the 'new geography' (as illustrated in Cosgrove's 1989a, 1989b, cogent presentations of that case). That opposition was clarified by Entrikin's (1976, p. 616) definition of what became known as humanistic geography as:

> ... a reaction against what they believe to be an overly objective, narrow, mechanistic and deterministic view of [the human being] presented in much of the contemporary research in the human sciences. Humanist geographers argue that their approach deserves the appellation 'humanistic' in that they study the aspects of [people] which are most distinctively 'human': meaning, values, goals and purposes.

Cloke, Philo and Sadler (1991, p. 69) expressed the critique more fully:

> It almost goes without saying that the geographers referenced here were unhappy about the tendency of spatial science to treat people as little more than dots on a map, statistics on a graph or numbers in an equation, since the impression being conveyed was of human beings 'whizzing' around in space – travelling from place X to place Y; shopping in centre X rather than in centre Y; selling produce in market X rather than at market Y – in a fashion little different from the 'behaviour' of stones on a slope, particles in a river or atoms in a gas. Indeed, it was complained that such exercises ... effectively converted human beings into 'dehumanised' entities drained of the very 'stuff' (the meanings, values and so on) that made humans into humans as opposed to other things living or non-living.

The nature of those criticisms, the alternatives advanced and the developing practices of humanistic geography are the subject of the present chapter.

Cultural and historical behavioural geography

As indicated in earlier chapters, very few cultural and historical geographers were attracted by the so-called quantitative and theoretical revolutions. There was some application of statistical procedures to make work in these fields appear more 'modern', but few substantive changes were adopted by adherents working within the traditional approaches (despite the efforts of the *ad hoc* committees established to chart ways forward for the 'new geography': see above, p. 93). By the 1970s, however, some historical and cultural geographers had taken the initiative, and were proposing alternative philosophies to positivism which were humanistic in their orientation: according to Hugill and Foote (1994, p. 12), prior to the Second World War, 'cultural geography was more advanced in its theories than was the rest of human geography', but the challenge of the 'revolutions' outlined in the previous two chapters meant that 'Cultural geography ceased to be the most theoretically informed of the subdisciplines and embarked on a long search for theory that is still underway' (p. 14).

The beginnings of these changes can be traced to two papers, one of which had more impact than the other on the geographical discipline at large. In the first, John K. Wright (1947, p. 12) introduced the term *geosophy*, defined as the study of geographical knowledge:

> ... it covers the geographical ideas, both true and false, of all manners of people – not only geographers, but farmers and fishermen, business executives and poets, novelists and painters, Bedouins and Hottentots – and for this reason it necessarily has to do with subjective conceptions (p. 12).

Wright conceded that study of such subjective ideas could not employ the strict scientific principles of physical geography, but claimed that it provided indispensable background and perspective to geographical work:

> ... geographical knowledge of one kind or another is universal among men, and is in no sense a monopoly of geographers ... such knowledge is acquired in the first instance through observations of many kinds. ... Its acquisition, in turn, is conditioned by the complex interplay of cultural and psychological factors ... nearly every important activity in which man engages, from hoeing in a field or writing a book or conducting a business to spreading a gospel or waging a war, is to some extent affected by the geographical knowledge at his disposal (pp. 13–14).

These words could well have heralded an earlier start to behavioural geography than that chronicled earlier, but the lack of reference to them in later published works suggests that they had little impact until taken up by Wright's colleague at the American Geographical Society, David Lowenthal (1961, p. 259), in a widely cited paper, 'concerned with *all* geographic thought, scientific and other: how it is acquired, transmitted, altered and integrated into conceptual systems'. Lowenthal argued in a wide-ranging survey that the world of each individual's experience is intensely parochial and covers but a small fraction of the total available. There are consensus views about many aspects of the world, but individuals will often mistakenly assume that their view is the consensus. We all live in personal worlds, which are 'both more and less inclusive than the common realm' (p. 248). Our perceptions of these worlds are personal too; they are not fantasies, being firmly rooted in reality, but because 'we elect to see certain aspects of the world and to avoid others' (p. 251) behaviour based on such perceptions must have its unique elements. Different cultures have their own shared stereotypes, however, which are often reflected in language, and attempts are made to create environments fitting into these stereotypes:

> The surface of the earth is shaped for each person by refraction through cultural and personal lenses of custom and fancy. We are all artists and landscape architects, creating order and organizing space, time, and causality in accordance with our apperceptions and predilections (p. 260).

His ideas were implemented in papers concerned with the interpretation of landscapes as reflections of societal norms and tastes (e.g. Lowenthal, 1968; Lowenthal and Prince, 1965), thereby belatedly bringing Wright's ideas before a wider, and perhaps more readily appreciative, audience.

The second of the original papers was by a British geographer, although it was published in India (Kirk, 1951; it is reprinted in Boal and Livingstone, 1989; see also Johnston, 1993c), the main arguments were reiterated in a later article (Kirk, 1963). Kirk stressed that the environment is not simply a 'thing' but rather a whole with 'shape, cohesiveness and meaning added to it by the act of human perception' (Kirk, 1963, p. 365); once this meaning has been ascribed, it tends to be passed to later generations. Thus he recognized two, separate but not independent, environments: a *phenomenal environment*, which is the totality of the earth's surface, and a *behavioural environment*, which is the perceived and interpreted portion of the phenomenal environment: 'Facts which exist in the Phenomenal Environment but do not enter the Behavioural Environment of a society have no relevance to rational, spatial behaviour and consequently do not enter into problems of the Geographical Environment' (p. 367). Since much geography is concerned with decision-making and its consequences, appreciation of the behavioural environment should be central to its study. Indeed, according to Ley (1977a) one cannot proceed without such awareness of what is in the behavioural environment: even an apparently neutral statement such as 'Pittsburgh is a steel town' is, he argued, a value-laden view of a geographer-outsider, which may not accord with the perceptions of the resident-insiders, so that:

> Too often there is the danger that our geography reflects our own concerns, and not the meanings of the people and places we write of ... The geographical fact is as thoroughly a social product as the landscape to which it is attached (Ley, 1977a, p. 12).

Scientific disciplines, as indicated in Chapter 1, usually comprise a number of 'invisible colleges', groups of scholars working on the same topic who refer to each other's publications. Wright, Lowenthal and Kirk were not members of any major college during the early 1960s, and so had very little impact on the first phase of behavioural work identified in the previous chapter. None of the three is in Pred's (1967, 1969) bibliographies, for example, nor referred to by Wolpert. Golledge, Brown and Williamson (1972, p. 75) make only a passing reference to Lowenthal's work:

> *Pursued by insightful researchers, the analysis of literary and other artistic data of past and present can have strong explanatory power. The subjective element in these attempts to assess the impact of spatial perception is acknowledged, but its presence in many other studies is more subtle and potentially damaging.*

Kirk (1978, p. 388) referred to his influence on non-geographers who adopted the concept of the behavioural environment, however, and Spate (1989, p. xix) commented on Kirk's initial paper, and its discussion at an IBG Conference, as 'the Catalytic Crystal in the Saturated Solution' (for a detailed exegesis of Kirk's work, see Campbell, 1989). The behavioural work of the mid-1960s was in the positivist mould; that of Wright, Lowenthal and Kirk just discussed was not, however, and so they were ignored by the former, who were in the ascendancy.

Several cultural and historical geographers took up the concept of the behavioural or perceived environments. One of the leaders was Brookfield, a British geographer with field experience, by the mid-1960s, of South Africa, Mauritius, New Guinea, and several Pacific Islands. In reviewing work by cultural geographers on other societies, he noted (Brookfield, 1964, p. 283):

> *A difference of approach is apparent between those who have an overtly chorographic purpose, who scarcely ever seek explanations in matters such as human behaviour, attitudes and beliefs, social organization, and the characteristics and interrelationships of human groups, and those whose inquiries are not primarily chorographic, and who are more inclined to undertake a search for processes as a means of reaching explanation.*

Social organization provides the key to many explanations, he argued, so that:

> *... when an individual human geographer is sitting down in one small corner of a foreign land, and seeks to interpret the geography of that small corner, then it is difficult for him to do so without trying to comprehend the perception of environment among the inhabitants* (p. 287).

Geographers had largely failed to delve into such details of social organization, however, because of the broad areal scale at which they tended to work, their concern with distributions rather than with processes, and their avoidance of what he terms 'micro-geography'. Inquiry in human geography should involve three stages:

1. General statements about areal patterns and inter-relationships;
2. Detailed local inquiries which follow up the questions about processes raised by these general statements; and
3. Organization of the general and local material to produce explanatory generalizations.

Brookfield argued for more micro-geographical studies at the second of these stages, to provide the foundation for the development of comparative methods with which generalizations could be forged (Brookfield, 1962; on comparative study in social science, see Taylor, 1996).

Brookfield's (1969, p. 53) later literature survey showed that, 'decision-makers operating on an environment base their decisions on the environment as they perceive it, not as it is. The action resulting from decision, on the other hand, is played out in a real environment'. Referring to the 'modern' behavioural work, as well as studies by cultural geographers, he pointed out the great problems involved in isolating the perceived environment – something which is 'complex, monistic, distorted and discontinuous, unstable and full of unwoven irrelevancies' (p. 74) – and of building it into an analytical methodology. Further data are needed, too, on such topics as work organization, time allocation, and budget allocation, on the meaning of consumption and of distance – all necessary tasks for the full understanding of people-environment systems.

The concept of the perceived environment has a considerable pedigree in historical-geographical scholarship, though without the current terminology, as illustrated by Glacken's (1956, 1967) seminal survey of societal attitudes to environments (see also Smith, N., 1984, and Pepper, 1984). Historical geographers, Prince (1971a) suggested, must study a trilogy of worlds:

1. The *real world*, as recorded in documents and in the landscape (though see Harley's, 1989, 1990, seminal papers on maps as selective documents);
2. The *abstract world*, as depicted by general models of spatial order in the past; and
3. The *perceived world*: 'Past worlds, seen through the eyes of contemporaries, perceived according to their culturally acquired preferences and prejudices, shaped in the images of their assumed worlds' (p. 4).

Using all three, it may be possible to explain landscape changes, which cannot be done by assuming processes from investigations of continua of data over time (see also Moodie and Lehr, 1976). Thus, 'it [is] the province of the intellect to observe the facts, to reduce them to order and to discover relationships among them, but it [is] the imagination which [gives] them meaning through the exercise of judgement and insight' (Prince, 1961–2, p. 21). Reconstruction of past environments is extremely difficult, however, for it involves seeing the written record through the cultural lens of the writer:

> A study of past behavioural environments provides a key to understanding past actions, explaining why changes were made in the landscape. We must understand man and his cultures before we can understand landscapes; we must understand what limits of physical and mental strain his body will bear; we must learn what choices his culture makes available to him and what sanctions his fellows impose upon him to deter him from transgressing and to encourage him to conform (Prince, 1971a, p. 44).

Perhaps the enormity of such a task explains why most successful reconstructions have concerned the relatively recent past, such as the perceptions which guided the settlement of the American West (e.g. Lewis, 1966), although Wright (1925) essayed a similar task for Europe at the time of the Crusades. More recently, representations of nineteenth-century Egypt have been explored (Godlewska, 1995; Gregory, 1995a) to illustrate how representations of that country were implicated in the development of imperial ideologies: Gregory (1994, p. 169) refers to the 'extraordinary importance' of Edward

Said's (1978) *Orientalism* for the development of critiques of those ideologies (see also Gregory, 1995b, 1997 and p. 293).

Not all perceived worlds refer to either past or present; some landscapes have been fashioned out of Utopian views of the future (Porter and Lukermann, 1975; Powell, 1971). In general, however, and whether of past, present or future, geosophy has not become a popular field of study, despite some intriguing essays (see Lowenthal and Bowden, 1975). But directly or indirectly, it has led to arguments for alternative approaches in human geography to those of the positivist, and those arguments form the material for the rest of this chapter.

The attack on positivism

From the early 1970s on, some cultural and historical geographers attacked the positivism of spatial science. To replace it, a variety of humanistic approaches has been proposed, focusing on decision-makers and their perceived worlds and denying the existence of an objective world which can be studied by positivist methods. The intent is to reorient human geography towards a more humanistic stance, to resurrect its synthetic character, and to re-emphasize the importance of studying unique events rather than the spuriously general.

Anti-positivism, idealism and historical geography

The various humanistic approaches have much in common, but they can be separated into different proposals in the present context. The first discussed here is associated with two workers who were together at the University of Toronto at the end of the 1960s; both are historical geographers.

The initial paper's basic theme (Harris, 1971) was that geography is a synthetic discipline, concerned with particular assemblages of phenomena and not with the science of spatial relations (see Cosgrove, 1996). Thus:

> When the history of North American geography in the 1950s and 1960s is written, a paradox with which it will have to deal is how, with little argued, logical justification, so many geographers came to see their subject as a science of spatial relations (Harris, 1971, p. 157).

With May and Sack (p. 135), Harris saw the spatial perspective producing a dismemberment of geography, as specialists communicate more with their contemporaries in other disciplines than with other geographers, and develop theories that are descriptions of how the world might operate under certain conditions, rather than of how it actually works:

> The difficulty in conceiving of geographical theory comes down to this. The development of theory is necessarily an exercise in abstraction and simplification in which the complexities of particular situations are eliminated to the point which common characteristics become apparent. But if geography is thought to have a particular subject matter, it is certainly not individual phenomena or categories of phenomena which other fields do not study. Rather it is a whole complex of phenomena, many or all of which may be studied individually by other fields but which are not studied elsewhere in their complex interactions (p. 162).

The clear parallel is with history, for 'Few historians would attempt to develop a general theory of revolutions. In so doing they would lose grasp of the type of insight that characterizes good historical synthesis' (p. 163). The goal of both history and geography is synthesis, therefore. In developing syntheses, positivist methods may be applicable: historians may be law-consumers, applying the generalizations of other social scientists to particular events, and geographers could operate likewise. Alternatively, both historians and geographers could apply the idealist method, arguing that all activity is based on personal theories. Thus Harris (1978, p. 126) – who gained his PhD at the University of Wisconsin where he was supervized by Andrew Clark (see p. 67) and was also clearly influenced by Hartshorne – wrote of a 'historical mind':

Such a mind is contextual, not law-finding. Sometimes it is thought of as law-applying but, characteristically, the historical mind is dubious that there are overarching laws to explain the general patterns of human life.

It is open and eclectic, he argued, uses no formal research procedures, sees things in context, is sensitive to motives and values, excludes little, and is wary of sweeping generalizations. Its goal is understanding, not planning, and this should be the case with the 'geographical mind' too. To understand an event is to appreciate why it took place, which is the humanistic goal: to explain an event is to predict it, as an instance of a general law or suite of such laws, and that is the positivist goal. (Interestingly, few others have addressed this issue of a 'geographical mind'. Two have been attracted to a parallel concept of 'geographical imagination'. To Harvey – 1990 – the geographical imagination focuses on 'the historical geography of social conceptions of space and time', with the goal of stimulating critical reflection on the spatial and temporal components of alternative societies to capitalist; to Gregory – 1994, p. 11 – it involves the roles of space and time, plus nature, in everyday life, just as Mills's – 1959 – sociological imagination involves the dialogue of biography and history.)

Developing his theme of the parallel between history and geography, Harris (1971, p. 167) identified four points of agreement concerning the nature of history:

1. Its primary concern is with the particular;
2. Explanation may take into account the thoughts of relevant individuals;
3. Explanation may make use of general laws; and
4. 'Explanation in history relies heavily on the reflective judgement of individual historians.'

From these, he concluded that, 'If geography aims to describe and explain not so much particular events or peoples, as particular parts of the surface of the earth, then these points of agreement about history also apply to geography' (p. 167). (The term 'particular parts' can be widely interpreted, it would seem, and Harris (1977) himself sought to understand the nature of northwestern European colonizing societies 'by a model': the implication is that colonists had a common reaction to the 'new world'.) The landscape results from actions; behind those actions lie thoughts; study of thoughts allows understanding of landscape. Thus synthesis is crucial, since:

the idea of synthesis itself becomes more important as it becomes obvious that our larger problems transcend narrow subject-matter fields … integration … in a larger understanding is still achieved, however aided by statistical methods and computers, by the judgement of wise men who have cultivated the habit of seeing things together (p. 170).

Geographers are presumably to be those wise individuals. This was not an original claim for, according to Buttimer (1978a, p. 73), the basis of Paul Vidal de la Blache's work was that:

The task which no other discipline with the possible exception of history claims is to examine how diverse phenomena and forces interweave and connect with the finite horizons of particular settings. Temporality and spatiality are universal features of life so historical and geographical study belong together.

Positivist work seeks the same end — interweaving parts of a whole — but its parts are instances of general laws, not unique events.

Many of Harris's arguments were extended by his Toronto graduate student, Leonard Guelke, whose first paper was a strong criticism of the 'narrowly conceived scientific approach' (Guelke, 1971, p. 38) to geography using the positivist method. He argued against geography as a law-seeking activity by asking the proponents of the positivist approach to indicate how their laws would meet the basic standards of scientific acceptability, particularly with regard to prediction. Whereas they might be able to produce generalizations concerning the phenomena which they actually studied, he felt it very unlikely that they could generate laws applicable to all examples of the relevant phenomena. Statistical regularities are not laws and:

Until the new geographers have shown that the laws that might conceivably be discovered in geography will be more than generalizations, which describe common but non-essential connections between phenomena, their claims must be treated cautiously … there is little cause for optimism, especially as the statistical methods widely employed by geographers cannot be considered appropriate law-finding procedures (p. 42).

Regarding geography as a law-applying science, Guelke argued that laws of human behaviour are virtually impossible to conceive in anything but the most generalized form, because so much behaviour is culturally specific; an *a priori* statement of the determining conditions for their operation is thus not feasible so that, 'Human geographers cannot consider themselves to be law-applying scientists … because they have no laws to apply' (p. 45).

Turning to the use of theories and models in geography, Guelke pointed out that for them to serve a valid purpose in the pursuit of understanding, criteria must be specified which indicate how such devices are testable against reality (see also Newman, 1973, on the vague use of the term 'hypothesis'). Such criteria have not been, and cannot be, stated, Guelke claimed; for example, studies purporting to test central place theory seemed to operate on the rule that 'one counts one's hits but not one's misses' (p. 48; see also Guelke, 1978, p. 50). Too often, failure to reproduce reality was explained by claims that the test environment was not entirely suitable, and *ad hoc* hypotheses are frequently adduced to account for observed disparities. Models and theories may have heuristic value for human geographers, clarifying certain aspects, therefore, but they can have no explanatory power. Guelke (1971, pp. 50–1) concluded that:

> The new geography ... has not yet produced any scientific laws and ... appears unlikely to produce them in the future. ... The theories and models ... are not amenable to empirical testing. ... The new geographers insisted on ... logical and internally consistent theories and models. Yet, none of their theoretical constructs were ever complex enough to describe the real world accurately. They had achieved internal consistency while losing their grip on reality.

His offered alternative to that discredited procedure was the idealist approach mentioned by Harris, which is 'a method by which one can rethink the thoughts of those whose actions he seeks to explain' (Guelke, 1974, p. 193). All actions, according to the idealist, are the result of rational thought, the parameters of which are constrained by a theory, which is, 'any system of ideas that man has invented, imposed, or elicited from the raw data of sensation that make connections between the phenomena of the external world' (p. 194). Many such theories are part of the individual's society and culture; they include its religions, myths and traditions. Using them, 'the explanation of an action is complete when the agent's goal and theoretical understanding of his situation have been discovered. ... One must discover what he believed, not why he believed it' (p. 197; but see Sayer, 1981). Thus human geographers do not need to develop theories, since the relevant theories, which led to the action being studied, already exist (or existed) in the minds of the actors involved. The analyst's task is to isolate those theories (a task of considerable difficulty, according to Curry, 1982a, because people cannot always identify the reasons for their actions). Some of them may be unique to particular individuals, but most are shared in large part by (sometimes great) numbers of actors; they represent the order which people themselves have stamped on the world, and do not require further theories in order to be understood.

Guelke's argument was challenged by Chappell (1975), who pointed out that by focusing on the individual actor alone the idealist omitted any reference to the environmental constraints and influences on that person's actions (see also Gregory, 1978a). Guelke (1976) accepted the existence of such constraints and influences, but claimed that their investigation lay outside the geographer's domain. Study of environmental causes would, he felt, lead into physiology and psychology and deviate attention from 'the most critical dimension of human behaviour, namely the thought behind it' (p. 169). Chappell (1976) responded that, 'to go so far as to say that there is no possible respectable theory to explain man's rational theories and the actions which flow from them' (p. 170) is to be myopic: 'paradigms not only explain facts but they guide the research of whole disciplines' (p. 171). To him, Guelke's contention that the ultimate causes of actions lie outside the scope of human geography places geographers in an inferior position in the academic division of labour.

In a further essay, Guelke (1975) promoted his ideas on idealist approaches to historical geographers, as a counter to the arguments that they should adopt the approaches and techniques of positivism. He argued that:

It is obvious that quantitative techniques will often be useful. . . . Statistical methods put in harness with positivist philosophy are a dangerous combination. . . . Historical geographers need to rethink not their techniques but their philosophy. . . . This can best be achieved by moving from problem-solving contemporary applied geography towards the idealist approach widely adopted by historians (p. 138).

Gregory (1976) agreed with the first part of this statement, but not with the proposed solution. Like Chappell, he saw the need to investigate individual action within its constraining structures (see p. 242 and Curry, 1982a).

Positivist approaches in human geography were defended against the idealist attack by Hay (1979a), who both responded to the criticisms and raised points of contention with the proposed alternative. He argued that Guelke's case is ill-founded and rests on misconceptions of the nature of positivism, such as:

1. That all theory must be both normative and based on conceptions of optimal decision-making;
2. That to be scientific is to be nomological; and
3. That prediction is the same as prophecy (rather than simply testing, from the known to the unknown).

He also claimed that Guelke presented an anti-positivist argument by using a positivist test, and failed to realize the value of *ad hoc* hypotheses in the improvement of theory (the basis of Lakatos's concept of a research programme and its positive heuristic − p. 12): Guelke should not, according to Hay, ask 'does this theory explain Y?' but rather, 'does this theory contribute to an understanding of Y?' − again, a pragmatic approach to knowledge (does it work?).

Regarding the idealist alternative, Hay raised the problem of studying groups rather than individuals. To Guelke (1978, p. 55):

The assumption that thought lies behind human action is not related to the numbers involved. . . . If thousands of people drive motor cars to their places of work the idealist assumes that each of these journeys is a considered action involving thought. In such situations the investigator will not be able to look at each case individually, but he will seek to isolate the general factors involved in typical circumstances . . . [for which he] might well make use of statistical procedures . . . the value of statistical analysis will largely depend on its successful integration in the general interpretation or explanatory thesis being developed.

This procedure is akin to that employed by the behavioural geographers. Such a procedure, Hay contends, does not give ontological status to groups as collections of individuals in which, as with 'traditional' regions, the whole is greater than the sum of the parts. Second, Hay points out that objective facts must influence behavioural outcomes, in addition to the thoughts of the actors: Columbus found America, because it was there (although he didn't recognize it as such). Third, he claims that the idealist position ignores the possibility of either unconscious or subconscious behaviour. In sum, idealism is reductionist, but the world is more than a large number of independent decision-makers.

Idealism was also criticized by Mabogunje (1977), who claimed that, 'Such a retreat from objective theory formulations as a means of seeking explanation to certain events would exclude from our consideration the exploration of the consequences of societal actions' (p. 368). Instead of retreating to a focus on particular cases – 'seek[ing] special explanation for each situation in which a different value system can be shown to be operative' (p. 370) – geographers should attempt to build better theories encompassing these differences in value systems. Others asked how an idealist interpretation can be verified. (Mercer and Powell, 1972, raised the same question regarding phenomenology – p. 201; they wondered whether two phenomenologists can ever have the same 'intuitions' of a phenomenon, or indeed know whether they have.) Guelke was prepared for this argument, presenting the analogy of the court of law, rather than the positivist's laboratory, for his Popperian procedure. A well-verified idealist explanation is one in which a 'pattern of behaviour can be shown to be consistent with certain underlying ideas. Where data are presented which are not in accordance with a proposed explanation a new hypothesis will be needed' (Guelke, 1978, p. 55), which contradicts somewhat his earlier statements that theory should not be imposed from without by the observer. Even so, 'one cannot guarantee mistake-free interpretations. The complex nature of human societies and lack of pertinent data make it inevitable that many idealist interpretations will be of a tentative character' (p. 55), a position which is very similar to Moss's (1977) outline of deductive procedures in historical explanation.

The idealist philosophy, according to Guelke (1981b, p. 133), combines two positions: a metaphysical argument that 'mental activity has a life of its own which is not controlled by material things and processes'; and an epistemological argument, 'that the world can only be known indirectly through ideas ... all knowledge is ultimately based on an individual's subjective experience of the world, and comprises mental constructs and ideas. There is no "real" world that can be known independently of mind'. Positivist spatial science is criticized because it believes in the existence of a 'real' world, whose nature it seeks to explain via general laws of behaviour. Behavioural geography is similarly criticized, not for its acceptable (to Guelke) premise that behaviour is a response to perceived images and subjective evaluations, but rather because of two assumptions within this field: 'that identifiable environmental images exist that can be measured accurately ... [and] that there are strong relationships between revealed images and preferences and actual (real-world) behaviour' (Bunting and Guelke, 1979, p. 453). Such an approach traps human geographers into single-cause models, much like environmental determinism, and even if one accepted this model, research in behavioural geography has failed to validate it. They argued for an idealist perspective, which focuses on overt behaviour and its interpretation: 'In searching for the truth a scholar conducts a critical dialogue with his evidence and in due course he puts the results before his colleagues for their appraisal' (p. 458). In response, Downs (1979), Rushton (1979) and Saarinen (1979) claimed that Bunting and Guelke misrepresented much behavioural geography and argued that although the study of overt behaviour may give clues as to the answers to 'Why?', only the study of decision-making can provide understandings of value in planning, as in the work on environmental hazards. Golledge (1981a, p. 1328), also responding to Bunting and Guelke, claimed that to qualify as behavioural geography research may focus on the overt act, but more importantly the set of explanatory variables must include 'one or more process variables'.

Curry (1982a) criticized Guelke's idealist programme on a number of grounds. Central to Guelke's argument is the claim that positivist science methods are irrelevant to the study of human behaviour; the latter results from rational thought, and thus can only be explained by reconstructing that thought. There is then a single answer to the question 'Why did you do that?', which forms the explanation. But, according to Curry:

> First, in our daily lives we do many things for which, at the time, we consciously entertain no reason; at the same time, we hardly consider these actions to be non-rational. Second, we often, both at the time and after the fact, give reasons that are not the 'real' reasons for our actions. And, third, we can often attribute reasons to behaviour in which they were patently not involved (p. 43).

Those reasons, which may not be readily explored, may be examples of individuals following rules, whether consciously or not, and such rules need not be determinate – as in chess, where the rules identify what moves are possible in a given situation but do not define which will be followed in any particular game. Thus we must study behaviour in its context:

> Without appeal to rules human action would be random and, hence, incomprehensible. The idealist geographer … must consider the human world as a whole as imbued with the same sort of normative significance as that found in the more limited area of rules or maxims of actions (p. 46).

In response, Guelke (1982) restated his position that geography is an ideographic discipline seeking to understand the 'complexity of human activity on the land' (p. 52), drawing the boundaries such that, 'The geographer is not concerned with explaining fluctuations in wheat prices or the level of interest rates, but he is concerned with the impact that these factors might have on, say, farming in western Canada' (p. 53). In seeking to understand the reasons for any action, he accepted that stated reasons may not always help and that a 'historical reconstruction of thought' is necessary to explicate the learned response which is 'part of an individual's cultural heritage' (p. 54); this does not require exploring the subconscious forces that may have influenced the composition of that heritage, however.

Nevertheless, Guelke accepted much of Curry's case, claiming that, 'for both of us human geography is concerned with understanding the meaning of human activity on the earth's surface in its unique cultural contexts' (p. 57). Curry (1982b) disagreed, however, arguing that 'we remain very much farther apart than he believes' (p. 59), because he wishes to understand the processes that produce the thoughts behind actions that are Guelke's sole interest. Pickles (1986, p. 34) followed Curry in arguing that idealism, as promoted by Guelke, is not concerned with understanding that is 'empathetic in an emotional sense' but rather requires conformity 'to rules of inference and evidence'. Guelke remained committed to his cause, however, and two decades later wrote in a review of Gregory's (1994) discussion of European colonization in *Geographical Imaginations* that (Guelke, 1995, p. 185):

The geostrategic thinking of both the colonists and the colonized needs to be reconstructed in a way that provides a convincing explanation of how one group subdued others and how colonization itself was sustained within ideologies of white supremacy. This task involves explorations of how people saw themselves in societies and in relation to the earth, and of the contrasts that existed between different systems of knowledge and territorial control and exploitation as they actually articulated themselves in specific geographical circumstances.

Phenomenology and related approaches

Phenomenology attracted more attention from human geographers than idealism. The first direct advocacy for a phenomenological approach was by Relph (1970), who was also associated with the Department of Geography at the University of Toronto. Despite a variety of specific interpretations, he noted that phenomenology's basic aim is to present an alternative methodology to the hypothesis-testing and theory-building of positivism, an alternative grounded in people's lived world of experience. Phenomenologists argue that there is no objective world independent of human existence – 'all knowledge proceeds from the world of experience and cannot be independent of that world' (p. 193). Thus, according to Entrikin (1976, p. 617), 'phenomenologists describe, rather than explain, in that explanation is viewed as [an observer's] construction and hence antithetical to the phenomenologist's attempt to "get back" to the meaning of the data of consciousness'. (Seamon, 1984, p. 4, defines phenomenology as a 'descriptive science'.)

Phenomenology in human geography is concerned with what Kirk termed the phenomenal environment (p. 191). That environment's contents are unique to every individual, for each of its elements is the result of an act of intentionality – it is given meaning by the individual, without which it does not exist but through which it influences behaviour. Phenomenology is the study of how such meanings are defined. It involves researchers identifying how individuals structure the environment in an entirely subjective way; the researchers are presuppositionless, using no personal ideas in seeking to understand their subjects' ideas. (Thus the subjectivity is that of the focus of the study, not that of the researcher who, in the positivist method, imposes a personal subjective view of the world: Ley, 1980.) Phenomenologists may be satisfied with such empathetic understanding, but some seek to go further, however, and identify essences – elements in individual consciousness which control the allocation of meanings (Johnston, 1983b; Pickles, 1988, p. 252, distinguishes between 'transitional essences' and 'invariant and universal structures (understood carefully)'). Phenomenology, then, studies human appraisals. It works at the individual level, but may search for the common (imprinted not agreed) elements among those appraisals.

Relph's paper was followed by one from another geographer briefly associated with the University of Toronto, Yi-Fu Tuan (1971), for whom geography is a mirror, revealing the essence of human existence and human striving: to know the world is to know oneself, just as careful analysis of a house reveals much about both the designer and the occupant. The study of landscapes is the study of the essences in the societies which mould them, in just the same way that the study of literature and art reveals much of human life. Such geographical study has its foundations in the humanities, rather than the social or physical sciences. Tuan (1974, 1975b) illustrated it in a number of essays, giving, for example, insights into such topics as the sense of place (Tuan, 1976, pp. 266–7):

> Humanistic geography achieves an understanding of the human world by studying people's relations with nature, their geographical behavior as well as their feelings and ideas in regard to space and place … Scientific approaches to the study of man tend to minimize the role of human awareness and knowledge. Humanistic geography, by contrast, specifically tries to understand how geographical activities and phenomena reveal the quality of human awareness.

Tuan exemplified this with five themes: the nature of geographical knowledge and its role in human survival; the role of territory in human behaviour and the creation of place identities; the inter-relationships between crowding and privacy, as mediated by culture; the role of knowledge as an influence on livelihood; and the influence of religion on human activity. Such concerns are best developed in historical and in regional geography; their value to human welfare is that they clarify the nature of the experience (see also Appleton, 1975, 1994). Indeed, Tuan (1978, p. 204) claimed that, 'The model for the regional geographers of humanist leaning is … the Victorian novelist who strives to achieve a synthesis of the subjective and the objective', and quoted the first two pages of E. M. Forster's *A Passage to India* as a paradigm example.

Tuan's corpus of work has not involved philosophical explorations, and he rarely claims allegiance to any particular approach. Rather, he has been involved in a variety of explorations of the inter-relationships between people and environments:

> … my point of departure is a simple one, namely, that the quality of human experience in an environment (physical and human) is given by people's capacity – mediated through culture – to feel, think and act … I have explored the nature of human attachment to place, the component of fear in attitudes to nature and landscape, and the development of subjective world views and self-consciousness in progressively segmented spaces (Tuan, 1984, p. ix).

Thus, for example, he shows that fear is both a representation of the environment and an influence on the creation of environments (Tuan, 1979), that the creation of residential segregation reflects the retreat of individuals from wholes to segmented parts (Tuan, 1982), and that the construction of gardens reflects a desire to dominate the environment (Tuan, 1984). Such works are implicitly phenomenological in that they suggest the existence of general essences, or behavioural stimuli, but the term is not in the index to any of his books. Indeed, as Gregory (1994, pp. 79–80) argues:

> One of the most persistent motifs in Tuan's writings is an appeal to common sense and common experience: to a 'we' whose inclusive address presumes a shared human condition to which 'we' have access without theoretical mediation. His humanistic geography is, in essence, a moral-aesthetic discourse; it is contemplative, at once reflective and speculative, and yet – despite the model of the ideal conversation – at best studiously indifferent to the wider conversations that might be made possible through the theoretical.

These explorations by Tuan have covered a wide range of topics within what Gregory (1994, p. 385) terms 'ways of being-in-the-world'. Tuan, whose first work (including his

PhD) was in geomorphology, grounds his work in his desire to answer his wonderings, since childhood, regarding 'the meaning of existence: I want to know what we are doing here, what we want out of life' (Tuan, 1999, p. 94) – what he terms 'the big woozy questions' and which he related to his own individuality – 'my apartness from others' – which aroused in him both pride and anguish, and which resulted him being comfortable in the open environments of deserts but dreading rain forests. The title of his autobiographical chapter on his research interests is 'Salvation by geography', because the discipline has 'directed my attention to the world, and I have found there, for all the inanities and horrors, much that is good and beautiful' (p. 115). His books and other essays illustrate those discoveries from the point of view of (p. 10):

> ... a maverick in the discipline to the degree that, unlike most other geographers, my landscapes are 'inscapes', as much psychological conditions as material arrangments.

They are thus individual and particular, but assist others in illuminating their own 'inscapes'.

Tuan's 'inscapes' mean that he focuses more on place than space, from that binary pair of major geographical concepts (as in Tuan, 1977), thus to some extent seeking to correct the bias towards space that characterized 'geography as spatial science, and seeks to present them as complementary perspectives'. (For Taylor – 1999, p. 10 – Tuan's 'generally undervalued' 1977 book, which provides 'explicit treatment of what are arguably geography's two core concepts by unarguably one of the discipline's leading thinkers' has 'featured only marginally in the stories told of geography's recent past'; it was reprinted in 2001). In a volume dedicated to Tuan and produced to mark his retirement, however, Adams et al. (2001) focus on place, something with texture, with a shape and feel which 'provides a glimpse into the processes, structures, spaces and histories that went into its making' (p. xiii), suggesting a weaving of the terms text and context and which is conveyed through conversations (or communication acts: p. xiv). For them *Textures of Place* (p. xiv) involves highlighting:

> ... the geographic tradition of trying to understand the meanings and processes of place – their material and symbolic qualities – as well as the range of peoples and social relations that continuously define and create social and spatial contexts.

In this mould, knowing the world involves knowing oneself – a goal that they associate with Tuan's (1974) writings on topophilia. But for Tuan it is more than just 'knowing oneself'. For him (Tuan, 2002a, p. 323; see also Tuan, 2002b):

> Geography is indispensable to survival. All animals, including American students who consistently fail their geography tests, must be competent applied geographers. How else do they get around, find food and mate, avoid dangerous places? History, in striking contrast, is an esoteric field of knowledge, and for that reason it plays only a small, indeed negligible role in the common tasks of life. It is not too far-fetched to call animals geographers, but it is to call them historians. With animals and probably most human beings, knowledge of the past is folded into present time and space – into geography, where the challenges of living lie.

Among other advocates for phenomenology, Mercer and Powell (1972, p. 28) argued that the use of positivism in geography 'left the subject with too many technicians and a dearth of scholars'; they claimed that land-use patterns can never be understood 'by the elementary dictates of geometry and cash register' (p. 42) and the world can only be comprehended through people's intentions and attitudes towards it. In a lengthy discussion of phenomenology and its development in other disciplines, notably sociology, they pointed to 'a very real danger of the research worker assuming that concepts which are cognitively organized in his own mind "exist" and are equally clearly organized in the minds of his respondents' (p. 26). They argued instead for research methods involving empathy between researcher and researched, which for geographers means 'that we make every effort to view problems and situations not from our own perspective, but from the actor's frame of reference' (p.48) – a position that they term 'disciplined naiveté'.

Buttimer (1974) made a similar case for geographers studying the values which permeate all aspects of living and thinking. The order, precision and theory produced by positivists are dearly bought – 'we often lose in adequacy to deal with the values and meanings of the everyday world' (p. 3) – and behavioural geography similarly fails to break away from the mechanistic, natural scientific view of humans as preconditioned responders to stimuli. Ley (1981) also identified the positivist elements in behavioural geography and the suggestions of operand conditioning: people are assumed to act in predetermined ways to particular stimuli, and so can be manipulated accordingly. On the other hand, 'An existentially aware geographer is ... less interested in establishing intellectual control over man through preconceived analytical methods than he is in encountering people and situations in an open, inter-subjective manner' (Buttimer, 1974, p. 24). Such activity results in 'a meditation on life', with geographers providing more comprehensive mirrors than their colleagues from more specialized disciplines can achieve, thereby clarifying the structural dynamics of life. Prediction would be impossible, apart from 'the most routinized aspects of experience' (p. 29), but the deeper appreciation achieved would allow much more vital social action and planning than is possible using spatial science and behavioural approaches.

Buttimer (1976) also directed geographers' attention to the concept of 'lifeworld', an amalgam of the worlds of facts and affairs with those of values in personal experience – 'the pre-reflective, taken-for-granted dimensions of experience, the unquestioned meanings, and routinized determinants of behavior' (p. 281). Positivism should be rejected for analysing the lifeworld because it separates the observer from the object of study and thus constrains appreciation of the human experience. Idealism should also be rejected, because it accepts the existence of a 'real world' outside the individual's consciousness. Phenomenology, on the other hand, provides a path to understanding, on which informed planning can be built:

> It helps elucidate how ... meanings in past experience can influence and shape the present ... extremely important as preamble not only to scientific procedure, but also as a door to existential awareness. It could elicit a clearer grasp of value issues surrounding one's normal way of life, and an appreciation of the kinds of education and socialization which might be appropriate for persons whose lives may weave through several milieux (p. 289).

The result is an understanding of actions as those involved understand them, rather than in the terms of abstract, outsider-imposed models and theories. Having achieved that understanding, human geographers can transmit it, thereby helping the subjects of their investigation to understand themselves better and realize their potential. In this way, the applied geographer acts as a provocateur, stimulating human development but not forcing it (Buttimer, 1979).

Berry (1973b, p. 9) backed this phenomenological orientation, calling for 'a view of the world from the vantage of *process metageography*. By metageography is meant that part of geographic speculation dealing with the principles lying behind perceptions of reality, and transcending them, including such concepts as essence, cause and identity' (p. 9). But not all accepted that phenomenology can entirely replace the positivist approach. Walmsley (1974), for example, accepted the merits of Buttimer's case because so many human decisions are based on 'experiential' rather than 'factual' concepts, but argued that the scale of geographical enquiry, and its long tradition of certain types of empirical work, required maintaining the positivist orientation. That the perceived world is not necessarily the same as the real world must be realized, but 'logical consistency and empirical truth will remain central to geographical enquiry provided the importance of values is recognized' (p. 106).

Gregory (1978a) criticized both positivism and phenomenology. Those favouring the former were condemned for making 'social science an activity performed *on* rather than *in* society, one which portrays society but which is at the same time estranged from it' (p. 51) and for supporting a procedure which, because it so often assumes *ceteris paribus* in testing its models, can never be sure why these fail to replicate reality (p. 66). He recognized the need for humanistic approaches, but argued that these would not be sufficient to provide a satisfactory foundation, because they ignore the 'constraints on social action which are so much part of the taken-for-granted life-world of the actors' (Gregory, 1978b, p. 166). Thus, 'A geography of the life-world must therefore determine the connections between social typifications of meaning and space-time rhythms of action and uncover the structures of intentionality which lie beneath them' (Gregory, 1978a, p. 139). But, 'A major deficiency ... is [the] restricted conception of social structure: in particular, it ignores the material imperatives and consequences of social actions and the external constraints which are imposed on and flow from them' (*ibid.*). Phenomenology and idealism must be incorporated with investigations of those imperatives and constraints; such incorporation produces a critical science, whose nature is discussed in Chapter 6.

Whereas a key feature of the positivist/spatial-science approach was a great numerical superiority of practitioners over preachers, the phenomenological movement (like the idealist) was initially characterized by the converse – much preaching but relatively little practice (Relph, 1981a, pointed to the absence of substantive applications of the phenomenological approach in geography, though see Jackson and Smith, 1984, p. 44):

> There is an essential difference between the contemplative intentions of this transcendental philosophy and the practical concerns of a social science, so that it is scarcely surprising that ... geographers' ... efforts have been directed towards the destruction of positivism as a philosophy rather than the construction of a phenomenologically sound geography (Gregory, 1978a, pp. 125–6).

Tuan's interpretative essays exemplify its use, and Relph, who 'would much prefer to see substantive applications rather than discussions of the possible uses of phenomenology'

(1977, p. 178), published his thesis on *Place and Placelessness* in which – implicitly, he says – phenomenological methods are used 'to elucidate the diversity and intensity of our experiences of place' (Relph, 1976, p. i). His essential themes are the sense of place and identity in the human make-up and the destruction of this through the growing placelessness of modern design (see also Porteous, 1988). Other work generally quoted as phenomenological includes pieces on European settlement of the New World. Powell (1972), for example, has written on images of Australia; his major work on the settlement of Victoria's western plains (Powell, 1970) examined the conflict between official and popular environmental appraisals, the dialogue between these, and the learning process which resulted in the final settlement pattern (see also Powell, 1977, where he presents the study of eiconics, or image-making, in the context of colonization processes). Billinge (1977, p. 64) queried whether such works are really phenomenological, however:

> ... the idea has spread that since certain branches of our discipline are less susceptible to quantitative reduction (and, so the argument continues, by false extension, to scientific analysis), we can justify our partially formulated hypotheses, exploit the atypicality of our data, cease worrying about the validity of our reconstruction and within some weakly articulated framework label the whole exercise phenomenological.

The study of perceived environments represents an 'important and vigorous movement' (p. 65), but Billinge argued that phenomenology is not just the study of such environments: its method is presuppositionless, concerned with the human consciousness and not only its output, thus 'phenomenological we have by no means become' (p. 67) since geographers have paid little attention to consciousness. Much work claimed as phenomenological is probably closer to the idealist position, since it does not seek to isolate essences.

Geographers' attempts to adopt a phenomenological approach were trenchantly criticized by Pickles (1985), not because he opposed them in principle but rather because he believed that those undertaken were misconceived. He accepted that, if for no other reason than its attack on positivism, 'It cannot be denied that the founding and guiding intuitions of a phenomenological approach in geography as it exists at the moment are in the main sound and well intentioned' (p. 68), but argued that work such as Buttimer's and Relph's 'is ungrounded method, unfounded claims, and the actual imposition of unexamined propositions' (p. 71). His criticisms led him to contend that 'we now need to move from what passes for phenomenology in the geographical literature, *towards* what is actually the case in phenomenology itself' (p. 89). Quoting substantially from Husserl's and Heidegger's original works, he argued that phenomenology is not concerned to explicate subjective meanings as an end in itself, but rather 'to be the science of science through explicating the science of beginnings' (p. 97). Its goal is to identify the essences that underpin individual meanings:

> The essential relation between an individual object and its essence – such that to each object there corresponds its essential structure, and to each essential structure there corresponds a series of possible individuals as its factual instances – necessarily leads to a corresponding relationship between sciences of fact and sciences of essence (p. 111).

The subjectivity of the lived world is to be explored for the insights that it can provide on those essential structures, the underpinnings of knowledge itself.

According to this interpretation, phenomenology has much in common with certain forms of structuralism in its basic concern with neither empirical appearances nor actual decision-making but rather with the deep structures of consciousness (see p. 228; Johnston, 1986f; Pickles, 1988, p. 252, implies this too). Thus it does not fit easily into the humanistic concerns of most geographers who have espoused phenomenology, which Pickles identifies as the search for those essences that give rise to the necessity for geography, as the empirical science concerned with particular facets of behaviour. (Each empirical science should be grounded in such an essence.) Thus:

> we seek an ontological, existential understanding of the universal structures characteristic of man's spatiality as the precondition for any understanding of places and spaces as such. That is, we seek to clarify the original experiences on the basis of which geography can articulate and develop its regional ontology if geography as a human science, concerned with man's spatiality, is to be possible at all (p. 155).

Spatiality is that essence, he claims, best represented by the German noun *Raum* and verb *raumen*, 'which means to clear away, to free from wilderness or to bring forth into an openness. *Raumen* is thus a clearing away or release of places, a making room for the settling and dwelling of man and things' (p. 167). In this context, space and place are closely related concepts (see also Gould, 1981b).

Phenomenology is closely associated with existentialism, and some geographers have experienced difficulty in separating the two (Entrikin, 1976). Whereas phenomenology assumes the primacy of essence – the allocation of meanings results from the existence of consciousness – for existentialists the basic dictum is 'being before essence – or man makes himself'. The process of defining oneself (creating an essence) involves creating an environment. Thus Samuels (1978, p. 31) argued that environments can be read as biographies – 'for every landscape or every existential geography there is someone who can be held accountable'. Generalization may be possible from analysing such landscapes. Appleton (1975), for example, suggested that landscapes reflect two primal needs – prospect (the need to search for the means of survival), and refuge (the need to hide from threatening others) – although individuals and groups may satisfy these in particular ways (as he illustrates from his autobiography: Appleton, 1994). Lowenthal (1975; see also Lowenthal, 1985) argued that individuals rewrite their biographies, and those of their ancestors, by their choices of what to preserve in the landscape.

All of this suggests that humanistic geography is concerned either with the study of individuals and their construction of, plus behaviour in, phenomenal environments (as in Rowles, 1978) or with the analysis of landscapes as repositories of human meaning. As such, it is separate from the subject matter of much human geography, notably behavioural geography and its investigation of everyday activity within environments. But the phenomenological perspective has been adapted to the latter type of work also, in the application of Schutz's writings on the 'taken-for-granted' world (Ley, 1977b). Much everyday behaviour is unconsidered, in that it involves no original encounters with new situations. The behaviour is habitual, because all of the stimuli encountered can be processed as examples of particular types. Those types are not externally defined for the individual, but are personally created. The phenomenology of the taken-for-granted world is the study of those individually defined typifications – of the unconsidered 'world of social reality' rather than 'a fictional non-existing world constructed by the scientific observer' (Ley, 1980, p. 10, quoting Schutz; see also Curry's (1982a, p. 38) discussion of 'the ordinary, everyday actions of individuals' which create for the geographer 'a complex world of complex places and actions' in which the role of the individual decision-maker 'can be determined only on an individual basis, case by case'). Interaction within communities may lead to shared typifications, which quantitative methods may be used to identify descriptively.

Humanistic geography is based on a profound critique of positivist work, which it claims makes major unwarranted assumptions about the nature of decision-making, and seeks inductive laws of human behaviour that can be scientifically verified (Ley and Samuels, 1978; Powell, 1980b). Its counter-argument promotes understanding of the individual as a 'living, acting, thinking' being. To some, however, it is just a criticism – Entrikin (1976, p. 616) argues that:

> humanist geography does not offer a viable alternative to, nor a presuppositionless basis for, scientific geography as it is claimed by some of its proponents. Rather the humanist approach is best understood as a form of criticism. As criticism the humanist approach helps to counter the overly objective and abstractive tendencies of some scientific geographers.

For others, however, the human condition can only be discerned through humanistic endeavour, for attitudes, impressions and subjective relations to places (the 'sense of place') cannot be revealed by positivist research. As Pickles (1986, p. 42) put it, 'The value of humanism has been its resilience in consistently raising questions which do not fit within other frameworks ... humanism has been the voice of man against reason, against science'.

Some critics argue that humanistic geography focuses on relatively trivial matters and not on the major foci of an applied geography concerned with improving the world. To Buttimer (1979, p. 30) the latter form of applied geography is managerial, manipulating individuals and their environments rather than seeking to advance the process of 'human becoming'. To Relph (1981b, pp. 139–41) it implies geographism: 'the view that people should behave rationally in geographical, two-dimensional space ... that cities and industries and transportation routes should be arranged in the most efficient way' which, when used as a basis for planning, 'will diminish the distinctiveness and individuality of ... communities and places. Geographism involves the imposition of generalizations onto specific landscapes; it breeds uniformity and placelessness'. Both of them argued that planning should emphasize subjectivity and individuality. Scientists, engineers, and planners may seek to improve well-being, but in so doing they make people rootless and deny them individuality. Planning must be allied with environmental humility, by which 'places and communities would increasingly become the responsibility of those who live and work in them instead of being objects of professional disinterest' (Relph, 1981b, p. 201). In this context, humanistic geography is not only a reaction against the dehumanizing treatment of people in spatial science and behavioural geography, but also an argument against an applied geography which imposes that treatment on the landscape, and for a form of anarchism in which individuals are encouraged to realize what they are and how they can control both themselves and their environments (see also Pickles, 1986, p. 47). Seamon (1984) has reviewed a substantial volume of phenomenological work, illustrating that it is 'a learning tool which can help us to discover more about ourselves, others, and the world in which we live' (p. 21), and which may then have practical value in environmental design.

The practice of humanistic geography

Much of the practice of humanistic geography has been concerned with exploring and explicating the subjectivity of human action and its base in meanings (both individual and shared), with relatively little concern for the claims of idealist, phenomenological, existentialist, and other philosophies. (Curry, 1996, p. 16, claims that although the earliest figures involved in the break from positivism all referred to phenomenology, for example, 'it seems fair to say that none took it very seriously'.) To the extent that such work is explicitly influenced by philosophical and methodological writings, the (albeit usually implicit) stimulus is more often the *pragmatism* (and symbolic interactionism) developed by the Chicago school of sociologists in the 1920s and 1930s (and largely overlooked by human geographers who paid much more attention to the relatively small amount of spatial analysis undertaken by that school, as typified by the Burgess model of the internal structure of cities: Johnston, 1971). Pragmatism portrays life as a continuous process of experience, experiment and evaluation through which beliefs are continually reconstructed; such reconstruction is a social process, whereby individuals learn and behave in the context of the beliefs of those with whom they interact (hence the term interactionism: see Jackson and Smith, 1984, Chapter 4; both Smith, 1988, and Jackson, 1988, illustrate this in their own research).

Understanding social life within this broad framework involves participatory field work (as detailed in Evans, 1988), the methodology of which (according to Smith, S., 1984, p. 353) is 'a hallmark of much geographic humanism'. This, she continues,

> ... requires a commitment to fieldwork, with the aim of securing data lodged in the meanings ascribed to the world by active social subjects. The strength of this strategy derives from the unique insight it offers into 'lay' or 'folk' perceptions and behaviors. True to the pragmatic maxim, the method allows the truth of a social reality to be established in terms of its consequences for those experiencing it (pp. 356–7).

How local societies work is thereby explicated, which was the goal of the ethnographic work of the Chicago school (Jackson, 1984, 1985); Ley's (1974) detailed portrayal of a Philadelphia community illustrates this, as does his general textbook on urban social geography (Ley, 1983).

Field studies, involving interaction with residents over long or short terms, provide only one source of information about how people structure their lives. There are other *texts*, other repositories of meanings: Pocock (1983) described humanistic strategies ranging 'from library search, to the observational, to the experiential' (p. 356). The landscape, the creation of those who live/have lived in it, is an important text, and Lowenthal (1985) provides a perspective on its study: he portrays it not as a mirror of the past but rather as an insight to the present:

> Traditions and revivals dominate architecture and the arts; schoolchildren delve into local history and grandparental recollections; historical romances and tales of olden days deluge all the media. The past thus conjured up is, to be sure, largely an artifact of the present. However faithfully we preserve, however authentically we restore, however deeply we immerse ourselves in bygone times, life back then was based on ways of being and believing incommensurable with our own. The past's difference is, indeed, one of its claims: no one would yearn for it if it merely replicated the present. But we cannot help but view and celebrate it through present-day lenses (p. xvi).

The present landscape is a conglomerate of relics from many different periods in most cases, and by preserving only parts of it we bias our representation of the past:

> Every act of recognition alters survivals from the past. Simply to appreciate or protect a relic, let alone to embellish or imitate it, affects its form or our impressions. Just as selective recall skews memory and subjectivity shapes historical insight, so manipulating antiquities refashions their appearance and meaning. Interaction with a heritage continually alters its nature and context, whether by choice or by chance (p. 263).

Thus, when use of the landscape as a text involves reading the outcome of a long sequence of selective retentions of earlier forms, so that we learn about what parts of their history people wanted to build into their own presents and futures, 'We must concede the ancients their place … But their place is not simply back there, in a separate and foreign country; it is assimilated in ourselves, and resurrected into an ever-changing present' (p. 412). The past does not exist independently of those who seek to interpret it (as Taylor, 1988, makes clear in a very different context); the landscape may tell us more about the past which people wanted to preserve than about the past as it was experienced. (It also tells us much about the people who describe it, as Porteous, 1986, illustrates in his discussion of body imagery as a metaphor for landscape description.) Study of current processes of landscape-creation illustrate this process, as with the creation of various types of 'living museum' and the promotion of places as 'cities of spectacle' (as in Crang, 1994; Jacobs, 1994).

An increasingly-used text for the explication of meanings is literature – or 'creative literature' in White's (1985) term; Porteous (1985, p. 117) refers to 'imaginative literature', with which geographers have been highly selective:

> Plays are not considered, poetry is but occasionally used, the novel reigns supreme. The advantages of the novel lie in its length (meaty), its prose form (understandable), its involvement with the human condition (relevant), and its tendency to contain passages, purple or otherwise, which deal directly with landscapes and places in the form of description (geographical).

He argued that when using novels as texts, geographers have concentrated on nineteenth-century, rural contexts (as in Darby's, 1948, paper on Hardy's Wessex). To correct this, he proposed a two-variable categorization of situations according to whether the subject is an insider or an outsider and whether the place being described is 'home' or 'away'. The 'home-insider' provides material on sense of place, whereas the much less frequently reported 'away-outsider' refers to those experiencing alienation in a placeless world. (White's, 1985, use of novels to describe migrants' situations fits readily into this category.) 'Home-outsiders' are people who fail to develop insider relationships with their milieux, whereas 'away-insiders' are travellers reporting their experiences (as in 'road, tramp, and down-and-out novels'; Porteous, 1985, p. 119). Such distinctions are reflected in a collection of essays about literature and migration (King, Connell and White, 1995), which distinguishes between migrants' autobiographical accounts and general fiction about migration (Duffy, 1995). These are used to explore the renegotiation of identity that accompanies migration experiences (White, 1995), but as texts they are subjected to less critical scrutiny than that undertaken by deconstructionists (p. 285). Similarly, science fiction and related literature gives insights to imaginative geographies of the future: it 'maps out possible future spatialities of the postmodern condition, and provides cognitive spaces which are being used by individuals and institutions in conceiving and making future society' (Kitchin and Kneale, 2001, p. 32).

Much humanistic geography has been written to describe and appreciate the variety of the human condition, as it is experienced. (Eyles's, 1989, essay, in a volume designed to 'introduce some of the most exciting challenges of the contemporary subject to a wider audience' writes of place and landscape without reference to philosophy.) It has been relatively unconcerned with philosophical issues, such as the origins of meanings in human consciousness, and has focused almost entirely on the empirical worlds of experience, even if these have to be interpreted from secondary sources, although Watson (1983), himself a prize-winning poet, claimed that literature is not a secondary source but 'primary source material for the whole world of images' (p. 397) that illustrates the 'soul' of a place. Its relevance, according to Pocock (1983), is that:

> ... it attempts to unravel the nature of being-in-the-world, as it explores the existential significance of place as an integral part of human existence. In short, it is a geographical contribution to the most fundamental of questions, 'what is man?' (p. 357).

Meinig (1983, p. 325) expresses this more vigorously:

> By limiting ourselves to describing and measuring and analyzing certain aspects of the world as it seems geographers have denied themselves the possibility of probing very deeply into what it all means. Being unable to convey what it means we cannot help shape it toward what it might become.

Explicating what it means involves practising geography as art – placing the discipline firmly in the humanities as well as the sciences and the social sciences – as illustrated by Meinig (2002) in a biographical essay.

One problem for such work, brought home to geographers by Olsson in a series of iconoclastic essays (Olsson, 1978, 1979, 1982; see also Pred, 1988), is that the medium of the text is constraining as well as enabling. He focuses on language as the most frequently used medium, with the constraints that word definitions and usages put on their application, hence the modes of thought that they support. Thus (Olsson, 1982, p. 227):

. . . any social scientist is handicapped by the methodological praxis which requires him to be more stupid than he actually is. Thus, in the interests of discipline, verification and communication he relies mainly on the two senses of sight and hearing: what counts is what can be counted: what can be counted is what can be pointed to; what can be pointed to is what can be unequivocally named. Accumulation of knowledge about the nameable is consequently the point of the scientist's game.

Thus ambiguity is translated into certainty; describing a phenomenon in words allocates it to a category, and can over-simplify its complexity. Hence our ability to think is made possible by the richness of language, yet also constrained by the categorizations that it imposes; the former aids our understanding but the latter can hinder it (as critical theorists and poststructuralists have explored: see Chapter 7).

Geographers' involvement in humanistic work involves more than interpretation of texts, however, since they themselves create new texts in transmitting their appreciations to others, usually in writing but also through maps, lectures and other media. This involves what is sometimes referred to as a double hermeneutic. Initially developed for the exegesis of biblical texts, *hermeneutics* was developed by Dilthey (Rose 1980, 1981) to embrace all studies which involve scrutinizing an author's intentions when evaluating a text. This involves what Dilthey termed *Verstehen* (interpretative understanding), which not only enables students of a text to appreciate its author but also to increase their own self-awareness (Giddens, 1976, p. 17):

Understanding a text from a historical period remote from our own . . . or from a culture very different from our own is . . . essentially a creative process in which the observer, through penetrating an alien mode of existence, enriches his own self-knowledge through acquiring knowledge of others.

Thus an applied humanistic geography promotes both self-awareness and awareness of others. A double hermeneutic is involved because it is not only: 'the job of human geographers to interpret such texts as a spectator in order to make certain statements about actors operating within the texts', but also 'to communicate the meanings of such phenomena as he should deem important back to the actors involved' (Rose, 1981, p. 124) as well as to others who wish to understand those meanings. Thus the reader of a research paper by a humanistic geographer is only interrogating those meanings through their interpretation by an intermediary – the humanistic geographer. The latter's selection of those items 'deemed important' means that different geographers may transmit different interpretations of the same text, in the same way as two biographers might interpret a novelist's texts differently and two artists may differ in their portrayal of the same landscape. (On hermeneutics in geography, see Livingstone, 2002.)

Humanistic and cultural geography
Detailed debates about philosophy and methodology in geography have engaged only a minority of the discipline's practitioners, so far as the empiricist/positivist approaches are concerned, whereas a majority have conducted their own empirical inquiries informed by those debates but only marginally connected to them. To a considerable extent this has been the case with humanistic geography too, with Hugill and Foote (1994, p. 18)

contending that whereas humanistic geographers turned to such philosophies and methodologies as 'ethnomethodology, existentialism, idealism, phenomenology, symbolic interactionism, and transactionalism ... [although] successful applications of each of these can be found in the geographical literature ... none captured the imaginations of more than a handful of geographers at a time'.

A small number of writers have been concerned with philosophical underpinnings and the relative merits of different humanistic approaches, but more have accepted the general tenor of the argument, described by Boal and Livingstone as (1989, pp. 7–8):

> We can give up the need to find direct empirical connections between terms and objects in the world; we can view knowledge not as presenting the world in some correct way, but as just helping us to get along in it, or to change it. Truth, to repeat, has nothing to do with accurately representing, or, as Rorty has it, mirroring reality; it is just, according to Rose [1987], 'what we are well advised, given our present beliefs, to assert'. The purpose of geography, then, is not to tell us about how the world 'really' is: it tells us nothing about regions or landscapes or economic structures or human agency, because these are mere linguistic fictions; it is just the search for the right vocabulary, the right jargon, the best discourse in which to pursue the kinds of account which help us, in the most basic sense, decide what to do.

Doing that, according to Pickles (1986, p. 29), involves 'archaeology', uncovering the layers of human behaviour to identify the experience that underpins it, which involves the explication of texts – the 'written records, cultural artefacts, urban landscapes or whatever' (Boal and Livingstone, 1989, p. 15) – which are the repositories of human meanings, and whose interpretation is the goal of humanistic geography.

Some of the work undertaken within this humanistic framework, and without the explicit philosophical underpinnings, goes under the rubric of *cultural geography*, which has a long and distinguished background, notably in the United States, based on the work of Sauer. The suggestion of a break between an 'old' and a 'new' cultural geography was denied in the review in *Geography in America*: Rowntree, Foote and Domosh (1989, p. 215) argued that, 'Although traditional cultural geography has preferred topics with historical depth, there is increasing interest and emphasis on the study of everyday life and landscapes'. They recognized that trends originating in Britain, as promoted by Cosgrove and Jackson (1987), differed substantially from the more traditional concerns (as represented in the chapter on cultural ecology in the same volume: Butzer, 1989; see also Turner, 1989). 'Whether the British trajectory becomes an integral part of North American cultural geography remains to be seen': quoting Kofman (1988), they suggested that 'the "new" cultural geography is more talked about than done' (p. 209). Hugill and Foote (1994, p.18), however, saw the introduction of humanistic approaches (as exemplified by Ley and Samuels', 1978, anthology) as 'an attempt to define a "new" cultural geography' in an 'attempted coup' which failed. Furthermore, they also portrayed a conflict between traditional cultural geography as practised in North America and that promoted in the United Kingdom:

> ... a large number of [American cultural] geographers had continued to cultivate the traditional themes of the Berkeley school ... These geographers felt little need to accept humanistic geography and resented its new agenda. Humanistic research had little to say about traditional concerns. The

unfortunate mismatch between American cultural geography and British social geography compounded problems of assimilation. The contributions of British social geography to recent advances in humanistic cultural geography have been increasing . . . but the overlap is slight.

Duncan (1994, p. 401) refers to this debate as:

. . . a civil war [that] has been going on in cultural geography since the early 1980s. This struggle has largely, though not exclusively, had an intergenerational character, younger cultural geographers trained in the late 1970s and 1980s assailing the positions of an older generation trained in the 1950s and 1960s.

The main issue, he argued, was theory:

The younger generation launched its attacks using an arsenal of theory-seeking weapons provided by suppliers in the humanities and social sciences. Some direct hits were scored on the lightly camouflaged theories of the older generation, but such hits proved indecisive in the war for a number of reasons. Many of the older generation were unaware that they had any theories in their camp: others insisted that these were relic theories long since abandoned. Still others claimed that the theoretical targets had in fact been surreptitiously inserted into their camp by the younger generation to discredit them. At any rate, they argued that no meaningful losses had been sustained.

Others (e.g. Price and Lewis, 1993a) argued that the older generation was far from homogeneous in its views, however, and that 'traditional cultural geography' was being misrepresented by those advancing an alternative position.

Cosgrove and Jackson (1987) pointed not only to the continued vitality of cultural geography as the interpretation of past and present landscapes and other texts (for which they appropriated the term iconography, as in Cosgrove and Daniels, 1988; see also Powell, 1977, to whom they do not refer), but also to growing contacts with contemporary social geography. (Soon after they wrote, the Social Geography Study Group of the IBG was renamed the Social and Cultural Geography Study Group.) The field of contemporary cultural studies offered 'alternative ways of theorising culture without specific reference to the landscape concept' (p. 98), they claimed, with its emphasis on contemporary sub-cultures and their political struggles rather than 'the elitist and antiquarian predilections of traditional cultural studies'. This is illustrated in a special issue of *Society and Space* (Gregory and Ley, 1988), and in Jackson's (1989) text *Maps of Meaning* which begins with a definition of culture that characterizes the 'new' cultural geography (p. ix):

This book employs a more expansive definition of culture than that commonly adopted in cultural geography. It looks at the cultures of socially marginal groups as well as the dominant, national culture of the elite. It is interested in popular culture as well as in vernacular or folk styles: in contemporary landscapes as well as relict features of the past.

The work of Sauer and the Berkeley school (p. 106) is criticized for being relatively narrow; culture is instead linked by Jackson to the contested concept of ideology, and his substantive chapters cover popular culture, gender and sexuality, racism and language (see Chapter 7). An agenda for future work suggests an even wider coverage, into aspects of social relations that impinge upon the economic organization of society and thus link cultural geography more firmly with aspects of radical geography (as discussed, in Chapter 6). Work in this mould will presumably further the challenge to the content of traditional cultural geography as 'innocent' (Rowntree *et al.* 1989, p. 214).

More recently, the concept of culture has itself been examined. The definition adopted by Duncan and others, in contrast to the 'superorganicism' of the Berkeley school and its followers, is described as, 'socially constructed, actively maintained by social actors, and supple in its engagement with other "spheres" of human life and activity' (Mitchell, 1995, p. 102). For those who adopt this position, culture exists as, according to Cosgrove and Jackson (1987, p. 95), 'the very medium through which change is experienced, contested and constituted'. To Mitchell (1995, p. 103) this means that:

> *Culture, therefore, can be specified as something which both differentiates the world and provides a concept for understanding that differentiation. Culture itself is a sphere of human life every bit as important as, yet somehow different from, politics, economy and social relations. It is an important ontological category which must be theorized and understood if we hope to understand human differentiation, behaviour, experience and contest.*

Against this, he argues that, 'there is no such (ontological) thing as culture. Rather there is only a very powerful *idea* of culture, an idea that has developed under specific historical conditions and was later broadened as a means of explaining material differences'. As with the superorganic conception, he contended, the concept of culture promoted by the 'new cultural geography' involves reification and its adherents have reached 'something of a dead end' (p. 104): 'While important empirical work exploring the social creation of many aspects of life continues, none of this work has been able adequately to explain what culture is. Cultural geography has remained incapable of theorizing its object'.

Attempts to define culture, according to Mitchell, involve an infinite regress, using terms which themselves are neither internally coherent nor inclusive (see the later discussion on metaphors, p. 285). The regress is ended by claims that cultures exist and the term is used as part of a strategy to define and control:

> *The naming and representation of cultures create partial, yet globalizing, truths. By localizing social interaction into discrete cultures … contentious activities are abstracted into the partial truth contained in the idea of culture: namely that there are true and deep differences between people.*

This strategy is crucial in many aspects of life, such as geopolitics (see p. 291) and the promotion of consumerism (p. 307): indeed, as the essays in Lee and Wills (1997) illustrate (see also Thrift and Olds, 1996; Wheeler, 2002b), it is increasingly difficult to separate out the cultural from the economic. For Mitchell, therefore, (1995, p. 112):

> *… like 'race', 'culture' is a social imposition on an unruly world. What does exist, and very importantly, is the historical development of the idea of culture as a means of ordering and defining the world … Culture is an idea that integrates by dividing; it is a strategy for control, like territoriality, and its study calls for investigations of how the concept of culture has been used to promote both positive and negative views of societies (of 'us' and 'them').*

As such, many cultural geographers have been deeply involved in developments during the 1990s characterized below as 'the cultural turn'.

We return to these issues in Chapter 7. For now, it is sufficient to note that whereas traditional cultural geographers pay little explicit attention to methodological concerns, those linked to the more recent developments have addressed a range of issues involved in the collection of 'data', through the interrogation of both texts and people's lived experiences. In this respect, Cook and Crang equate (a renewed) cultural geography with humanistic geography in terms of the methods adopted. There is a sense that one of the preconditions for such renewal, however, was the legacy of human-orientated research in geography which came to the fore in humanistic geography's critique of positivism and spatial science. 'Doing humanistic, or cultural, geography' involves a variety of methods often characterized as ethnographic and contrasted to the positivist approach (Cook and Crang, 1995, p. 4) as 'reading, doing and writing ... thoroughly mixed up' during the course of a piece of research rather than the 'conventional read-then-do-then-write sequence' of other approaches.

Cook and Crang note that one author has identified 43 different ways of conducting ethnographic research (Tesch, 1990), but focus on just four:

1. *Participant observation*, in which the researcher(s) lives in and/or works among a selected community in order to appreciate its values and ways of life, and then interprets that culture to a wider audience – the process involves researchers and community developing mutual (or inter-subjective) understandings;
2. *Interviewing*, which involves conversations between researcher(s) and researched, which can vary in the degree to which they are structured with pre-determined questions by the interviewer;
3. *Focus groups*, whereby researchers initiate information-collection by bringing together groups who interact as they discuss the issues raised by the researcher (and perhaps others which lead from them), thereby treating people as members of interacting communities that influence their behaviour rather than as isolated individuals; and
4. *Filmed approaches*, wherein visual material obtained from the research subjects indicate meanings and values which are not readily expressed in words (Rose, 2001).

Preparing for each of these approaches is a major task, as is the follow-up construction of the information obtained. A number of ethical issues is involved (geographers have paid much less attention to these than other social scientists, such as anthropologists, psychologists and sociologists, who depend on such approaches for their information, and whose learned societies have developed ethical codes of practice for field investigations) and the continued relationship between researcher(s) and the researched is of considerable importance. (On ethics in geography, see p. 339.) As Cloke, Philo and Sadler (1991, p. 92) put it, 'doing ethnography' lacks neither rigour nor academic merit: it is not, as some imply, a 'soft option' compared to the 'hard' spatial science:

. . . rather, it is to engage very honestly with both the enchantment and the problems associated with researchers trying to gain an insight into the worlds of other peoples in other places, and it is also to insist that this insight emerges not by supposing (as might a philosophically inclined phenomenologist or existentialist) that these peoples are basically the same as us but by letting them and their version of humanity simply be different.

Conclusions

A common thread links the material discussed in this chapter and the behavioural work discussed in the preceding chapter; both are concerned with positive rather than normative investigations, with attempts to uncover how humans behave in the world rather than with contrasts between actual patterns of behaviour in space and those predicted from normative theories. Both are also part of a more general trend towards an anthropocentric focus within the social sciences, which reflects reorientations in the external environment. From the mid-1960s on, there was a growing disillusion with science and technology, especially among students, and the popularity of the social sciences boomed. Within the latter, there was a shift in emphasis from study of the aggregate to the individual, an increase in the relative volume of research conducted at the micro-scale, and growing unease about the role of social scientists in planning mechanisms. Both behavioural (or behaviourist) geography and the various humanistic approaches reflect these trends.

Beyond the general concern with the individual as a decision-maker, little else connects the two types of work, however. Behavioural geography has maintained strong ties with the positivist/spatial-science tradition. Data are collected from individuals, but these almost all concern the conscious elements in action and their outcomes; they are usually aggregated in order to allow statistically substantive and significant generalizations to be made about spatial behaviour. In the humanistic strand, on the other hand, the intent has been to understand and to recognize the dignity and humanity of the individual, but there has not been a widespread embracing of the philosophies discussed in this chapter. Many (perhaps most) investigations in human geography from 1970 onwards have involved some behavioural concepts other than those of 'economic man', but relatively few human geographers have become humanistic geographers.

The two approaches remain distinctive. Behavioural geography treats people as responders to stimuli, and investigates how different individuals respond to particular stimuli (and also how the same individual responds to the same stimulus in different situations): by isolating the correlates of those varying responses it builds models that can account for, and potentially predict, the probable impact of certain stimuli. The end product is input to processes aimed at either providing environments to which people respond in a preferred way or at changing behaviour by changing the stimuli. (Such environmental planning is considered social engineering and control by some.) The other approach – humanistic geography – treats the person as an individual constantly interacting with the environment and with a range of communities, thereby continually changing both self and milieu. It seeks to understand that interaction by studying it, as it is represented by the individual and not as an example of some scientifically defined model of behaviour. And then by transmitting that understanding, it seeks both to reveal people to themselves, enabling them to develop the interactions in self-fulfilling ways, and to promote their appreciation by others.

The two approaches are thus not readily combined, since the concept of behavioural laws is out of sympathy with the humanist view centred on people's views and experiences.. Few adherents of either approach totally denigrate the other. Humanists recognize that behavioural geography and spatial science may be valid approaches to certain aggregate phenomena – such as trade flows (Ley, 1981; see also Tuan, 1977) and the planning of transport systems – and behaviouralists recognize that their methods are irrelevant to the study of emotions and aspects of landscape (as suggested in the two main ways of studying space: Sack, 1981). But the two have little in common and are competing for central positions as the philosophy of *human* geography.

For D. M. Smith (1988a, p. 266), humanistic work involved a 'new movement', and the chapters in the book that he edited with Eyles:

> ... have provided persuasive accounts of ways of interpreting the geographical world which are capable of challenging if not displacing prevailing orthodoxy or at least of providing a convincing alternative. The positivist and empiricist paradigm fixated by mathematical process modelling with a promise of policy relevance ... is already yielding to approaches more sensitive to actual human achievement.

For him, the struggle between paradigms continues, with humanistic interpretative work now being rich in empirical example as well as strong in philosophical criticism; as subsequent chapters here illustrate, it has also been integrated with other approaches to provide a wider appreciation of 'individuals in society'. But it has attracted relatively few adherents because, according to Gregory (1994, p. 78), too many humanistic geographers have been reluctant to 'engage more directly with theoretical concerns'. As the following chapters illustrate, setting human behaviour in a sharpened theoretical (and hence, for many, a geographical and political) context became a prime focus of much geographical work from the 1970s on.

6
'Radical' Geographies

Everyone who studies Marx, it is said, feels compelled to write a book about the experience.

(Harvey, 1982, p. 1)

... during the 'summer of love' (1967) geography was perhaps the least sexy subject, certainly in the English-speaking world. The influence of the intellectually conservative Richard Hartshorne ... still weighed heavily on US geography even as a new generation of positivists in Britain and the US were installing themselves as the next new thing. It is difficult to conceive of a discipline more uncool than geography in 1967. And yet, the influence of the anti-war movement in the US, the feminist and environmental movements, the Prague Spring of 1968, the anti-imperialist movement, radicals discovering socialism and Marx – all of these wider social eruptions in the late 1960s and early 1970s completely transformed the discipline. They had a greater effect on geography than on any other social science in the Anglophone world.

(Smith, 2001, p. 6)

Since the late 1960s a group of interrelated politicized approaches has developed within human geography, which are nevertheless hard to classify under an all-embracing single, descriptive adjective. The term initially favoured was 'radical' (see Peet, 1977, 1978, 1985b; Smith 1971), but this became less popular in the 1980s as that term was being applied to the political movements associated with the 'new right', 'Thatcherism' and 'Reaganomics'. More recently Blunt and Wills (2000, p. xi) use the term 'dissident geographies' for their textbook 'about radical ideas and practices, their geographical origins and manifestations and their implications for geographical thought'.

Today, the more common term is 'critical geography', although this includes a considerably wider range of work and influences than those of prior radical geographies (see Castree, 1999, for more on this relationship). Subsequently, much of the spirit of earlier radical geography has been incorporated into such 'critical', postmodern, poststructuralist and feminist geographies, as Chapters 7 and 8 detail. Anarchism has also had some influence via a radical rediscovery and celebration of the works of Kropotkin and Reclus, both late-nineteenth-century Russian and French anarchist geographers (see the summary in Blunt and Wills, 2000). In the late 1960s and 1970s however, radicalism was more clearly associated with the adoption of a Marxist (or Marxian: on the difference, see Harvey, 1973) approach. Thus in Gibson's (1991, p. 75) words:

It appears that the stature of human geography within the social sciences has changed dramatically over the last 20 years. From its location as a field of study uneasily straddling the earth sciences-social sciences divide and whose contribution to debates central to the study of society were rather defensively limited to spatial impacts and effects, geography has become 'flavour of the month', especially within left social science discourse. This shift has partly been produced by others 'discovering' geography – Giddens and Foucault, for example. But more importantly, I would say, it has been produced by changes within the discipline itself, particularly those wrought by the marrying of aspects of marxist and geographic theory and the incredible burst of vitality and productivity to which this gave rise. The work of geographers such as Harvey, Soja, Massey and Sayer is now almost as well known outside the discipline as within. Many of us have been surprised, and I suppose rather chuffed, by the way in which human geography has become more broadly validated. But even more surprising over this period has been the acceptance into 'mainstream geography' of significant elements of marxist theory.

For a few years – mostly during the 1980s – radical approaches also became caught up with debates about the merits of an approach to research known as 'philosophical realism' and about the potential for human geography of 'structuration theory' which had been developed by the sociologist Anthony Giddens. Embodying these, Cloke, Philo and Sadler's (1991) text contained an entire chapter on realist approaches in human geography and another on structuration theory. In Peet's (1998) more recent text these approaches are relegated to a wider chapter on 'Structuration, Realism and Locality Studies'. But Walker (1989a, p. 135) went as far to claim that, 'While not every realist is a Marxist as regards theory of society ... every Marxist must be a realist'. However, not all (indeed not most) of those geographers influenced by Marxism would agree with Walker (Lawson and Staeheli, 1991, characterize critical realism as an 'arcane sect') and, as this chapter (and the subsequent two) will show, geographers' adoptions of Marxism and the influence of other radical currents, such as feminism and anti-racism, have produced an enduring and heterodox radical presence in geography.

In his evaluation of their contribution to American geography, Walker (1989b) wrote of 'Geography from the left', which involved 'bringing the analytic framework and progressive social agenda of Marxism and allied schools of thought into most of the traditional subject areas of the discipline' (p. 619). The goal of achieving a 'more explicitly spatialized theory of capitalist societies' involved some scholars developing Marxist theory more fully, whereas others concentrated on methods and welcomed 'the clarifications that realism, critical theory, and structuration theory might add to the understanding of social processes and how to grasp them' (p. 620); others focused on 'middle level' theories of such topics as local labour markets. Walker (p. 620) argued that:

Left geographers can be proud of their achievements in a discipline that is not always noted for its explanatory depth or overriding concern with human oppression and liberation. The left can claim a good deal of credit for broadening the intellectual respectability of the geographic enterprise.

His review clearly illustrates the breadth of enquiry undertaken by 'the left' in geography over the preceding couple of decades. Also embodying these contributions, but no longer favouring the adjective 'radical', Peet and Thrift (1989, p. 3) selected the term 'political economy':

... to encompass a whole range of perspectives which sometimes differ from one another and yet share common concerns and similar viewpoints. The term does not imply geography as a type of economics. Rather economy is understood in its broad sense as social economy, or way of life, founded in production ... Clearly, this definition is influenced by Marxism ... But the political-economy approach in geography is not, and never was, confined to Marxism ... So while political economy refers to a broad spectrum of ideas, these notions have focus and order: political-economic geographers practise their discipline as part of a general, critical theory emphasizing the social production of existence.

This group of approaches began, however, as 'radical geography' in the 1960s, largely as a reaction to the crises of capitalism made clear in increased concern about the persistence of deep pockets of poverty within the supposedly affluent Western societies, the domestic and international response to the American war in Vietnam, the US Civil Rights movement (beginning with a call for an improved status for African-Americans, but later encompassing other 'racial', 'ethnic' and 'cultural' minorities), the nascent Green (ecological and conservation) movement, and the wider rise of a 'counter-culture' (perhaps epitomized by the 'hippies' of the late 1960s and early 1970s) that questioned the 'mainstream' way of life. These were accompanied by the 'sexual revolution': changing social mores and a sense of increased sexual freedom in Western societies – although it would be a few years more before these mores were further questioned by the women's and gay liberation movements (see Chapter 8). The late 1960s and 1970s also saw a period of creative reinterpretation of Marx(ism) in the aftermath of the Stalinist orthodoxy which prevailed in preceding decades. This was both an intellectual movement, led by scholars in Western universities, and a practical politics of revolution and social change, especially in those parts of the Third World where national liberation and revolutionary movements came or aspired to power. Looking back to this moment, Harvey (1999, p. xi) notes that:

Marx seemed to speak to those of us (always a minority of course) who were seeking a theoretical basis to understand the chaos and political disruptions surrounding us at the time (the imperialist war in Vietnam, the strikes and urban unrest, the civil rights movement, the student movements of 1968 that shook the world from Paris to Mexico city, the Czech 'spring' and its subsequent repression by the Soviets, the war in the Middle East – just to name a few of the signal events that made it seem as if the world as we knew it was falling apart).

The Spanish geographer Horacio Capel, (1981 pp. 426–7 – our translation) thus notes how, in American geography of the late 1960s:

That which just a few years before [quantitative geography] had been received as the truly scientific method, seemed now clearly unsatisfactory or a mystification.

Capel designates 1969 as a significant moment in the emergence of radical geography:

Firstly, the 1969 annual meeting of the Association of American Geographers at Ann Arbor saw a critical mass of radical papers and manifestos. Secondly, in 1969 commenced the publication of a journal which, in its very title already expressed its aspiration to situate itself in the antipodes of geography as it was then practised: Antipode. A Radical Journal of Geography.

Capel also notes that at the same time William Bunge initiated his so-called 'geographical expeditions' to 'marginal urban areas' (see Merrifield, 1995, and p. 337) and that other geographers increasingly participated in political and citizens' movements. Finally, Capel notes that while the actual numbers of radical geographers were never large, radical geography constituted:

> ... an extraordinarily active movement that has extended its critique to very diverse fields of academic geography and forced it to encounter authentically radical alternative trajectories (p. 427).

Subsequently, as the revolutionary pressures of the late 1960s became a distant memory, the ideas and critical insights of radical geography percolated into and then – to a significant extent – became part of the intellectual mainstream of Anglo-American human geography. However, what, two decades on, Peet and Thrift (1989) termed geography as 'political economy' had became 'more sober and less combative' (p. 7). There was a number of reasons for this. In the first place, Marxism was subjected to renewed criticism. Secondly, the recession and restructurings of the 1980s (which included cuts in academic budgets) led to a more sober and cautious intellectual atmosphere than the heady days of the late 1960s when everything seemed possible. At the same time, greater awareness of the problems of state socialist economies and a wider sense that the tide of history had tipped against statist and socialist projects made the prospects of revolutionary or radical change more precarious. Finally, radical geography became more narrowly professional, and some of the 'radical, anti-establishment Young Turks' joined the establishment (see Barnes, 1996, p. 49). Nevertheless, Peet and Thrift conclude (p. 7) that:

> The political-economy approach ... has survived counterattack, critique, and economic and professional hard times, and has matured into a leading and, for many, the [their emphasis] leading school of contemporary geographic thought.

Radical beginnings

Peet (1977) has claimed that the early 'radical' work by geographers in the late 1960s was mostly liberal in its interpretations and aspirations:

> Radicals investigated only the surface aspects of these questions – that is, how social problems were manifested in space. For this, either we found the conventional methodology adequate enough or we proposed only that existing methods of research must be modified to some extent if they are to serve the analytic and reconstructive policies of ... radical applications (Wisner, 1970, p. 1) ... we were fitting into an established market ... we were amenable to established ways of thinking ... we were useful in providing background ideas for the formulation of pragmatic public policy directions, and so could not, and were not, engaging in radical analysis and practice (p. 245).

Initially, the purpose of much writing in the emerging radical framework was to demonstrate the shortcomings and lacunae of positivist-inspired (and related behavioural) research. Gray (1975), for example, presented a critique of studies of the operations of housing markets which mapped people's residential moves and inferred that these were the outcomes of choice and the expressions of preferences. He argued that such research:

1. Assumes that people are free to choose in which homes (including where) they live, when most are constrained to particular types of dwellings in certain parts of urban areas only;
2. Accepts that residential patterns are the consequence of a large number of residents' decisions rather than those of a few developers and institutional managers; and
3. Implies that the study of consumers provides the key to understanding the structure of urban areas.

People are not free to choose, however: 'Instead, many groups are constricted and constrained from choice and pushed into particular housing situations because of their position in the housing market, and by the individuals and institutions ... controlling the operation of particular housing systems' (p. 230). Research in line with Gray's critique focused on the controllers of access to housing, individuals who became known as 'urban managers'. According to Pahl's (1969) influential paper, urban residential patterns are the consequence of two basic sets of constraints: the spatial constraints on access to resources and facilities, which are usually expressed in terms of time/cost distance; and the social constraints – the bureaucratic rules and procedures operated by gatekeepers – that govern access and reflect the distribution of power in society. Study of the latter focused on the key managerial groups, such as building societies and their lending policies (Boddy, 1976; Dingemans, 1979), the managers of local government housing stock (Gray, 1976; Taylor, 1979), the local authority officials who influence the redevelopment of private housing (Duncan, 1974a, 1975), and the real-estate agents who structure access to housing sub-markets (Palm, 1979). Subsequently therefore, urban geography became a key entry point of radical ideas into the discipline. This was given further impetus by the evolution of radical perspectives in the neighbouring field of urban sociology and the inauguration of the multidisciplinary *International Journal of Urban and Regional Research* (IJURR) which was founded under the auspices of the International Sociological Association (ISA) research committee on the sociology of regional and urban development in 1977.

The reception of Pahl's work is a case in point (he was trained as a geographer, with a PhD from the LSE, but then worked in a sociology department). In the 1970s, Pahl was widely read and cited among radical geographers (especially in the UK and Europe). Pahl himself continued to revise his ideas, pointing out that planners, for example, are merely 'the bailiffs and estate managers of capitalism, with very little power' (1975, p. 7; see also Pahl, 1979) so that focusing on them and other gatekeepers tends to:

> ... view the situation through the eyes of disadvantaged local populations and to attribute more control and responsibility to the local official than, say, local employers or the national government ... such 'a criticism of local managers of the Caretaking Establishment' and 'of the vested interest and archaic methods of the middle dogs' may lead to an uncritical accommodation to the national elite and society's master institutions (pp. 267–8).

Whereas the managerial approach focuses on the agents who interpret and activate the real mechanisms, producing patterns of residential segregation, Harvey paid much more attention to the mechanisms themselves (though with reference to particular outcomes: Harvey, 1974e). Residential separation is one means of reproducing class differences in a capitalist society. It is produced by those who manage finance capital, interpreting the basic mechanisms of the capitalist mode of production (i.e. the need to generate profits), and it results in a series of spatially separated housing sub-markets within which individual households may express their preferences, producing micro-scale migration patterns:

> But there is a scale of action at which the individual loses control of the social conditions of existence … [sensing] their own helplessness in the face of forces that do not appear amenable, under given institutions, even to collective political mechanisms of control (Harvey, 1975a, p. 368).

In the American context the promotion of suburbanization was a major means of stimulating consumption (of housing, automobiles, consumer durables, etc.) at a time of dangerous latent over-production (Harvey, 1975b, 1978; Walker, 1981a; for the particular outcomes, see Johnston, 1984b). Thus, urban geographers who accepted the Marxist argument saw their basic task as integrating discussions of the mechanisms that drive capitalist (and other) societies, the interpretations of those mechanisms by key agents (the managers and gatekeepers), and the empirical outcomes and experiences. They focused on how and why society operates, not on generalizations regarding the empirical outcomes (as in Bassett and Short, 1980; Badcock, 1984; Johnston, 1980b). However, the study of urban residential patterns is just one element of the wider study of urbanization, which Scott (1985, p. 481) – in ways that echoed Harvey's developing work on the urbanization of capital – related to the complex nature of capitalism:

> … the mechanisms of production, the interlinkages of firms, and the formation of local labor markets … combine to create a process in which the profit-seeking (cost-reducing) proclivities of producers lead directly to the dense spatial massing of units of capital and, as a corollary, of labor.

The influence of the initial move to radical urban geography has thus been long and enduring. Subsequent work has explored how cities are both labour markets and places for the reproduction of labour, involving what Castells (1977) and others term 'collective consumption' of commodities produced by the state rather than purchased in the market place (see also Pinch, 1985, 1997) – although the shift to 'privatize' these has itself become a domain of critical analysis, amidst other regulatory shifts (see p. 232). Here, however, we are getting ahead of the story of the formation of radical geography in the late 1960s and early 1970s.

The move from liberal interpretation to radical and Marxist critique was also illustrated in Peet's (1971) paper on poverty in the United States – in which, like Morrill and Wohlenberg (see p. 337), he argued for a series of growth centres in the poverty areas to stimulate economic development and job creation – and also by the tenor of the articles in early issues of the radicals' journal, *Antipode*. Morrill (1969, pp. 7–8), for example, argued:

> … against the 'New Left' premise that a revolution is the only route to progress … the dreams of revolution are naive … the 'New Left' vastly exaggerates potential support … a 'revolutionary program' is hopelessly dated and simplistic … the 'New Left' underestimates the capacity of our

society for change. . . . All revolutions seem to have been betrayed by incompetents who preferred exercising power to executing reform.

Again, he argued (Morrill, 1970b, p. 8) that:

A simple Marxist-type change in the ownership of business from private to a government (or union) bureaucracy would in all probability decrease production, and would not necessarily bring any improvement in basic conditions. The key is to retain the institution of private property while instituting social control over its exchange and circumscribing its power over people.

The case for a Marxist approach was first presented formally by Folke (1972) in a critique of Harvey's (1972) paper on ghetto formation and counter-revolutionary theory. Folke represented geography and the other social sciences as:

. . . highly sophisticated, technique-orientated, but largely descriptive disciplines with little relevance for the solution of acute and seemingly chronic societal problems . . . theory has reflected the values and interests of the ruling class (p. 13).

Liberal cases like Morrill's were dismissed as unlikely to succeed. Morrill's two papers in *Antipode* argued for change to be brought about by political consensus, producing a capitalist-socialist convergence. But this is the social democrat method practised in Sweden (and then also influential in other left of centre parties, such as the French socialists, German Social Democrats and British Labour Party) where, according to Folke (1972, p. 15):

. . . it has been shown over and over again that the idea of equal influence for employers and employees is an illusion. After half a century of social-democratic rule injustices and inequalities still prevail. . . . No small group of experts can accomplish anything . . . when it runs counter to the interests of the dominant social forces. These are not interested in equality or justice, but in profit.

Radical change requires mass mobilization and so, to Folke, Harvey's call for a new paradigm within geography was insufficient. What was needed was a new paradigm for a unified social science, containing geography, which deals with problems in all their complexity and provides not only theory but also the basis for action: 'Revolutionary theory without revolutionary practice is not only useless, it is inconceivable . . . practice is the ultimate criterion of truth' (p. 7; see also Eliot Hurst, 1980, 1985).

The major contribution to the case for a Marxist-inspired theoretical development within geography was subsequently made by David Harvey, initially in his collection of essays *Social Justice and the City* (Harvey, 1973). The book is presented as autobiographical, illustrating the evolution of Harvey's views towards an acceptance of Marx's analysis:

. . . as a guide to enquiry . . . I do not turn to it out of some a priori sense of its inherent superiority (although I find myself naturally in tune with its general presupposition of and commitment to change), but because I can find no other way of accomplishing what I set out to do or of understanding what has to be understood (p. 17).

The first part of the book, entitled 'Liberal Formulations', comprises essays which analyse problems of inequality within societies in terms of income-allocating mechanisms; the role of accessibility and location in those mechanisms is stressed. This leads into an attempt at defining territorial social justice, which separates the processes allocating incomes from those which produce them. Only in the second part of the book – 'Socialist Formulations' – is it:

> . . . finally recognized that the definition of income (which is what distributive justice is concerned with) is itself defined by production. . . . The collapse of the distinction between production and distribution, between efficiency and social justice, is a part of that general collapse of all dualisms of this sort accomplished through accepting Marx's approach and technique of analysis (p. 15).

Harvey (2000, pp. 77–8) has recently noted how he had become disillusioned with the evident limits to the socialism of the British Labour party in the late 1960s (the government of Harold Wilson). However, it was his move to the United States (from the University of Bristol to Johns Hopkins University, Baltimore) at the end of the 1960s that sharpened his political commitment. Thus, when he wrote *Explanation in Geography* (Harvey, 1969a) in 1968 (which, as Chapter 4 above charts, was a key text setting out the prospects for a positivist and quantitative geography):

> . . . my politics at that time were closer to a Fabian progressivism, which is why I was taken with the ideas of planning, efficiency and rationality. . . . So in my mind, there was no real conflict between a rational scientific approach to geographical issues, and an efficient application of planning to political issues. But I was so absorbed in writing the book that I didn't notice how much was collapsing around me. I turned in my magnum opus to the publishers in May 1968, only to find myself acutely embarrassed by the change of political temperature at large. By then, I was thoroughly disillusioned with Harold Wilson's socialism. Just at that moment, I got a job in the US, arriving in Baltimore a year after much of the city had burnt down in the wake of the assassination of Martin Luther King. In the States, the anti-war movement and the civil rights movement were really fired up; and there was I, having written this neutral tome that seemed somehow or other just not to fit. I realized I had to rethink a lot of things I had taken for granted in the sixties (Harvey, 2000, p. 78).

That political stance did not disappear: when Harvey returned to England to a senior post at Oxford University in 1987:

> I was forcefully reminded of what I had long ago rebelled against. The smugness of much of Oxford repelled me, and I could not understand how the left in Britain, within geography and without, was taking such wishy-washy positions in relation to Thatcherism (Harvey, 2002, p. 179).

The transition in Harvey's approach is marked by his paper on ghetto formation (Harvey, 1972). He begins with a critique of Kuhn's model of scientific development (p. 7), asking how anomalies to the current paradigm arise and how they are translated into crises. The problem with Kuhn's analysis, he claims, is the assumption that science is independent of its enveloping material conditions, when in fact it is very much geared to its containing and constraining society. Recognition of this point is important for geographers because:

> . . . the driving force behind paradigm formulation in the social sciences is the desire to manipulate and control human activity in the interest of man. Immediately the question arises as to who is going

> to control whom, in whose interest is the controlling going to be exercised, and if control is going to be
> exercised in the interest of all, who is going to take it upon himself to define that public interest?
> (Harvey, 1973, p. 125).

To Harvey, Marxist theory provides 'the key to understanding capitalist production from the position of those not in control of the means of production ... an enormous threat to the power structure of the capitalist world' (p. 127). It not only enhances an understanding of the origins of the present system, with its many-faceted inequalities, but also propounds alternative practices which would avoid such inequalities: 'we become active participants in the social process. The intellectual task is to identify real choices as they are immanent in an existing situation and to devise ways of validating or invalidating these choices through action' (p. 149). In such a context, geography can no longer be merely an academic discipline, isolated in its 'ivory towers'. Its practitioners must become politically aware and active, involved in the creation of a just society which involves not only reform but rather replacement of the present one. The remainder of Harvey's (1973) book does not make this commitment clear, however; it contains one essay on land use and land-value theory, investigating the difficult concept of rent, and another on the nature of urbanism, presenting a Marxist interpretation of the process of urbanization. His later (1984) historical materialist manifesto is a very clear statement of that goal, however, and his (1982, second edition 1999) *The Limits to Capital* is presented as a venture to extend Marx's theory, excavating the centrality of the production of space and geographically uneven development to the reproduction of capitalist society, in a similar spirit to Smith's (1994) equally ambitious excavations of the essential – but highly complex – relations between capitalist (re)production and *Uneven Development*. (Interestingly, Harvey – 2002, p.176 – claimed that it was 'far easier to bring Marxism into geography than to take geographical perspectives back into Marxism'.)

Harvey's work continued to develop these themes during the 1980s and 1990s. Two further volumes of essays extended his analyses of urbanization under capitalism (Harvey, 1985a, 1985c; see also Harvey, 1996b) followed by an interpretation of the socio-economic and geographical backdrop to 'postmodern' forms of culture (1989a). Other essays addressed issues of geopolitics (Harvey, 1985b) and relationships with nature (Harvey, 1994). He then returned to issues of justice (Harvey, 1993a, 1996a) and the imperative for and possibility of alternatives to capitalist urbanization and 'globalization' (Harvey, 2000), while at the same time defending his approach against a variety of critiques. Throughout, he has advanced the case for Marxism (as a creative and open-ended historical dialectical materialism), as a *holistic* approach that necessarily puts material issues at the core of its analysis (Harvey, 1989b). Over the years, Harvey's understanding of this materiality has broadened (Harvey, 2000, thus has an extended consideration of 'the body' as a site of accumulation) but remained always resolute and ambitious in the face, as Harvey (2000, pp. 87–8) would see it, of 'The ubiquity and volatility of money as the impalpable ground of contemporary existence'.

Peet had also moved from a liberal to a Marxist position, replacing his earlier paper on poverty (Peet, 1971) by a Marxist interpretation (Peet, 1975a) based on the assumption that inequality is inherent in the capitalist mode of production. This led to a 'metatheory dealing with the great forces which shape millions of lives' (p. 567) within which: 'Environmental, or geographic, theory deals with the mechanisms which perpetuate inequality from the point of view of the individual. It deals with the complex of forces, both stimuli and frictions, which immediately shape the course of a person's life' (pp. 567–8). Environmental resources act as constraints because they define the milieux within which individuals are socialized and are presented with opportunities for participation within the capitalist system (see also Soja, 1980). Redistribution of income through liberal mechanisms, based on taxation policies, will not solve the problems of poverty, therefore; according to Peet, alternative environmental designs, with removal of central bureaucracies and their replacement by anarchistic models of community control, are needed and geographers should work towards their creation. (Harvey – 1973, p. 93 – disagreed with the latter, pointing out that unless resources are equalized among communities and territories, community control will only result in 'the poor controlling their own poverty while the rich grow more affluent from the fruits of their riches'. See, however, Harvey, 2000.)

To Eliot Hurst (1980), however, embracing Marxism would be insufficient to make geography relevant. In a subsequent essay he argued that by circumscribing their discipline geographers were severely constraining what they could contribute towards understanding the world: their discipline was presented as a technical practice only, which 'is merely descriptive of self-selected phenomena and is scientifically bankrupt' (Eliot Hurst, 1985, p. 62). He examined eight separate definitions of geography, all of which were guilty of what he termed spatial fetishism (after Anderson, 1973), whereby space is accorded a separate and substantial reality with its own distinctive powers, and he followed Slater (1977) in arguing that geography cannot be incorporated within Marxism but has to be transcended and superseded by it: to become Marxist, geographers as a professional group must commit suicide. He concluded that 'geography is irrelevant to contemporary society on two basic grounds' (Eliot Hurst, 1985, p. 85):

1. In terms of substantial content, it has developed 'certain types of ideography, method/technique-strong, but lacking theory in a strict sense' to provide the sort of material which underpins contemporary capitalism; and
2. In philosophical terms it occupies 'an untheorized point of entry to knowledge' because its dominant: 'categories of concern, such as space, spatial differentiation, spatial interaction and uneven development, are mere fetishisms and unscientific'.

Radical reconfiguration is needed in order to promote full understanding of capitalist society, not just of geography but of the entire body of 'bourgeois social science'.

Structuralist Marxisms and regulation theory

Structuralisms

The reinvigorated Marxism which influenced radical geographers has sometimes been presented as a variant of the philosophy of structuralism (of which there are many different forms: cf. Johnston, 1983b, Peet 1998), but which are most indebted to the French Marxist Louis Althussuer who published a number of influential reinterpretations of Marx in the 1960s and early 1970s. Structuralism is certainly not the only strand of Marxist geography, for Sheppard and Barnes (1990) have also set out the possibilities of an 'analytical Marxism' in geography (of which more below) and David Harvey has very much charted his own course to an historical geographical materialism. On Harvey, Castree (1996, p. 344) therefore argues that:

> ... what is distinctive about Harvey's Marxism ... is how little indebted it is to other readings of Marx: reading Capital has for him long been preferred to Reading capital (Althusser and Balibar 1970). ... This is quite unusual among Anglophone Marxian theorists: few appropriate Marx in an 'unreconstructed' way and far more read him through interpretations provided by earlier heirs of Marx's legacy ... This is why Harvey ... sees both Althusserian and analytical Marxism – perhaps the two leading Marxist paradigms of the last two decades – as radical reworkings of Marx. ... Harvey, by contrast, very much regards his own work as a more or less direct, 'faithful' continuation and extension of Marx's own practices and ideas: in short, as a peculiarly classical version of Marxism bought forward from the last fin de siècle to our own.

Meanwhile, analytical Marxism seeks to evaluate Marx's work and insights using tools available from contemporary social sciences. Influential within radical branches of economics, for geography it has amounted to:

> ... the use of analytical methods ... to construct a wide-ranging model of the capitalist space economy incorporating commodity production, natural resources, the built environment, class formation, technical change and industrial organization. (Sheppard and Barnes, 1990, pp. 1–2)

Describing some of the inspiration to this project, Sheppard and Barnes (1990, p. 1) also note how:

> As a model for the kind of account we wish to present, we pay homage to David Harvey's (1982) Limits to Capital, from which we drew many insights and ideas. Yet our argument is different in style from his, and indeed from many others whose ideas we share. For at the core of this book is the belief that a clear account of the political economic approach is obtained by interrogating our subject matter with an analytical (mathmatical) logic.

Nevertheless, structuralism merits further consideration here, in part because of its indirect impacts as an influence on the regulationist approaches that we will also consider.

Perhaps where structuralism had the most direct impact within Anglophone geography has been in reactions to the work of the the Catalan theorist, Manuel Castells (whose original work was mostly written in French). Peet (1989, p. 112) notes how:

> ... structural[ist] work on cities and urban planning (Preticeille 1976; Pickvance 1976) began to appear in English in the middle 1970s. ... Most importantly, a translation of Manuel Castells's (1977) structuralist work on cities, The Urban Question, had a profound effect, especially on urban geography.

Peet, however, goes on to note how:

The move towards structuralism, never complete in geographical thought, represented a search for greater theoretical coherence and rigor. It is also the most misrepresented and underappreciated period in social and geogrphical thought (p. 112).

Structural Marxism was also an influence in Massey's (1984a) account of *Spatial Divisions of Labour: Social Structures and the Geography of Production*. In turn this soon proved to be an influential book (see below), even if its debt to structural Marxism was only set out explictly in the second (1995) edition. Structural Marxism also came to influence a generation of work on the uneveness, contradictions and limits of capitalist development in the 'Third World' (for example, Blaut, 1975; Canon, 1973; Slater, 1973, 1977) – even if its influence on development geography was soon being criticized for its percieved 'economism'. Thus Corbridge (1986, p. 64) claimed that:

Althusserians have not escaped the sins of economic determinism. . . . In their curiously changless theories, capitalism is endowed with an endless and ageless capacity to secure its own perpetuation.

In response, Watts (1988) stressed the continued relevance and richness of Marxist perspectives on geographies of (uneven) development. Althusser's work can thus be read as creating radically new formulations of Marxism, especially his development of the concepts of 'overdetermination' and 'condensation'. In this he adapted terms from psychoanalysis ('condensation' is used in Freud's interpretations of dreams) to refer to the way that elements of a complex whole are expressed in each of its parts and vice versa. The potential application of these to human geography was not quickly realized, however (despite Massey, 1995, noting Althusseur's influence in the introduction to the second edition of her influential *Spatial Divisions of Labour*). Moreover, the sense that structural Marxism has often been *misrepresented* or caricatured as unduly rigid and mechanistic is also a point of critique for Castree (1994, 1995a). Castree reminds us of both the continued *diversity* of Marxist writings, their considerable nuances and differences, and the range of works in geography that they lend themselves to. Moreover, as Peet shows, the impacts of structuralism within and beyond Marxist-influenced geography have been complex. Perhaps the most significant influence has been a rather indirect one, via the way that structuralist ideas shaped regulation theory, which in turn became an influential strand of geographical work in the 1990s. We will consider this strand in a moment.

Firstly, however, it should be noted that structuralism more widely has had a long-standing concern with the dynamics and rules of systems of meaning and power. In particular, structuralism proceeds through examining the relations and functions of the smallest constituent elements of such systems in relation to each other. The emphasis is on this relation, on the relationship of parts to the whole. The work of Ferdinand de Saussure, undertaken just prior to the First World War in the field of linguistics, has been a prototype and inspiration. Setting the agenda for wider structuralist analysis, Saussure's study was centered less on speech itself, but rather on the fundamental rules and conventions enabling language to operate. Structuralism has since found further application in the fields of linguistics and textual analysis as well as anthropology and wider studies of culture, prior to coming into fruitful interactions with Marxism in the form of Althussers's work. The fact that Marx's method contained a parallel commitment to study the dynamic relations between the whole and parts of the capitalist system enabled this encounter between structuralism and Marxism. Marxism adopts a dialectical approach to its subject matter, since this represents how societies develop. It involves the resolution of opposites, usually represented by the trilogy of:

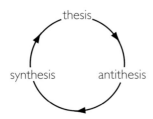

in which each synthesis becomes the next thesis; thus there is no permanent resolution, each synthesis containing within itself the seeds of its own destruction. Dialectic processes operate at a variety of spatial and temporal resolutions (Castree, 1996; Harvey, 1996b; Ollman, 1993). Indeed, Castree (1996, p. 344) reminds us that:

> Just as Marxism has developed into a complex discursive tradition [and we might add complex political practice too] — that is, a variegated set of distinct but related intellectual positions and practices whose particularity and specific genealogies must be respected — dialectics too has assumed manifold forms and accumulated multiple meanings within [and we might add beyond] this Marxist tradition. Strictly speaking, then, the language of 'Marxism' and 'dialectics', in the singular, must be abandoned for a more discriminating attention to Marxisms and dialectics, in the plural.

To return to structuralism, however, a key theme is that of relations between levels of analysis:

1. The level of appearances, or the superstructure;
2. The level of processes, or the infrastructure; and
3. The level of imperatives, or the deep structure.

Most forms of structuralism have no deterministic relationship between these levels. A process can result in a considerable number of outcomes, depending on a variety of enabling and constraining factors, most of them within the superstructure. To illustrate this, the French social anthropologist Claude Lévi-Strauss used the analogy of the cam-shaft driving a machine for cutting the outlines of jigsaw puzzles (Figure 6.1). The machine is constrained to certain movements only, but the order in which they come is random, which means that it can produce a large number of unique puzzles. Study of one of these puzzles alone could not reveal the nature of the machine; only study of the machine could do that. Structuralism is the study of the machines but, unlike the analogy, these are not available for investigation. Structuralist researchers must develop a theory of the machine, and test whether the contents of the superstructure are consistent with that theory; the contents of the superstructure cannot be predicted, however, because, to continue the cam-shaft analogy, the particular operation of the machine cannot be foreseen.

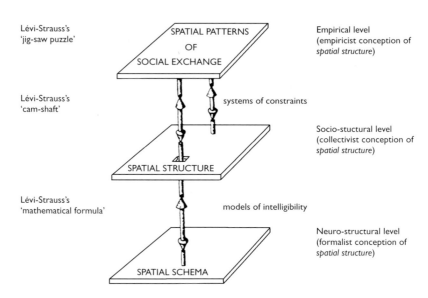

Lévi-Strauss's 'jig-saw puzzle'

SPATIAL PATTERNS OF SOCIAL EXCHANGE

Empirical level (empiricist conception of *spatial structure*)

Lévi-Strauss's 'cam-shaft'

systems of constraints

Socio-stuctural level (collectivist conception of *spatial structure*)

SPATIAL STRUCTURE

Lévi-Strauss's 'mathematical formula'

models of intelligibility

Neuro-structural level (formalist conception of *spatial structure*)

SPATIAL SCHEMA

Figure 6.1 *A geographical interpretation of Lévi-Strauss's cam-shaft analogy for structuralism (Source: Gregory, 1978a, p. 100)*

In some forms of structuralism, such as Lévi-Strauss's social anthropology (E. R. Leach, 1974), it is further argued that the processes operating in the infrastructure reflect imperatives located in the deep structure. Theoretical study of the patterns in the superstructure should reveal the nature of the deep structure, therefore (in somewhat similar fashion to the identification of essences in phenomenology: p. 201). Thus, according to Lévi-Strauss, all incest taboos are variants of a basic taboo which is imprinted in everybody's conscience. That basic form occurs in different forms in separate societies and cultures, but careful comparison of all taboos should reveal their common elements, and thus that aspect of human neural structure.

Few geographers have taken structuralism this far, although it might be claimed that the imperatives of deep structures have often appealed to geographers as a domain of analyis (see Golledge, 1981a; Sack, 1983; Sibley, 1998). Moreover, there are those who would point to the the consequences – in their view problematic ones – of Marxist geography (in the form of David Harvey's work) replicating this appeal to structure at the percieved expense of agency and contignecy (Jones, 1999). We return to this theme later in this chapter.

Regulation theory

As we have noted, one way in which structuralism has found productive expression has been via geographers' adoption of regulation theory. This studies the procedures and practices whereby capitalism is reproduced ('regulated'); the sets of checks and balances that keep the system going, albeit from one period of crisis to another. It thus draws on a nuanced understanding of both ideology and power – drawing on the rediscovery and translation of the (pre-Second World War) works of the Italian Marxist Antonio Gramsci – as well as the concepts of multiple determination (so called overdetermination) which shape the balances between 'state', 'society', production, consumption, and social and technological forces which are seen to propel and embody socio-spatial transformations (this owes much to Louis Althusser, see Lipietz, 1993). This is much more than a formal interest in govenment rules and regulations; what is understood by regulation in the common sense of the word. Instead, as Peck and Tickell (1995, p. 16) note:

> Although by no means a completed theoretical project, it has nevertheless matured to the extent that proponents now work from a well-established set of conceptual foundations. The theory holds that capitalist development proceeds through a succession of historically specific phases of stability and crisis, sustained growth and intense restructuring. Emphasis is placed on the role of state forms, social mores, laws and habits; the so-called mode of social regulation (MSR) in underwriting sustained phases of growth. These phases, in which the schema of reproduction (the complex of production, consumption, and distibution systems) is broadly in synchronisation are termed regimes of accumulation.

Though regulation theory first developed in France outside geography (see Boyer and Saillard, 1995; Macleod, 1997), 'Anglo-American' human geographers and allied social scientists have since added greatly to it through careful attention to the relationships between reconfigurations in systems of production, different geographical scales and their roles in regulatory reconfigurations (e.g. Amin, 1994; Amin and Robins, 1990; Clark, 1992; Dunford, 1990; Gertler, 1992; Goodwin, Duncan and Halford, 1993; Peck and Tickell, 1992), including reconfigured rural geographies (Cloke and Goodwin, 1992). In turn, this has reinvigorated geographical literature on the intersection and *production* of different scales of social and political life (Herod and Wright, 2002, review these debates). Related notions of the 'geographies of governance' have noted how they are today less clearly organized along state lines (and national boundaries – hence such work has consequences for political geography) within the context of rescalings (e.g. Brenner, Jessop, Jones and MacLeod, 2003; Clark, 1992; Herod et al., 1998; Herod and Wright, 2002) and the shifting regulation and scales of state policy (see the reviews by Painter, 2000, and Peck, 2000).

At the same time as regulation theory has offerered fruitful pathhways to renew radical geography's concern with the structural dynamics of capitalism, other work has returned to the points and relations of production (though not just industrial production), charting labour geographies (see the review in Wills, 2002) and changing geographies of class relations (e.g. Herod, 2001, and Peck, 1996) – including those of universities in which academic geographers and many relatively low paid support and technical staff work (Roberts, 2000).

'Localities'

The localities research programme originated in part from Massey's (1984a) work on the changing geography of economic activity in the UK. (A measure of the significance of *Spatial Divisions of Labour* is the series of ten commentaries produced by Australian-based authors in Volume 12, Number 5 (May 1989) of *Environment and Planning A*.) Her central argument was that understanding changing locational patterns of industries requires appreciation of the links between economic and social change. Local social structures vary in how the labour process is organized, and from comparing two case study regions she concluded that (p. 194):

> ... although both ... are now being drawn into a similar place in an emerging wider division of labour, their roles in previous spatial divisions of labour have been very different; they have different histories. They bring with them different class structures and social characteristics, and, as a result, the changes which they undergo ... are also different.

Thus, changing industrial geography is linked to a changing social geography as new 'layers of investment' (and disinvestment) are superimposed on those of earlier eras (see too, Anderson, Duncan and Hudson, 1983).

Those processes generate uneven development; a regional mosaic of unique areas reflecting the interpretations of local contexts by the actors involved in creating the UK's changing geographies of production. Massey (1984b) generalized this in her essay 'Geography matters', in terms of each of its three traditional concerns – space, environment, and place. Regarding space, for example, she argued that, 'aspects of "the spatial" are important in the construction, functioning, reproduction and change of societies as a whole and of elements of society. *Distance* and separation are regularly used by companies to establish degrees of monopoly control'(p. 5). Regarding the environment, she argued that conceptions of the 'natural', and thus interpretations of local environmental potentials, are socially produced, and could vary among areas as a reflection of their separate social systems, whereas with regard to place she contended that general processes can have particular outcomes in unique areas. Thus, the study of geography involves unravelling the unique and the general: 'the fact of uneven development and of interdependent systems of dominance and subordination between regions on the one hand, and the specificity of place on the other' (p. 9) is thus a central concern for the discipline.

Massey illustrated her general contention by a number of case studies in *Spatial Divisions of Labour* (1984a), and provided others in an essay on women in the labour force (McDowell and Massey, 1984: see also Rose, 1987). Her work was also instrumental in the establishment of a major research programme (financed by the British Economic and Social Research Council), into the *Changing Urban and Regional System (CURS)*: this was introduced by its co-ordinator (Cooke, 1986) and summarized in a volume that reported on the programme's seven case studies (Cooke, 1989a). The substantive focus was the spatially varying processes of economic restructuring taking place in Britain during the 1980s. Thus (Cooke, 1989a, p. ix):

> The overall objectives of the programme were to explore the impact of economic restructuring at national and local levels, and to assess the role of central and local government policies in enabling or constraining localities, through their various social and political organizations, to deal with processes of restructuring.

In addition:

. . . an important dimension of the research involved seeking to establish the conceptual status of the idea of 'locality' by taking account of a wide range of social scientific theory and research.

The concept of *locality* was chosen after both the traditional terms 'community' and 'locale' were rejected:

There is a gap in the social science literature when it comes to a concept dealing with the sphere of social activity that is focused upon place, that is not only reactive or inward-looking with regard to place, and that is not limited in its scope by a primary stress on stability and continuity (Cooke, 1989a, p. 10).

Locale was rejected because its spatial scope is vague; it suggests a passive rather than an active context for action and lacks any specific social meaning. (Giddens, 1984, defined a locale as a 'setting for interaction' which implies a spatial component, but no more: an e-mail 'chatroom' could be described as a locale on that definition.) A locality, on the other hand, is 'the space within which the larger part of most citizens' daily working and consuming lives is lived' (p. 12) and in which their citizenship rights are defined. Citizenship, according to recent debates, involves: individuals having obligations to their community (via the state) as well as entitlements from it – or duties as well as rights (Smith, 1989; see also Bennett, 1989a). The contest over rights and duties is fought out in places, at a variety of scales: their nature involves 'the construction of an identity, complete with a related package of known rights and obligations, which posits residence in a definable place or (commonly quite sizeable) territory as the basis for the nurturing and preservation of this identity' (Painter and Philo, 1995, p. 111). We become what we are because of where we are and the categories used in the structuring of civil society there (and we are implicated in those local struggles over our rights, obligations and identities).

At the end of his summary volume on the localities project, Cooke argued that the seven case studies sustained his earlier contention regarding the crucial role of localities in the restructuring process and in the creation and recreation of uneven development; they illustrate (Cooke, 1989a, p. 296):

. . . the argument that the relationship between the different scales is not simply a one-way street with localities the mere recipients of fortune or fate from above. Rather localities are actively involved in their own transformation, though not necessarily as masters of their own destiny. Localities are not simply places or even communities: they are the sum of social energy and agency resulting from the clustering of diverse individuals, groups and social interests in space. They are not passive or residual but, in varying ways and degrees, centres of collective consciousness. They are bases for intervention in the internal workings of not only individual and collective daily lives but also events on a broader canvas as affecting local interests.

This conclusion, and the path towards it, became the subject of considerable debate, however, much of it unfavourable on conceptual grounds because what is necessarily local and what is contingently so has not been defined (Cox and Mair, 1989).

One of the initial critiques was Neil Smith's (1987a) argument that the CURS programme as formulated was likely to be submerged in a morass of statistical information; it contained within itself the potential for producing no more than those earlier empiricist studies, 'which deliberately examined individual places for their own sake, and [did] not attempt to draw out theoretical or historical conclusions' (p. 62; see also Jonas, 1988). He was also concerned about the vagueness of the spatial scale in defining localities, but welcomed the attempt to blend theoretical analysis with local understanding. Cooke (1987a) refuted the charge of empiricism, arguing that the objective of the CURS initiative was 'theorised interrogation' (p. 75) of available data. His general position was supported by Urry, who initially argued that 'there are some significant locality-specific processes' (Urry, 1986, p. 239), which he followed with a list of ten different ways in which social scientists have addressed them (Urry, 1987; see also Urry, 1985).

Cochrane (1987, p. 355) wondered whether CURS was 'just a cover for structural Marxism with a human face, or . . . the cover for a return to empiricism with a theoretically sophisticated face', and concluded that the programme contained the danger that as a guide to political action it might suggest that local struggle could suffice (what he termed 'micro-structuralism') rather than the realization that parts cannot readily be isolated from wholes. Gregson (1987a) was perhaps even less sanguine, arguing that the theoretical rationale for the seven case studies was far from clear, thus making the likelihood of falling into the empiricist trap high; without a properly articulated theoretical core, 'CURS simply replicates the mistakes of previous local studies; with such a core it could be so much more' (p. 370). Beauregard (1988) claimed that the programme lacked any clear directions for practice, for using the radical theory to achieve social change.

Duncan's (1989) full critique accepted that the concept refers to something important – spatial variability and specificity – but he concluded that 'the locality concept is misleading and unsupported' (p. 247; he concluded elsewhere – Duncan and Savage, 1989, pp. 202–4 – that it is 'confused, unsatisfactory, and largely redundant . . . a mystification'). He accepted that 'space makes a difference', in three ways:

1. Social processes are constituted in places, which may differ because of previous 'layers of investment' (to use Massey's term);
2. Actions take place locally and so can vary spatially; and
3. Spatially varying actions can create spatially varying contexts.

But the concept of locality implies 'social autonomy and spatial determinism' (p. 247), both of which he rejects. He is not convinced that local differences are very important in creating uneven development, relative to more general processes: 'Locality is . . . only important if and when locality effects are part of the causal group explaining any event. And locality may well not be important', which implies a verdict of 'not proven' (p. 248).

Cooke's (1989b, p. 272) response to these critiques (and to the Duncan and Savage paper in particular) was trenchant:

> Local social processes are clearly an abiding feature of contemporary social life. Duncan and Savage's injunction to ignore them and settle on the structural level, supra-local, supra-national or whatever, in order to describe spatial variation in terms which deny agency to the social groups comprising localities, is both dated and redundant.

And he concluded that:

'Locality' can be seen to be a fascinating, complex concept of considerable value to geographical theory and empirical research.

Griffiths and Johnston (1991) outlined a clearer framework for studying how localities differ, using three components of local economic, social, and political structures drawn from their study of responses to the 1984–5 National Union of Mineworkers' strike in the UK. Johnston (1991) later applied this framework to a range of studies of uneven development at a number of scales, including the southern United States.

The debate over 'localities' was part of a much wider range of work which addressed the role of place in the creation of social scientific understanding. Agnew and Duncan (1989, p. 1), for example, opened their introduction to *The Power of Place* with the statement that the book is:

... an attempt to make the case for the intellectual importance of geographical place in the practice of social science and history ... [through] bringing together what can be called the geographical and sociological 'imaginations'.

Agnew (1989) analysed why place had been devalued in 'orthodox social science' in recent decades, focusing on the confusion of place with community (itself a term with many definitions: Bell and Newby, 1976). The orthodox treatment identifies a decline in community with 'modernisation' and its replacement by a 'placeless' society, a transition seen as 'natural, lawful, and universal' (Agnew, 1989, p. 16), with nationalism growing as a 'place-transcending ideology'. Similarly, the alternative view derived from Marxism devalued place with its emphasis on 'freeing people from places' (p. 22; Entrikin, 1989, provides a parallel, elegant argument.) The goal of *The Power of Place* is to correct those tendencies, and, through both theoretical argument and empirical illustration, 'argue against the prevalent tendency in history and social science to overvalue the sociological imagination at the expense of the geographical' (Agnew, 1989, p. 7; see also Agnew, 1990). He adduced five reasons for a place perspective (Agnew, 1987b):

1. It allows abstract categories – such as class – to be analysed in the context of everyday situations;
2. It avoids the search for 'universal' laws;
3. It allows a focus on structure–agency inter-relations;
4. It shows that societies in different places change at different rates and along different trajectories, thereby removing any tendency to identify 'historical stages' to which all should conform; and
5. It illustrates the operation of cultural agents acting outside economic determinism.

A 'new regional geography'

The debate over locality research is part of a wider literature on the importance of studying the specific characteristics of places. The numerous works using an implicit contextual approach include Agnew's (1984, 1987b) argument that voting behaviour is strongly influenced by the electorate's local context (see also Johnston, 1986e) and a detailed analysis of variations between local states in their provision of public housing (Dickens et al., 1985). Some translated this general concern into a plea for a revived, but restructured, regional geography. Massey (1984b, p. 10), for example, ended such a plea with the argument that it is:

> ... necessary to reassert the existence, the explicability, and the significance, of the particular. What we [must do] ... is take up again the challenge of the old regional geography, reject the answers it gave while recognizing the importance of the problem it set (p. 10).

This echoes Gregory's (1978a, pp. 171–2) contention that:

> Ever since regional geography was declared to be dead ... geographers, to their credit, have kept trying to revive it in one form or another ... This is a vital task ... we need to know about the constitution of regional social formations, of regional articulations and regional structures. ... [producing] a doubly human geography: human in the sense that it recognizes that its concepts are specifically human constructions, rooted in specific social formations, and capable of – demanding of – continual examination and criticism; and human in the sense that it restores human beings to their own worlds and enables them to take part in the collective transformation of their own human geographies.

This call was not immediately taken up, although Fleming (1973), Steel (1982) and Hart (1982) all called for a revival of traditional regional geography, which to Hart meant; 'producing good regional geography – evocative descriptions that facilitate an understanding and an appreciation of places, areas and regions' (p. 2). Some have followed Gregory's lead (see also Gregory, 1985b), however, and argued – as do Lee (1984, 1985) and Johnston (1984c, 1985a) – for a reconstituted regional geography which recognizes (Lee, 1985) that:

1. Social processes operate in historically and geographically specific circumstances, so their understanding requires a sensitivity to geographical variations (regional mosaics);
2. Society is not a fixed phenomenon but something that is constantly being recreated by human actions. Since those actions occur in historically and geographically specific contexts, then societal recreation is similarly historically and geographically variable;
3. Those local transformations occur in the context of wider social relationships; and
4. The regions that emerge are not fixed divisions of territory but changing social constructions.

A major goal of geography should be to uncover the nature of those regions, as illustrated by some of the essays in Johnston, Hauer and Hoekveld (1990).

The emphasis on change in these arguments implies the absence of a distinct niche for historical geography within the discipline's overall programme. The claim that a major route to understanding the present lies in study of the past is not new, but adoption of approaches based on structuration and contextual theory clarifies the importance of an historical perspective. Not surprisingly, therefore, historical geographers have made major contributions to the debates (see Baker and Gregory, 1984), drawing on such sources as the writings of the French *Annales* school of history (Baker, 1984; Pred, 1984c, draws on Braudel, for example). Thus, interpretations of the long-term evolution of a society (e.g. Dunford and Perrons, 1983) and its regional components (Langton, 1984), of basic transformations in a region, whether industrial (e.g. Gregory, 1982a) or agricultural (Pred, 1985, 1986), and of the constitution of particular places (as in Harvey's, 1985c, detailed analysis of nineteenth-century Paris as an example of how consciousness is created in a particular context) all illustrate how changes take place as the result of general tendencies being played out in specific milieux by particular human agents. (Not all historical geographers agreed however: see Meinig, 1978, especially p. 1215, and Dodgshon, 1998.)

The differences between the 'new' and the 'traditional' approaches to regional geography are clarified by Pudup (1988, p. 374), who characterized the latter as empiricist:

> Theoretically neutral observations are the basis for areal description. A reconstructed regional geography has foundations that rest in a clarified status of regions as objects of study – put simply, why geographers bother to study regions in the first place (p. 379).

The answers to that 'Why?' question are provided in works such as Pred's (1984c) on southern Sweden and Gregory's (1982a) on West Yorkshire: regions are territorial entities, produced, reproduced, and transformed through human agency. This argument is similar to Taylor's on the scale of experience and Giddens' on structuration (see p. 243); regions are the places in which people learn a culture, and contribute to its continuation (what Thrift, 1983a, after Giddens, calls 'settings for interaction': p. 235). The nature of those processes is appreciated through a theorized approach, with the appreciation being provided through a narrative that draws on a defined vocabulary and permits 'theory to speak through subsequent empirical accounts' (Pudup, 1988, p. 383; see also Sayer, 1989a, 1989b). What those empirical accounts should focus on is still debated, and the need for a sub-discipline called regional geography has been contested. Warf (1988, p. 57) contended that with the replacement of traditional regional geography by positivism, 'a geography of "regions without theories" quickly became a geography of "theories without regions"', but Johnston (1990a, p. 139) argued that whereas 'we do not need regional geography ... we do need regions in geography'.

Pudup's characterization of the 'new' regional geography was extended by Gilbert (1988), who identified three separate concerns with regional specificity in recent writings:

1. A concern with regions as *local responses to capitalist processes*, which she identified as probably the most prominent among English-speaking writers, who set the study of local variations within a political economy (usually Marxist) framework;
2. A concern with the region as *a focus of identification* (or 'sense of place'), which is especially strong among French writers concerned with the analysis of culture. To them, appropriation of a place (or region) is part of the creation and recreation of cultural identity; and

3. A concern with the region as *a medium for social interaction*, playing 'a basic role in the production and reproduction of social relations' (p. 212). The work on 'localities' fits into this concern.

All three represent a break from 'traditional' regional geography, Gilbert claimed, through their recognition that the persistence of regional diversity in the face of the homogenizing tendencies within capitalism provides regional geography with a practical significance, in the mobilization of resistance to those tendencies (see also Peet, 1989). The 'new' work depends on structuralist theory (as illustrated in Agnew's, 1987a, book on the United States within the capitalist world economy); on the recognition that regional processes rely on dialectical rather than naturalistic theories; and on the importance of human agency in the creation, recreation and transformation of regions. Together, these suggest a mode of study committed to understanding and achieving social change, which provides the challenge of making 'geography a science useful for society' (Gilbert, 1988, p. 223).

More recently, regulationist work (see p. 232) has also informed accounts of regions and regional configurations of governance and accumulation (e.g. MacLeod, 1998; MacLeod and Goodwin, 1999) – as well as making what Ward (2001, p. 130) terms 'a substantial contribution to the study of urban politics'. Both strands of work – on regions and on urban localities – have been informed by (and blended with) social, cultural and political geographies, and wider social and political theory (e.g. Murphy, 1991; Paassi, 1991; Thrift, 1990, 1991, 1993, 1994). Thus, according to MacLeod and Jones (2001, p. 671):

> ... geographers were encouraged to embrace elements of social theory, sociology, anthropology, and political economy in order to transcend the purported limitations of an earlier regional geography, not least its emphasis on the natural environment as the key factor in establishing the regional shape of society ... for the new regional geographers, amid a range of rapid economic and political restructuring, regions were being presented as arenas through which to view the movements and dramas of individuals and groups in a whole series of economic, political and cultural contexts.

Realism and structuration

Marxism has long been interested in exploring different levels of analysis and relations; between economy and culture, for example, or between production and reproduction as well as between different scales and places – classically the contrast between the 'country and the city', but also between 'core' and 'periphery' and the spatial and temporal dynamics of growth and decline. While Marxism has a materialist base, arguing that society comprises a set of economic processes, these may only be reproduced through social, cultural and political processes, and in turn those also become aspects of what Marxists characterize as means and forces of production. Debates about the relations between these and their 'relative autonomy' have long characterized Marxist thought. Most recently – in the 1990s and since – regulation theory has promised geographers a path through these.

In the 1980s however, human geographers also explored two approaches which claimed to offer advances in the way that structure and agency (and the role of space) could be conceptualized. The first of these, the philosophy of *realism*, is based on the separation out of three domains (Bhaskar, 1978):

1. *The domain of the empirical* is concerned solely with experiences, with the world as it is perceived;
2. *The domain of the actual* is concerned with events as well as experiences, accepting that an event (a particular item of human behaviour, for example) may be interpreted in different ways by individuals (by the actor, perhaps, and by another person experiencing it); and
3. *The domain of the real* is concerned with structures that cannot be apprehended directly, but which contain the mechanisms that lead to the events and their empirical perception.

Realists argue that all science incorporates these three domains, but the natural and the social sciences differ in the type of mechanism with which they deal. In particular, natural science deals with 'closed systems' in which the same inter-relationships can be observed on innumerable occasions, allowing the development of universal laws based on replicable results. Social science rarely if ever deals with such closed systems, however, both because of the difficulties of abstracting independent parts from the whole (most attempts to do this produce what Sayer, 1985a, terms 'chaotic conceptions') and because some components of the system — people — learn from their experiences, so that experiments can never be replicated.

The goal of realism, like that of positivism, is to explain events, to discover their causes by 'finding out what *produces* change, what *makes* things happen, what *allows or forces* change' (Sayer, 1985a, p. 163). It differs from positivism because it contends that, 'what causes something to happen has nothing to do with the matter of the number of times it has happened or been observed to happen and hence with whether it causes a regularity' (p. 162). Indeed 'regularities' (i.e. laws and law-like generalizations) are very unlikely to occur in the social sciences. Sayer (1984) argues that two conditions are necessary if regularities are to occur:

1. The mechanisms must be invariant; and
2. The relationships between the mechanisms and the conditions in which they occur must be constant.

If both hold, then scientists will be studying closed systems, with identical conditions leading to identical events (either naturally or in laboratory conditions). If one or both is absent, however, the object of study is an open system, and regularities will then not occur. The social sciences study open systems:

> ... we can interpret the same material conditions and statements in different ways and hence learn new ways of responding, so that effectively we become different kinds of people. Human actions characteristically modify the configuration of systems, thereby violating the ... [first] condition ... while our capacity for learning and self-change violates the ... [second] condition (Sayer, 1984, p. 113).

The mechanisms underpinning the operations of human societies are interpreted in different ways, therefore, with the outcomes of those interpretations creating new sets of conditions within which future interpretations will be constrained. The mechanisms are abstract concepts which are actualized in contingently-related conditions as, for example, with:

> ... the law of value, which concerns mechanisms which are possessed necessarily by capital by virtue of its structure (as consisting of competing and independently directed capitals, each producing for profit and being reliant on the production of surplus value, etc.), produces effects which are mediated by such things as the particular kinds of technology available, the relative power of capital and labour and state in[ter]vention. No theory of society could be expected to know the nature and form of these contingencies in advance purely on the basis of theoretical claims (pp. 128–30).

Thus, whereas the mechanisms can be theorized, their particular realizations cannot, since they depend on human agency, on individuals interpreting the mechanisms in the context of their interpretations of the empirical world (see Johnston, 1989a). Furthermore, those individuals learn, with every decision and its outcomes feeding forward into future decision-making, so that even if the external milieu does not change, the nature of the decision-maker (and his or her culture) does (this was also taken up by Pred, see p. 285).

A major issue for those adopting a realist approach concerns the role of space – does it, as asked in the title of Sayer's (1985b) essay, 'make a difference'? In realist terms, that question can be pitched at the level of either the necessary or the contingent – is space important in theoretical work, or only in concrete realizations of the outcome of general processes? Regarding the former, he noted that, 'Abstract social theory need only consider space insofar as *necessary* properties of objects are involved, and this does not amount to very much' (p. 54). All matter has a spatial location and so all events occur in space but, while recognizing this, abstract theory need say very little about actual spatial forms, 'Hence, while it is important for abstract theory to be aware of the existence of space, the claims that can be made about it are inevitably rather indifferent ones' and refer to concrete realizations only. He concludes that to claim that space is contingent in its operation does not mean that it is unimportant: 'The difference that space makes in concrete situations can never be ignored, and therefore in that sense "geography matters" ' (p. 109).

The study of causation in a realist context involves what Sayer and Morgan (1985) term *intensive* research programmes, whose questions take the form 'What did the agents actually do?'; answering them involves examining causal processes in a particular case or group of cases. The answers cannot be generalized beyond those cases, in contrast to those produced in *extensive* research programmes, commonly adopted in empiricist/positivist human geography, which are 'mainly concerned with discovering some of the common properties and general patterns in a population as a whole' (p. 150).

A second path which some geographers advocated in the 1980s, as an overall framework to research and as a means to explore the constitutive role of space in social life, was *structuration* – a theoretical approach first developed by Giddens (1984) to account for the ways in which people learn about and transform social structures. This a place-bound (and time-bound) process; one's context (including one's language: see p. 281) is a major influence on one's individual development. (For exegeses and applications by geographers, see Moos and Dear, 1986; Dear and Moos, 1986; Phipps, 2001.)

Structuration, as an example of a contextual approach, clarifies the falseness of any distinction between social relations and spatial structures; as Gregory and Urry (1985, p. 3) express it, 'spatial structure is now seen not merely as an arena in which social life unfolds, but rather as a medium through which social relations are produced and reproduced'. Together they produce the process of *spatiality* (or socio-spatial dialectic), used by Soja (1980, 1985) to characterize the conjoint social production of space (*à la* Harvey, 1982) and the spatial construction of society. Giddens and others identify much common ground between his conception of structuration and Hägerstrand's of time geography (though see Gregson, 1986), and Pred has used the two in a number of essays to illustrate their relevance to understanding both the unfolding of his own career (Pred, 1979, 1984a) and the development of particular places (Pred, 1984b, 1984c). Thus:

> The meanings of interpretations I have imposed upon the past, the there and then in Berkeley and Sweden, are a result of the knowledge, attitudes and values I hold now, the ever fading here and now in Berkeley. Yet, the knowledge, attitudes and values I hold here and now are rooted in my past path, my past participation in projects and the institutional and societal context which generated those projects (Pred, 1984a, p. 101).

Also, 'Biographies are formed through the becoming of places, and places become through the formation of biographies' (Pred, 1984b, p. 258).

In the end, relatively few geographers adopted structuration as a research methodology (although, as we have noted, it did appear promising and Cloke, Philo and Sadler's 1991 text contained an entire chapter on structuration theory, juxtaposed to the one on realism, and Phipps, 2001, has more recently explored structuration theory's empirical applications). Gregson (1987b), for example, identified 'some quite major, and unresolved, problems in front of us before Giddens' theory of structuration can be demonstrated to be of real import for empirical enquiry' (p. 89). She discussed Moos and Dear's (1986) use of two levels of analysis: analysis of the individuals involved in the production of a particular event (level 1); and the higher-order analysis of the structural properties within which those agents are operating (level 2). They argue that these are tied together by Giddens' concept of the 'duality of structure', the inter-dependent relationships among structure and agency, which they term 'abstraction'. Gregson doubts whether they have provided a way of moving 'between what are often universal theoretical categories and the specifics of the events which occur in particular times and places' (p. 81): they have provided 'abstraction without specification'. Further, she argued that (p. 83):

> ... it would be unreasonable to expect structuration theory to generate either empirical research questions or appropriate categories for empirical analysis as it stands, and ... to transfer structurationist concepts directly into empirical analysis is misconceived.

Structuration is about second-order questions, questions *about* social science that cannot be answered by an appeal to methods of obtaining facts, rather than about first-order questions concerning the domain of the actual.

Gregson's argument that 'structurationist concepts and categories will not, and should not, be expected to specify particular empirical research projects' (p. 84) appears to have been adopted by others, who take it as an organizing framework within which empirical work can be set rather than a methodological protocol. Locales are presented as the social systems that provide the contexts within which individuals become 'knowledgeable actors'. Sarre *et al.* (1989, p. 43) define 'knowledgeability' as: 'individuals' ability to infer from the complex and contradictory situations and processes of society both the prevailing rules and the most advantageous strategies and tactics'. The ability to apply knowledge reflects 'capability' to act in the ways that they wish. Their locale is thus both enabling and constraining: enabling in its provision of resources – knowledge – on which they can base action, and constraining because it limits how they can act (through both the knowledge provided and the milieux in which it is interpreted and used). As they act, they reproduce the local knowledge, and thus ensure that the social system continues to constrain and enable further actions (theirs and others'). But their actions and choices will change the knowledge somewhat, creating a (probably very slightly) different set of enabling and constraining conditions for future action.

The production of 'nature'

The holistic conception of relations and dynamics in Marxist thought has also lent itself to work on one of the oldest of concerns in geography – human–environment relations. Marxist work on uneven development thus includes work on the relationships between society and nature. Liberal concerns over environmental issues had increased substantially during the late 1960s and early 1970s (see p. 341). Harvey (1974d) introduced a Marxist perspective to this issue, arguing that contemporary statements on resource–population ratios are ideologically based, an argument sustained through examination of the works of Malthus, Marx and Ricardo. Resources are not defined outside the context of societal appraisals of nature, and those appraisals reflect the current mode of production. Thus, predictions such as those of the *Limits to Growth* study (p. 342) represent a *status quo* theoretical perspective (p. 331), whereas employment of other perspectives may lead to different conclusions:

> ... let us consider a simple sentence: 'Overpopulation arises because of the scarcity of resources available for meeting the subsistence needs of the mass of the population'. If we substitute our definitions [of subsistence, resources and scarcity] into this sentence we get: There are too many people in the world because the particular ends we have in view (together with the form of social organisation we have) and the materials available in nature, that we have the will and the way to use, are not sufficient to provide us with those things to which we are accustomed (p. 272).

With the first version of the sentence, the policy option seems clear – population reduction. The second allows Harvey to identify three possibilities, however: (i) changing both the desired end and the social organization; (ii) changing technical and cultural appraisals of nature; and (iii) changing views about the capitalist system and its scarcity basis. The Ehrlich–Commoner arguments regarding the origins of current environmental problems (p. 341) accept the first version of the sentence, however, and Harvey claimed that they have been grasped by the elite of the capitalist world to provide an underpinning for a popular ideology (the need for birth control). Similarly, Buchanan (1973) argued that the arguments for birth control in the Third World are part of the 'white north's' imperialist policy of ensuring its continued access to the resources of the international periphery (even to the extent of stimulating environmental destruction and famine: Bradley, 1986; Blaikie, 1986), and Johnston, Taylor and O'Loughlin (1987) have explored the geography of what Buchanan (1973, p. 9), along with other peace scientists, terms structural poverty: 'The poverty which is regarded as symptomatic of reckless population growth is rather a *structural poverty* caused by the irresponsible squandering of world resources by a small handful of nations'.

Under capitalism, the environment (or nature) is treated as a commodity, to be bought, exploited, and sold. N. Smith (1984) points out that nature is presented in capitalism's ideology as external to society, as the 'antithesis of human productivity . . . the realm of use-values rather than exchange values' (p. 32). But a 'second nature' is produced by capitalism:

> In its uncontrolled drive for universality, capitalism creates new barriers to its own future, it creates a society of needed resources, impoverishes the quality of those resources not yet devoured, breeds new diseases, develops a nuclear technology that threatens the future of all humanity, pollutes the entire environment that we must consume in order to reproduce, and in the daily work process it threatens the very existence of those who produce the vital social wealth (p. 59).

Nature, like spatial organization and reorganization, becomes a product of the continuing processes of capitalist accumulation (Fitzsimmons, 1989); as an abstract concept it is of no value to society and it is of interest only as a sphere of human activity (Pepper, 1984, 1996). This representation of nature as a social construction is not new: Zimmerman's (1972) classic work on natural resources defined a resource as only existing when it was perceived as such, and Glacken's (1967) classic survey shows how cultural conceptions of nature have varied. In his adaptation, however, Pepper (1984) separates the 'historicity of nature' (how the concept of nature in a particular time and place is related to the human activities there) from the 'naturalness of history' (the relationship between natural conditions and human activity – a relationship crudely expressed in theories of environmental determinism, p. 46). Part of the creation of a society involves its historicity of nature:

> Labour is the means whereby man converts nature into forms useful to him. In the main nature does not offer ready-made subsistence to man, neither does man take direct possession of nature's resources. He has to transform them. This process of transformation is a social one – it is done with other people who are organized in a particular way . . . Thus through shaping nature, men shape their own society and their relations with their fellows (p. 162).

Thus, just as the creation of social relations (the means of exploiting surplus value from labour by capital) is part of the making of a society, so too is the creation of society–nature inter-relations; and just as those social relations contain within them the seeds of crisis for capital accumulation (the class conflict) so too do the society–nature inter-relations (environmental problems). Johnston (1989b, 1996c) has carried this argument forward in an account of society–nature relationships under various modes of production and of the role of the state in their regulation (see also Taylor, 1994); the essays in Blaikie and Brookfield (1987) illustrate the general theme.

Harvey's (1974d) early Marxist work on ideology, social and economic life, and their complex inter-relationships with nature has since been extended by others into a holistic conception of the the social mediation of nature and the inevitability and necessity of (geographically) uneven development (e.g. Braun and Castree, 1998; Castree, 1995, 2003; Castree and Braun, 2001; Peet and Watts, 1996; Smith, 1984). In turn, such relationships have been problematized in Marxist-influenced work on 'landscapes'. Daniels (1989) thus stressed how conceptions of landscape were rooted in western capitalist society (see the recent review by Cosgrove, 2003). Building on this, but in a more direct line to Marx, Mitchell (2003, p. 238) notes that:

> ... the landscape can be understood to be a product of human labor, of people going to work on the land to make some thing out of it.

Thus:

> To understand landscape, and to understand the 'culture' within which it exists, requires an examination of human practices – of forms of labor. Through labor the landscapes is both made and made known. And in the process of working on and in landscape so too are people changed, whether that change is understood at the level of culture. ... or at the level of the individual human body (p. 239).

Radicals in debate

The 'radical camp' was never a united body of scholars, therefore, and although Marxism has remained the focus of some workers' activities it has been attacked by others, who are themselves associated with 'radical' stances. In 1986, for example, Saunders and Williams equated the recent literature in urban studies with an unchallenged 'taken for granted orthodoxy ... [that] thrives on an unspoken and largely unexamined political and theoretical consensus' (p. 393). They claimed that this has opposition to positivism as its linchpin, and arguments within it occupy 'a very narrow spectrum embracing left Weberianism and the different varieties of Marxism, but excluding almost everything else'. They concluded that, as a consequence, urban studies currently:

> ... makes little pretence of being 'value-free' or 'ethically neutral' and ... is sheltered from the possibility of empirical disconfirmation. This in turn means that approaches (such as the philosophy of the so-called 'New Right') which cannot be subsumed under the orthodoxy can be dismissed almost a priori. Such work is rarely read, still less seriously considered on its own terms. Rather a pejorative label is attached to it (for example, 'Thatcherism', 'Reaganism', or 'authoritarian populism') which enables us to pigeonhole it within our existing conceptual apparatus ... without ever having to engage with its intellectual content. In this way alternative ideas are dismissed but never discussed, explained away but never critically evaluated (pp. 393–4).

Elements of both Marxism and realism were then criticized, with the latter being characterized as a 'justification for subordinating history to theory' (p. 394) and the source of 'causes which can only be identified theoretically and which are guaranteed immunity from falsification even where there is no manifest evidence for their existence' (p. 395):

works which are explicitly anti-positivist are therefore castigated for not being subjected to positivist and critical rationalist procedures.

According to this critique, theories of structures have primacy in realist and Marxist approaches and as such are outdated: some major changes (such a changing gender relations and reconfigurations of culture, 'race', and identity) in British society over the last century are ignored, it is claimed – 'we still employ an essentially outdated class theory in our analyses' (p. 397) – and these approaches are also criticized as:

> . . . having done little or nothing to change the essential features of capitalism. As social change takes place under our noses, so we risk a situation where our methods and theories ensure that we pay it little heed. The orthodoxy is safeguarded and reproduced as the society changes.

One of the strongest adherents to a Marxist position, and a major focus of the Saunders-Williams critique, is Harvey, who characterized the goal of 'my academic concerns these last two decades . . . [as] to unravel the role of urbanisation in social change, in particular under conditions of capitalist social relations and accumulation' (Harvey, 1989b, p. 3). He responded to Saunders and Williams by noting 'a marked strategic withdrawal from Marxian theory within the field of urban analysis and a broadening reluctance to make explicit use of Marx's conceptual apparatus in articulating arguments' (Harvey, 1987, p. 367), and launched an attack against those whom he identified as abandoning the 'tough rigour of dialectical theorizing and historical materialist analysis', because:

> The case for retiring Marx's Capital to the shelves of some antiquarian bookstore . . . is not yet there. Indeed, in many respects the time has never been more appropriate for the application of Marx's conceptual apparatus to understanding processes of capitalist development and transformation. Furthermore, I believe the claim of Marxian analysis to provide the surest guide to the construction of radical theory and radicalizing practices still stands.

His critics have caved in too readily to right-wing pressures, he argued.

Harvey (1987, p. 368) agreed with Saunders and Williams that realism and the conceptualization of agency and structure 'are nothing more than weak disguises, soft versions of a traditional left orthodoxy ranging from left Weberianism to "different varieties of Marxism"'. But he disagreed with their identified way forward. He claimed that three 'myths' have pervaded the critique of Marxist scholarship. The first is *economism*, as illustrated by Duncan and Ley's critique (1982; see below, p. 253). The second is the claim that 'The abstractions of Marxian theory cannot explain the specificities of history and the particularities of geography' (p. 370), to which he took great exception. Harvey believes that, 'it is in principle possible to apply theoretical laws to understand individual instances, unique events' (p. 371), particularly since Marx's most interesting law-like statements were about capitalist processes, not events. He illustrated this with the chapter in *Capital* on 'The Working Day', arguing that such a detailed empirical description of how humans respond to their conditions on a daily basis allow 'categories like money, profit, daily wage, labour time, the working day, and ultimately value and surplus value [to] arise through an examination of historical materials' (p. 372), thereby illustrating how theory is both derived from and developed through the unravelling of particular situations.

Harvey saw the second myth being advanced from 'within the ranks of the left itself' (p. 373); Massey and Sayer's 'very deep and serious concerns for the particularities of places, events and processes' were noted. Sayer's realist approach was presented as involving a combination of 'wide-ranging contingency with an understanding of general processes', but:

> The problem with this superficially attractive method is that there is nothing within it, apart from the judgement of individual researchers, as to what constitutes a special instance to which special processes inhere or as to what contingencies (out of a potentially infinite number) ought to be taken seriously. There is nothing, in short, to guard against the collapse of scientific understandings into a mass of contingencies exhibiting relations and processes special to each unique event (Harvey, 1987, p. 373).

This, Harvey feared, is a path to 'simple empiricism' (p. 374), which he believed Saunders and Williams (1986) were also promoting; he characterized their agenda as 'nothing short of an abrogation of scientific responsibility and a caving in of political will'. Against that, Harvey insisted on 'the viability of the Marxist project', with its focus on 'universalising statements and abstractions' (p. 375) and its ability to guide political practice.

Finally, the third myth (the 'never-never land of nontotalizing discourses into which Marxists cannot enter because they insist on talking about totalities', p. 374) was presented as an attack on 'totalizing discourses', meta-theories and meta-narratives. While rejecting the notion that Marxism is 'inherently totalizing', Harvey nevertheless argued that, 'nothing appears more totalizing to me than the penetration of capitalist social relations and the commodity calculus into every niche and cranny of contemporary life'. If social theory can look only at the parts, then the whole can never be apprehended and challenged (part of Harvey's argument against postmodernism: see p. 276). To Harvey (p. 375):

> ... every single local study I read ... points to how locality is caught up in universal processes of financial flows, international divisions of labour, and the operations of global financial markets'. Claims to the contrary are dangerous, for they involve avoiding confrontations with 'the realities of political economy and the circumstances of global power'.

As Harvey (2002, pp. 184–5) later recorded, he rarely responded to critiques – 'because it had always seemed to me that the general stance of opposition to capitalism was best served by making creative contributions rather than engaging in destructive slanging matches'. But he 'had been somewhat taken by surprise' by the feminist critiques of *Condition of Postmodernity* (Harvey, 1989a: cf. Deutsch, 1991; Massey, 1991) and felt he had little option but to reply: this was published in *Antipode* (Harvey, 1992) – 'Nobody took much notice'.

Harvey's stance was supported by Smith (1987b), who defended Marxism as providing both a broad analytical framework and a 'quintessentially political discourse'; he found that the 'realist project ... has become the theoretical justification for the belief that there can be no general theory *at all* concerning questions of geographical space, and that any attempt to devise such a theory is fundamentally misconceived' (p. 379).

Others were less supportive, however; Ball (1987, p. 393), for example, took issue with Harvey's

> ... total dismissal of anyone who does not repeatedly declare their Marxist label, who does not believe that everything Marx said is unambiguous and correct, and who fails directly to apply the most abstract propositions of Marxist theory to the empirical situations they are investigating.

Sayer (1987, p. 395) also resented Harvey's impugning of motives, and responded to both Saunders and Williams and Harvey that, 'even if it means breaking off from what I had hoped and still hope for is a broad but common project, the search for a social science with an emancipatory potential'. Sayer agreed very much with Harvey that empirical research enables a clarification of theoretical understanding, it being 'partly responsible for making me revise my abstract ideas about the nature of capital, competition, class and the division of labour' (1987, p. 397: see also Sayer, 1995). He also defended realism against the charges of both reductionism and theoreticism (exemplified by Saunders and Williams), on the one hand, and of empiricism (Harvey), on the other.

Saunders and Williams (1987, pp. 427–8) began their response with the following categorization:

> Harvey eschews fraternization with the enemy, and he adopts a quasi-religious, almost messianic tone in delivering his epistle. He tells us ... of his unswerving belief that Marxism provides the surest guide to radical salvation ... Harvey's statement provides a good example of precisely that tendency in contemporary urban studies which we suggested could stifle fresh initiatives and hamper intellectual debate. If you believe, as Harvey apparently does, that the eternal verities have largely been established by Marx's Capital, then you have effectively closed off the possibility of open debate, and even more the possibility of learning from others who disagree.

Gould (1988) similarly criticized Marxist writers in general and Harvey in particular for what he termed their 'claim to exclusiveness'. Saunders and Williams then attacked Harvey for sustaining a 'totalizing' form of theory, which embraces the whole of society and thus has a privileged starting-point (or set of initial assumptions) which is not open to empirical refutation/confirmation:

> It is difficult to see how you can get to the whole by studying the parts and building up from there ... Totalising discourses are thus always unalterably committed to a priori assumptions – Marx's theories of exploitation, class struggle, and historical evolution came, not from studying people in Manchester, but from ideas about society 'as a whole', and these ideas were then mapped onto existing empirical observations (Saunders and Williams, 1987, pp. 428–9).

Thus Harvey's Marxism is not susceptible to effective falsification; nor, they assert, despite Sayer's arguments, is realism. Both are presented as 'closed' approaches, and although Saunders and Williams share the same goal as Harvey and Sayer, they believe that 'you will not develop an emancipatory social science before social science itself is opened up' (p. 430). Hence the debate, which the editor argued was necessary because capitalist society is changing; the nature of politics is altering and 'social theory has to take account of these cumulative changes' (Dear, 1987, p. 363).

Liberals, radicals and postmarxists in debate

Alongside debates *within* the 'radical' approach there have been others which, in the published contributions at least, have been much more heated than that generated by the 'quantitative revolution'. They have also been developed in more depth and detail, using forums, such as the journal *Area*, which were not available 20 years earlier, when publication outlets for 'views and opinions' were few. Whereas the behaviourists caused little real concern within the discipline, and their views were soon co-opted within the corpus of acceptable approaches, the radicals had much more impact, because they attacked not only the basis of most prior geographical work but also, in the clear inter-disciplinarity of their approach, both the bureaucratic structure of the discipline and the existence of geography itself (Johnston, 1978c); some, such as Eliot Hurst (1980, 1985), argued explicitly for the abolition of geography as a separate discipline (see also Taylor, 1996). A clear early example of the liberal–radical polarization was a debate on the geography of crime initiated by Peet (1975b), who argued that in attempting to make their work relevant geographers avoided asking 'relevant to whom?' (on which, see Harvey, 1974c); the political consequences of their work were ignored. The studies of crime reviewed (e.g. Harries, 1974) referred only to the surface manifestations of a social problem and could not provide solutions, only ways of ameliorating the problems: 'So it is that "useful" geography comes to be of use only in preserving the existing order of things by diverting attention away from the deepest causes of social problems and towards the details of effect' (Peet, 1975b, p. 277). Furthermore, geographers study only the crimes for which statistics are collected, thereby accepting the definition of crime by the elite; their maps, which are useful to police patrols, can therefore be employed to help maintain the *status quo* of power relations within society. The implicit position of the geographers involved is one of protecting the 'monopoly-capitalist state'.

Harries (1975) responded by attacking the simplistic nature of Peet's arguments, claiming that geographers would have no influence at all if they argued merely that crime is a consequence of monopoly capitalism. He contended that it is best to work within the system, to make the administration of justice more humane and equitable, to protect the potential victims of crime, and to provide employment opportunities for graduate geographers. Approaches based on crime control are likely to be more influential than polemics relating its cause to the mode of production: as Lee (1975, p. 285) also pointed out, Peet 'failed to provide us with any clues as to how he or other radical geographers would study crime' (p. 285).

Peet (1976a) responded to Lee's challenge, outlining a radical theory which would 'contribute directly, through persuasion, to the movement for social revolution' (p. 97). Capitalism harnesses human competitive emotions and generates inequalities in material and power rewards. Aggression is an acceptable part of being competitive, and is often released on the lower classes, who are encouraged to consume but provided with insufficient purchasing power. As the contradictions of this paradox increase, so does the pressure to turn to crime. Thus, crime occurs where the lower classes live, and at their spatial interface with the middle class. Harries (1976) replied that being a radical was a luxury few academics could afford, because working at a publicly-fnanced university demanded a pragmatic rather than a revolutionary approach. To him, Peet's theory is overly economic and deterministic; it fails to account for cultural elements, such as the disproportionate criminal involvement of blacks, the sub-culture of violence in the southern United States and other areas, and the fact that all economic systems produce minorities disadvantaged in terms of what they want and what they can get by socially legitimate means. He could offer no alternative theory, however: 'I do not carry in my head a theory of crime causation, and I am quite incapable of synthesizing and attaching value judgements to existing theoretical formulations within a couple of pages of typescript' (p. 102). He encouraged Peet to come off the fence, and to get involved in the production of change within the present system. Wolf (1976), on the other hand, claimed that by concentrating on the traditional concerns of Marxism Peet was not radical enough.

Two geographers who were involved in a considerable, often virulent, debate in the 1970s were Brian Berry and David Harvey. Berry (1972b) initiated the exchanges with comments on Harvey's (1972) paper on revolutionary theory and the ghetto. He wondered whether Harvey's rational arguments on the need for a revolution would be accepted, 'because of "commitment", the opposition will quietly drift into corners, the world will welcome the new Messiah, and social change will somehow, magically, transpire' (p. 32). The power to achieve change, he contended, needs more than logical argument – 'nothing less than cudgels has been effective' (p. 32) – and Harvey's belief in logical rationalism will be to no avail. He also argued that Harvey was wrong about the ghetto, for liberal policies were succeeding and the inequalities between blacks and whites were being reduced (Berry, 1974a). Harvey (1974a) responded that scarcity must continue in a capitalist economy, which will leave some people – probably those in the inner city – relatively disadvantaged.

Berry's (1974b) review of *Social Justice and the City* (Harvey, 1973) criticized Harvey's dependence on economic explanations. Based on Daniel Bell's (1973) characterization of post-industrial society, Berry (1974b, p. 144) claimed that the economic function is now subordinate to the political:

> . . . the autonomy of the economic order (and the power of the men who run it) is coming to an end, and new and varied, but different, control systems are emerging. In sum, the control of society is no longer primarily economic but political.

Harvey (1974b) responded that Marxism could not be considered as *passé* while the selling of labour power and the collusion between the economically and the politically powerful continue, and that the state has to be considered within a Marxist framework too (Harvey, 1976). Berry (1974b, p. 448) retorted:

> I believe that change can be produced within 'the system'. Harvey believes that it will come from sources external to that system, and then only if enough noise is produced at the wailing wall. . . . The choice, after all, is not that hard: between pragmatic pursuit of what is attainable and revolutionary romanticism, between realism and the heady perfumes of flower power.

Harvey's (1975c) response came in a review of Berry's (1973a) *The Human Consequences of Urbanization* – a study of urbanization processes at various times and places and of the planning responses they stimulated – which concluded that the book is 'all fanfare and no substance' (p. 99), revealing that Anglo-American urban theory is 'substantively bankrupt' and that 'it is scholarship of the Brian Berry sort which typically produces such messes' (p. 99):

> It is doubtful if it makes any sense even to consider urbanisation as something isolated from processes of capital formation, foreign and domestic trade, international money flows, and the like, for in a fundamental sense urbanisation is economic growth and capital accumulation – and the latter processes are clearly global in their compass (p. 102).

To Harvey, Berry has nothing to say of any substance, but he recognized that Berry 'is influential and important ... his influence is potentially devastating' (p. 103 – whether he meant this influence as within geography only, or beyond it too, is not clear). Berry's only response at the time was a general comment on the Union of Socialist Geographers (Halvorson and Stave, 1978, p. 233):

> ... there's no more amusing thing than goading a series of malcontents and kooks and freaks and dropouts and so on, which is after all what that group mainly consists of. There are very few scholars in the group.

Nearly 30 years later, Berry (2002c, p. 443) revisited that debate, claiming that Harvey's 'approach was that of the armchair intellectual contrarian ... [he] came to exemplify the tenured radical who lives comfortably on the rewards provided by the society that is the objective of his disdain'. Harvey (2002, p. 173), on the other hand, recorded that, 'I had a relatively secure position in the field. I could use my intellectual resources and powers to a political end and was fiercely determined ... to do so to the hilt, much as I had as an undergraduate when confronted by aristocratic privilege' at Cambridge.

Apart from these very polarized exchanges, several others indicated that whereas some 'liberals' were prepared to consider the radical case seriously, others tended to avoid the issues. Chisholm, for example (1975a, p. 175), claimed that:

> ... while I am fully sympathetic to the view that the 'scientific' paradigm is not adequate to all our needs, and must be supplemented by other approaches, I am not persuaded that it should be replaced. ... Harvey wants us to embrace the marxist method of 'dialectic'. This 'method' passes my understanding; so far as it has a value, it seems to be as a metaphysical belief system and not – as its protagonists proclaim – a mode of rational argument.

More frequently, reviewers accepted that the radical view added to their appreciation, but argued that is was not, for them at least, tenable in its entirety. Thus Morrill (1974) wrote of *Social Justice and the City* that, 'I am pulled most of the way by this revolutionary analysis but I cannot make the final leap that our task is no longer to find truth, but to create and accept a particular truth' (p. 477). King (1976, pp. 294–5) also sought a middle course:

> An economic and urban geography that will be concerned explicitly with social change and policy. ... Such a middle course will not find favour with the ideologues, who will see it either as another obfuscation favouring only 'status quo' and 'counter-revolutionary' theory, or as a distraction from the

immediate task of building elegant quantitative-theoretic structures, but some paths are being cut through the thicket of competing epistemologies, rambling lines of empirical analysis, and gnarled branches of applied studies that now cover the middle ground.

He accepted that much quantitative-cum-theoretical geography had sought mathematical elegance as an end in itself, at the sacrifice of realism; he believed that social science must feed into social policy and generate social change; and he accepted the 'intellectual power' of Marxist analysis but believed that prescriptions based on it are acceptable only if the ideological framework is also. His conclusion suggested the need for more quantification, which was operationally useful rather than mathematically elegant (see also Bennett, 1985a, 1985b), and later noted that, '*space* ... should be seen as an element in the political process, an object of competition and conflict between interest groups and different classes' (King and Clark, 1978, p. 12). Finally, Smith (1977, p. 368) concluded that:

Marx may have been able to dissect the operation of a capitalist economy with particular clarity, and see the essential unity of economy, polity and society that we so often miss today. But Marx does not hold the key to every modern problem in complex, pluralistic society.

The debates continued, with many geographers unable/unwilling to accept both the Marxist analysis of society and the Marxist programme for action. In part, this reflected a partial reading of Marxism – in particular a concentration on strict structural interpretations which neither allow for the activities of knowing individuals nor accept or acknowledge the considerable heterogeneity of Marxism. Ley (1980, p. 12), for example, saw in Marxism not only 'some hidden transcendental phenomenon ... directing the course of human society' – which commits an epistemological error, by denying or at least suppressing the subjective – but also a theoretical error that devalues the power of human action to redirect the course of events, and a moral error, which makes humans into puppets and threatens basic freedoms of speech, assembly and worship. Muir (1978) attacked interpretations of Marxism, and similarly implied that it threatens individual freedom of the academic 'to pick and choose from among the ... literature' (p. 325). Respondents pointed to the lack of such 'intellectual orthodoxy' and 'sterilized geography' (Manion and Whitelegg, 1979; Duncan, 1979), but Muir (1979, p. 127) remained convinced of the threat implicit in 'the commands from such little men as Marx, Lenin, Trotsky, Stalin and Mao concerning the primacy of activism, the obligations of party membership and the necessity to subordinate individual judgement to the will of the party'. He claimed that radical geography is contributing to understanding, but to call it Marxist is to give it a certain programmatic base. Walmsley and Sorensen (1980), on the other hand, presented Marxism as just irrelevant, deflecting attention from 'reformism and relevance'.

Duncan and Ley (1982) published an extensive critique of Marxism in geography, containing four major themes.

1. Marxist analysis is a form of holism, in which the whole – variously termed capital, the economic structure, economic processes, etc. – is given a life of its own: an abstraction is assumed to exist. This reification (see also Gould, 1988) offended their belief in individuals as conscious, free agents (see Duncan, 1980, on holism in

cultural geography, and Agnew and Duncan, 1981) – although they did not proclaim an idealist alternative, and accepted that 'individual action cannot be fully explained without reference to the contexts under which individuals act' (p. 32);

2. Individuals are represented as agents of the whole – the means of implementing its goals – not as free decision-makers in their own right;
3. The materialist infrastructure of Marxism is a form of economism – it presents economic processes as the ultimate cause of all behaviour, which excludes many other influences and leads to the final theme; and
4. 'The attempt to cast explanation continually and everywhere in terms of economic imperatives, [leads] . . . to a crisis in empirical exposition' (p. 47).

The last comprises what is essentially a positivist critique: 'the form of the explanations is both tautological and empirically untestable. The result is a mystification in explanation of how real processes operate' (p. 55). They concluded that structural Marxism in human geography presents a passive view of the individual, offering explanations in terms of abstract wholes which are obfuscatory and not verifiable. Later work by Duncan (1985) showed that he was attracted to the structuration approach, however, which allows for human agency operating within structural constraints – as indeed do most interpretations of Marxism.

Others who criticized structural Marxism disagreed with its treatment of the individual, and wanted more convincing models of the inter-relationships between infrastructure and superstructure in the process of societal change. Gregory (1981) presented four such models (Figure 6.2):

Figure 6.2 *Models of the relationships between society and individual (Source: Gregory, 1981, p. 11)*

1. *Reification*, in which the individual's actions are entirely determined by the whole – as in a structural Marxism that denies human agency;
2. *Voluntarism*, in which society has no separate identity but is constructed from the actions of free individuals;
3. *Dialectical reproduction*, in which the whole creates the individuals, whose actions then influence the whole – which in turn creates the next generation of individuals; and
4. *Structuration*, which starts with individuals rather than with the whole, and portrays them in a continuous dialectic with society from then on.

These different approaches are based on a variety of conceptions of the nature of the human agent (see Barnes, 1988; Claval, 1983; Harrison and Livingston, 1982; and van der Laan and Piersma, 1982). Gregory opted for the fourth, because it integrated humanist and materialist (or structuralist) perspectives, in a way that critiques such as Duncan and Ley's did not (see also Thrift, 1983a). Such an integration would recognize the materialist base to society (the infrastructure) while accepting the important role of human agency in the superstructure; humanistic geography should not compete with a scientific approach, but should acknowledge 'the recurrent and recursive relations between the individual and society as being fundamentally implicated in the production and reproduction of both social life and social structure' (p. 15).

Alongside debates on the relevance of Marxist ideas, other geographers were defending quantitative spatial science against critiques such as Gregory's (1978a, 1980). Bennett (1981d, p. 24), for example, argued that much of the critique of quantitative geography as 'positivism' had been misplaced and accepted uncritically the representation of science as positivism given by Harvey in 1969. This has had a pernicious and destructive effect on the subject in three main ways: first, it has suggested that scientific and empirical enquiry is largely socially worthless; second, it has often rejected the links between physical and human geography; and third, it has often rejected the existence of geography as a discipline at all. (Elsewhere, he characterized the critique as 'at best a mis-representative irrelevance, and at worst a fatuous distraction': Bennett and Wrigley, 1981, p. 10.) Quantification need not be allied with positivism according to Bennett, who identified three messages from Harvey's *Explanation in Geography*: geography is primarily inductive; geography is an objective science; and geography seeks universal laws. But 'each is only a partial representation of the literature and ideas it seeks to describe' (Bennett, 1981d, p. 13). Radical and quantitative approaches must be integrated 'by empirical analyses, from the integration of environmental, social, political, and economic aspects with space, historical stimuli, and specific modes of thought and their spatial-political manifestations . . . by the re-establishment of the geographical subject matter' (p. 24). A separate discipline of geography (human plus physical), in which quantitative geography – 'never . . . truly positive' (Bennett and Wrigley, 1981, p. 10) – occupies a central place, would answer: 'the fundamental questions of social norms, social distribution, policy impacts and humanistic concerns which the critics rightly emphasize' (p. 10). Many 'radicals' would categorize this as a *status quo* approach (p. 331).

In a later provocative essay, Bennett (1989a) argued that much 'radical geography' was out of touch with what he termed the 'spirit of the times'. He claimed that the welfare state, with its emphasis on rights, had led geographers to concentrate not only on inequalities but also to adopt a welfarist view that '*morally* they should be overcome or at least ameliorated' (p. 279). This leads to the argument that all differences imply relative deprivation and automatic entitlements to state action which would remedy them. But the newly dominant social theories (associated in the UK with 'Thatcherism') stress not 'the negative aspects of capitalism's capacity to create new wants and hence new "relative deprivation" but rather the liberating potential of markets'. According to his argument (see also p. 352), geographers should reorient their work to focus on the proper role of the state in such a society, identifying when it should interfere with market forces to ensure basic human rights, rather than promoting a welfare-corporate state that must eventually fail (see Johnston, 1992a, 1993e).

Thrall (1985) reported on a conference on 'scientific geography', which reached the consensus that, 'Research in the unified areas of theory and modelling, data measurement and simulation, estimation and verification is central to the discipline of geography' (p. 254); such a perspective, he contended, should be used to promote the image of geography among the sciences and the 'acceptance of scientific approaches within geography'. His equation of science with mathematics, statistics and computer literacy was challenged by Driver and Philo (1986), who argued that 'science is more than a matter of technique' (p. 161) and that a clearly technocratic approach 'effectively marginalizes all other modes of interpretation and explanation' (p. 162). Thrall's (1986) response identified three major geographical traditions: humanistic, scientific and pure theoretical. Scientific geography, he claimed, is a 'philosophy of research … clearly distinct from the earlier quantitative geography movement' (p. 162); he advocated research involving hypothesis-testing leading to theory-creation and verification, rather than either the empiricism of regional geographies or the sterile output of pure theoretical research.

This presentation of geography as an applied, quantitative discipline, but one which does not accept the canons of positivism, faced continuing criticism. David Smith (1984, p. 132), for example, concluded an autobiographical essay with the statement that:

> To be quite honest, I no longer care very much about geography, with its smug self-satisfaction and nauseating narrow-minded chauvinism. Who else but geographers would dignify their puerile pursuit of statistics, models and paradigms as a 'revolution' as though it mattered to anyone but themselves? … And who else would want to read such trivia? How can we take it all so seriously, when it contributes so little to the improvement of the human condition? Most geography is inconsequential claptrap, and never more so than during the 'quantitative revolution'.

Mercer (1984, p. 194) argued in the same vein, though noting that:

> … the last few years have witnessed a small – though perhaps temporary – retreat from the more lunatic excesses of flat earth quantitative geography towards a growing recognition that reality is not in fact beautifully ordered but that it is characterized much more by contradictions, tension and

disharmony. The daunting ... task for the critical geographer – whether 'Marxist' or humanist – [includes] ... the fight against the hegemony of naive, blinkered, technocratic thinking.

He wanted to unmask 'technocratic geography' and divert attention away from topics such as 'Where are the regions of health care need based on access to hospitals?' to more fundamental questions like 'What leads to ill health?'. His basic theme was that selection of a particular research style, with the connotations of how its output may be used, involves an (albeit possibly unconscious) ideological choice: different conceptions of science are based on different views of both its utility and the social order within which that utility is to be employed.

Other writers sought to integrate elements of the positivist, humanistic and structuralist approaches to human geography (e.g. Christensen, 1982; for a fuller review, see Johnston, 1986f). Some attempts have been short-lived, such as an essay on the links between catastrophe theory and the discontinuities central to Marxist economic theory (Day and Tivers, 1979, pp. 54–8; Alexander, 1979, pp. 228–30). Hay (1979a, p. 22) argued for an empirical, analytical geography that is:

... at the same time a nomological geography which seeks, for example, to understand the workings of urban rent theory as positivistically observed, a hermeneutic geography which seeks to identify the meaning of the urban rent system for those who are participants (active or passive) within it, and a critical geography which points to the extent to which present urban rent systems are themselves transformations of the capitalist system, but which admits that some of its features may indeed be 'invariant regularities'.

Livingstone and Harrison (1981, p. 370) somewhat similarly presented a case for 'a humanistic geography which is, at the same time, critical, in questioning rather than bracketing our presuppositions, hermeneutic, in interpreting the meanings behind action, and empirical, in examining the subjectively interpreted objective world'. But, unlike Hay, they included no nomological – or generalizing – component.

Some, particularly the critics of positivism, argued that such attempts at integration are not feasible because the approaches are incompatible: Gregory (1978a, p. 169) terms it 'inchoate eclecticism'. (See also Gregory, 1982b; Eyles and Lee, 1982; Hudson, 1983. Positivist and structuralist approaches sit unhappily together in Rhind and Hudson, 1981.) The biggest problem is with positivism – not quantification (Walker, 1981b; though see Sayer, 1984, 1992a, and the response in Johnston, 1986a, 1993f) – because of its nomological orientation and belief that human geographers can discover 'invariant regularities'.

Increasingly these debates were not directly concerned with different philosophies of geography, but rather with their utility. As a consequence of the demands on education and research from governments of the 'New Right', considerable pressure to advance the study and practice of applied geography built up. (Taylor, 1985c, sets such pressures in historical context; themes to which we shall return in Chapter 9.) Some, such as Bennett (1985b) and Openshaw (1989), saw geographers' technical competence being applied to situations in the public and private sectors without any necessary reference to philosophical issues; applied geographers are thus technicians (as in Gatrell, 1985), who implicitly accept the context within which their skills are used. The philosophical issues remain important to others, however; Golledge *et al.* (1982) countered Hart's (1982, p. 5) case for regional geography that 'We cannot allow ourselves to be intimidated by those who flaunt the banner of science' with:

> We equally cannot allow ourselves to be intimidated by those who flaunt the banner of anti-science, those who would reject all that is scientific about the discipline, and those who would urge a return to the descriptive morass from which we have recently emerged (Golledge *et al.*, 1982, p. 558).

Most arguments for applied geography implied that it should be based in empiricist/positivist philosophies, however; the counter-arguments that humanistic science can be applied to improve self- and mutual awareness and that realistic science can be applied to advance social transformation were rarely presented (Johnston, 1986a).

Others believed that an eclectic pluralism is possible (see the discussion in Johnston, 1986f): some conducted empiricist work (often in the behavioural geography mould) unconcerned with any philosophical ramifications of that practice (see Flowerdew, 1986), however, whereas others generally accepted the realist case and situated their activities within that context. Gould (1985a, p. 296), for example, contended that:

> There is no question in my mind that the appearance of Marxist concern in geography, and its concomitant shaping of the lens through which the world is seen, have greatly enriched our methodological approach. There is an insistence that the things at the surface are not always what they seem, and that it is crucial to dig down underneath the superficial appearances to get at the deep structures. I think this is quite right.

But he criticized Marxists for their claims to truth, their condescending attitudes to 'non-believers', their over-concentration on economic forces, and the 'messianic claims that seem to lead so readily and so often to the sacrifice of human beings today for some promise tomorrow' (p. 300). Finally, there were geographers who, while not convinced of the case for an eclectic pluralism, nevertheless saw the need for a *rapprochement* of the 'radical' and humanistic approaches: their arguments are the focus of the next chapter.

Just as wider political pressure for radical transformations around the world provided the initial backdrop to the emergence of radical geography at the end of the 1960s, so the relative eclipse of socialism in the Third World and its collapse in what was hitherto the Second World produced a new context. The political events of the late 1980s and early 1990s in Eastern Europe thus demanded critical reflection. As Sayer (1995, p. 13) notes:

> For the Right they were a vindication: communism was defeated, capitalism had won. . . . Strangely, it was assumed by many that it also meant that Marxism was defeated, as if Western Marxists ought to have recanted as soon as the statues of Lenin and Marx started being toppled. This ignored the fact that the vast majority of Marx's work and most Western Marxism is concerned with capitalism and that most Western Marxists were overwhelmingly critical of the state socialist regimes.

This, he argued, diverted attention to capitalism's continued failings and to the failure of what he termed radical political economy to suggest viable alternatives. Hence his detailed analysis of work in that genre, which he located within 'Marxism's lack of a sufficiently materialist understanding of the social division of labour and its associated division and dispersion of knowledge in advanced economies' (p. 12). Instead of attacking this problem, researchers (in the context of the 'cultural turn' — see the next chapter) have switched their attention away from issues of power, domination, and subordination linked to class and capital (p. 13):

> This seems an entirely reasonable response, as analysis of these matters was long overdue. The uncharitable explanation is that faced with the challenge of the New Right and the weakening of Marxism, radicals shifted their attention to new concerns which did not require them to make any painful concessions to the Right. Socialism as an alternative political system was increasingly difficult to articulate and defend, but in any case there were other important issues to turn to which provided a convenient escape. While understandable, this escapist response is surely less defensible. In my view, both of these explanations of the shift from economy to culture — charitable and uncharitable — are right. Although post-Marxism has been generally a progressive development in terms of broadening radical interests it has neglected political-economic theory. There is therefore much unfinished business.

His approach to that unfinished business concentrates on the complexity of the social division of labour within contemporary capitalism (see also Sayer and Walker, 1992). Social divisions occur between enterprises involved in the creation of a vast range of products and services, whereas technical divisions (on which Marx and his followers concentrated) occur within enterprises, and are concerned with their ownership and structure and the nature of labour contracts (see Rose and Pevalin, 2003). Individual enterprises can be planned in terms of how much will be produced and marketed, by how many people, and at what cost. Whole conglomerations of enterprises — Sayer follows Hayek in terming them catallaxies — cannot be so planned because of their internal variety and complexity, however; their activities must be coordinated in other ways, which at present means the market economy celebrated by the New Right's identification of the 'end of history' (Fukuyama, 1992; Peet, 1993; Johnston, 1994a). But the inequalities that follow pose major challenges (Sayer, 1995, p. 210):

> Political economy ... has to address issues of division of knowledge and catallaxy, horizontal control, coordination, allocation and economizing, which generally elude democratic control ... To ignore these issues is simply to duck the most serious problems of political economy.

So that (p. 252):

> Radical political economy cannot continue to follow Marxism in standing apart from the debates of normative political theory, nor can it embrace a postmodernist celebration of fragmentation and rejection of the search for a better social framework. It is now more clear than ever that struggles which are directed against domination and oppression but which lack any normative direction in terms of alternative frameworks are unlikely to be successful. Though it has recently suffered from neglect we need a radical political economy more than ever before.

The events of 1989 and the early 1990s in the former Soviet Union and its client regimes in eastern Europe (and their variants in the Third World) thus posed both difficulties and an opportunity for geographers of a Marxist persuasion, as many of their opponents argued that the collapse of the communist states indicated the fallibility of Marxist political programmes. (Smith, 1991, p. 406, noted that, 'it has become a common argument in left circles that the crumbling of Communist Party control throughout Eastern Europe and the Soviet Union provides definite proof that planning and state control of the economy don't work and can't work'.) Folke and Sayer (1991) argued that to claim that 'they weren't really socialist' anyhow is an unsatisfactory response, although they recognize that the events mean that 'genuine socialist visions and utopian dreams will have a hard time in Eastern Europe in the coming years' (p. 248): new blueprints of how to manage complex societies in the interests of all are needed (see Sayer, 1995), and they must recognize, as Smith (1991, p. 416) argued, that '1989 teaches us the profound depth of human resistance to all forms of economic, social and political repression': successful revolutions must be broadly based and sustained. Sayer (1992b, p. 217) responded that:

> The problems that the left now faces are not just a consequence of the rise of the right, or of mistakes made in the 1920s; they are also a result of the vacuum on the left concerning socialist alternatives which are feasible as well as desirable. I think we would do better to confront that fatal weakness.

Moreover, work in a political economy tradition has also charted the contradictions and unevenness of the capitalist transition in post-communist societies (see Pickles and Smith, 1998). Such works claim the continued relevance of Marxist and allied political economy approaches in an avowedly post-Marxist world. Notable too is the online and activist 'People's Geography Project':

> The major goal of the People's Geography Project is to popularize and make even more relevant and useful to ordinary people the important, critical ways of understanding the complex geographies of everyday life that geographers have and continue to develop. Our contention is that such knowledge is an important tool not just in learning to cope with constantly developing and transforming relations of power that are deeply geographical, but in learning how to actively transform those relations in the name of social and economic justice (http://www.peoplesgeography.org/).

On another scale, the role of 'global cities' that are the 'control centres' of the international (or 'globalizing') corporate economy (Beaverstock, Smith and Taylor, 2000; Knox and Taylor, 1995) has become a significant theme of contemporary research (see the online *Globalization and World Cities Study Group and Network* at http://www.lboro.ac.uk/gawc/), whose origins can partly be traced to radical geography's attention to power and inequality and its understanding of urbanization and uneven development as integral to capitalist dynamics.

Others reclaim Marxism within a critique of the globally hegemonic ideas and practices of 'neo-liberalism' (see the special issue of *Antipode* 2002 – Volume 34, 3 – especially Peck and Tickell, 2002). Thus Wills (2002, pp. 96–7) feels able to claim that:

Political-economic geographers are seeking to develop new theory and analysis to understand capitalism and political change. Encouragingly, I detect a move back to the big picture, to unpacking capitalism, while also developing a more sophisticated theorization of political agency, which incorporates economy and culture, class and identity. ...There is a huge canvas on which a new generation of geographers could get to work and it is critically important that new students are attracted into political-economic research within the discipline. Indeed this may happen through an initial engagement with cultural and social geography as much as through economic or political geography.

And while, as Wills points out, Marxism also continues as an important influence in reconstituted cultural geography (see Chapter 7), on the part of others there is also continued caution and sober reassessment about the limits to Marxism (e.g. Jones, 1999; Storper, 2001) and/or the value of supplementing it with other approaches and qualifications. Recent debates in *Antipode* about the future of radical geography have reviewed its status and roles, as well as reconsidering the commitment of geographers to progressive social change and the policies and politics that might be most productive in such a project, and the role of 'theory' therein (see Hague, 2002, and Castree, 2002). For example, while Waterstone (2002, p. 666) claimed that:

What we have is, once again, a radical critique from the margins of a truly staid discipline that moves along mostly untouched by what happens in the pages of this journal.

Wills and Peck (2002, p. 669) responded:

... the fact that radical geography can no longer be dismissed as a fringe concern represents a remarkable victory for the project, even if in the process it has taken on some 'mainstream' connotations.

Throughout virtually all of human geography, the scale and force of the radical contribution and legacy means that it has proven hard to ignore. It may now be the case that, as Taylor (2003, pp. 55–6) states:

Soon after its emergence, radical geography, whether of Peet, of Harvey, of Blaut, or of Bunge, became explicitly Marxist in nature ... to be a radical scholar no inevitably means taking a Marxist, 'neo' or otherwise, approach to understanding social change. In the contemporary academy there is an array of schools of thought that aspire 'to turn the world upside down'.

However, it is a measure of the ongoing presence of radical geography and of Marxism within it that avowedly 'post-Marxist' geographers such as Smith and Doel (2001, p. 137) allow that 'it is clear that many postmodernists and poststructuralists have extended or reacted to Marxism in a number of useful and interesting ways which do not necessarily mean the jettisoning of a radical left-wing politics'. Such possibilities are the subjects of our next chapters here.

Conclusions

This chapter has illustrated the depth and breadth of discussions that occupied much of the 1970s and 1980s and continued into the 1990s. Peet (1998, p. 294) feels that:

A discipline can support only a few true radicals; the rest have functional utility, oblique though this often may seem.

Yet in these turbulent decades, a growing proportion of geographers wished to be involved in reshaping societies, either through ameliorative correction of current problems and trends or by designing desirable spatial organizations (Berry, 1973a): some saw this as necessary if human geography was to retain its institutional position. Their motives ranged from 'pure altruism' to 'devoted self-seeking'; their methods varied from those who accept the present mode of production and see humanitarian goals as achievable within its constraints, to those who subscribed to the phenomenological view (Buttimer, 1974, p. 29) that:

> ... the social scientist's role is neither to choose or decide for people, nor even to formulate the alternatives for choice but rather, through the models of his discipline, to enlarge their horizons of consciousness to the point where both the articulation of alternatives and the choice of direction could be theirs, to those who believed that a revolution is necessary to remove the causes of society's myriad problems and replace them by an equitable social structure.

Perhaps paradoxically, the 'revolutionaries' in the above classification are not 'activists' in the sense of being deeply involved in contemporary issues. The 'liberals' advanced the strongest arguments for geographical contributions to the solution of societal problems, particularly those which involve public sector intervention (e.g. Bennett, 1983), and pressed for academic engagement in policy-making; many of the 'radicals', on the other hand, argued that their longer-term goals were best served through educational programmes (e.g. Huckle, 1985), although some were involved in policy-making activities for institutions (such as local governments) that promoted alternative (socialist) strategies, especially in the support for employment initiatives (e.g. Duncan and Goodwin, 1985; see, however, Harvey, 1995, and Massey, 2001, on the tensions this can create). The two groups are members of the same discipline, and practise in the same academic environments, yet their goals and methods seem totally incommensurate. Alongside them are many others who continue to research and teach in an empiricist context, with some recognition of the range of the philosophical arguments but little detailed consideration of their implications for the practice of geography. (Flowerdew, 1986, argues that, on the basis of papers submitted to him as Editor of *Area* over a three-year period, the vast majority of geographical work is empiricist, with 'unexamined value positions, no explicit theory and no clear criteria for establishing the truth of statements', p. 263.) For them, perhaps the majority of human geographers, the task is to assemble material, thereby to sensitize their readers to the world as they perceive it.

In this context, perhaps the key to the influence of radical geography within the discipline is that Marxist work was able to set many of its leading intellectual agendas. Thus Neil Smith (2001, p. 9) comments that:

> Within 'establishment geography', the dramatic rise of Marxism in the early 1970s was first ignored, later despised, and eventually resented, even if it was eventually if begrudgingly accomodated. Yet there was little that establishment geographers, who completely controlled the discipline in North America,

Britain, and Australia, could do to prevent it. Responses to marxist work in this period invariably lacked the intellectual sophistication that marxist theory brought, and criticisms often came across as shallow and contradictory. ... A medical metaphor captures the situation. The allergy of English-speaking geography (as a discipline) to social theory throughout most of the twentieth century now meant that the discipline had no immune system against Marxism. Marxism in the 1970s and 1980s ... offered powerful insights concerning the political questions of the day, and offered a breathtaking global vista of of the geographies of exploitation, oppression and and injustice – and their causes. ... Just as important, it provided the most sophisticated social theory that many geographers had come in contact with, and its opponents had few if any social theoretical resources for counteracting its influence. Unlike anthropology or sociology where various major figures had been socialists, geography as a discipline lacked all immunity against Marxism. Intellectually if not institutionally, the old guard was defeated almost before the struggle began.

Yet by the 1980s, Anglo-American geography as a whole was still characterized by a plurality of approaches (Gould and Olsson, 1982), which can perhaps be classified into three intertwined philosophical strands (or sets of strands), each with a distinctive epistemology, or theory of knowledge.

1. First was the positivist philosophy, with its belief in the objectivity of scientific description (empiricism) and analysis of the world, its goal of formulating laws about that world, and its assumption that explanation (causal laws) can be derived by studying the outcomes of the laws; the laws of spatial organization and behaviour can be revealed by analysing spatial patterns. At least some of those who promoted the empiricist foundation to this philosophy denied that it necessarily leads to the full positivist commitment. They disagreed over the use of scientific procedures for the evaluation of hypothesis, however, as in the critical rationalism usually associated with Popper (Hay, 1985a; Marshall, 1985; Bird, 1989).
2. Second were the humanistic philosophies based on a belief that people live in subjective worlds of their own creation, within which they act as free agents. Their actions cannot be explained (predicted) as examples of general laws of behaviour, but only understood – or appreciated – through methodologies that pierce their subjectivity.
3. Finally there were various structuralist-influenced philosophies (and other broadly allied variants of Marxism) that argued that explanations for observed patterns cannot be discovered through analysis of the patterns themselves, but only by the development of theories of the underlying processes that generate the conditions within which human agents can create those patterns. Foremost within this group is Marxism, which argues that the processes are themselves changing – and can be altered by concerted political action – so that no universal laws of spatial organization are possible; at least not outside an understanding of the social dynamics of particular societies and modes of production. The trajectory of Marxism through geography has, however, been complex (and with detours such as realism and structuration theory) and the trajectories (as in the case of structuralist Marxisms influence via the work of Massey and regulation theory)

have not always been clear to all or contributed to and contested in a variety of Marxist geographies.

Weaving across these was also a nascent feminist critique (the focus of Chapter 8).

Such plurality provided a focus of debate, and even a source of confusion, among human geographers. For some, it presented a polarization that can only be solved when one approach (paradigm?) is proved triumphant. Others argued that this cannot be done logically, since there are no common criteria for comparing the approaches. For many, the plurality offered potential for developing a newer, more robust human geography (e.g. Wilson, 1989a), though the nature of that development remained unclear to many. (The summaries of the statements made by six geographers – Hall *et al.*, 1987 – to a review by the British Economic and Social Research Council on *Horizons and Opportunities in Social Science* clearly illustrated the pluralism.) However complex and uncertain this may have looked to many, geography had undoubtedly been transformed, and although it was still a relatively small discipline (especially in the US), its relative status among the social sciences was greatly enhanced.

But the world in which geographers work, and which they study, and the political and philosophical influences upon them continued to change so that, without any definitive resolution of the debates outlined in this chapter, by the 1990s geographers were presented with further intellectual and practical challenges. Thus, further developments outside the discipline influenced it by the mid-1980s, and within a decade these were the source of further significant reorientations in what many human geographers did, and why. They are the focus of the next two chapters.

7
Postmodern geographies

Posts- and turns

It might perhaps be rather un-postmodern of us to give our readers the clear structure of things in advance. We also might rearrange things, like Soja's (1989) text on *Postmodern Geographies* which begins on page one with a combined Preface and Postscript – 'to shake up the normal flow of the linear text to allow other, more "lateral" connections to be made'. Alternatively, like Dear and Flusty's (2002, p. xiii) *The Spaces of Postmodernity*, we might 'forego a "Conclusion" for an "Inconclusion", refusing even to contemplate a closure that, like so many previous (anti)climaxes, would function only to suppress different ways of knowing'. But like many geographers, a variety of (modernist) structured narrative might be what you have come to expect from diagrams, texts, tables, maps and published papers in the discipline – so allow us some pointers here.

This chapter is concerned with a number of influences and transformations which informed human geography in the 1980s and 1990s and that show little sign of losing their senses of possibility and potential for re-working human geography in the twenty-first century. These include postmodernism, poststructuralism and a putative 'cultural turn'. The latter has seen a reinvigoration not only of cultural geography, but also a bringing to bear of cultural themes on a wider range of human geographies (including economic geography: see Lee and Wills, 1997). Feminist geography (and allied work on sexuality) also had a substantial and growing impact in the 1980s and 1990s; we will consider this in the next chapter. In this chapter, however, we also consider the impact of postcolonialism, in particular a reconsideration of geography's complicity in colonialism and tentative moves to decolonize geography. The former – geography's colonial history – is something that radical geographers and positivists had both sought, in different ways, to put behind them. Positivists had advocated a new scientific geography which would have little or nothing to do with geography's prior trajectory of regional description and narration of difference (geography as an inventory of regions and their peoples). For their part, radicals had often proclaimed their anti-imperialism. Postcolonialism builds on this sense of critique.

Beyond the discipline, the 1980s and 1990s saw rapid changes in the economic, social and political contexts within which academic geography was set and in the practices employed in other social science and humanities disciplines. The former comprised the globalization and flexible accumulation trends within capitalism described earlier (and the eclipse of communism – at least that form of it which had been known through most of the twentieth century), along with major changes in the nature and role of the state apparatus which had profound effects on the funding and expectations of research in higher education. The latter involved attempts to come to terms intellectually with those changes, in the context of widespread disillusion with current academic practices. On both sides of the North Atlantic and in the other Anglophone contexts that are the focus of this book, the private and public sector structures in place since the 1940s were being partly dismantled, and replaced by others which appeared much less permanent. In the private sector, for example, many of the large manufacturing industries were very significantly 'downsized', if not totally eliminated, and their replacements were often in service industries, usually offering less job security and fewer fringe benefits, and with much weaker trades unions representing worker interests. In the public sphere, social democratic and 'left' political parties appeared to have lost some of their core support: the Democratic party's hegemony in the American southern states rapidly dwindled away, for example, and in the UK a majority of skilled working-class trades unionists (a class faction in relative decline and increasingly out-manoeuvered) voted for the Conservative party at the 1983 and 1987 general elections – and then a decade later a large proportion of the middle classes switched their support to 'New Labour'. Change was rapid and was everywhere; understanding why it was happening and what was replacing it provided human geographers with major challenges (as suggested by the essays in Johnston, 1993d) – but the changes were also affecting the institutions in which they worked, often increasing pressures associated with such rapid changes, combined with increased audit and so called 'efficiency' gains (see Chapters 1 and 10). At the same time, however, many of the demographic and social changes and pressures of the 1960s were also working through the system – with attendant generational shifts and a sense of new possibilities. The radical geography which began then had also come of age and continued to be a point of departure and reference – it had opened up new ways of thinking and new engagements for human geography – and would be re-evaluated by new generations of geographers. Hence, in Neil Smith's (2001, p. 10) words:

> The rapid deepening of Marxist research in that decade [of the 1980s] was therefore matched by an even more rapid broadening as Marxist work explored and eventually fused with all kinds of social theory.

For Hubbard, Kitchin, Bartley and Fuller (2002, p. 63) however:

> ...much contemporary critical human geography (though not all) is fundamentally different from the more homogeneous radical geography practised in the late 1960s and 1970s. ...As such, structural and materialist accounts have been complemented (and in many instances replaced) by positions more sensitive to human agency and questions of culture.

Cultural turns?

Although it might also partly be summarized by reference to the growth of qualitative methods (Crang, 2002), a more frequent way of summarizing new trends in human geography during the later part of the 1980s and the 1990s has been to adopt the label of 'cultural turn'. Chris Philo, who had earlier (1991) identified a nascent cultural turn in human geography, had the following to say in the year 2000 of that earlier moment (and of the 1991 collection of essays *New Words, New Worlds: Reconceptualising Social and Cultural Geography* which he had compiled and which contributed to the sense of new departures):

> ... the main achievement was arguably to heighten our senses of how all things cultural might be raised to a much more prominent position in studies throughout the corpus of human geography (and not just in one or two neatly parceled-off subdisciplines). It was to take much more seriously than hitherto all manner of things that might be construed as constituting the cultural 'stuff' of human life, not just phenomena routinely designated as cultural ... but also the complete panoramo of meaning systems both collective (e.g. religions and nationalisms) and more individual (built up in personal psychic economies). ...This was to anticipate the amazingly rich arc of the cultural turn within human geography as it has now arisen: a turn which obviously had great ramifications for both social and cultural geography, but one too which has undoubtedly sent shockwaves throughout the length and breadth of human geography, leading to debates (more or less explicit, more or less heated) about the merits of a cultural turn within (say) economic geography, political geography, population geography, environmental geography and elsewhere (Philo, 2000, p. 28).

For Philo, the cultural turn had been many years in the making. Thus, what he terms the 'valuable manouvers' (p. 32) and 'twin routes out of spatial science after *circa* 1970 signposted by, respectively, radical/Marxist geography (with its focus on social structure) and behavioral/humanistic geography (with its focus on human agency)' (p. 31) together:

> ... paved the way for the cultural turn of more recent vintage ... the wider horizons of late 1980s human geography which gave birth to the cultural turn included a variety of developments which extended, and in many cases recast, the Marxist and humanistic revolutions of the previous decade. ... The reworkings of Marxist geography – the spatializing of Marxist concepts; the restructuring, spatial divisions of labour and locality studies debates; the advent of regulation and regime theories; the critical realist encounter; the agitations around post-Marxism ... have all created a receptiveness to the ways in which ... cultural processes become implicated in political-economic spaces ... [and] the reworkings of humanistic geography – the reappraisal of the landscape tradition; the growing attention to intersubjective meaning systems; the fragmenting of the singular figure of 'Man' in recognizing the sheer dioversity of peoples occupying this planet; the new mapping of the human subject(s); the alterness to the psycho-dynamics of gender and sexuality – have all fostered a sensitivity to the many dimensions of immaterial culture which enter into the making of virtually all human spaces imaginable.

This use of the term 'cultural turn' suggests a link with the sub-discipline of cultural geography, as traditionally practised – what was widely known as the Berkeley School, associated with the work of Carl Sauer (see p. 57). Price and Lewis (1993a), however, suggested that beyond the use of the adjective 'cultural', the 'old' and the 'new' 'share precious little' (p. 2). They argued that the 'new cultural geographers' (they cite Cosgrove, Duncan and Jackson as 'standard bearers') have 'reinvented' the nature of 'old' cultural geography, in order to criticize it, with the Berkeley school (see p. 106) as 'its currently most misinterpreted form' (p. 3). In return, Cosgrove (1993) accused them of inventing a conspiracy, claimed that he had not wholeheartedly embraced the term 'new cultural geography', and welcomed the growing accommodation between the 'theory-free' Berkeley school and the theoretically grounded approaches. Jackson (1993b) was also accommodating, while pointing to a wide range of other traditions. More stridently, Duncan (1993b, p. 518) responded that 'I cannot accept that it is possible to employ the term culture in one's work and yet employ no theory of culture', to which Price and Lewis (1993b) responded by re-stressing their case that Duncan misrepresented the Berkeley canon (as in Duncan, 1980), both in its orientation and in its implicit acceptance of 'the tiresome superorganic debate' (p. 521). Since then, debates about the dynamics and merits (or otherwise) of the cultural turn(s) have continued (notably in Mitchell's, 1995, work as detailed in Chapter 5; see too, Barnett 1998a, 1998b, and Sayer 2000): we return to aspects of these debates in what follows.

Meanwhile, the cultural turn runs through the themes that follow – but these are not contained by it (or *them*, for as Cook, Crouch, Naylor and Ryan, 2000, p. xii, point out, 'there has been less a *cultural turn* than a series of cultural insights, turns, multiple circuits'). So this chapter will be somewhat more disjointed than its predesssors as we work through a series of interwoven, postmodern, poststructuralist and postcolonial strands of contemporary human geography.

Postmodernism

Perhaps the best – and last – bit of advice that can be given to readers of this book is to not accept anyone else's definition of postmodern geographical praxis.

(Soja, 2001, p. 294)

Postmodernism has become increasingly popular in the social sciences and humanities over the last couple of decades and has attracted considerable attention from geographers. Its rise, according to Soja (1989), represented an attack on the predominance of historicism in modern thought, with its emphasis on biography (both individual and collective) and time and the consequent neglect of spatiality and geography. He defined historicism as (p. 15):

... an overdeveloped historical contextualization of social life and social theory that actively submerges and peripheralizes the geographical or spatial imagination ... [and which produces] an implicit subordination of space to time that obscures geographical interpretations of the changeability of the social world.

Because of this, he claimed that geographers had failed to attain their 'rightful position' within the social sciences for much of the twentieth century. A 'superficially similar historical rhythm' (p. 33) was assumed to occur across all places, rather than a realization – as stressed in the localities project and new regional geography projects discussed above (p. 237) – that social processes are differently constituted in different places, so that the historical flow is not the same everywhere; not surprisingly, some sought to link the localities project to postmodernism (see Cooke, 1990). Thus, for example, postmodern novels have either a non-linear or an apparently chaotic structure when they try to represent different things happening simultaneously in different places, and postmodern architecture does not rely on the kinds of clear functional structure that characterized most modern architecture (Knox, 1987).

This problem of synchronicity has long been recognized by geographers (as well as poets, novelists and film makers), as Massey (1992) observed with reference to Darby's (1962) paper on 'The problem of geographic description'. Darby pointed out that (p. 2):

A series of geographical facts is much more difficult to present than a sequence of historical facts. Events follow one another in time in an inherently dramatic fashion that makes juxtaposition in time easier to convey through the written word than juxtaposition in space. Geographical description is inevitably more difficult to achieve than is historical narrative.

But histories have geographies, and relating concurrent changes over both time and space simultaneously provides particular problems, especially since all mapped distributions are simply static snapshots of continuing processes (Blaut, 1962). In a sense then, in his concern for the combinations of place and space Soja was returning to an old theme in the geographical tradition. He did so, however, in the context not of a rural or isolated region but of what he described (adopting a slogan from the *Los Angeles Times*) as:

... the place where 'it all comes together' ... the sprawling urban region defined by the sixty mile (100 kilometer) circle around the centre of the City of Los Angeles a prototopos, a paradigmatic place; or,

pushing inventiveness still further, a mesocosm, an ordered world in which the micro and the macro, the idiographic and the nomothethic, the concrete and the abstract, can be seen simultaneously in an articulated and interactive combination (p. 191).

So, Soja writes a 'free-wheeling essay on Los Angeles. ... a decidedly postmodern landscape, a search for revealing "other spaces" and hidden geographical texts' (p. 2). He captures the putative postmodernism of these spaces by drawing upon the Argentinean writer Jorge Luis Borges. Thus Soja (p. 2) quotes from Borges' [originally published in Spanish in 1945] short story of:

'The Aleph' – the only place on earth where all places are, a limitless space of simultaneity and paradox, impossible to describe in less than extraordinary language. Borge's observations crystallize some of the dilemmas confronting the interpretation of postmodern geographies:

Then I saw the Aleph ... And here begins my despair as a writer. All language is a set of symbols whose use among its speakers assumes a shared past. How, then, can I translate into words the limitless Aleph, which my floundering mind can scarely encompass? ... Really what I want to do is impossible, for any listing of an endless series is doomed to be infinitesimal. In that single gigantic instant I saw millions of acts both delightful and awful; not one of them amazed me more than the fact that all of them occupied the same point in space, without overlapping or transparency. What my eyes beheld was simultaneous, but what I shall write down will be successive, because language is successive. Nonetheless, I will try to recollect what I can.

While for Soja it is found in Los Angeles, whose 'spatiality and historicity are archetypes of vividness, simultaneity, and interconnection' (p. 248), postmodernism has been attributed a wide range of explicit and implicit meanings, and its core is hard to identify; Cloke *et al.* (1991, p. 19) write of it as 'infuriatingly difficult to define'.

According to Dear (1994, p. 3):

Postmodernity is everywhere, from literature, design and philosophy, to MTV [Music Television], ice cream and underwear. This seeming ubiquity only aggravates the problem in grasping its meaning. Postmodern discourse seems capable of instant adaptation in response to context and choice of interlocutors.

Nevertheless, he believes 'we can cut to the heart of the matter by identifying three principal constructs in postmodernism: style, epoch and method', with the first having provided the source of the initial explosion of interest.

1. *Postmodernism as style* originated in literature and literary criticism, and spread to other artistic fields such as design, film, art, photography and architecture; the general trend involved the promotion of difference and the lack of conformity to overriding structural imperatives. Dear found trends within architecture especially revealing:

   ... the search for the new was associated with a revolt against the formalism and austerity of the modern style epitomized by the unadorned office tower ... The burgeoning postmodern architecture was disturbingly divorced from any broad philosophical underpinnings, taking the

form of an apparently-random cannibalizing of existing architectural archetypes, and combining them into an ironic collage of (or pastiche) of previous styles.

2. *Postmodernism as epoch* portrays current developments within society as a major radical break with the past – hence use of the term 'postmodernity' to contrast it with the modernity of the previous epoch. These 'new times' are characterized by difference, so that study of the postmodern epoch involves grappling with the fundamental problem of theorizing contemporaneity, i.e. the task of making sense out of an infinity of concurrent social realities. Any landscape is simultaneously composed of obsolete, current and emergent artifacts; but how do we begin to codify and understand this variety?

3. *Postmodernism as method* is, according to Dear, likely to be the most enduring of the three main trends. It eschews the notions of universal truths and meta-theories which can account for 'the Meaning of Everything'. No portrayal can claim dominance over another; separate theories are incommensurable and so their evalation is always relative and contingent: 'even the attempt to reconcile or resolve the tensions among competing theories should *a priori* be resisted'.

Epoch, style and method are undoubtedly tangled-up and can be differentiated in a variety of ways. Such tangles are what led Cloke *et al.* (1991) to propose a two-fold approach to postmodernism – as an approach or method and as object of analysis – while Demeritt (cited in Hoggart, Lees and Davies, 2002, p. 3) locates three strands of postmodernism:

1. A concern for new and non-universalist models of *human subjectivity* and rationality (e.g. Pile 1991, 1993; Sibley, 2000) that emphasize complexity and diversity;

2. An *epistemological project* critiquing concepts of Truth and claims of universal knowledge; and

3. An emphasis on 'the *radical phenomenological* and *social constructivist* implications of postmodernism in suggesting that our knowledge of nature, and, in some sense, the nature of reality itself (and of nature), are culturally relative' (see Demeritt, 1998).

Either way, postmodernism's emphasis on 'heterogeneity, particularity and uniqueness' (Gregory, 1989a, p. 70) undoubtedly attracted some human geographers to it. Human geographers under the sway of modernism had emphasized order in their promotion of spatial science, when their empirical observations (as their critics pointed out: see p. 198) could really only identify disorder, which suggested the absence of generally applicable theories and universal truths (Barnes, 1996). Postmodernism gave them a philosophical hanger, recognizing that (Gregory, 1989a, pp. 91–2):

. . . there is more disorder in the world than appears at first sight is not discovered until that order is looked for . . . we need, in part, to go back to the question of areal differentiaion: but armed with a new theoretical sensitivity towards the world in which we live and to ways in which we represent it.

With regard to theory, Dear (1988) observed that postmodernism suggests that geographers should be wary of aspirations to 'grand theory' (p. 272). Yet recognition that all knowledge is not only time–space specific but also expressed in language which reflects that such specificity (see below) meant, to him, that geography can 'claim its place alongside history as one of two key disciplines concerned with the time–space reconstruction of human knowledge' (p. 272).

Understanding the attractions of this postmodern stance to geographers requires prior appreciation of why modernist spatial science came to dominate their discipline. According to Gregory (1989b), throughout much of the nineteenth and twentieth centuries geographical practice has been influenced by particular aspects of, first, anthropology, then sociology, and finally economics. Two features dominated the adopted modernist paradigm:

1. Its firm base in *naturalism,* which was likely to have 'special significance in a discipline like ours, where human geography is yoked to physical geography' (p. 352) and the consequent reliance on the aims and procedures of the natural sciences as relevant to the study of humans and their societies; and
2. A *totalization* conception of space, which involves the search for a 'systematic order whose internal logic imposes a fundamental coherence on the chaos of our immediate impressions', hence the dominance of spatial science within that project.

Postmodernism presents a substantial critique to the approaches that dominated much of geography in the period from the 1950s through the 1980s, with their emphases on order and 'grand theory'. As Cloke *et al.* (1991, p. 200) express it:

> … *human geographers will increasingly come to recognise the gravity of the challenge that postmodernism as attitude poses to the most conventional theorisations of the human world, and will begin to appreciate that a sensitivity to the geography of this world – to its fragmentation across multiple spaces, places, environments and landscapes – is itself very much bound up with (and an impetus for) a postmodern suspicion of modernist 'grand theories' and 'metanarratives'. … These manoeuvres will doubtless cause much unease and controversy, however, given that they cast doubt on the stability of the foundations from which most human geography had proceeded over the last thirty years or so.*

Soja's (1989) book represented mostly an engagement with what it identifed as postmodernism as a place (or assembly of places). As we noted above, the Los Angeles metropolitan area is, he argued, difficult to represent in a narrative because its many images seem 'to stretch laterally instead of unfolding sequentially' (p. 222), and because 'it too seems limitless and constantly in motion, never still enough to encompass, [it seems] too filled with "other spaces" to be informatively described'. All he says he can offer is 'a succession of fragmentary glimpses' into a 'particularly restless geographical landscape' (p. 223) – what he terms an 'interjacent medley' (p. 247). Its environment is too multi-layered, created by too many authors to be identified: there are too many 'discordant symbols drawing out the underlying themes'.

Soja's work was subjected to an engaged critique by Gregory (1990; see also Chapter 4 of Gregory, 1994). He argued that *modernist* theories of the capitalist city also stressed 'geographically uneven development via simultaneous tendencies towards homogenization, fragmentation and hierachization' (Soja, 1989, p. 50). He accepted that the Los Angeles landscape contains 'an economic order, an instrumental nodal structure, an essentially exploitative spatial division of labor', but claimed that these cannot be summarized into a 'totalising description'; all that can be offered is a 'series of fragmentary glimpses' (p. 246). And yet, Gregory stressed, Soja advised those wishing to explore the metropolis that 'it must be reduced to a more familiar and localized geometry to be seen' (Soja, 1989, p. 224) and its emphases are (Gregory, 1994, pp. 300–1):

> *Towers and freeways, sites and districts, zones and areas, enclaves and pockets, gradients and wedges: a landscape without figures … Soja's essay becomes a morphology of landscape that, like Sauer's original, is rarely disturbed by the human form … Soja's essay [is] so astonishingly univocal. We never hear the multiple voices of those who live in Los Angeles – other than Soja himself – and who presumably learn rather different things from it.*

To Gregory, Soja excluded much of the *difference* which is supposedly at the heart of a postmodern approach; he ignored the various social struggles that underpin the making and remaking of the Los Angeles landscape, plus the distinctive urban cultures of ordinary people's everyday lives. Thus, whereas Gregory applauded Soja's thesis that 'it is impossible to recover human geographies from a contemplation of their abstract geometries' (p. 304), nevertheless he concluded that Soja 'renders the landscape of Los Angeles as a still life'. Soja had demonstrated that 'postmodernism can have an insistently critical edge' (Gregory, 1990, p. 312), but there is a clear hermeneutic problem in his work: 'his master-narrative is sometimes so authoritarian that it drowns out the voices of other people engaged in making their own human geographies'. Indeed, according to Duncan (1996, p. 443) Soja's 'goal of reconstructing geography along postmodernist lines … belies the fact that Soja is not really postmodernist!'.

Dear's work has also attracted considerable criticism, notably a paper on 'postmodern urbanism' (Dear and Flusty, 1998), which uses the case of Los Angeles – and the work of a 'Los Angeles School' of urbanists (which they contrast with the 'Chicago School' of the 1920s–1940s: see p. 81) – to argue that a new form of urbanism is emerging. They contrasted five features of 'modern' townscapes (those analysed by the Chicago School) – mega-structural bigness; straight-space; rational order and flexibility; hardness and opacity; discontinuous serial vision – with five characteristics of their postmodern successors – quaintspace (or cuteness); textured facades; stylishness; reconnection with the local; and pedestrian–automobile split. They then identify ten features of 'Southern Californian urbanisms' which are synthesized into a 'theory' of protopostmodern urbanism: globalization and restructuring are generating both political-economic polarization and cultures of heteropolis (i.e. increased cultural variety stimulated by immigration). Together these are leading to the development of interdictory spaces – or segregation – and a greater variety of spatial forms, such as edge cities and fortified enclaves, as well as a new politics of nature. The result is that (p. 67):

> *Conventional city form, Chicago-style, is sacrificed in favor of a noncontiguous collage of parcelized, consumption-oriented landscapes devoid of conventional centers yet wired into electronic propinquity and nominally unified by the mythologies of the disinformation superhighway. Los Angeles may be a mature form of this postmodern metropolis; Las Vegas comes to mind as a youthful example.*

Nijman (2000, p. 135) offered Miami as an alternative 'paradigmatic city' illustrating the 'fundamental traits and trends' of the emerging urban system.

Critiques of Dear and Flusty included arguments that they had not identified a clear modern–postmodern break: 'The theory of postmodern urbanism is a mixture of the old and the new, of breaks and continuities. It is indebted to and rooted in modernism, just as Los Angeles is less of the sheer novelty than its devotees proclaim' (Beauregard, 1999, p. 398). Jackson (1999) contended that the contrast with the Chicago School was poorly drawn, given the lack of ethnographic studies of life in these paradigmatic cities (on which see Amin and Thrift, 2002). Sui (1999) went further, arguing that postmodernism was likely to lead geographers into a new 'Dark Age of intellectual inquiry' because of its 'assumed or implied ontological relativism, epistemological nihilism, and methodological neologism' (p. 408; see also Symanski, 1994). Dear and Flusty's (1999) response not only defended their position against Beauregard and Jackson's criticisms, but also argued, contra Sui, that postmodernism will not go away (p. 415):

> To encompass the full richness of urban life requires much more work and that we invent new ways of writing, because conventional academic writing is singularly ill-equipped for this task.

More generally, Dear (1994, p. 299) has argued that postmodernism has encountered such hostility from those geographers (as it has within other disciplines too) who

> . . . perceived their intellectual authority being threatened; [plus] incomprehension on the part of those who (for whatever reason) failed to negotiate its arcane jargon; and the indifference of a majority who ignored what was presumably perceived as the latest fad. . . . [yet] despite the combined armies of antipathy and inertia, postmodernism has flourished.

In some cases, it seems, the debate has been conducted in highly personal terms (Dear, 2001). To others, it is just a reflection of changes not only in theoretical positions but also substantive concerns (see, for example, Peach's, 2002, comparisons of the 'old' and the 'new' cultural geography). Whatever the language and concerns, however, new textbooks (in the classic Kuhnian sense – p. 7) now see postmodernism as an integral part of 'new theories, new geographies' (Hubbard et al., 2002).

Time–space compression

Other geographical work considering postmodernism and putatively postmodern landscapes explores a diversity of postmodernisms, refusing to draw clear boundaries around who or what is or is not 'postmodern' (Amin and Thrift, 2002; Dear 2000; Dear and Flusty, 2002). Leaving aside who and what is and is not 'really' modern or postmodern (for it should be clear that these terms are contested and defined with reference to each other), the most influential geographical treatment of postmodernism turned out to be a wide-ranging critique of it launched by Harvey (1989a) in *The Condition of Postmodernity* (on which see Harvey, 2002). This soon became an academic bestseller: Smith (2001, p. 10) notes that it 'went on to sell almost 100,000 copies in various languages, was widely influential throughout the social sciences and humanities, and was voted one of the best 100 books of the second half of the twentieth century by the *New Stateman/New Society*'.

Harvey drew on his prior Marxist work (see Chapter 6) on the dynamics of capitalism to argue that the epoch and phenomenon of postmodernism was less a break with the modernism that had supposedly gone before and instead might be interpreted as a variant on a old theme. Harvey's basic thesis on postmodernism is clearly expressed in his brief summary page, entitled 'The argument' (p. vii), which is reproduced here in full:

There has been a sea-change in cultural as well as in political-economic practices since around 1972.

This sea-change is bound up with the emergence of new dominant ways in which we experience space and time.

While simultaneity in the shifting dimensions of time and space is no proof of necessary or causal connection, strong a priori grounds can be adduced for the proposition that there is some kind of necessary relation between the rise of postmodernist cultural forms, the emergence of more flexible modes of capital accumulation, and a new round of 'time–space compression' in the organization of capitalism.

But these changes, when set against the basic rules of capitalistic accumulation, appear more as shifts in surface appearance rather than as signs of the emergence of some entirely new postcapitalist or even postindustrial society.

The observed changes, especially but not only in modes of economic organization and much facilitated by technological changes (notably but not only, in information technology), are the outcomes of the processes of continual restructuring by which capitalism seeks to overcome crisis tendencies (on which see Harvey, 1982; Harvey and Scott, 1989: their term for this restructuring was 'flexible accumulation') and within which cultural forms are produced and reproduced (as set out in Harvey, 1985c). For Harvey, geography matters in understanding the arrival of a postmodern epoch, style or landscape. Indeed the key is the way that capitalism and its attendant means of production and circulation have *compressed* space and time in pursuit of 'spatial fixes' to the ever-present capitalist tendency to crisis and overaccumulation (and hence declining profits). Thus, next to a figure indicating a sense of a shrinking world (see Figure 7.1), Harvey (1989a, p.) notes:

In what follows I shall make frequent use to the concept of 'time–space compression'. I mean to signal by that term processes that so revolutionize the objective qualities of space and time that we are forced to alter, sometimes in quite radical ways, how we represent the world to ourselves. I use the word 'compression' because a strong case can be made that the history of capitalism has been characterized by speed-up in the pace of life, while so overcoming spatial barriers that the world sometimes seems to collapse inwards upon us. … The experience of time-space compression is challenging, exciting, stressful, and sometimes deeply troubling, capable of sparking, therefore, a diversity of social, cultural and political responses.

Harvey's assessment of postmodernism identified some positive elements (pp. 113–15):

… in its concern for difference, for the difficulties of communication, for the complexity and nuances of interests, cultures, places and the like, it exercises a positive influence. The meta-languages, meta-theories, and meta-narratives of modernism … did tend to gloss over important differences, and failed to pay attention to important disjunctions and details.

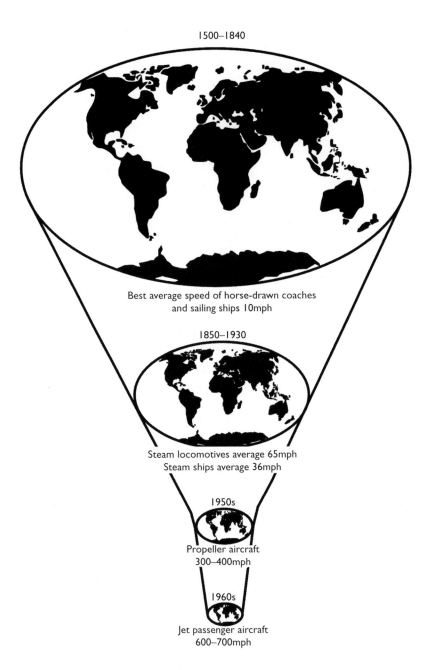

1500–1840

Best average speed of horse-drawn coaches
and sailing ships 10mph

1850–1930

Steam locomotives average 65mph
Steam ships average 36mph

1950s

Propeller aircraft
300–400mph

1960s

Jet passenger aircraft
600–700mph

Figure 7.1 *The shrinking map of the world through innovations in transport that 'annihilate space through time' (Source: Harvey, 1989, p. 241)*

But he also rejected what he identified as the negative elements, with postmodernism presented as 'a wilful and rather chaotic movement to overcome all the supposed ills of modernism'. Postmodernism, to him, reflects (p. 116):

> ... a particular kind of crisis within ... [modernism], one that emphasizes the fragmentary, the ephemeral, and the chaotic side ... (that side which Marx so admirably dissects as integral to the capitalist mode of production) while expressing a deep scepticism as to any particular prescriptions as to how the eternal and immutable should be conceived of, represented, and expressed.

And so it gets the balance wrong, because its adherents are unwilling to grapple with the need for a theory which promotes appreciation of the nature of capitalism and its manifest contradictions, especially, for geographers, those relating to time–space compression through changed transport and other technologies and the political strategies which promote the fortunes of people in different places. The shifts identified in the first sentence of his summary require a dynamic theory of historical materialism, within which he identified four main agenda items (p. 355):

1. The treatment of difference and 'otherness' (see p. 293) within the dialectics of social change, thereby 'recuperating such aspects of social organization as race, gender, religion, within the overall frame of historical materialist enquiry (with its emphasis on the power of money and capital circulation) and class politics (with its emphasis upon the unity of the emancipatory struggle)';
2. Recognition of the importance of cultural practices, including the production of images and discourses, on the reproduction of the social order;
3. Recognition of the importance of space and time in the geopolitics of capitalism, now that 'Historical materialism is finally beginning to take its geography seriously'; and
4. Acceptance that historical-geographical materialism is an open-ended and dialectical mode of enquiry rather than a closed and fixed body of understandings. Meta-theory is not a statement of total truth but an attempt to come to terms with the historical and geographical truths that characterize capitalism in general as well as in its present phase.

Harvey, in turn, has been critiqued. Deutsch (1991) criticized his 'totalizing vision' of society, with aspects of difference merely appended to Marxist theory, and Massey (1991) similarly pointed out that the book fails to consider the possibility of a feminist interpretation of postmodernism (and of the images that Harvey uses to illustrate modernism and postmodernism in *The Condition of Postmodernity*). Massey points out that 'gender is a determining factor in cultural production' (p. 51), but Harvey promotes a form of Marxism, within which gender differences can be subsumed. Likewise, Dear (1991b) claimed that Harvey 'seems incapable of tolerating difference' (p. 536) so that 'The catalogue of different voices that are consequently denied relevance in Harvey's discourse is long and depressing' and his goal appears to be to 'dissolve differences' (p. 537).

Much of the postmodern literature is ignored, Dear argued – 'Harvey is a much better political economist than he is cultural critic'. He summarized Harvey's position as follows:

1. All aspects of social processes can be encompassed within historical materialism; so that
2. No alternatives need be addressed;
3. The shift to flexible accumulation accounts for recent social, economic and political changes; and
4. There is no need for any other theory beyond historical materialism.

He then concluded that, 'Perhaps it is time that Harvey tried to transform his Marxism, rather than obliging the world to fit into it'. Harvey recognizes difference, but refuses to incorporate it to his thinking.

In response, Harvey (1992) noted that he was influenced by some feminist writers, and that incorporation of their insights would have strengthened his book; the work of Young (1990) in particular had considerably shaped his later work on justice (Harvey, 1993a). He accepted the role of situation and position in the production of knowledge (see p. 292) but found some of their applications in feminist work 'rather more vulgar' because their focus on individual biographies is not dialectically placed in an evolving mode of production and because of their denial of the veracity of other accounts. Thus his book was written from a particular (privileged, white male) position and (p. 304):

> ... emphasized the commonality of our condition as users of commodities and money and as participants in labor markets and the circulation processes of capital. But emphasizing commonality does not deny difference. Properly done, it can enhance the understanding of differences at the same time as it provides a critical basis from which to evaluate the work of those who purport to write critical theory outside the confines of what capitalism as a social system is all about.

In this context, he found the critiques 'unnecessarily personalized, hurtful and sometimes abusive' (p. 308), part of a strategy of creating a feminist position which he claims shows that 'they exhibit not the slightest hint of concern to grapple with the deeper problematic' involved with dissolving gender differences. He wants debate to focus on these and finishes by pointing to a major paradox regarding truth and generalization in all postmodern writing (p. 322):

> ... postmodernists ... cannot criticise The Condition as wrong, misguided, or fundamentally misconceived without deploying truth terms of their own which presuppose they have an ultimate line on a truth they theoretically claim cannot exist. I am reminded here of William Blake's great aphorism: 'to generalise is to be an idiot; to particularise is to achieve the greatest distinction of merit', which sounds great ... until it is recognized as a generalization and thereby self-condemned as idiotic.

Elsewhere, Dear (1991a, p. 549) criticized both Harvey and Soja, claiming that each rejects the pluralism and celebration of difference that characterizes postmodernism:

> By insisting on their totalizing and reductionist visions, Soja and Harvey squander the insights from different voices and alternative subjectivities. Difference is relegated to the status of an obstacle hindering 'our' view of a coherent theoretical and political praxis.

Barnes, too, concluded that Harvey's commitment to what he terms the Enlightenment project – 'a belief in rational progress, the individual subject, a monolithic order, and universal truth' (Barnes, 1996, p. 3) – runs counter to prevailing trends:

> Although [Harvey] wants to recognize that truths are socially constructed at a given moment in time and space, he also wants to claim that his theory is a valid and accurate representation of the capitalist world.

Dear's evaluation of postmodernism's promise for human geography is unequivocally positive (1994, p. 9):

> Simply stated, we live in an era of postmodern consciousness; there is no choice in this matter, unless we are prepared to declare in favor of ignorance or the status quo. I believe that a revolution of sorts is occurring in geographical thinking.

He supported this last claim by arguing that since 1984 we have witnessed: (a) a truly unprecedented increase in quality scholarship devoted to the relationship between space and society; (b) reassertion of the significance and role of space in social theory and social process; (c) an effective reintegration of human geography with mainstream social science and philosophy; (d) the establishment of theory and philosophy as the *sine qua non* for the discipline's identity and survival; (e) a new appreciation of diversity and difference, and a consequent diversification of theoretical and empirical interests; and (f) a self-conscious questioning of the relationship between geographical knowledge and social action. He further claimed that a large number of publications that appeared in 1989 or later 'reveal a significant postmodern consciousness' (p. 7) in seven areas:

1. Cultural landscapes and 'place-making';
2. The economic landscapes of flexible accumulation and post-Fordism;
3. Philosophical and theoretical disputes about space and language;
4. Problems of representation in geographical writing and image-making;
5. The politics of postmodernity and difference;
6. The construction of the individual; and
7. A realization of the importance of nature and the environmental question.

This leads him to an optimistic conclusion, provided that geographers are prepared to grapple with the postmodern challenge (p. 9):

> Postmodernism places the construction of meaning at the core of geography's problematic. The key issue here is authority; and postmodernism has served notice on all those who seek to assert or preserve their authority in the academic or everyday world. And yet I understand that geographers, like everyone else, cling tenaciously to their beliefs. Knowledge is, after all, power, and we are all loathe to relinquish the basis for our claims to legitimacy.

Thus:

> To ignore the postmodern challenge is to risk disengaging geography once more from the mainstream. To accept it is to encourage new ways of seeing, to relish participating at the cutting edge

of social and philosophical inquiry, to convince our peers of the significance of space in contemporary social thought and social process, and to help forge a new politics for the twenty-first century.

Many human geographers remained concerned as to how these could be achieved, as Dear (1995) recognized in responding to an evaluation of developments since his 1988 paper. Graham (1995, p. 175) accepted that in evaluating Dear's (1994) claim that postmodernism has flourished:

If judged by the volume of literature which mentions postmodernism then this is certainly true. Postmodernism has become the lingua franca of intellectual discourse (Ley, 1993). As yet, however, few are fluent and communication easily breaks down, inevitably producing a disturbingly disorganised discussion (a concern also of Warf, 1993).

Such debates continue (see Minca, 2001) and are tangled up with others; about consumption and its roles in the (post)modern economy and society (e.g. Gregson, Crewe and Brooks, 2002; Glennie and Thrift, 1992; Gregson, 1995; May, 1996a; Thrift and Olds, 1996), for example, and concerning the merits, possibilities (or otherwise), pitfalls and problematics of poststructuralism and postcolonialism. But there is possibility here, too, in the startling recognition that all geographical (and other) interpretations:

. . . are local and contingent, and that any conclusions represent no more than a temporary hegemony of a favoured belief. Such studied relativism makes it a condition of knowing and practice that we make explicit the conditions and criteria under which knowing is to occur and decisions to be deliberated. (Dear, 1995, pp. 179–80)

Such a notion of knowing one's position has been problematized in poststructuralist (and many feminist) conceptions of the individual a complex and sometimes contradictory or divided subject. It is to such reconceptualizations that we now turn.

Poststructuralism: power, language, texts and discourse

What has come to be known as 'poststructuralism' has its own geography. It is hard to say where postmodernism and poststructuralism divide – and for many the latter is viewed as variant of the former. We have already noted that for one geographer, the fragmented city of Los Angeles becomes a place to investigate postmodernity. And whilst Smith (2003, p. 71) warns us that 'the term was not widely used in France' and that the label poststructuralism 'obliterates the differences between quite different authors', Peet (1998, pp. 194–5), however, begins his account of 'Poststructuralism, Postmodernism and Postmodern Geographies' across the Atlantic, in a city that has at times been presented as an archetype of modernity:

Poststructuralism and postmodernism in their theoretical guises are very much the direct products of events in France. In May 1968, a Parisian alliance of student agitators and working-class militants rose in spontaneous revolutionary upheaval. It seemed for a short while that the dreams of radical modernism were about to be realized in their ultimately radical, social-anarchistic form (worker self-management, participatory democracy. . .). But the eventual, eternal return of bourgeois rational normalcy to Paris began a period of contemplative reaction on the left. This turned against structuralism and Marxism immediately, hence a series of poststructural and post-Marxist ideas. But thinkers began also to react once more against the aspirations of modernism as a whole, hence the postmodern aspect to poststructural philosophy.

A key concern of 'poststructuralist' work has been the issue of struggles over *representation:* the complex of linguistic, cultural and symbolic processes which, poststructuralists argue, is intimately tied up with (both express and constitute) power. Although humanistic geography (see Chapter 5) and some of the debates about regional geography (see p. 239) did raise issues about how language (and other modes of geographic description) embody, enable and constrain power, poststructuralism makes this a more central concern. Thus, as indicated, writing was for long considered not a problematic issue within geography; the task was just the mechanical one of bolting words together in the right order so that the final construction represents the thought or object modelled. In this sense 'earth writing', rather than 'writing about the earth', was a good description of what geographers thought they were doing. Earth came with its own labels, and provided that they were in the correct sequence one's written account was always a mirror representation. Anyone could do it as long as a dictionary and style manual were at hand. Writing is now viewed as a highly problematic task, however:

> *Pieces of the world . . . do not come with their own labels, and thus representing 'out there' to an audience must involve more than just lining up pieces of language in the right order. Instead it is humans that decide how to represent things, and not the things themselves.* (Barnes and Duncan, 1992, p. 2)

Thus, writing is integral to the complex and contested social construction of knowledge and meaning. If the written word is not a mirror of the world it seeks to represent, but is itself understood as a social creation, several consequences follow (Gregory and Walford, 1989).

1. Severing the assumed mirror link between 'reality' and 'text' means that reality cannot be apprehended outside the language used to describe it: the world is always narrated. The texts that we produce draw on other texts, which are the sources of the images that we are trying to convey, such as the metaphors that we use to describe the 'unknown' (Barnes, 1996). This is termed intertextuality: meanings are created in a continual transition process from text to text (Barnes and Duncan, 1992, p. 3):

   > *. . . new worlds are made out of old texts, and old worlds are the basis of new texts. In this world of one text careening off another, we cannot appeal to any epistemological bedrocks in privileging one text over another. For what is true is made inside texts, not outside them.*

2. Writing reveals as much about the writer, and his or her position, as it does about what is being written about. We write, Barnes and Duncan argue, from our own local setting; thus the worlds we represent are inevitably stamped with our own particular set of local interests, views, standards, and so on. To understand critically our own representations, and also those of others, we must therefore know the

kinds of contexts bearing upon an author that makes an account come out the way that it does.

3. All writing involves the use of literary apparatus, such as metaphors and other rhetorical devices, whose use we must appreciate since they are central to the construction and circulation of meanings.

These are illustrated by Barnes and Duncan, and in the essays in their edited volume, with reference to landscape descriptions. Landscapes, following Cosgrove and Daniels (1988, p. 1), may be 'represented in a variety of materials and on many surfaces – in paint on canvas, in writing on paper, in earth, stone, water, and vegetation on the ground. A landscape park is more palpable but no more real, nor less imaginary, than a landscape painting or poem'. Thus the 'texts' to be appreciated may be produced through the medium of words, drawings, paintings or other media, or may be inscribed in the landscape itself. (This is illustrated by Harvey's, 1979, paper on the Sacré Cœur monument in Paris; by Daniels', 1991, interpretation of 'Constable country'; by work on film, produced both commercially – e.g. Aitken, 1991, and in communities – e.g. Rose, 1994; and in studies of music – Leyshon *et al.*, 1995.)

Barnes and Duncan (1992) identify three major concepts as central to the study of representation: text, discourse and metaphor. *Text* embraces a wide range of cultural products (see also p. 286) that involves the author rewriting what has been 'read' in a hermeneutic exercise (p. 34). Texts give fixity, or concrete expression, to many aspects of social life; they represent the author's intentions but also illustrate the wider context in which they were composed and their author(s) socialized. They are also open to a range of interpretations (p. 6):

> . . . the meaning of a text is unstable, dependent upon the wide range of interpretations brought to bear upon it by various different readers. Similarly, social productions and institutions also address a wide range of possible interpreters. But those interpreters are not free to make of the text what they like, but are subject to discursive practices of specific textual communities. Thus both how we produce a text and how we interpret one depends upon our textual community – on the language (even the particular form of a language) that we use, reflecting our individual compositional and contextual positions.

Discourses are the larger structures from within which texts are constructed and within which others are read. They comprise (p. 8):

> . . . frameworks that embrace particular combinations of narratives, concepts, ideologies and signifying practices, each relevant to a particular realm of social action. Between discourses words may have different connotations, causing people who ostensibly speak the same language to talk past one another, often without realizing it.

The relationship between a component of the text, such as a word (the signifier), and that to which it refers (the signified) is a complex social construction, undertaken within the specific textual community. Thus:

> . . . discourses are practices of signification, thereby providing a framework for understanding the world. As such, discourses are both enabling as well as constraining: they determine answers to

questions, as well as the questions that can be asked. More generally, a discourse constitutes the limits within which ideas and practices are considered to be natural . . . These limits are by no means fixed, however. This is because discourses are not unified, but are subject to negotiation, challenge and transformation.

Metaphors are major devices for representing meanings. The world is apprehended and known through study, which requires a language, or some other form of textual representation, for the transmission of meanings. Metaphors are extremely valuable, since they provide a means of describing the unknown using the vocabulary of the known; the unfamiliar is illuminated by comparing it to the familiar. In much science, for example, the use of metaphor steers the study of the unknown, providing a framework for its investigation – as was the case with applications of the gravity model in spatial science (p. 120: Barnes, 1996). Understanding a discourse therefore involves appreciating its metaphors.

If metaphors dominate textual discourse, however, they also ensure instability in the ongoing transmission of meanings, or the reproduction of knowledge. As Barnes (1996, p. 166) argues, drawing on the work of Derrida:

> . . . the meaning of words and concepts (signifiers) can never be directly tied to particular things (signified). For meaning is derived from a signifier's position with respect to all other signifiers in the system [i.e. a metaphor can only be understood in the context in which it was developed]. According to Harland (1987, p. 135), 'In Derrida's conception, one signifier points away to another signifier, which in turn points away to another signifier, which in turn points away to another signifier, and so on ad infinitum'. There is no anchor of some final presence or some ultimate origin point of meaning. Meaning, rather, is always produced through displacement and deferral, shaped as much by what is absent as by what is present.

If meaning can only be conveyed through 'an orchestration of signifiers' (metaphors), therefore, then we are led 'to deny identification of an unimpeachable presence. For, if there is no ultimate signified and only a shifting system of signifiers . . . there can only ever be the flux of meaning and no constant presence' (Barnes, 1996, p. 166).

A recent text on *Thinking Geographically* by Hubbard et al. (2002, p. 87) similarly registers the developing impacts of Derrida in geography and how 'deconstruction' (which also refuses clear distinction between the metaphorical and the literal) opens up the meanings of geography:

> For Derrida, when we describe something as having a certain characteristic ('x'), we inevitably recognize that it lacks another characteristic (i.e. is not 'y') and we are able to speak the difference between these (so that one becomes deemed as lacking in relation to the other: 'x' > 'y') . . . language is a play of signifiers that cannot articulate absolute difference, only lack or excess. The implication of Derrida's thinking is that the meaning of texts can never be [definitively] pinned down; language is seen to defer, rather than yield, truth and meaning.

They illustrate this through looking up the word 'geography' in the *Oxford English Dictionary*. They note that it contains three definitions (referring to places, area and arrangement). In turn, they look up the words (such as climate) that crop up in one of these definitions, only to find that each also has several meanings:

> *Tracking through the dictionary highlights how meaning is always intertextually deferred, always reliant on words that are themselves reliant on others and so on. Only when located in discourse and grounded in context do words take on meanings* (Hubbard et al., 2002, p. 88).

In turn, however, the limits to such contexts are hard to specify. In other words, any geographical categories that construct boundaries are susceptible to deconstruction, whereby the boundary is shown to be to profoundly arbitrary and to rest on excluding what is held to belong (usually difference and diversity) only on the 'other' side of the boundary.

Metaphor is not the only device used in geographical writing, however. According to Jonathan Smith (1996), geographers use four different modes in their story-telling: *Romance* – as in biographical narratives of individual and group struggle, especially where it leads to radical change; *Tragedy* – as in representations of deterministic systems, many of which involve prognostications of doom; *Comedy* – which represents harmony and reconciled conflict; and *Irony* – in which the detached observer occupies a superior position. These represent release, resignation, reconciliation and removal respectively, and in them the author employs one or more tropes, or figures of speech:

1. *Metaphor* involves the use of comparisons to introduce concepts, describing 'the remote in terms of the immediate, the exotic in terms of the domestic, the abstract in terms of the concrete, and the complex in terms of the simple' (p. 12);
2. *Metonymy* uses technical terms to provide (accurate) descriptions for specialized audiences;
3. *Synecdoche* promotes understanding through synthesizing the general and the particular to impart meanings; and
4. *Irony* suggests that representation and understanding are futile, and that general apprehensions can never be produced.

Duncan and Ley (1993, pp. 2–3) identified four major modes of representation within Anglo-American human geography:

1. *Description of observations obtained through fieldwork*, which dominated cultural geography until relatively recently: its underpinning assumption was that 'trained observation transcribed into clear prose and unencumbered by abstract theorizing produces an accurate understanding of the world';
2. *Mimesis*, whereby the world is reflected in media other than words, as with the mathematical modelling of spatial science that had little impact upon cultural geography;
3. *Postmodernism*, which 'distrusts and interrogates all meta-narratives including those of the researcher' and, as indicated earlier, rejects the search for 'universal truths'; and
4. *Hermeneutic interpretation*, which acknowledges the role of the interpreter, and therefore rules out mimesis – 'reality' cannot be faithfully reproduced:

Yet, however many discrete styles are identified and whatever way they are classified, the rhetorical styles produced by geographers reflect both the general approach to their subject matter and the audiences they consider themselves to be writing for: irony is characteristic of many postmodernists, for example; metonymy (and perhaps tragedy) of many analysts of spatial systems; and metaphor and romance of the educator seeking to open eyes to the world. Above all, language is crucial in the construction and transmission of meanings, for, as Barnes (1996, p. 167) explains:

> ... we can never have direct access to things in and of themselves. This is because in order to understand those terms, they must already be expressed in language. But if they are part of language, then their meaningfulness only becomes about through a play of difference among signifiers, which ... exclude any fundamental signifieds or presences.

Appreciation of those meanings involves understanding the metaphors employed (as Olsson, 1980, did when exploring the gravity model metaphor which underpinned his early spatial science). This involves appreciating the translation process, represented by Olsson (1992, p. 86, and 1991) as distortion, and therefore an exercise in the use of power (see the sympathetic review by Philo, 1994). Doel (1993), for example, uses irony in his characterization of the futility of much geographical writing's failure to represent the world the author claims to portray, whereas Pred (1989, 1990) has explored a variety of linguistic repertoires ('words, variable meanings, pronunciation, grammar, sign-tactical arrangements, rules of interpretation and expressive bodily gestures at one's command'; 1990, p. 33) to show how their production and reproduction are inherent to local struggles. Further, like Olsson, he has employed various writing strategies in order to 'subvert the taken-for-granted (and thereby ideology-riddled and power-laden) nature of the academic printed word' (Pred, 1990, p. 48). This:

> ... seeks to make the taken-for-granted format of representation appear strange and yet comprehensible, that seeks to make the reader understand and mentally see what she otherwise might not understand or mentally see, that seeks, somehow, to push through the filter of preconceptions and interpretative predispositions deeply inset in the reader's social, biographical and disciplinary past. Thus, I occasionally resort to chameleon like (mis)spellings, hyphenations and word-couplings that are de- or re-signed either so as to trigger previously unmade associations, or so as to convey the ambiguity, the shifting subtleties, the multiplicity of meanings characteristic of on-the-ground practices and social relations in any place.

Thus, as Barnes and Gregory (1997, pp. 3–4) note, attention to the poetics of geographical writing is also attention to their politics:

> It might seem odd that we foreground 'poetics'. Some geographers read and write poetry during their off-hours, and occasionally use it in their books and articles, but there is nothing conventionally poetic about most contemporary geographical writing. Some critics would say that post-positivist geographers are among the least poetic of all: that their prose is all too often stilted, leaden, inflated, and opaque. ... By poetics we have in mind the interpretation provided by the anthropologist and cultural critic James Clifford. ... For Clifford, all ethnographic accounts – and, we would argue,

geographical ones too – are rhetorical constructions, textual artefacts that seek to persuade us of their claims through an amalgam of 'academic' and 'literary' genres. But such accounts are not just texts; they also reach out to wider contexts of power and resistance, institutional constraint and innovation. . . . Words, as poets and contributors to this volume know very well, are extraordinarily powerful. We need to use them with care, with sensitivity, and above all with a critical passion: a poetics of inquiry is thus also a politics of inquiry.

Of course geography is not only expressed through writing – words-(and sometimes numbers and formulae)-in-order-on-a-page – but also mapping. Although it may be particularly evident in the case of propaganda maps (see Monmonier 1996; Pickles 1992), all maps (and Geographical Information Systems, see Curry 1998; Pickles, 1995a; Flowerdew, 1998) are interpretations, a point stressed in a series of papers by a cartographic historian, Brian Harley. His starting-point was that (Harley, 1989, p.1):

. . . we still accept uncritically the broad consensus, with relatively few dissenting voices, of what cartographers tell us maps are supposed to be. In particular, we often tend to work from the premise that mappers engage in an unquestionably 'scientific' or 'objective' form of knowledge creation. Of course, cartographers believe that they have to say this to remain credible but historians do not have that obligation. It is better for us to begin from the premise that cartography is seldom what cartographers say it is.

Cartographers' 'scientistic rhetoric' was becoming more strident with the development of computer-assisted map-making, he claimed, but he used deconstruction procedures 'to break the assumed link between reality and representation which has dominated cartographic thinking' (p. 2); by 'reading between the lines' of maps, he sought to identify their 'silences and contradictions', their metaphors and rhetorical flourishes.

Cartographers have traditionally tended to accept that the objects they wish to represent on their maps are 'real and objective' pregivens. Their goal is to display these accurately, hence their search for ever greater scientific precision; they can come closer to an exact mirror in their representation and can reject maps (especially old ones) that fail to conform to their canons of conforming to the rules. But, Harley argued, the production of maps is governed by cultural as well as scientific rules. Thus, for example, most societies are ethnocentric in producing maps which have their territories at the centre of their world, thereby helping to promote geopolitical world views. In selecting what to show, and what prominence to give it, cartographers frequently employ a 'hierarchicalization of space' (p. 7):

. . . it is taken for granted in a society that the place of the king is more important than the place of a lesser baron, that a castle is more important than a peasant's house, that the town of an archbishop is more important than that of a minor prelate, or that the estate of a landed gentleman is more worthy of emphasis than that of a plain farmer. Cartography deploys its vocabulary accordingly so that it embodies a systematic social inequality. The distinctions of class and power are engineered, reified and legitimated in the map by means of cartographic signs.

Thus, partial representations are undertaken 'behind a mask of a seemingly neutral science', and yet the 'rules of society will surface. They have ensured that maps are at least as much an image of the social order as they are a measurement of the phenomenal world of objects'.

If we accept maps as cultural texts, Harley contends, we can interrogate them and come to learn of their functions within the society for whom they were created. Map-making involves a series of steps, he argues – selection, omission, simplification, classification, the creation of hierarchies, and 'symbolization' – all of which are rhetorical devices. Cartographic rhetoric is involved in the production of all maps, and is implicated in the exercise of power:

> Power is exerted on cartography. Behind most cartographers there is a patron; in innumerable instances the makers of cartographic texts were responding to external needs. Monarchs, ministers, state institutions, the Church, have all initiated programs of mapping for their own ends. In modern Western society maps quickly became crucial to the maintenance of state power – to its boundaries, to its commerce, to its internal administration, to control of populations, and to its military strength.

Thus mapping became a state business, and the publication of maps became subject to laws regarding state security.

The map becomes 'juridical territory': it facilitates surveillance and control. Maps are still used to control our lives in innumerable ways. A mapless society, though we may take the map for granted, would now be politically unimaginable. All this is power *with* the help of maps. It is an external power, often centralized and exercised bureaucratically, imposed from above, and manifest in particular acts or phases of deliberate policy. As a consequence, cartography (and cartographers) are not just one element in a power structure (p. 13):'Cartographers manufacture power: they create a spatial panopticon. It is a power embedded in the map text'. Their power is not exercised over people directly, but rather over the knowledge made available to them; 'maps, by articulating the world in mass-produced and stereotyped images, express an embedded social vision' (p. 14; Harley, 1992, exemplified this in his essay on the role of maps in the Columbian encounter with the 'new world'; see also Schulten, 2001).

Deconstructing maps serves three functions (Harley, 1989, p. 15):

1. It challenges the myth that technological improvements 'always produce better delineations of reality';
2. It allows appreciation of the role of maps in the historical processes of creating a socially constructed order to the world; and
3. It promotes the understanding of other texts as the meaning of maps is discovered.

He later extended this argument, asserting that, 'As a discourse created and received by human agents, maps represent the world through a veil of ideology, are fraught with internal tensions, provide classic examples of power-knowledge, and are always caught up in wider political contexts' (Harley, 1990, p. 1). This is illustrated by a range of examples including, for example, cartographic complicity in racial stereotyping through place-name labelling, and the exclusion of 'places to avoid' (such as the *barrios pobres/favelas* which are absent from the maps of most South American cities). Cartographers' interests, he claimed, are dominated by mechanical issues related to 'efficiencies' associated with new technologies, so that the ethical issues of what is and is not depicted go largely unconsidered.

Harley concluded his 1990 paper by noting that, 'The challenge to and continual crisis of representation is universal and not peculiar to cartography' (p. 18). Earlier, he had referred to GIS as extending the crisis of representation to the crisis of the machine. GIS are new ways of presenting the world, new texts to be deconstructed to illustrate meanings and power relationships. This argument has been taken up by Pickles (1995a, p. 3), who identified as a central characteristic of all GIS that they involve 'the production of electronic spatial representations' of data. Those media not only facilitate data capture, entry and reproduction and speed up operations on the data but also allow new forms of representation.

Thus, like maps and other texts, the use of GIS relies on signs and representations (signifiers and signified) which call for deconstruction: 'We are ... entering a potential new phase of ways of *worldmaking* for which we desperately need new ways of *wordmaking*' (p. 5) because GIS are much more than counting machines with greatly increased efficiency; they are enabling new ways of representing the world, and hence new 'realities', and their use by the technically skilled involves new power relationships. Curry (1998) and Gilbert (1996), however, encourage geographers associated with the cultural turn and critical geography not to reject all developments in modern information technology because of the association of GIS with statistics, spatial analysis, military applications and positivism (contra Smith, 1992).

According to Curry (1998, p. 143):

> ... the literature on the systems has come to be more balanced, or perhaps more forgiving. Nonetheless ... there has remained in the literature a strongly critical element. But this criticism has increasingly come to involve not Luddite calls for an abolition of the systems, but rather calls for a new GIS, for what some have called a GIS2. Connected in part to another goal, of developing systems that might be more appropriate to public participation, by neighborhood and environmental groups for example, advocates of GIS2 have suggested the possibility of a reformulation that will meet the needs of these groups ...

For Gilbert (1996, p. 7), wider developments of hypermedia (within which GIS can be situated) allow exactly the sorts of explorations of textual and other media that postmodernists and others promote:

> In a computer hypertext the reader can use a mouse to point and click on a word, and be instantly taken to related ideas elsewhere in the text. The freedom created for the reader to jump from place to place, to compare, contrast, or simply juxtapose different elements radically changes the nature of writing (or 'authoring' ...) and of reading. ... the hypertext form marks a move away from a modernist concern for 'objects, positions, order and stability' towards a postmodern emphasis on 'processes, relations, chaos, and instability'.

Images (still and moving), diagrams, sounds and other media can be incorporated, allowing a 'polyphonic' (Crang, 1992) approach to geographical writing and study similar to the postmodern novel: the 'reader' becomes an 'active co-author'.

Others have also set-out the consequences and possibilities of a deconstructive approach in geography, in particular through more careful engagement with the works of the French philosopher Jacques Derrida (Barnett, 1999; see also p. 283) and such approaches (in fertile combination with Foucault's work and the legacies of radical geography) have also enabled a *critical* reengagement with geopolitical discourses (Dodds and Atkinson, 2000; Ó Tuathail, 1996; Dalby and Ó Tuathail, 1998) that examines the imagination, narration and scripting of global and strategic spaces. Thus, according to Ó Tuathail and Dalby (1998, p. 3):

> *Critical geopolitics bears witness to the irredeemable plurality of space and the multiplicity of possible constructions of space. Thus … it pays particular attention to the boundary-drawing practices and performances that characterize the everyday life of states. In contrast to conventional geography and geopolitics, both the material borders at the edge of the state and the conceptual borders designating this as a boundary between a secure inside and an anarchic outside are objects of investigation. Critical geopolitics is not about the 'the outside' of the state but about the very construction of boundaries of 'inside' and 'outside,' 'here' and 'there,', the 'domestic' and the 'foreign'.*

Such work has examined both elite (government and state) and popular (e.g. media) geopolitical narratives and the connections between them (Sharp, 2000).

A similar critical sense of the taken-for-granted spaces of (geo)politics and cartography informs Lewis and Wigen's (1997) critique of conventional notions of continents (Europe distinct from Asia, for example, or the notion of Australia as a continent apart from Asia and the Pacific); the 'commonsense' and naturalized view of the world, which they show to be historically contingent, rather than eternal and fixed. And whilst some have wondered if any rendition of geopolitics ('critical' or otherwise) is compatible with a cosmopolitan, multi-cultural society (Heffernan, 2000), Ó Tuathail (writing under both the anglicized and Irish spellings of his name), responds that:

> *… 'critical geopolitics': a project that involves commitments, subjectivities and positions which can be described. … as a positional geo-politics which 'one cannot not want'* (Toal/Ó Tuathail, 2000, p. 386).

Whilst 'critical geopolitics' has offered a rich vein of ideas and poststructuralist departures and others have revisited complex and wider entanglements of power (see the survey by Allen, 2003), probably the most far-reaching and sustained geographical engagement with poststructuralism and geography is Doel's (1999) *Poststructuralist Geographies: The Diabolical Art of Spatial Science*. Doel's book defies easy summary. So we will allow it to speak to for 'itself' here (if such a thing is possible):

> *Letting space take place: that is the ambition of geography. … geography is simply an inclination towards the event of spacing. This is not spacing in the paranoiac sense of dissociating one position from another, of forcing distanciated identities onto space – a tendency that I have dubbed 'pointallism'. Rather than a poststructuralism that could get taken up by geography and geographers, I want to demonstrate that poststructuralism is always already spatial: that it attends from the off to the 'difference that space makes'* (p. 10).

Doel makes clear that his explorations of poststructuralism and geography are operating in the spaces opened by Marxist geography (he thus engages creatively with Harvey's work), yet the result is not reducible to a reworking (or even a post-) Marxist geography. For example, he posits a 'Deleuzian' notion of origami rather than socio-spatial dialectics:

> ... the world can be (un)folded in countless ways, with innumerable folds over folds, and folds within folds, but such a disfiguration never permits one (or more) of those folds to become redundant, nor for one (or more) of them to seize power as a master-fold. Every fold plays its part in lending consistency to the thing that is folded and since every fold participates in the lending of consistency to 'something = x' without ever belonging to it ... folds cannot be distinguished in terms of the essential and the inessential, the necessary and the contingent, or the structural and the ornamental. Every fold plays its part: every fold spays 'it' apart. The event of origami is in the (un)folding, just as the gift is in the wrapping: not as content, but as process (p. 18).

The book is subsequently divided into three sections: (a) the space of poststructuralism: a review of the spatiality of selected writings by Baudrilliard, Deleuze, Foucault, Irigaray and Lyotard; (b) a schizoanalysis of the geographical tradition – exploring spatial science and the drawing of lines; and (c) a move to a 'Poststructuralist geography'. Doel however explains that:

> Accordingly what I want to achieve in this book is neither a secure identity for poststructuralist geography, which one or two readers may attest to being the 'Real Thing', nor a justification for reducing the geographical idiom in all of its heterogeneity to the theoretical practices of figures such as Deleuze, Derrida, Lyotard, Irigary, Baudrillard and Olsson. I hope that my actual aim is much more modest. I want to participate in generating a different way of feeling about events, about the world, about others, and about theoretical practice.

Doel's book, and similar works by him and his collaborators elsewhere (e.g. Doel and Clarke, 1999), elicited a variety of reactions from hostility to fascination and bemusement. Thus Peet (1998, p. 241) labels it an 'Amoral geography': 'an extreme form of the postmodern position in the discipline of geography, which does manage to lose virtually all connection with any project of emancipatory politics'. Responding to an earlier paper by Clark and Doel (1995) (in this case on transpolitical geography), however, Philo (1994, p. 525) begins with an observation that:

> It goes without saying that papers by David Clarke and Marcus Doel are tricky to read, and that many readers – whether they would call themselves political geographers, cultural geographers, urban geographers or whatever – are wary about the effort required to see if anything valuable can be recovered from them. Questions immediately arise as to whether readers can fully understand the papers, whether they are indeed supposed to be able to, whether the onus is deliberately being shifted from the author(s) to the reader(s), and about whether the latter can ever achieve more than one creative 'misreading' after another.

Philo concludes with a mixture of reservations and possibility:

> I ... would want to be less cavalier than Clarke and Doel in consigning large portions of existing political geography to dustbin of outdated or untenable geographical inquires, but I nonetheless have sympathy for a paper which is so consistently unnerving and unswerving in its commitment to finding the 'holes' in an established geography ... (p. 531).

Philo (1992) had earlier sought to explore the geographies in the influential works of the French poststructuralist thinker Michel Foucault (*cf.* Matless, 1992). Philo presents this as:

> Not a matter of 'creating yet another intellectual base to defend' ... but of stirring another voice into the richness of recent 'geographical' debates ... (p. 138).

Foucault is interpreted as suspicious and subversive of supposed historical (and geographical) certainties. Foucault's heterodox notions of order and power (the former as highly contingent to different times, societies and places and the latter as diffuse; not something which is simply held, so much as enacted and exercised) provide us with:

> ... a blueprint for ... a postmodern geography in which details and difference, fragmentation and chaos, substance and heterogeneity, humility and respectfulness feature at every turn, and an account of social life which necessarily brings with it a sustained concern for the geography of things rather than a recall for the formal geometries of spatial science (p. 159).

Moreover:

> Foucault's geography emerges directly from his own suspicion of the certainties (the order, coherence, truth, reason) supposed by most historians and social scientists to lie at the heart of social life, and as such I think that it can be adjudged a 'truly' postmodern human geography in a manner that, say, Edward Soja's postmodern geographies cannot. We might not like this Foucauldian version of a postmodern human geography, but I think that there is much we can learn from it, even if we then chose to retain our faith in a more obviously modernist conceptual, practical, and political geographical project (p. 137).

In some complementary ways, other strands of work also drawing loosely and in various ways on poststructuralism have recently enlivened human geography. Thus *actor-network theory*, which was first developed in (very broadly poststructuralist inspired) work on the histories and applications of science and technology (see Law and Hassard, 1999, for a summary) has been proposed as:

> ... a useful way of thinking about how spatial relations come to be wrapped up into complex networks. Moreover, the theory is also believed to provide a means of navigating those dualisms, such as nature/society, action/structure and local/global, that have afflicted so much geographical work (Murdoch, 1998, p. 357).

The study of networks has long been a domain of human geography – especially when it became spatial science and spatial analysis (see Chapter 4) and the notion of complex relational spaces has been explored earlier in humanistic and radical geographies (Chapters 5 and 6). Actor-network theory, however, interprets 'actors' (or actants as they are termed) as complex assemblages of humans and artifacts:

> What ANT [Actor-Network Theory] adds to the more commonplace understandings of relational spaces is a concern with networks. While the term network is commonly utilised in social science to describe technological relations, economic forms, political structures and social processes, ANT uses the term in a way which is quite distinct from such applications. Or rather, it might be argued that

ANT bundles all these network applications together for it concerns itself with the heterogeneity of networks; that is, ANT seeks to a analyse how social and material processes (subjects, objects and relations) become seamlessly entwined within complex sets of association (Murdoch, 1998, p. 359).

ANT has therefore been drawn upon by geographers interested in cyberspaces and more mundane technologies (Bingham, 1996; Hinchliffe, 1996) as well as another fruitful means to explore human-nature interactions (Whatmore, 1999). Indeed, for Thrift (2000, p. 5):

... all the usual boundaries from which and with which western knowledge is constituted – between humans and things, NATURE and CULTURE, tradition and MODERNITY, inside and outside – must be put aside. These divides have made it impossible to see the world for what it really is: a collection of heterogeneous activities which are constantly in formation.

Another strand of broadly poststructuralist work in human geography has coalesced around the themes of *performance* and representation (Thrift and Dewsbury, 2000). Even more so than actor-network theory, this defies easy summary (and some of it is informed by feminist work and as such will be considered in Chapter 8). It has, however, seen renewed debates about the difficulties, potentials, pitfalls of geographical representation (an old theme, given new twists by poststructuralism) – see for example Smith (2003), who draws on Baudrillard, and Harrison (2002) who draws on Wittgenstein; both stressing the limits of (geographical) explanation/representation of practices.

Summing up such departures, Dewsbury, Harrison, Rose and Wylie (2002, p. 439) provide the following indications:

... in the performances that make us, the world comes about. This is about giving space to the event of the world, to make primary its emergent nature, and to the active role we too play in actualizing that which happens – we are thinking here specifically of what we make visible by what we cite as significant. In particular, an awareness of the coming-to-be, the badly formed, the seemingly inconsequential, the ephemerally felt; the desire that lights up a room, the turning you didn't take (but which still haunts you), the anxiety of completing the next task. ... These are not arcane concerns; they speak directly to our practices as social scientists, to the way our techniques are attentive to aspects of the world's unfolding. We are thinking of an expanded socio-logic, of mobilising other sources of expression (literature, art, performance), and above all of rearticulating what counts.

Postcolonialism: decolonizing human geography?

As Chapter 2 charted, geography has long had a close relationship to colonialism and racism. Some radical geographers raised this legacy in their demands for a new, more critical geography. In recent years such calls have multiplied.

Part of this has developed from a more explicit awareness of the class, 'racial' and gendered backdrop to geographical work (inseparable from the impact of feminism, which will be considered in Chapter 8), an enhanced and politicized sense of the 'positionality' of the author. Thus, according to Jackson (1993a, p. 210–11):

Contemporary society is characterized by multiple forms of exploitation and oppression, which suggests that our politics should also be increasingly positional. ... Those of us who wish to change the discipline and have ambitions to change the world should start from modest beginnings, recognizing our own positionality with respect to the fundamental inequalities of gender, 'race' and class. For if those dimensions are a source of power to us, they are as surely a source of oppression to those around us. If our geographical imagination is to develop in ways that are genuinely and constructively oppositional, we should begin by changing ourselves.

Gregory (1994, p. ix) claims that he recognized this need when he moved from the University of Cambridge to the University of British Columbia (Vancouver, Canada) while writing *Geographical Imaginations*. He had to come to terms with what he calls his own 'situatedness', clarified to him by three features of his new home:

1. Canada had a double colonial legacy, linked to both England and France, plus close ties to the USA;
2. Canada is an 'avowedly multicultural society' and many of his students had cultural roots different from his own; and
3. The University of British Columbia was taking issues of gender and sexuality much more seriously than he had been accustomed to.

As a consequence he abandoned his first draft of the text and began again, although Guelke (1995, p. 185) argued that:

... in the text there is scarcely a hint of Canadian culture or intellectual life. This work could have been written anywhere but Canada ... Gregory has a desk in Canada, but he has ignored its artists and intellectuals as thoroughly as any British colonial official might have kept his focus on London in the heart of Africa. Canada for Gregory is an invisible country and its peoples have evidently produced little of importance for him.

However, Gregory claims to have been awakened to issues of positionality in North America, such as colonial status and equal rights, which altered his stance on the issues and literature that he addressed without requiring a particular 'Canadian position'.

For Gregory, a major source for geographers' appreciation of their own positionality and hence partial representation of the world (in every sense of the term partial) has been the writing of Edward Said, especially his classic *Orientalism* (Said, 1978), which argued that 'Westerners' created an 'imaginative geography' of the Orient as part of the imperialist project. Orientals were presented by 'Westerners' as 'others', with different (implicitly if not explicitly inferior) cultures that contrasted with themselves (for examples and elaborations, see Kasbarian, 1996, and Taylor, 1993). The Orient did not exist as a straightforward pre-given object. It was imagined by the British and French in the nineteenth century (an activity promoted by the various geographical societies which transmitted this view of the Oriental 'other' to home audiences: see Bell, Butlin and Heffernan, 1995), for example, in part to promote its colonial dispossession and exploitation (Gregory, 1994, p. 171): 'Orientalism was an active process of othering, the exhibiting of "the" Oriental in a profoundly worldly set of texts which, in a quite fundamental sense, made colonization and dispossession possible' (see also Gregory, 1995b).

The 'othering' of the Orient (and the wider non-West) also provided its residents with a position from which they could later challenge the imperial and colonial hegemonies, not only politically but also culturally and intellectually. This includes, for example, the field of 'subaltern studies' whose goal is to enable the voice and recognize the experience of hitherto marginalized colonial subjects, thereby challenging the intellectual hegemony of 'Western' narratives. That 'Western' hegemony is based on partial views of the rest of the world, often promoted for political and other reasons (see Sharp, 1993). Emancipation and exchange requires that such partiality be countered. Gregory (1994, p. 205) argued that:

> To assume that we are entitled to speak only of what we know by virtue of our own experience is not only to reinstate an empiricism: it is to institutionalize parochialism. Many of us have not been very good at listening to others and learning from them, but the present challenge is surely to find ways of comprehending those other worlds – including our relations with them and our responsibilities toward them – without being invasive, colonizing and violent. If we are to free ourselves from universalizing our own parochialisms, we need to learn how to reach beyond particularities, to speak to the larger questions without diminishing the significance of the places and the people to which they are accountable.

Thus the call for postcolonial perspectives in geography that:

> . . . highlight the importance of representing people and places across different cultures, traditions and contexts but also point to the difficulties of such endeavours. At the same time, postcolonial critiques stress the need to destablise what might be taken for granted and assumed in our own cultures, traditions and contexts. So for example, postcolonial studies challenge the production of knowledges that are exclusively western and ethnocentric by not only focusing on the world beyond 'the West' but also by destabilising what is understood and taken for granted about 'the West' (Blunt and Wills, 2000, p. 168).

Others, such as Clayton (2001, 2002), Crush (1994), Pawson (1999) and Sidaway (2000) have similarly characterized the possibilities and difficulties of a postcolonial geography. For example, Crush (1994, pp. 336–7) also specifies what the aims of a post-colonial geography might be:

> . . . the unveiling of geographical complicity in colonial dominion over space; the character of geographical representation in colonial discourse, the de-linking of local geographical enterprise from metropolitan theory and its totalizing systems of representation; and the recovery of those hidden spaces occupied, and invested with their own meaning, by the colonial underclass.

Blunt and McEwan (2002, p. 3) detect a possibility for geography here, in so far as 'an emphasis on the spatiality of postcolonial thought can help us move beyond the impasse of thinking [about postcolonialism] primarily in temporal terms'. Whilst geography has traditionally been associated with Western knowledge and colonialism they stress 'the diversity of postcolonial perspectives in analyzing space, power, identity and resistance' (p. 6). Moreover:

> Although postcolonialism might not have had much impact on the power imbalances between North and South, the diverse body of approaches identified as postcolonial are a significant advancement and offer a great deal to the possibilities of a meaningfully decolonized geography.

Clayton (2001, pp. 749–50) suggests the following departures for 'postcolonial-geographical lines of enquiry that (variously and among other things)':

1. Seek to document and theorize multiple, contradictory and fragmented spaces of identity;
2. Work with postcolonial theory in grounded ways;
3. Be attuned to the discordant postcolonial politics of places studied;
4. Acknowledge that all studies of colonialism are 'situated knowledges' that stem from and feed into particular sites of study, learning and memory;
5. Work at a variety of scales and seek to build 'middle range' narratives;
6. Treat colonial contact as a two-way and contradictory process;
7. Take archives and the past seriously, but use them to question or transform understandings of the present; and
8. Have an anti-colonial effect.

However for Clayton, this list:

> ... does not amount to some sort of postcolonial template for geography. Rather, we have here the rudiments of a postcolonial-geographical way of thinking, and one that I think needs to be explored and debated in much greater depth, not least because there is considerable disagreement about the appropriate aims and methods of postcolonial studies and the status of colonialism as a spatial problematic (p. 750).

'Race' and racisms

Jacobs and Jackson (1996) have argued that postcolonialism demands sustained argument with geographies of 'race' and racism. This raises both the complicity of the discipline in the racist categorizations of colonialism (and all the attendant debates about environmental determinism considered in Chapter 2) as well as the contemporary whiteness of the discipline (see Bonnett, 1997; McGuiness, 1999) and therefore, in Peake and Kobayashi's (2002, p. 50) terms:

> ... the various (and often hidden) racist practices and discourses that permeate the epistemological foundations of geography and the institutional structures and practises that shape our work and environment

For them, an antiracist geography embraces:

1. Research on the geographies of racism;
2. Extending antiracist principles throughout the 'institutional practices' of the discipline, particularly in the classroom;
3. Increasing the participation and presence of non-white geographers in the discipline; and
4. Linking all of these to activism beyond (but building on insights offered by) the discipline, academic life and the University.

For these geographers (and others contributing to the same, 2002, special issue of *The Professional Geographer* on 'Race, Racism and Geography') the key is a less white discipline.

Echoing the ways that the increased presence, power and visibility of women in the discipline since the 1970s has played a role in the making of feminist geographies (see Chapter 9), Pulido (2002, p. 45–6) argues that:

We need sufficient scholars to generate an intellectual synergy around race. A similar process can be seen in feminist geography. Only after women gained access to academia did the study of gender flourish. Men could have taken the lead, but they did not. Because patriarchy was a problem for female geographers, they studied it seriously.

She insists, therefore, that while white geographers have produced incisive and critical work on race and that there is *no* inherent reason why 'scholars of color are more likely to have more penetrating insights and analyses' (p. 45), 'more people of color could create a "critical mass", which currently does not exist'.

Thus a call to change the culture of a discipline that institutionally:

. . . is nearly as white an enterprise as country and Western music, professional golf, or the supreme court of the United States (Delaney, 2002, p. 12).

And whiteness itself should be seen as marker of difference, rather than the often taken-for-granted norm against which supposed minorities (in global terms, arguably majorities) are defined. Thus Bonnett and Nayak (2003, p. 309) argue that:

. . . it is only by understanding such normative terms as 'white' and 'western' – the ones against which others are defined as exotic – that wider systems of racial privilige can be bought into view. By making it clear that categories such as whiteness are also the products of racialization, that they too have a history and a geography and, hence, are changeable, we can help transform the critique of race and ethnicity from a 'subfield' into an essential theme running throughout a rigorous geographical education.

Meanwhile, however, 'ideas about "race(s)" (and their relationship to territorially-bounded nations) remain among the most powerful sources of human identity and division within the contemporary world', according to Jackson and Penrose (1993, p. 1). But although they are often taken for granted they are social constructions rather than natural categories, 'the product of specific historical and geographical forces, rather than biologically given ideas whose meaning is dictated by nature'. Thus those who speak from a 'racial' or national position are doing so within categories defined by imperial and colonial histories and geographies – in many cases (notably with regard to racism) from a position of assumed superiority. Such is the power of these constructions that 'resistance is often couched in terms which do not challenge such dominant modes of representation' (Penrose and Jackson, 1993, p. 203). Only when the social construction of identity is recognized does a politics of identity emerge, whereby individuals and groups 'attach significance to certain dimensions and contest the relevance of other designations'.

The politics of identity, like all politics, is a struggle for power and, as Penrose and Jackson (1993, p. 207) argued, 'takes place within a hegemonic system of social relations':

. . . at any given place and time positions of hegemony are being employed to exercise and preserve power [which] . . . includes the capacity to set the parameters for negotiation within any given society.

It also gives the freedom to define 'difference' and to enforce this vision through hegemonic institutions of government, law and education. In a system where 'sameness' and conformity are rewarded, the power to define 'difference' becomes the power to disadvantage and disempower.

Such complex geographies of power, domination and resistance (Pile and Keith, 1997), or 'entanglements of power' as one collection (Sharp, 2000; Routledge, Philo and Paddison, 2000) termed them, have thus become rich domains of geographical enquiry. Moreover, it has become more a matter of regard that the practice of geography; the circulation of its texts and journals and the structure and sociology of the academic discipline:

... as much a product of specific social, cultural and geographical constructions as the taken-for-granted geographies they [geographers] wish to contest and transform and this affects their analyses (and their disagreements with each other). Such geographies are always constructed within relations of power in which some spaces (and ways of understanding them) are effaced by dominant and hegemonic geographies (Berg, 2003, p. 308).

We return to some of the issues this raises in Chapters 9 and 10.

Conclusions

Postmodernism, poststructuralism, postcolonialism and the 'cultural turn' continue to work through human geography in complex and intertwined ways and are themselves subject to a wide variety of definitions, (mis?)understandings and interpretations. Some geographers voice concern over what these mean for the identity and social relevance of the discipline or draw attention to the degree of fashionability associated with geography's 'cultural turn' (Barnett and Low, 1996; Barnett, 1998a, 1998b; Castree, 1999; Mohan, 1994), and some have condemned the 'excesses' of the cultural turn (and associated encounters) for its neglect of urgent social questions about inequality and social justice or for its lack of application (e.g. Sayer, 2000). While herself sympathetic to many of its departures, McDowell (2000) also notes that there is considerable unease and angry reactions from some regarding the 'cultural turn'. Thus Hamnett (2003, p. 1) is concerned:

... that the rise of a 'post-modern' human geography, with its stress on textuality and texts, deconstruction, critique, 'reading' and interpretation, has led human geography into a theoretical playground where its practitioners stimulate or entertain themselves and a handful of readers, but have in the process become increasingly detached from contemporary social issues and concerns. The risk is that much of human geography will cease to be taken seriously in the world beyond the narrow confines of academe. It will be seen simply as a corner of the post-modern theoretical playground, possibly entertaining to study for a while, but something which can be safely ignored while the grown ups get on with the business of changing the world, often for the worse.

Others, notably Mitchell (1995), criticize what they see as the reification of culture in geography's putative cultural turn:

Like 'race', 'culture' in itself possesses no explanatory value ... Our goal, therefore, should be one of figuring out how the idea of culture becomes socially solidified as a thing, ream, attribute or domain (p. 113).

Some others might sympathize with Mikesell's (1999, p. 441) claim that 'Most of what has been written by self-styled radical, new, or social-cum-cultural geographers is superficial or worse'; similar sentiments are voiced by Gould (1999). Yet many have welcomed and take pride in a human geography which is more engaged with (and in some ways contributing to) wider social theory. In the mid 1990s, Derek Gregory (1994, p. 4) thus claimed that:

Many of those working in other humanities and social sciences have also become interested in questions of place, space and landscape. ... Their studies have multiple origins, but they treat the production of social space, of human spatiality, in new and immensely productive ways.

Gregory goes on to state – in tones which reflect a human geography more deeply informed by and situated within a wider social theory, but which also betray both a sense of optimism and limits about what human geography has achieved – that:

The production of space is not an incidental by-product of social life but a moment intrinsic to its conduct and constitution, and for geography to make a difference – politically and intellectually – it must be attentive to difference (p. 414).

In complementary terms, Amin and Thrift (2000) argued that economic geography was currently 'narrowly specialised' (p. 4) and drew on only a thin range of work within the contemporary discipline of economics – what they saw as its 'certain type of rigour; its emphasis on well-defined models of limited domains' (p. 5). Geographers should look beyond those traditional areas of economic scholarship to the 'new areas of economic study that are currently both flourishing and provided a genuine ground for the kind of contributions we can make' (p. 8). This stimulated a number of responses, several of which – like Martin and Sunley's (2001) – warned against 'throwing out the baby with the bathwater' by abandoning contacts with 'traditional' economic geography: one of the headings in their response – 'Beware of vague theory and thin empirics' – was repeated by others in a variety of guises. Rodríguez-Pose (2001) warned of the possibility of 'killing economic geography' with a 'cultural turn overdose', for example, and Plummer and Sheppard (2001) asked 'Must emancipatory economic geography be qualitative?'. Elsewhere, Plummer (2001, p. 761) argued that increasingly geographers' 'visions of the economic landscape are being constructed on the basis of, at best, vaguely formulated and strictly imposed theoretical constructs' which are only evaluated by either 'casual empiricism or self-selected case studies' – leading him to align himself with Markusen's (1999) query – 'How do I know it when I see it?'.

We have perhaps not been able to do proper justice in this chapter to all aspects of the developments of the last decade or two in human geography, for we are mindful of Philo's (2000, p. 27) point that:

It is important, I feel, to resist the impression of sitting in some kind of satellite circling human geography's cultural turn, claiming the 'scopic power' to see clearly all that is taking place but which others closer by cannot themselves comprehend.

Moreover, part of what the cultural turn (and perhaps postmodernism) has been about has been the reconfiguration of many subdisciplinary boundaries (epitomized in the scope and heterodoxy of recent edited 'companions' to and handbooks for economic, cultural and political geography; Anderson, Domosh, Pile and Thrift, 2002; Agnew, Mitchell and Ó Tuathail, 2003; Sheppard and Barnes, 2000) as well as some inter- and trans-disciplinary trends. Hubbard, Kitchen, Bartley and Fuller (2003, p. 61–2) provide a useful *précis* of these intricate turns – and their limits:

> ... the importance of culture has been seized upon widely across the discipline, with social, political and economic geographers seeking to undertake culturally sensitive analyses [they cite Lee and Wills, 1997, as an example of such engagements by economic geographers for instance] ... while the combination of the 'cultural turn' in geography and a wider 'spatial turn' across the social sciences and humanities might create the semblance of a more fluid, post-disciplinary landscape, disciplinary boundaries do continue to exist as administrative units within institutions and within the popular (academic) imagination.

Similar thoughts lead Crang and Thrift (2000, p. xi) to reflect that:

> Within the discipline there has been a burgeoning interest in social thought that has both extended and pluralized the influences drawn upon by geographers. Beyond the discipline social thought appeared to be increasingly smitten with a geographical idiom of margins, spaces and borders. However, this spatial turn was not a cause for disciplinary triumphalism that others were turning to geography since much of it seemed resolutely ignorant of geography and geographers as a discipline. Indeed, it seemed at various times to show both deliberate ignorance of geography while – lest anyone might become chauvinistic or proprietary over the claims of the discipline – also displaying how limited much geographical thought had been.

Indeed, their book illustrates the wide range of philosophical and social-theoretical sources on which geographers and others now draw in their considerations of space. They identify five 'spaces' within this corpus of work: spaces of language; spaces of the self and other; metonymic spaces; agitated spaces; spaces of experience; and spaces of writing. Furthermore, 'exotic new hybrids continue to be produced' (pp. 24–5), and the interactions among geographers, social scientists and scholars in the humanities over issues of space and spatiality are likely to increase, even though many contemporary treatments by the last group are undertaken in apparent ignorance of geographical interest in such topics (as in Miller and Hashmi, 2001).

So, despite all the complex twists and turns, polemics and departures and although they may also circulate now on the internet (witness, for example the recent arrival of *ACME: An Online Journal for Critical Geographies*: http://www.acme-journal.org) as well as in traditional academic journals (themselves increasingly accessed online), lectures, conferences and texts, there is ultimately little to differentiate these recent developments within human geography from those charted earlier in this book. They are based on dissatisfaction with what has been, and is being, done in the name of the discipline, and a wish to change it, at least by adding new perspectives if not by also expunging some of their predecessors.

8
Feminist geographies

Geography, could you be my world?
. . . By looking within and without, upside down and inside out,
Come alive geography, come alive!

(Clare Madge 1997, p. 32–3)

In 1984, when feminist geography was just getting going, and when the field was characterised by a relatively small number of individuals, the WGSG [Women and Geography Study Group, established in 1980 within the professional Institute of British Geographers] produced the text Geography and Gender. *Aimed at first year undergraduates, this ground-breaking book was also important for the collective way in which it was written. Rather than being written by one or two named individuals, the book was written by several people working and writing together, as 'a collective', and has as its 'author' the WGSG. Taking their cue from wider feminist politics, the feminist geographers who wrote* Geography and Gender *wished both to challenge the accepted conventions of academic writing (conventions which celebrate and reward the individual, apparently working in glorious isolation) and to acknowledge the genuinely collaborative and supportive ways in which feminist geography was emerging in Britain.*

(Gillian Rose, Nicky Gregson, Jo Foord, Sophie Bowlby, Claire Dywer, Sarah Holloway,
Nina Laurie, Avril Maddrell, Tracy Skelton, 1997, p. 1–2)

To the pioneers of the 1970s, a journal devoted to feminist geography must have seemed a distant dream. Although the women's liberation movement motivated many to take action in the streets, few dared to move that action into the halls of the academy. Yet feminist voices persisted and slowly gained momentum. And from these modest yet courageous beginnings, feminist geography has now permeated most, if not all, corners of the discipline and has become a force that cannot be ignored in accounts of contemporary geographical knowledge. Our hope is that Gender, Place and Culture *– a journal devoted to feminist geography – will serve to celebrate and consolidate that presence.*

(Bondi and Domosh, 1994, p. 3)

Although for many years and in most places at least half of geography undergraduate students have been women, research and teaching in both human and physical geography have long tended to be performed mostly by men. This is still true in a number of university geography departments. While long taken for granted (rather like the references to *man* and the environment that were usually taken for granted as somehow including the half of humanity who are women or girls), over the past few decades this male dominance (and the wider 'masculinity' of geographical scholarship) has become a theme of extensive debate and a focus of demands for progressive transformation. For example, in the UK of the early 1980s – a period when many of the changes associated with the radical and humanistic critiques of positivism made for a lively human geography – only 25 per cent of graduate students in geography (the data were for both physical and human geography) were women (Johnston and Brack, 1983). Johnston and Brack went on to quantify some other facts and trends relating to the relative status of women in the discipline:

> . . . of the 1106 [UK-based] academic geographers identified in this survey, only 126 (11.4 per cent) were female. Furthermore, the percentage of females obtaining posts has declined. In the 1930s, 16.8 per cent of geographers obtaining their first posts (plus those in post in 1933) were female. In the 1940s, the figure was 30.4 per cent, but it fell from then on, to 11.6 per cent in the 1950s, 8.5 per cent in the 1960s and 7.9 per cent in the 1970s. . . . Of the 142 geographers who have held readerships [between 1933 and 1983] only 6.3 per cent were females (the chances of a male becoming reader were 1 in 7.4, whereas for a female they were 1 in 14). Of the 142 who have occupied chairs, only 6 (4.3 per cent) have been women (p. 110).

Even in those few departments where larger numbers of women entered postgraduate training and research in geography they frequently found limited prospects for employment as academic geographers. Monk (1998), claims that Clark University in Massachusetts – where in the 1920s, Ellen Churchill Semple (see p. 48) spent the later part of her influential career – was an 'original hearthland' of women geographers from the 1920s to the 1970s), but nevertheless:

> Even though Clark was 'welcoming', when the when the women graduated they found restricted opportunities. Occupational segregation was quite evident. Realistically, women geographers, even those with doctorates, could aspire to positions in teacher education institutions, the few women's colleges, high schools, or outside academia . . . University positions were almost exclusively open to men. (p. 28)

Today, despite the fact that in many departments there remains a numerical prevalence of men (particularly in more senior positions), some things have changed (although see the papers in the special issue of *The Professional Geographer* on this topic: Falconer al-Hindi, 2000). For feminist geography is now a rich field. In addition to frequent papers in all the main disciplinary journals and the prominent, specialist, journal *Gender Space and Culture*, there are many collections and texts. For example, a recent text on *Methods and Techniques in Human Geography* (Robinson, 1998) has a chapter on 'Feminist Geographies' among others on 'multivariate analysis', 'generalised linear models' and 'categorical data analysis'. Other collections such as *A Feminist Glossary of Human Geography* (McDowell and Sharp, 1999), *Space, Gender and Knowledge: Feminist Readings* (McDowell and Sharp, 1997), *Full Circles: Geographies of Women Over the Life Course* (Katz and Monk, 1993), *Thresholds in Feminist Geography* (Jones III, Nast and Roberts 1997) and others bear witness to the wealth of feminist work in geography. It was not always so.

The first paper raising the issue of the relative status of women in the discipline appeared in 1973 (Zelinksky 1973a) – and was penned by a man – although around this time the first papers on feminist geography appeared in *Antipode* (Burnett, 1973; Hayford, 1974). Subsequent papers tended to focus on the facts and consequences of the exclusion and isolation both of women geographers and of the distinctive geographies of women (for example differing experiences and uses of urban, paid work and 'home' spaces). The titles of subsequent papers that used terms such as 'sex discrimination in geography' (Berman, 1974), 'the other half', 'geographical study of women' (Tivers, 1978), and 'on not excluding half of the human in human geography' (Monk and Hanson, 1982) reveal the concern to produce a more inclusive human geography.

Early feminist analyses stressed that the different experiences that structure women's views of the world are created in contexts that have a clear power gradient between the oppressors (men) and the oppressed (women): the collective experiences of men and women are distinctive and unequal. Thus the feminist project is necessarily a political one, seeking to remove the power gradient through emancipatory and other processes. Just as Marx argued that his project involved the emancipation of the working classes, providing them with the means to control their own destinies, so the feminist project is the basis for 'identity politics' – 'an emancipatory politics of opposition ... resisting and challenging the fraudulent claims of dominant groups' (Bondi, 1993, pp. 86–7). This calls for 'consciousness raising' and transformation, out of which identities can be constructed and reconstructed (in places) as bases for action. While it came late to geography, feminism has a long history as an intellectual and political movement and there are diverse strands of feminist thought and politics.

In the 1980s, however, an engaged and diverse feminist geography had emerged and was establishing itself as a vibrant domain of research and teaching. According to McDowell (1986a, p. 151), such a feminist geography project 'emphasizes questions of gender inequality and the oppression of women in virtually all spheres of life', and its goal includes uncovering and countering such inequality and discrimination within the geographical profession itself (on which see that early essay by Zelinsky, 1973a, plus Zelinsky, Monk and Hanson, 1982; Jackson, Smith and Johnston, 1988; Johnson, 1989). That is part of a much larger task (McDowell, 1989, p. 137):

> ... to demonstrate that women do matter in geography, and to argue that the failure to take gender differences into account impoverishes both geographical teaching and scholarship ... [in addition] it is not enough just to add women in as an additional category. Feminist geography, as opposed to a geography or geographies of women, entails a new look at our discipline. It poses several awkward questions about how we currently divide the subject matter into convenient academic parcels and also challenges current practice in teaching and research.

However, McDowell (1993b, p. 305) also noted how:

> As in feminist scholarship more generally, that part of our discipline subsumed under the heading 'feminist geography' has become such a diverse and pluralistic enterprise that it is increasingly inaccurate to define feminism as a single perspective.

Refining this a few years later, McDowell (1999, p. 93) identified 'the specific aim' of feminist geography as:

> ... to investigate, make visible and challenge relations between gender divisions and spatial divisions, to uncover their mutual constitution and problematise their apparent naturalness. Thus the purpose is to examine the extent to which women and men experience spaces and places differently and to show how these differences themselves are part of the social construction of gender as well as that of place.

Diverse strands

In the 1990s diverse strands of encounters between feminism and geography have led to even broader critiques and concerns. Pratt (2000, p. 261) thus notes how:

> Since the late 1980s, many feminist geographers have moved away from an exclusive focus on gender and class systems. This new phase can be identified as feminist geographies of difference.

She identifies three characteristics of this new phase:

1. *The contestation of gender categories of man and woman.* Feminist geography has refused to take such categories for granted, instead exploring the ways that humans learn to perform the accustomed roles of being a man or a woman and how these vary across time and space. Such concern has led feminist geography to be 'increasingly attentive to the differences in the construction of gender relations across races, ethnicities, ages, religions, sexualities [the differing experiences and meanings of gay, lesbian bisexual and heterosexual roles for example], and nationalities, and to exploitative relations among women who are positioned in varying ways along these multiple axes of difference' (p. 261). In other words, the commonality of women's position and experiences – something that was often taken for granted in earlier renditions of feminist geography – is replaced with a more nuanced understanding of the diversity of what it means to be a man or a woman in different places, amongst different classes and ethnicities, and at different times.

2. *The resort to a broader array of social and (reflecting 'the cultural turn') cultural theory.* This includes both poststructuralist thought and psychoanalysis, seeking a deeper appreciation of how gender relations and identities (including sexuality) are formed and shaped. While this has produced a flow of works (and some attention to feminist geography in wider feminist studies), another consequence of these developments is that 'theoretical differences among feminist geographers are more obvious than in the past' (p. 261). In other words, it is perhaps no longer appropriate (if it ever was) to speak of a singular feminist geography. Rather *feminist geographies* have come to embody the wider debates and polemics across the more or less marxist, poststructuralist and postcolonial positions that earlier chapters have examined. So, while feminist geography has often had to struggle to establish itself against sexist and sometimes misogynist dismissal on the part of other geographers, ideological differences among feminist geographers have

sometimes surfaced (see Valentine, 1998; Johnston, 1994; McDowell, 1990; and Peake, 1994, on different 'personal' aspects of all this), indicating a continuing debate.

3. *A move towards the concept of 'situated (feminist) knowledges'.* This has meant exploring the basis of different geographical claims and the diversity of vantage points from which they are made. While this shares much with a wider postmodernism and poststructuralism in geography and social sciences, in feminist geographies it has also led to a stress on what is a stake in creating feminist alliances across differences of class and 'race' (Gibson-Graham, 1994; Jacobs, 1994).

Pratt illustrates these (and prior) developments through tabulating three strands of feminist geography that have evolved very broadly in sequence (Figure 8.1). She describes the first phase as a concern to bring the effects of gender inequality into geography, hence

THE GEOGRAPHY OF WOMEN

Topical focus	Theoretical influences	Geographical focus
Description of the effects of gender inequality	Welfare geography, Liberal feminism	Constraints of distance and spatial separation

SOCIALIST FEMINIST GEOGRAPHY

Topical focus	Theoretical influences	Geographical focus
Explanation of inequality, and relations between capitalism and patriarchy	Marxism, Socialist feminism	Spatial separation, Gender, Place, Localities

FEMINIST GEOGRAPHIES OF DIFFERENCE

Topical focus	Theoretical influences	Geographical focus
The construction of gendered, hetero(sexed) indentities; differences among women;	Cultural, poststructural, postcolonial, psychoanalytic theories;	Micro-geographies of the body;
Gender and constructions of nature; heteropatriarchy and geopolitics	Writings of women of colour, lesbian women, gay men, women from 'developing countries'	Mobile identities; Distance, separation and place; Imaginative geographies; Colonialisms and postcolonialisms; Environment/nature

Figure 8.1 *Strands of feminist geography (Source: Pratt, 2000, p. 260)*

'*the geography of women*'. A second strand, influenced by Marxism, seeks to theorize these inequalities in terms of their relationships to the capitalist economy, hence '*socialist feminist geography*'. Finally there has been a wider stress on construction of gendered differences, both of men and women, straight, gay and bisexual, from different places, classes and 'races', hence '*feminist geographies of difference*'.

These strands do not always divide clearly or neatly. For example, Gibson-Graham's (1996) influential work *The End of Capitalism (As We Knew It): A Feminist Critique of Political Economy* is simultaneously Marxist, feminist and poststructuralist. Yet throughout the many departures of feminist geography, the original concern with the sociology of the discipline has endured (and the concern with the hitherto relatively marginal position of women within its power structures). Blunt and Wills (2000, p. 91) thus note that:

> *While feminist geographies are diverse, they share several common themes. ... One important site of resistance is against sexism within the discipline, departments and other institutions of geography. Resisting the status of detached and disembodied analyses, feminist geographies often share a commitment to situating the production of knowledge in more embodied and contexualised ways. Finally, just as feminist theory and politics transcend disciplinary boundaries, they also transcend the subdisciplinary boundaries within geography, inspiring a wide range of connections within and between economic, social, cultural, historical, political and urban fields of geographical interest.*

Rethinking histories of geography

The aspiration of feminist geographers is not simply to add a further fragment to the academic discipline, with the potential for its ghettoization, therefore, but rather to ensure that a feminist perspective informs all work within human geography. Feminist geography, according to Johnson (1989), involves recognizing women's common experience of, and resistance to, oppression by men, and a commitment to end it 'so that women can define and control themselves' (p. 85). Evaluation of geographical practice will demonstrate that it is 'sexist, patriarchal and phallocentric' and will open the way to emancipation, by providing a guide to political practice (Bowlby et al., 1989). One of the fullest such evaluations has been undertaken by Rose. In a critique of histories of the discipline, for example, she argued that (Rose, 1995, p. 414):

> *The writing of certain kinds of pasts is legitimated by, and legitimates, only certain kinds of presents. ... Traditions are constructed: written, spoken, visualized, taught, lived ... certain people or kinds of people are included as relevant to the tradition under construction and others are deemed as irrelevant.*

This is a procedure which, she claimed, allowed Stoddart (1991) to dismiss the writings of Victorian women travellers (Domosh, 1991a) as outside what he interpreted as the geographical tradition, and thereby irrelevant to any history he might write. Women have been written out of geography's history, and not only by Stoddart, so that:

> *... even if we can no longer be certain exactly what geography was in the past, in virtually all histories of geographical knowledges one apparently incontrovertible fact remains: geography, whatever it was, was almost always done by men* (Rose, 1995, p. 414).

Stoddart (1991) argued against the perceived need for a 'feminist historiography' of geography expressed in Domosh's (1991a) critique of the treatment of women in his *On Geography* (Stoddart, 1986). He argued that such an enterprise is unnecessary for an understanding of the work of the small number of women who were influential on nineteenth-century geography: 'No feminist historiography is required to analyse their contributions: they looked after themselves, their careers and their scholarship perfectly well without such assistance' (p. 485), and to do other is to impose 'the explanatory whims of an evanescent present on an increasingly distant past' (p. 486). Domosh (1991b) responded that women should not be 'tacked on to the list of heroes'; their particular viewpoints and experiences should be explored through a feminist approach.

Domosh (1991b) and Rose (1995) thus force us to question the delimitation of geographical tradition – how it is that which is classified as geography became defined in such a way that its tradition is so male dominated, a 'patriarchy'? Citing this work and others leads McEwan (1998, p. 373) to comment how:

Stoddart's delimitation of the discursive boundaries of geography produces a definition that is both epistemologically narrow and contestable. As Blunt [1994] points out, institutions outside the academy were [also] important in shaping views of women and their travels, and produced a wider constituency for geographical knowledge. Rose's suggestion that a strategy is required to unsettle the traditional boundaries of geography is both radical and holds out the potential of producing more inclusive histories of the discipline. The real problem, it seems, in (re)writing histories of geography lies with the apparent need to position women (and subaltern groups) and their 'knowledges' at various historical junctures within or beyond the 'tradition', or within an alternative 'tradition'. The fact remains that women travellers, for example, were not geographers, nor did they define themselves as such.

Out of these tangles, McEwan (p. 374) proposes that:

A particular problematic in writing feminist histories of geography has been the apparent need to claim women travellers in a disciplinary sense, in order that they can be located in the 'geographical tradition(s)'. A critical feminist approach need not concern itself with such myopic considerations.

For:

Despite a recognition of their exclusion from the traditions and practice of scientific geography, however, the experiences of nineteenth-century women [travellers] are nonetheless of relevance to the histories of geography and imperialism.

She notes that women were both actively involved in imperialism – in a variety of roles – and influenced imperial policies as well as making notable contributions (through travel writing) to imperial discourse. Thus:

Their status as writers, rather than their place in 'heroic' histories of geography, lends significance to the works of women travellers.

Moreover, influenced by postcolonial arguments (see Chapter 7), McEwan argues that the very notion of a Western patriarchial geographical tradition demands deconstruction, which would show it to have drawn extensively (and often without admitting it) on many others ('native' and women's labour and knowledges, for example).

Focusing on its more recent history (especially the period since 1945 that is also our main concern here), Rose's (1993a) major contribution to the debate on the role of women, masculinity and men within geography involves the argument that:

1. '... the academic discipline of geography has historically been dominated by men' (p. 1);
2. Within the profession, women have been patronized, harassed and marginalized;
3. Feminism remains 'outside the project' of geography (p. 3); and
4. '... the domination of the discipline by men has serious consequences both for what counts as legitimate geographical knowledge and who can produce such knowledge. [men] ... have insisted that geography holds a series of unstated assumptions about what men and women do, and that the discipline concentrates on spaces, places and landscapes that it sees as men's' (p. 2). Moreover, 'to think geography – to think within the parameters of the discipline in order to create geographical knowledge acceptable to the discipline – is to occupy a masculine subject position' (p. 4).

This leads her to conclude that the social construction of the discipline of geography is such that it is now necessarily 'masculinist' – it concerns itself primarily with the issues classically of interest to men (p. 4; see also Pile, 1994). This is not presented as a straightforward conscious strategy, even if at times it may have been such. Rather, geography has adopted a particular set of positions and practices which attract both men and women who subscribe, often either subconsciously or by default, to masculinist positions. Most of her book details the four points of her main argument – via a series of careful and creative engagements with many of the aspects of and 'paradigms' within human geography that have also concerned us here (hence Rose examines work on landscape, for example, on spatial science as well as political economy, structuration, locality, and so on). The final chapter sets out the basis for a feminist approach to geography via thinking about the complexity and richness of what Rose terms 'paradoxical space', and considers alternatives on which resistance to the masculinist hegemony can be based.

Elsewhere, Rose (1993b, p. 531) has pointed to the ways in which feminist work continues to face marginalization. She thus points out how 'two recent books discussing – and thus implicitly constituting – geography as an academic discipline' either disregard or incorporate feminist work:

The first of these, Livingstone's (1992) account of The geographical tradition, *is a roll call of great men which completely ignores over a decade of work on gender issues; both the women who write on gender, and their work, are simply erased as if they never happened. The second adopts a different strategy towards feminist work; Unwin's (1992)* The place of geography *devotes one paragraph to feminist work in the discipline, which has the effect of rendering feminism as just one more, rather small, example of the rich diversity of, well, the geographical tradition: any possibility that feminism might offer a fundamental critique of the discipline is thus lost.*

Similarly, Mayer (1989) felt that the representation of women in basic human geography textbooks was still charcterized by 'consensus and invisibility'. While more recent books describing the changing structure of human geography (Hubbard et al., 2002; Holloway and Hubbard, 2001; Peet, 1998), do accord feminist critiques more attention, Cloke, Philo and Sadler's (1991) earlier and influential *Approaching Human Geography: An Introduction to Contemporary Theoretical Debates* does not. Instead, they self-consciously note both the exclusion of geographical debates conducted in languages other than English (a theme that we shall return to in Chapter 10) and the limited attention that they pay to feminist geography, 'and to the very real difference feminist arguments are undoubtedly making to the theory and practice of human geography more generally' (p. x). They note that feminist arguments are at least as influential in human geography – and in some ways more so – than the series of debates (Marxist, humanist, postmodernist etc.) that their book concentrates upon. However, they feel that feminist geography 'is itself influenced by and to some degree fragmented into Marxist, humanist, structurationist, realist and postmodernist approaches' (p. x–xi). Their wish is not to 'ghettoise' feminist geography through according it a separate chapter, on grounds both of its importance throughout human geography (they say that 'feminism in geography should surely be seen as more than just "another" approach', p. xi) and, because they feel that while men can meaningfully discuss feminism in geography, 'at present such discussion is most ably pursued by women within the discipline who are developing new ways of theorising and practising a human geography sentitised to gender issues' (p. xi).

Rose (1993a, p. 3) claims that Cloke et al.'s (1991) position only 'demonstrates and sustains' the continued exclusion of feminism, by refusing to address its impact on geography, and thus relates 'to the very nature of hegemonic geographical knowledge itself'. Nearly a decade on, Cloke, Philo and Sadler's tactic is less sustainable and Peet's (1998) book on *Modern Geographical Thought* culminates with a chapter on feminist theory and the geography of gender. Peet notes the initial close association of feminist geography with radical geography although, as he goes on to chart the range of debates that has characterized feminist geography since the 1970s, he recognizes that the latter soon developed its own set of debates and sense of purpose and directions. Although Peet recognizes that by the 1980s there were differences 'between feminist and masculinist radical geography' (as well as 'between perspectives in feminist geography': p. 271), he reminds us that while some radical geography may have been as sexist in its language and assumptions as the mainstream, feminist and radical arguments were 'often made by the same people, simultaneously radical and feminist' (p. 270). It is thus no accident that the earliest papers formulating what became feminist geography appeared in *Antipode: A Journal of Radical Geography* or that today, according to the 'notes for contributors' (inside every back cover) that invite submissions, '*Antipode* publishes articles that offer a radical (Marxist/socialist/anarchist/antiracist/feminist) analysis of geographical issues and whose intent is to contribute to a new and better society'. Here too, extensive debates can be found within feminist geography about the relationship of capitalism to patriarchy and the spaces through which this is mediated.

From the geography of women to socialist feminisms

By the mid-1980s, a rich debate about the relationship between class and gender relations had developed (see, for example, Foord and Gregson, 1986, and subsequent elaboration and responses by L. Johnston, 1994; Lauria and Knopp, 1985, and the reviews of the debates in Rose, 1993a, and Peet, 1998). These debates embodied a range of approaches and positions. Walby (1986) identified five approaches to the study of gender inequality:

1. The demonstration that it is either theoretically insignificant or non-existent;
2. Indications that it is derivative of capitalist relations, and has no independent status;
3. Suggestions that it results from an autonomous patriarchal system that is the primary form of social inequality;
4. Demonstrations that it results from patriarchal relations that are so intertwined with capitalist social relations that they comprise a single system of capitalist patriarchy; and
5. Arguments that it results from the interaction of autonomous systems of patriarchy and capitalism.

Bowlby et al. (1989) showed that the second and fourth of these have been more commonly adopted among geographers, thus focusing on ways in which patriarchy is structured by capitalism's imperatives. Foord and Gregson (1986) adopted the fifth strategy, however, arguing that although patriarchy and capitalism are empirically linked they are theoretically separate. Just as capitalism can be presented as a particular example of a necessary condition (a mode of production within which economic and social life is structured), with unique individual instances at separate times and places, so, they argued, patriarchy can be represented as a particular example of a general condition (gender relations) which also has its time- and space-specific realizations.

Foord and Gregson (1986, p. 199) argued that the necessary inter-relationships between humans and nature call for a form of social organization to ensure human survival and social reproduction, so that 'all social relations must involve gender, and gender ... relations will be embedded in all forms of social relations'. They could not conceive of a society lacking gender relations, therefore, so that the latter are independent of any mode of production, let alone any particular instance of it. Patriarchy is a particular form of gender relations, in which men dominate the processes of species reproduction; empirical work focuses on the nature of that domination 'in particular periods and places' (p. 206): 'Just as other relations vary and combine differently over time and space, so too must the practices of which comprise these relations' hence the professed importance of studying them within the context of the localities programme (see p. 233), as illustrated by McDowell and Massey (1984). The assumption that politics and social relations could be read-off the socio-economic characteristics of the locality is, however, problematized by Rose (1989), who takes into account the roles of unwaged women's labour and thus disturbs the assumption that a locality is reducible to the structure of its paid employment alone (cf. Jackson's, 1991, wider cultural critique of locality studies).

Similarly, because they regard gender and social relations as semi-autonomous spheres of activity, Foord and Gregson contended that Marxist and feminist theories could not easily be integrated. Against this view, McDowell (1986b) advanced a class analysis and rejected the notion of a universal female experience. Biological reproduction is part of the process of capitalist reproduction, and 'Patriarchal social relations are further strengthened by the political and ideological functions of the state that has a vested interest in supporting the domination of individual women in the exploited class by individual men in that class' (p. 313). The contradiction underpinning the need to create surplus value within capitalism is thus the source of women's oppression, not any necessary gender relations: 'the social construction of male sexuality and the dominance of family forms based on sexuality and kinship networks to class societies are historical resolutions of the contradiction' (p. 317). Subsequently, McDowell has insisted on supplementing regulationist approaches (see p. 232) with an understanding of the importance of unwaged work (overwhelmingly performed by women) in the home and the significance of gendered subjects in the (paid) workplace. In terms of the overall relationships between gender, space and society, Gier and Walton (1987, pp. 56–7) took a slightly different approach, disagreeing with Foord and Gregson's contention that gender relations are necessary to all social relations:

> *Evidence from anthropology and history as well as other disciplines indicates that gender has not always been used to identify male and female sexual difference and its attendant physical and psychological archetypes ... [so that] the very identification of the concept is the product of human consciousness and human society.*

According to this view, significant gender differences need not always be present (see also Knopp and Lauria, 1987). Gregson and Foord (1987, pp. 373–4) responded by defending their position that mode of production and gender relations are 'distinct and separate objects of analysis which interlock as particular forms (capitalism and patriarchal gender relations) but not as conceptual categories', but were unprepared to admit that this was a preface to the creation of a universal theory of women's oppression.

Although some of the earlier work presented as feminist geography involved demonstrating that women are subordinated and thereby have distinctive spatialities in contemporary societies (e.g. Women and Geography Study Group, 1984; Little, Peake and Richardson, 1988), wider issues were soon introduced. Pratt and Hanson (1994), for example, moved from demonstrating differences between men's and women's commuting patterns to analyses of how those patterns were exploited by capital to reproduce segmented labour markets (see Hanson and Pratt, 1995). Indeed, the issue of mobility and gendered differences in its range and mode continues, albeit redefined and expanded by incorporating broader social and cultural geographies of mobility (associated with the 'cultural turn': Law, 1999), including work on the gendered geography of urban fear and danger, and its consequences for women's experience and use of space (Pain, 1991).

The variety of perspectives adopted in feminist geography is illustrated in McDowell's (1993a, 1993b) review articles. During the 1980s and early 1990s feminist geography, while addressing the discipline's three main concepts of space, place and nature, shifted from analyses of gender differences to concerns over the social creation of gendered beings in particular places, which brings *feminist* geography (as distinct from feminist geography) closer to the wider feminist project – 'the study of the lives, experiences and behaviour of women' (1993a, p. 161). Three main themes are identified in the early work:

1. *Spatial differences in women's status* – demonstrating 'man's inhumanity to women' (p. 163) – a largely empirical task that emphasized western experience and was increasingly criticized for its ethnocentrism;
2. *Gender and place: women and the urban environment,* which stressed that most women were excluded from analyses of urban areas that focused on public rather than private activities, at scales which were larger than the individual household, and so ignored the gender relations that underpinned the home, childbirth and the unpaid labour involved in social reproduction (pp. 165–6):

> ... in common with the other social sciences, geography takes for granted the Enlightenment distinction between the public and the private, and, implicitly, the gendered associations of those spheres ... [which involves the patriarchal assumptions that] women are the angels of the hearth, to be confined to domesticity preferably in sylvan and suburban surroundings, while men join the fray of public life in the bustling city centres, returning home for emotional and sexual solace, and hot meals to fit them for their continuing labours;

3. *Patriarchal power,* which illustrated the 'blindness' of (urban and other) geographers to the 'embodiment of conventional gender divisions' (p. 167) in the built environment on both large (the structuring of urban land-use patterns) and small (the design and layout of buildings) scales.

Thus gender inequalities were added to the others identified by those involved in portraying 'unfairly structured cities' (e.g. Badcock, 1984) as major elements in the reproduction processes of 'patriarchal capitalism'. This 'feminist empiricism' (McDowell, 1993a, p. 174) paralleled concerns of other geographers for social justice, and stimulated a 'common focus on excluded or oppressed groups – be they women, the working class or ethnic minorities – [that] united "radical" geographers'. These concerns needed to be linked to wider theoretical considerations, however. McDowell (like Sheppard, 1995) saw a bifurcation within human geography (McDowell, 1993a, p. 174):

> It is perhaps not too much of a caricature to argue that throughout the 1970s and early 1980s human geography consisted of two phalanxes going off in sharply different directions. In the early part of the period, the opposing forces consisted of those who held on to mathematically modelled, rational choice, context-free notions facing the grand theoreticians of structuralism whose forward march in a single direction admitted women only in the tail position. Despite their relegation, it was in this camp that feminists found common interests, not least because of its intellectual and political attraction ... [nevertheless] Despite an enormous shift over the last 15 years or so within economic and urban geography from a structuralist Marxism influenced by Althusser towards a geohistorical materialism alive to specificity, complexity and local struggles ... gender issues remained marginal to the concerns of 'left' geographers.

Yet in 1989 Susan Christopherson was moved to publish a critical reflection on the ways in which feminism and feminists still remained outside what she saw as the geographical project. Feminist empiricism was a foundation for a challenge to the masculinist domination, even epistemological foundations, of human geography (p. 175):

> ... this diverse set of theoretical and empirical books and papers published throughout the 1980s succeeded in placing gender divisions on the geographical agenda. It made women and men visible as both academic authors and subjects, thus challenging the implicit masculinity of the discipline. It also succeeded as geography, documenting some of the range of variation in women's social position and circumstances in different parts of the world and raising questions about gender identity and place.

It also laid the groundwork for advance on other fields:

> ... this work has enabled more complex theoretical questions about the extent of variety in the spatial constitution of gender and the specific ways in which the characteristics of masculinity and femininity vary between spaces, classes and ethnicities to begin to be raised. Thus by the end of the decade the particular geographic interest in variety coincided with a more widespread interest in the deconstructionism in social theory to enlarge the scope of the agenda for feminist geography in the forthcoming years

in which it was joined by those interested in other sources of difference, such as sexual orientation (see p. 314) and race.

Notably, feminist work on the intersections of race, class and gender has explored how these are registered in the lives of migrant women workers (e.g. England and Stiell, 1997; Kofman and England, 1997; Pratt, 1999; Radcliffe, 1990; Stiell and England, 1997), extending socialist-feminist influenced works on geographies of social class, patriarchy, maternity and childcare (e.g. Dyck, 1990; England, 1996; Gregson and Lowe, 1994) and wider reworkings of gender, class and space (Pratt and Hanson, 1988). In tandem, work on the geographies of children (Holloway and Valentine, 2000) and on different forms and geographies of illness, impairment and disability (Butler and Parr, 1999; Imrie, 2000), while not simply reducible to feminist geography, have certainly been influenced by its concerns and methods and are a measure of its broad impacts. In particular, feminist geography has more recently registered a growing concern with 'the body' (e.g. Longhurst, 2000), both as a subject in space – produced through a variety of discourses (think of the role of advertising and televisual representations):

> ... in order to understand questions around sexual specificity, the differences between bodies, women's social subordination to men, and the mutually constitutive relationships that exist between bodies and spaces (Longhurst, 1997, p. 486)

and also about how geography (in tandem with other western social sciences) has assumed a masculinist separation between mind and body:

> Cartesian dualism underlines our thinking in a myriad of ways, not least in the divergence of the social sciences from the natural sciences, and in a geography which is based on the separation of people from their environments. Thus while geography is unusual in its spanning of the natural and social sciences and in focusing on the interrelations between people and their environments, it is still

assumed that the two are distinct and one acts on the other ... Geography, like all of the social sciences, has been built upon a particular conception of the mind and body which sees them as separate, apart and acting on each other (Johnson, 1989, cited in Longhurst, 1997, p. 492).

Thus, too, feminist work has sought to transform approaches to the study of landscape by relating it to the way that it is represented ('appreciated' so to speak), in ways that are analogous to the heterosexual male gaze directed towards the female body (Nash 1996). Both of these concerns (and others) – about the body as a contested site and for the Cartesian distinction between mind and body – have been challenged in postmodern and poststructuralist feminist geographies.

Feminist geographies of difference

Although explorations of postmodernism and poststructuralism in geography have sometimes proceeded without due attention to gendered and sexual differences, the postmodern impulse to accommodate and give voice to difference has been seen as a possibility for feminist perspectives and feminist geographies. Building on that foundation involved two other feminist perspectives emerging alongside the 'rationalist or empiricist feminism' (McDowell, 1993b):

1. *Anti-rational, or feminist standpoint theory* celebrates gender differences and, rather than present them as unfair or unjust, promotes them and has as its goal the elimination of the traditional allocation of superiority to everything associated with masculinity. Knowledge is socially created, in context, so that women's experiences of, for example, menstruation, childbirth and lactation lead to the construction of different self-identities from those involved in masculine experience, which also vary between places, because of their separately constructed gender relations. Such different standpoints provide a basis not only for understanding but also for practice, hence the development of various forms of radical feminism, including ecofeminism.

2. *Postrational or postmodern feminism* argues that treatment of women as a single category involves linking together very different groups with separate experiences and needs. Many feminists initially identified this as a threat to the project, but McDowell argues that the encounter with postmodernism stimulated a debate about 'situated knowledge' which has led to the situation (McDowell, 1993b, p. 310) whereby:

   ... geographers sympathetic to the postmodern deconstructive project are ... reluctant to abandon gender as a difference that makes a difference, if no longer the difference. The current aim within feminist geography is a move towards ... 'partial' or 'situated knowledges' that recognize that the positionings of white British women in the academy, to take but one example, are not the same as those of other women, women from different ethnic or class backgrounds, and that this makes a difference to knowledge construction.

For geographers, this emphasis on difference within the 'oppressed' group raises important issues regarding the role of place in identity-creation. Knowledge is both local and gendered – and also linked to other socially constructed categories. Feminists argue that 'some differences are more significant than others' (McDowell, 1993b, p. 315):

> ... their work demands a theoretical analysis of differences, building up an understanding of the mutual interrelations of gender ... of sexuality, household and family structures and the political economy of domestic and workplace relations within and between places. It is a feminism located in a theoretical understanding of differences between women, rejecting both the transhistorical and cross-class search for the origins of patriarchy that concerned us at an earlier moment ... and notions of a cultural feminist essentialism that denies the structure of power relations between women. It is a feminism that recognizes the existence of a material world, or women living in different social formations, engaged in struggles in which their interests may converge or diverge.

This presents a major challenge to all geographers, who, as this chapter and the preceding one have illustrated, are having to come to terms with a wide range of situated knowledges. Bondi and Domosh (1992, p. 210) have argued, however, that although postmodernism attacks universal truth claims and so should sustain feminist arguments, its application has failed to do so because, 'there is a major impulse within postmodernism that continues a tradition of masculine discourse in which the stereotyping of women is intrinsic to its operation'. However, both these writers and other feminist geographers have welcomed aspects of postmodernism. Thus, Duncan (1999, p. 212, capitals in the original), writing on postmodernism/postmodernity in *A Feminist Glossary of Human Geography* (itself a marker of the dynamism of the field) notes how:

> Many feminist geographers are attracted to postmodernism's rejection of REASON as being gendered, historical and ethnocentric rather than disembodied and neutral, as is usually claimed. Others agree with postmodernism's refusal of ESSENTIALISM and the replacement of POSITIVIST and empiricist theories of representation and truth with a diversity of viewpoints.

Sexuality and space

Feminism has been a major foundation on which a wider geographical focus on difference has been built since the late 1980s (as illustrated by Jackson's, 1991, essay on the social construction of masculinism, Valentine's, 1993, essay on sexual identities, and Forrest's, 1995, essay on the role of place in the construction of gay identity). Pratt (1992), for example, promoted a postcolonial feminism (see too Radcliffe, 1994) which:

1. No longer focuses solely on male–female differences but incorporates other sources such as race, class and sexual orientation;
2. Employs social theory to appreciate how differences are created socially, and what power relations they incorporate; and
3. Argues, therefore, that all knowledge is 'situated'.

Among all this, feminist geography (and allied work) has stimulated more attention to masculinity, not only within geography as a discipline but also within wider society. Ways of performing manhood and heterosexuality have thus come under scrutiny (e.g. Hubbard, 2000; McDowell, 2002; McDowell and Court, 1994; Nayak, 2003; Peck and Tickell, 1996;

Jones, 1998; Jackson, 1991) as well as their relationship to nationalism and the geopolitical (Dalby, 1994; Hyndman, 2001; Radcliffe, 1996; Radcliffe and Westwood, 1996; Sparke, 1994, 1996) plus the 'public' or political sphere of citizenship (e.g. Staeheli and Cope, 1994) together with work on the diversity of (or 'new') femininities (Laurie, Dwyer, Holloway and Smith, 1999).

Other work has also examined the intersections of sexuality, gender and class and space (Duncan, 1996; Knopp, 1992) for, as we noted earlier, in the last decade or so the human *body* has become an explicit domain of geographical analysis, and with this has come a plethora of works on sexuality and spaces. Reflecting on a decade of such works on sexuality and space, Hubbard (2000, p. 191) notes that:

> Although traditionally regarded as 'squeamish' about sexual matters ... [see too Symanski, 2002] recent research by geographers has begun to demonstrate that space is inevitably sexed in a variety of complex ways, placing issues of sex and sexuality firmly on the geographical agenda. As such, there is now a substantial body of critical geographic scholarship which has indicated that space is fundamentally shaped by the dynamics of human sexuality, reflecting the ways in which sex is represented, perceived and understood.

In similar terms, England (1999, p. 95) records that:

> The 1990s have seen a rapid expansion of published research on sexualities and sexual identities. Most major English language geography journals have published articles related to sexualities (although there are notable holdouts). There is certainly no longer a shortage of materials that can be used to teach the geographies of sexualities although there is a shortage of materials looking explicitly at heterosexualities.

The first papers on sexuality and space appeared at the end of the 1970s and in the early 1980s (Weightman, 1981). These, and much of the subsequent work on sexuality and space, focused at first on the spaces and places associated with expressions and geographical consequences of lesbian and gay male sexuality. Such research and associated manifestations of lesbian, gay and bisexuality within geography did not establish themselves without resistance. Citing Carter's (1977) objections, Brown and Knopp (2003, p. 314) note that in the mid-1970s:

> The simple act of arranging meetings of gay and lesbian geographers at Association of American Geographers' meetings precipitated extraordinary nasty public (and published) denouncements from established and secure figures in the discipline.

More recent cases of harassment (Valentine, 1998) reveal continued discord and ill feelings.

However, a critical mass of scholarship and degree of wider acknowledgement of sexuality and space as a challenging field of study was evident by the mid-1990s. A mark of this was the publication of an influential collection on *Mapping Desire: Geographies of Sexuality* (Bell and Valentine, 1995). In this and other work that accompanied or preceded it (e.g. Adler and Brenner, 1992; Brown, 1995; Forest, 1995; Valentine, 1993), the parameters of work on sexuality and space both work with the early concerns about gay and lesbian spaces (and their experiences in mainstream 'heterosexual space') as well as complementing this with a wider sense of the paradoxical spaces of sexuality (Bell, Binnie, Cream and Valentine, 1994). Much of the earlier work was on urban quarters or zones associated with the gay and lesbian 'scene', including the role of gay men as agents in the wider gentrification of urban neighbourhoods, supplementing established Marxist work on gentrification (Knopp, 1990). Subsequently, work in rural geographies and on migration has also been enriched by attention to the roles of sexualities. Summarizing all this, Binnie and Valentine (1999, p. 182) conclude that:

> . . . geographies of sexualities have come a long way in the last decade. Progress in the study of lives of dissident sexualities has been most striking, most notably in three key areas: urban geography, rural lesbian and gay geographies; and the geography of sexual citizenship. In each of these areas, there have been significant developments in both geographical understandings of lesbian, gay and bisexual lives and signs that sexual dissidents are beginning to have an impact on the heteronormative nature of the geographical knowledge.

The latter is an open challenge, to which we will return in a moment. However, at this point we should add that Binnie and Valentine also note the unevenness of geographical work on sexuality (something which has also been evident in terms of the development and impacts of feminism in geography). In terms of sexuality and space, they note two dimensions with respect to this. Firstly, 'the ethnocentricity of the literature on sexuality and space remains largely unchallenged' (p. 183). In other words the sexualities and spaces studied have mostly tended to be western and white (though see Mohammad, 1999). Secondly, they note how some subdisciplines have been much more receptive than others:

> Indeed, there are many areas within the discipline of geography where discussion of sexuality has been notable for its absence, for example, transport geography and population geography. The different philosophical approaches that dominate different subdisciplinary areas may explain the uneven impact of work on dissident sexualities within geography. Geography remains a highly contested enterprise. While social and cultural geography have been very receptive towards contemporary developments in social theory (particularly with respect to the postmodern emphasis on 'difference') and therefore towards dissident sexualities, many other fields of geographical enquiry remain wedded to their positivist tradition. However this does not explain why the hegemonic sexual identity, heterosexuality, has thus far received so little attention from geographers . . .

They note partial exceptions, such as Crang (1995) and McDowell (1995) – both perhaps better known as social-cultural and economic geographers, however – amidst this relative lack of attention to 'mainstream' heterosexuality. Moreover, more geographers have recently begun to map and theorize *heterosexuality*. Rather like feminist geography concerned itself first with the status of women before turning to consider wider constructions of femininity and masculinity (and thus men), so the work attentive to sexuality and space tended first to focus on the relative invisibility of the geographies associated with male homosexuality, lesbianism and bisexuality ('insignificant others' to mainstream human geography according to Bell, 1991) before turning either to examine the construction and problems associated with such categories or to the wider geographies of sexuality – 'straight', gay, or whatever. One aspect of this is 'queer theory' (representing a subversion of a hitherto mostly pejorative term) which begins with, but then goes beyond, the issue of sexuality. Thus as Elder (1999, p. 88) – a South African-born, white male geographer working in the United States who represents his sexuality as 'gay' – notes:

> I see queerness as a theoretical and personal insistence to study the relationships between social boundaries (like 'race', gender, sexuality and class). Queerness is not only a device for thinking through issues related to sexuality. . . . It follows that for me the attraction to queer theory is an obvious one; the language of geography as well as the queer geography that shapes my daily life. The queer geography that I refer to is learning to perform on boundaries (coming out) and realizing the consequences and effects of those performances . . . I am not only referring to the sexual aspects of my identity: I am perceived by students to be too white to be 'African' and too foreign to be 'American'. As a condition, queerness captures a delightful sense of unbounded chaos and uncertainty and it helps me to think about identity.

For Kitchin and Lysaght (2003, p. 490):

> Queer theory, a theoretical position founded on poststructuralist ideas, posits that sexual identity is never fixed, but is always in the process of becoming. . . . it critiques the notion of being able to draw coherent boundaries around sexual identities.

What role then, and possibility for, a queer geography?

> . . . an extension of queer theory suggests that, given . . . that all space is sexed, all space is inherently queered and it is only ever temporarily fixed as heterosexual (or homosexual for that matter). That is, the sexing of space is in a constant process of 'becoming', created through the (re)production of (sexual) discourse and practice (p. 491).

In turn, however, for others too sexuality (be it 'queer' or not) is, like the gender relations of which it forms a part, seen to be caught-up with wider economic, social, cultural and political geographies. For Hubbard (2000, p. 211), this is:

> . . . beginning (belatedly) to clarify the importance of heterosexuality in maintaining and reproducing geographical order, particularly in their attempts to elucidate the importance of domestic space in maintaining the 'family values' which lie at the heart of heteronormality.

Geography too as a discipline has been seen as embodying similar heteronormality; an often taken for granted assumption that the spaces and lives we study and the outlook of the geographers who do the studies are 'straight'.

This leads Binnie (1997, p. 223) to ask the following questions:

> How have systems of (geographical) thought from positivist social science to poststructuralism treated sexual dissidence? Are they inherently, essentially heterosexist? Are some systems of thought and theoretical frameworks more damaging or better at promoting the interests of an antihomophobic 'project' than others?

It does not take Binnie long to conclude that spatial science was problematic, by virtue of its indirect association with a scientific discourse that assigned deviance to homosexuality ('the medicalisation and pathologicalisation of homosexuality' in his words, p. 224). Binnie recognizes more potential in postmodern, feminist and poststructuralist geographies. Yet he remains wary of the 'cultural turn', declaring that:

> I remain deeply suspicious of the 'cultural turn' in geography and social theory more generally, as the post-modern emphasis on difference (although opening up a space for work on sexuality) has also been guilty of skirting around the edges of sex and sexuality, preferring a more abstract engagement with, for example, Lacanian pyschoanalysis (p. 225).

Binnie also takes issue with much feminist geography. For example, he is concerned that otherwise 'invaluable, insightful critique of the masculinism of the discipline ... [here he refers to Rose, 1993a, 1995] ... does have a tendency to rant about "men and their theories" '. The use of the term 'rant' here resorts to a pejorative language that has often been applied by sexist men to feminism and feminists. But perhaps it is indicative of how strongly Binnie perceives a relative failure of some feminist geography to recognize diversity among men and masculinities. For Binnie, there seems to be a world of difference within what maleness and especially 'male' sexuality means (queer, bi, straight, camp, sado-masochist, for example). He feels therefore that those feminist geographies that, for example, posit landscape as a domain of sexualized masculine vision foreclose other ways that men and women might look and be seen, amidst 'the celebration of queer pleasure, sexual diversity, and exuberance' (p. 227).

Conclusions

Things have changed since the end of the 1980s when Jackson (1989, p. 104) remarked that:

> ... gender and sexuality are still too rarely regarded as part of the central agenda of human geography ... regarded as peripheral, private, and personal issues, not suitable for academic debate or public discussion ... What could possibly be geographical, critics imply, about such intimate personal subjects as gender and sexuality?

Feminist geography has undoubtedly made a difference. There are, however, some significant limits to this. Firstly, the challenge to feminist geographies from working across cultures remains (Radcliffe, 1994; Staeheli and Nagar, 2002). While one of the key insights of feminist geography has been to bring home (so to speak) the social and cultural contingency of gender relations, it has hardly begun to accommodate the global range of these (think of the different expectations and norms of gender roles – and of gendered spaces – in different societies around the world), notwithstanding feminist work on geographies of globalization (Nagar, Lawson, McDowell and Hanson, 2002). Secondly, the impact of feminism in human geography has developed unevenly; it took longer for political geography to register feminist themes (see Drake and Horton, 1983; Hyndman, 2001; Kofman and Peake, 1990) than social and cultural, urban and economic geography, for example. And other subdisciplines hardly seem to notice it all. Much human geography continues as usual, outside (but a subject of criticism from) the influences of feminist traditions. And there are resistances, tensions and 'backlashes'. For example, a senior male geographer complained that in feminist geography, especially work focused on language, he claimed to have encountered 'not just anger, which is perfectly understandable, but something close to hate' (Gould, 1994, p. 197). This was countered by Peake (1994, p. 205), who characterized Gould's position as:

> ... woe betide any feminist who adopts a mode of expression that offends his notions of clearness, effectiveness, and beauty ... this situation is fine only if we accept the male prerogative to legislate language ... a proprietary attitude that could be espoused only by someone who has appointed himself as the arbiter of language. ... He is refusing women the right to make linguistic changes because, in his dominant subject position, he cannot admit to change, to the recognition of difference.

Gould (1999, p. 82) responded that although:

> ... the various genres of writing emerging out of an excitingly refurbished social and cultural geography are frequently enlightening, thought-provoking, and intellectually satisfying, in that they help us to see something in a different way, from a perspective or viewpoint we had not taken before ... some throw up (the image is deliberate) writing that is so totally biased, shrill and predictable that it eventually becomes boring.

Feminist concerns and influences are now visible across almost all human geography, however. The relative success (partial victories) of feminist geography in transforming human geography has also served as inspiration for others seeking other transformations (as we documented in Chapter 7 with respect to the 'whiteness' of the discipline). Others, however, have still felt themselves to be excluded from 'the project' (a reference to Christopherson's, 1989, paper designating how feminist work was poised to play a defining role in 'the project' of reconstituting human geography) – as in the case of the concerns and insights of disabled geographers (Chouinard and Grant, 1995), who complained of 'not being anywhere near the project' (see too the paper by Butler and Bowlby, 1997, and others in that special issue of *Environment and Planning D: Society and Space* on Geography and Disability). Some of the impetus to social geographies of childhood (Aitkin, 2001; Holloway and Valentine, 2000), as well as *non-human* geographies of other sentient life in relation to humans (e.g. Philo and Wilbert, 2000; Whatmore, 2002) also registers the *example* and impact of feminism in broadening the range and understanding of what constitutes human geography.

Three decades of feminist and allied work in geography have enabled qualitative methodologies as well as renewed debates about the oldest of geographical concerns – fieldwork (a debate usefully summarized in Peet's, 1998, chapter on 'Feminist Theory and the Geography of Gender' in his *Modern Geographical Thought*) including work on hetrosexuality and experiences and assumptions in geographical fieldwork (Cupples, 2002). Part of this has been an ongoing debate about 'positionality' – the vantage points (class, gendered, national and 'racial' formations) from which geographers write and teach (see England, 1994; the debates between Sidaway, 1992, and Madge, 1993; and McDowell, 1992, and Schoenberger, 1992, plus Herod, 1999, and other papers in that 1999 special issue of *Geoforum*). While such debates have not been confined specifically to feminist geography, they have certainly been greatly enhanced by feminist critiques (see Rose,

1997, for a critical review). Moreover, the backdrop of several decades of feminist geography enabled and encouraged such debates. Moves to revive ethnography (*participant* observation in which the researcher observes and interacts closely with the society under study: see the articles in a special issue of *The Professional Geographer* on critical feminist perspectives: Nast, 1994), as a method in human geography also partly rests upon feminist groundings (Jackson, 1985; Herbert, 2000). There seems no end to the potential for feminist geographies to make a difference to the assumptions and norms of human geography. Thus quantitative geographies (Falconer Al-Hindi, 2001; Mattingly and Falconer Al-Hindi, 1995; Rocheleau, 1995) as well as issues such as remote sensing and GIS methodologies have come under distinctively feminist scrutiny. Summarizing a set of papers (published in *Gender, Place and Culture*) on feminist geography and GIS, Hanson (2002, p. 301) notes how:

> ... denying one's connections to, embeddedness in, and complicity with an intellectual tradition facilitates classifying that tradition as 'the other'; such denial legitimizes intellectual boundary maintenance and dismissing the other tradition as irrelevant. Years ago, the idea that feminism and quantification were incompatible had to be dispelled by feminist geographers carefully demonstrating how quantitative approaches could support a feminist analysis. Similarly, this collection of articles effectively refutes the notion that feminism and GIS have nothing to offer each other.

And there can be little doubt that other work in a psychoanalytic tradition in geography (e.g. Pile and Thrift, 1995; Sibley, 1995) has been enabled by feminist geography even if it is not necessarily confined to it. Moreover, feminist geography (frequently in affinity with postmodernism) has further encouraged attention to 'writing practices' (Bondi, 1997) and the development of alternative narrative styles, genres and methods (e.g. England, 1994; Nast, 1996: see also Bondi *et al.*, 2002). Thus, Gregson and Rose (1997, p. 23) note how:

> The pre-eminence of the dispassionate, distant and disembodied voice is something which has been challenged repeatedly in human geography over the past 20 years or so, for example by those who initiated the first critiques of positivism. Humanistic geographers, for example, argued that such a writing voice simply could not evoke the creative and emotional senses of place. ... Marxist geographers suggested that the supposed neutrality of that voice served merely to hide its lack of critique of capitalism; it was a voice whose apparent objectivity masked a conservative and reactionary set of values. More recently, feminist geographers have also criticized that voice as expressive of certain kinds of masculinities. Particularly in the academy, where cool and calm rationality is the desired norm of both behavior and debate (which is not to suggest that this is what actually happens!), to be masculine often means not to be emotional or passionate, not to be explicit about your values, your background, your own felt experiences.

In other words, some of the very norms of an academic discipline (the universality, universalism and so on that we briefly considered in Chapter 1) embody masculine assumptions and routine.

As we recorded in one of the opening citations to this chapter, therefore, the conventional process of academic writing (which foregrounds the *names* and therefore authority of individual or joint authors) has sometimes been challenged by more collective modes held to be in the spirit of feminist politics. Thus two key textbooks of feminist geography were authored by a collective, the Women and Geography Study Group (WGSG, 1984, 1997). Yet Gregson and Rose (1997) detect a tension for feminist geography here. On the one hand, the possibility that to write in alternative, embodied or personalized positions risks having feminist work which does this being dismissed by the mainstream. But, on the other hand, the potential and power of a human geography that explicitly draws on personal experiences and feelings is evident.

There are other strategic tensions, as between the idea that feminist geography should (or has) become mainstream and its sense of being on the margins and therefore iconoclastic and more critical. There is also a tension between the importance of differences between the genders and acknowledging differences among women (Rose, 1993b). While the latter may now be more evident than in the formative days of feminist geography, it would be wrong to emphasize these at the expense of missing the wider changes that feminist geography has wrought. Feminist geography also challenges notions of progress and a neat sequence of paradigms in human geography. For feminist geography operates both within their logic, but is also critical of disciplinary and academic norms. Gregson, Rose, Cream and Laurie (1997, pp. 199–200) argue that:

> ... to position feminist geography entirely on the margins of contemporary human geography is misplaced. Rather for this collective [that is the authors of WGSG, 1997], feminist geographies occupy the centre and margins simultaneously: another example of paradoxical space.

9

Applied geography and the relevance debate

*Geography is by its nature **applied**. Geographers' systems of interest are of such direct concern to people, businesses, government, other organisations, and NGOs that any understanding achieved within the discipline is likely to be applicable.*

(Bennett and Wilson, 2003, p. 463: their emphasis)

The history of geography is one of a subject and an academic discipline with a strong applied value – or relevance, as it is often termed. Indeed, the subject matter from which the discipline emerged comprised useful knowledge – maps, information about environmental conditions, material on trade potential etc. And as that information was collated, so it was put to wider uses in the service of the state apparatus – to Mackinder, one of the discipline's founders in the United Kingdom, geography was an 'aid to statecraft' (Parker, 1982). As Bennett and Wilson (2003) point out, applied geography was being promoted there very early in the twentieth century (Keltie, 1908), with another book having the same title appearing soon after the First World War (Stevens, 1921). Nevertheless, and despite much 'applied work' by individuals (both academic geographers and those with geographical training working in other professions), notably though not only in key subdisciplines such as medical and health geography (Mohan, 2000; Cliff and Haggett, 2003), more explicit concerns about geography's applicability and relevance did not take centre stage within academic debates until well after the Second World War.

The period since the late 1960s has contained traumatic years in the countries being studied here. The underlying problem has been economic uncertainty. After two decades of relatively high rates of economic growth and a sense of increasing prosperity, the American and British economies began to experience serious difficulties. At times, the 1980s and the 1990s both appeared to offer a return to growth, only for the booms to be punctuated – in some areas at least – by sudden reversals. Further, it became increasingly clear that the prosperity was not being shared by all, even within the richest countries let alone at a global scale; this was highlighted in the United States by the growing tempo of the civil rights movement and in the United Kingdom by the turmoil in Northern Ireland, which began as a civil rights movement (and violent state reactions to it), and a series of 'inner-city riots', which were in part responses to racism and deprivation/discrimination. Student and youth protest erupted in both countries (as well as elsewhere) during 1968, related both to protest against the American war in Vietnam and its neighbours and a wider upsurge in militancy, plus increasing concern about human-induced degradation of the physical environment. Discrimination against women in all parts of western societies was also brought to the forefront of attention (including the geographical profession: Zelinsky, 1973a).

Much of the protest of the late 1960s centred on particular issues and was relatively ephemeral. For many of those involved, the aim was to win reforms within society, in the classical liberal manner, while leaving its major structure untouched. For some, however, disillusion stimulated what Peet (1977) termed a 'breaking-off' from liberalism and a move to more radical political stances:

> The starting point was the liberal political social scientific paradigm, based on the belief that societal problems can be solved, or at least significantly ameliorated, within the context of a modified capitalism. A corollary of this belief is the advocacy of pragmatism – better to be involved in partial solutions than in futile efforts at revolution. Radicalization in the political arena involved, as its first step, rejecting the point of view that one more policy change, one more 'new face', would make any difference (p. 242).

The substantive concerns of those termed 'radicals' from the late 1960s on were treated in detail in Chapter 7. Although there are some overlaps with that, the current chapter is concerned with general issues of applied geography and its role within the discipline. As noted in Chapter 1, the pressures for more applied work built up from the 1970s on in response to economic, social and political conditions. In addition, government policies towards higher education, especially in the United Kingdom, placed an increased emphasis on applied work, both in terms of providing vocational and professional training for students and in the pressure to cover institutional costs through 'earnings' from research activity, whereas in the United States there was an increasing emphasis on geographic education providing students with technical skills (notably though not solely in GIS) to enhance their employment and career potentials. Thus the debate over applied geography concerned pragmatic issues of disciplinary survival as well as concerns with regard to relevance.

Tracking the development of applied geography is not as easy as study of other aspects of the discipline, because relatively little of its output is published in academic journals. This is partly because of the nature of the research contracts and the associated funding for researchers. Some contracts make publication in academic journals difficult, because of commercial sensitivity of the research results, and even where this is not a particular problem the time pressures on those involved – to complete one project and then go on to the next, if for no other reason than to secure a continuing salary for the contract researchers – militate against preparation of academic papers and mature reflection on the theoretical and other implications of particular (usually empirical) research findings. As universities have been pressed to do more of this type of work, however, and as geographers have identified commercial niches for themselves, so the practice of applied geography has somewhat disappeared from general view. Nevertheless, its nature and validity have been debated, and that forms the focus of the present discussion.

Disenchantment and disillusion in academic geography

A forthcoming revolution in human geography, against the innate conservatism of behavioural studies and spatial science, was foreseen by Kasperson (1971, p. 13):

> *The shift in the objects of study in geography from supermarkets and highways to poverty and racism has already begun, and we can expect it to continue, for the goals of geography are changing. The new men see the objective of geography as the same as that for medicine – to postpone death and reduce suffering.*

Through the 1970s, an important aspect of debates about the application and relevance of geography concerned the status of 'radical geography'. This can be illustrated by one senior geographer's writings in the 1970s. Wilbur Zelinsky was president of the Association of American Geographers (AAG) in 1973; his views may not be entirely typical, and are certainly more firmly stated than those of his peers, but they reflect both growing disillusion within geographical circles with past achievements (see also Cooke and Robson, 1976) and a concern about future directions. Zelinsky's (1970, p. 499) first statement began:

> *This is a tract ... The reader is asked to consider what I have come to regard as the most timely and momentous item on the agenda of the human geographer: the study of the implications of a continuing growth in human numbers in the advanced countries, acceleration in their production and consumption of commodities, the misapplication of old and new technologies, and of the feasible responses to the resultant difficulties.*

He developed three basic arguments:

1. That people are inducing for themselves a state of acute frustration and a crisis of survival;
2. That these conditions originate, and can only be solved, in the 'advanced' nations; and
3. That the current 'growth syndrome' has profound geographical implications.

Material accumulation can no longer be considered progress, he argued, because it is unsustainable; effort is currently misallocated on a massive scale, and there is a major geographical task involved in its sensible reallocation.

Zelinsky identified five typical academic reactions towards the problems of the 'growth syndrome':

1. Ignore them;
2. Accept that major consequences will occur, but only eventually;
3. Admit that problems exist, but argue that they are easily solved by the free market, perhaps with state guidance;
4. Claim that nothing can be done, but that in any case we will survive; and
5. Realize the potential for immediate, unprecedented trouble.

His own reaction clearly fell into the fifth type, but many others suggested that it was (and remains) an over-reaction, as illustrated by Beckerman's (1995) critique of the 'sustainable development' thesis. Zelinsky identified three roles which geographers could play in facing up to perceived oncoming disasters. The first – which involves a minimal political commitment and 'should not offend even the most rock-ribbed conservative scholar' (p. 518) – is the *geographer as diagnostician*, applying 'the geographic stethoscope to a stressful demography' (p. 519), mapping what he calls geodemographic load, environmental contamination, crowding and stress. The second involves the *geographer as prophet*, projecting and forecasting likely futures. Finally, there is the *geographer as architect of utopia*, educating with regard to problems and possible solutions and providing support for the unknown leaders who have the political will to guide society through the coming 'Great Transition'.

Ending his 'declaration of conscience' on a pessimistic note, Zelinsky argued regarding geographers:

> ... how woefully deficient we are in terms of practitioners, in terms of both quantity and quality, how we are still lacking in relevant techniques, but most of all that we are totally at sea in terms of ideology, theory and proper institutional arrangements (p. 529).

Those criticisms were not confined to geographers, however; he applied them to scientists *en masse* in his AAG presidential address (Zelinsky, 1975). Science, he contended, is the twentieth-century religion, and has failed to avert the oncoming crisis. (See also Harvey, 1973, 1989a, 1994, discussed on pp. 331 and 333.) Its disciplinary specialisms and separatism 'fog perception of larger social realities' (p. 128), while 'fresher, keener insights, along with much better prose' (p. 129) are produced by the brighter contemporary journalists.

Zelinsky identified five crucial axioms as the foundations of science:

1. That the principle of causality is valid for studying all phenomena;
2. That all problems are soluble (see Johnston's, 1990b, response to Pacione, 1990a);
3. That there is a final state of perfect knowledge;
4. That findings have universal validity; and
5. That total scientific objectivity is possible.

The social sciences have failed to live up to these, he claims, for several reasons: their immaturity; their use as a refuge for mediocre personnel; the difficulty of their subject matter concerning interpersonal relationships; their problems of observation and experimentation; and the political and other problems involved in applying their proposed solutions. Furthermore, and the major cause of their failure, the natural science model is irrelevant to the study of society:

> If we are in pursuit of nothing more than information or knowledge, then there is some value in copying the standard formula of a research paper in the so called hard sciences. ... But if we are in pursuit of something more difficult and precious than just knowledge, namely understanding, then this simple didactic pattern has very limited value (p. 141).

The natural science approach adopted by positivist spatial scientists helps to describe the world, he claims, but not to understand it. For Berry, on the other hand, all other approaches are flawed: science, as he defines it, 'is the basis for rational action' (Berry,

2002d, p. 502). If geographers practise it, then they may have substantial influence on 'how environmental influences modify thought and behavior by modifying brain structure and functioning . . . provided . . . we resist the linguistic excesses and the seductive but ultimately self-defeating siren song of self-congratulatory postmodernism' (Berry, 1999, p. 590). For him, following Wilson (1998), science is differentiated from pseudo-science on four criteria: the repeatability of its findings by independent analysis; the economy of its explanations; its unambiguous statements; its heuristic power for future work; and its consilience – its appreciation that 'all living phenomena are ultimately obedient to the laws of physics and chemistry . . . and that all biological phenomena are products of evolution by natural selection' (Berry, 1998, p. 95). Geography needs to meet all of these criteria if it is to contribute to constructing a better world. In a later piece (Berry, 2002e, p. 1) he presents a 'toolkit' for detecting whether a claim is valid as a series of four questions – 'Can it be tested?'; 'Is it supported by evidence?'; 'Has it been confirmed?'; and 'Is it logical?' – and wonders, 'how much of what we see published in our flagship journals meets the test of my Cheshire cat's smile, and of that which does not, how much is pseudo-science, anti-science, or pure baloney' (p. 2).

There are two major components to Zelinsky's case: geographical research should be relevant to the solution of major societal problems; and the positivist-based spatial-science methodology may be inappropriate for such a task. Several were quick to point out that neither was particularly new, especially the first. House (1973), for example, reviewed the tradition of involvement in public policy by British geographers, and Stoddart (1975b, p. 190) identified the late nineteenth-century views of Reclus and Kropotkin as 'the origins of a socially relevant geography' – the latter was later rediscovered by the 'radicals' (Peet, 1978). Nor was the more 'revolutionary' approach of those who had 'broken off' from liberalism particularly novel: Santos (1974) reminded English-speaking geographers of the Marxist-inspired works of Jean Dresch on capital flows in Africa and Jean Tricart on class conflict and human ecology, both prior to the Second World War, for example, and Keith Buchanan's presidential address to the New Zealand Geographical Society on the need for studying 'the absolute geographical primacy of the state; especially in the non-Western world' (Buchanan, 1962) produced an acid response from Spate (1963).

Zelinsky's views were echoed in another AAG presidential address, with Ginsburg (1973, p. 2) writing that:

> Much so called theory in geography . . . is so abstracted from reality that we hardly recognize reality when we see it. . . . The increasing demand for rigor to cast light on trivia has come to plague all of the social sciences . . . the most important questions tend not to be asked because they are the most difficult to answer.

At about that time, the Association established a Standing Committee on Society and Public Policy (Ginsburg, 1972), which White (1973, p. 103) hoped would 'be alert to distinguishing the fatuous problems and the activities that are pedestrian fire-fighting or flabby reform'. This statement was made at a session on geography and public policy at the Association's 1970 conference; a similar theme was chosen for the 1974 conference of the Institute of British Geographers (IBG). Not all geographers accepted White's aim – using learned societies to influence public policy – while not denying the value of geographic method in social engineering. Trewartha (1973, p. 79) stated that:

> I must demur when he proposes that it should be a corporate responsibility of our professional society to become an instrument for social change. … From the beginning, the unique purpose of the Association of American Geographers has been to advance the cause of geography and geographers; it was never intended to be a social-action organization. … All kinds of research, pure as well as applied, should be equally approved and supported by the AAG.

Relevance, to what and for whom?

Claims that geographical work should be more relevant to major societal problems raised queries about the nature of that relevance, and it soon became apparent that there was no consensus on what should be done, and why. The ensuing debate is illustrated by a number of contributions to the British journal *Area* during the early 1970s.

Chisholm (1971b) opened it, identifying differences between governments, with their interests in cost-effective research and their primacy in decision-making, and academics, some of whom are concerned to protect their academic freedom and their right to be the sole judges of what they study and publish. Traditionally, geographers had advised governments in the roles of information-gatherers and 'masterful synthesizers' and they had not been involved in the final stages of policy-making: they had been delvers and dovetailers, but not deciders. On the latter role, unfortunately:

> The magic of quantification is apt to seem rather less exciting when the specifications of the goods it can deliver are inspected at close quarters (p. 66). … The danger with empirical science is the absence of guidance at the normative level as to which of various options one should take (pp. 67–8).

The challenge to human geography, according to Chisholm, was to define such norms. Chisholm himself later worked for several British governments in a role which was neither delver nor dovetailer: as a member of independent commissions (the Local Government Boundary Commission in the 1970s and the Local Government Commission in the 1990s) he was involved in advising governments on the best way to redraw important components of England's administrative map (Chisholm, 1975b, 1995) – though he has been critical of many of the procedures with which he was involved, and was apparently not re-appointed to the latter Commission because of this (Chisholm, 2000). Eyles (1971) responded that the focus of relevant research should be 'some of the social and spatial inequities in society' (p. 242), and the first challenge is to study the distribution of power in society, thereby identifying the mechanisms for allocating scarce resources. Research could then isolate the disadvantages of relative powerlessness and provide the basis for policy aimed at redistributing resources.

British geographers were introduced to the ongoing debates in American geography in two reports on the 1971 AAG conference. (This was not the first at which major social issues had been raised. The 1969 meeting should have been in Chicago but was transferred to Ann Arbor as a protest over police violence directed at anti-war protesters at the 1968 Democratic Party Convention in Chicago. The radical journal *Antipode* was launched there in 1969, and those attending were confronted by the problems of the inhabitants of Detroit's black ghetto, small groups of whom 'invaded' several of the sessions to present their concerns at the academics' 'unworldliness'.) By 1971, 'many geographers were deeply frustrated by a sense of failure' to deal with major social issues (Prince, 1971b, p. 152), but although some members were taking notice of 'the sufferings of the outside world' (p. 152) other scholars remained 'locked in private debates, preoccupied with trivia, mending and qualifying accepted ideas' (p. 153).

Smith's (1971) report suggested that American geography was about to undergo another revolution, to counter a situation in which 'geography is overpreoccupied with the study of the production of goods and the exploitation of natural resources, while ignoring important conditions of human welfare and social justice' (p. 154). This forthcoming revolution would involve a fundamental re-evaluation of research, teaching activities and basic social philosophies, and was represented at the conference by activities such as the foundation of SERGE (the Socially and Ecologically Responsible Geographer) by Zelinsky and others and by a motion at the Annual General Meeting condemning United States' involvement in Vietnam. Smith (1971) was unsure whether this revolution, with its emphasis on social as against economic concerns, would spread to Britain, however:

> The conditions which have helped to spawn radical geography in the United States include the existence of large oppressed racial minorities, inequalities between rich and poor with respect to social justice, a power structure and value system largely unresponsive to the needs of the underprivileged, and an unpopular war which is sapping national economic and moral strength. These conditions do not exist in Britain or exist in a less severe form, and the stimulus for social activism in geography is thus considerably less than in America (pp. 156–7).

Smith would almost certainly have changed his mind a decade later: by the mid-1990s he was writing of the need 'to place social justice at the heart of human geography' (Smith, 1994, p. 1). Dickenson and Clarke (1972) responded to his 1971 claim by arguing that British geographers had long been concerned with 'relevant' issues, with particular respect to the Third World.

Another commentary on AAG's 1971 conference came from Berry (1972c), who felt that what he had observed was just a new fad involving 'new entrants to the field seeking their "turf"'. He could identify no real commitment:

> The majority of the new revolutionaries, it seems, are essentially white liberals – quick to lament the supposed ills of society and to wear their bleeding hearts like emblems or old school ties – and quicker to avoid the hard work that diagnosis and action demand. A smaller group of hard-line marxists keeps bubbling the potage of liberal laments. In neither group is there any profound commitment to producing constructive change by democratic means. . . . If either of these will be the 'new geography' of the 1970s, count me out (pp. 77–8, emphasis in the original. See also Berry, 2002c).

To him, academic geographers should provide a knowledge base on which policy can be built, which implies close involvement with the education of future generations of policy-makers (on which see Yeates, 2001). To Blowers (1972), however, 'The issue is not how we can cooperate with policy-makers, but whether and in what sense we should do so. It is a question of values' (p. 291); he argued that the sort of activities proposed by Berry would be strongly supportive of the *status quo*, and unlikely to produce fundamental social reform.

Smith's (1973a, p. 1) response to Berry was that, 'bleeding hearts sometimes help to draw attention to important issues, and marxists can make valuable contributions in the search for alternatives to existing institutions and policies', and he pointed out that the current 'fad' was no more pronounced than that of the quantifiers a decade earlier. The results of their 'revolution' offered little for the solution of social problems, however, and Smith doubted the value of the large projects established by the AAG as part of its geography and public policy drive. (One of those projects produced a major series of books on Metropolitan America: Adams, 1976.) Research should highlight particular problems, and teaching should place emphases on 'a man in harmony with nature rather than master of it, on social health rather than economic health, on equity rather than efficiency, and on the quality of life rather than the quantity of goods' (p. 3). Chisholm (1973) advocated caution in the corridors of power, because geographers had done insufficient substantive research to back up a 'hard sell' (a point made three decades earlier by Ackerman: see p. 63); Eyles (1973, p. 155) argued that, 'any entry to those corridors assumes that the structure underlying policy alternatives is basically sound'; and Blowers (1974) wrote that in the corridors one can only influence, not decide, and that for the latter task geographers must develop their political convictions and act accordingly. (Blowers was active in English local government for some decades, focusing on environmental issues, on which he has also written major academic works: Blowers, 1984.)

This debate on if, and how, geographers should contribute to the solution of societal problems was a major issue at the 1974 IBG annual conference. Coppock's (1974) presidential address presented the challenges, opportunities and implications of geographical involvement in public policy, an involvement which he felt the current generation of students welcomed. He argued that policy-makers were largely ignorant of potential geographical contributions, while at the same time geographers seemed unaware that, 'there is virtually no aspect of contemporary geography which is not affected to some degree by public policy' (p. 5). Coppock wanted to change this, to have geographers identify the contributions that they could make, to encourage research relevant to those contributions, and to enter a dialogue with those who advise on and implement public policy.

Other conference contributors were neither as optimistic nor as committed as Coppock. Hare (1974), himself an adviser to the Canadian government, reacted to cries that geographers were not consulted enough with the reply 'Thank goodness': geography, as a discipline, is irrelevant to the separate domain of public policy-making, although geographers, as individuals, because of the breadth of their training, could offer much that was valuable, so his conclusion was 'Geography no, geographers yes' (p. 26). His was a different response to mounting social concerns from Steel's, who told the British Geographical Association (Steel, 1974, p. 200):

As geographers we often get hot under the collar over the number of theoretical economists who are called on to advise the governments of developing countries. We comment on how much better World Bank surveys of countries would be if they were prepared, at least in part, by geographers. . . . We wonder why university departments of geography are not engaged on a consultancy basis more often than they are, and we marvel that the Overseas Development Administration in London has only a handful of geographers on its staff where, we feel, an army would be more appropriate.

Hare (1977) subsequently argued that a major reason for a lack of geographical contributions to public policy may be the poverty of their academic training: in recent years we have 'swept geography departments into the social-science divisions of faculties of arts and sciences where, from playing second fiddle to geologists or literary critics, we learned to play second fiddle to economists and sociologists' (p. 263). Geographers would have to rebuild their discipline based on the centrality of society–environment interactions, he argued, with a new brand of physical geography that leans heavily on biological ideas and sources: 'We must reassert the old, essential truth that geography is the study of the earth as the habitat of man, and not some small sub-set of that gigantic theme' (p. 266). (See also Steel, 1982; Hart, 1982.) Hare's views on the current irrelevance of geography to public policy were supported by Hall (1974, p. 49), who argued that:

. . . geography, most clearly of all the social sciences, has neither an explicit nor an implicit normative base . . . spatial efficiency . . . is rather a description of what men seek to do in actuality . . . not . . . an objective to be achieved or objective function to be maximized.

Policy-makers must seek their norms elsewhere; geographers, meanwhile, must develop a new political geography which will aid them in understanding the crucial role of political decisions in structuring spatial systems (Johnston, 1978b).

Two other papers given at the 1974 IBG conference argued against Coppock's programme. Leach (1974), for example, claimed that governments, as paymasters, already constrained what geographers could do research on, and as a result geographers were being used; their only alternative was political action. Harvey's (1974c) contribution was entitled 'What kind of geography for what kind of public policy?'. Individuals wishing to become involved in policy-making were, he argued, stimulated by motives such as personal ambition, disciplinary imperialism, social necessity and moral obligation: at the level of the whole discipline, on the other hand, geography had been co-opted, through the universities, by the growing corporate state, and geographers had been given some illusion of power within a decision-making process designed to maintain the *status quo*. He portrayed the corporate state as 'proto-fascist' (p. 23), a transitional step on the path to the barbarism depicted in Orwell's *Nineteen Eighty-Four*. The function of academics, he claimed, was to counter such trends, to expunge the racism, ethnocentrism and condescending paternalism from within their own discipline and to build a humanistic subject, thereby assisting all human beings 'to control and enhance the conditions of our own existence' (p. 24).

Harvey (1973, p. 129) had previously argued that the current mode of analysis in geography offered little for the solution of pressing societal concerns:

There is an ecological problem, an urban problem, an international trade problem, and yet we seem incapable of saying anything of depth or profundity about any of them. When we do say anything, it appears trite and rather ludicrous. ... It is the emerging objective social conditions and our patent inability to cope with them which essentially explain the necessity for a revolution in geographic thought.

He recognized three types of theory:

1. *Status quo*, which represents reality accurately but only in terms of static patterns, and therefore cannot make predictions which will lead to fundamental social change;
2. *Counter-revolutionary*, which also represents reality, but obfuscates the real issues because it ignores (either deliberately or accidentally) the important causative factors and so can be used to promote changes that will not bring about significant alterations to the operation of those factors. It is, 'a perfect device for non-decision making, for it diverts attention from fundamental issues to superficial or non-existent issues' (p. 151); and
3. *Revolutionary*, which is grounded in the reality it seeks to represent, and is formulated so as to encompass the contradictions and conflicts which produce social change.

Harvey wished to write revolutionary theory, thereby overthrowing the current paradigm; his blueprint for geography:

... does not entail yet another empirical investigation. ... In fact, mapping even more evidence of man's patent inhumanity to man is counter-revolutionary in the sense that it allows the bleeding-heart liberal in us to pretend we are contributing to a solution when in fact we are not. This kind of empiricism is irrelevant. There is already enough information. ... Our task does not lie here. Nor does it lie in what can only be termed 'moral masturbation' of the sort which accompanies the masochistic assemblage of some huge dossier of the daily injustices. ... This, too, is counter-revolutionary for it merely serves to expiate guilt without our ever being forced to face the fundamental issues, let alone do anything about them. Nor is it a solution to indulge in that emotional tourism which attracts us to live and work with the poor for a while. ... These ... paths ... merely serve to divert us from the essential task at hand.

This immediate task is nothing more nor less than the self-conscious and aware construction of a new paradigm for social geographic thought through a deep and profound critique of our existing analytical constructs. This is what we are best equipped to do. We are academies, after all, working with the tools of the academic trade ... our task is to mobilize our power of thought, which we can apply to the task of bringing about a humanizing social change (pp. 144–5).

To Harvey, then, relevant geography involves building new geographic theory on a Marxist base, and its dissemination will achieve social reform through the education process. (This gradualist view, promoting reform through education, is only implicit in Harvey's work; Johnston, 1974, p. 189; 1986g. Harvey later discussed the problems of creating a new society, and outlined a scenario of how that might come about, and with what effects: Harvey, 2000). Blaut (1979) contended that Marxist theory offered benefits because it can handle two crucial issues which positivist theory cannot: increased injustice and heightened economic and social instability.

Harvey (1984) presented a forceful elaboration of his views in a paper subtitled 'an historical materialist manifesto'. Geography, he contended, not only records, analyses and stores information about society but also 'promotes conscious awareness of how such conditions are subject to continuous transformation through human action' (p. 1). The nature of the knowledge that it produces and propagates reflects the social context of place and time, hence the role of geography in the 'Bourgeois era' as an 'active vehicle for the transmission of doctrines of racial, cultural, sexual, or national superiority' (p. 3). The positivist movement had sought to establish a universal science of spatial relations, which was countered by both humanistic and Marxist critiques. Together the latter suggested the development of a revitalized geography, but they lacked:

> ... a clear context, a theoretical frame of reference, a language which can simultaneously capture global processes restructuring social, economic and political life in the contemporary era and the specifics of what is happening to individuals, groups, classes, and communities at particular places at certain times (p. 6).

Historical materialism provides that framework, he argues (though see Eliot Hurst's, 1985, argument that, if Harvey accepted his own (1972) contention that disciplinary boundaries are counter-revolutionary, then it is hard to understand how he can later promote a disciplinary-based manifesto).

Harvey argued that geographers cannot be neutral; their work must be of value to some special interest group within society. For him, that group should not be 'generals, politicians, and corporate chiefs' (p. 7) but the disenfranchised. A people's geography, 'threaded into the fabric of daily life with deep taproots into the well-springs of popular consciousness', 'must also open channels of communication, undermine parochialist world views, and confront or subvert the power of the dominant classes or the state. It must penetrate the barriers to common understanding by identifying the material base to common interests' (p. 7). It would not only reveal to the disenfranchised how societies are structured and restructured so that, 'centers exploit peripheries, the first world subjugates the third, and capitalist powers compete for domination of protected space (markets, labor power, raw materials). People in one place exploit and struggle against those in another place' (p. 9), but would also help them to:

> Define a political project that sees the transition from capitalism to socialism in historico-geographical terms ... we must define, also, a radical guiding vision: one that explores the realms of freedom beyond material necessity, that opens the way to the creation of new forms of society in which common people have the power to create their own geography and history in the image of liberty and mutual respect of opposed interests. The only other course ... is to sustain a present geography founded on class oppression, state domination, unnecessary material deprivation, war, and human denial (p. 10).

Harvey returned to this theme in 1989, in a retrospective volume reporting on a conference held to mark the twentieth anniversary of the publication of *Models in*

Geography (see p. 101). He set out a brief critique of the scientific approach adopted in the earlier book, claiming that the type of modelling adopted could not be used to tackle what he identified as the major geographical questions (such as the 'evolutionary path of capitalism itself' – Harvey, 1989b, p. 212: in this context, he portrays 'all geography as historical geography'). Indeed, 'when put in the context of these grander questions, the modelling effort appeared both puny and not particularly revealing'. Many geographers retained that modelling approach, however, by fragmenting the discipline and focusing on narrow questions. They had restricted the nature of the questions asked, and as a consequence (pp. 212–13):

> ... we can now model spatial behaviour like journey-to-work, retail activity, the spread of measles epidemics, the atmospheric dispersion of pollutants, and the like, with much greater security and precision than once was the case. And I accept that this represents no mean achievement. But what can we say about the sudden explosion of third world debt in the 1970s, the remarkable push into new and seemingly quite different modes of flexible accumulation, the rise of geopolitical tensions, even the definition of key ecological problems? What more do we know about major historical-geographical transitions (the rise of capitalism, world wars, socialist revolutions and the like)? Furthermore, pursuit of knowledge by the positivist route did not necessarily generate usable configurations of concepts and theories. There must be thousands of hypotheses proven correct at some appropriate significance level in the geographical literature by now, and I am left with the impression that in toto this adds up to little more than the proverbial hill of beans.

He found it hard to understand why Marxism had had such little influence on geography until the 1970s, and noted that when it did, 'geographers who turned to Marx were swept up in that, and many were so submerged in it that they entirely forgot their own disciplinary identity' (p. 215). The submersion was necessary, but so was the identity: the production of knowledge is a political project, and the history and future of the discipline have to be appreciated in that context. Thus (p. 216):

> ... any project to 'remodel' contemporary geography must take the achievements of the Marxist thrust thoroughly into account at the same time as it recognizes the limits of positivism and the restricted domain of the modelling endeavours that derived therefrom. This is not to rule all forms of mathematical representation, data analysis and experimental design out of order, but to insist that those batteries of techniques and scientific languages be deployed within a much more powerful framework of historical-materialist analysis.

This, he accepts, must be ideological, 'because it is necessarily political and built upon some conception of our collective agency in history'.

The liberal contribution

Liberalism is defined as here the idea 'shared by many modern American liberals who, characteristically, combine a belief in democratic capitalism with a strong commitment to executive and legislative action in order to alleviate social ills' (Bullock, 1977, p. 347). Associated in the USA with the left of the Democratic party, and in Canada, the UK and parts of Europe with social democratic, socialist and Labour parties, liberals are concerned that all members of society do not fall below certain minimum levels of well-being (variously defined), and are prepared for state action within the capitalist structure in order that this can be achieved. Within geography, much of the work conducted in this ethos focused on description rather than theory-construction: Chisholm's (1971a) investigation of the potential of welfare economics as a basis for normative theory which does not involve profit-maximization goals was one of the few exceptions (see also Wilson, 1976b).

There is a long tradition of liberal contributions by 'applied geographers', both in their research and associated activities and in their teaching (see House, 1973; Hall, 1981b, 2003, reviews UK geographers' work in the fields of urban planning, for example, and Hudson, 2003, similarly outlines their work on issues of regional development and planning). In Britain, applied geography as information-gathering and -synthesizing has a substantial record, starting with Stamp's Land Utilization Survey of Britain in the 1930s, and his subsequent involvement in the preparation for post-war land-use planning (Stamp, 1946: see p. 54). Other aspects of land-use planning were of interest to geographers in the 1930s and 1940s, and were discussed several times at the Royal Geographical Society (Freeman, 1980b); similar geographical involvement occurred in the United States (Kollmorgen, 1979). During the Second World War geographers made many contributions as information synthesizers and gatherers, the latter including the development of air-photo interpretation (on British contributions see Balchin, 1987, and Clout and Gosme, 2003; on US activity see several of the essays in Miller, 1993).

After the Second World War land-use and transport planning were established on a large scale, and trained geographers provided a substantial proportion of its personnel. Many academic geographers were active in applied work in other ways. Technical developments in cartography and data handling saw them involved in redistricting for Congressional elections (Morrill, 1981), a wide range of mapping activities (Rhind and Adams, 1980; Rhind later became the first academic to head the British national mapping agency – the Ordnance Survey: Rhind, 2003), and developing regional bases for the presentation of census statistics (Coombes et al., 1982; Berry, Goheen and Goldstein, 1969), for example, while developments in GIS during the 1980s and 1990s stimulated very substantial increases in mapping and enumeration (Charlton, Rao and Carver, 1995; Martin, 2002). Alongside this, various policies have been evaluated, such as those aimed at changing the distribution of industrial activity, and much of the entropy-maximizing systems modelling (p. 129) was intended to provide procedures for planning the joint activities of land-use and transport planning (Wilson, 1974; Bennett and Wilson, 2003; on whether it did, see Batty, 1989).

Most of this work used an empiricist and (usually implicit) positivist framework. Geographers are perceived as having valuable skills in the collection and ordering of data, as in land-use surveys, for example, and the presentation of such data frequently assumed the existence, and desirability of maintaining, certain causal relationships; planning agricultural land use, for example, often assumed a clear causal link between the physical environment and agricultural productivity and that of industrial location assumed the need for efficiency via the minimization of total travel costs. (Interestingly, some critics pointed out that the greatest use of such optimizing models occurred not in the 'capitalist west' but rather in the 'socialist east'.) As positivist work on the allocation of land uses and traffic flows increased, so the potential for geographic inputs to spatial planning was promoted (and many people initially trained as geographers became professional planners). Most of this was pragmatic application of technical skills, though there were also evaluations of policy impacts (e.g. Hall *et al.,* 1973) and attempts to develop decision-making theories in this context (Hall, 1981a, 1982, 1998).

Geographers' empiricist role continued to be advanced in response to economic crises and the perceived need for valid data. In Britain, for example, the government introduced a three-year programme in 1983 to provide 'new blood' for university research efforts; 792 lectureships were available, in open competition between universities, with a further 146 in the fields of information technology. Geography departments received 11.5 per cent of these posts (1.1 per cent of the total; the staff of geography departments comprised 2 per cent of all university posts in 1982–3). D. M. Smith (1985) argued not only that geography lost out relatively in that contest (the 'winners' were engineering, technology, and the physical and biological sciences) but also that within geography the posts allocated were selectively focused on certain aspects of the discipline: five were for research in remote sensing/digital mapping, for example, and three more were for various aspects of mathematical modelling (two in physical geography); only one reflected 'place-specific' issues, a post in historical-cultural geography. Smith interprets this as follows:

> The predominance of remote sensing (and associated digital mapping) reflects a view of geography as a technologically sophisticated means of gathering and displaying information, in the tradition of the geographer as map-maker linked to the contemporary preoccupation with information technology . . . [that] appears to conflate the needs of the discipline with a conception of the needs of society in which the emphasis is much more economic than social. It is hard to see more than one or two of the posts contributing much to the solution of social problems. The predominant impression is of an a-social view of the world, in which social relations, class structure and political power seem strangely absent (p. 2).

Clayton (1985a) responded that this was unlikely to be the only example of more direct state influence on the direction of academic research (see also his analysis of how geographers should react to that: Clayton, 1985b). In 1986 the University Grants Committee produced its first rating of the research record of every university department – on criteria that included externally earned research income as well as publications, information on which was subjectively examined by 'expert panels' which graded every department – and began a selective allocation of funds to universities that reflected those ratings (see Smith, 1986). Similar rating exercises were undertaken in 1989, 1992, 1996, and 2001 (each using peer review, and more transparent than the first: Thorne, 1993); virtually all of the research money distributed to the universities by the funding councils (some £20 million annually in 2003 across geography departments) is now allocated by a formula linked to those ratings, with most money going to the largest departments whose research records and plans win the highest ratings (on the funding implications, see Johnston, 1993b, 1995b; on the ethics of such a distribution, see Smith, 1995, 1996; Rhind,

1996; Curran, 1996; Curran, 2000, 2001a, has modelled the distribution of 'success' in these exercises). In the early twenty-first century, this allocation procedure was made even more selective, with only a minority of the country's geography departments (basically those in the top three grades – by then 6*, 5* and 5) getting any allocation, with the implication that the remainder were largely being funded for their teaching activities only.

Alongside those who argued for a greater commitment to applied geography in the empiricist/positivist mould, and therefore for an implicit acceptance of a particular ideology (Johnston, 1981a), others challenged this as the best way to respond to pressing societal problems. They argued for a reappraisal of how geographers could assist in understanding the genesis of those problems rather than in the suggestion of solutions which rarely tackled the root causes. The major contributions of the two groups are the subject of the next sections.

Mapping welfare

Much research was published in the 1960s and 1970s under the general title of factorial ecologies (p. 97), applications of multivariate statistical procedures to large data matrices as a means of representing spatial variations in population characteristics. These, according to Smith (1973b, p. 43), were over-reliant on certain types of census data and therefore provided little information on social conditions. Earlier attempts had been made to structure analyses of such data towards particular ends, as in the work of rural sociologists on farmers' levels of living (Hagood, 1943) – a concept introduced to the geographical literature by Lewis (1968) and in Thompson et al.'s (1962) investigation of variations in levels of economic health among different parts of New York State.

Factorial ecology procedures were adapted to the task of portraying spatial variations in social welfare in the 1970s, led by two workers. Knox (1975) promoted the mapping of social and spatial variations in the quality of life as a fundamental objective for geography, to provide both an input to planning procedures and a means of monitoring policies aimed at improving welfare. He divided the concept of 'level-of-living' into three sets of variables – physical needs (nutrition, shelter and health); cultural needs (education, leisure and recreation, and security); and higher needs (to be purchased with surplus income) – and used statistical procedures to portray their spatial variations. With the resultant maps, geographers must then decide whether they are playing a sufficient role in awakening human awareness of the extent of the disparities or are 'under an obligation to help society improve the situation' (p. 53).

Similar work by Smith (1973b) was set in the context of the American social indicators movement and the growing belief there that GNP and national income 'are not necessarily direct measures of the quality of life in its broadest sense' (p. 1). He initiated the collation and dissemination of territorial social indicators, in order to illustrate the extent of discrimination by place of residence which occurs in the United States; multivariate statistical procedures generated the maps, on inter-state, inter-city and intra-urban scales. (Cox, 1979, extended the treatment to the international scale.) Smith's (1979, p. 11) goal was to present: 'the basis for a better understanding of the origins of inequality as a geographical condition and of the difficulties in the way of plans to promote greater equality in human life chances'.

In Chisholm's terms (p. 328 above), these two works represented the geographer as delver and dovetailer, producing information on which more equitable social planning could be based. Other studies performed similar roles, and also suggested spatial policies which could lead to improvements. Harries (1974), for example, analysed spatial variations in crime rates and the administration of justice, and argued that predictive models of criminal patterns could assist the organization of police work; Shannon and Dever (1974) and Phillips and Joseph (1984) investigated variations in the provision of health-care facilities and argued for spatial planning that would improve the services offered to the sick (which is different from a geography of prophylaxis: Fuller, 1971); and Morrill and Wohlenberg (1971) studied the geography of poverty in the United States, proposing both social policies – higher minimum wages, guaranteed incomes, guaranteed jobs, and stronger anti-discrimination laws – and spatial policies (such as an extensive programme of economic decentralization to a network of regional growth centres) that would alleviate this major social problem.

An alternative, highly personal, programme of mapping variations in human welfare was advanced by Bunge (1971), who prepared a 'geobiography' of his home area in Detroit's black ghetto. His deeply humanitarian concern for the future was interpreted as a need to ensure a healthy existence for children; he proposed a 'dictatorship of the children' (Bunge, 1973b, p. 329) with regions – 'may the world be full of happy regions' (p. 331) – designed for them. This requires a reduction in the worship of machines, which are inimical to children's health (Bunge, 1973c), and a mapping of the sorts of variables never collected by external agencies and therefore requiring the development of geographical expeditions within the world's large cities. These maps would include roach regions, parkless spaces, toyless regions, and rat-bitten-children regions (Bunge, 1973d), and some were prepared for both Detroit and Toronto (Bunge and Bordessa, 1975). This work was later described by Merrifield (1995, p. 57) as involving excursions 'beyond the cloisters of the academy' and, 'a redefinition of the research problematic and intellectual commitment of the researcher away from a smug campus career to one incorporating a dedicated community perspective'. The task of empathizing with and situating oneself authentically within an impoverished community is difficult, and the researcher's own biography is likely to influence the process of learning about and becoming committed to such a community. This raises the issues of voice that have increasingly concerned those studying various forms of representation (see p. 282). By becoming involved, the geographer will become 'a person of action, a radical problem-raiser, [and] a responsible critical analyst participating *with* the oppressed' (Merrifield, 1995, p. 63), but:

> ... there is always an immanent hazard that the voice heard in the supposed symbiosis between academic geographer and folk geographer is skewed towards the overzealous – though well-meaning – academic geographer. As the voice of the oppressed is muted, the expedition program degenerates into a paternalism reminiscent of 19th century Western missionaries and settlement houses.

More mapping has been undertaken since the pioneering efforts – as in Seager's (Seager and Olson, 1986; Seager, Reed and Stott, 1995) atlases – but increasingly, in line with Harvey's critique of such descriptive analyses, efforts have been re-directed towards an appreciation of the underlying processes generating such geographies – not just describing 'who, gets what, where' but also analysing 'who gets what, where ... and why' (Johnston, 1975).

Attempts at understanding

The mapping investigations just discussed were very largely descriptive, and any prescriptions offered based on limited theoretical foundations. Attempts were made to develop the necessary theoretical understanding, however. Cox (1973), for example, looked at the urban crisis in the United States – the racial tensions and riots, municipal bankruptcies, and the role of the government in the urban economy – presenting his analysis in terms of conflict over access to sources of power (see also Adams, 1972 on the role of spatial constraints as a generating influence on ethnic unrest in US cities in the late 1960s). This was intended by Cox as part of an educational exercise, for:

> It would be utopian to think that we can propose solutions on the basis of our analysis. The locational problems and locational consequences of policies weave too intricate a web for that to be possible. All we can hope to do is inform. To be aware of the problems and of their complexity may induce some sensitivity in a citizenry which has shown as yet precious little tolerance for the other point of view (p. xii).

Nevertheless, his final chapter, entitled 'Policy implications', discussed two imperatives towards greater equity in the provision of public services – moral and efficiency (the latter applies to the total level of welfare in society as well). The policies presented involve spatial reorganization to achieve the desired equity (including metropolitan government integration), community control, population redistribution and transport improvements. Massam's (1976) review of geographical contributions to social administration also focused on spatial reorganization: he evaluated service provision using the spatial variables of distance and accessibility, with major chapters on the size and shape of administrative districts and on the efficient allocation of facilities within such districts (see also Hodgart, 1978).

Cox's work heralded an increased geographical interest in a much neglected field, the role of the state in capitalist society (see also Cox, Reynolds and Rokkan, 1974; Dear and Clark, 1978; Johnston, 1982a; Cox, 1979). Political geography had traditionally been mostly concerned with the state at the macro-scale only, dealing with (geo-)political regions, with national and intra-federal boundaries, and with the operations of the international political system (e.g. Muir, 1975). The similarly under-developed field of electoral geography had highlighted spatial variations in voting, but there had been little work on either the geographical inputs to voting or the geographical consequences of the translation of votes into political power (Taylor, 1978, 1985a; Taylor and Johnston, 1979). The state is involved in many aspects of economic and social geography, however, as both Buchanan (1962) and Coppock (1974) had stressed, but few geographers had investigated this involvement in any detail, or the electoral base on which it is founded (Brunn, 1974; Johnston, 1978b).

A framework for understanding spatial variations in well-being was presented by Coates, Johnston and Knox (1977). They defined the components of well-being, whose variations were mapped at three scales (international intra-national and intra-urban), and argued that those variations reflected three sets of causes: the spatial division of labour; accessibility to goods and facilities; and the political manipulation of territories. (See also Cox, 1979.) Spatial policies aimed at the reduction of spatial inequalities were evaluated, such as various forms of positive discrimination by areas, leading to the conclusion that the division of labour is the primary determinant of levels of social well-being. Creation of this division is a social and not a spatial process, though it has clear spatial consequences, so that:

> The root causes of spatial inequalities cannot be tackled by spatial policies alone, therefore. Inequalities are products of social and economic structures, of which capitalism in its many guises is the predominant example. Certainly inequalities can be alleviated by spatial policies . . . but alleviation is not cure: whilst capitalism reigns, however, remedial social action may be the best that is possible . . . the solution of inequalities must be sought in the restructuring of societies (pp. 256–7).

Smith (1977 – see also Smith, 1979) essayed a more ambitious attempt at explaining such spatial variations, arguing that, 'the well-being of society as a spatially variable condition should be the focal point of geographical enquiry . . . if human beings are the object of our curiosity in human geography, then the quality of their lives is of paramount interest' (pp. 362–3). This was the foundation of his case for 'a restructuring of human geography around the theme of *welfare* . . . to provide both positive knowledge and guidance in the normative realm of evaluation and policy formulation' (p. ix). His book proceeded from theory through measurement to application. The theoretical section is an amalgam of normative welfare economics with Marxian perspectives on the creation of value, plus the political conflict for power:

> The analysis will inevitably reveal certain fundamental weaknesses of the contemporary capitalist-competitive-materialistic society, but the temptation to offer a more radical critique of existing structures has been resisted, in favour of an approach that builds on the discipline's established intellectual tradition (p. xi).

He concluded that:

> As geographers we have a special role – a truly creative and revolutionary one – that of helping to reveal the spatial *malfunctionings and injustices, and contributing to the design of a spatial form of society in which people can be really free to fulfil themselves. This, surely, would be progress in geography* (p. 373).

Inequality, justice and ethics

Smith's (1994) *Geography and Social Justice* took forward his concerns with inequality and welfare, reflecting changing circumstances (p. xiii). He had been:

> . . . involved [in] a variety of engagements with geographical aspects of inequality and human welfare. Reflecting the dominant mood of the times, explicit concern for social justice remained muted, for the most part. But the theme was still there, and increasingly required reassertion as social change on the world stage – east, west and south – began to resurrect some basic questions concerning the distribution of benefits and burdens under alternative economic and political arrangements.

He determined to explore those aspects of moral philosophy related to the issue of distributive justice, to 'see what can be made of this in the geographical context'. This involved a return to normative thinking, 'with how we conceive of what is right or wrong, better or worse, in human affairs lived out in geographical space'. He concluded that 'social justice should not be left to market forces' because 'to commend observed market outcomes on the grounds that they are the results of a just process is not credible' (p. 279), and he argued instead for a foundation in egalitarianism which, despite postmodern critiques, should embrace certain universal needs (see also p. 269). Harvey (1993a, 1993b, 1996a) also addressed issues of justice, focusing on the interplay between universal conceptions and local circumstances.

Smith took this agenda forward in a series of essays on 'moral geographies', at a time when ethical issues came to the fore in debates within UK geography, as illustrated by the controversies related to Shell's sponsorship of the RGS (see below, p. 349: similar issues had previously been debated at American geography conferences – see p. 327 – but much less so in the UK). He identified this 'contemporary geography and ethics movement' (Smith, 1997a, p. 584) as involving a greater interrogation of the literature of philosophy than previously, with particular reference to the role of space and place therein – what he terms, 'the contextual thickening of moral concepts in the particular (local) circumstances of differentiated human being' (p. 587), an area that philosophers tend to ignore. (See Miller and Hashmi, 2001, who don't ignore it – but do ignore the work of geographers.) The study of ethics thus required appreciation of the place(s) in which people were morally socialized. Space too was important, as illustrated by essays on the spatial scope of care and beneficence: is there a distance–decay effect to moral action (Smith, 1994, 1998)? As with others (e.g. Sayer and Storper, 1997), Smith also found stimuli for this turn to ethical and normative concerns in the writings of environmentalists and feminists as well as philosophers (see also Whatmore, 1997, on the ethics of care).

For Smith (1997b), an 'ethical turn' in geography was necessary because of the pressing need for public debate on moral issues, 'Otherwise, humankind risks losing any residual grip on the meaning of the good life, any capacity to recognise and challenge evil' (Smith, 2000a, p. vii). For him, concepts central to geographic inquiry – 'landscape, location and place, locality, proximity and distance, space and territory, development and nature' (p. viii: these are the subject matter of the book's main chapters) – are significant to debates about 'questions of justice and the good life'. Difference is highly significant in ethics, not so much difference at an individual level (relevant though this is to fair treatment of all) but rather difference between groups, much of which is rooted in places, hence the importance of geography in what Smith terms 'geographically [or context-]sensitive ethics'. He sees the choice between universal ethical principles universally applied and local particularity lacking any transcendent values as a false dualism: with either (p. 202):

> … it would be hard to see how anything resembling moral truth might be discovered, or created, except universals so vacuous as to be impotent in the face of our sorry reality, or beliefs so restricted in scope as to be part of the problem rather than part of the solution of human conflict.

His final message advances (p. 208):

> ... the imperative of developing more caring relations with others, especially those most vulnerable, whoever and wherever they are, within a more egalitarian and environmentally sustainable way of life in which some of the traditional strengths of community can be realised and spatially extended.

Cloke (2002) made a similar argument for 'living ethically and acting politically', though his search for the geographies that might underpin and secure this is based on spiritual beliefs and his focus is on the recognition of what he terms 'ordered evil'.

Others have joined Smith in his effort to develop a 'moral (or ethical) imagination' within geography (Proctor, 1998a), which includes calls for reconsidering the human/nature binary division that underpins so much of contemporary geography (Proctor, 1998b; Whatmore, 2002). Apart from Smith's (2000a) book, several other contributions have addressed a broad range of issues in and exemplars of geographically-sensitive ethics (see Proctor and Smith, 1999, which includes essays on space, place, nature and knowledge; Bondi et al., 2002; Valentine, 2003). For Sack (1997, p. 1), for example, the fact that as humans we are geographical beings, transforming the earth and then ourselves being transformed by the altered environments that we inhabit, requires a moral focus to our work: the nature and force of geographical agency calls for moral agency, for an 'understanding of the consequences of our actions on nature and culture, locally and globally' (p. 2). The impact of these arguments was almost immediate: in 1998 a new journal on *Ethics, Place and Environment* was launched to carry material that illustrated and advanced the case for a more theoretically-developed and explicit moral commitment within geography.

Environmentalism

The late 1960s saw a rapid increase in concern about environmental problems; in the United States (Mikesell, 1974, p. 1):

> Towards the end of the 1960s the American public was overwhelmed with declarations of an impending environmental crisis. ... Since that time, crisis rhetoric and a yearning for simple answers to complicated questions have given way to a more sophisticated and deliberate search for environmental understanding. Ecology has been institutionalized.

Two of the leaders of the public debate disagreed over the cause of the problems (O'Riordan, 1976, pp. 65–80). Ehrlich argued for the primacy of population increase, and popularized the concept of zero population growth; Commoner claimed that technological advances and the consequent rapid depletion of resources plus deposition of pollutants created the major problems. Both arguments have clear geographical components, and it was stressed that geographers have a strong record of activity in resource conservation: George Perkins Marsh had written on the topic in 1864 (Lowenthal, 1965, 2001) and the climatologist Warren Thornthwaite had been closely involved in the 1930s' soil conservation movement established as a consequence of the Dust Bowl phenomenon. The interest in landscape modification was advanced by Sauer and his followers, and reflected in the symposium *Man's Role in Changing the Face of the Earth*. Similar interest elsewhere was exemplified by Cumberland's (1947) pioneering classic on soil erosion in New Zealand. Nevertheless, Mikesell argued that, 'developments in geography have been such that the several phases of national preoccupation with environmental problems have not produced a general awareness of our interests and skills' (p. 2). Similarly, Eden (2003, p. 213; see also Castree, 2004) has argued that because of 'a detour to other topics even as other disciplines discovered the environment as a topic of interest', British geographers were not prominent in the early years of this movement, leaving them 'playing "catch-up" in the late twentieth century, as the discipline sought to reoccupy the ground previously abandoned'. (Turner, 2002, on the other hand, has argued that human-environment inter-relationships now form a viable core area of geographical scholarship in the United States.)

As part of the AAG's increased commitment to public affairs in the early 1970s, its Commission on College Geography established a Panel on Environmental Education and sponsored a Task Force on Environmental Quality. The latter reported (Lowenthal *et al.*, 1973) that geographers would make excellent leaders for the educational tasks in hand because of:

1. The breadth of their training and their ability to handle and synthesize material from a range of sources;
2. Their acceptance of the complexity of causation;
3. The range of information which they are trained to tap;
4. Their interest in distributions; and
5. Their long tradition of study in this area.

All had fostered expertise in work on environmental perception, on vegetation succession, and on relationships between land use and soil erosion, which could be used as the bases for environmental impact statements, the elaboration of environmental choices, and international research collaboration.

Two types of work characterized geographers' activities on society–environment inter-relationships at this time. The first involved the traditional geographical concern with description and analysis. Review volumes such as *Perspectives on Environment* (Manners and Mikesell, 1974) were prepared, and a particular interest in problems of the physical environment of urban areas was generated (Detwyler and Marcus, 1972; Berry and Horton, 1974; Berry *et al.*, 1974; a later, British, addition was Douglas, 1983). The second type focused on issues of environmental management (O'Riordan, 1971a, 1971b), with particular emphasis on its economic aspects and on societal response to environmental hazards (Hewitt, 1983): as Kates (1972, p. 519) pointed out, economics provided the theories and prescriptions of the 1960s (and later, see Rees, 1985). A topic of special interest was leisure, particularly the growing demand for recreational facilities, and the impact of recreational and tourism activities on the environment (Patmore, 1970, 1983; see the critique of much of that work in Owens, 1984).

Despite such activity, Mikesell concluded that geographical contributions to environmentalism had not been great up to 1974. He commented regarding the prognostications of *The Limits to Growth* (Meadows *et al.*, 1972), for example, that, 'the debate on this most relevant of all issues has attracted remarkably little attention from geographers' (Mikesell, 1974, p. 19 – though see Eyre 1978). He concluded more generally that: 'one must add hastily that many of the environmental problems exposed in recent years and also many of the social and philosophical issues debated during the environmental crusade have not been given adequate attention by geographers'. This conclusion was supported by analysis of the contents of recent geographical journals and O'Riordan's (1976) lengthy bibliography, and sustained by Goudie (1993) nearly two decades later. Turner (2002) has suggested that this has now been rectified, however, with work on the human–environment interface now a major component of (American) geography.

A powerfully argued case not only for more work on the society–environment interface but also for its centrality to the whole of geographical activity was presented by Stoddart (1987), who contended that instead of celebrating the achievements of a century of professional geography, many of his colleagues were 'despondent, morose, disillusioned, almost literally devoid of hope, not only about Geography as it is today but as it might be in the future' (p. 328). This, he believed, was because so many of them 'have either abandoned or failed ever to recognize what I take to be our subject's central intent and indeed self-evident role in the community of knowledge' (p. 329). For him, geography had become diffuse and lacked a central focus, which should be 'Earth's diversity, its resources, man's survival on the planet'(p. 331). This requires a unified discipline, human and physical, in which 'The task is to identify geographical problems, issues of man and environment within regions – problems not of geomorphology or history or economics or sociology, but geographical problems: and to use our skills to work to alleviate them, perhaps to solve them'. Focusing on 'the big questions, about man, land, resources, human potential' would involve geographers reclaiming 'the high ground' (p. 334: examples include Williams, 1989, 2003) and abandoning much that is currently done:

> Quite frankly I have little patience with so-called geographers who ignore these challenges. I cannot take seriously those who promote as topics worthy of research subjects like geographical influences in the Canadian cinema, or the distribution of fast-food outlets in Tel Aviv. Nor have I a great deal more time for what I can only call the chauvinist self-indulgence of our contemporary obsession with the minutiae of our own affluent and urbanized society … We cannot afford the luxury of putting so much energy into peripheral things. Fiddle if you will, but at least be aware that Rome is burning all the while.

Bird (1989, p. 212) pointed out, however, that although Stoddart called for a geography that is 'real, united and committed . . . we are not told exactly what it is, though for Stoddart such a geography obviously exists'.

Similar, though less strident, calls have been made by others (e.g. Douglas, 1986; Goudie, 1986b; see also Cosgrove and Daniels, 1989); in response, the relevance of much that Stoddart would disregard in contemporary social science has been promoted as necessary to an appreciation of society–environment relations (Blaikie, 1985; Blaikie and Brookfield, 1987; Johnston, 1989b – the latter was written to counter the relative naiveté of much writing by physical geographers regarding the potential role of the state in the resolution of environmental problems: Trudgill, 1990; see also Johnston, 1996c). The nature of risk has been closely scrutinized by Adams (1995), for example, as have varying perceptions of nature (Simmons, 1993) and political approaches to environmental problems (Pepper, 1996); a successor to the 1954 Wenner-Gren Symposium explored human exploitation of the environment in considerable depth (Turner *et al.*, 1990) as have others on specific issues such as desertification (Granger, 1990; Middleton and Thomas, 1994, discuss the extent to which it was a political construction).

Stoddart's argument was clearly set in the cultural ecology mould. A similar case was made in the same year by Kates (1987, p. 526), who regretted the dominance of spatial science within geography and argued that when environmental issues became important on the public and political agenda in the early 1970s:

> No discipline was better situated than was geography to provide intellectual and scientific leadership. The natural science for the environmental revolution should have been the science of the human environment. Instead, intellectual leadership was split among biology, economics, and engineering, each of which transferred onto the human environmental realm their own theories of nature, of economy, or of technology, but none of these offered a truly integrated view ... The theory of the human environment, then, was the theory of plant or animal ecosystems, or of pervasive externalities, or of technological and managerial fixes.

For geographers, a perceived inability to respond to the demand for environmental scientists (producing 'geographers who can sit astride the natural and social science boundary to provide analysis, integration and leadership') was an opportunity lost, a 'road not taken'. But the Malthusian dilemma remains, posing great questions for society to which geographers can bring their special disciplinary advantages to in the search for answers (p. 532):

> We possess more than passing knowledge of both the natural and social sciences ... We have some useful tools for organizing data and information ... We possess a strong tradition of empirical field research ... And perhaps most important we have and we teach a respect for other peoples' theories. Our answer, then, as to why geography ... is that we are needed and that we are useful. When they go forth, our students understand the nature of the great questions, have more than a passing knowledge of natural and social science, have been in the field, have collected and organized new data, and have placed these data into a theoretical perspective.

To be sure that they will be called upon to perform in this way, geographers must put their house in order and some university departments should rebuild centres of expertise in the human environment tradition. The University of Oxford established an Environmental Change Centre alongside its School of Geography, for example, and its first director had an established international reputation in the study of the interactions between climatic change and human activity (Parry and Duncan, 1995). Other universities have similarly created 'environmental institutes' within which geographers play important roles: in some countries, such as Australia, geography has somewhat disappeared as a separate academic discipline, instead only being present in universities as part of some institutional structure focused on environmental science/studies (Holmes, 2002).

One of the major concepts to emerge from the increased concern over environmental problems in the late 1980s was sustainable development, a considerably ambiguous term that is generally taken to imply continual increases in material living standards without any diminution in environmental capacity to meet the needs of future generations (Turner, 1993). This was a focal concern of the 1992 Earth Summit at Rio de Janeiro, but the difficulties of implementing global environmental policies have been frequently stressed (see the essays in Johnston, Taylor and Watts, 1995, 2002), although others believe that the problems have been over-stated and can readily be addressed, within a satisfactory time scale, using instruments of economic policy that promote continued development (Beckerman, 1995; see also Kates, 1995).

While these broader concerns were being aired, geographers were continuing to be active in the tradition established by White (see p. 141). In 1937, for example, White's memorandum to President Roosevelt had helped to convince him, against Congressional advice, not to make the Secretary of War responsible for flood control projects, thereby bypassing local and regional planning bodies, and in 1965 he prepared a paper for the Bureau of the Budget on national policy options for dealing with floods and similar hazards. The result was the National Flood Insurance Program, after which White held annual seminars in Boulder to bring public-sector officials and academics together to discuss disaster response and mitigation policies (Platt, 1986). In this, he and the many others who have studied environmental policy and contributed to its implementation have adopted what Feldman (1986, p.189) termed the citizen-scholar model:

> The scholar chooses his or her research concerns on the basis of perceived social need but attempts to conduct the inquiry free of influence from outside the inquiry itself. The scholar is committed to social and political action as follow-up to the research, based on the findings and quality of the inquiry. But political activity is, during the course of the scholarship, kept separate … [In addition] the citizen-scholar teaches public affairs both within a curriculum and by example, letting her or his own activities demonstrate good citizenship and good scholarship without being didactic.

Earlier, White (1972, p. 322) had asked, 'What shall it profit a profession if it fabricate a nifty discipline about the world while that world and the human spirit are degraded?', and in seeking to avoid that problem he developed an approach which Wescoat (1992) compares to that of the philosopher of pragmatism, John Dewey. It had four components, he argued:

1. Recognition of the precariousness of existence;
2. A pragmatic conception of the nature of inquiry – problems arise and are tackled within situations, for there are no absolute truths; hence
3. A tradition of learning from experience; and
4. A belief in public discourse and democracy.

All of these fitted White's deep involvement with the work of the Society of Friends. (For a fuller discussion of his career, see White, 2002.)

The breadth of study in modern environmentalism is illustrated by O'Riordan's (1981) work, much of it set in the liberal humanitarian tradition already illustrated here, and from which he drew four conclusions:

1. Modern environmentalism challenges many aspects of Western capitalism;
2. It points out paradoxes rather than clear solutions;
3. It involves a conviction that better modes of existence are possible; and
4. It is a politicizing and reformist movement, based on a realization of the need for action in the face of impending scarcity and a lack of faith in the western democracies (pp. 300–1).

A new social, environmental order is required and O'Riordan identified three possibilities: centralized, authoritarian and anarchist. He chose a middle of the road, liberal option:

> . . . we must individually and collectively seize the opportunities of the present situation to end the era of exploitation and enter a new age of humanitarian concern and cooperative endeavour with a driving desire to re-establish the old values of comfortable frugality and cheerful sharing (p. 310).

Such a new era, involving a new political order based on a combination of local self-determination and supra-nationalism, can be achieved through education, he claimed, so environmental education will form a preparation for citizenship. Others are more doubtful: Pepper (1996, pp. 324–5), for example, is sceptical about the liberal arguments that, 'a basic unselfishness and communalism which is human nature would come to the fore in ecotopia's unalienated society, as it has never been allowed to do in industrial capitalism' (arguments that he terms 'simply hard to believe') and promotes instead the view 'that by making humanist, egalitarian and socialist aspirations a prerequisite for an ecological society, rather than something that is supposed automatically to follow, we can avoid making ecological society a repressive dystopia'. Social change must precede the resolution of environmental problems.

Some writers have argued that the revival of interest in environmental issues – mainly through the study of resources and their management – provides a contemporary linking of human and physical geography. Relatively little of the research and textbook writing indicates any integration of the two, however (Johnston, 1983a, 1989b), because the focus is almost invariably on the processes studied in one of the sub-disciplines only (as illustrated by most of the papers in the journal *Applied Geography*, which focuses on such issues, and by those in the *Geographical Journal*, which the RGS decided would concentrate on such topics from 2001 on). Physical geographers portray trends such as demographic growth, technological sophistication, urbanization, and demands for resources as catalysts for environmental processes and changes, but they take those trends for granted and do not address what processes generate them. Similarly, human geographers take the resources of the physical environment as given and do not inquire about the physical and chemical laws underpinning their genesis. Thus, while connections have been made across the human–physical geography interface, there has been no integration of the study of physical and societal processes. For human geographers their links with other social scientists are very much stronger than those with environmental scientists (as illustrated, for example, by the lack of references to the physical geography literature in O'Riordan, 1976, and Pepper, 1996); physical geographers, in turn, direct much of their scientific activity away from geographical journals towards work by their peers in other disciplines such as geology (especially of the Holocene), glaciology and hydrology (Johnston, 2003f).

Geographers have also turned their attention to other 'great questions' within contemporary society, such as nuclear weapons and nuclear power. They have criticized attitudes to civil defence policies and likely deaths from nuclear blast and fall-out (Openshaw, Steadman and Green, 1983), for example, with others setting that concern within a developing geographical contribution to peace studies (Pepper and Jenkins, 1985), and they have addressed issues relating to the siting of nuclear power stations (Openshaw, 1986) and the transport of nuclear waste. (Openshaw's work on these topics involved innovative prototypes of GIS technology: see p. 172.) Arguments for geographical contributions to other aspects of peace studies, such as international relations (van der Wusten and O'Loughlin, 1986), were advanced (Pepper and Jenkins, 1983), none more forcibly than Gilbert White's (1985, p. 14), which saw the human family 'tortured and driven by its newfound capacity to throw the whole set of processes out of kilter by more violent action'. The two editions of *A World in Crisis?* (Johnston and Taylor, 1986a, 1989; see also Johnston, Taylor, and Watts, 1995, 2002) focused on many of these issues, ranging from the macro-scale in the study of geopolitics to the investigation of individual human rights. And at the beginning of the twenty-first century, the impact of the attacks on New York's World Trade Center and the Pentagon led American geographers – under the auspices of the AAG – to address issues of geography's role in the promotion of 'homeland security' (Cutter, Richardson and Wilbanks, 2003).

Geographers and policy

Many of the studies referred to here have been concerned with identifying problems and suggesting solutions. Underlying their varied approaches has been the basic thesis that geographers should be much more involved in the creation and monitoring of policies. But what sort of policies, and what sort of involvement?

Berry (1973a) categorized planning policies into four types:

1. *Ameliorative problem-solving* involves identifying problems and proposing immediate solutions, as with the removal of a traffic bottleneck. Such solutions are likely to stimulate further problems in the future, since it is only the proximate cause that is tackled (the features of the bottleneck) rather than the real cause (the growth of traffic).
2. *Allocative trend-modifying: planning towards the future* involves identifying trends, evaluating what is likely to be the best outcome of the several which they imply, and then allocating resources to steer the system being planned towards that end.
3. *Exploitative opportunity-seeking: planning with the future* identifies trends and then seeks to gain the maximum benefit from them, irrespective of the possible long-term consequences. Compared with the previous category, this one has a dominantly short-term focus.
4. *Normative goal-oriented planning for the future* begins with a statement of goals, a vision of the future, and then prepares a strategy which will ensure that they are achieved.

Relatively little policy-making is of the fourth type; most involves elements of the other three, with general statements about goals but no clear strategy regarding a foreseeable future. Some critics interpret this as meaning that geographers who become involved in policy-making and evaluation are likely to accept the dominant forces in society uncritically, which leads to arguments that their claimed scientific objectivity and neutrality are an (often unrealized) cloak for ideological political judgements about the nature of society. Whatever their individual motives, such geographers are acting on behalf of interest groups (private and public) whose sustenance depends on maintaining an unjust and unequal structure to society.

Clark (1982, p. 43) accepted that, 'the academic community is not independent: there are no objective standards between competing explanations and thus policy advice'. Nevertheless he agreed 'with the principle of policy analysis and the involvement of academics in policy-making' (p. 48). That involvement cannot be presented as neutral and objective, however, since all social science 'explanations' are incomplete and compete with others to provide plausible accounts and prescriptions. He suggested that academic contributions to policy analysis should be guided by four propositions (pp. 55–9):

1. Academics must acknowledge their own values and beliefs in presenting policy alternatives and impact assessments;
2. Policy analysts must be advocates for particular causes rather than supposedly independent and objective adjudicators of knowledge;
3. Policy science should be critical of the *status quo*; and
4. Sponsoring institutions must encourage advocate briefs and make those briefs accessible to the public.

In accepting these, academics who become involved in policy analysis should be considered 'part of the political process' (p. 57) whose role would be to ensure that, 'Choices would be brought squarely into the open and be dependent upon the political, as opposed to expert, process' (p. 59).

The present situation idolises experts, and promotes a myth of social science as objective, neutral knowledge – although most governments carefully choose those experts who fit their own ideological presuppositions and whose advice is therefore very likely to be consistent with the desired direction of 'evidence-based policy'. Clark argues that social scientists cannot be neutral experts, because their 'values, interests and normative views of the world' mean that their presentations, although scholarly and rigorous, are necessarily partial. Sayer (1981) made a similar case in a slightly different context, arguing that any rigorous social scientific inquiry must be based on rationally defended value judgements; objectivity does not require neutrality. (Clark, 1991, has illustrated this from his experience as an expert witness in US court cases.)

In an essay on the role of urban geographers in applied work, Pacione (1990a) argued that practitioners have paid insufficient attention to conceptual issues underlying what they do. He derived the following 'principles or guidelines' to remedy those failings:

1. The notion of value-free research is an illusion;
2. Towns, as examples of places, are meaningful entities on which to work;

3. A spatial perspective is of substantial value;
4. The main emphasis of applied urban geography is on problem-solving;
5. A realist position provides the context for such work (see above, p. 240);
6. Analysis must integrate various spatial scales;
7. A wide methodological tool-kit of quantitative and qualitative procedures must be employed; and
8. Geography must integrate the findings of many disciplines.

Johnston (1990b) responded by posing six questions to Pacione: What is a problem? Are problems always soluble? What is science? What is a geographic perspective? Who solves? What sort of society? He concluded that some of the principles/guidelines are trivial and/or irrelevant, some are unsupported, and some are wrong; unless Pacione is prepared to tackle the fundamental issues of what problems are and how they can be tackled, he is unlikely to help those who want *both* an end to currently perceived problems *and* a society which would no longer produce such problems. Furthermore, few problems are soluble in the true sense of that term, which points to the need for resolution between opposing points of view, none of which have any straightforward or absolute claim to *absolute* truth. This point is made in another way in debates between Palestinian and Israeli geographers over the geography of Israel/Palestine (Waterman, 1985; Soffer and Minghi, 1986; Newman and Portugali, 1987; Falah, 1989; Waterman and Kliot, 1990; Falah and Newman, 1995; Newman, 1996).

Undertaking research characterized as 'relevant' – pertinent to tackling societal problems – raises major issues for the individuals concerned. Mitchell and Draper (1982, p. 2) argued that, 'when functioning as an advocate or consultant, the geographer must consciously decide how to resolve a conflict which may arise regarding the promotion of one perspective versus critical assessment and balanced judgement about all viewpoints'. There are also issues of ethics: 'when functioning as a pure researcher, the geographer must balance a concern for obtaining necessary information against a concern for respecting the dignity and integrity of those people or things being studied' (p. 3), which also applies to 'relevant' research. They claimed that geographers have largely ignored these ethical issues, and their professional bodies, unlike those of other disciplines, have promulgated no codes of conduct. Conflict is frequently likely between striving to 'discover truth' and respecting the rights of those being studied, however, and they advocated individual, institutional and external controls.

An example of the problem was raised in 1996 within the newly-merged RGS-IBG. The Shell oil company was one of the RGS's commercial sponsors prior to the merger, donating £40,000 per annum towards the costs of its Expeditions Advisory Service; this was presented as an example of the sort of commercial sponsorship for geographical work which academic geographers could benefit from within the merged society. In late 1995, however, several members of the Ogoni people in the Niger delta region of Nigeria, including a well-known author Ken Saro-Wiwa, were sentenced to death by a military tribunal (in a trial which Western observers claimed violated their basic human rights) and were subsequently executed, despite political pressure on the Nigerian government, which culminated in its exclusion from the Commonwealth Heads of Government conference held in New Zealand in November 1995. Their 'crimes' were related to protests over Shell's treatment of the Ogoniland environment, where it was involved in exploiting major oil and gas fields. A number of academic geographers argued that Shell's corporate patronage of the RGS-IBG should be ended because of its environmental record there and its alleged complicity in the trial of the Ogoni leaders. A motion to that effect was passed by a very substantial majority at the Research Section (formerly the IBG) conference in January 1996 (an event that attracted considerable media attention worldwide) and the RGS-IBG as a consequence set up a working party to consider all aspects of corporate sponsorship, which proposed a code of practice and ethical guidelines but had little apparent long-term impact. (On the debate, see Gilbert, 1999. See also Watts, 2000.)

Most of the critiques of the arguments for greater involvement by geographers in policy analysis are entirely sympathetic. They make a case for *sensitive* geographical involvement; others question the grounds for such involvement and instead focus on the development of revolutionary theory (see p. 332). The latter focus almost entirely on applied work in the tradition of positivist, empirical science, in which the goal is perceived to be to improve well-being through contributing to one or more of:

1. The preparation of public (i.e. state) policies;
2. The development of commercial (i.e. profit-making) strategies; and
3. The attack on environmental problems.

Virtually none of this work is concerned with the applied 'arms' of the two other types of science identified in Chapter 1, leading to either greater self- and mutual awareness (see Chapter 5) or emancipation (Chapter 6). To that extent, most applied geography in the English-speaking world accepts, and seeks to serve, the ruling ideas.

The nature of applied geography has been restricted by some to work at the 'society–environment interface'. When launching the journal *Applied Geography* in 1981, for example, its founding editor followed Stamp (1960, p. 10), who defined the discipline's applied role as addressing 'some of the great world problems – the increasing pressure of population on space, the development of underdeveloped areas, or the attempt to improve living conditions'. Two decades later, according to Briggs (1981, p. 2), 'These problems remain. Indeed, they are growing; environmental problems such as pollution, damage to wildlife, destruction of habitats, soil erosion and resource depletion; the problems of human deprivation and inequality'. He set out the fundamental basis of applied geography as use of resources:

> The exploitation of scarce resources represents a dominating theme to human existence. It is from the pursuit of these resources and from the attempt to decide between alternative policies of exploitation, that not only environmental damage, but also the greater part of political, social and economic problems emerge; they can be seen as expressions of man's inability to organize himself and his world to his best, long-term advantage.

To overcome that inability, the applied geographer must be brave (p. 6): 'He needs to commit himself before he knows all the answers. He needs to be able to make public mistakes. But he must also be prepared to learn from them'.

Much of the applied work undertaken by academic geographers has been commissioned by one or more arms of the public sector and most geographers who have applied their skills in non-academic careers have probably entered the public sector too. Given the importance of the welfare state in the first four post-Second World War decades, this has not been surprising. Nevertheless, much work has always been done for the private sector too: for example, geographers such as Applebaum (1954) were involved in work for supermarket and similar companies in the United States during the 1950s and geographers were central to the establishment of an Institute for Retail Studies at the University of Stirling in the mid-1980s. Others, building on their expertise in spatial data handling, have moved into information management, including some who work in prestigious university business schools.

The pressure on university academics to obtain more external financial support for research activities in the 1980s and 1990s has stimulated much more work for the private sector – a trend accentuated by the attempts to reduce the size of the public sector and to increase competitiveness and efficiency in the provision of public goods (including, of course, higher education). Some of this work has involved spatial analysis in its various forms – as by the GMap company established at the School of Geography at the University of Leeds, which has applied and developed Alan Wilson's pioneering work on location-allocation models to a wide range of problems in, for example, operations research for health-care providers and the location of franchises for major car firms (Birkin, Clarke, Clarke and Wilson, 1990, 1996; Birkin, Clarke and George, 1995; Birkin, Clarke and Clarke, 2002). Much more of it has used geographers' skills in spatial data handling (what Openshaw and others refer to as 'adding value' to geocoded data) in the growing field of geodemographics, whereby marketing and other campaigns are spatially targeted to people living in areas where demand for particular goods and services is most likely to be generated (Batey and Brown, 1995; Birkin, 1995). Other work is in the areas of resource and environmental management.

Changing contexts and applied geography

The demands for greater involvement in what is generally termed applied geography have grown in recent decades, largely as a response to changes in the societal contexts within which Anglo-American human geographers work. This is not a surprising trend, according to Taylor's (1985c) analysis of the history of geography. In periods of economic recession, cutbacks in public funding for higher education and research can be expected, and to counter the loss of support geographers are forced to seek financial backing elsewhere (including arms of the state which contract for research); that backing is only likely to come if individuals within the discipline, and even organizations representing it, can convince potential sponsors of the value (i.e. potential 'profitability') of investing in geography and geographers. From this observation, and following Grano (1981), Taylor identified two external influences on disciplinary developments: 'Within academia geographers had to be given an intellectual foundation to satisfy intellectual peers, and outside in the wider world geography had to be justified as a useful activity on which to spend public money' (p. 100). These produce 'pure' and 'applied' geography respectively.

Both are necessary to a discipline's future, but the relative emphasis placed on each will vary over time and space:

> Outside pressures will be particularly acute in periods of economic recession when all public expenditure has to prove its worth. All disciplines will tend to emphasize their problem-solving capacity and we can expect applied geography to be in the ascendancy. . . . In contrast in a period of expanding economies and social optimism outside pressures will diminish and academia can be expected to be under less external pressure. Geographers will thus be able to contemplate their discipline and feel much less guilty about this activity. We can expect bursts of pure geography to occur in these periods.

Taylor identified cycles of pure and applied geography corresponding to cycles in economic prosperity, and Hägerstrand (1977, p. 329) reached a similar conclusion: 'When the world is stable and/or unhampered liberalism prevails, then there is probably not much to do for geographers except surviving in academic departments trying to keep up competence and train schoolteachers in how wisely arranged the world is'.

The period since the late 1970s should demonstrate applied geography in the ascendancy, according to Taylor's analysis, an expectation generally supported by experience of those years. Pressure to justify the discipline in terms of utility to economic goals was strong, and the search for research contracts of all types became much more determined (so that learned journals and newsletters began to list new grants and contracts won by geographers, and institutions such as the IBG prepared documents to promote the discipline that emphasized its utilitarian aspects, including one which graduates could show to potential employers). That pressure for applied geography has continued. Indeed, academic departments were continually required to canvass for research funds from research councils and outside sponsors (which they were apparently very successful at: Johnston, 1995b).

Changing the focus

The desirability of a continued period within which applied geography is in the ascendancy has been the focus of further debate of the type discussed above. Some clearly accepted and argued for that ethos, but their main concern was either with geography using its perceived particular skills in what Harvey (1973; see p. 327) termed the application of *status quo* theory (as in Pacione, 1990a, 1990b) or with exploring how geographers could make a committed contribution towards the achievement of change (Clark, 1982).

Bennett (1989a) based a case for a reorientation of what geographers do on a belief that there has been a major shift in the 'culture of the times', away from 'welfarism' – a consensus ideology aimed at 'improving the quality of life and provision of needs through collective and governmental intervention' (p. 273) – towards what he terms 'post-welfarism', which emphasizes individual rather than collective decision-making, and the role of markets rather than states (p. 286):

> . . . the emergent 'culture of the times' has been happier to see the market as both the creator and the provider of new wants. Rather than markets being seen as an inhumane and exploitative system, socialism and even corporatist social democracy have come to be associated with the odious and paternalistic treatment of individuals.

This led him to criticize geographers who work with 'social theory', and who accept the welfarist ethos, as being necessarily of the 'political left', and he challenged their 'core concept of relative deprivation and its consequential focus on relative inequality and hence "social" and "spatial" justice' (p. 285). Rather than a society in which 'every difference in outcome is translated into an entitlement to state intervention', which inevitably leads to a situation of 'total state intervention in everything', Bennett (p. 286) argued that:

> Where the Thatcher era has heralded consumer choice and economic change, social theory and socialist politics have sought to defend the mode of production and to trap people in labour-intensive work practices and unattractive jobs vulnerable to technological change. The spirit of market freedom of individuals has heralded a consumer and service economy which has offered the release from the least attractive toils and labours, and has seemed to offer the potential to satisfy many of people's most avaricious dreams.

This market-oriented society poses an important challenge to geographers' applied role. It has been embraced by a number of geographers, including some who work with GIS (see p. 176). Longley (1995, p. 127), for example, argues that spatial analysis using GIS technology can enhance business management systems enabling users 'to gain competitive advantage in sophisticated consumer-led markets'. He criticizes the 'deskilling of geography and planning' associated with arguments such as Harvey's (1989b; see p. 333) that quantitative research has produced little relevant output. Not only does the development and teaching of GIS equip students with 'a range of flexible skills for use in continually restructuring labour markets' (p. 129: see also NRC, 1997), but in addition the range of applications:

> ... provides clear testimony that quantitative spatial analysis is most certainly not preoccupied with techniques that do not work to analyse problems that do not matter. Social science that does not show interest in real world issues of popular concern is doomed to remain on the sidelines of academic respectability and perceived social relevance, and reinvigorated spatial analysis is central to the measurement and modelling of economic and social aspects of human behaviour.

Bennett portrayed the geographical research he criticized as focused on aiding government intervention in economy and society, without questioning its validity. He believed such intervention to be no longer viable, and he also rejected its underpinning critical stance, based on a critique of capitalism. He identified the intellectual challenge for geographers to involve dismissing notions of a welfare state founded on a social theory which emphasizes rights and relative needs, because policies based on such theory 'cannot be proved to work ... Even social democracy offers no easy solutions' (p. 287). But markets do fail, so:

> The two key questions for a post-welfarist society are: first how can support be improved by practical policies that can be demonstrated to work and are reasonably cost-effective; and second at what point does governmental action end . . . Hence what is needed is a better definition of what is 'socially' possible through collective action and what is not. Social theory and social democracy have, perhaps, promised too much and hence led to disillusionment in its own promises (pp. 287–8).

Answering those questions is central to the role he casts for geographers: 'The grand objective of the discipline should be to contribute to the debate around these issues. But it must be a contribution to practice'. This implies a discipline in which practical concern with means is more important than theoretical debate about ends. In a post-welfarist society:

> The welfare state, and its associated public decision-making, no longer have the privileged status that it can be justified by mere statements of belief in public or governmental goods: public goods and the policy that provides them have to be demonstrated to be effective in meeting social needs; policies have to work and be more effective than alternatives (pp. 288–9).

Bennett provided no detail regarding what such a post-welfarist geography would contain, though he referred approvingly to Openshaw's (1989) arguments (see p. 180). He offered two brief suggestions, however. The first is a criticism of Marxist and related work (p. 289):

> The key aspect ... is a better understanding of the structure of economic incentives and rights, rather than class ... We need to identify a new language not of class but of 'rights' or nature. By which I mean choice conceptions of rights which promote autonomy, freedom, self-determination and human development, and not 'interest' conceptions of rights which make people passive beneficiaries of the services of others.

The other is a recommendation that:

> For the academic discipline of geography this means adaptation of its frameworks of teaching and research. I would argue that one aspect of this requires more intensive training in analytical methods including model-based approaches, information systems and elementary analytical skills.

Thus geographers are called upon to participate in a re-evaluation of the welfare state, focusing attention on the limits to both individual choice and collective action, and to develop the analytical skills which will advance policy appraisal and so contribute 'useful knowledge to the research process, to policy debate and to practice' (p. 290). The extent to which the call will be followed, in the creation of a new form of applied geography, waits to be seen: in his commentary at the end of the book in which Bennett's chapter appears, Macmillan (1989b, p. 306) comments that 'the idea that the welfarist tradition is in terminal decline seems highly debatable'.

The 1990s did not see a return to the 'traditional' welfare state, however, but rather a continuation of the trends set by Thatcherism in the UK and Reaganism in the USA. The hegemonic ideology is now presented as 'neo-liberalism' (Brenner and Theodore, 2002a, p. 350), underpinned by a:

> ... belief that open, competitive and unregulated markets, liberated from all forms of state interference, represent the optimal mechanism for economic development.

As they point out, however, this belief is generally associated with new sets of policies of state interference in non-economic spheres – usually conceived as associated with promotion of economic success (Brenner and Theodore, 2002b) – as illustrated by the rise of the 'workfare state' (Peck, 2001; Painter, 2002) and increased levels of prison incarceration in the US (Gilmore, 2002).

Continuing debates

Geographers have undertaken a great deal of applied work over recent decades, in both public and private sectors and across a wide range of subject matter. In addition to the activities of those working within academia, many trained geographers are putting their expertise into practice – not least in the deployment of GIS, in which geographers play central roles in the training of students and practitioners and the development of software for a wide range of applications. This latter activity is probably more visible in the United States, where the AAG has a large applied geography specialty group and holds regular conferences as well as sessions at the Association's annual meetings.

Despite all of this, however, and in part reacting to contemporary changes in the discipline, a number of (mainly British) geographers have recently bemoaned their discipline's apparent relative failure to address major contemporary issues within society – i.e. to be sufficiently applied and relevant, and therefore influential. Peck (1999), for example, argued in an editorial entitled 'Grey geography?' that, 'human geographers have on the whole been conspicuous by their absence from substantive policy debates' (p. 131). Academic practice increasingly privileges research outputs in the form of journal papers (which enhance career prospects and a department's ratings) over 'practical and policy-oriented research':

> Policy research seems to have become the grey 'other' of academic research. While academic research appeals, with its cerebral and 'pure' processes of library-based learning and thoughtful contemplation, to the privileged scientific canon, policy research is often tainted by its association with cash, clients, contracts and reports-in-cardboard-covers. An appropriate analogy here might be with the distinction between manual and mental labour, where policy research is associated with 'getting one's hands dirty'.

The division between 'academic' and 'practical' research is potentially damaging to geography, he claims, with the latter being significantly neglected and undervalued. Such research need not be constructive – using the term in the sense of sustaining the *status quo* distribution of wealth and power, but it should be engaged and effective – 'Active participation in the formal policy process, and in the wider political domain in which this is embedded, is surely something that geographers would dispense with at their peril' (p. 133). He cautions, however, that some policy-research is 'shallow and simple' (p. 134) – aimed at quick fixes – as compared with that which is 'deep and complex': unfortunately, the former is more likely to have an immediate impact within policy communities, so that geographers wishing to influence policy have to find ways of being influential without compromising their ('deep and complex') academic strengths.

Massey (2000) expanded this argument. She noted that there had long been an antipathy towards the social sciences within political and policy communities, especially towards the 'soft' social sciences (i.e. all but economics), but that the UK's New Labour government (elected in 1997) was seeking to change that in its drive towards 'evidence-led policy'. However, one of the problems with such a stance is that the politicians and policy-makers remain those who pose the questions and call for the evidence which – in Peck's terms – may call for 'shallow and simple' responses. She argues that social scientists (including geographers) should be involved in both reformulating the questions and raising others that are rarely, if ever, asked. To do that requires a 'more in-depth and sustained relationship with policymakers' (p. 132) than has been the norm. She further exemplified her case regarding geographers' lack of impact with regard to regional uneven development in the UK, suggesting that public debates about this in 2000–1 were being conducted as if no research had been done on the issue. A government adviser had said in her presence that academics were 'a waste of time' who 'never came up with anything of real use to those involved in "real politics"' (Massey, 2001, p. 11). To some extent this confirmed her view that much of what we write as academics for academics (and perhaps their students) has no wider impact, but it also implied that the only research valued by policy-makers and politicians and, 'the only way to be politically or socially relevant was to come up with advice or answers on government policy' (p. 12). There is a need for a much wider engagement, deploying geographic theories and evidence to promote policy initiatives rather than accepting the agenda of others, but to do that geographers needed to tackle the negative public image of their discipline as 'boring, as being a joke subject, as being all about capes and bays'. Geographers have to tackle their intellectual image if they are to be heard and respected in the policy-making corridors.

A similar theme was developed by Leyshon (1995) and reiterated by Martin (2001a), who were concerned that geographers were not making a greater impact in debates about major contemporary issues, such as growing inequality (though see Philo, 1995). To Martin (2001a, p. 267), important but rarely asked questions include 'what are we doing geography *for*?' and '*for whom* are we doing it?'. In this context:

> Part of our endeavour must surely be to expose and explain the inequalities and injustices that our socio-economic and [sic] system produces and reproduces. And following from this, we have an obligation, indeed a duty, to assess and debate policy responses to those inequalities and injustices, with a view to exposing the limitations of existing approaches and helping to reshape political and public opinion as to possible alternatives. In short, there is a key role for the geographer as social critic, and a strong case for making geography a more activist endeavour.

But, it seems, we aren't, so that there is a missing agenda with regard to geography and public policy (Martin, 2001b) – and associated with this is a failure to meet what he sees as a 'moral duty' (p. 190). That duty involves an agenda with three main items: exposing and explaining inequalities; interrogating and evaluating existing policies and practices; and 'seeking to exert a direct influence on policy-making processes, at all scales, with the aim of producing more appropriate and more effective forms of policy intervention'. (The implication is that this should be an organized collective response, but later – p. 194 – he acknowledges that there is a case that such policy activity should be a separate response by individual geographers operating within their own academic and political agenda.). The main reason why we currently lack influence, he argues, is neither because we publicize our work insufficiently nor because we lack confidence in arenas beyond our immediate profession. Rather, it is because 'much of what is done under the banner or human geography is unlikely to be seen by policy-makers as being remotely germane to policy issues. The fundamental problem is that there is no readily discernible policy research agenda in the discipline' (p. 191). (In the United States, three senior figures sought to show geography's relevance to contemporary issues, following the events of 11 September 2001, with a book on the contributions geography could make to tackling the modern problems of terrorism: Cutter *et al.*, 2003.)

A major cause for geography's policy irrelevance, Martin argues (p. 194), is 'the postmodern/textualist/discursive and cultural "turns" that have had such a pervasive impact across the subject in the last few years'. These have enriched the discipline in a number of ways but nevertheless resulted in its further retreat from policy research and modes of inquiry: 'it is difficult to envisage how the vague abstractions and epistemic and ontological relativism of much of human geography research ... can form the basis of a critical public policy analysis' (p. 196). Hamnett (2003: see also Hamnett, 1997) agreed, claiming that geographers are not addressing major issues of global and national significance to anything like the level they should. For him, too, 'much recent cultural geography ... has been a retreat from substantive political engagement and social analysis in favour of superficial academic radicalism' (p. 2):

> ... *parts of geography are the new intellectual dilettanti: relevance has been replaced by irrelevance, reality by representation and social criticism by theoretical critique. For some, contemporary human geography has become an arena for theoretical play, little more. Regrettably, such frothy theoretical constructions are likely to be viewed in the outside world as ... nice to look at, nice to taste but insubstantial and not to be taken seriously* (p. 3).

Their prognoses differ, however. For Martin, human geography is suffering from a lack of empirical and explanatory rigour, as well as an intellectual bias against policy issues and a lack of political commitment. Insufficient numbers of geographers lack one or more of these. As he notes, to many empirical rigour implies 'positivistic, quantitative methods and formal (statistical and mathematical) analysis, and what is widely regarded as a misplaced search for general principles' (p. 197). It may, but it need not: rigour calls for a 'sustained attempt to interrogate ... evidence critically, to contextualize it thoroughly, to test propositions or to assess its wider relevance'. For Hamnett, on the other hand, 'Quantitative techniques and aggregate social research have been largely abandoned ... Analysis of large data sets has become totally *passé*, the object of suspicion or even derision as "empiricist" ' (p. 2; but see Johnston *et al.*, 2003).

In responding to these critiques, several authors have presented partial defences of the contemporary situation, while at the same time agreeing with the force of much that has been written. Several, too, highlight the constraints on academic work in this area, given other career pressures (e.g. Pollard *et al.*, 2000). Thus, for example, both Banks and MacKian (2000) and Pollard *et al.* (2000) argue that Peck focused too narrowly on a particular genre of policy research – emphasizing macro-economic issues to the neglect of others in social, environmental and cultural policy realms on which much is being done, especially at local scales: 'geographers are not abandoning policy – it is simply that we are approaching it from many more angles, guises and positions than Peck gives us credit for'

(Banks and McKian, 2000, p. 253). Peck (2000) responded positively, while at the same time stressing his preference for engaged policy research, 'which gets behind the backs – and, if necessary, under the feet or up the noses – of policy makers and elite actors' (p. 255). This involves creating a different image for geographers and their fundamental concerns: in contemporary society, neo-classical economic thinking is generally accepted as 'the commonsense of our age' (p. 256), whereas critical geographical thinking is not.

The response from Dorling and Shaw (2002) called for geographers to participate more in debates beyond their academic discipline and spend less time on 'internal discussions'. In order to get their arguments across to such wider audiences, they claim, geographers need concrete (i.e. empirical, quantitative) not abstract arguments, presented without any deployment of 'élitist jargon': the former are more likely to be reported in the press and eventually to infiltrate the policy-making arena. Geographers also need, according to their prescription, to interact more with other social scientists. At present, they do not value policy-related work, and are not very good at it when they try: they are also too inclined to jump on new bandwagons – and perhaps geography 'is an intellectual safety net, an academic refugee camp – a place where academics can work on whatever they wish to work on and not be disturbed by the need to conform to the traditions of other disciplines . . . a home for intellectual anarchists' (p. 638). Nevertheless, on a positive note they also conclude that (pp. 637–8):

> *Academic research does influence policy. . . . It also helps to form the values of both individuals and institutions. Most current policies are informed in some way by findings which were derived from university-based research at some point in the past. Most individual views are now very much informed by what children learn in schools from teachers, almost all of whom are to some degree influenced by what they learned at university. Similarly, academics in universities may perhaps have their greatest impact through their teaching rather than publication.*

So, as long as enough geography is taught in universities, eventually it will trickle through the educational system and influence later generations of policy-makers. Martin (2002) largely agreed with them, pointing to a malaise within geography – its 'inferior standing and profile in the wider academic, educational and public domains' (p. 643; see also Powell and Boyne, 2001, and the response by Mohan, 2003). For Massey (2002), however, Dorling and Shaw have a narrow conception of the 'political': one can become embedded in civil society in a wide variety of ways and arenas, gaining influence indirectly as a consequence. A discussion of British urban policy illustrates one such route (Amin, Massey and Thrift, 2000), whereas Smith's (1986) classic monograph on the geography of crime also illustrates the wider applicability of geographic research, and Pain (2003) illustrates a wide range of action-oriented research involved with 'bottom-up' activism rather than 'top down' policy initiatives. Meanwhile, Bonnett (2003) has called on university geographers to capitalize on public interest in their subject matter and connect with this in critical and engaging ways.

Conclusions
Many of the arguments for applied geography locate it within the spatial-science approach to the discipline; that which is applicable is that which is based on empiricism, as illustrated

in Pacione's (1999) substantial overview of 'useful knowledge' in geography. But each of the three types of science identified in Chapter 1 has its 'applied arm' (see p. 20): hermeneutic sciences have as their goal the development of self- and mutual understanding, a project shared with the critical sciences, whose emancipatory aspirations seek similar understanding within the wider context of appreciation of the economic, social, cultural and political contexts within which individuals and groups are embedded. Whereas radical geography sought emancipation largely in the context of class interests, therefore, that imbued with the cultural turn promotes a wide range of identity politics, within which class is only of the foundations (May, 1996b), and which the gender and sexual politics that feminist and allied work in geography brought to the fore within the discipline. Such emancipatory intentions may extend further, both opening people's eyes to the nature of the world and leading them towards alternative scenarios. Thus Blunt and Wills (2000, p. x) introduce their book on dissident geographies by classifying them as sharing 'a political commitment to overturning prevailing relations of power and oppression', aiming to change both geography and the world.

Such applied goals are political and ideological to those who oppose them – but no more so than those promoted within the constraints of empirical science: the difference is that whereas the latter are largely supportive of the *status quo* – in particular its reliance on market mechanisms founded on the ideology of private property – the former challenge it, and argue for altered economic, social and political arrangements. As Harvey argued in 1974, the crucial questions to be asked about any work claiming to be 'relevant' are 'relevant to whom?' and 'for what?' (Harvey, 1974c). Nearly thirty years later, Wills and Peck (2002, p. 667) argued that, 'In some ways, there has never been a better time to practice radical geography', with the discipline and its core concepts central to debates on issues such as the injustices of globalization, 'the erosion of democratic and progressive institutions and the inequities and repressions of daily life'.

10
A changing discipline?

It must be considered that there is nothing more difficult to carry out, nor more doubtful of success, nor more dangerous to handle, than to initiate a new order of things. For the reformer has enemies in all those who profit by the old order, and only lukewarm defenders in all those who would profit by the new order.

Niccolò Machiavelli, *The Prince*

I was only fifteen when I chose geography as my field. Twelve years later, in 1957, I received my doctoral degree. So ended my long period of formal training. Ever since, I have not only taught and done research in geography but I have breathed and lived it. How was (is) that possible? How can geography, a rather down-to-earth-subject, have such a hold on me, offer me 'salvation' when, from time to time, my personal life seemed to be the pits? I couldn't have answered properly as a teenager or even as a newly minted PhD. I can give a well-rounded answer only late in life – in retrospect, for the meaning of geography has expanded over a lifetime. It grew as I grew.

Yi-Fu Tuan (1999, p. 93)

The preceding chapters have outlined the major debates among Anglo-American human geographers since 1945 regarding their discipline's contents – what it studies, how, and why. The chapter titles themselves indicate that several very different approaches to the discipline have been advocated; their contents suggest a large number of academics promoting new arrangements but being resisted by defenders of the old order – to a greater or lesser extent! The purpose of this final chapter is not to assess progress within those approaches (Lowe and Short, 1990), let alone to establish whether they have contributed towards the attainment of 'higher levels of intellectual, social and physical well-being for [our] fellow men [and women]' (Wise, 1977, p. 10); indeed, according to some interpretations, progress in the Enlightenment sense of that term is not feasible (Barnes, 1996). For, as Bassett (1999, p. 28) sets out in detail, one's determination of whether there has been progress depends on how that concept is defined. Geography may have made one or more of: *institutional progress* – becoming more firmly established and influential within academia; *empirical progress* – in that it can better predict some aspects of the 'reality' it studies; *explanatory progress* – being better able to explain through concepts and theories that which it studies; *conceptual progress* – with its theories having wider scope and greater internal consistency; *progress in inter-subjective understanding* – we can now appreciate better how we and others see the world; *pragmatic progress* — our understanding allows better public policy; and *emancipatory progress* — we are freed from illusions about how the world works.

Over the period discussed in this book, progress along several — if not all — of those dimensions may have been achieved. Assessing that is not the basic concern here, however. Rather, the evaluation returns to the issues raised in Chapter 1, where several different models of the development of scientific disciplines were presented. No formal testing of those models is presented, for no methodology has been outlined that would allow such a task. Instead, the general relevance of the ideas presented there is assessed against the material outlined above.

Human geographers and models of disciplinary progress

Along with members of almost every other scientific and social science discipline, human geographers have been attracted to the ideas and language of Kuhn's paradigm model (Harvey and Holly, 1981, p. 11):

> ... the use of the word paradigm has become fashionable in geography as well as having become a pivotal concept for courses in geographic thought on both sides of the Atlantic. Thomas Kuhn has become as familiar to students of geography as Hartshorne or Humboldt.

Kuhnian ideas were applied in the 1960s and 1970s with relatively little reference to the major debates they had stimulated throughout Anglo-American academia, however. Most human geographers relied, it seems, on the first (1962) edition of *The Structure of Scientific Revolutions*; they seemed unaware either that, 'The loose use of "paradigm" in his book has made [it] amenable to a wide variety of incompatible interpretations' (Suppe, 1977a, p. 137) or that, 'Kuhn's views have undergone a sharply declining influence on contemporary philosophy of science' (1977c, p. 647). Furthermore, Kuhn (1977) substantially revised his ideas later (see also the exegesis of his work in Barnes, 1982, and the recently-published books on Kuhn referred to on p. 7) and argued that it would be rare for a paradigm as he understood it (puzzle-solving within a normal science framework) to appear in the human sciences because their goal is 'new and deeper interpretations' (Kuhn, 1991, p. 23). Geographers at that time displayed a general tendency to adopt ideas from other disciplines rather uncritically. Agnew and Duncan (1981, p. 42), for example, argued that:

> Recent reviews and programmatic statements concerning trends in Anglo-American human geography leave the impression that little attention has been given by geographers to the philosophical compatibility of borrowed ideas ... that the political implications of different ideas have largely been ignored ... and that controversy on source disciplines or literatures has not excited much interest.

Their examples do not include the import of Kuhnian ideas into geography, but their conclusions certainly hold in this case. (For a critical discussion of geographers' importing Kuhnian ideas, see Mair, 1986. It could have been used as one of the examples in Symanski and Agnew's — 1981, p. 2 — treatment of 'order and scepticism in geography', in which they argue that 'geographers have given too much attention to the search for order and not enough to skepticism'.)

Kuhnian concepts were first used in the geographical literature by Haggett and Chorley (1967), as part of a normative argument for a revolution in geographical method – and, perhaps surprisingly, in a book that they produced from a conference designed to introduce school-teachers to their 'new geography'. The book was reprinted in several paperback sections and widely used as an undergraduate text. Nevertheless, the context of its production does have echoes of Goodson's (1988) claim that geography is one of the few academic disciplines for which the pressure for its establishment in universities came largely from school-teachers (on which see our discussion in Chapter 2). Chorley and Haggett argued that the then dominant paradigm, as they defined it (discussed in Chapter 2 of the present book), could not handle either the explosion of relevant data for geographical research or the increasing fragmentation and compartmentalization of the sciences. They proposed a new 'model-based' paradigm (p. 38):

> ... able to rise above this flood-tide of information and push out confidently and rapidly into new data-territories. It must possess the scientific habit of seeking for relevant pattern and order in information, and the related ability to rapidly discard irrelevant information.

The new paradigm had been launched more than a decade previously (see Chapter 3 above); Haggett and Chorley's goal was to spread the new ideas, and to win British converts to a new orientation of work within geography. In the same book, Stoddart (1967b, p. 512), used the concept to promote an 'organic paradigm' – as a 'general conceptual model'. When that essay was reprinted in 1986, he added as a footnote 'that I would now take a less enthusiastic view of Kuhn's analysis' (Stoddart, 1986, p. 231).

Haggett and Chorley were attracted by the concept of scientific revolutions. A similar argument was presented by Burton, whose paper appeared at almost the same time as Kuhn's book. Burton (1963, p.113) introduced the term 'quantitative and theoretical revolution', and argued that:

> An intellectual revolution is over when accepted ideas have been overthrown or have been modified to include new ideas. An intellectual revolution is over when the revolutionary ideas themselves become part of the conventional wisdom. When Ackerman, Hartshorne and Spate are in substantial agreement about something, then we are talking about the conventional wisdom. Hence, my belief that the quantitative revolution is over and has been for some time. Further evidence may be found in the rate at which schools of geography in North America are adding courses in quantitative methods to their requirements for graduate degrees.

Davies (1972b) also used Kuhnian terminology in the title of his book, *The Conceptual Revolution in Geography*. He identified a change from contemplation of the unique to adoption of 'the more rational scientific methodology' (p. 9) as a revolution: none of the contributions reprinted in his collection refer to Kuhn, but their context is clearly influenced by Kuhnian ideas. A year later, Harvey (1973) used the term, like Haggett and Chorley, in a normative sense in his search for a new world view: the goal was to promote a revolution in geographical practice rather than – as Kuhn portrayed it – describing a revolution emerging from the anomalies thrown up by failures in normal-science puzzle-solving.

The authors cited so far used the paradigm concept (probably unwittingly) at either the macro-scale of a world view or the meso-scale of a disciplinary matrix (see above, p. 11, and Mair, 1986). Others employed it either as a general descriptive tool (e.g. Buttimer, 1978b, 1981; Holt-Jensen, 1981, 1988 – see also Asheim, 1990; paradigm has the largest number of entries in the index to James and Martin, 1981, and remains one of the most-commonly cited terms in the later edition – Martin and James, 1993), or as a framework for summarizing sub-disciplinary changes (Herbert and Johnston, 1978). Kuhn's micro-scale concept of a paradigm as an exemplar has also been deployed: Taylor (1976), for example, identified seven separate revolutions during the preceding decades and Webber (1977) proposed an entropy-based paradigm (see p. 129).

Harvey and Holly (1981, p. 31) identified five paradigms within geography during the last century, associating each with an individual scholar:

. . . we can tentatively assign paradigmatic status to . . . Ratzel with the paradigm of determinism, Vidal with that of possibilism, Sauer with the landscape paradigm, Hartshorne with the chronological paradigm and Schaefer with the spatial organization paradigm.

They were focusing on 'schools of thought' associated with particular scholars, some of which ran concurrently rather than consecutively. They claimed that a single paradigm dominated the 1960s. Whether it was stimulated by Schaefer, as they claim, is open to question, despite the views of Bunge, 1979, and others; Cox (1995, p. 306) claimed that, 'Schaefer arguably was rescued from intellectual oblivion only in order to provide some philosophical justification for what was happening in human geography at that time', though Getis (1993), reported that Schaefer's paper was widely read at the University of Washington in the late 1950s (see also Berry, 1993). Some of Wheeler's (2002a) data cast doubts on Harvey and Holly's claim regarding dominance. The 1970s were then characterized by a 'diversity of viewpoints' (Harvey and Holly, 1981, p. 37), within which spatial organization remained important. Zelinsky (1978, p. 8) called that decade one:

. . . of confused calm, or rather of pluralistic stalemate, as geographers explore a multiplicity of philosophical avenues and research strategies . . . without that single firm conviction as to destination that guided most of us in the past.

The discipline was technically more capable, substantively more catholic, philosophically more mature, internationally more merged, socially more relevant, and academically more linked to other disciplines, he claimed, and these would probably lead to a continued plurality of approaches: 'I happen to believe that, more than anything else, this philosophical coming of age, this rising above the superficiality and tunnel vision that blemished so much geographical work earlier in this century, justifies' (p. 10) the title of his edited collection – *Human Geography: Coming of Age*.

Although some were uncertain about the relevance of Kuhn's concepts to changes in the 1970s and 1980s, in comparison with the 1950s and 1960s, others were less equivocal. In his introduction to a collection of essays on *The Nature of Change in Geographical Ideas*, Berry (1978a, pp. vii, ix) claimed that 'The changes in geographical ideas that we have discussed are distinctly Kuhnian'. The other contributors' essays provided little supporting evidence for this claim, however, and Berry's own contribution suggested that pluralism and inter-paradigm conflict were much more common than periods of normal science. Writing of geographical theories of social change, he noted (Berry, 1978b, pp. 19–22):

... a diversity arising from the mosaic quality of modern geography ... they have ... moved from one paradigm to another, and in the last decade they have been extremely dynamic. ... With multiple ideas and multiple origins, modern geography could rightly be characterized as a mosaic within a mosaic (Mikesell, 1969).

Gauthier and Taaffe (2003) also use the term 'revolutions' to describe what they identify as three major changes in American geography during the twentieth century according to six criteria – type of change; pace of change; intensity of accompanying debate; operational characteristics (or core concepts); impact of the change; and context for the change. Paradigms were also the core organizing framwork of a discussion of changes in geomorphology (Orme, 2002).

Human geographers' critiques of Kuhnian applications

Kuhnian concepts and terminology have been widely used by human geographers, therefore, although some treatments of recent disciplinary history entirely ignore this literature (Freeman, 1980a, 1980b) and others make little use of it: Buttimer (1993, p. 70) has a single, brief reference to Kuhn, for example. Livingstone (1992), after noting that (p. 14), 'In the wake of Kuhn's treatise, a batch of historians working in various disciplines set out on a paradigm hunt, looking for paradigms, paradigm-shifts, and what not. Geographers were no exception', concluded that some, like Haggett and Chorley, Berry, and Harvey, used the concept of a paradigm as 'little more than a flag for rallying the troops' (p. 24) to a new cause. Gould (1994, p. 196) argued that, 'They challenge, sometimes with deliberate overstatement, using polemic to grab the ear of an established coterie, and rhetoric to persuade it of its folly'. Berry claimed that this was necessary: in the context of Hartshorne's responses to Schaefer (p. 65) those promoting the new approach in the late 1950s were engaged in a debate with the 'discipline's luminaries' (Berry, 1993, p. 438):

Mainline geographers were suspicious, threatened, antagonistic; and we reciprocated. We felt we had to fight and fight we did, earning reputations for brashness and abrasiveness. So be it: if we had not been aggressive, geography would have rolled over us. Instead, we tried to roll geography.

In that fight they sought support from the emerging field of regional science (see p. 91), and as a consequence of their victory, according to Morrill (1993, p. 442):

I believe we saved geography from extinction as a serious university discipline, by attracting and training good students, by writing articles and books that developed theory and method, by gaining a foothold in science at large, and by applying these methods and theories to contemporary social problems.

Nevertheless, he still finds geography's position 'weak, fragile and almost invisible' (p. 443), 'we survived but did not succeed in the goal of propelling geography into the mainstream' because 'much of geographic work ... was not good enough' and some of the best spatial scientists 'defected'.

Livingstone's (1992, p. 24) attitude to discussions of Kuhn and the revolutionary fervour of some spatial scientists was that, 'The details of these (and other similar cases) need not be reviewed here. Suffice to say that their revolutionary gung ho spirit of triumphalism was scarcely what Kuhn had in mind as he portrayed the mega-level Gestalt-shifts in the history of science'. Many of the presentations were superficial, however (see Graves, 1981), both cavalier and uncritical in basing their descriptions on Kuhnian foundations. Mair (1986, p. 357) includes previous editions of this book in that category, claiming that it 'rarely reaches beyond a superficial comparison of the Kuhnian model and the recent history of human geography'. Nevertheless, he does recognize that it, like other evaluations, concludes 'either that Kuhn's ideas are irrelevant to the historiography of geography, or that they 'fit' only when stretched almost beyond recognition' (p. 345). Hubbard *et al.* (2002, p. 26) are also critical of the use of the paradigm concept in geography and its treatment in earlier editions of this book (although we should clarify here that the fifth edition of *Geography and Geographers* had also concluded on page 389 that 'Kuhn's model does not fit the experience of human geography since 1945 therefore.') . They note (p. 26) that:

> In particular, the idea that geography has moved through unified (and generational) paradigms glosses over the ideas and practices associated with those who did not conform to the dominant or fashionable way of doing things. The consensus among geographers at any one time that there is a best way of doing things has seldom been complete or stable, and to pretend that it has been so is to obliterate the voices of many researchers. In relation to the recent history of Anglo-American human geography, we therefore need to be mindful of the fact that it is often white, English-speaking, middle-class, heterosexual, able-bodied male academics who seek to define the Zeitgeist and identify which ideas are most useful to progress. The net result of this is that dissenting voices – and alternative traditions within geography – are often maginalised or obliterated in the pages of geographical history. . . . you should be wary that most histories of geography can serve to legitimate the careers of an academic elite while obliterating the views of others regarded as insignificant.

Livingstone (1992, p. 25) found that, 'it became plain that much of this writing [about the applicability of the paradigm concept] amounted to misdirected effort', but agreed with Mair that 'even among [the] ... critics the flavour of Kuhn's work still lingers. The Kuhnian ghost, it seems, is proving rather hard to exorcize from the history of geography'. Nevertheless, he welcomed the sociological approach to disciplinary history which the adaptation of Kuhn's ideas heralded; it countered the belief in 'conceptual cumulation, disciplinary progress, and internal chronology', and encouraged contextual readings in its stead.

Other geographers have been very sceptical of the value of a Kuhnian interpretation, with two claiming that it has 'distorted even perverted the development of geography' (Haines-Young and Petch, 1978, p. 1). The concepts of revolutions and normal science have been criticized as providing poor descriptions of geography in recent decades (e.g. Holt-Jensen, 1988). Individual geographers may have experienced personal revolutions and rapid shifts from one paradigm to another – at the meso- if not the macro-scale. (Harvey, 1973, 2002, indicates this for himself: see the essays in Billinge, Gregory and Martin, 1984; the editors – p. 11 – quote Cox, Gould, Olsson, Scott and D. M. Smith as additional examples). Sheppard (1995, p. 287), employing citation data, contrasted a drastic shift in the discipline's 'master weavers' (the term is drawn from Bodman's, 1991, 1992, depiction of the most-cited human geographers) from spatial science to social theory during the 1980s, and also argued that:

It is of interest to note that 8 of the 12 social theorists [all of the geographers discussed are classified by him as either spatial scientists or social theorists], as well as a large number of other influential individuals in the social-theory group, began their careers within the research traditions of spatial analysis.

Among them, he identified three cohorts:

1. Those who wrote classic spatial analysis papers of the 1960s (he cites Bunge, Cox, Harvey, Johnston, Olsson, Pred, Scott, Soja and Webber);
2. Those: 'whose early work was solidly within spatial analysis, and recognized as such, but for whom this work did not represent a major period in research careers that shifted rapidly from spatial analysis to Marxism and social theory' (he lists Dear, Massey, Peet, Taylor and Thrift); and
3. Those whose careers began in the late 1970s with contributions to spatial analysis when it was already under heavy criticism, 'only to re-identify themselves prominently with the concerns of social theory' (the names given, and trajectories discussed, are Gordon Clark, John Paul Jones – and himself!).

For Sheppard, therefore, there have been only two major competing world views – the spatial scientists' versus the social theorists': most of the debates discussed in this book can presumably either be encapsulated within that competition or involve controversy within a world view (over disciplinary matrices and/or exemplars, but not basic orientation, which Barnes – 1996 – portrays as for or against the Enlightenment project with its belief in progress and universal truths).

To claim that such individual experiences can be amalgamated into disciplinary revolutions strikes some observers as both inapt and inconsistent with the evidence (Bird, 1977, p. 105): 'Perhaps so many revolutions in so short a time indicate in themselves either a continuously rolling programme, or something basically wrong with the overturning metaphor'. Bird (1978, p. 134) suggested that mono-paradigm dominance of a discipline is inconsistent with 'the fact that society itself is organized around more than one major principle'. The focus of Bird's criticism is not clear, however: it is much more convincing on the world-view scale than at that of the disciplinary matrix, for example, and even less so at the scale of the exemplar.

Stoddart's criticism was even more pointed; he initially saw some value in the paradigm model (Stoddart, 1967b) but later argued (Stoddart, 1977, p. 1) that:

. . . the concept sheds no light on the processes of scientific change, and readily becomes caricature. I suggest that as more is understood of the complexities of change in geography over the last hundred years, and especially of the subtle interrelationships of geographers themselves, the less appropriate the concept of the paradigm becomes.

His analysis showed both the absence of consensus (normal science) and the slow pace of change (which is more readily represented in Lakatos's schema: p. 12). In his view the paradigm concept became part of the 'boosterism' image with which geographers conducted debates (Stoddart, 1981a):

> ... the paradigm terminology has been used to illuminate either the establishment of views of which a commentator approved, or to advocate the rejection of those he did not (p. 72) ... the concept of revolution bolsters the heroic self-image of those who see themselves as innovators and who use the term paradigm in a polemical manner ... those who propound the Kuhnian interpretation have done so in ways which tend to make it self-fulfilling (p. 78).

He argued (Stoddart, 1977, p. 2) that, 'There is scope for sociological enquiry into the extent to which the concept has been used in recent years as a slogan in interactions between different age groups, schools of thought, and centres of learning'.

Billinge, Gregory and Martin (1984, p. 6) claimed that Chorley and Haggett's initial use of Kuhn's terminology was 'In some measure ... only gestural' because although they clearly distinguished between normal science and extraordinary research 'the "anomalies" within the traditional paradigm which were central to Kuhn's thesis were never identified in any detail'. Chorley and Haggett were pressing for a revolution in the nature of geography, but it was not a revolution generated by the failure of the previous paradigm (using failure in a Kuhnian context). Billinge et al. pointed out that the term 'paradigm' was being used more for propaganda than for historiography – thereby potentially gaining prestige by locating their would-be revolution alongside those in physics described by Kuhn (Taylor, 1976). With regard to the latter, they accepted that the Kuhnian model should be rejected, but argued that since Kuhn himself did not expect the model to fit the social sciences, such a conclusion is hardly surprising. Nevertheless, they did identify insights in Kuhn's work that may be of value in the study of a social science like human geography, such as his concept of the paradigm as what constitutes, or 'gives form to' (Billinge et al., 1984, p. 16), scientific activity by providing the 'maps' with which scientists are socialized into a discipline or sub-discipline. Science takes place in 'heterogeneous settings' with their own 'rules and resources' (p. 17): it is a 'localised' activity, which occurs within communities and hence its study is necessarily a study of community sociology.

Mair (1986, p. 359) took the criticism further, contending that, with the single exception of Billinge, Gregory and Martin:

> ... geographers have entirely misinterpreted Kuhn's contributions. They have been wrong on Kuhn in the simple sense that the skeletal Kuhnian model is misrepresented as Kuhn's major contribution. More fundamentally, however, they have been wrong on Kuhn in misconceiving his entire project.

For him, the main values of Kuhn's work are:

1. The concept of the exemplar as an analogy to be used in the creative process;
2. The notion of incommensurability in the comparison on competing paradigms; and
3. The clear need to study the sociology of scientific communities.

Geertz (1983 – see above, p. 6) has also stressed the last of these points. For others, the important issue is the absence of clear 'revolutions': Chisholm (1975a, p. 89), for example, concluded that:

> ... by using prose as the medium of exposition and by concentrating on the essential underlying ideas, it is manifest that continuity of thought dominates over the apparent discontinuity which some have called the 'quantitative revolution'.

Slightly later, however, he admitted that, 'in respect of analytical techniques geography has indeed experienced a revolution. However, in terms of the subject-matter studied the position has changed less rapidly' (p. 173: there is a confusion of scales implicit here, between exemplars and disciplinary matrices, if not world-views) – and it was only later that the problems addressed by geographers 'caught up' with their analytic ability to handle them. (See also Gregory, 1978a, pp. 52–3, and 1994, p. 55.) Although they use the term revolutions, Gauthier and Taaffe (2003, p. 523) are close to Chisholm in their characterization, writing of a

> ... continuity model with surges superimposed to represent the three "revolutions". During the surges the weaknesses of the previous paradigm are usually stressed and caricatured. ... Later, as the surge subsides, we begin hearing more about hapless conceptual babies being thrown out with the bathwater of the old paradigm. The merits of some aspects of the previous paradigm are discussed and recognized, and a certain amount of continuity sets in – perhaps only leading to a wave of enthusiasm about a new paradigm.

Despite such criticisms, relatively little has been done until recently to suggest an alternative sociology, either one based in another model of the history of science or one developed specifically to represent the situation in human geography. Wheeler (1982) found Lakatos's work attractive, arguing that several separate programme cores could be identified in contemporary human geography (he cites areal differentiation, spatial science, cognitive-behavioural approaches and Marxist structuralism), in each of which the operation of positive heuristics (see p. 12) can be identified. These research programmes are in continuing competition, whose nature will change over time (Wheeler, 1982, p. 4):

> Given the deficiencies in Kuhn's scheme and the rather ill-defined nature of geography, it seems unlikely that the future of the discipline will be characterized by sequences of revolutionary change interspersed with efficient problem solving. Moreover expectations of revolutionary progress appear to be unjustified. Instead it seems that a variety of approaches, which will undoubtedly wax and wane in popularity, will continue to be employed.

Mohan (1994), drawing on the notion of a product cycle that has informed much work in economic geography, suggested that a rapid turnover of theories had recently occurred within geography as a consequence of pressures within the academic profession. He identified 'four "big" approaches over the preceding decade hailed as capable of explaining social reality' alone (p. 387: the four were critical realism, structuration, postmodernism, and postcolonialism). He associates this with the growing 'commodification of knowledge' and the competition for status within academia, so that:

… these ideas were not paradigmatic and their diffusion into geography uneven. Likewise some of these intellectuals [those promoting the 'big approaches'] have persisted with their theoretical frameworks and have not continually experimented with new ones … [nevertheless] Many academics fight for currency and exploit 'new markets' in knowledge. This increased competition has, in the spirit of flexible specialisation, resulted in the 'niching' of academic thought despite the recent emphasis on trans-disciplinary pursuits.

Some of the forces impelling these trends are general within academia, but one at least is specific to geographers (p. 389):

As a trans-disciplinary subject geography has often lacked kudos in wider social theory. The result is that geography has tended to borrow and incorporate any social theory that appears spatial or contains spatial metaphors. The increased commodification of knowledge has served to heighten this tendency. For example, we have had Giddens' locales, Foucault's disciplinary spaces and Mohanty's contested cartographies. It seems that few have time to actually apply any of these potentially useful ideas before the next theoretical innovation superseded them.

Disciplinary matrices and exemplars come and go at an alarming rate according to this view, with geography equated to a supermarket in its concern for 'turnover time' and short shelf lives as its practitioners seek status through the novelty of their approaches.

One alternative sociology of science that has been addressed (and found wanting by some: Bassett, 1999) is actor-network theory (see Barnes, 2001a). This takes the notion of a community of scholars linked together in networks, but takes it further by extending the nodes on that network to inanimate objects as well – such as publications – many of which may be mobile rather than fixed, and immutable rather than transient. A discipline, in this context, is thus an inter-locked network of entities, 'material and non-material', 'social' and 'natural' (Barnes, 2001a, p. 528) and understanding its development involves studying how strong network links are developed: the powerful entities (probably though not necessarily individuals) in those networks are those that have greatest influence on disciplinary change – as Barnes (2001a, 2001b) illustrates for two different periods in economic geography.

Geography and its environment

Some geographers have argued (in similar terms to ours here) that the major influence on their discipline's content and approaches comes from a combination of its wider environment, particularly its economic, social and political milieux, and changes in other subjects: in general, it is believed that geography is more likely to change because of developments in other disciplines than vice versa. Stoddart (1981b, p. 1), for example, introduced a book of essays as demonstrating 'that both the ideas and the structure of the subject have developed in response to complex social, economic, ideological and intellectual stimuli'. Evidence for this was presented, as a second theme of the essays, in the reciprocal relationship between geographers and their milieux: 'throughout its recent history geographers have been not only concerned with narrowly academic issues, but have also been deeply involved with matters of social concern'. For Hubbard *et al.* (2002, pp. 25–6), for example:

*. . . contemporary theoretical approaches to human geography need to be understood contextually,
in relation to at least three things. . . .*

1. *The* history *of geography – how geography has actually developed in terms of what geographers
have studied (and how).*
2. *The* sociology *of geography – how institutions, social networks, journals and educational structures
(particularly universities) have shaped the development of geography.*
3. *The* psychology *of geography – how individual geographers have adopted ways of thinking about
and interpreting the world, whether conformist or confrontational.*

One of the most detailed deployments of the contextual approach is Livingstone's (1992)
The Geographical Tradition, in which he refers to the history of geography as 'situated
messiness' with the absence of any 'essential nature' (p. 28). In the discussion of any
particular theory within geography, therefore, this means that (p.29):

*. . . it will never be wrong to ask of any theory: Why was it put forward? Whose interests did it advance
or retard? In what kind of milieu was it conceived and communicated? How adapted was it to its
cognitive and social environment?*

His chapters on geography in the late nineteenth century ('A sternly practical pursuit;
geography, race and empire'), the first half of the twentieth ('The regionalizing ritual:
geography, place and particularity') and the 1950s–1960s ('Statistics don't bleed:
quantification and its detractors') illustrate his theme that (p. 347):

*. . . geography changes as society changes, and that the best way to understand the tradition to which
geographers belong is to get a handle on the different social and intellectual environments within
which geography has been practised.*

Within those environments, the character of geography was contested, though not necessarily
by all of its practitioners within the particularities of any one time and place: 'Sometimes the
conversations have admitted a range of geographers, from time to time only a select group
were equipped, or permitted, to take part' (p. 358). But as we get closer to the present, the
latter condition became rarer, with fewer 'partisan apologists . . . [striving] to monopolize the
conversation in order to serve their own sectarian interests'. Likewise, Gregory (1994, p. x)
writes that the concept of a 'discipline' such as geography implies 'a set of sovereign concepts
. . . [and] a rigorous policing operation' when in effect it involves individuals and groups
traversing 'nomadic tracks. . .[and] new lines of flight' as they explore alternative ways of
producing and reproducing knowledge – as fully illustrated in the various chapters of
Geographical Imaginations. Elsewhere he has argued for the importance of studying both 'life
geographies' (the career trajectories of individual geographers, including their spatial
movements) and 'intellectual spaces' – the places in which ideas are crystallized and developed
(Livingstone, 2000b; Johnston, 2004c): Barnes (2003) has undertaken this in his exploration
of the history of locational analysis, emphasizing that rather than be characterized by
inexorable, linear progress 'halting, local contingent, factors . . . shaped it' (p. 91).

Many geographers who employ a contextual approach stress that any changes in a
discipline's contents (revolutionary or not) are associated with significant events in its

milieux. Thus Berdoulay (1981, p. 10) wrote of the role of the *Zeitgeist* (or spirit of the age) influencing what geographers do. Gräno (1981) took this much further (Figure 10.1); geographers are a sub-set within the community of scientists, which is itself a sub-set of wider society, whose culture includes a scientific component that strongly influences the content of geography. The community of geographers is an 'institutionalizing social group' (p. 26), providing the context within which individual geographers are socialized and defining their disciplinary goals within the constraining and enabling characteristics of the external structures. A major goal when geography was established as an academic discipline was to create an identity, to 'establish an object of study that could be regarded as geography's own and that differed from that of other disciplines' (p. 30). This, he claimed, was a 'passive education role' (p. 32) disseminating knowledge of society-environment inter-relationships, but it was replaced in the 1970s when 'geography began to contribute actively to a transformed and replanned world. Applied geography was created and geography became a *profession* outside the small world of the university' (p. 32).

Geographers made and continue to remake geography: 'It was the external goals of society that brought the establishment of geography as an academic discipline. This took place without any noticeable contribution from any other scientists' (Gräno, 1981, p. 30; see however, Stoddart, 1986). The initial period of institutionalization involved geography operating largely as a pedagogic subject, meeting the needs for training teachers whose activities would promote the interests of the expanding 'nation-states' (Capel, 1981; Taylor, 1985c; Goodson, 1981, 1988; Fuller, 2000). Capel (1981, p. 36) referred to the creation of geography as a discipline resulting from:

> . . . the presence of geography in primary and secondary education at the time when the European countries began the rapid process of diffusion of elementary education; the necessity to train geography teachers for primary and middle schools was the essential factor which led to the institutionalization of geography in the university and the appearance of the scientific community of geographers (p. 36).

(See also Freeman 1961, 1980a, and, for a more critical account, Rieser, 1973.) As the context changed, however, so did geography for (Capel, 1981, p. 66):

KNOWLEDGE   ACTION   SOCIAL STRUCTURE

Figure 10.1 *Geography's context (Source: Gräno, 1981, p. 19)*

The established community employs strategies tending to reproduce and amplify itself. Never will it opt for self-liquidation; the community will defend its survival, even if other communities of scientists investigate similar problems with like methods, or if the logical incoherence of the conceptions that they defend is revealed ... Everything will be sacrificed for the reproduction and growth of the community, including the coherence of the very conception of the discipline: different conceptions can defend themselves in distinct moments or even simultaneously, without putting into doubt the continuity of the science practised.

The promotion of national interests, especially national commercial interests, by nineteenth-century geographical societies provided the context for the creation of geography as an academic discipline (see the essays in Bell, Butlin and Heffernan, 1995), and subsequent changes in economic, social and political structures and needs generated new demands, to which geographers responded. (See, for example, Taylor's, 1993, evaluation of different geographical perspectives on 'the global' during the twentieth century.)

Scott's (1982) answer to the question, 'why do geographers, regional scientists, urban economists and others study the spatial patterning of social events?' (p. 141) provides an example of disciplinary reconstruction in the context of changed circumstances. He concentrated on the ways in which late capitalism is organized, not through market relations but rather involving bureaucratic intervention by an all-embracing state. (Note that this was written in 1982 in North America; a decade later, the context was very different.) Because 'the geography of late capitalist society is shot through with problems and predicaments' (p. 145: Scott uses geography there in the vernacular sense – Johnston, 1986b – rather than the professional) state action is required in 'more subtle forms of social, cultural, and psychological management' (p. 146) on which science thrives. By participating in those managerial tasks, however, scientists contribute to the creation of countervailing forces, with which they may also become involved:

... the endemic crisis of economic production and growth in late capitalist society creates the need for specific problematics and policy discourses out of which technical control may be accomplished. But technical control creates an advanced set of social conditions in which a countervailing set of human predicaments makes its appearance – alienation, the destruction of affective human relations, the repoliticization of human and regional planning, and so on (p. 152).

Hence the radical and humanistic responses to spatial science.

The link between the external environment and the practice of economic geography was examined further in a later essay, in which Scott (2000, p. 18) began by claiming that:

Over time, economic geography has behaved in a manner quite different from that which might be expected of a rationally ordered discipline pursuing some pre-ordained epistemological mission. Its historical course has been notably responsive to changes in external economic conditions, to the unfolding of political events, and to the play of professional ambitions and rivalries. ... These imply that any answer to the question 'what are the central problems of economic geography?' is likely to be historically contingent, even if the inertia of tradition and its institutionalization in a system of higher education means that important continuities can be deciphered over time.

In this context, 'one of the few general principles that seems to be reasonably evident in this connection is that the concrete questions and problems that society faces at any given historical moment tend also – in one way or another – to become burning questions and problems for practising social scientists' (p. 19) – though it is not clear whether this simply reflects social scientists responding to the perceived world or rather social scientists being required to reorient their concerns by external 'paymasters'. Thus economic geography can be characterized by a series of episodes – spatial analysis and regional science; behavioural geography (a 'brief interlude'); political economy; localities (another 'brief interlude'); and a world of regions within globalisation (see also Clark *et al.*, 2000b). Scott eschews Kuhnian terminology – neither paradigms nor revolutions are identified – in part because none of his episodes or interludes has entirely ended (pp. 32–3):

> ... I have tended to treat the main episodes in the postwar history of economic geography as occurring in relatively discrete blocks of historical time. To be sure, each of these episodes can be described in terms of a moment of emergence, a subsequent period of rapid efflorescence, and a period of decline, where the latter period is often extended over a number of decades. As a consequence, almost all of the episodes identified here continue to leave traces on the work of practicing economic geographers today, just as adherents of this or that tendency whose heyday is long past continue to produce and publish scholarly work right down to the present. The intellectual landscape of economic geography at any given moment in time is therefore best represented as a sort of intellectual palimpsest rather than as a unified front.

Scott doesn't assess the value of work published long after the episode's heyday, however. Further, he implies – in part by his criticism of Barnes' (1996) work – that the response to economic changes by economic geographers is largely determined by those changes, leaving relatively little room for debate and decision-making (with just a few economic geographers left practising an obsolescent craft long after others have moved on). For Barnes (2000, p. 12), context is both constraining and enabling (see the discussion of structuration on p. 242):

> The discipline arose because of a set of contextual factors, and as those factors changed so did economic geography. Further, those factors ... entered into economic geography's very constitution, shaping the questions it asked, the methods and tools it used, and the range of answers it deemed acceptable. For sure, the discipline had its own geniuses, people who were brilliant in thinking up new ideas, but their creativity was always ... informed and tempered by a wider context.

Thus, for him, economic geographers 'invented' and 're-invented' economic geography through the accepted practices of the sub-disciplinary community(ies). Scott (2000, p. 34), too, accepts that changes in disciplinary practices are invariably subject to 'a welter of critique and counter-critique' and may reflect 'the changing fortunes of different professional groups as those whose human capital is sunk in waning problematics engage with those pressing forward with new approaches in the endless struggle to come out on top in the stock-market of ideas', but seems less prepared than Barnes to identify particular individuals having a significant role in this struggle.

For Thrift (2000, p. 692), the cultural turn – Scott's final episode – 'saved economic geography from what might otherwise have been a musty oblivion. By the 1980s, economic geography was in a pretty moribund state, at risk of boring its audience to death'. Now, however, work in economic geography – and other social science disciplines too – no longer takes place on economists' terms: the nature of the economic, and the assumptions and principles of the discipline which studies it, is open to debate (see also Amin and Thrift, 2000).

There is no necessity for geography, however, no 'specific necessities in scientific knowledge' (Gräno, 1981, p. 65). Rather, according to Taylor (1985c, p. 93):

> Geography is a social institution. Like all such institutions its value to society varies over time and place. The creation of any social institution is a result of a group of people who identify a particular need and are able to find the resources to meet that need. As needs change the institution has to adopt to survive.

It may fail; the forms of scientific discourse created and practised may not command sponsorship and resources. Scott (1982, p. 151) argued strongly that success requires identification of clear social needs: 'only discourses that are posited upon existing problems of social life and practice, and upon existing political interests, stand any likelihood of commanding a significant consensus of scholars and scientists'.

There is nothing deterministic in these arguments, for they depend on geographers identifying what is and is not sustainable in a particular context and successfully promoting themselves as able to meet the perceived needs. How they do this will reflect what Berdoulay (1981) calls their individual 'circles of affinity', social networks extending outside their disciplinary base. To appreciate those one must appreciate biographies, as Buttimer (1981) argued and several volumes of autobiographical recollections illustrate (Buttimer, 1983; Billinge, Gregory and Martin, 1984; Moss, 2001; Gould and Pitts, 2002; see also the fuller presentations in Haggett, 1990, and Gould, 1999). Buttimer (1983, p. 3) defends such an approach because, 'each person's life echoes the drama of his or her times and milieu; in all, to varying degrees, the propensity to submit or rebel. Through our own biographies we reach toward understanding, being and becoming'. Autobiography provides what she terms 'choreographic awareness', the 'moral, esthetic, and emotional commitments which are related to lived experience and which underpin a scholar's eventual choice of epistemological presentation and style of practice' (p. 12). It can indicate aspects of disciplinary history that are absent from the written record of research papers and student texts, isolating the influence of 'pioneers of geographic thought whose inspiration flowed through their teaching and field experiences, through their counselling and listening' (Buttimer, 1981, p. 88). Biographies offer an alternative source, but there are few on geographers who have contributed significantly to the contemporary period – Paterson, 1985; Johnston, 1986g, 1993a, 1996b, 2000b, 2002a – and the few biographical dictionaries available are limited in their treatment of geographers' intellectual contributions relative to their career paths (Larkin and Peters, 1993).

Geographers and their networks

The autobiographical theme was taken up explicitly by Pred (1979, 1984a), using the language of time geography (p. 148). For him (1979, p. 175),

... under contemporary circumstances, the 'life content' and the spatial and temporal attributes of an individual's life path are apt to be highly influenced by the sequence of independently existing specialized roles — created by institutions and technology — that a person is able to occupy. ... For the academic whose writings are rooted complexly in the past, it is evident that the content of those works would be different if the individual's life path had been linked differently with a variety of specific, independently existing limited-access roles of both an academic and a non-academic character.

Thus he was able to trace the evolution of his academic interests from his interactions with people who were with him in particular places at certain times — their 'path convergences' — as well as items that he read and appreciated.

A particular feature of a scientist's autobiography, however, is that the encounters which influence career development and change need not be inter-personal. Bird (1975, 1985) used Popper's concept of World Three (the world of recorded knowledge) to show how geographers can be strongly influenced by reading both ancient and contemporary sources, so that our milieux are not as bounded (in time and space) as are those of people who rely much more on inter-personal transmission of information (see Johnston, 1984e, 2004a) — though, of course, we are reliant on what materials are, or can be, made available to us locally, which is increasing very rapidly through developments in information technology (Adams, 1995). As noted earlier with regard to actor-network theory (p. 369), non-human artefacts — notably though far from solely published items — are crucial elements in the circulation of knowledge and as influences on individual's academic developments. Technological developments have speeded up this circulation process, with major impacts on changes in knowledge construction — although, as always, uneven accessibility to relevant items can have a significant influence: items that are widely circulated are more likely to be influential, as was the case with the mimeographed discussion papers circulated by graduate students at the heart of the 'quantitative revolution' in Seattle in the 1950s (Johnston, 2004a). Nevertheless, whether such 'knowledge communities', many of which are located in a particular place (Pinch, 1998), eventually significantly influence the direction that their discipline takes depends on their relative power to change others' research practices.

Geographers have extended their work on contextual influences on their discipline's content and direction by drawing on the ideas of sociologists of science regarding 'situated, or local, knowledge'. In presenting an 'alternative history' of economic geography, for example, Barnes (1996, p. 105) argued that understanding geographers' practices requires knowing 'something about the local context and not overarching principles of rationality'. Thus (p. 124):

Economic geographers will continue to do economic geography in the way that they have always done, that is, by creatively drawing upon existing ideas and beliefs and responding — sometimes with great originality and imagination, other times with less of each — to the concerns of their own local context. ... this is all there is to practice. There is no foolproof method of directing inquiry.

The nature of the 'local' is not addressed in depth, however, so that the interaction of 'place as context' with 'World Three as context' remains unexplored. (For Barnes himself, for example, the key local context was the department of geography at the University of Minnesota in the late 1970s where he was a graduate student, working with Fred Lukermann and Eric Sheppard and alongside Michael Curry. A decade later, he was working in Vancouver and still writing with Curry and Sheppard, who were in Los Angeles and Minneapolis respectively.) But his later work illustrates his theme through the examples of economic geography and locational analysis: rather than linear sequences of individuals building on their predecessors' work, he emphasizes the 'halting, local, contingent factors that shaped it' (Barnes, 2003, p. 91). While there may be progress in the technologies deployed – as with computing power and communications – there is no 'relentlessly progressive' trajectory of thought but rather a series of 'enormously bright, imaginative, intellectually vibrant and creative' individuals carving out their own histories 'reflecting the particular circumstances of their origins'. Like Livingstone (2000a), Barnes argues that all knowledge is locally produced, geographically and historically bounded in its generation – though as communication without travel becomes easier, one wonders for how long the local can be defined in terms of places rather than as networks – the 'locales' (or settings for interaction) of knowledge-production within geography may increasingly be a punctiform set of sites (themselves far from permanent) among which there are frequent flows, rather than a relatively small, bounded space such as the Department of Geography at the University of California, Berkeley in the 1930s.

The case for understanding the changing nature of geography contextually closely parallels that promoted by structurationists for appreciating all human activity; the operation of human agency must be analysed within the constraining and enabling conditions provided by its environment. Thus Johnston (1983d, p. 4) enlisted structuration theory as a framework for analysing the changes in human geography that are the concern of this book, arguing that, 'the content of a discipline at any one time and place reflects the response of the individuals involved to external circumstances and influences, within the context of their intellectual socialization'. Mikesell (1981) took a similar position, though without the language of structuration, describing the history of geography in the United States as a sequence of 'temporary enthusiasms or episodes' (p. 9), which he claimed were responses to contemporary stimuli – hence the popularity of urban studies in recent decades, the relative decline in foreign-area studies for some years after the American retreat from Vietnam, and the impact of national concern about the physical environment in the 1970s. He also suggested that physical milieux influenced the culture of individual geographers:

> The first generation of American geographers grew up in a country that was still strongly influenced by the mores of small towns. Most of the students now attracted to geography are products not only of an urban but increasingly of a suburban environment ... the geographical profession has changed and is changing as a consequence of the suburban, middle-class origin of most of its current members (p. 12).

Porter (1978) advanced similar arguments, identifying two types of American geography: a midwest version that 'was a characteristically optimistic, action-oriented, "can-do" kind' (p. 17); and a Californian geography, based on Sauer, 'historical, uncompromisingly academic, speculative, suspicious of government, keenly interested in cultures other than the dominant Anglo culture of the United States' (p. 18).

This environmental influence thesis should not become environmental determinism, however: Mikesell noted that urban geography flowered in the 1950s and 1960s not only in Chicago but also in Iowa. But it stresses the importance of studying human geography and human geographers in context and, as Capel (1981) noted, the disciplinary community (or major elements within it) will seek to maintain its identity by bending to perceived shifts in their milieux (as clearly demonstrated for anthropologists by Patterson, 1986). Mikesell (1981, p. 13; see also Johnston, 1996d) also argued – following Harvey (1973) and others – that reactions to environmental shifts involve individual scholars seeking not only to defend and promote their chosen discipline but also to defend and promote their own status and careers within it:

> ... innovation will continue to be regarded as a virtue. Much of the development that has already taken place in American geography is a consequence of the attempt of individual scholars to stake a claim for themselves, to be or at least to seem to be different from their rivals. The fact that most academics see virtue in innovation means that there is reward for innovation.

Mikesell did not discuss the scale of the innovation, however; does it have to involve developments within the positive heuristic of a research programme, to use Lakatos's terms, or does it require the launch of a new research programme? Can one bring potentially greater rewards, and disasters, than the other?

One little explored aspect of this sociological approach is that it focuses on the winners rather than the losers, on those whose ideas have a major impact on at least parts of their discipline. Many ideas are not taken up at the time they are initially published, but are later revived, whereas others are never followed through because the published versions languish largely unread. Why some individuals and their ideas are much more influential than others is an intriguing aspect of a discipline's history, as illustrated by: the belated recognition of Hägerstrand's seminal work (Duncan, 1974b: Morrill, 1984, p. 62, notes that his visit to Seattle in 1959 'had an electrifying impact'); the slight impact of Wreford Watson's ideas regarding the social geography of cities, which predated the studies referred to earlier (p. 92) by several years but were almost ignored (Robinson, 1991; Johnston, 1993a); the focus on only one aspect of Gottmann's voluminous writings (Johnston, 1996b); and the lack of influence that Dickinson's pioneering work on functional regions and urban areas had on 1950s–1960s urban geography (Johnston, 2000b, 2002a). In general, it seems that the most influential are those who are well-networked with other influential scholars, especially those who have been trained in large graduate schools with a clear agenda for the discipline. Morrill recognized this with regard to the developments he was involved in during the 1950s and 1960s, at both the University of Washington (see p. 75, and also Berry, 1993, on the depth of the resources available there, outwith as well as inside the geography department) and Northwestern University (Morrill, 1993, p. 442):

> This happened when and where it did because at a few universities there was a fortunate combination of an emphasis on interdisciplinary study, existing development of theory in these related fields, notably regional economics and sociology, some students ready for change, and some faculty ready to encourage them.

Following this, leading proponents of the new approach were able to promote the discipline more widely within the social sciences, thus achieving what King (1993, p. 545) refers to as 'the professionalization of geography as a social science'.

Context is not deterministic, of course: it provides opportunities. Thus Hanson's (1993) reflections on graduate school at Northwestern University, whilst stressing the positive aspects of the education provided (such as the concern for theory and explanation, the importance of space, and the emphasis on standards of evidence), also noted that (p. 553):

> Coexisting with these considerable strengths, counterbalancing and – at the time – sometimes overwhelming them, were blind spots and inflexibilities bred in revolutionary fervor and in earlier bruising conflicts with the reigning paradigm. Our mentors exuded a certain intolerance, a certain hubris, a certain arrogance, a certain certainty that there was only one way to the Truth, and they knew it. There was a caricaturing and a trivializing of the idiographic/regional approach, much as today critical social theorists caricature and demean spatial analysis and scientific geography.

Hanson and some of her contemporaries were involved in the emergence of behavioural geography as a counter to some of the 'certainties' being advanced by the 'space cadets' (her term for the Seattle-trained spatial scientists then on the staff at Northwestern, p. 534): 'By dethroning economic man and replacing him with a variety of decision makers, behavioral geography ignited the first glimmer of the notion that each viewpoint is partial, incomplete and dependent on the subject's [i.e. the decision-maker's] location'. She was led, by her questioning of the assumptions which underpinned the then popular theories, to the realization that (pp. 555–6) 'people's decision making and behavior are not immune to context but are conditioned, *inter alia*, by time, place, class and gender', an argument which applies as much to geography itself as to that which it studies – indeed the recent growth of GIS reflects geographers (among others) capitalizing on what they have seen as a major opportunity for their discipline.

A structure for the discipline?

The structure of geography can be represented as a network of nodes and flows – very much like Haggett's representation of the spatial economy (p. 113). The nodes are individual geographers and the flows are the ideas and research findings they share with others in formal situations such as teaching and conference sessions, during informal conversations, and in their publications. Some of those flows are situated – in classrooms, conference halls, and the informal settings for conversations; others are widely available in many places, such as the libraries of geography books and journals; an increasing proportion is even more generally available, to anybody with access to the World Wide Web. Individuals move between settings, and as they do so may be either or both influenced by others or influential on them. They also refer to the flow material, again hoping to be influenced by what they access, and submit further material to the network, hoping to influence others indirectly through what they write.

Within those networks, some individuals and some flow materials are more important than others – i.e. the network nodes can be structured into a hierarchy of influence. In part, the degree to which either an individual or a flow material is influential reflects settings. With regard to direct inter-personal contact, for example, it is often suggested that dense concentrations of workers with linked interests are more likely to stimulate important developments through interaction: there are intellectual economies of scale and scope. This is the basis for the growth of major graduate schools, and of research groups of staff in many university geography departments: they provide the critical mass whereby ideas are generated, refined and disseminated – both within the school and outwards, as graduates get posts elsewhere and convey the message to new settings. Examples of this can be found in the twentieth century history of human geography, as with the 'Berkeley school' under Sauer (Spencer, 1979), the historical geographers trained by Darby (Prince, 2000), the 'Washington school' under Garrison (see p. 75), the 'Chicago school' of urbanism (Yeates, 2001; Berry, 2002c), plus a number of more specialized groupings (see, e.g., Peach, 2003). To some extent the influence may be serendipitous: a student may enrol in a department not expecting to be supervised, or even influenced, by a particular staff member (or even other students) there. Unanticipated conversations at a conference may have a similar impact, and so forth.

The degree to which individuals may influence each other's mode of working is likely to vary, however, even if other possible factors are held constant. Some individuals may not be appointed to a large graduate school, for example, and so lack the access to a potential band of disciples: others are, but for some reason or another do not capitalize on that access – they may be 'lone scholars', difficult to work with, or studying topics that are currently relatively unpopular. Chance, charisma, and a number of other factors can result in some individuals having much more influence over the development of their discipline than others.

The same argument can be made about the impact of various publications: some are widely read and influential; others may attract few readers and be largely ignored (whatever their potential merits). To some extent this may also reflect the settings in which they are placed: a paper in a relative obscure publication that has a small circulation will be relatively invisible and may pass largely unnoticed, compared to one in a widely-circulated and referred-to journal. Similarly, some publishers are better able to get books widely purchased and adopted as texts. But there is more to the distribution of influence than such material conditions. There is little doubt that some authors are considered more innovative and stimulating than others – especially, perhaps, those who challenge the conventional wisdoms and whose writings can not be categorised, in a general sense, as simply contributing to normal science activity within the context of a given exemplar. They may move work on in a small way along established paths, but not stimulate wider debates about means and ends. Thus some authors' writings are more likely to be read and referred to (i.e. through formal – class reading lists; book reviews – and informal media) than others' – as is suggested by the large variations in the numbers of citations to particular authors and works. Given the pressure on time, and the great explosion of publications in recent decades, selectivity is necessary: people choose to read that which looks most relevant to their current concerns – whether that is a course that has to be taught or a research project advanced. Such selectivity is based on a number of criteria, such as whether the potential reader knows the author and rates her/his work highly, or the author's reputation, or advice that a piece is worth consulting – or just chance while browsing along a bookshelf (or through a bookseller's website) or through the pages of a journal (including the book reviews).

What we have, then, in the continuing operation of an academic discipline is a massive network of potential contacts only some of which are actualized. Knowing which have been, when and where, is not easy to discover. Some clues are given in published material – many authors acknowledge individuals who have helped them in their work, for example; references in a paper indicate the sources considered worthy of mention (although not necessarily all those accessed); and known biographical details (where a person was in graduate school, and when, for example) are suggestive. Autobiographical and biographical essays may fill in gaps – though these are relatively few – as also might obituaries. But in most cases we have only circumstantial evidence of who influenced whom, who read what and to what effect, and so forth: and such evidence is the stuff of books like this. (The items we have referred in this book to indicate our own selectivity in deciding what was of value to read and use in compiling our account.) Almost certainly, detailed studies of disciplinary networks would find them divided up into sub-communities – Geertz's (1983 – see p. 6 above) 'intellectual peasant villages'.

All of these contacts – direct and indirect, positive and negative – are not only the basic evidence for books like this, therefore: they are also the foundation of disciplinary change. Almost all intellectual endeavour involves and results from inter-personal interaction of some form, usually mediated by the written word (World Three in Popper's terminology: p. 375). What is of interest, however, even if difficult to determine, is how those micro-level contact patterns have any significant impact on the directions that a discipline takes at the macro-level. Or, in other words, do some individuals and groups (or individual written pieces) have a disproportionate impact – so that if they had not been on the networks the discipline might have taken other directions? There seems little doubt that in the early days of geography as an academic discipline this was indeed the case: among the small number of practitioners a few powerful professors, by virtue of a combination of and ability to disseminate ideas, were highly influential on geography's foundations (on which, see Lichtenberger, 1984). Since then, as the number of geographers has grown and the size of the network expanded exponentially, influence has been much more widely dispersed. Nevertheless, it may well be that certain paths would not have been followed – at least when and where they were, and with what effect – if particular events had not occurred. Almost certainly geography would have taken a quantitative turn at some stage in the 1960s, but would it have taken the particular form that it did if, for example, Hudson and Garrison had not taken up posts at the University of Washington in the 1950s, if a group of talented graduate students had not clustered there at the same time (some of them attracted there by Ullman's presence rather than Garrison's), if they had been unable to spread their ideas through discussion papers (Johnston, 2004a), and so forth? And would this book have taken its particular form – even been written at all! – if Chorley and Haggett had not been influenced by Kuhn's ideas in the mid-1960s (and a publisher had not perceived a potential market for it)?

Such questions are, of course, ultimately unanswerable counterfactuals, although by posing them it is possible to illuminate what did happen. They also illustrate the all-important contingency of academic life. A discipline like human geography is not a disembodied phenomenon with a life and trajectory of its own: it is shaped and continually re-shaped by geographers reacting to circumstances in particular milieux, the temporal and spatial situations in which they are placed and place themselves. We can present the history of geography as a changing melange of ideas and approaches, but that melange is a (far from planned) human creation: it is the sum of a large number of biographies.

The current context

The impact of external circumstances on geographical practice has been illustrated several times in this book. It has been very noticeable since the late 1970s as a consequence of economic recessions, cut-backs in higher education funding, attacks on social-science research (in 1996 the US House of Representatives voted to end funding for the social-science divisions of the National Science Foundation – although this was not enacted; a decade earlier the UK Secretary of State for Education insisted on the term social science being removed from the title of the Social Science Research Council, and sought to make its successor – the Economic and Social Research Council – more responsive to government and commercial agenda), and the policy prescriptions of the 'New Right' designed to sustain what has become widely known as 'flexible accumulation' (Hudson, 1988) through a 'free economy and a strong state' (Gamble, 1988; Johnston and Pattie, 1990).

Many have reacted to this by promoting human geography as an 'applied discipline', offering relevant skills for the attack on contemporary problems. In the December 1981 issue of the Association of American Geographers' (AAG) *Newsletter* an article entitled 'A survival package for geography and other endangered disciplines' indicated that (Kish and Ward, 1981, p. 8), 'On 19 June, 1981, the Board of Regents of the University of Michigan decided, by unanimous vote, to terminate the Department of Geography at the end of the 1981–82 academic year'. Their experience of this decision led Kish and Ward to suggest how other departments of geography could counter similar attacks. They emphasized the teaching role, recognizing the need to attract students in a competitive market and present 'our wares in a stimulating and excellent way' involving 'the virtues of applied geography. As students become more conscious of careers, there may be a corresponding need to increase a skill-oriented curriculum. This could demonstrate the relevancy of geography and enhance its appeal to students' (p. 14). Kish and Ward – 'To appease some traditionalists' – did not advocate reorganizing the entire corpus of geography, 'but only [an] attempt to broaden the appeal of geography to the student population'. (See also Ford, 1982; Powell, 1981.) Their prescriptions were written at a time in North America when, according to Haigh (1992, p. 185), geographers' peers saw their discipline as 'small, marginal and perhaps immature': the late 1970s had seen a net loss of 32 university departments, including one-sixth of those in 'private and denominationally funded institutions'. Avoiding the discipline's demise was presented as a crucial task (Wilbanks and Libbee, 1979), a problem stimulated by the absence of geography in most American high schools and the very small number of undergraduate students intending to take geography courses. Despite the vitality of geographical research, therefore, 'Geographical education is still regarded as a marginal activity by American schools and colleges' (Haigh, 1992, p. 189); the discipline there is a not only 'small, often beleaguered' (Koelsch, 2002, p. 274) but:

> ... it would be difficult to identify any other university study that in the course of the 20th century had achieved full departmental independence and programmatic recognition at the doctoral and research level in so many leading American universities, only to lose both by the end of that same century. At the pre-college level ... geography remains largely a minor component of social studies or of global education, taught most often by teachers with little or no background in the discipline.

Koelsch puts this parlous state down to the 'fracturing of any consensual view of what the discipline and its practitioners should be about'. In Australia recently, almost all of the separate university departments of geography have been merged into larger units, thereby losing a separate identity for the discipline in some cases (Holmes, 2002). And in the UK, too, similar mergers and closures characterized the first years of the millennium with more than one-tenth of the country's geography departments 'disappearing' — as separate entities, if not totally — causing concern among disciplinary leaders (Cooke, 2002), not least because the trends appear to be linked with a reduction in the number of secondary (high) school students taking geography, which for more than a century was the foundation for successful university departments (see below, p. 386).

Promotion of geography as an applied discipline was heavily emphasized in research as well as teaching in the USA. The announcement of a new editorial policy for *The Professional Geographer* in the AAG *Newsletter* for April 1992 reported that (p. 1), '[The new editor] hopes to emphasize work in applied geography and to include information on corporation activities, state and local government projects, Federal government activities, activities by United Nations and other international agencies, and research projects'. The need for more applied work has been widely accepted among American human geographers as a necessary means for their discipline's vitality. Mikesell (1981, p. 14) suggested that:

> ... geographers fortunate enough to have secure teaching positions will worry about what they should do. The best response to this concern could be a decision to do what they have been doing, but with a keener appreciation of context and a greater willingness to be influenced by environment.

The response has taken a variety of forms, with many arguing for a greater concentration on cartographic, remote sensing and geographical information systems skills.

This response is illustrated by a group of papers published by the AAG in 1995. In 1993, the National Academy of Sciences/National Research Council undertook its first major review of geography for nearly three decades (see p. 95). It established a committee of 16 charged with 'Rediscovering geography: new relevance for the new century' and given five objectives (Wilbanks, 1995):

1. Identify critical issues and constraints for the discipline of geography;
2. Clarify priorities for teaching and research;
3. Link developments in geography as a science with national needs for geography education;

4. Increase the appreciation of geography within the scientific community; and
5. Communicate with the international scientific community about future directions of the discipline in the United States.

Within this context, a report was commissioned from the AAG on the supply and demand for geographers. Introducing papers based on that report, Wilbanks (1995, p. 316) noted some challenges and opportunities:

> ... many geography programs in universities across the United States are already experiencing unprecedented growth in student demand. ...A major concern for geography should be that, because of supply limitations (e.g. a lack of additional faculty positions in geography departments) the demand will be artificially and arbitrarily truncated by limitations on course enrollments.

This is described as a 'very welcome but very difficult disciplinary transition from relative penury to relative abundance'.

The committee's report on the supply side of the equation (Gober et al., 1995a) referred to an earlier study (Goodchild and Janelle, 1988) on the internal structure of the discipline which found that (Gober et al., 1995a, p. 317), 'Technical expertise and interest in geographical information systems (GIS) were burgeoning, especially among young geographers, while regionally oriented specialities were shrinking'. (Turner and Varlyguin's, 1995, report on foreign-area dissertations in the same issue of *The Professional Geographer* shows that the latter trend was relative, not absolute.) To identify which skills and interests university departments of geography were focusing on, department chairs were asked about specializations and the occupations students were being prepared for. Of the 212 respondents, 139 identified at least one specialization, and the full list was:

> ... led by programs in environmental/resource management, techniques (GIS, cartography, and remote sensing), and urban planning. These tracks appear to be designed to prepare students for the occupations in which geographers traditionally have found work rather than to develop their interests in regional geography or the systematic specialties like urban, economic or physical geography that have traditionally formed the core of the academic discipline.

More specifically:

> We also asked chairs to indicate the specific occupations for which students were being prepared. The occupations indicated by the highest numbers of departments were (1) GIS/remote sensing specialist, (2) secondary school teacher, (3) cartographer, (4) environmental manager/technician, and (5) urban/regional planner. ... GIS was by far the most popular occupational trajectory (involving almost 11% of students enrolled in programs offering GIS training).

The committee also surveyed the labour market experiences of recent graduates (Gober et al., 1995b, p. 331), finding that, 'Among those who were employed and listed occupations closely related to geography, respondents clustered into five predictable occupations: teacher (15.6%), environmental manager/technician (12.9%), GIS/remote sensing specialist (10.5%), cartographer (8.2%), and planner (6.7%)'. They also studied the employers and job-seekers using the placement service at the AAG's 1994 annual meeting: 45 per cent of

the employers were looking for candidates with technical qualifications, and they comprised 80 per cent of all non-academic employers using the service.

Finally, the committee surveyed the future labour market by asking department chairs the areas of expertise of staff who would be retiring over the next decade, and also of those which they would be recruiting (Gober *et al.*, 1995c). Technical areas of the discipline predominated in the latter category, with GIS specified in 17 per cent of the cases – nearly 12 times more frequently than it was among the retirements. As the discipline reproduces itself over the next decade, according to these figures, the relative number of technical specialists would increase substantially, whereas traditional areas, such as agricultural, historical, political, cultural and economic geography, would decline substantially. The committee's conclusions, based on interviews with the AAG's corporate sponsors, implied a major shift in the nature of the discipline, as taught to undergraduates (p. 346):

> *The debate over geography as a broad-based liberal arts discipline or as a technical, semiprofessional field ignores the realities of the current labor market. Sponsors told us they want employees who can combine technical skills with a broad-based background. Geography's comparative advantage over other social sciences lies in its ability to combine technical skills with a more traditional liberal arts perspective. Successful geography programs will be those that are able to find the appropriate balance of field-based technical skills like GIS, cartography and air-photo interpretation with competence in literacy, numeracy, decision making, problem solving, and critical thinking.*

(See also Miyares and McGlade, 1994.) In this context, the review's conclusions – indeed its whole tenor – focused on technical skills: its first recommended response was that the discipline should:

> *Improve geographic analysis in a new era of data and analytical tool availability, related to broader needs of science* (NAS-NRC, 1997, p. 162).

Its student base could be enhanced if it were to:

> *Implement programs to support and assure the quality of the science content in kindergarten through grade 12 geography education . . .*

and:

> *Foster conceptually sound general education courses in geography as part of a liberal arts college education . . .*

while at the same time it should:

> *Develop programs that bring geographic perspectives to bear more effectively on business, government and other organizations at national to community levels* (p.164).

Little of this has occurred, however, and although geography was recognized in the mid-1990s as a 'core discipline' for contemporary education, no funding to develop school geography programmes had been made available (Richardson, 2003); in the 1920s, according to Schulten (2001), geography academics in the USA distanced themselves from their discipline's status in the country's schools, and this still appears very largely to be the case.

External pressures became just as great in the UK during the 1980s, with expression of the need for applied geography and the development of what are known as 'transferable skills' (problem-solving, group-working, IT awareness, etc.) within undergraduate curricula (see Matthews and Livingstone, 1996). Bennett (1982, p. 69), for example, found at the 1982 conference of the Institute of British Geographers, that it was:

> ... possible to discern a strong and growing set of foci which, if they do not yet demark a new core, at least show an emerging commonality of interest. For this writer these foci were a widespread assertion of 'relevant' research, the reassertion of quantitative and analytical methods, and the rejection of recent anti-empirical movements.

He welcomed these, noting that, 'hot [i.e. relevant] issues are not ones which British geographers are particularly noted for tackling en masse – and, as a result, the discipline has suffered a lack of public exposure, and a marked inability to influence public and private decisions'. Furthermore:

> ...At a time when higher education as a whole is under considerable challenge, and when geography as a discipline may suffer particularly severe pressure in some institutions it is heartening to see the emergence of concern with the hot issues expressed at this meeting (p.71).

Beaumont (1987, p. 172) echoed this a few years later:

> ... the issues raised for the next twenty years are a practical and developmental, rather than a research, orientation. The future is unknown, but it could be exciting, if geographers are prepared to become involved (probably with new partners) in doing geography.

Richards and Wrigley (1996, p. 41) presented the early 1990s as a period of even greater and faster change, arguing that in contrast earlier periods

> ... seem in retrospect almost to have been years of relative stability and calm, prefacing the maelstrom of change which swept through the whole British education system in the early to mid-1990s. ... This period has been one of system-wide expansion, of curriculum and quality control through external review ... and of institutional change. ... These have combined to alter, quite fundamentally, the size, nature and structure of British geography.

The assessment of teaching in university departments of geography was set in the context of a national agenda concerned not only with the quality of the education provided (that some believe conflicts with an over-emphasis on research: Gibbs, 1995; Johnston, 1996e) but also with the development of 'transferable skills' beyond the traditional focus on subject-based knowledge and a critical intellect (Johnston, 1996b). The assessment of research has produced not only a grading of all departments but also substantial differentials in funding (Johnston, 1993b), while government directives on research funding make it (Richards and Wrigley, 1996, p. 47):

> ... likely that future research will be constrained to ask specific questions, will be increasingly 'applied', and will be manipulated by government, business and industry for ends which are unlikely to assist the less material aspects of the quality of civilized life; and critical (social or environmental) science will be marginalized.

On the last point, however, it is important to note a considerable 'culture of resistance' among many geographers against such imperatives, as exemplified by the burgeoning work discussed in Chapters 6–8. To a considerable extent, this is because geographers in UK universities have been able to rely on a continuing stream of potential undergraduates wanting to read for degrees in geography. At the end of the twentieth century, for example, there were some 7,000 or so places available each year on geography honours degrees (in which the majority of the student's time will be spent on geography courses, especially in the final years), compared to only 4,000 or so who major in geography from all US universities. This large stream of UK would-be geographers results from the discipline's strength in the country's secondary schools and place in national curricula – itself a product of successful political lobby by bodies such as the Geographical Association (Goodson, 1988; Balchin, 1993; Walford, 2001; Johnston, 2003a). Almost all of the 7,000 students arriving at UK universities each year to study geography have a strong foundation in the subject having studied it for the previous ten years – a situation very different from that in the USA where most students arriving at university have not encountered geography at high school, and their understanding of the discipline rarely extends beyond basic geographical knowledge of where places are. Geography has not been a 'problem discipline' in most British universities, therefore; (most of) its departments can recruit good students and their graduates can get good jobs. There is relatively little need to focus on courses that will attract students by the 'employability value added' they might provide – though there is attention to this. The breadth of material in cultural geography and related subject matter taught in many of the departments currently reflects this: academic geographers in the UK are freer to teach a wide range of material at undergraduate level than is the case for their North American counterparts.

Despite this important difference between the two sides of the North Atlantic, reflecting long-established differences in the role of geography in the respective school systems, in the UK, as elsewhere, there is a need for continual vigilance in order to protect and promote the discipline's interests. In his 2002 Presidential Address to the Royal Geographical Society, Cooke (2002) identified several challenges facing the discipline in the UK. Key among these was the potential reduction of time given to geography in the school curriculum: the Society was working to sustain geography's central role, because it is 'unquestionably fundamental to public understanding of such enduring issues as social equity, globalization and the relations between environment and society' (p. 260; see also Thrift, 2002; Johnston, 2002b).

A generational model?

The importance of context as an influence on the nature of the practice of human geography suggests that the paradigm model might be rephrased as a generational model (Johnston, 1978c, 1979b; Taylor, 1976). Changes in the external environment provide necessary, but not sufficient, stimuli to changes within the discipline which may be interpreted as attempts to develop new research programmes, if not to launch a revolution and create a new normal science (see the discussion of Scott's work above, p. 372).

Associated with the external changes must be a set of conditions within the discipline itself which is sympathetic to the new demands of the milieux. In most cases, these conditions are best met by younger members of the discipline. Stegmuller (1976, p. 148) argues that, 'it is mostly young people who bring new paradigms into the world. And it is young people who are most inclined to champion new causes with religious fervour, to thump the propaganda drums'. To win influence, however, especially in times of resource shortage within higher education, younger workers need the patronage of some established members of the discipline (see Chapter 1). According to Lemaine *et al.* (1976, p. 5), for example:

> Mendel's work [on what is now termed genetics], and that of his successors, was a response to scientific problems. But the scientific implications of their results were not pursued until there existed a strong group of scientists who, owing to their academic background and their position in the research community, were willing to abandon established conceptions.

Such responses may involve attempts to create a new paradigm or new research programme, or they may only require new branches of an existing paradigm/programme. Whichever it is, even when establishment support has been obtained, success is more likely when certain criteria are met, including (van den Daele and Weingart, 1976):

1. An autonomous system of evaluation and reputation;
2. An autonomous communication system;
3. Acknowledgement of the new ability to solve puzzles within the confines of the disciplinary matrix;
4. A formal organization providing training programmes which allow reproduction and expansion of the new group's membership;
5. An informal structure with leaders; and
6. Resources for research.

These rarely create problems if resources are available; Capel (1981), Mikesell (1981) and Taylor (1976) all indicated that innovation is encouraged if it brings status, charisma and resources to the discipline. During periods of stagnation and retrenchment, however, conditions are less favourable and major shifts are more likely to be achieved by revolutions among existing members of the discipline. The generational model suggests that the latter is rare. With regard to the research record, Law (1976, p. 228) has counselled that:

> ... it may well be the case that scientists do lay special emphasis on the accounts in scientific papers, but my hunch is that there is immense (and non-trivial) variation between scientists on this count. For some, science is something you do in the laboratory, something you talk about, and something you get excited about. For others, science is what they write and what they read in the journals. I would even hypothesize (in conformity with the invisible college notion) that those who are generally felt to be of higher status locate science less in their journals than in their own and other people's heads.

Many academics are less active as researchers, and some get 'left behind' as changes proceed. The 'normal science' that they continue to teach is probably based on the world view, disciplinary matrix, and exemplars into which they were socialized. But their colleagues, socialized later and influenced by different environmental conditions, operate in different ways. The academic career cycle, in combination with a changing milieu, can produce a multi-paradigm teaching discipline, at least in terms of what is taught.

The key elements in the generational model (modified after Johnston, 1978c) are:

1. The external environment is a major influence on a discipline's contents, especially in the social sciences that are closely linked with that environment;
2. At times, the nature of this environment may change significantly, provoking a reaction among a minority of members of the discipline who try to stimulate change in disciplinary practice by its established members and to generate interest in that change among the youngest generation of research workers – the latter is usually much more successful than the former;
3. Together, this grouping presents a new 'school of thought', although in some cases opposing new schools may be stimulated;
4. The new school is co-opted into the disciplinary career structure;
5. The publications of the new school come to dominate the disciplinary research output, as the productivity of the earlier generation declines;
6. Students face two or more separate generational schools in a department's teaching syllabus; and
7. Over time, members of the new school attain seniority and political influence within the discipline.

Several consequences may follow. If a discipline fails to react to a changing milieu it could stagnate, and so innovators are encouraged. Another is that some potential innovators may be unable to influence their discipline, either because conditions are not conducive, the 'establishment' does not react positively to their suggestions, or they cannot obtain permanent positions within the academic career structure. Duncan (1974b, p. 109) illustrated these 'processes of resistance' using the example of Hägerstrand's (1968) ideas on spatial diffusion that were originally published in 1953; citation analysis shows that widespread recognition was much delayed, compared to the average for all publications in geography (Stoddart, 1967a). This was not, Duncan claims, because of either language or Hägerstrand's relative isolation in Sweden (though see Getis, 1993, p. 519, on the 'excitement' generated by Hägerstrand's visit to Seattle in 1960, which led to Morrill doing his PhD. work in Sweden), but the apparent irrelevance of his work to those steeped in another paradigm. Only when spatial science had been established was Hägerstrand's contribution recognized:

> Hägerstrand's own attempts to disseminate his work met rejection from adherents to orthodoxy, but later enthusiasm from those pioneering spatial science. The eventual relay of information to this community owed more to dogged personal effort than to the formal communication system of normal science, and general recognition was not achieved until professional allegiances were reorganized (p. 130: see also Johnston, 1993c, 1996b).

Even when a new idea has been recognized, however, several virtually independent groups may be involved in its development (Gatrell, 1982).

In all of these debates about changing communities within geography and orientations to the discipline, the threefold hierarchy introduced by Kuhn should be remembered (see p. 7). Changes – whether revolutionary or not – are much more likely to occur at the lowest level of the exemplar than at the level of the disciplinary matrix, and even less likely with regard to the world review: charting an evolving discipline involves separating the changes that occur regularly within communities – almost as part of normal science – from those which involve much more radical rethinks of what is done, and why.

Geographies of geography?

Given the importance of context being stressed by observers of geography's recent history, it should not be surprising to find that there are significant differences in how the discipline has been (and is being) practised, at a variety of scales and across a range of cleavages. It has been suggested, for example, that there are four main cleavage lines within contemporary geography (Johnston, 1997b, pp. 30–1):

1. The *substantive divisions* according to subject matter studied;
2. The *epistemological divisions* according to views on the nature of knowledge and its production;
3. *Divisions in rationale*, reflecting the reasons for undertaking work; and
4. *Community divisions* which can be found at a variety of scales – language used (macro-scales); national schools (meso-scales); and intellectual schools (local communities at the micro-scale).

To a considerable extent these all overlap, creating a myriad academic communities within the discipline with points of contact and interaction, but also considerable difference and distance.

One of the clearest axes of contemporary differentiation in geographical practices is that provided by different meso-scale linguistic communities. In the nineteenth century, when geography was being launched as an academic discipline, there was considerable international contact and developments in several linguistic realms – not least the English-speaking world – were much influenced by pioneering ideas emanating from Germany and France (see Chapter 2). These contacts waned, however; they were fairly weak by the time that the Second World War ruptured international intellectual communities, and were not re-established in the early post-war decades.

During the second half of the twentieth century, geography as practised in countries where the English language was the norm (including Sweden and the Netherlands) came to dominate: 'International' journals almost invariably published in English only, which created difficulties for 'outsiders' – not only in reading the material but, even more so, in getting their research findings and ideas before wide audiences (Gutiérrez and López-Nieva, 2001). For some commentators this has amounted to the formation of an Anglo-American disciplinary hegemony. Minca (2000, p. 285), for example, reported that, 'the past fifteen years or so of the postmodern debate in geography have been an almost exclusively Anglo-American domain', marginalizing those who 'navigate only on the edges of the Anglo-American academic empire – but are firmly placed within other geographical traditions', with a joint conference of Italian and Anglo-American geographers providing (p. 287):

> ... further confirmation of the essentially undisputed dominion of Anglo-American geography. ... today the boundaries as well as the rules/coordinates of what passes for 'international' debate within our discipline are determined from within the Anglo-American universe.

For many (especially younger) European geographers this created problems of co-location in their home academic traditions and the 'languages and methodologies of Anglo-American geography', with the (so-called) 'international' journals published in English offering a 'formidable instrument of internal regulation and legitimation for the Anglo-American community [but] ... not a propitious terrain for encounter and debate among diverse geographical traditions'. The result was a claimed 'hegemonic closure': all debates in 'international journals' were 'essentially internal to the Anglo-American geographical community' (p. 288) from which others were effectively excluded:

> It is therefore deceiving, if not intellectually dishonest, to identify these leading journals as the locus of international debates – unless, of course, one retains the belief that the entirety of relevant contemporary theoretical contributions in geography can be limited to the Anglo-American world and to English-language publications.

Sidaway and Samers (2000) took up this cause, citing a wider literature and pointing out the relative marginalization of some scholars within the English-language realm; they related the Anglo-American (i.e. North Atlantic) apparent intellectual hegemony to the wider post-1945 US economic and geopolitical influence. The period was marked by an upsurge of influence of British geography (Whitehand and Edmondson, 1977). Nevertheless, they argued that work in other traditions had influenced that undertaken in the Anglo-American realm (citing regulation theory as an example; see p. 232), and that all geographical traditions were inherently hybrid (or 'trans-national'). Garcia-Ramon (2003, p. 1) was unconvinced by this argument, however, and re-stated the case regarding Anglo-American hegemony. For Simonsen (2002, p. 391) there is the paradox that growing cultural globalization is associated with Anglo-American predominance within human geography, in which 'a presumed universality is constructed that tends to conceal a particularity based, to a large extent, on specific experiences of the USA and United Kingdom'.

There are also significant differences within the Anglo-American realm, however, not least between the UK and the USA. To some extent these reflect the different inheritances – the intellectual palimpsests identified by Scott (p. 372) – as with the cultural geography developed by Sauer and the Berkeley School for several decades from the 1920s on and the parallel school of historical geographers, with its emphasis on cross-sections, established by Darby in the UK at about the same time. They also reflect the different educational contexts. In the UK, as noted above (p. 386), geography has long been a strong discipline in the schools, because of successful lobbying campaigns by institutions such as the Royal Geographical Society and the Geographical Association: indeed, according to Fuller (2000, p. 228) – who based his argument on Goodson (1988) – 'geography ... is perhaps the only major academic discipline to have been built from the grassroots of sub-university-level teachers', although his claim that it 'did not have a clear research agenda until elementary- and secondary-school teachers lobbied Parliament to get the subject established in the Universities' is historically inaccurate.

This strength in the country's schools has ensured a continued flow of students to the UK universities who wish to take a degree in the subject and have a firm foundation in it. This not only allows more specialist teaching from an early stage than is the case where many students come to geography new when they reach university but also, because the discipline has little difficulty recruiting undergraduates, means less direct pressure on its departments to offer 'relevant' curricula. In the United States, on the other hand, geography has typically been weak in the country's high schools, and most students have had little exposure to the discipline beyond some basic learning of locational facts in primary classes. Geography departments are therefore few (being present in only a small minority of the country's universities), and they need to attract students once they get to the campus by offering courses that are attractive – not least because they suggest career paths and benefits that a geographical training might bring. Thus, introductory courses are usually pitched at a very general level, and much emphasis is currently put (as discussed on p. 384) on providing courses on 'saleable, transferable skills', notably those associated with GIS. Graduate programs also recruit widely – whereas most academic geographers in the UK have first degrees in the subject, many in the USA do not (as shown by the autobiographical accounts in Gould and Pitts, 2002) – and many American graduate programmes have particular orientations, not least because most of them are small, in terms of the numbers of staff (faculty), when compared with the major UK departments. Furthermore, in the United States geography is competing for status within the social sciences with a number of much larger disciplines – notably economics, political science and sociology – which considerably constrains its promotion and growth. In the UK, on the other hand, the creation of significant university geography departments largely pre-dated that of sociology and politics departments (if not economics), giving it a comparative advantage, alongside that provided by its school presence, in promoting itself to potential students.

There are, then, complex geographies of geography, some of whose parameters we have started to map here. Few departments (even the largest in the UK) cover the full range of the current subdisciplines in their teaching programs, for example, let alone in their research concentrations. Most specialize, reflecting the interests of senior staff at particular times in their development and institutional resourcing decisions. Thus the practice of geography as an academic discipline itself reflects its own fundamental precepts. There are general features that apply to most geography programs but also particularities that reflect local characteristics and individual decision-making. In geography, as in so much else, place matters.

Human geography: paradigms, or research programmes, or . . . ?

Several models of scientific progress have been applied to the task of interpreting changes within human geography over the last five decades, therefore. This final discussion otes the general relevance of Kuhn's concept of a paradigm (at all three scales of tion), without necessarily suggesting either substantial periods of mono-paradigm dominance and normal science for the discipline as a whole or major revolutionary events that involved large numbers of geographers switching from one paradigm to another. (In some ways, paradigms as disciplinary matrices can be equated with research programmes in Lakatos's terminology; the Kuhnian term is preferred here.) In seeking to understand the relative popularity of various paradigms at different times, however, it is necessary to employ the contextual approach largely ignored by advocates of a Kuhnian approach within geography.

The 1950s and 1960s

Regionalism, with its empiricist and implicit exceptionalist philosophy, dominated the discipline until the 1940s, though in several versions. In the United States, for example, areal differentiation was stressed by geographers emanating from the midwest, notably Chicago and Madison, whereas those from Berkeley focused on the evolving cultural landscape, with a third distinct school based in Clark University (Bushong, 1981; Prunty, 1979; Koelsch, 1988; Martin, 1998; Monk, 1998). The regional theme dominated in Britain, too, though with a greater emphasis on physical geography and less evidence of distinct 'schools' (Freeman, 1979; Johnston and Gregory, 1984).

Systematic studies increasingly replaced regional descriptions through the 1950s; their stated (though often unrealized) aims were to increase the content of regional descriptions, advancing the understanding of particular places through knowledge of the general processes which interact to produce unique characteristics. Nevertheless, regional synthesis remained the central focus of many (senior) geographers' conception of their discipline, and regional courses predominated in many undergraduate degree programmes.

Regionalism was a disciplinary matrix with several competing exemplars, therefore. In the 1950s and 1960s, there was what Entrikin (1981, p. 1) terms 'transition between reigning orthodoxies ... in which the spatial theme superseded the regional theme'. This was marked by the further growth of systematic studies, the distancing of many geographers from the core belief in regional synthesis, and an increasing emphasis on finding laws of spatial organization, involving distance as a basic influence on human behaviour. As Guelke (1977a, 1977b, 1978) and Entrikin (1981) have indicated, the distancing was not rapid – in part no doubt because of the political need to sustain the unity and identity of the discipline – and some of those promoting the new paradigm only argued that quantitative analysis and spatial science offered better and more rigorous procedures for identifying and understanding regions (as in Berry, 1964b). This was seen by some as a methodological shift only (Chisholm, 1975a), which involved new exemplars but not a new disciplinary matrix, let alone a new world view.

The methodological shift alone was increasingly portrayed as insufficient, however, and a philosophical shift slowly emerged (elsewhere termed a 'quiet revolution': Johnston, 1978c, 1979b, 1981b). Regional synthesis as the disciplinary core was unattractive to many younger geographers (e.g. Gould, 1979), for whom contact with other social scientists introduced the excitements of systematic specialisms practised according to the positivist model of science, which implied the search for laws and applicable research findings. The links with the regional core were severed and a new disciplinary matrix of spatial science established, although Batty (1989) argued that by the time its models were well developed and applicable the demand for them had declined: 'It is an irony of history that such good models finally exist which could well have produced excellent advice in their day had they been available. But that day has passed' (p. 156). The term 'region' took on a very different meaning (Johnston, 1984d). The shared values of the new disciplinary matrix differed from those of regionalism, and to the extent that the adherents of spatial science, most of them from the new generation of geographers who were part of the educational boom of those decades, came to dominate the discipline (see Mikesell, 1984, on whether they did) so a revolution can be said to have occurred. Whether it was a revolution in Kuhnian terms is doubtful, however, since, as noted above (p. 361), the shift hardly fits into the 'response to anomalies' component of Kuhn's model. That would involve not only a shift in disciplinary matrix but also a shift in world view, in the conception of the nature of science but, as Hartshorne made clear (p. 67), traditional regional geography as he conceived it did not deny the possible relevance of generalizations about processes for the understanding of places. Bird (1989) identified a 'one and only' revolution, however, dating it to June 1966 with the publication of Bunge's (1966) note which criticized those who argued that the uniqueness of location meant that positivism was inapplicable in human geography.

The new disciplinary matrix of spatial science was firmly established in Anglo-American human geography by the end of the 1960s, and has been sustained since. Over nearly 40 years it has seen many shifts in exemplars, a lot of them linked to methodological – especially technical – developments in data collection, collation, analysis and display. (Compare, for example, Haggett, 1965c, with Haggett, Cliff and Frey, 1977, for shifts in the general orientation; Cliff and Ord, 1973 with Cliff and Ord, 1981, for a single methodological issue; and Hägerstrand, 1968, with Cliff et al., 1987, and Haggett, 2000, for a particular substantive topic.) Such paradigm shifts at the level of exemplar are closer to Kuhn's original presentation (and later clarified intention), with new ways of doing research accepted as superior to those previously used. They brought greater substantive success, too: Haggett (1978, p. 161), writing on 'The spatial economy', claimed that it:

> ... is more carefully defined than before, we know a little more about its organization, the ways it responds to shocks, and the way some regional sections are tied to others. There now exist theoretical bridges, albeit incomplete and shaky, which span from pure, spaceless economics through to a more spatially disaggregated reality.

In addition to the shifts among methodological exemplars there were also changes within the spatial science disciplinary matrix which had a wider import. The first was the reorientation away from normative modelling, which involved testing observed spatial organization against a priori models, and towards behavioural studies; as Cox (1981) and Hanson (1993) indicate, the disciplinary matrix was not queried but there were major shifts in emphasis and style. (See also the discussion of Openshaw's views on p. 351.) The second was the advocacy for 'welfare geography' (p. 337), described by Eyles and Smith

(1978) as a response to social conditions and a desire to make contemporary human geography more relevant to them.

The 1950s and 1960s saw the establishment of a new disciplinary matrix for human geographers, therefore, with twin concentrations on the spatial organization of society and human spatial behaviour. During those decades, and much more so since, particular exemplars have waxed and waned. They have introduced new methodological procedures and new substantive foci, in part as reactions to anomalies thrown up within the discipline (the failure of certain normative models, for example, and the shortcomings of some quantitative procedures) and in part as responses to trends in society, as illustrated by the many branches and sub-branches of the disciplinary matrix, reflecting the substantive interests of geographers (urban social, agricultural, etc.) and the technical arsenal that they deploy. A review of American geography published at the end of the 1980s is almost entirely structured within those systematic specialisms (Gaile and Willmott, 1989).

The 1970s and 1980s

The spatial-science disciplinary matrix expanded rapidly in the 1960s and early 1970s and in many departments it was relatively unchallenged until the mid-1970s (Taylor, 1976). Responses to the output from that disciplinary matrix and to events and issues elsewhere in society then stimulated two major challenges, contesting not just the exemplars, nor even the disciplinary matrix, but the world view implicit in the disciplinary matrix of spatial science.

The first of these challenges – termed humanistic here – was a response both to the nature of spatial science and to the ideology of society that it reflected. Spatial science is technocratic in its orientation and application; it tends to reduce people to terms in equations; it thereby ignores their individuality and freedom of action (Ley, 1981) and ignores the immense variety among places in favour of a universalistic view of how people think and act. As Barnes (1996, p. 6ff.) describes it, spatial scientists adhered (implicitly in most cases) to the 'Enlightenment project' launched in seventeenth-century Europe, which emphasized:

1. The *notion of progress* in the development of scientific understanding, through the application of the power of reason and the rationality of scientific methods;
2. A belief in *autonomous, sovereign, self-consciously directed individuals*, so that all are in essence the same, able to make the same moral and other judgements;
3. A belief that *'the world had order and humans could find it'* through application of their rational methods, notably those based on logic and mathematics; and
4. An acceptance that there are *universal truths*, which hold at all times and in all places, and whose discovery is the goal of all scientific endeavour.

These tenets are questioned by humanistic geographers, whose reading in other social sciences and philosophy led them to argue for a focus on subjectivity, which was clearly incommensurable with positivistic spatial science, so that the choice of which to practise was ideological (Johnston, 1986a). According to Barnes (pp. 8–10), they had their own core beliefs (shared with other counter-Enlightenment scholars) which:

1. Rejected 'both the epic of progress and the power of rationality and reason' (p. 8);
2. Contended that individuals are 'shaped from the outside rather than from the inside' (p. 9; i.e. by their context);
3. Rejected any notions of a 'monolithic order'; and
4. Argued that science advances not through the use of universal constructs but rather through 'a set of local social practices of a given time and place'.

Cloke et al. (1991) sustained this case, and criticized spatial science on the grounds that the can involve treating individuals as members of categories, which they saw as denigrating to the individual – at best, it is only 'a partial treatment of people' and at worst it involves their 'complete neglect' (Cloke, Philo, and Sadler, 1991, p.67). It treats them as 'little more than dots on a map, statistics on a graph or numbers in an equation … exercises … that effectively convert […] human beings into "dehumanised" entities drained of the very "stuff" (the meanings, values and so on) that made humans into humans as opposed to other things living or non-living' (p. 69).

Humanistic geography was introduced as an alternative science of geography, therefore, and not as a reorientation of the existing way, though some proponents claimed roots in earlier geographical practices such as those of the French geographer Vidal de la Blache (Buttimer, 1978a). It had its own disciplinary matrix, and its own variety of exemplars – in terms of both their philosophy and their subject matter, as set out in Chapter 5. Its introduction did not stimulate a major switch in the contents of the discipline as a whole, however. Rather, it offered an alternative conception of human geography and competed (ultimately unsuccessfully) with the others on that basis.

The second challenge – from radical geography – was also a response to the contents of the spatial-science disciplinary matrix, but was much more influenced by the wider political conjuncture than was the humanistic. As detailed earlier (Chapter 6), those who launched what was initially known as radical geography were concerned with the failure of positivist spatial science to tackle and solve pressing societal problems. They advocated applied geography, but defined relevance in a very different way (Harvey, 1974c; Johnston, 1981a). As with humanistic geography, this involved promoting a scientific revolution at the level of the world view; the realist science that they advanced was incommensurable with both positivist and humanistic science.

Once reasonably well-established, radical geography also became a kind of disciplinary matrix with a variety of exemplars. The core of its programme is the desire to uncover the mechanisms that drive society, providing accounts of how people act and how the empirical world is organized. How such understanding can be achieved, and how the knowledge should be used, has been the subject of much debate – both between Marxists and non-Marxists and among various types of Marxist – and exemplars have waxed and waned rapidly in recent years as a consequence. The debates within the realist conception of science are about how to achieve agreed scientific goals; the debates with positivist and humanistic geographers are about the nature of science. The former produce internal revolutions; the latter seek to promote major disciplinary revolutions. (Note, however, Barnes', 1996, critique of both Harvey – the leading advocate of Marxism within geography

– and Sayer – the leading advocate for realism – as both implicit part-adherents to the Enlightenment project, and hence to the same world view as the spatial scientists: 'my argument is that as with Harvey, Sayer totters between Enlightenment and anti-Enlightenment views' – p. 23.)

These decades were turbulent for human geography, which Ley (1981) found both exciting and confusing, in part because of the rapidity with which human geographers explored new ideas. He believed that such exploration was often superficial, with ideas discarded almost as soon as they had been adopted – 'In true North American fashion, obsolescence is setting in more and more speedily' (p. 209). Others argued that ideas were often divorced from their original context, and that geographers who imported them may have been unaware of the controversies surrounding their use (Agnew and Duncan, 1981; Duncan, 1980; Mohan, 1994). Some sought to reconcile the various world views (Harrison and Livingstone, 1982; Hay, 1979a; Johnston, 1980a, 1982c; Livingstone and Harrison, 1981); some argued that is impossible (Eyles and Lee, 1982); and others still contended that each of the various world views is informed by the others (e.g. Thrift, 1987, p. 401 and his claim that Marxist political economy now 'forms a vital subtext to most theorising'), so that geographers should use their synthesizing powers to integrate the various perspectives (Brookfield, 1989, p. 314).

Whatever the detailed interpretations and attempts to reconcile the competing world views, it is clear that the 1980s was characterized by a pluralism that not only challenged the would-be hegemony of the approaches launched in the 1960s but also presented problems for geographers in presenting their discipline to others. The intense conflicts that these debates engendered is exemplified in a retrospective essay by Berry (2002c, p. 441). His hope was that:

> Urban geography, with a rapidly developing reputation within the social sciences and a penchant for transdisciplinary inquiry, was to be directed towards and receive its inspiration from a commitment to help meeting national needs. It was my hope that the challenges of use-oriented research would stimulate new rounds of theoretical development and leverage the field to new levels of understanding. I took seriously the notion that geography is the science of which planning is the art.

But:

> By 1980 the excitement had waned, however. The paradigm appeared lost. There was a new fragmentation as young geographers did what so many have dome in earlier epochs of the discipline's history – they changed the channel to a different program. The common interest that seemed to be at hand succumbed to bickering and feuds.

Urban geography – until then in the disciplinary vanguard according to Berry's view – diverged along a series of 'incommensurate paths' (p. 443) as a result of both internal and external forces. The latter reflected the sentiments associated with the anti-Vietnam war protests, with many graduate students mobilized, according to Berry, by 'left-wing activists' who turned their antiwar sentiment into an 'anti-American anticapitalist radicalism'. Instead of 'use-inspired basic research', these radicals took the stance of the 'armchair intellectual contrarian', as exemplified for him by David Harvey:

There could be no meeting of the minds, no common ground. David disavowed our fumbling attempts to build a social science, positioning his agenda squarely within the realm of politics and imprinting in the minds of many young geographers the idea that science is merely one political viewpoint among many.

The new generation that followed the radical and humanistic geographers 'rejected the Enlightenment ideal of the perfectibility of the human mind – the ideal of an ever-progressing rationality – devaluing the speaking subject in favor of a highly theoretical linguistic and cultural determinism' (p. 444). As a result Berry shifted away from geography as an institutional base, whilst remaining active within his chosen orientation. Twenty years later, he was identifying with 'a political economy that we are trying to enrich with an emergent geographic information science that offers the prospect for new rounds of use-oriented investigation supported by new and more powerful forms of spatial analysis'. The potential is exciting for him, and 'once again the social and environmental sciences are looking to us'; however, although:

There is great promise in the idea of spatially integrated social science, but geography's traditional threat, the congenital inability to pull together, remains with us. We should not fritter away yet another opportunity because we lack the fortitude to withstand the contrarian responses of our professional dialecticians.

For him, at least, the debates of the 1970s and 1980s are not past history: the world view that he and others pioneered some 40 years ago remains central to their view of the discipline's future. For others, the debate seems to have been lost. Ford (2002, p. 438) identifies a polarization of urban geography between 'social theory and software' with no central ground between them: 'most of the [current] applicants for urban positions are interested in the city only tangentially, and instead present themselves as experts is aspects of either theory or technology'.

The 1990s and beyond

The 1990s witnessed yet more turbulence, again reflecting both dissatisfaction with the various world views and a rapidly changing external environment – economically, socially, politically, technically and culturally. Within it, the challenge of humanistic geography very substantially withered, in that very few followed the postulates of idealism, phenomenology and the other approaches discussed in Chapter 5, although, as stressed in Chapter 6, rejection of the Enlightenment model of the individual was at the core of the various critiques of Marxism. The 'new generation' emphasized difference, although – in part via the 'cultural turn' and the influences of feminism and poststructuralism – in a rather different way from that promulgated by Hartshorne some half a century earlier (Campbell, 1994). Spatial science did not wither, let alone disappear, however: its world view remained strong, although more marginal to the discipline, many of whose members (in part on political-ideological grounds) rejected not only the implicit positivism but also the emphasis on technical rigour in data analysis. Some commentators claim otherwise, according to Hamnett (2003, p.2), 'Quantitative techniques and aggregate social research have been largely abandoned ... Analysis of large data sets has become totally passé, the object of suspicion or even derision as "empiricist". (Similar arguments appear in, *inter alia*, Cloke, Philo, and Sadler, 1991, and Peet, 1998; for a response, see Chapter 4 and Johnston *et al*, 2003.)

By the 1990s, the discipline was substantially fragmented, not only in its world view and disciplinary matrices but also in its substantive concerns. It comprised a variety of approaches held together as much by the *realpolitik* of university politics and funding as by any adherence to core beliefs, and relatively few of its practitioners interact across sub-disciplinary frontiers (Johnston, 1991, 1996a). There are signs that some of those frontiers are increasingly being crossed by the latest generation of human geographers (as illustrated in Chapter 7), but only some of them (Johnston, 1996d): the relative peripheralization of much of the technical work in GIS and spatial statistics remains. This view was challenged by Gould (1994, p. 194): 'I find the idea of fragmentation absurd, and too frequently raised by people who long for others to conform to their monolithic ideological positions'. He argued that geographers with different specialist interests (as reflected, for example, by their affiliations to institutional study groups) nevertheless are following his advice of 'don't specialize ... read eclectically' and:

> Despite some contrary opinion, [there] is no evidence that they are disconnecting from the rich body of ideas that constitute the geographic 'way of looking' today. For their research, they may be using remotely sensed images, geographic information systems, structural-Marxist concepts, hydrological science, socially constructed ideas of the environment, Michel Foucault and the power of surveillance, deconstructions of official government reports, goal programming, a heightened awareness of gender issues ... I mean, you name it! ... to illuminate the spatio-temporal human condition at a place ... embedded in a larger regional and national space. With all that conceptual and methodological integration, where, literally on earth, is the fragmentation?

Others were much more concerned about fragmentation, however. When the AAG Council decided to initiate a follow-up volume to that edited by James and Jones (1954) 30 years earlier, it rejected a proposal from Gaile and Willmott (subsequently published independently: Gaile and Willmott, 1989) because it drew largely on the AAG's specialty groups and so reflected a fragmented view of the discipline rather than focus on 'cross-cutting and unifying concepts and methods' (Abler, Marcus and Olson, 1992a, p. xvii). The book which they edited for the AAG (*Geography's Inner Worlds: Pervasive Themes in Contemporary American Geography*) had four main sections:

1. *What geography is about* – geography's worlds, places and regions, representations of the world;
2. *What geographers do* – observation, visualization, analysis, modelling, communication;
3. *How geographers think* – location, place, region and space, movements, cycles and systems, the local-global continuum, scale in space and time; and
4. *Why geographers think that way* – paradigms for inquiry?, humanism and science in geography, applications of geographic concepts and methods, the peopling of American geography.

This was done to counter the perceived fragmentation (Abler, Marcus and Olson, 1992b, p. 2):

> Specialization and specialty groups foster better communication in a multi-faceted discipline. They permit scholars and practitioners with common interests to achieve identity without forming independent associations ... [but they also] foster intellectual isolation by retarding the cross-fertilization that occurs when geographers encounter unexpected ideas. Despite the fact that the fission evident within geography is common in the physical and social sciences, specialization may have gone as far as it can or should go in American geography.

Hence their book was structured to bring geographers together:

> ... to highlight the common elements within a discipline whose practitioners are in danger of forgetting their shared heritage and ideals. In their preoccupation with the great diversity of geographic problems with which they deal on a day to day basis, geographers are prone to overlook how much they share emotionally and intellectually with other geographers that they do not share with colleagues in other disciplines.

A few of the chapters are multi-authored, presumably as a way of bringing individuals with diverse interests together to identify common elements, and the outcome led the editors to conclude that the discipline is shown to be 'simultaneously less fragmented than we had feared it would be and less coherent than we had hoped' (Abler, Marcus and Olson, 1992c, p. 391), but nevertheless 'wonderfully diverse in substance, method and philosophy' (p. 395):

> Compared with other disciplines, geography has always been tolerant of variety, and often enthusiastic about multiplicity. With the possible exception of the period before 1920 when environmental determinism achieved a measure of intellectual hegemony, American geography has never been a normal, paradigmatic science of the kind postulated by Thomas Kuhn.

Thus, although concerned about fragmentation they also promote it as a 'geographical good thing':

> American geography was postmodern long before the term was invented. It has historically been eclectic and self-contradictory in many respects. It has often playfully delighted in juxtaposing dissonant substantive interests and intellectual traditions. American geography will prosper in the 1990s not so much because geography will change radically, but rather because the discipline's social and intellectual environments have now evolved to where geography has long been. Geographers are at last professing and practicing a postmodern discipline in a postmodern age.

Nevertheless, if geography is to prosper, the basis for coherence (necessary in a postmodern discipline?) has to be realized, which they argued involves: overcoming the indifference to physical geography among some human geographers; finding 'the language and narrative forms that will engage the attention of American society' (p. 398); and ensuring mutual recognition between the two main 'camps' within human geography – termed spatial scientists and social theorists elsewhere in this chapter ('The critical matter is that all parties avoid the wholesale rejection of each others' viewpoints that occurred in geography after 1920 and again after 1955': p. 400).

A second feature of the contemporary world, which is particular to academic life in many of its aspects yet at the same time linked to changes in the wider milieux, relates to the contexts within which universities operate. Since the 1980s, as illustrated earlier with regard to the pressures for applied work and skills-based training (see Chapter 9), universities have come under increasing pressure to adopt a range of business-like practices and to be accountable for their activities – including research. This has stimulated what has been termed an 'audit and accountability culture' and a 'quality industry' in the United Kingdom (Johnston, 1994b), and many have claimed that it has redirected research (some would say skewed it) in particular directions.

Luke (2000, p. 216) has recently referred to many aspects of this restructuring of the academic milieu in the United States as a 'discipline of reputational development'. Within academic networks power is exercised to ensure conformity to both general academic and specific disciplinary norms, and access to positions of power and influence is in general restricted to those who conform and win reputation points as a consequence. Thus:

> Academic life is an existence pegged to perpetual examinations: seminar discussions, research papers, dissertation defenses, conference papers, journal submissions, book contracts, teaching evaluations, committee assignments, tenure hearings, academic promotions, annual reports. . . . these facts about the routines of continual judgment in the disciplinary operations of the discipline [are] . . . those necessities that 'constitute a recurrent aspect of academic life'.

As we noted in Chapter 1, academic life is a chosen career, and those involved want to get their share of its rewards, which involves facing up to the continual judgements posed by the 'perpetual examinations' – and to a considerable extent this means conformity, since the allocation of those rewards is very largely in the hands of others.

Such conformity operates at two levels. At the first it operates within the discipline – or at least a significant section of it. As Luke expresses it, professional training and acculturation from graduate school onwards inculcates norms of conformity: each discipline is a 'powerful regime of normalizing thoughts and behaviors' which is 'intent on creating the correctly disciplined disciple of its knowledge via personal surveillance and methodological instruction' (p. 217). This, among other things, involves a great deal of ranking, of both individuals and departments, according to their reputations:

> The professionally correct gauge the value and position of individual persons and departments, willingly and openly, as 'names'. One is 'a big name', 'a name', or 'a no-name'. . . . Reputation and its development in rankings, therefore, boil down, first, to building one's meganymic profile, and, second, avoiding anymic obscurity or micronymic ineffectuality.

For Luke, this building a reputation for oneself – and the building of a collective departmental reputation based on those of its individual members – is not a function of what one studies (of disciplinary substance) but simply of successful performance on the key reputational indicators, which may be grant/contract income obtained, for example, or publications in certain journals, or citations to one's published work, or . . . . To some extent, even, an individual's scholarly reputation is a function of the university and/or department that he/she works in (p. 218):

Who gets what, where, when, and why in university departments, professional associations and grant competitions depends on these ranking systems of invidiously ranked distinction. While the intrinsic worth of any widely sought after rewards – pay raises, tenure, promotion, corner offices, or administrative powers – are declining, the battle for them continues at full tilt. And, the strategies for winning success or evading failure totally are denominated in these codes of professional correctness: the normalizing judgment of superiors, peers, and inferiors iterate their evaluations in matrices or performative success and failure.

This, in turn, influences the content of the discipline, at least in the short term, since the works of those who win in the ranking contests are presumably considered as providing the best exemplars to follow by those still seeking reputational preferment (unless they perceive that greater renown as likely to result from successfully challenging the conventional wisdom and power bases). Thus a discipline is divided into a range of sub-communities, each of which has its 'meganyms' whose ideas and opinions have a substantial impact on not only the allocation of rewards and resources (leading to claims of overweaning power in some instances: Short, 2002) but also what is considered good and bad practice within that community.

Many of Luke's claims relate to the internal operations of disciplines and subdisciplines but increasingly, as we have already suggested, those operations are subject to external audit and constraint. This is especially marked in the UK, where reputational rankings of departments (and therefore, at least implicitly, of their members) are the basis for the allocation of large sums of public moneys – especially with regard to research: teaching quality is also evaluated but the results are not used in selective disbursements. Although these judgements are made by peer review procedures involving academics (mainly 'meganyms') evaluating each other, they are constructed to meet political agenda regarding accountability and self-reliance (through the attraction of external support for research work, including contracts for applied work for public and private sector contractors). Thus they are informed, at least, by reputational metrics such as income earned and citations to papers published, and the quality of research publications is to some extent conditioned by the standing of the journals in which they appear. These leads to pressures on such journals and on individuals to publish in them: it also stimulates greater frequency of publication in order to attract metanymic status – which to some involves putting means before ends and can result in a deterioration in research quality.

An abundance of turbulence

Evaluating these turbulent years, when the turbulence shows little sign of abating, is not easy. Kuhn's model, sometimes presented to geographers as periods of normal scientific progress punctuated by major revolutions, is not sufficient to account for what has happened within their discipline since 1945. But each of the basic Kuhnian definitions of a paradigm (world view, disciplinary matrix, and exemplar) is relevant to appreciating what has occurred and is occurring within geography, as Mair (1986) argued for the concept of the paradigm as a scientific community (or *disciplinary matrix*) with shared values.

At the lowest definitional level of a paradigm, the *exemplar*, human geographers socialized within any of the available disciplinary matrices have shifted the orientation of their work as 'better' ways have been suggested to them and different topics have come to the foreground; minor revolutions have occurred – frequently. Such shifts have gone in a variety of directions, presenting an apparent anarchy – not chaos, which is the vernacular use of that term, but 'free and voluntary cooperation of individuals and groups' (Labedz, 1977, p. 22). But the core values hold.

There is also considerable evidence of the relevance of the largest scale definition of a paradigm, the *world view*, to recent changes in human geography. Very different and entirely incommensurable conceptions of the nature of science are competing for geographers' attention. They differ in their scientific and their societal goals, and demand choice. Some have made a very clear choice, switching from one conception of science to another because, as Harvey (1973, p. 17) expressed it with regard to Marxism, 'I can find no other way of accomplishing what I set out to do or of understanding what has to be understood': 30 years later, he noted 'now, when the [Marxist] text is so pertinent, scarcely anyone cares to consider it' (Harvey, 2000, p. 8).

Some argue that the choice is really between two world views only (spatial science and social theory: Sheppard, 1995): others identify three and, according to Duncan and Barnes (1993, p. 248), one of them has triumphed:

> R. J. Johnston's Geography and Geographers Since 1945 [sic] … could have been subtitled 'Modernism and its Discontents'. For its narrative structure is compellingly organized around the contest for intellectual supremacy among the triad of approaches: empiricist, positivist and modernist social theory. Although from Johnston's perspectives the social theorists win the day, and the others are relegated to the dustbin of geographical history, it is only modernism that really triumphed, because it is the only game in town.

Each of those positions, they contend, seeks to provide the 'one best method to explain geographical phenomena' and 'None has seriously entertained the notion that there is no best method' (p. 249). The differences among the three approaches are, they claim, 'relatively minor when compared to their shared assumptions', and they fear that the most radical aspects of postmodern epistemology have been rejected by geographers who 'wish to incorporate certain of its important insights into a reconstructed modernist [i.e. Enlightenment] project'. If the postmodern project was fully embraced, they argue, then the discipline would become much more varied since it would no longer be characterized by the views of 'trained academics':

> The problem lies in our conceptualization of difference. Difference for geographers is other spaces, other places, other regions or other landscapes. To embrace difference is in Gregory's … words to embrace 'areal differentiation'. It is instructive, however, to compare the postmodernist geographers' conception of difference to that of postmodernist ethnographers. For the latter, difference is other people and, to be more precise, other peoples' voices. Their plea is for an end to monovocality and authorial authority. Let us hear direct, they say, from those from whom we as academics have for so long spoken (p. 253).

Such a shift in the nature of geography is politically threatening because of its challenge to the academics' authority. Furthermore:

> Multivocality (taking others' voices seriously) is not something that can be easily accomplished in geography, for we have no tradition of ethnography. Unless we begin to focus more of our energies on developing our techniques for listening to others our calls for difference are highly suspect, for we will continue systematically to silence difference. Those outside the academy have no voice in our work other than the one we choose to give them … to speak for another is not a politically innocent act. We have appropriated their voice – colonized their perspective.

To adopt their agenda would be to increase the turbulence exponentially (as is the case in teaching as well as research: McDowell, 1994, Johnston, 2000d).

Buttimer (1993), drawing on Pepper (1942), identified four 'root metaphors', or world views, underpinning the practice of geography, each of which 'projects a distinct interpretation of reality':

1. The *world as a mosaic of patterns and forms*, which she sees as the 'central root metaphor for geography's chorological tradition, the most practiced of all four' (p. 22);
2. The *world as a mechanism* of causally integrated interacting systems;
3. The *world as an organism*, as a whole which comprises unity in diversity; and
4. The *world as arena*, as the context within which 'spontaneous and possibly unique events may occur' (p. 23).

To which could be added a fifth:

5. The *world as text*, as which the landscape is a means of understanding its creators' intentions and cultures (an activity also associated with both archaeology and, in different ways, some forms of theology).

Buttimer did not present her four as exclusive, nor are they treated as such: 'Most creative scholars … avail themselves of more than one root metaphor in the course of a career. Only the rare dogmatist clings to one throughout'. Nevertheless, she sees them as 'vectors of distinct *thought styles* whose appeal has varied through different moments in Western social history' (p. 24). Which styles are dominant when depends on the interaction of people and context:

> Acceptance or rejection of a particular paradigm, model, or method within the discipline of geography has as much to do with the aesthetic, emotional or moral connotations of a root metaphor as it does with purely epistemological reasoning. The succession of metaphors within any tradition raises questions about the interplay of internal and external circumstances. Career stories of geographers reveal important clues about their succession and relative appeal. At any moment of disciplinary history, all four root metaphors … may be simultaneously co-present, although one or more may appear dominant within particular periods.

Her descriptions of the metaphors, based to a considerable extent on autobiographical data, does not lead to a detailed appreciation of why one or more has been more visible in some periods than others. Instead, she identifies a major tension between, on the one hand, 'the integrated approaches of *organism* and *mechanism* [which] have invited research of wider scale and have apparently enhanced the status of geography within the academy' which is desirable given 'the political expediency of the times' and the 'political economy of research grantsmanship', and, on the other, 'The dispersed approaches of *mosaic* and *arena* [to which we can add *text*] have yielded more sensitive accounts of life and landscape at local and regional scales of inquiry' (p. 212). Her own preference is clearly for the latter pair, for 'the humanist's emancipatory hope' and 'communication and understanding' (p. 219). Humanism must be 'the leaven in the dough and not a separate loaf in the smorgasbord of geographic endeavor' (p. 220), but she does not seek to impose (p. 212):

> The integrity of disciplinary practice ... demands a flexibility to changing educational needs and to new substantive research challenges. Ideally each individual, department or research team, given its resources, aims and context, should assume responsibility for designing and adapting its agenda to such changing demands.

Each world view's *disciplinary matrices* identify the framework within which research is conducted. The shift from regionalism to spatial science involved a change of disciplinary matrix, for example; whilst the world view remained constant – that of positivist science with its foundation in empiricism (although it was hidden until relatively late in the shift) – the shared goals altered very considerably. The relative popularity of Marxism, realism, structuration, and postmodernism at different times reflects changes in the disciplinary matrix of the 'geography as social theory' world view.

Kuhn's model as usually presented cannot accommodate the intricate experience of human geography since 1945, therefore. But its major components have some value in appreciating much of what has happened within the discipline over that period. In summary, the salient elements of the period have been:

1. Relative mono-paradigm dominance at the level of the world view until the late 1960s, with empiricism as the foundation and an increasingly explicit acceptance of positivism;
2. A steady switch within that period from one disciplinary matrix (regionalism) to another (spatial science), but with the former never entirely ousted by the latter;
3. A substantial number of exemplars providing frameworks for conducting research within the spatial science disciplinary matrix, reflecting both technical developments and the systematic sub-division of the discipline;
4. Further world views promoted from the late 1960s on representing two very different views of science, both from each other and from spatial science. One ('radical' or, later, a broader 'social theory') is now well established within the discipline, with substantial numbers of adherents, but has not achieved disciplinary hegemony: the other ('humanistic') informed the shift away from the search for 'universal truths', but its particular research routes are rarely travelled now (and a case could be made that its various components – idealism, phenomenology, etc. – are now no more than exemplars within the social theory world view); and

5. During the 1980s and 1990s a new group of disciplinary matrices developed within the social theory world view, each emphasizing 'difference' within structural constraints.

Peet (1998) also maps some of these trends – and earlier 'schools of geographical thought' – as a set of movements, flows and channels in 'disciplinary space' (see Figure 10.2). Though his comments in the text of the page in which his chart appears indicates some self-consciousness at such a bold and clear sketch of geography:

> *Theoretical organizational devices are political tools of power formation. So the map may give a 'bird's-eye' view but the bird is an eagle, symbol of the state, and soaring on high, rather than a working sparrow pecking up the crumbs of its localized existence* (p. 10).

A relatively rare attempt to (re)narrate the history of geography from such other viewpoints – drawing upon a departmental geographical magazine produced by students at the University of Glasgow – has been produced by Philo (1998). He notes that:

> *... little appears to have been said about how academic visions of geography have been received by the countless students who filter through 'our' lecture theatres, tutorial rooms and libraries. It seems to me that this is an omission of some magnitude, and that therefore more might be done to ascertain how all manner of shifts in academic geography, as fostered by small numbers of 'visible' professional geographers translate into the thinking, writing, fieldworking and murmurings of the many 'invisible' student geographers whose responses are almost never afforded sympathetic scrutiny* (p. 345).

More recently, Lorimer and Spedding (2002) stress the wealth, complexity, and value of departmental histories, reconstructing something of the contextual histories of geography – as practised by staff and students – at another Scottish department (Aberdeen) and Withers (2002b, p. 306) has pursued a similar task at Edinburgh:

> *... kindled by hearing stories from older colleagues ... [and] motivated by the 'discovery' at one time and another of large amounts of textual material relating to an earlier department: students' work, personal papers of former staff, photographs, examination papers and old glass slides. I say 'discovery' for a reason: colleagues in my department knew of its existence, but not until an interest was expressed in 'that old stuff' was any value attached to it as a nascent department archive.*

Either way, human geography is currently characterized by a multi-paradigm situation at the world-view level, by competition between disciplinary matrices within at least two of those world views, and by a wealth of exemplars on which research is based in all three. It is because of the last element, and because many human geographers have not been deeply schooled into any one disciplinary matrix, let alone the use of any one exemplar, that the discipline appears replete with fickle allegiances, as individuals explore various ways of practising geography (Johnston, 1981b, pp. 313–14):

> *Much geographical work is exploratory, and is conducted by individuals who operate independently. Indeed, many, although influenced by what they read, are in no sense socialized into a particular matrix or set of exemplars which might be associated with a 'research school' and its leader. The charisma of certain individuals and their published works may occasionally produce the prophet and disciple situation. Much more usual, however, is a situation of fickle allegiances.*

Such fickleness suggests anarchy, in the sense used by Feyerabend (1975; Johnston, 1976b, 1978c). Some human geographers shift frequently among exemplars, sometimes between disciplinary matrices, and just occasionally between world views.

The last five decades have seen individual human geographers occasionally promoting a particular paradigm (world view, disciplinary matrix or exemplar) in opposition to prevailing practice. That has rarely been done in isolation; either contacts with others or reading (or both) suggest the argument, and support is then sought within the discipline, and perhaps resources and sponsorship from within society too. Why are some people better able to promote paradigm change than others? Little work has been done on such aspects of the sociology of geography as a discipline, especially with regard to power over the acceptance/rejection of proposed paradigm shifts and the ability to convince others of the 'rightness' of any approach. Studies have been undertaken on influential figures in the discipline's early development (e.g. in Blouet, 1981, in the biobibliography series edited by Freeman, 1977, and in Smith, 2003) and the nature of the profession in Britain has been explored (Johnston and Brack, 1983; Sidaway, 1997), but the dynamics of the discipline in recent years have not been the subject of detailed analysis. Nor, interestingly, has the impact of the 'commercialisation of knowledge' by publishing houses been scrutinized (Barnett and Low, 1996), although the increased stress on research publications in the UK from the mid-1980s on led to problems for textbook publishers (Davey et al., 1995).

Within the discipline, analysis of citations (mostly from the data base constructed by the Institute of Scientific Information in Philadelphia) has been used:

1. To identify frequently referenced works that can be categorized as exemplars (e.g. Whitehand, 1985; Wrigley and Matthews, 1986; Bodman, 1991, 1992; Yeung, 2002);
2. To isolate research communities, groups of scholars who refer to each other's writings on a particular topic and so occupy a disciplinary matrix focused on particular exemplars (Gatrell, 1984a, 1984b);
3. To rate journals and chart their interdependence (e.g. Whitehand, 1984; Gatrell and Smith, 1984);
4. To rank departments in the United States and the United Kingdom in terms of publications produced, publications cited and peer evaluation, for example (see Morrill, 1980; Jones, Lindsey and Coggeshall, 1982; Turner and Meyer, 1985 on the US; on the UK, see Bentham, 1987; Smith, 1988b; Johnston, 2003d); and
5. To conduct exploratory studies of particular sub-disciplines and the main exemplars which have stimulated how individuals practise (e.g. Phillips and Unwin, 1985).

All describe aspects of the discipline's structure but tell us little of its processes; like spatial science they provide valuable descriptive data, but not necessarily much understanding.

For that understanding, it is necessary not only to appreciate the contexts in which people worked but also to realize that those contexts are not straightforwardly determinate. A change in a country's economic, social and/or political trajectories will not necessarily bring forth a certain reaction from geographers; individuals may respond to their interpretations of that change, and their responses may stimulate others to follow

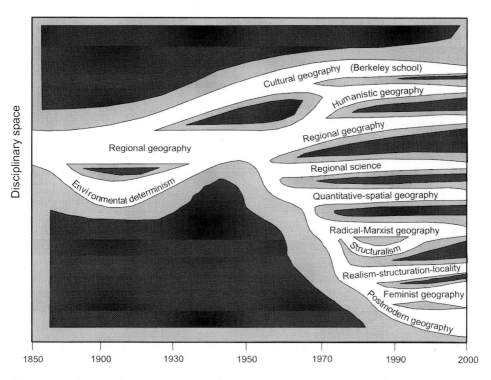

Figure 10.2 *Schools of modern and postmodern thought (Source: Peet, 1998, p.10)*

them. This is the most likely reason for shifts at the level of the world view and, probably, the disciplinary matrix too, as exemplified by the introduction of a radical/structuralist world view and by the shift within the empiricist world view from regionalism to spatial science. But such shifts can stimulate counter-reactions, as with the advancement of humanistic geography as a response to spatial science; those promoting the latter cause were influenced both by currents of thinking outwith geography and by their explorations of World Three. At the level of the exemplar, shifts are most likely to occur as a response to events within the discipline, as Kuhn suggests; this occurred within the spatial-science disciplinary matrix with the movement from normative to behavioural analyses, but the later move towards welfare geography was strongly influenced by external factors.

No simple model can be applied to the changes within human geography to provide an explanation of why the discipline has altered in the ways described here. Kuhn's work provides a valuable vocabulary and organizing framework within which to describe the communities, but what has occurred reflects the perceptions and actions of individual human geographers. Like all other aspects of society, geography is a discipline created by and for geographers, and is continually fought over and recreated by them, at a variety of scales and in social, economic and political contexts that vary over space and through time. The last point is crucial, for – as the structuration approach stresses – people are socialized in particular contexts and they then create part of the milieux within which others are socialized; these processes are presented by Bourdieu (1988, 1990) as the construction and evolution of 'fields' (see the exegeses by Bassett, 1996, and Painter, 2000) and by Purcell (2003) as 'islands of practice'. Those places (fields and islands) are not isolated, and changes in one can influence changes in others. But, as illustrated here, there have been substantial differences from one place to another within Anglo-American human geography regarding how the discipline is practised, reflecting both the nature of those places and the people in them; on the broader international scale, the differences are even greater (Johnston and Claval, 1984).

And the future?

> ... human geography is a profoundly trendy subject, in part because it still tends to import most of its ideas from outside the discipline. New generations of postgraduates therefore tend, rather more than in other and larger disciplines, to follow new trends. The discipline is therefore characterized by generational cycles which leave little room for much work outside the norm (Thrift, 2000, p.692).

In the early 1970s, several leading geographers were asked their views of the discipline's future (Chorley, 1973a). Little of what they suggested is reflected in what happened; the contents of a similar book produced twelve years later (Johnston, 1985c) are very different. Debates about how geography should be practised and taught continue, reflecting not only internal divisions but also trends in the societies to which human geographers belong. The contents and contexts of those future debates cannot be predicted; one could suggest with some certainty, however, that human geography will not be characterized by mono-paradigm dominance in the next decade.

In the introduction to an autobiographical essay, David Smith (1984, p. 118) wrote that:

> ... my own professional activities seem to have been a continual struggle to come to terms with (or keep up with) the rapidly shifting focus of human geography. The struggle arises in large measure from the difficulty of breaking free from one's own intellectual heritage. ... If my own struggles represent anything more than one half-life experience, it may well be the theme of the geographer or social scientist as creature of his or her times.... If anything is to be learned from the instant replay of such recent events ... it is that 'scientific' advance is not conducted in a social vacuum but as an integral part of human history, within which the element of chance arising from individual personality and creativity plays an important part. So let us proceed with the recollection of one of the random variables.

We are all random variables, it seems: Robson (1984, p. 104) used a similar turn of phrase – 'it is clear how small a part in my own development seems to have been played by clearly guided aims and how much has been contributed by the collage of rather random influences and serendipitous events to which I both responded and contributed'. Hence our 'individual' and collective projects and life-paths (our 'geographies') can be appreciated and set in context, but no more. We are therefore often uncertain where we, as individuals, are going, let alone exactly where geography as a set of linked yet anarchistic communities is heading. We are making the future of geography as we practise it, just as we have been remaking its past by writing this book.

Bibliography

ABLER, R. F. 1971: Distance, intercommunications, and geography. *Proceedings, Association of American Geographers* **3**, 1–5.

—— 1993a: Everything in its place: GPS, GIS, and geography in the 1990s. *The Professional Geographer* **45**, 131–9.

—— 1993b: Personal perspectives on the fiftieth anniversary of the founding of the ASPG. In E. W. Miller (ed.), *The American Society for Professional Geographers*. Washington DC: Association of American Geographers, occasional Publication 3.

ABLER, R. F., ADAMS, J. S. and GOULD, P. R. 1971: *Spatial organization: the geographer's view of the world*. Englewood Cliffs, NJ: Prentice-Hall.

ABLER, R. F., MARCUS, M. G. and OLSON, J. M. 1992a: Preface. In R. F. Abler, M. G. Marcus and J. M. Olson (eds) *Geography's inner worlds: pervasive themes in contemporary American geography*. New Brunswick, NJ: Rutgers University Press, xv–xx.

—— 1992b: Contemporary American geography. In R. F. Abler, M. G. Marcus and J. M. Olson (eds) *Geography's inner worlds: pervasive themes in contemporary American geography*. New Brunswick, NJ: Rutgers University Press, 1–8.

—— 1992c: Afterword. In R. F. Abler, M. G. Marcus and J. M. Olson (eds) *Geography's inner worlds: pervasive themes in contemporary American geography*. New Brunswick, NJ: Rutgers University Press, 391–402.

ACKERMAN, E. A. 1945: Geographic training, wartime research, and immediate professional objectives. *Annals of the Association of American Geographers* **35**, 121–43.

—— 1958: *Geography as a fundamental research discipline*. Chicago: University of Chicago, Department of Geography Research Paper 53.

—— 1963: Where is a research frontier? *Annals of the Association of American Geographers* **53**, 429–40.

ADAMS, J. S. 1969: Directional bias in intra-urban migration. *Economic Geography* **45**, 302–23.

—— 1972: The geography of riots and civil disorder in the 1960s. *Economic Geography* **48**, 24–42.

—— (ed.) 1976: *Urban policymaking and metropolitan dynamics: a comparative geographical analysis*. Cambridge MA: Ballinger.

—— 1994: *Risk*. London: Routledge.

—— 2002: The quantitative revolution in urban geography. *Urban Geography* **22**, 530–9.

ADAMS, P. C. 1995: A reconsideration of personal boundaries in space-time. *Annals of the Association of American Geographers* **85**, 267–85.

ADAMS, P. C., HOELSCHER, S. and TILL, K. E. 2001: Place in context: rethinking humanistic geographies. In P. C. Adams, S. Hoelscher and K. E. Till, (eds), *Textures of Place: Exploring Humanist Geographies*. Minneapolis: University of Minnesota Press, xiii–xxiii.

ADLER, S. and BRENNER, J. 1992: Gender and space: lesbians and gay men in the city. *International Journal of Urban and Regional Research* **16**, 24–34.

AGNEW, J. A. 1984: Place and political behaviour: the geography of Scottish nationalism. *Political Geography Quarterly* **3**, 191–202.

—— 1987a: *The United States in the world-economy: a regional geography.* Cambridge: Cambridge University Press.

—— 1987b: *Place and politics: the geographical mediation of state and society.* Boston: Allen and Unwin.

—— 1989: The devaluation of place in social science. In J. A. Agnew and J. S. Duncan (eds) *The power of place.* Boston: Unwin Hyman, 9–29.

—— 1990: Sameness and difference: Hartshorne's *The Nature of Geography* and geography as areal variation. In J. N. Entrikin and S. D. Brunn (eds) *Reflections on Richard Hartshorne's The Nature of Geography.* Washington: Association of American Geographers, 121–40.

—— 1993: Representing space: space, scale and culture in social science. In J. S. Duncan and D. Ley (eds) *Place/culture/representation.* London: Routledge, 251–71.

—— 1994: The territorial trap: the geographical assumption of international relations theory. *Review of International Political Economy* **1**, 53–80.

AGNEW, J., MITCHELL, K. and TOAL, G. (eds) 2003: *A companion to political geography.* Oxford: Blackwell.

AGNEW, J. A. and DUNCAN, J. S. 1981: The transfer of ideas into Anglo-American human geography. *Progress in Human Geography* **5**, 42–57.

—— 1989: Introduction. In J. A. Agnew and J. S. Duncan (eds) *The power of place.* Boston: Unwin Hyman, 1–8.

AGNEW, J. S. 1997: Commemoration and criticism: fifty years after the publication of Harris and Ullman's 'The nature of cities'. *Urban Geography* **18**, 4–6.

AITKEN, S. C. 1991: A transactional geography of the image-event: the films of Scottish director, Bill Forsyth. *Transactions, Institute of British Geographers* **NS16**, 105–18.

—— 2001: *Geographies of young people: the morally contested spaces of identity.* London and New York: Routledge.

AITKEN, S. C., CUTTER, S. L., FOOTE, K. E. and SELL, J. S. 1989: Environmental perception and behavioral geography. In G. L. Gaile and C. J. Willmott (eds) *Geography in America.* Merrill, Columbus, 218–38.

ALEXANDER, D. 1979: Catastrophic misconception? *Area* **11**, 228–30.

ALEXANDER, J. W. and ZAHORCHAK, G. A. 1943: Population-density maps of the United States: techniques and patterns. *Geographical Review* **33**, 457–66.

ALKER, H. R. 1969: A typology of ecological fallacies. In M. Dogan and S. Rokkan (eds), *Quantitative ecological analysis in the social sciences.* Cambridge MA: The MIT Press, 69–86.

ALLEN, J. 2003: *Lost geographies of power.* Oxford: Blackwell.

ALTHUSSER, L. and BALIBAR, E. 1970: *Reading 'Capital'.* London: New Left Books.

AMEDEO, D. and GOLLEDGE, R. G. 1975: *An introduction to scientific reasoning in geography.* New York: John Wiley.

AMERICAN ASSOCIATION OF GEOGRAPHERS (AAG) 1946: Lessons from the wartime experience for improving graduate training for geographic research. *Annals of the Association of American Geographers* **36**: 195–214.

AMIN, A. (ed.) 1994: *Postfordism: a reader.* Oxford: Blackwell.

AMIN, A. and ROBBINS, K. 1990: The reemergence of regional economies: the mythical geography of flexible accumulation. *Environment and Planning D: Society and Space* **8**, 7–34.

AMIN, A. and THRIFT, N. J. 2000: What kind of economic theory for what kind of economic geography? *Antipode* **32**, 4–9.

—— 2002: *Cities: reimagining the urban.* Cambridge: Polity Press.

AMIN, A., MASSEY, D. and THRIFT, N. J. 2000: *Cities for the many not the few.* Bristol: The Policy Press.

ANDERSON, J. 1973: Ideology in geography: an introduction. *Antipode* **5(3)**, 1–6.

ANDERSON, J., DUNCAN, S. and HUDSON, R. 1983: *Redundant spaces in cities and regions?: studies in industrial decline and social change* (special publication series, Institute of British Geographers No. 15). London: Academic Press.

ANDERSON, K. 1995: Culture and nature at the Adelaide Zoo: at the frontiers of 'human' geography. *Transactions, Institute of British Geographers* **NS20**, 275–94.

ANDERSON, K., DOMOSH, M. PILE, S. and THRIFT, N. (eds) 2003: *The handbook of cultural geography*. London, Thousand Oaks, CA and New Delhi: Sage.

ANON, 1968: A preliminary contribution to the geographical analysis of a Pooh-scape. *IBG Newsletter* **6**, 54–63.

ANSELIN, L. 1988: *Spatial econometrics: methods and models*. Dordrecht: Kluwer.

—— 1995: Local indicators of spatial association – LISA. *Geographical Analysis* **27**, 93–115.

—— 1998: Exploratory spatial data analysis in a geocomputational environment. In P. A. Longley, S. M. Brooks, R. MacDonnell, and B. Macmillan (eds) *Geocomputation: a primer*. Chichester: John Wiley, 77–94.

APPLEBAUM, W. 1954: Marketing geography. In P. E. James and C. F. Jones (eds) *American geography: inventory and prospect*. Syracuse: Syracuse University Press, 245–51.

APPLETON, J. 1975: *The experience of landscape*. London: John Wiley.

—— 1994: *How I made the world: shaping a view of landscape*. Hull: University of Hull Press.

ARCHER, J. C. and TAYLOR. P. J. 1981: *Section and party*. Chichester: John Wiley.

ARMSTRONG, M. P. 1993: On automated geography. *The Professional Geographer* **45**, 440–2.

—— 2000: Geography and computational science. *Annals of the Association of American Geographers* **90**, 146–156.

ARMSTRONG, P. 1999: Charles Darwin's image of the world: the influence of Alexander von Humboldt on the Victorian naturalist. In A. Buttimer, S. D. Brunn and U. Wardenga (eds) *Text and image: social construction of regional knowledges*. Leipzig: Institut für Länderkunde Leipzig, Beiträge zur regionalen Geographie **49**, 46–53.

ASHEIM, B. T. 1990: How to confuse rather than guide students: a review of Holt-Jensen's *Geography – history and concepts. Progress in Human Geography* **14**, 281–92.

BADCOCK, B. A. 1970: Central-place evolution and network development in south Auckland, 1840–1968: a systems analytic approach. *New Zealand Geographer* **26**, 109–35.

—— 1984: *Unfairly structured cities*. Oxford: Basil Blackwell.

BAHRENBERG, G., FISCHER, M. M. and NIJKAMP, P. (eds) 1984: *Recent developments in spatial data analysis: methodology, measurement, models*. Aldershot: Gower Press.

BAILEY, T. C. and GATRELL, A. C. 1995: *Interactive spatial data analysis*. London: Longman.

BAKER, A. R. H. 1972: Rethinking historical geography. In A. R. H. Baker (ed.), *Progress in historical geography*. Newton Abbott: David & Charles, 11–28.

—— 1979: Historical geography: a new beginning? *Progress in Human Geography* **3**, 560–70.

—— 1981: An historico-geographical perspective on time and space and on period and place. *Progress in Human Geography* **5**, 439–43.

—— 1984: Reflections on the relations of historical geography and the *Annales* school of history. In A. R. H. Baker and D. Gregory (eds). *Explorations in historical geography*. Cambridge: Cambridge University Press, 1–27.

BAKER, A. R. H. and GREGORY, D. 1984: Some terrae incognitae in historical geography: an exploratory discussion. In A. R. H. Baker and D. Gregory (eds) *Explorations in historical geography*. Cambridge: Cambridge University Press, 180–94.

BALCHIN, W. G. V. 1987: United Kingdom geographers in the Second World War. *The Geographical Journal* **153**, 159–180.

—— 1993: *The Geographical Association: the first hundred years, 1893–1993*. Sheffield: The Geographical Association.

BALL, M. 1987: Harvey's Marxism. *Environment and Planning D: Society and Space* **5**, 393–4.

BALLABON, M. B. 1957: Putting the economic into economic geography. *Economic Geography* **33**, 217–23.

BALLAS, D., CLARKE, G. P. and TURTON, I. 2002: A spatial microsimulation model for social policy micro-spatial analysis. In B. Boots, A. Okabe and R. Thomas (eds.) *Modelling geographical systems: statistical and computational applications*. Dordrecht: Kluwer,

BANKS, M. and MacKIAN, S, 2000: Jump in! The water's warm: a comment on Peck's 'grey geography'. *Transactions of the Institute of British Geographers* **NS25**, 249–254.

BARNES, B. 1974: *Scientific knowledge and sociological theory*. London: Routledge & Kegan Paul.

—— 1982: *T. S. Kuhn and social science*. London: Macmillan.

BARNES, T. J. 1985: Theories of international trade and theories of value. *Environment and Planning A* **17**, 729–46.

—— 1988: Rationality and relativism in economic geography: an interpretive review of the *homo economicus* assumption. *Progress in Human Geography* **12**, 473–96.

—— 1989a: Place, space and theories of economic value: contextualism and essentialism in economic geography. *Transactions, Institute of British Geographers* **NS14**, 299–316.

—— 1989b: Structure and agency in economic geography and theories of economic value. In A. Kobayashi and S. Mackenzie (eds) *Remaking human geography*. Boston: Unwin Hyman, 134–48.

—— 1996: *Logics of dislocation: models, metaphors and meaning of economic space*. New York: The Guilford Press.

—— 2000: Inventing Anglo-American economic geography, 1889–1960. In E. Sheppard and T. J. Barnes, (eds), *A companion to economic geography*. Oxford: Blackwell Publishers, 11–26.

—— 2001a: 'In the beginning was economic geography' – a science studies approach to disciplinary history. *Progress in Human Geography* **25**, 521–544.

—— 2001b: Lives lived and lives told: biographies of geography's quantitative revolution. *Environment and Planning D: Society and Space* **19**, 409–430.

—— 2001c Retheorizing economic geography: from the quantitative revolution to the 'cultural turn'. *Annals of the Association of American Geographers* **91**, 546–65.

—— 2002: Critical notes on economic geography from an aging radical. Or radical notes on economic geography from a critical age. *ACME* **1**, 8–14. www.acme_journal.org.

—— 2003: The place of locational analysis: a selective and interpretive history. *Progress in Human Geography* **27**, 69–95.

BARNES, T. J. and DUNCAN, J. S. 1992: Introduction: writing worlds. In T. J. Barnes and J. S. Duncan (eds) *Writing worlds: discourse, text and metaphor in the representation of landscape*. London: Routledge, 1–17.

BARNES, T. J. and GREGORY, D. (eds) 1997: *Reading human geography: the poetics and politics of enquiry*. London: Arnold.

BARNETT, C. 1995: Awakening the dead: who needs the history of geography? *Transactions, Institute of British Geographers* **NS20**, 417–19.

—— 1998a: The cultural turn: fashion or progress in human geography. *Antipode* **30**, 379–94.

—— 1998b: Cultural twist and turns. *Environment and Planning D: Society and Space* **16**, 631–4.

—— 1999: Deconstructing context: exposing Derrida. *Transactions, Institute of British Geographers* **NS24**, 277–93.

BARNETT, C. and LOW, M. 1996: Speculating on theory: towards a political economy of academic publishing. *Area* **28**, 13–24.

BARROWS, H. H. 1923: Geography as human ecology. *Annals of the Association of American Geographers* **13**, 1–14.

BARTON, R. 2003: 'Men of science': language, identity and professionalization in the mid-Victorian scientific community. *History of Science* **41**, 73–119.

BASSETT, K. 1996: Postmodernism and the crisis of the intellectual: reflections on reflexivity, universities and the scientific field. *Environment and Planning D: Society and Space* **14**, 507–27.

—— 1999: Is there progress in human geography? The problem of progress in the light of recent work in the philosophy and sociology of science. *Progress in Human Geography* **23**, 27–47.

BASSETT, K. and SHORT, J. R. 1980: *Housing and residential structure: alternative approaches.* London: Routledge & Kegan Paul.

BATEY, P. and BROWN, P. 1995: From human ecology to customer targeting: the evolution of geodemographics. In P. Longley and G. Clarke (eds) *GIS for business and service planning.* Cambridge: GeoInformation International, 73–103.

BATTY, M. 1976: *Urban modelling: algorithms, calibrations, predictions.* London: Cambridge University Press.

—— 1978: Urban models in the planning process. In D. T. Herbert and R. J. Johnston (eds) *Geography and the urban environment,* vol. 1. Chichester: John Wiley, 63–134.

—— 1989: Urban modelling and planning; reflections, retrodictions and prescriptions. In B. Macmillan (ed.) *Remodelling geography.* Oxford: Basil Blackwell, 147.

BATTY, M. and LONGLEY, P. 1994: *Fractal cities: a geometry of form and function.* London: Academic Press.

BEAUMONT, J. R. 1987: Quantitative methods in the real world: a consultant's view of practice. *Environment and Planning A* **19**, 1441–8.

BEAUMONT, J. R. and GATRELL, A. C. 1982: *An introduction to Q-analysis.* CATMOG 34, Norwich: Geo Books.

BEAUREGARD, R. A. 1988: In the absence of practice: the locality research debate. *Antipode* **20**, 52–9.

—— 1999: Break dancing on Santa Monica Boulevard. *Urban Geography* **20**, 396–399.

BEAVERSTOCK, J., SMITH, R. G. and TAYLOR, P. J. 2000: World city network: a new metageography of the future? *Annals of the Association of American Geographers* **90**, 121–34.

BECHER, T. and TROWLER, P. R. 2001: *Academic tribes and territories* 2nd edn. Buckingham: Open University Press.

BECKERMAN, W. 1995: *Small is stupid: blowing the whistle on the greens.* London: Duckworth.

BECKINSALE, R. P. 1997: Richard J. Chorley: a reformer with a cause. In D. R. Stoddart (ed.) *Process and Form in Geomorphology.* London: Routledge, 3–14.

BELL, C. and NEWBY, H. 1976: Community, communion, class and community action: the social sources of new urban politics. In D. T. Herbert and R. J. Johnston (eds) *Social areas in cities,* volume 2: *Spatial perspectives on problems and policies.* Chichester: John Wiley, 189–208.

BELL, D. 1973: *The coming of post-industrial society.* New York: Basic Books.

—— 1991: Insignificant others: lesbian and gay geographies. *Area* **23**, 323–29.

BELL, D., BINNIE, J., CREAM, J. and VALENTINE, G. 1994: All hyped up and no place to go. *Gender, Place and Culture* **1**, 31–47.

BELL, D. and VALENTINE, G. (eds) 1995: *Mapping desire: geographies of sexualities.* London and New York: Routledge.

BELL, M., BUTLIN, R. J. and HEFFERNAN, M. (eds) 1995: *Geography and imperialism: 1820–1940.* Manchester: Manchester University Press.

BENNETT, R. J. 1974: Process identification for time-series modelling in urban and regional planning. *Regional Studies* **8**, 157–74.

—— 1975: Dynamic systems modelling of the Northwest region: 1. Spatio-temporal representation and identification. 2. Estimation of the spatio-temporal policy model. 3. Adaptive parameter policy model. 4. Adaptive spatio-temporal forecasts. *Environment and Planning A* **7**, 525–38, 539–66, 617–36, 887–98.

—— 1978a: Forecasting in urban and regional planning closed loops: the examples of road and air traffic forecasts. *Environment and Planning A* **10**, 145–62.

—— 1978b: *Spatial time series: analysis, forecasting and control.* London: Pion.

—— 1979: Space-time models and urban geographical research. In D.T. Herbert and R. J. Johnston (eds) *Geography and the urban environment: progress in research and application,* vol. 2. London: John Wiley, 27–58.

—— 1981a: Quantitative geography and public policy. In N.Wrigley and R. J. Bennett (eds) *Quantitative geography.* London: Routledge & Kegan Paul, 387–96.

—— 1981b: A hierarchical control solution to allocation of the British Rate Support Grant. *Geographical Analysis* **13**, 300–14.

—— (ed.) 1981c: *European progress in spatial analysis.* London: Pion.

—— 1981d: Quantitative and theoretical geography in Western Europe. In R. J. Bennett (ed.) *European progress in spatial analysis.* London: Pion, 1–32.

—— 1982: Geography, relevance and the role of the Institute. *Area* **14**, 69–71.

—— 1983: Individual and territorial equity. *Geographical Analysis* **15**, 50–87.

—— 1985a: A reappraisal of the role of spatial science and statistical inference in geography in Britain. *L'Espace Géographique* **14**, 23–8.

—— 1985b: Quantification and relevance. In R. J. Johnston (ed.) *The future of geography.* London: Methuen, 211–24.

—— 1989a: Whither models and geography in a post-welfarist world? In B. Macmillan (ed.) *Remodelling geography.* Oxford: Basil Blackwell, 273–90.

—— 1989b: Demography and budgetary influence on the geography of the poll tax: alarm or false alarm? *Transactions, Institute of British Geographers* **NS14**, 400–17.

BENNETT, R. J. and CHORLEY, R. J. 1978: *Environmental systems: philosophy, analysis and control.* London: Methuen.

BENNETT, R. J. and HAINING, R. P. 1985: Spatial structure and spatial interaction: modelling approaches to the statistical analysis of geographical data. *Journal of the Royal Statistical Society A* **148**, 1–36.

BENNETT, R. J., HAINING, R. P., and WILSON, A. G. 1985: Spatial structure, spatial interaction and their integration: a review of alternative models. *Environment and Planning A* **17**, 625–46.

BENNETT, R. J. and THORNES, J. B. 1988: Geography in the United Kingdom, 1984–1988. *The Geographical Journal* **154**, 23–48.

BENNETT, R. J. and WILSON, A. G. 2003: Geography applied. In R. J. Johnston and M. Williams (eds), *A Century of British Geography.* Oxford: Oxford University Press for the British Academy, 463–501.

BENNETT, R. J. and WRIGLEY, N. 1981: Introduction. In N. Wrigley and R. J. Bennett (eds), *Quantitative geography.* London: Routledge & Kegan Paul, 3–11.

BENTHAM, G. 1987: An evaluation of the UGC's rating of the research of British university geography departments. *Area* **19**, 147–54.

BERDOULAY, V. 1981: The contextual approach. In D. R. Stoddart (ed.) *Geography, ideology and social concern.* Oxford: Blackwell, 8–16.

BERG, L. D. 1993: Between modernism and postmodernism. *Progress in Human Geography* **17**, 490–507.

—— 2003: (Some) spaces of critical geography. In A. Rogers and H. R. Viles (eds) *The students' companion to geography,* 2nd edn. Oxford: Blackwell.

BERG, L. D. and KEARNS, R. A. 1998: America Unlimited. *Environment and Planning D: Society and Space* **16**, 128–32.

BERMAN, M. 1974: Sex discrimination in geography: the case of Ellen Churchill Semple. *The Professional Geographer* **26**, 8–11.

BERRY, B. J. L. 1958: A critique of contemporary planning for business centers. *Land Economics* **25**, 306–12.

—— 1959a: Ribbon developments in the urban business pattern. *Annals of the Association of American Geographers* **49**, 145–55.

—— 1959b: Further comments 'geographic' and 'economic' economic geography. *The Professional Geographer* **11(1)**, 11–12.

—— 1964a: Cities as systems within systems of cities. *Papers, Regional Science Association* **13**, 147–63.

—— 1964b: Approaches to regional analysis: a synthesis. *Annals of the Association of American Geographers* **54**, 2–11.

—— 1965: Research frontiers in urban geography. In P. M. Hauser and L. F. Schnore (eds) *The study of urbanization*. New York: John Wiley, 403–30.

—— 1966: *Essays on commodity flows and the spatial structure of the Indian economy*. Chicago: University of Chicago, Department of Geography, Research Paper 111.

—— 1967: *The geography of market centers and retail distribution*. Englewood Cliffs, NJ: Prentice-Hall.

—— 1968: A synthesis of formal and functional regions using a general field theory of spatial behavior. In B. J. L. Berry and D. F. Marble (eds) *Spatial analysis*. Englewood Cliffs, NJ: Prentice-Hall, 419–28.

—— 1969: Review of B. M. Russett *International regions and the international system*. *The Geographical Review* **59**, 450–1.

—— (ed.) 1971: Comparative factorial ecology. *Economic Geography* **47**, 209–367.

—— 1972a: Hierarchical diffusion: the basis of development filtering and spread in a system of growth centers. In N. M. Hansen (ed.) *Growth centers in regional economic development*. New York: The Free Press, 108–38.

—— 1972b: 'Revolutionary and counter-revolutionary theory in geography' – a ghetto commentary. *Antipode* **4(2)**, 31–3.

—— 1972c: More on relevance and policy analysis. *Area* **4**, 77–80.

—— 1973a: *The human consequences of urbanization*. London: Macmillan.

—— 1973b: A paradigm for modern geography. In R. J. Chorley (ed.) *Directions in geography*. London: Methuen, 3–22.

—— 1974a: Review of H. M. Rose (ed.) *Perspectives in geography 2. Geography of the ghetto, perceptions, problems and alternatives*. *Annals of the Association of American Geographers* **64**, 342–5.

—— 1974b: Review of David Harvey, *Social Justice and the City*. *Antipode* **6(2)**, 142–5, 448.

—— 1978a: Introduction: a Kuhnian perspective. In B. J. L. Berry (ed.) *The nature of change in geographical ideas*. de Kalb: Northern Illinois University Press, vii–x.

—— 1978b: Geographical theories of social change. In B. J. L. Berry (ed.) *The nature of change in geographical ideas*. de Kalb: Northern Illinois University Press, 17–36.

—— 1993: Geography's quantitative revolution: initial conditions, 1954–1960: a personal memoir. *Urban Geography* **14**, 434–41.

—— 1995: Whither regional science? *International Regional Science Review* **17**, 297–306.

—— 1998: On consilience. *Urban Geography* **19**, 95–97.

—— 1999: Beyond postmodernism. *Urban Geography* **20**, 589–590.

—— 2002a: Clara voce cognito. . In P. Gould and F. R. Pitts, (eds), *Geographical voices: fourteen autobiographical essays*. Syracuse: Syracuse University Press, 1–26.

—— 2002b: The Chicago School in retrospect. *Urban Geography* **22**, 559–61.

—— 2002c: Paradigm lost. *Urban Geography* **23**, 441–5.

—— 2002d: Big tents or firm foundations? *Urban Geography* **23**, 501–2.

—— 2002e: My Cheshire cat's smile. *Urban Geography* **23**, 1–2.

BERRY, B. J. L. and BAKER, A. M. 1968: Geographic sampling. In B. J. L. Berry and D. F. Marble (eds) *Spatial analysis*. Englewood Cliffs, NJ: Prentice-Hall, 91–100.

BERRY, B. J. L. and GARRISON, W. L. 1958a: The functional bases of the central place hierarchy. *Economic Geography* **34**, 145–54.

—— 1958b: Recent developments in central place theory. *Papers and Proceedings, Regional Science Association* **4**, 107–20.

BERRY, B. J. L. and HORTON, F. E. (eds) 1974: *Urban environmental management: planning for pollution control.* Englewood Cliffs, NJ: Prentice-Hall.

BERRY, B. J. L. *et al.* 1974: *Land use, urban form and environmental quality.* Chicago: Department of Geography, Research Paper 155, University of Chicago.

BERRY, B. J. L., GOHEEN, P. G. and GOLDSTEIN, H. 1969: *Metropolitan area definition: a re-evaluation of the concept and statistical practice.* Washington DC: US Bureau of the Census.

BHASKAR, R. 1978: A *realist theory of science.* Brighton: Harvester Press.

BILLINGE, M. 1977: In search of negativism: phenomenology and historical geography. *Journal of Historical Geography* **3**, 55–68.

—— 1983: The mandarin dialect: an essay on style in contemporary geographical writing. *Transactions, Institute of British Geographers* **NS8**, 400–20.

BILLINGE, M., GREGORY, D. and MARTIN, R. L. (eds) 1984: *Recollections of a revolution: geography as spatial science.* London: Macmillan.

BINGHAM, N. 1996: Object-ions: from technological determinism towards geographies of relations. *Environment and Planning D: Society and Space* **14**, 635–7.

BINNIE, J. 1997: Coming out of geography: towards a queer epistemology? *Environment and Planning D: Society and Space* **15**, 223–37.

BINNIE, J. and VALENTINE, G. 1999: Geographies of sexuality – a review of progress. *Progress in Human Geography* **23**, 175–87.

BIRD, A. 2000: *Thomas Kuhn.* Chesham: Acumen Books.

BIRD, J. H. 1975: Methodological implications for geography from the philosophy of K. R. Popper. *Scottish Geographical Magazine* **91**, 153–63.

—— 1977: Methodology and philosophy. *Progress in Human Geography* **1**, 104–10.

—— 1978: Methodology and philosophy. *Progress in Human Geography* **2**, 133–40.

—— 1985: Geography in three worlds: how Popper's system can help elucidate dichotomies and changes in the discipline. *The Professional Geographer* **37**, 403–9.

—— 1989: *The changing worlds of geography: a critical guide to concepts and methods.* Oxford: Clarendon Press.

BIRKIN, M. 1995: Customer targeting, geodemographics and lifestyle approaches. In P. Longley and G. Clarke (eds) *GIS for business and service planning.* Cambridge: GeoInformation International, 104–49.

BIRKIN, M. and CLARKE, M. 1988: SYNTHESIS: a synthetic spatial information system: methods and examples. *Environment and Planning A* **20**, 645–71.

—— 1989: The generation of individual and household incomes at the small area level using SYNTHESIS. *Regional Studies* **23**, 535–48.

BIRKIN, M., CLARKE, G. P. and CLARKE, M. 2002: *Retail geography and intelligent network planning.* Chichester: John Wiley.

BIRKIN, M., CLARKE, G., CLARKE, M. and WILSON, A. G. 1990: Elements of a model-based GIS for evaluation of urban policy. In L. Worrall (ed.) *Geographic information systems: development and applications.* London: Belhaven Press, 131–62.

—— 1996: *Intelligent GIS: location decisions and strategic planning.* Cambridge: Geoinformation International.

BIRKIN, M., CLARKE, M. and GEORGE, F. 1995: The use of parallel computers to solve nonlinear spatial optimisation problems: an application to network planning. *Environment and Planning A* **27**, 1049–68.

BIRKIN, M. and WILSON, A. G. 1986: Industrial location models 1. a review and integrating framework and 2. Weber, Palander, Hotelling and extensions within a new framework. *Environment and Planning A* **18**, 175–206 and 293–306.

BLAIKIE, P. M. 1978: The theory of the spatial diffusion of innovations: a spacious cul-de-sac. *Progress in Human Geography* **2**, 268–95.

—— 1985: *The political economy of soil erosion.* London: Longman.

—— 1986: Natural resource use in developing countries. In R. J. Johnston and P. J. Taylor (eds) *A world in crisis? Geographical perspectives*. Oxford: Basil Blackwell, 107–26.

BLAIKIE, P. M. and BROOKFIELD, H. C. (eds) 1987: *Land degradation and society*. London: Methuen.

BLALOCK, H. M. 1960: *Social statistics*. New York: McGraw Hill.

BLAUG, M. 1975: Kuhn versus Lakatos, or paradigms versus research programmes in the history of economics. *History of Political Economy* **7**, 399–419.

BLAUT, J. M. 1962: Object and relationship. *The Professional Geographer* **14**, 1–6.

—— 1975: Imperialism: the Marxist theory and its evolution. *Antipode* **7**, 1–19.

—— 1979: The dissenting tradition. *Annals of the Association of America Geographers* **69**, 157–64.

—— 1987: Diffusionism: a uniformitarian critique. *Annals of the Association of American Geographers* **77**, 30–47.

BLOUET, B. W. (ed.) 1981: *The origins of academic geography in the United States*. Hamden CT: Archon Books.

—— 1987: *Halford Mackinder: a biography*. College Station TX: Texas A & M University Press.

BLOWERS, A. T. 1972: Bleeding hearts and open values. *Area* **4**, 290–2.

—— 1974: Relevance, research and the political process. *Area* **6**, 32–6.

—— 1984: *Something in the air: corporate power and the environment*. London: Harper and Row.

BLUMENSTOCK, D. I. 1953: The reliability factor in the drawing of isarithms. *Annals of the Association of American Geographers* **43**, 289–304.

BLUNT, A. 1994: *Travel, gender and imperialism: Mary Kingsley and West Africa*. New York: Guilford.

BLUNT, A. and McEWAN, C. (eds) 2002: *Postcolonial geographies*. New York and London: Continuum.

BLUNT, A. and WILLS, J. 2000: *Dissident geographies: an introduction to radical ideas and practice*. Harlow: Pearson.

BOAL, F. W. and LIVINGSTONE, D. N. 1989: The behavioural environment: worlds of meaning in a world of facts. In F. W. Boal and D. N. Livingstone (eds) *The behavioural environment*. London: Routledge, 3–17.

BODDY, M. J. 1976: The structure of mortgage finance: building societies and the British social formation. *Transactions, Institute of British Geographers* **NS1**, 58–71.

BODMAN, A. R. 1991: Weavers of influence: the structure of contemporary geographic research. *Transactions, Institute of British Geographers* **NS16**, 21–7.

—— 1992: Holes in the fabric: more on the master weavers in human geography. *Transactions, Institute of British Geographers* **NS17**, 108–9.

BONDI, L. 1993: Locating identity politics. In M. Keith and S. Pile (eds) *Place and the politics of identity*. London: Routledge, 84–101.

—— 1997: In whose words? On gender identities, knowledge and writing practices. *Transactions, Institute of British Geographers* **22**, 245–58.

BONDI, L. and DOMOSH, M. 1992: Other figures in other places: on feminism, postmodernism and geography. *Environment and Planning D: Society and Space* **10**, 199–213.

—— 1994: Editorial. *Gender, Place and Culture* **1**, 3–4.

BONDI, L. et al. 2002: *Subjectivities, knowledges and feminist geographies: the subjects and ethics of social research*. Lanham MD: Rowmna and Littlefield.

BONNETT, A. 1993: Contours of crisis: anti-racism and reflexivity. In P. Jackson and J. Penrose (eds) *Constructions of race, place and nation*. London: UCL Press, 163–80.

—— 1997: Geography, 'race', and whiteness: invisible traditions and current challenges. *Area* **29**, 193–99.

—— 2003: Geography as the world discipline: connecting popular and academic geographical imaginations. *Area* **35**, 55–63.

BONNETT, A. and KNOOP, A. 2003: Cultural geographies of racialization – the territory of race. In K. Anderson, M. Domosh, S. Pile and N. Thrift (eds) *The handbook of cultural geography*. London, Thousand Oaks, CA and New Delhi: Sage, 300–12.

BONNETT, A. and NAYAK, A. 2003: Racialization – the territory of race. In K. Anderson, M. Domosh, S. Pile and N. Thrift (eds) *The handbook of cultural geography*. London, Thousand Oaks, CA and New Delhi: Sage, 300–12.

BOOTS, B. N. and GETIS, A. 1978: *Models of spatial processes*. Cambridge: Cambridge University Press.

BORGES, J. L. 1949: *El aleph*. Buenos Aires: Losado.
http://usarios.lycos.es/bibliotecario/relatos/ALEPH.htm.

—— 1988: *Homo academicus*. Cambridge: Polity.

BOURDIEU, P. 1990: *The logic of practice*. Cambridge: Polity.

BOWEN, M. 1970: Mind and nature: the physical geography of Alexander von Humboldt. *Scottish Geographical Magazine* **86**, 222–33.

—— 1981: *Empiricism and geographical thought from Francis Bacon to Alexander von Humboldt*. Cambridge: Cambridge University Press.

BOWLBY, S. R., FOORD, J. and MCDOWELL, L. 1986: The place of gender in locality studies. *Area* **18**, 327–31.

BOWLBY, S. R., LEWIS, J., McDOWELL, L. and FOORD, J. 1989: The geography of gender. In Peet, R. and Thrift, N. J. (eds) *New models in geography*, vol. 2. London: Unwin Hyman, 157–75.

BOWMAN, I. 1921: *The New World: problems in political geography*. New York: Harrap.

BOYER, R. and SAILLARD, Y. (eds) 1995: *Regulation theory: the state of the art*. London and New York: Routledge.

BOYLE, M. J. and ROBINSON, M. E. 1979: Cognitive mapping and understanding. In D. T. Herbert and R. J. Johnston (eds) *Geography and the urban environment*, vol. 2. Chichester: John Wiley, 59–82.

BRACKEN, I., HIGGS, G., MARTIN, D. and WEBSTER, C. 1990: *A classification of geographical information systems literature and applications*. CATMOG 52, Norwich: Environmental Publications.

BRADLEY, P. N. 1986: Food production and distribution – and hunger. In R. J. Johnston and P. J. Taylor (eds) *A world in crisis? Geographical perspectives*. Oxford: Basil Blackwell, 89–106.

BRAUN, B. and CASTREE, N. (eds) 1998: *Remaking reality: nature at the millennium*. London and New York: Routledge.

BREITBART, M. M. 1981: Peter Kropotkin, the anarchist geographer. In D. R. Stoddart (ed.) *Geography, ideology and social concern*. Oxford: Blackwell, 134–53.

BRENNER, N., JESSOP, B., JONES, M. and MacLEOD, G. (eds) 2003: *State/space: a reader*. Oxford: Blackwell.

BRENNER, N. and THEODORE, N. 2002a: From the 'new localism' to the spaces of neoliberalis. *Antipode* **34**, 341–7.

—— 2002b: Cities and the geographies of 'actually existing neoliberalism'. *Antipode* **34**, 349–379.

BRIGGS, D. J. 1981: The principles and practice of applied geography. *Applied Geography* **1**, 1–8.

BRITTAN, S. 1977: Economic liberalism. In A. Bullock and O. Stallybrass (eds) *The Fontana dictionary of modern thought*. London: William Collins, 188–9.

BROOKFIELD, H. C. 1962: Local study and comparative method: an example from Central New Guinea. *Annals of the Association of American Geographers* **52**, 242–54.

—— 1964: Questions on the human frontiers of geography. *Economic Geography* **40**, 283–303.

—— 1969: On the environment as perceived. In C. Board et al. (eds) *Progress in Geography 1*. London: Edward Arnold, 51–80.

—— 1973: On one geography and a Third World. *Transactions, Institute of British Geographers* **58**, 1–20.

—— 1975: *Interdependent development*. London: Methuen.

—— 1989: The behavioural environment: how, what for, and whose? In F. W. Boal and D. N. Livingstone (eds) *The behavioural environment*. London: Routledge, 311.

BROWETT, J. 1984: On the necessity and inevitability of uneven spatial development under capitalism. *International Journal of Urban and Regional Research* **8**, 155–76.

BROWN, L. A. 1968: *Diffusion processes and location: a conceptual framework and bibliography.* Regional Science Research Institute, Bibliography Series 3, Philadelphia.

—— 1975: The market and infrastructure context of adoption: a spatial perspective on the diffusion of innovation. *Economic Geography* **51**, 185–216.

—— 1981: *Innovation diffusion: a new perspective.* London: Methuen.

BROWN, L. A. and MOORE, E. G. 1970: The intra-urban migration process: a perspective. *Geografiska Annaler* **52B**, 1–13.

BROWN, M. 1995: Ironies of distance: an ongoing critique of geographies of AIDS. *Environment and Planning D: Society and Space* **13**, 159–83.

BROWN, M. and KNOPP, L. 2003: Queer cultural geographies – We're here! We're queer! We're over there, too! In K. Anderson, M. Domosh, S. Pile and N. Thrift (eds) *The handbook of cultural geography.* London, Thousand Oaks, CA and New Delhi: Sage, 313–29.

BROWN, R. H. 1943: *Mirror for Americans: likenesses of the eastern seaboard 1810.* New York: American Geographical Society.

BROWN, S. E. 1978: Guy-Harold Smith, 1895–1976. *Annals of the Association of American Geographers* **68**, 115–18.

BROWNING, C. 1982: *Conversations with geographers: career pathways and research styles.* University of North Carolina at Chapel Hill, Department of Geography, Occasional Paper 16.

BROWNING, C. E. 1982: *Conversations with geographers: career pathways and research style.* Chapel Hill: University of North Carolina Press.

BRUNN, S. D. 1974: *Geography and politics in America.* New York: Harper & Row.

BRUSH, J. E. 1953: The hierarchy of central places in southwestern Wisconsin. *Geographical Review* **43**, 380–402.

—— 1973: The white north and the population explosion. *Antipode* **5(3)**, 7–15.

BUCHANAN, K. M. 1958a: Review of R. J. Harrison Church, *West Africa: a study of the environment and man's use of it.* London: Longman, 1957. *Economic Geography* **34**, 277–8.

—— 1958b: Review of R. W. Steel and C. A. Fisher (eds), *Geographical essays on British tropical lands.* London: George Phillip, 1956. *The Geographical Review,* 48, 447–9.

—— 1962: West wind, east wind. *Geography* **47**, 333–46.

—— 1966: *The Chinese people and the Chinese earth.* London: Bell.

BUCHANAN, K. M. and PUGH, J. C. (1958) *Land and people in Nigeria: the human geography of Nigeria and its environmental basis.* London: University of London Press.

BUCHANAN, R. O. 1968: The man and his work. *Land use and resources: studies in applied geography.* London: Institute of British Geographers, Special Publication 1, 1–12.

BULLOCK, A. 1977: Liberalism. In A. Bullock and O. Stallybrass (eds) *The Fontana dictionary of modern thought.* London: William Collins, 347.

BUNGE, W. 1962: second edition, 1966. *Theoretical geography.* Lund Studies in Geography, Series C 1, Lund: C. W. K. Gleerup.

—— 1966: Locations are not unique. *Annals of the Association of America Geographers* **56**, 375–6.

—— 1968: Fred K. Schaefer and the science of geography. *Harvard Papers in Theoretical Geography,* Special Papers Series, Paper A, Laboratory for Computer Graphics and Spatial Analysis, Harvard University, Cambridge, MA.

—— 1971: *Fitzgerald: geography of a revolution.* Cambridge, MA: Schlenkman.

—— 1973a: Spatial prediction. *Annals of the Association of American Geographers* **63**, 566–8.

—— 1973b: Ethics and logic in geography. In R. J. Chorley (ed.) *Directions in geography.* London: Methuen, 317–31.

—— 1973c: The geography of human survival. *Annals of the Association of American Geographers* **63**, 275–95.

—— 1973d: The geography. *The Professional Geographer* **25**, 331–7.

—— 1979: Fred K. Schaefer and the science of geography. *Annals of the Association of American Geographers* **69**, 128–33.

BUNGE, W. and BORDESSA, R. 1975: *The Canadian alternative: survival, expeditions and urban change*. Geographical Monographs, Atkinson College, York University, Downsview, Ontario.

BUNTING, T. E. and GUELKE, L. 1979: Behavioral and perception geography: a critical appraisal. *Annals of the Association of American Geographers* **69**, 448–62, 471–4.

BURNETT, K. P. (ed.) 1981: Studies in choice, constraints, and human spatial behavior. *Economic Geography* **57**, 291–383.

BURNETT, P. 1973: Social change, the status of women and models of city form and development. *Antipode* **5**, 57–62.

BURTON, I. 1963: The quantitative revolution and theoretical geography. *The Canadian Geographer* **7**, 151–62.

BURTON, I., KATES, R. W. and WHITE, G. F. 1978: *The environment as hazard*. New York: Oxford University Press.

BUSHONG, A. D. 1981: Geographers and their mentors: a genealogical view of American academic geography. In B. W. Blouet (ed.) *The origins of academic geography in the United States*. Hamden, CT: Archon Books, 193–220.

BUTLER, R. and BOWLBY, S. 1997: Bodies and spaces: an exploration of disabled people's experiences of public space. *Environment and Planning D: Society and Space* **15**, 411–33.

BUTLER, R. and PARR, H. (eds) 1999: *Mind and body spaces: geographies of illness, impairment and disability*. London: Routledge.

BUTLIN, R. A. 1982: *The transformation of rural England c. 1580–1800*. Oxford: Oxford University Press.

BUTTIMER, A. 1971: *Society and milieu in the French geographical tradition*. Chicago: Rand McNally.

—— 1974: *Values in geography*. Commission on College Geography, Resource Paper 24, Association of American Geographers, Washington.

—— 1976: Grasping the dynamism of lifeworld. *Annals of the Association of American Geographers* **66**, 277–92.

—— 1978a: Charism and context: the challenge of *La Geographie Humaine*. In D. Ley and M. S. Samuels (eds) *Humanistic geography: prospects and problems*. Chicago: Maaroufa Press, 58–76.

—— 1978b: On people, paradigms and progress in geography. Institutionen for Kulturgeografi oeh Eeonomisk Geografi vid Lunds Universitet, *Rapporter och Notiser* **47**.

—— 1979: Erewhon or nowhere land. In S. Gale and G. Olsson (eds) *Philosophy in geography*. Dordrecht: D. Reidel, 9–38.

—— 1981: On people, paradigms and progress in geography. In D. R. Stoddart (ed.) *Geography, ideology and social concern*. Oxford: Blackwell, 70–80.

—— 1983: *The practice of geography*. London: Longman.

—— 1993: *Geography and the human spirit*. Baltimore: Johns Hopkins University Press.

—— 1995: Book review. *Annals of the Association of American Geographers*, **85**, 406–7.

BUTTIMER, A. and FAHY, G. 1999: Imagining Ireland through geography texts. In A. Buttimer, S. D. Brunn and U. Wardenga (eds) *Text and image: social construction of regional knowledges*. Leipzig: Institut für Länderkunde Leipzig, Beiträge zur regionalen Geographie **49**, 179–91.

BUTTIMER, A. and HÄGERSTRAND, T. 1980: *Invitation to dialogue: a progress report*. DIA Paper 1, Lund: University of Lund.

BUTZER, K. W. 1989: Cultural ecology. In G. L. Gaile and C. J. Willmot (eds) *Geography in America*. Columbus, OH: Merrill, 192–208.

—— 1990: Hartshorne, Hettner, and *The Nature of Geography*. In J. N. Entrikin and S. D. Brunn (eds) *Reflections on Richard Hartshorne's The Nature of Geography*. Washington: Association of American Geographers, 35–52.

CADWALLADER, M. 1975: A behavioral model of consumer spatial decision making. *Economic Geography* **51**, 339–49.

——— 1986: Structural equation models in human geography. *Progress in Human Geography* **10**, 24–47.

CAMERON, I. 1980: *To the farthest ends of the earth.* London: Macdonald.

CAMPBELL, C. S. 1994: The second nature of geography: Hartshorne as humanist. *The Professional Geographer* **46**, 411–17.

CAMPBELL, J. A. 1989: The concept of 'the behavioural environment', and its origins, reconsidered. In F. W. Boal and D. N. Livingstone (eds) *The behavioural environment.* London: Routledge, 33–76.

CAMPBELL, J. A. and LIVINGSTONE, D. N. 1983: Neo-Lamarckism and the development of geography in the United States and Great Britain. *Transactions, Institute of British Geographers* **NS8**, 267–94.

CANON, T. 1975: Geography and underdevelopment. *Area* **7**, 212–6.

CAPEL, H. 1981: Institutionalization of geography and strategies of change. In D. R. Stoddart (ed.) *Geography, ideology and social concern.* Oxford: Blackwell, 37–69.

——— 1981: *Filosofía y ciencia en la geografía contemporánea: una introdución a la geografía.* Barcelona: Barcano.

CAREY, H. C. 1858: *Principles of social science.* Philadelphia: J. Lippincott.

CARLSTEIN, T. 1980: *Time, resources, society and ecology.* Lund: Department of Geography, University of Lund.

CARLSTEIN, T., PARKES, D. N. and THRIFT, N. J. (eds) 1978: *Timing space and spacing time* (three volumes). London: Edward Arnold.

CARR, M. 1983: A contribution to the review and critique of behavioural industrial location theory. *Progress in Human Geography* **7**, 386–402.

CARROLL, G. R. 1982: National city-size distributions: what do we know after 67 years of research? *Progress in Human Geography* **6**, 1–43.

CARROTHERS, G. A. P. 1956: An historical review of the gravity and potential concepts of human interaction. *Journal, American Institute of Planners* **22**, 94–102.

CARTER, G. 1977: A geographical society should be a geographical society. *The Professional Geographer* **29**, 101–2.

CASETTI, E. 1999: The evolution of scientific disciplines, mathematical modelling and human geography. *Geographical Analysis* **30**, 332–9.

CASTELLS, M. 1977: *The urban question.* London: Edward Arnold.

CASTREE, N. 1994: Teaching history, philosophy and theory: notes on representing Marxism and 'Marxist geography'. *Journal of Geography in Higher Education* **18**, 33–42.

——— 1995a: Review essay. The lonely hour of the last word: Marx, Althusser, and the critical critics. *Environment and Planning A* **27**, 1163–78.

——— 1995b: The nature of produced nature. *Antipode* **27**, 13–48.

——— 1996: Birds, mice and geography: Marxisms and dialectics. *Transactions, Institute of British Geographers* **NS21**, 342–62.

——— 1999: Editorial: situating cultural twists and turns. *Environment and Planning D: Society and Space* **17**, 257–260.

——— 2002: The antinomies of Antipode. *Antipode* **34**, 672–8.

——— 2003: Geographies of nature in the making. In K. Anderson, M. Domosh, S. Pile and N. Thrift (eds) *The handbook of cultural geography.* London, Thousand Oaks, CA and New Delhi: Sage, 168–83.

——— 2004: Environmental issues: signals in the noise? *Progress in Human Geography* **28**, 79–90.

CASTREE, N. and BRAUN, B. (eds) 2001: *Social nature: theory, practice and politics.* London: Blackwell.

CHAPMAN, G. P. 1977: *Human and environmental systems: a geographer's appraisal.* London: Academic Press.

—— 1982: *The green revolution game*. Cambridge: Marginal Context.

CHAPPELL, J. E., Jr. 1975: The ecological dimension: Russian and American views. *Annals of the Association of American Geographers* **65**, 144–62.

—— 1976: Comment in reply. *Annals of the Association of American Geographers* **66**, 169–73.

CHAPPELL, J. M. A. and WEBBER, M. J. 1970: Electrical analogues of spatial diffusion processes. *Regional Studies* **4**, 25–39.

CHARLTON, M., RAO, L. and CARVER, S. 1995: GIS and the census. In S. Openshaw (ed.) *Census users' handbook*. Cambridge: GeoInformation International.

CHISHOLM, G. G. 1895: *Handbook of Commercial Geography*. London: Longman.

—— 1899: *The Times Gazetteer of the World*. London: The Times.

CHISHOLM, M. 1962: *Rural settlement and land use*. London: Hutchinson.

—— 1966: *Geography and economics*. London: G. Bell & Sons.

—— 1967: General systems theory and geography. *Transactions, Institute of British Geographers* **42**, 45–52.

—— 1971a: In search of a basis for location theory: micro-economics or welfare economics? In C. Board *et al.* (eds) *Progress in Geography 3*, London: Edward Arnold, 111–34.

—— 1971b: Geography and the question of 'relevance'. *Area* **3**, 65–8.

—— 1971c: *Research in human geography*. London: Heinemann.

—— 1973: The corridors of geography. *Area* **5**, 43.

—— 1975a: *Human geography: evolution or revolution?* Harmondsworth: Penguin Books.

—— 1975b: The reformation of local government in England. In R. Peel, M. Chisholm and P. Haggett (eds) *Processes in physical and human geography: Bristol essays*. London: Heinemann, 305–18.

—— 1976: Regional policies in an era of slow population growth and higher unemployment. *Regional Studies* **10**, 201–13.

—— 1995: Some lessons from the review of local government in England. *Regional Studies* **29**, 563–9.

—— 2000: *Structural reform of British local government: rhetoric and reality*. Manchester: Manchester University Press.

—— 2001: Human geography joins the Social Science Research Council: personal recollections. *Area* **33**, 428–30.

CHISHOLM, M. and RODGERS, B. (eds) 1973: *Studies in human geography*. London: Heinemann.

CHISHOLM, M., FREY, A. E. and HAGGETT, P. (eds) 1971: *Regional forecasting*. London: Butterworth.

CHISHOLM, M. and MANNERS, G. (eds) 1973: *Spatial policy problems of the British economy*. London: Cambridge University Press.

CHISHOLM, M. and O'SULLIVAN, P. 1973: *Freight flows and spatial aspects of the British economy*. Cambridge: Cambridge University Press.

CHORLEY, R. J. 1962: Geomorphology and general systems theory. *Professional Paper 500–B*, United States Geological Survey, Washington.

—— 1964: Geography and analogue theory. *Annals of the Association of American Geographers* **54**, 127–37.

—— 1973a: Geography as human ecology. In R. J. Chorley (ed.) *Directions in geography*. London: Methuen, 155–70.

—— (ed.) 1973b: *Directions in geography*. London: Methuen.

—— 1995: Haggett's Cambridge: 1957–1966. In A. D. Cliff, P. R. Gould, A. G. Hoare and N. J. Thrift (eds) *Diffusing geography*. Oxford: Blackwell Publishers, 355–74.

CHORLEY, R. J. and BENNETT, R. J. 1981: Optimization: control models. In N. Wrigley and R. J. Bennett (eds) *Quantitative geography*. London: Routledge & Kegan Paul, 219–24.

CHORLEY, R. J. and HAGGETT, P. 1965a: Trend-surface mapping in geographical research. *Transactions and Papers, Institute of British Geographers* **37**, 47–67.

—— (eds) 1965b: *Frontiers in geographical teaching.* London: Methuen.

—— (eds) 1967: *Models in geography.* London: Methuen.

CHORLEY, R. J. and KENNEDY, B. A. 1971: *Physical geography: a systems approach.* London: Prentice-Hall International.

CHOUINARD, V., FINCHER, R. and WEBBER, M. 1984: Empirical research in scientific human geography. *Progress in Human Geography* **8**, 347–80.

CHOUINARD, V. and GRANT, A. 1995: On being not even anywhere near 'the project': ways of putting ourselves in the picture. *Antipode* **27**, 137–66.

CHRISMAN, N. R., COWEN, D. J., FISHER, P. F., GOODCHILD, M. F. and MARK, D. M. 1989: Geographic information systems. In G. L. Gaile and C. J. Willmott (eds) *Geography in America.* Columbus, OH: Merrill, 776–96.

CHRISTALLER, W. 1966: *Central places in southern Germany* (translated by C. W. Baskin). Englewood Cliffs, NJ: Prentice-Hall.

CHRISTENSEN, K. 1982: Geography as a human science. In P. Gould and G. Olsson (eds) *A search for common ground.* London: Pion, 37–57.

CHRISTOPHERSON, S. 1989: On being outside 'the project'. *Antipode* **21**, 83–9.

CIRINCIONE, C., DARLING, T. A. and O'ROURKE, T. G. 2000: Assessing South Carolina's congressional districting. *Political Geography* **19**, 189–212.

CLARK, A. H. 1949: *The invasion of New Zealand by people, plants and animals: the South Island.* New Brunswick NJ: Rutgers University Press.

—— 1954: Historical geography. In P. E. James and C. F. Jones (eds) *American geography: inventory and prospects.* Syracuse: Syracuse University Press, 70–105.

—— 1977: The whole is greater than the sum of the parts: a humanistic element in human geography. In D. R. Deskins *et al.* (eds) *Geographic humanism, analysis and social action: a half century of geography at Michigan.* Ann Arbor Michigan Geographical Publication No. 17, 3–26.

CLARK, D. and DOEL, M. 1995: Transpolitical geography. *Geoforum* **25**, 505–24.

CLARK, D., DAVIES, W. K. D. and JOHNSTON, R. J. 1974: The application of factor analysis in human geography. *The Statistician* **23**, 259–81.

CLARK, G. L. 1982: Instrumental reason and policy analysis. In D. T. Herbert and R. J. Johnston (eds) *Geography and the urban environment,* vol. 5. Chichester: John Wiley, 41–62.

—— 1985: *Judges and the cities.* Chicago: University of Chicago Press.

—— 1992: Real regulation reconsidered. *Environment and Planning A* **24**, 615–27.

CLARK, G. L. and DEAR, M. J. 1984: *State apparatus.* Boston: George Allen & Unwin.

CLARK, G. L, FELDMAN, M. P. and GERTLER, M. S. (eds.) 2000a: *The Oxford handbook of economic geography.* Oxford: Oxford University Press.

—— 2000b: Economic geography: transition and growth. In G. L. Clark, M. P. Feldmann and M. S. Gertler, (eds), *The Oxford handbook of economic geography.* Oxford: Oxford University Press, 3–17.

CLARK, K. G. T. 1950: Certain underpinnings of our arguments in human geography. *Transactions, Institute of British Geographers* **16**, 15–22.

CLARK, W. A. V. 1975: Locational stress and residential mobility in a New Zealand context. *New Zealand Geographer* **31**, 67–79.

—— 1981: Residential mobility and behavioral geography: parallelism or interdependence? In K. R. Cox and R. C. Golledge (eds) *Behavioral problems in geography revisited.* London: Methuen, 182–205.

—— 1991: Geography in court: expertise in adversarial settings. *Transactions, Institute of British Geographers* **NS16**, 5–20.

—— 1993: Applying our understanding: social science in government and the marketplace. *Environment and Planning A* anniversary issue, 38–47.

—— 2002: Pacific views of urban geography in the 1960s. *Urban Geography* **22**, 540–8.

CLARKE, G. P. (ed.) 1996: *Microsimulation for urban and regional policy analysis.* London: Pion.

CLARKE, K. C. 1998: Visualising different geofutures. In P. A. Longley, S. M. Brooks, R. MacDonnell, and B. Macmillan (eds) *Geocomputation: a primer*. Chichester: John Wiley, 119–37.

CLARKE, M. and HOLM, E. 1987: Towards an applicable human geography: some developments and observations. *Environment and Planning A* **19**, 1525–41.

—— 1988: Microsimulation methods in spatial analysis and planning. *Geografiska Annaler* **69B**, 145–64.

CLARKE, M. and WILSON, A. G. 1985a: A model-based approach to planning in the National Health Service. *Environment and Planning B: Planning and Design* **12**, 287–302.

—— 1985b: The dynamics of urban spatial structure: the progress of a research programme. *Transactions, Institute of British Geographers* **NS10**, 427–51.

—— 1989: Mathematical models in human geography. In R. Peet and N. J. Thrift (eds) *New models in geography*, vol. 2. London: Unwin Hyman, 30–42.

CLARKSON, J. D. 1970: Ecology and spatial analysis. *Annals of the Association of American Geographers* **60**, 700–16.

CLAVAL, P. 1981: Epistemology and the history of geographical thought. In D. R. Stoddart (ed.) *Geography, ideology and social concern*. Oxford: Blackwell, 227–39.

—— 1983: *Models of man in geography*. Syracuse: Department of Geography, Syracuse University, Discussion Paper 79.

—— 1999: Historians, geography and the general public in France. In A. Buttimer, S. D. Brunn and U. Wardenga (eds) *Text and image: social construction of regional knowledges*. Leipzig: Institut für Länderkunde Leipzig, Beiträge zur regionalen Geographie **49**, 70–6.

CLAYTON, D. 2001: Questions of postcolonial geography. *Antipode* **33**, 749–51.

—— 2002: Critical imperial and colonial geographies. In K. Anderson, M. Domosh, S. Pile and N. Thrift (eds) *The handbook of cultural geography*. London, Thousand Oaks, CA and New Delhi: Sage, 531–57.

CLAYTON, K. M. 1985a: New blood by (government) order. *Area* **17**, 321–2.

—— 1985b: The state of geography. *Transactions, Institute of British Geographers* **NS10**, 5–16.

CLIFF, A. D. and HAGGETT, P. 1988: *Atlas of disease distributions: analytical approaches to epidemiological data*. Oxford: Blackwell Publishers.

—— 1989: Spatial aspects of epidemic control. *Progress in Human Geography* **13**, 315–47.

—— 1995: Disease implications of global change. In R. J. Johnston, P. J. Taylor and M. J. Watts (eds) *Geographies of global change: remapping the world in the late twentieth century*. Oxford: Blackwell Publishers, 206–22.

—— 1998: On complex geographical space: computing frameworks for spatial diffusion processes. In P. A. Longley, S. M. Brooks, R. MacDonnell, and B. Macmillan (eds) *Geocomputation: a primer*. Chichester: John Wiley, 231–56.

—— 2003: The geography of disease distributions. In R. J. Johnston and M. Williams, (eds), *A century of British geography*. Oxford: Oxford University Press for the British Academy, 463–501.

CLIFF, A. D., HAGGETT, P. and ORD, J. K. 1987: *Spatial aspects of influenza epidemics*. London: Pion.

CLIFF, A. D., HAGGETT, P. and SMALLMAN-RAYNOR, M. 1993: *Measles: an historical geography of a major human viral disease from global expansion to local retreat, 1840–1990*. Cambridge: Cambridge University Press.

CLIFF, A. D. and ORD, J. K. 1973: *Spatial autocorrelation*. London: Pion.

—— 1981: *Spatial process*. London: Pion.

CLIFF, A. D. et al. 1975: *Elements of spatial structure: a quantitative approach*. London: Cambridge University Press.

—— et al. 1981: *Spatial diffusion*. Cambridge: Cambridge University Press.

CLIFFORD, N. 2002: The future of geography: when the whole is less than the sum of the parts. *Geoforum* **33**, 421–5.

CLOKE, P. J. 2002: Deliver us from evil? Prospects for living ethically and acting politically in human geography. *Progress in Human Geography* **26**, 587–604.

CLOKE, P. and GOODWIN, M. 1992: Conceptualising countryside change: from Post-Fordism to rural structural coherence. *Transactions, Institute of British Geographers* **NS17**, 321–36.

CLOKE, P., PHILO, C. and SADLER, D. 1991: *Approaching human geography: an introduction to contemporary theoretical debates*. London: Paul Chapman Publishing.

CLOUT, H. 2003a: Place description, regional geography and area studies: the chorographic inheritance. In R. J. Johnston and M. Williams (eds) *A century of British geography*. Oxford: Oxford University Press for the British Academy, 247–74.

—— 2003b: *Geography at University College London: A brief history*. London: Department of Geography, University College London.

CLOUT, H. and GOSME, C. 2003: The Naval Intelligence Handbooks: a monument in geographical writing. *Progress in Human Geography* **27**, 153–73.

COATES, B. E., JOHNSTON, R. J. and KNOX, P. L. 1977: *Geography and inequality*. Oxford: Oxford University Press.

COCHRANE, A. 1987: What a difference the place makes: the new structuralism of locality. *Antipode* **19**, 354–63.

COFFEY, W. J. 1981: *Geography: towards a general spatial systems approach*. London: Methuen.

COLE, J. P. 1969: Mathematics and geography. *Geography* **54**, 152–63.

COLE, J. P. and KING C. A. M. 1968: *Quantitative geography*. London: John Wiley.

COLLINS, M. J. 2002: *Cold War laboratory: RAND, the Air Force and the American State, 1945–1950*. Washington DC: Smithsonian Institute Press.

CONANT, J. B. and HAUGELAND, J. (eds) 2000: *The Road since structure: philosophical essays 1970–1993, with an autobiographical interview*. Chicago: University of Chicago Press.

CONZEN, M. P. 1981: The American urban system in the nineteenth century. In D. T. Herbert and R. J. Johnston (eds) *Geography and the urban environment*, vol. 4. Chichester: John Wiley, 295–348.

COOK, I. and CRANG, M. 1995: *Doing ethnographies. Concepts and techniques in modern geography* 58. Norwich: Geo Books.

COOK, I., CROUCH, D., NAYLOR, S. and RYAN, J. R. 2000: Foreword. In I. Cook, D. Crouch, S. Naylor and J. R. Ryan (eds) *Cultural turns/geographical turns: perspectives on cultural geography*. Harlow: Prentice Hall, xi–xii.

COOKE, P. N. 1986: The changing urban and regional system in the United Kingdom. *Regional Studies* **20**, 243–52.

—— 1987a: Clinical inference and geographic theory. *Antipode* **19**, 69–78.

—— 1987b: Individuals, localities and postmodernism. *Environment and Planning D: Society and Space* **5**, 408–12.

—— (ed.) 1989a: *Localities: The changing face of urban Britain*. London: Unwin Hyman.

—— 1989b: Locality theory and the poverty of 'spatial variation' (A response to Duncan and Savage). *Antipode* **21**, 261–73.

—— 1990: *Back to the future: modernity, postmodernity and locality*. London: Unwin Hyman.

COOKE, R. U. 1985a: Applied geomorphology. In A. Kent (ed.) *Perspectives on a changing geography*. Sheffield: The Geographical Association, 36–47.

—— 1985b: *Geomorphological hazards in Los Angeles*. London: George Allen & Unwin.

—— 1992: Common ground, shared inheritance: research imperatives for environmental geography. *Transactions, Institute of British Geographers* **NS17**, 131–51.

—— 2002: Presidential address. *The Geographical Journal* **168**, 260–3.

COOKE, R. U. and REEVES, R. W. 1976: *Arroyos and environmental change in the American south-west*. Oxford: Clarendon Press.

COOKE, R. U. and ROBSON, B. T. 1976: Geography in the United Kingdom, 1972–1976. *Geographical Journal* **142**, 3–22.

COOMBES, M. G. *et al.* 1982: Functional regions for the population census of Great Britain. In D. T. Herbert and R. J. Johnston (eds) *Geography and the urban environment*, vol. 5. Chichester: John Wiley, 63–111.

COOPER, W. 1952: *The struggles of Albert Woods*. London: Jonathan Cape.

COPPOCK, J. T. 1974: Geography and public policy: challenges, opportunities and implications. *Transactions, Institute of British Geographers* **63**, 1–16.

CORBRIDGE, S. 1986: *Capitalist world development*. London: Macmillan.

—— 1988: Deconstructing determinism. *Antipode* **20**, 239–69.

—— 1989: Marxism, post-Marxism, and the geography of development. In R. Peet and N. J. Thrift (eds) *New models in geography*, vol. 1. London: Unwin Hyman, 224–54.

—— 1993: Marxists, modernities, and moralities: development praxis and the claims of distant strangers. *Environment and Planning D: Society and Space* **11**, 449–72.

CORBRIDGE, S., MARTIN, R. L. and THRIFT, N. J. (eds) 1994: *Money, space and power*. Oxford: Blackwell Publishers.

CORMACK, L. B. 1997: *Charting an empire: geography at English universities, 1580–1620*. Chicago: University of Chicago Press.

COSGROVE, D. 2003: Landscape of the European sense of sight – eyeing nature. In K. Anderson, M. Domosh, S. Pile and N. Thrift (eds) *The handbook of cultural geography*. London, Thousand Oaks, CA and New Delhi: Sage.

COSGROVE, D. E. 1983: Towards a radical cultural geography: problems of theory. *Antipode* **15**, 1–11.

—— 1984: *Social formation and symbolic landscape*. London: Croom Helm.

—— 1989a: Geography is everywhere: culture and symbolism in human landscapes. In D. Gregory and R. Walford (eds) *Horizons in Human Geography*. London: Macmillan, 118–135.

—— 1989b: Models, description and imagination in geography. In B. Macmillan (ed.) *Remodelling geography*. Oxford: Blackwell, 23–44.

—— 1993: Commentary. *Annals of the Association of American Geographers* **83**, 515–17.

—— 1996: Classics in human geography revisited. *Progress in Human Geography* **20**, 197–9.

—— 2001: *Apollo's eye: a cartographic genealogy of the earth in western imagination*. Baltimore: Johns Hopkins University Press.

COSGROVE, D. E. and DANIELS, S. J. (eds) 1988: *The iconography of landscape*. Cambridge: Cambridge University Press.

—— 1989: Fieldwork as theatre: a week's performance in Venice and its region. *Journal of Geography in Higher Education* **13**, 169–82.

COSGROVE, D. E. and JACKSON, P. 1987: New directions in cultural geography. *Area* **19**, 95–101.

COUCLELIS, H. 1986a: Artificial intelligence in geography: conjectures on the shape of things to come. *The Professional Geographer* **38**, 1–10.

—— 1986b: A theoretical framework for alternative models of spatial decision and behavior. *Annals of the Association of American Geographers* **76**, 95–113.

COUCLELIS, H. and GOLLEDGE, R. G. 1983: Analytic research, positivism, and behavioral geography. *Annals of the Association of American Geographers* **73**, 331–9.

COURT, A. 1972: All statistical populations are estimated from samples. *The Professional Geographer* **24**, 160–1.

COWEN, D. J. 1983: Automated geography and the DIDS. *The Professional Geographer* **35**, 339–40.

COX, K. R. 1969: The voting decision in a spatial context. In C. Board *et al.* (eds) *Progress in Geography 1*. London: Edward Arnold, 81–118.

—— 1973: *Conflict, power and politics in the city: a geographic view*. New York: McGraw-Hill.

—— 1976: American geography: social science emergent. *Social Science Quarterly* **57**, 182–207.

—— 1979: *Location and public problems*. Oxford: Basil Blackwell.

—— 1981: Bourgeois thought and the behavioral geography debate. In K. R. Cox and R. G. Golledge (eds), *Behavioral problems in geography revisited*. London: Methuen, 256–79.

—— 1989: The politics of turf and the question of class. In J. Wolch and M. Dear (eds) *The power of geography*. Boston: Unwin Hyman, 61–90.

—— 1995: Concepts of space, understanding in human geography, and spatial analysis. *Urban Geography* **16**, 304–26.

COX, K. R. and GOLLEDGE R. G. (eds) 1969: *Behavioral problems in geography: a symposium.* Evanston: Northwestern University Studies in Geography 17.

—— (eds) 1981: *Behavioural problems in geography revisited.* London: Methuen.

COX, K. R. and McCARTHY, J. J. 1982: Neighbourhood activism as a politics of turf: a critical analysis. In K. R. Cox and R. J. Johnston, (eds) *Conflict, politics and the urban scene.* London: Longman, 196–219.

COX, K. R. and MAIR, A. 1989: Levels of abstraction in locality studies. *Antipode* **21**, 121–32.

COX, K. R., REYNOLDS, D. R. and ROKKAN, S. (eds) 1974: *Locational approaches to power and conflict.* New York: Halsted Press.

COX, N. J. 1989: Modelling, data analysis and Pygmalion's problem. In B. Macmillan (ed.) *Remodelling geography.* Oxford: Basil Blackwell, 204–10.

COX, N. J. and JONES, K. 1981: Exploratory data analysis. In N. Wrigley and R. J. Bennett (eds) *Quantitative geography.* London: Routledge & Kegan Paul, 135–43.

CRANE, D. 1972: *Invisible colleges.* Chicago: University of Chicago Press.

CRANG, M. 1994: On the heritage trail: maps of and journeys to olde Englande. *Environment and Planning D: Society and Space* **12**, 341–56.

—— 2002: Qualitative methods: the new orthodoxy? *Progress in Human Geography* **26**, 647–55.

CRANG, M. and THRIFT, N. J. (eds) 2000: *Thinking space.* London: Routledge.

CRANG, P. 1992: The politics of polyphony: reconfigurations in geographical authority. *Environment and Planning D: Society and Space* **10**, 527–49.

—— 1995: It's showtime: on the workplace geographies of display in a restaurant in southeast England. *Environment and Planning D: Society and Space* **12**, 675–704.

CREWE, L. 2000: Geographies of retailing and consumption. *Progress in Human Geography* **24**, 275–90.

CROMLEY, R. G. 1993: Automated geography ten years later. *The Professional Geographer* **45**, 442–3.

CROWE, P. R. 1936: The rainfall regime of the Western Plains. *Geographical Review* **26**, 463–84.

—— 1938: On progress in geography. *Scottish Geographical Magazine* **54**, 1–19.

—— 1970: Review of *Progress in Geography* 1. *Geography* **55**, 346–7.

CRUSH, J. 1994: Post-colonialism, decolonization and geography. In Godlewska, A. and Smith, N. (eds) *Geography and empire.* Oxford: Blackwell.

CULLEN, I. G. 1976: Human geography, regional science, and the study of individual behaviour. *Environment and Planning A* **8**, 397–411.

CUMBERLAND, K. B. 1947: *Soil erosion in New Zealand.* Wellington: Whitcombe & Tombs.

CUPPLES, J. 2002: The field as a landscape of desire: sex and sexuality in geographical fieldwork. *Area* **34**, 382–90.

CURRAN, P. J. 1984: Geographic information systems. *Area* **16**, 153–8.

—— 1996: Differential research funding. *Area* **28**.

—— 2000: Competition in UK higher education: competitive advantage and Porter's diamond model. *Higher Education Quarterly* **54**, 386–410.

—— 2001a: Competition in UK higher education: applying Porter's diamond model to geography departments. *Studies in Higher Education* **26**, 223–51.

—— 2001b: Remote sensing: using the spatial domain. *Environmental and Ecological Statistics* **8**, 331–44.

CURRY, L. 1967: Quantitative geography. *The Canadian Geographer* **11**, 265–74.

—— 1972: A spatial analysis of gravity flows. *Regional Studies* **6**, 131–47.

CURRY, M. 1982a: The idealist dispute in Anglo-American geography. *The Canadian Geographer* **26**, 37–50.

—— 1982b: The idealist dispute in Anglo-American geography: a reply. *The Canadian Geographer* **26**, 57–9.

—— 1991: Postmodernism, language and the strains of modernism. *Annals of the Association of American Geographers* **81**, 210–28.

—— 1992: Reply. *Annals of the Association of American Geographers* **82**, 310–12.

—— 1994: Image, practice and the hidden impacts of geographic information systems. *Progress in Human Geography* **18**, 460–90.

—— 1995: GIS and the inevitability of ethical inconsistency. In J. Pickles (ed.) *Ground truth: the social implications of geographical information systems.* New York: Guilford Press, 68–87.

—— 1996: On space and spatial practice in contemporary geography. In C. Earle, K. Mathewson and M. S. Kenzer (eds) *Concepts in human geography.* Lanham MD: Rowman & Littlefield, 3–32.

—— 1998: *Digital places: living with geographic information technologies.* London and New York: Routledge.

CUTTER, S. L., GOLLEDGE, R. and GRAF, W. L. 2002: The big questions in geography. *The Professional Geographer* **54**, 305–17.

CUTTER, S. L., RICHARDSON, D. B. and WILBANKS, T. J. (eds) 2003: *The geographical dimensions of terrorism.* London: Routledge.

DACEY, M.F. 1962: Analysis of central-place and point patterns by a nearest-neighbor method. In K. Norborg (ed.) *Proceedings of the IGU Symposium in Urban Geography, Lund 1960.* Lund: C. W. K. Gleerup, 55–76.

—— 1968: A review on measures of contiguity for two and k-color maps. In B. J. L. Berry and D. F. Marble (eds) *Spatial analysis.* Englewood Cliffs, NJ: Prentice-Hall, 479–95.

—— 1973: Some questions about spatial distributions. In R. J. Chorley (ed.) *Directions in geography.* London: Methuen, 127–52.

DALBY, S. 1991: Critical geopolitics: discourse, difference, and dissent. *Environment and Planning D: Society and Space* **9**, 261–83.

—— 1994: Gender and critical geopolitics: reading security discourse in the new world disorder. *Environment and Planning D: Society and Space* **9**, 261–83.

DALBY, S. and Ó TUATHAIL, G. (eds) 1998: *Rethinking geopolitics.* London and New York: Routledge.

DALE, A. 1993: Office of Population Censuses and Surveys longitudinal study. *Environment and Planning A* **25**, 83–6.

DANIELS, P. W. 1982: *Service industries: growth and location.* Cambridge: Cambridge University Press.

—— 1985: *Service industries: a geographical appraisal.* London: Methuen.

DANIELS, S. J. 1989: Marxism, culture and the duplicity of landscape. In R. Peet and N. Thrift (eds) *New models in geography,* vol. 2. London: Unwin Hyman, 196–220.

—— 1991: The making of Constable country. *Landscape Research* **16(2)**, 9–18.

DARBY, H. C. 1940a: *The medieval Fenland.* Cambridge: Cambridge University Press.

—— 1940b: *The draining of the fens.* Cambridge: Cambridge University Press.

—— 1948: The regional geography of Thomas Hardy's Wessex. *The Geographical Review* **38**, 426–43.

—— 1951: The changing English landscape. *The Geographical Journal* **117**, 377–98.

—— 1953: On the relations of geography and history. *Transactions and Papers, Institute of British Geographers* **19**, 1–11.

—— 1962: The problem of geographical description. *Transactions and Papers, Institute of British Geographers* **30**, 1–14.

—— (ed.) 1973: *A new historical geography of England.* London: Cambridge University Press.

—— 1977: *Domesday England.* London: Cambridge University Press.

—— 1983a: Historical geography in Britain, 1920–1980: continuity and change. *Transactions, Institute of British Geographers* **NS8**, 421–8.

—— 1983b: Academic geography in Britain, 1918–1946. *Transactions, Institute of British Geographers* **NS8**, 14–26.

—— 2002: *The relations of history and geography: studies in England, France and the United States* (edited by M. Williams, H. Clout, T. Coppock and H. Prince). Exeter: University of Exeter Press.

DAVEY, J., JONES, R., LAWRENCE, V., STEVENSON, I., JENKINS, A. and SHEPHERD, I. D. H. 1995: Issues and trends in textbook publishing: the views of geography editors/publishers. *Journal of Geography in Higher Education* **19**, 11–28.

DAVIES, R. B. and PICKLES, A. R. 1985: Longitudinal versus cross-sectional methods for behavioural research: a first-round knockout. *Environment and Planning A* **17**, 1315–30.

DAVIES, W. K. D. 1972a: Geography and the methods of modern science, In W. K. D. Davies (ed.) *The conceptual revolution in geography*. London: University of London Press, 131–9.

—— 1972b: Introduction: the conceptual revolution in geography. In W. K. D. Davies (ed.) *The conceptual revolution in geography*. London: University of London Press, 9–18.

DAVIS, W. M. 1906: An inductive study of the content of geography. *Bulletin of the American Geographical Society* **38**, 67–84.

DAWSON, J. A. and UNWIN, D. J. 1976: *Computing for geographers*. Newton Abbott: David and Charles.

DAY, M. and TIVERS, J. 1979: Catastrophe theory and geography: a Marxist critique. *Area* **11**, 54–8.

DAYSH, G. H. J. (ed.) 1949: *Studies in regional planning*. London: Philip & Son.

DEAR, M. J. 1987: Society, politics and social theory. *Environment and Planning D: Society and Space* **5**, 363–6.

—— 1988: The postmodern challenge: reconstructing human geography. *Transactions, Institute of British Geographers* **NS13**, 262–74.

—— 1991a: The premature demise of postmodern urbanism. *Cultural Anthropology* **6**, 538–52.

—— 1991b: Review of Harvey, The condition of postmodernity. *Annals of the Association of American Geographers* **81**, 533–9.

—— 1994: Postmodern human geography: an assessment. *Erdkunde* **48**, 2–13.

—— 1995: Practising postmodern geography. *Scottish Geographical Magazine* **111**, 179–81.

—— 1994: Who's afraid of postmodernism? *Annals of the Association of American Geographers* **84**, 295–300.

—— 2000: *The condition of postmodern urbanism*. Oxford: Blackwell.

—— 2001: The politics of geography: hate mail, rabid referees, and culture wars. *Political Geography* **20**, 1–12.

DEAR, M. J. and CLARK, G. L. 1978: The state and geographic process: a critical review. *Environment and Planning A* **10**, 173–84.

DEAR, M. J. and FLUSTY, S. 1998: Postmodern urbanism. *Annals of the Association of American Geographers* **88**, 50–72.

—— 1999: Engaging postmodern urbanism. *Urban Geography* **20**, 412–16.

—— 2002: Preface. In M. J. Dear and S. Flusty (eds) *Spaces of postmodernity: readings in human geography*. Oxford: Blackwell, ix–xiii.

DEAR, M. J. and MOOS, A. I. 1986: Structuration theory in urban analysis: 2. empirical application. *Environment and Planning A* **18**, 351–74.

DEAR, M. J. and SCOTT, A. J. (eds) 1981: *Urbanization and urban planning in capitalist society*. London: Methuen.

DELANEY, D. 2002: The space that race makes. *The Professional Geographer* **54**, 6–14.

DEMERITT, D. 1998: Science, social constructivism and nature. In B. Braun and N. Castree (eds) *Remaking reality: nature at the millennium*. London: Routledge, 177–97.

DENNIS, R. J. 1984: *English industrial cities in the nineteenth century: a social geography*. Cambridge: Cambridge University Press.

DERRIDA, J. 1976: *Of grammatology*. Baltimore: Johns Hopkins University Press.

DESBARATS, J. 1983: Spatial choice and constraints on behavior. *Annals of the Association of American Geographers* **73**, 340–57.

DESBIENS, C. 2002: Speaking in tongues, making geographies. *Environment and Planning D: Society and Space* **20**, 1–3.

DETWYLER, T. R. and MARCUS, M. G. (eds) 1972: *Urbanization and environment.* Belmont, CA: Duxbury Press.

DEUTSCH, R. 1991: Boy's town. *Environment and Planning D: Society and Space* **9**, 5–30.

DEWSBURY, J. D., HARRISON, P., ROSE, M. and WYLIE, J. 2002: Enacting geographies. *Geoforum* **33**, 437–40.

DICKEN, P. 1986: *Global shift.* London: Harper and Row.

—— 2003: *Global shift: transforming the world economy.* London: Sage.

DICKENS P., DUNCAN, S. S., GOODWIN, M. and GRAY, F. 1985: *Housing, states and localities.* London: Methuen.

DICKENSON, J. P. and CLARKE, C. G. 1972: Relevance and the 'newest geography'. *Area* **3**, 25–7.

DICKINSON, R. E. 1930: The regional functions and zones of influence of Leeds and Bradford. *Geography* **15**, 548–57.

—— 1933: The distribution and functions of smaller urban settlements of East Anglia. *Geography* **18**, 19–31.

—— 1938: Landscape and society. *Scottish Geographical Magazine* **55**, 1–15.

—— 1947: *City, region and regionalism.* London: Routledge & Kegan Paul.

—— 1976: *Regional concept: the Anglo-American leaders.* London: Routledge & Kegan Paul.

DINGEMANS, D. 1979: Redlining and mortgage lending in Sacramento. *Annals of the Association of American Geographers* **69**, 225–39.

DOBSON, J. E. 1983a: Automated geography. *The Professional Geographer* **35**, 135–43.

—— 1983b: Reply to comments on 'Automated geography'. *The Professional Geographer* **35**, 349–53.

—— 1993: The geographic revolution: a retrospective on the age of automated geography. *The Professional Geographer* **45**, 431–9.

DODDS, K. and ATKINSON, D. (eds) 2000: *Geopolitical traditions: a century of geopolitical thought.* London and New York: Routledge.

DODDS, K.-J. 1994a: Geopolitics and foreign policy: recent developments in Anglo-American political geography and international relations. *Progress in Human Geography* **18**, 186–208.

—— 1994b: Geopolitics in the Foreign Office: British representations of Argentine 1945–1961. *Transactions, Institute of British Geographers* **NS19**, 273–90.

DODDS, K.-J. and SIDAWAY, J. D. 1994: Locating critical geopolitics. *Environment and Planning D: Society and Space* **12**, 515–24.

DODGSHON, R. A. 1998: *Society in time and space: a geographical perspective on change.* Cambridge: Cambridge University Press.

DOEL, M. A. 1993: Proverbs for paranoids: writing geography on hollowed ground. *Transactions, Institute of British Geographers* **NS18**, 377–94.

—— 1999: *Poststructuralist geographies: the diabolical art of spatial science.* Edinburgh: University of Edinburgh Press.

DOEL, M.A. and CLARKE, D. B. 1999: Dark panopticon. Or, attack of the killer tomatoes. *Environment and Planning D: Society and Space* **17**, 427–50.

DOMOSH, M. 1991a: Towards a feminist historiography of geography. *Transactions, Institute of British Geographers* **NS16**, 95–104.

—— 1991b: Beyond the frontiers of geographical knowledge. *Transactions, Institute of British Geographers* **NS16**, 488–90.

DORLING, D. 1995: *A social atlas of Britain.* Chichester: John Wiley.

—— 1998: Human cartography: when is it good to map? *Environment and Planning A* **30**: 277–88.

DORLING, D. and FAIRBAIRN, D. 1997: *Mapping: ways of representing the world.* London: Longman.

DORLING, D. and SHAW, M. 2002: Geographies of the agenda: public policy, the discipline and its (re)'turns'. *Progress in Human Geography* **26**, 629–42.

DOUGLAS, I. 1983: *The urban environment.* London: Edward Arnold.

—— 1986: The unity of geography is obvious. *Transactions, Institute of British Geographers* **NS11**, 459–63.

DOWNS, R. M. 1970: Geographic space perception: past approaches and future prospects. In C. Board *et al.* (eds) *Progress in Geography 2.* London: Edward Arnold, 65–108.

—— 1979: Critical appraisal or determined philosophical skepticism? *Annals of the Association of American Geographers* **69**, 468–71.

DOWNS, R. M. and MEYER, J. T. 1978: Geography and the mind. *Human geography: coming of age. American Behavioral Scientist* **22**, 59–78.

DOWNS, R. M. and STEA, D. (eds) 1973: *Image and environment.* London: Edward Arnold.

—— 1977: *Maps in mind.* New York: Harper & Row.

DRAKE, C. and HORTON, J. 1983: Comment on editorial essay: sexist bias in political geography. *Political Geography Quarterly* **2**, 329–37.

DRIVER, F. 1998: *Geography militant: cultures of exploration in an age of Empire.* Oxford: Blackwell.

—— 2002: Geography as a visual discipline. *Antipode* **35**, 227–31.

DRIVER, F. and PHILO, C. 1986: Implications of 'scientific' geography. *Area* **18**, 161–2.

DRYSDALE, A. and WATTS, M. 1977: Modernization and social protest movements. *Antipode* **9(1)**, 40–55.

DUFFY, P. 1995: Literary reflections on Irish migration in the nineteenth and twentieth centuries. In R. King, J. Connell and P. White (eds) *Writing across worlds: literature and migration.* London: Routledge, 20–38.

DUNBAR, G. S. (ed.) 2002: *Geography: discipline, profession and subject since 1870.* Dordrecht: Kluwer.

DUNCAN, J. S. 1980: The superorganic in American cultural geography. *Annals of the Association of American Geographers* **70**, 181–98.

—— 1985: Individual action and political power: a structuration perspective. In R. J. Johnston (ed.) *The future of geography.* London: Methuen, 174–89.

—— 1993a: Representing power: the politics and poetics of urban form in the Kandyan Kingdom. In J. S. Duncan and D. Ley (eds) *Place/culture/representation.* London: Routledge, 232–50.

—— 1993b: Commentary. *Annals of the Association of American Geographers* **83**, 517–19.

—— 1994: After the civil war: reconstructing cultural geography as heterotopia. In K. E. Foote, P. J. Hugill, K. Mathewson and J. M. Smith (eds) *Re-reading cultural geography.* Austin: University of Texas Press, 401–8.

DUNCAN, J. S. and BARNES, T. S. 1993: Afterword. In T. J. Barnes and J. S. Duncan (eds) *Writing worlds: discourse, text and metaphor in the representation of landscape.* London: Routledge, 248–53.

DUNCAN, J. S. and LEY, D. 1982: Structural marxism and human geography: a critical assessment. *Annals of the Association of American Geographers* **72**, 30–59.

—— 1993: Introduction: representing the place of culture. In J. S. Duncan and D. Ley (eds) *Place/culture/representation.* London: Routledge, 1–21.

DUNCAN, N. 1996: Postmodernism in human geography. In C. V. Earle, K. Mathewson and M. S. Kenzer (eds) *Concepts in human geography.* Lanham MD: Rowman and Littlefield, 429–58.

—— 1996: *Body space: destabilizing geographies of gender and sexuality.* London: Routledge.

—— 1999: Postmodernism/postmodernity. In L. McDowell and J. P. Sharp (eds) *A feminist glossary of human geography.* London: Arnold, 211–13.

DUNCAN, O. D. 1959: Human ecology and population studies. In P. M. Hauser and O. D. Duncan (eds) *The study of population.* Chicago: University of Chicago Press, 678–716.

DUNCAN, O. D., CUZZORT, R. P. and DUNCAN, B. 1961: *Statistical geography.* New York: The Free Press.

DUNCAN, O. D. and SCHNORE, L. F. 1959: Cultural, behavioral and ecological perspectives in the study of social organization. *American Journal of Sociology* **65**, 132–46.

DUNCAN, S. S. 1974a: Cosmetic planning or social engineering? Improvement grants and improvement areas in Huddersfield. *Area* **6**, 259–70.

—— 1974b: The isolation of scientific discovery: indifference and resistance to a new idea. *Science Studies* **4**, 109–34.

—— 1975: Research directions in social geography: housing opportunities and constraints. *Transactions, Institute of British Geographers* **NS1**, 10–19.

—— 1979: Radical geography and marxism. *Area* **11**, 124–6.

—— 1981: Housing policy, the methodology of levels, and urban research: the case of Castells. *International Journal of Urban and Regional Research* **5**, 231–54.

—— 1989: What is a locality? In R. Peet and N. J. Thrift (eds) *New models in geography*, vol. 2. London: Unwin Hyman, 221–54.

DUNCAN, S. S. and GOODWIN, M. 1985: The local state and local economic policy. *Capital and Class* **27**, 14–36.

DUNCAN, S. S. and SAVAGE, M. 1989: Space, scale and locality. *Antipode* **21**, 179–206.

DUNFORD, M. 1990: Theories of regulation. *Environment and Planning D: Society and Space* **8**, 297–322.

DUNFORD, M. F. and PERRONS, D. 1983: *The arena of capital.* London: Macmillan.

DYCK, I. 1990: Space, time and renegotiating motherhood: an exploration of the domestic workplace. *Environment and Planning D: Society and Space* **8**, 459–83.

EDEN S. 2003: People and the contemporary environment. In R. J. Johnston and M. Williams (eds) *A century of British geography.* Oxford: Oxford University Press for the British Academy, 213–46.

EARLE, C. V. 1996: Classics in human geography revisited. *Progress in Human Geography* **20**, 195–7.

EILON, S. 1975: Seven faces of research. *Operational Research Quarterly* **26**, 359–67.

ELDER, G. S. 1999: 'Queering' boundaries in the geography classroom. *Journal of Geography in Higher Education* **23**, 86–93.

ELIOT HURST, M. E. 1972: Establishment geography: or how to be irrelevant in three easy lessons. *Antipode* **5(2)**, 40–59.

—— 1980: Geography, social science and society: towards a de-definition. *Australian Geographical Studies* **18**, 3–21.

—— 1985: Geography has neither existence nor future. In R. J. Johnston (ed.) *The future of geography.* London: Methuen, 59–91.

ELLIOTT, P., CUZICK, J., ENGLISH, D. and STERN, R. (eds) 1996: *Geographical and environmental epidemiology: methods for small-area studies.* Oxford: Oxford University Press.

ELLIOTT, P., WAKEFIELD, J., BEST, N. and BRIGGS, D. (eds) 2001: *Spatial epidemiology: methods and applications.* Oxford: Oxford University Press.

ENGLAND, K. 1994: Getting personal: reflexivity, positionality and feminist research. *The Professional Geographer* **46**, 80–9.

—— (ed.) 1996: *Who will mind the baby?: geographies of childcare and working mothers.* London and New York: Routledge.

—— 1999: Sexing geography, teaching sexualities [1]. *Journal of Geography in Higher Education* **23**, 94–101.

ENGLAND, K. and STIELL, B. 1997: 'They think you're as stupid as your English is': constructing foreign domestic workers in Toronto. *Environment and Planning A* **29**, 195–215.

ENTRIKIN, J. N. 1976: Contemporary humanism in geography. *Annals of the Association of American Geographers* **66**, 615–32.

—— 1980: Robert Park's human ecology and human geography. *Annals of the Association of American Geographers* **70**, 43–58.

—— 1981: Philosophical issues in the scientific study of regions. In D. T. Herbert and R. J. Johnston (eds) *Geography and the urban environment*, vol. 4. Chichester: John Wiley, 1–27.

—— 1989: Place, region, and modernity. In J. A. Agnew and J. S. Duncan (eds) *The power of place.* Boston: Unwin Hyman, 30–43.

—— 1990: Introduction: *The Nature of Geography* in perspective. In J. N. Entrikin and S. D. Brunn (eds) *Reflections on Richard Hartshorne's The Nature of Geography.* Washington: Association of American Geographers, 1–16.

ESRC 1988: *Horizons and opportunities in social science.* London: ESRC.

EVANS, M. 1988: Participant observation: the researcher as research tool. In J. Eyles and D. M. Smith (eds) *Qualitative methods in human geography.* Cambridge: Polity Press, 197–218.

EYLES, J. 1971: Pouring new sentiments into old theories: how else can we look at behavioural patterns? *Area* **3**, 242–50.

—— 1973: Geography and relevance. *Area* **5**, 158–60.

—— 1974: Social theory and social geography. In C. Board *et al.* (eds) *Progress in Geography 6.* London: Edward Arnold, 27–88.

—— 1981: Why geography cannot be Marxist: towards an understanding of lived experience. *Environment and Planning A* **13**, 1371–88.

—— 1989: The geography of everyday life. In D. Gregory and R. Walford (eds) *Horizons in human geography.* London: Macmillan, 102–17.

EYLES, J. and LEE, R. 1982: Human geography in explanation. *Transactions, Institute of British Geographers* **NS7**, 117–21.

EYLES, J. and SMITH, D. M. 1978: Social geography. *Human geography: Coming of Age. American Behavioral Scientist* **22**, 41–58.

EYRE, S. R. 1978: *The real wealth of nations.* London: Edward Arnold.

EYRE, S. R. and JONES, G. R. J. (eds) 1966: *Geography as human ecology.* London: Edward Arnold.

FALAH, G. 1989: Israelization of Palestine human geography. *Progress in Human Geography* **13**, 535–50.

—— 1994: The frontier of political criticism in Israeli geographic practice. *Area* **26**, 1–12.

FALAH, G. and NEWMAN, D. 1995: The spatial manifestation of threat: Israelis and Palestinians seek a 'good boundary'. *Political Geography* **14**, 689–706.

FALCONER AL-HINDI, K. 2000: Women in geography in the 21st century. *The Professional Geographer* **54**: 697–702.

—— 2001: Guest editorial. Do you get it? Feminism and quantitative geography. *Environment and Planning D: Society and Space* **19**, 505–13.

FAWCETT, C. B. 1919: *The provinces of England.* London: Williams and Norgate.

FELDMAN, E. J. 1986: The citizen-scholar: education and public affairs. In R. W. Kates and I. Burton (eds) *Geography, resources and environment,* vol. 2: *Themes from the work of Gilbert F. White.* Chicago: University of Chicago Press, 188–206.

FELLMANN, J. D. 1986: Myth and reality in the origin of American economic geography. *Annals of the Association of American Geographers* **76**, 313–30.

FERGUSON, R. I. 2003: Publication practices in physical and human geography: a comment on Nigel Thrift's 'The future of geography'. *Geoforum* **34**, 9–11.

FEYERABEND, P. 1975: *Against method.* London: New Left Books.

FIELDHOUSE, E., PATTIE, C. J. and JOHNSTON, R. J. 1996: Tactical voting and party constituency campaigning at the 1992 British general election in England. *British Journal of Political Science* **26**, 403–18.

FINGLETON, B. 1984: *Models of category counts.* Cambridge: Cambridge University Press.

FISCHER, M. M. and GOPAL, S. 1993: Neurocomputing – a new paradigm for geographic information processing. *Environment and Planning A* **25**, 757–60.

FISHER, P. F. 1989a: Geographical information system software for teaching. *Journal of Geography in Higher Education* **13**, 69–80.

—— 1989b: Expert system applications in geography. *Area* **21**, 279–87.

FITZSIMMONS, M. 1989: The matter of nature. *Antipode* **21**, 106–21.

FLEMING, D. K. 1973: The regionalizing ritual. *Scottish Geographical Magazine* **89**, 196–207.

FLEURE, H. J. 1919: Human regions. *Scottish Geographical Magazine* **35**, 94–105.

FLOWERDEW, R. 1986: Three years in British geography. *Area* **18**, 263–4.

—— 1989: Some critical views of modelling in geography. In B. Macmillan (ed.) *Remodelling geography*. Oxford: Basil Blackwell, 245–54.

—— 1998: Reacting to Ground Truth. *Environment and Planning A* **30**, 289–302.

FOLCH-SERRA, M. 1990: Place, voice and space: Mikhail Bakhtin's dialogical landscape. *Environment and Planning D: Society and Space* **8**, 255–74.

FOLKE, S. 1972: Why a radical geography must be Marxist. *Antipode* **4(2)**, 13–18.

—— 1973: First thoughts on the geography of imperialism. *Antipode* **5(3)**, 16–20.

FOLKE, S. and SAYER, A. 1991: What's left to do? Two views from Europe. *Antipode* **23**, 240–8.

FOORD, J. and GREGSON, N. 1986: Patriarchy: towards a reconceptualisation. *Antipode* **18**, 186–211.

FOOTE, D. G. and GREER-WOOTTEN, B. 1968: An approach to systems analysis in cultural geography. *The Professional Geographer* **20**, 86–90.

FORD, L. R. 1982: Beware of new geographies. *The Professional Geographer* **34**, 131–5.

—— 2002: Emerging political paradigms. *Urban Geography* **23**, 433–40.

FORER, P. C. 1974: Space through time: a case study with New Zealand airlines. In E. L. Cripps (ed.) *Space-time concepts in urban and regional models*. London: Pion, 22–45.

FORESMAN, T. W. (ed) 1998: *The history of geographic information systems: perspectives from the pioneers*. Upper Saddle River NJ: Prentice-Hall.

FOREST, B. 1995: West Hollywood as a symbol: the significance of place in the construction of a gay identity. *Environment and Planning D: Society and Space* **13**, 133–57.

FORRESTER, J. W. 1969: *Urban dynamics*. Cambridge, MA: MIT Press.

FOTHERINGHAM, A. S. 1981: Spatial structure and distance-decay parameters. *Annals of the Association of American Geographers* **71**, 425–36.

—— 1993: On the future of spatial analysis: the role of GIS. *Environment and Planning A* anniversary issue, 30–4.

—— 1997: Trends in quantitative methods: I Stressing the local. *Progress in Human Geography* **21**, 81–96.

FOTHERINGHAM, A. S. and MACKINNON, R. D. 1989: The National Center for Geographic Information and Analysis. *Environment and Planning A* **21**, 141–4.

FOTHERINGHAM, A. S., CHARLTON, M. E. and BRUNSDON, C. 2001: *Quantitative geography: perspectives on spatial data analysis*. London: Sage.

—— 2002: *Geographically weighted regression: the analysis of spatially varying relationships*. Chichester: John Wiley.

FOUCAULT, M. 1972: *The archaeology of knowledge*. London: Tavistock Publications.

FREEMAN, T. W. 1961: *A hundred years of geography*. London: Gerald Duckworth.

—— 1977: *Geographers: biobibliographical studies*. London: Mansell.

—— 1979: The British school of geography. *Organon* **14**, 205–16.

—— 1980a: *A history of modern British geography*. London: Longman.

—— 1980b: The Royal Geographical Society and the development of geography. In E. H. Brown (ed.) *Geography, yesterday and tomorrow*. Oxford: Oxford University Press, 1–99.

FUKUYAMA, F. 1992: *The end of history and the last man*. London: Penguin Books.

FULLER, G. A. 1971: The geography of prophylaxis: an example of intuitive schemes and spatial competition in Latin America. *Antipode* **3(1)**, 21–30.

FULLER, S. 2000: *Thomas Kuhn: a philosophical history for our times*. Chicago: University of Chicago Press.

GAILE, G. L. and WILLMOTT, C. J. (eds) 1984: *Spatial statistics and models*. Dordrecht: D. Reidel.

—— (eds) 1989: *Geography in America.* Columbus, OH: Merrill Publishing.

—— 2004: *Geography in America at the dawn of the 21st century.* New York: Oxford University Press.

GALE, N. and GOLLEDGE, R. G. 1982: On the subjective partitioning of space. *Annals of the Association of American Geographers* **72**, 60–7.

GAMBLE, A. 1988: *The free economy and the strong state.* London: Macmillan.

GARCIA-RAMON, M.-D. 2003: Globalization and international geography: the questions of languages and scholarly traditions. *Progress in Human Geography* **27**, 1–5.

GARRISON, W. L. 1953: Remoteness and the passenger utilization of air transportation. *Annals of the Association of American Geographers* **43**, 169.

—— 1956a: Applicability of statistical inference to geographical research. *Geographical Review* **46**, 427–9.

—— 1956b: Some confusing aspects of common measurements. *The Professional Geographer* **8**, 4–5.

—— 1959a: Spatial structure of the economy I. *Annals of the Association of American Geographers* **49**, 238–49.

—— 1959b: Spatial structure of the economy II. *Annals of the Association of American Geographers* **49**, 471–82.

—— 1960a: Spatial structure of the economy III. *Annals of the Association of American Geographers* **50**, 357–73.

—— 1960b: Connectivity of the interstate highway system. *Papers and Proceedings, Regional Science Association* **6**, 121–37.

—— 1962: Simulation models of urban growth and development. In K. Norborg (ed.) *IGU symposium in urban geography,* Lund Studies in Geography B 24. Lund: C. W. K. Gleerup, 91–108.

—— 1979: Playing with ideas. *Annals of the Association of American Geographers* **69**, 118–20.

—— 1995: Living with and loving a no-win situation. *International Regional Science Review* **17**, 327–32.

—— 2002: Lessons from the design of a life. In P. Gould and F. R. Pitts (eds) *Geographical voices: fourteen autobiographical essays.* Syracuse: Syracuse University Press, 99–123.

GARRISON, W. L., BERRY, B. J. L., MARBLE, D. F., NYSTUEN, J. D. and MORRILL, R. L. 1959: *Studies of highway development and geographic change.* Seattle: University of Washington Press.

GARRISON, W. L. and MARBLE, D. F. 1957: The spatial structure of agricultural activities. *Annals of the Association of American Geographers* **47**, 137–44.

—— (eds) 1967a: *Quantitative geography. Part I: economic and cultural topics.* Evanston, ILL Northwestern University Studies in Geography, Number 13.

—— (eds) 1967b: *Quantitative geography, Part II: physical and cartographic topics.* Evanston, ILL Northwestern University Studies in Geography, Number 14.

GATRELL, A. C. 1982: *Geometry in geography and the geometry of geography.* Discussion Paper 6, Department of Geography, Salford: University of Salford.

—— 1983: *Distance and space: a geographical perspective.* Oxford: Oxford University Press.

—— 1984a: The geometry of a research specialty: spatial diffusion modelling. *Annals of the Association of American Geographers* **74**, 437–53.

—— 1984b: Describing the structure of a research literature: spatial diffusion modelling in geography. *Environment and Planning B: Planning and Design* **11**, 29–45.

—— 1985: Any space for spatial analysis? In R. J. Johnston (ed.) *The future of geography.* London: Methuen, 190–208.

GATRELL, A. C. and LOVETT, A. A. 1986: The geography of hazardous waste disposal in England and Wales. *Area* **18**, 275–83.

GATRELL, A. C. and SMITH, A. 1984: Networks of relations among a set of geographical journals. *The Professional Geographer* **36**, 300–7.

GAUTHIER, H. L. 2002: Edward 'Ned' Taaffe (1921–2001). *Annals of the Association of American Geographers* **92**, 573–83.

GAUTHIER, H. L. and TAAFFE, E. J. 2003: Three 20th century 'revolutiuons' in American geography. *Urban Geography* **23**, 503–27.

GEARY, R. C. 1954: The contiguity ratio and statistical mapping. *The Incorporated Statistician* **5**, 115–41.

GEERTZ, C. 1983: *Local knowledge: further essays in interpretive anthropology*. New York: Basic Books.

GEHLKE, C. E. and BIEHL, H. 1934: Certain effects of grouping upon the size of the correlation coefficient in census tract material. *Journal of the American Statistical Association, Supplement*, 29, 169–70.

GERTLER, M. 1992: Flexibility revisited: districts, nation-states, and the forces of production. *Transactions, Institute of British Geographers* **NS17**, 259–78.

GETIS, A. 1963: The determination of the location of retail activities with the use of a map transformation. *Economic Geography* **39**, 1–22.

—— 1993: Scholarship, leadership and quantitative methods. *Urban Geography* **14**, 517–25.

GETIS, A. and BOOTS, B. N. 1978: *Models of spatial processes*. Cambridge: Cambridge University Press.

GIBBS, G. 1995: The relationship between quality in research and quality in teaching. *Quality in Higher Education* **1**, 147–57.

GIBSON, E. 1978: Understanding the subjective meaning of places. In D. Ley and M. S. Samuels (eds) *Humanistic geography: problems and prospects*. Chicago: Maaroufa Press, 138–54.

GIBSON, K. 1991: Considerations on northern Marxist geography: a review from the Antipodes. *Australian Geographer* **22**, 75–81.

GIBSON, K. and GRAHAM, J. 1992: Rethinking class in industrial geography: creating a space for alternative politics of class. *Economic Geography* **68**, 109–27.

GIBSON-GRAHAM, J. K. 1994: Stuffed if I know! Reflections on post-modern feminist social research. *Gender, Place and Culture* **1**, 205–24.

—— 1996: *The end of capitalism (as we knew it): a feminist critique of political economy*. Oxford and Cambridge, MA: Blackwell.

GIDDENS, A. 1976: *New rules of sociological method*. London: Hutchinson.

—— 1981: *A critique of contemporary historical materialism*. London: Macmillan.

—— 1984: *The constitution of society*. Oxford: Polity Press.

—— 1985: *The nation state and violence*. Oxford: Polity Press.

GIER, J. and WALTON, J. 1987: Some problems with reconceptualising patriarchy. *Antipode* **19**, 54–8.

GILBERT, A. 1988: The new regional geography in English- and French-speaking countries. *Progress in Human Geography* **12**, 208–28.

GILBERT, D. 1995: Between two cultures: geography, computing and the humanities. *Ecumene* **2**, 1–13.

—— 1996: Between two cultures: geography, computing and the humanities. *Ecumene* **2**, 1–14.

—— 1999: Sponsorship, academic independence and critical engagement: a forum on Shell, the Ogoni dispute, and the Royal Geographical Society (with the Institute of British Geographers). *Ethics, Place and Environment* **2**, 219–28.

GILMORE, R. 2002: Race and globalization. In R. J. Johnston, P. J. Taylor and M. J. Watts (eds), *Geographies of global change: remapping the world*. Oxford: Blackwell Publishers, 261–74.

GINSBURG, N. S. 1961: *Atlas of economic development*. Chicago: University of Chicago Press.

—— 1972: The mission of a scholarly society. *The Professional Geographer* **24**, 1–6.

—— 1973: From colonialism to national development: geographical perspectives on patterns and policies. *Annals of the Association of American Geographers* **63**, 1–21.

GLACKEN, C. J. 1956: Changing ideas of the habitable world. In W. L. Thomas (ed.) *Man's role in changing the face of the earth*. Chicago: University of Chicago Press, 70–92.

—— 1967: *Traces on the Rhodian shore: nature and culture in western thought from ancient times to the end of the eighteenth century.* Berkeley: University of California Press.

—— 1983: A late arrival in academia. In A. Buttimer, *The practice of geography.* London: Longman, 20–34.

GLEESON, B. 1996: A geography for disabled people? *Transactions of the Institute of British Geographers* **NS21**, 63–85.

GLENNIE, P. D. and THRIFT, N. J. 1992: Modernity, urbanism and modern consumption. *Environment and Planning D: Society and Space* **10**, 423–44.

GOBER, P. et al. 1995a: Employment trends in geography, Part 1: enrollment and degree patterns. *The Professional Geographer* **47**, 317–28.

—— 1995b: Employment trends in geography, Part 2: current demand conditions. *The Professional Geographer* **47**, 329–35.

—— 1995c: Employment trends in geography, Part 3: future demand conditions. *The Professional Geographer* **47**, 336–46.

GODDARD, J. B. and ARMSTRONG, P. 1986: The 1986 Domesday project. *Transactions, Institute of British Geographers* **NS11**, 279–89.

GODLEWSKA, A. 1995: Map, text and image. The mentality of enlightened conquerors: a new look at the *Description de l'Egypte*. *Transactions, Institute of British Geographers* **NS20**, 5–28.

GOHEEN, P. G. 1970: *Victorian Toronto.* Chicago: University of Chicago, Department of Geography, Research Paper 127.

GOLD, J. R. 1980: *An introduction to behavioural geography.* Oxford: Oxford University Press.

—— 1992: Image and environment: the decline of cognitive-behaviouralism in human geography and grounds for regeneration. *Geoforum* **23**, 239–47.

GOLINSKI, J. 1998: *Making natural knowledge: constructivism and the history of science.* Cambridge: Cambridge University Press.

GOLLEDGE, R. G. 1969: The geographical relevance of some learning theories. In K. R. Cox and R. G. Golledge (eds) *Behavioral problems in geography: a symposium.* Evanston: Northwestern University Studies in Geography 17, 101–45.

—— 1970: Some equilibrium models of consumer behavior. *Economic Geography* **46**, 417–24.

—— 1980: A behavioral view of mobility and migration research. *The Professional Geographer* **32**, 14–21.

—— 1981a: Misconceptions, misinterpretations, and misrepresentations of behavioral approaches in human geography. *Environment and Planning A* **13**, 1325–44.

—— 1981b: A critical response to Guelke's 'Uncritical rhetoric'. *The Professional Geographer* **33**, 247–51.

—— 1983: Models of man, points of view, and theory in social science. *Geographical Analysis* **15**, 57–60.

—— 1993: Geography and the disabled: a survey with special reference to vision impaired and blind populations. *Transactions of the Institute of British Geographers* **NS18**, 63–85.

—— 1996: A response to Gleeson and Imrie. *Transactions of the Institute of British Geographers* **NS21**, 404–11.

—— 2002: The nature of geographic knowledge. *Annals of the Association of American Geographers* **92**, 1–14.

GOLLEDGE, R. G. and AMEDEO, D. 1968: On laws in geography. *Annals of the Association of American Geographers* **58**, 760–74.

GOLLEDGE, R. G. and BROWN, L. A. 1967: Search, learning and the market decision process. *Geografiska Annaler* **49B**, 116–24.

GOLLEDGE, R. G. and STIMSON R. J. 1997: *Spatial behavior: a geographic perspective.* New York: Guilford Press.

GOLLEDGE, R. G., BROWN, L. A. and WILLIAMSON, F. 1972: Behavioral approaches in geography: an overview. *The Australian Geographer* **12**, 59–79.

GOLLEDGE, R. G. and COUCLELIS, H. 1984: Positivist philosophy and research in human spatial behavior. In T. F. Saarinen, D. Seamon and J. L. Sell (eds) *Environmental perception and behavior: an inventory and prospect.* Chicago: Department of Geography, University of Chicago, Research Paper 209, 179–90.

GOLLEDGE, R. G., COUCLELIS, H. and GOULD, P. R. (eds) 1988: *A search for common ground.* London: Pion.

GOLLEDGE, R. G. and RAYNER, J. N. (eds) 1982: *Proximity and preference: problems in the multidimensional analysis of large data sets.* Minneapolis: University of Minnesota Press.

GOLLEDGE, R. G. and RUSHTON, G. 1984: A review of analytic behavioural research in geography. In D. T. Herbert and R. J. Johnston (eds) *Geography and the urban environment: progress in research and application,* vol. 6. Chichester: John Wiley, 1–44.

GOLLEDGE, R. G. and STIMSON, R. J. 1987: *Analytical behavioural geography.* London: Croom Helm.

GOLLEDGE, R. G. and TIMMERMANS, H. (eds) 1988: *Behavioural modelling in geography and planning.* London: Croom Helm.

—— 1990: Applications of behavioural research on spatial problems: I. Cognition. *Progress in Human Geography* **14**, 57–100.

GOODCHILD, M. F. 1990: Comment: just the facts. *Political Geography Quarterly* **10**, 335–7.

—— 1992: Geographical information science. *International Journal of Geographical Information Systems* **6**, 31–46.

—— 1993: The years ahead: Dobson's automated geography in 1993. *The Professional Geographer* **45**, 444–6.

—— 1995: GIS and geographic research. In J. Pickles (ed.) *Ground truth: the social implications of geographic information systems.* New York: Guilford, 31–50.

GOODCHILD, M. F. and JANELLE, D. F. 1988: Specialization in the structure and organization of geography. *Annals of the Association of American Geographers* **78**, 11–28.

GOODCHILD, M. F. and MARK, D. M. 1987: The fractal nature of geographic phenomena. *Annals of the Association of American Geographers* **87**, 265–78.

GOODSON, I. 1981: Becoming an academic subject: patterns of explanation and evolution. *British Journal of Sociology of Education* **2**, 163–79.

—— 1988: *School subjects and curriculum change: studies in curriculum history.* Brighton: The Falmer Press.

GOODWIN, M., DUNCAN, S. and HALFORD, S. 1993: Regulation theory, the local state, and the transition of urban politics. *Environment and Planning D: Society and Space* **11**, 67–88.

GOSS, J. 1995: Marketing the new marketing: the strategic discourse of geodemographic information systems. In J. Pickles (ed.) *Ground truth: the social implications of geographic information systems.* New York: Guilford, 130–70.

GOTTMANN, J. 1951: Geography and international relations. *World Politics* **3**, 153–73.

—— 1952: The political partitioning of our world: an attempt at analysis. *World Politics* **4**, 512–19.

GOUDIE, A. S. 1986a: *The human use of the environment.* Oxford: Basil Blackwell.

—— 1986b: The integration of human and physical geography. *Transactions, Institute of British Geographers* **NS11** P, 464–7.

—— 1993: Land transformation. In R. J. Johnston (ed.) *The challenge for geography. A changing world: a changing discipline.* Oxford: Blackwell Publishers, 117–37.

GOULD, P. R. 1963: Man against his environment: a game theoretic framework. *Annals of the Association of American Geographers* **53**, 290–7.

—— 1965: Wheat on Kilimanjaro: the perception of choice within game and learning theory frameworks. *General Systems Theory* **10**, 157–66.

—— 1966: On mental maps. Michigan Inter-University Community of Mathematical Geographers, Discussion Paper 9. Reprinted in R. M. Downs and D. Stea (eds) 1973, *Image and environment.* London: Edward Arnold, 182–220.

—— 1969: Methodological developments since the fifties. In C. Board *et al.* (eds) *Progress in Geography 1,* London: Edward Arnold, 1–50.

—— 1970a: Is *statistix inferens* the geographical name for a wild goose? *Economic Geography* **46**, 439–48.

—— 1970b: Tanzania 1920–63: the spatial impress of the modernization process. *World Politics* **22**, 149–70.

—— 1972: Pedagogic review. *Annals of the Association of American Geographers* **62**, 689–700.

—— 1975: Mathematics in geography: conceptual revolution or new tool? *International Social Science Journal* **27**, 303–27.

—— 1977: What is worth teaching in geography? *Journal of Geography in Higher Education* **1**, 20–36.

—— 1978: Concerning a geographic education. In D. A. Lanegran and R. Palm (eds) *An invitation to geography.* New York: McGraw-Hill, 202–26.

—— 1979: Geography 1957–1977: the Augean period. *Annals of the Association of American Geographers* **69**, 139–51.

—— 1980: Q-analysis, or a language of structure: an introduction for social scientists, geographers and planners. *International Journal of Man-Machine Studies* **12**, 169–99.

—— 1981a: Letting the data speak for themselves. *Annals of the Association of American Geographers* **71**, 166–76.

—— 1981b: Space and rum: an English note on espacien and rumian meaning. *Geografiska Annaler* **63B**, 1–3.

—— 1985a: *The geographer at work.* London: Routledge & Kegan Paul.

—— 1985b: Will geographical self-reflection make you blind? In R. J. Johnston (ed.) *The future of geography.* London: Methuen, 276–90.

—— 1988: The only perspective: a critique of marxist claims to exclusiveness in geographical inquiry. In R. G. Golledge, H. Couclelis and P. R. Gould (eds) *A ground for common search.* Santa Barbara: The Santa Barbara Geographical Press, 1–10.

—— 1993: Why not? The search for spatiotemporal structure. *Environment and Planning A* anniversary issue, 48–55.

—— 1994: Sharing a tradition – geographies from the enlightenment. *The Canadian Geographer* **38**, 194–202.

—— 1999: *Becoming a geographer.* Syracuse: Syracuse University Press.

GOULD, P. R and OLA, D. 1970: The perception of residential desirability in the Western Region of Nigeria. *Environment and Planning* **2**, 73–8.

GOULD, P. R. and OLSSON, G. (eds) 1982: *A search for common ground.* London: Pion.

GOULD, P. R. and PITTS, F. R. (eds), 2002: *Geographical voices: fourteen autobiographical essays.* Syracuse: Syracuse University Press.

GOULD, P. R. and WHITE, R. 1974: *Mental maps.* Harmondsworth: Penguin Books.

—— 1986: *Mental maps* (second edition). London: George Allen & Unwin.

GRAHAM, E. 1986: The unity of geography: a comment. *Transactions, Institute of British Geographers* **NS 11**, 464–7.

—— 1995: Postmodernism and the possibility of a new human geography. *Scottish Geographical Magazine* **111**, 175–8.

GRAHAM, J. 1988: Postmodernism and marxism. *Antipode* **20**, 60–5.

—— 1992: Post-Fordism as politics: the political consequences of narratives on the left. *Environment and Planning D: Society and Space* **10**, 393–420.

GRANGER, A. 1990: *The threatening desert.* London: Earthscan.

GRÄNO, O. 1981: External influence and internal change in the development of geography. In D. R. Stoddart (ed.) *Geography, ideology and social concern.* Oxford: Blackwell, 17–36.

GRAVES, N. J. 1981: Can geographical studies be subsumed under one paradigm or are a plurality of paradigms inevitable? *Terra* **93**, 85–90.

GRAY, F. 1975: Non-explanation in urban geography. *Area* **7**, 228–35.

—— 1976: Selection and allocation in council housing. *Transactions, Institute of British Geographers* **NS1**, 34–46.

GREEN, N. P., FINCH, S. and WIGGINS, J. 1985: The 'state of the art' in Geographical Information Systems. *Area* **17**, 295–301.

GREENBERG, D. 1984: Whodunit? Structure and subjectivity in behavioral geography. In T. F. Saarinen, D. Seamon and J. L. Sell (eds) *Environmental perception and behavior: an inventory and prospect.* Chicago: Department of Geography, University of Chicago, Research Paper 209, 191–208.

GREER-WOOTTEN, B. 1972: *The role of general systems theory in geographic research.* Department of Geography, Toronto: York University, Discussion Paper No. 3.

GREGORY, D. 1976: Rethinking historical geography. *Area* **8**, 295–9.

—— 1978a: *Ideology, science and human geography.* London: Hutchinson.

—— 1978b: The discourse of the past: phenomenology, structuralism, and historical geography. *Journal of Historical Geography* **4**, 161–73.

—— 1980: The ideology of control: systems theory and geography. *Tijdschrift voor Economische en Sociale Geografie* **71**, 327–42.

—— 1981: Human agency and human geography. *Transactions, Institute of British Geographers* **NS6**, 1–18.

—— 1982a: *Regional transformation and industrial revolution. a geography of the Yorkshire woollen industry.* London: Macmillan.

—— 1982b: Solid geometry: notes on the recovery of spatial structure. In P. R. Gould and G. Olsson (eds) *A search for common ground.* London: Pion, 187–222.

—— 1985a: Suspended animation: the stasis of diffusion theory. In D. Gregory and J. Urry (eds) *Social relations and spatial structures.* London: Macmillan, 296–336.

—— 1985b: People, places and practices: the future of human geography. In R. King (ed.) *Geographical futures.* Sheffield: The Geographical Association, 56–76.

—— 1989a: Areal differentiation and post-modern human geography. In D. Gregory and R. Walford (eds) *Horizons in human geography.* London: Macmillan, 67–96.

—— 1989b: The crisis of modernity? Human geography and critical social theory. In R. Peet and N. J. Thrift (eds) *New models in geography,* vol. 2. London: Unwin Hyman, 348–85.

—— 1990: *Chinatown,* Part Three? Soja and the missing spaces of social theory. *Strategies: A Journal of Theory, Culture and Politics* **3**, 40–104.

—— 1994: *Geographical imaginations.* Oxford: Blackwell Publishers.

—— 1995a: Between the book and the lamp: imaginative geographies of Egypt, 1849–50. *Transactions, Institute of British Geographers* **NS20**, 29–57.

—— 1995b: Imaginative geographies. *Progress in Human Geography* **19**, 447–85.

—— 1997: *Explorations in critical human geography.* Heidelberg: Department of Geography, University of Heidelberg.

GREGORY, D. and LEY, D. 1988: Culture's geographies. *Environment and Planning D: Society and Space* **6**, 115–16.

GREGORY, D. and URRY, J. 1985: Introduction. In D. Gregory and J. Urry (eds) *Social relations and spatial structures.* London: Macmillan, 1–8.

GREGORY, D. and WALFORD, R. 1989: Introduction: making geography. In D. Gregory and R. Walford (eds) *Horizons in human geography.* London: Macmillan, 1–7.

GREGORY, K. J. 1985: *The changing nature of physical geography.* London: Edward Arnold.

—— 2000: *The changing nature of physical geography (second edition).* London: Arnold.

GREGORY, S. 1963: *Statistical methods and the geographer.* London: Longman.

—— 1976: On geographical myths and statistical fables. *Transactions, Institute of British Geographers* **NS1**, 385–400.

GREGSON, N. 1986: On duality and dualism: the case of structuration and time geography. *Progress in Human Geography* **10**, 184–205.

—— 1987a: The CURS initiative: some further comments. *Antipode* **19**, 364–70.

—— 1987b: Structuration theory: some thoughts on the possibilities for empirical research. *Environment and Planning D: Society and Space* **5**, 73–91.

—— 1995: And now it's all consumption. *Progress in Human Geography* **19**, 135–41.

GREGSON, N. and FOORD, J. 1987: Patriarchy: comments on critics. *Antipode* **19**, 371–5.

GREGSON, N. and LOWE, M. 1994: *Servicing the middle classes: class, gender and waged domestic labour in contemporary Britain*. London and New York: Routledge.

GREGSON, N. and ROSE, G. 1997: Contested and negotiated histories of feminist geographies. In Women and Geography Study Group (eds) *Feminist geographies: explorations in diversity and difference*. Harlow: Longman, 13–48.

GREGSON, N., CREWE, L. and BROOKS, K. 2002: Retailing, space and practice. *Environment and Planning D: Society and Space* **20**, 597–617.

GREGSON, N., ROSE, G., CREAM, J. and LAURIE, N. 1997: Conclusions. In Women and Geography Study Group (eds) *Feminist geographies: explorations in diversity and difference*. Harlow: Longman, 191–200.

GRIBBIN, J. 2002: *Science: a history 1543–2001*. London: Penguin.

GRIFFITHS, M. J. and JOHNSTON, R. J. 1991: What's in a place? An approach to the concept of place as illustrated by the British National Union of Mineworkers' strike, 1984–1985. *Antipode* **23**, 185–213.

GRIGG, D. B. 1977: E. G. Ravenstein and the laws of migration. *Journal of Historical Geography* **3**, 41–54.

GROSSMAN, L. 1977: Man-environment relationships in anthropology and geography. *Annals of the Association of American Geographers* **67**, 126–44.

GUDGIN, G. and TAYLOR, P. J. 1979: *Seats, votes and the spatial organisation of elections*. London: Pion.

GUELKE, L. 1971: Problems of scientific explanation in geography. *The Canadian Geographer* **15**, 38–53.

—— 1974: An idealist alternative in human geography. *Annals of the Association of American Geographers* **14**, 193–202.

—— 1975: On rethinking historical geography. *Area* **7**, 135–8.

—— 1976: The philosophy of idealism. *Annals of the Association of American Geographers* **66**, 168–9.

—— 1977a: The role of laws in human geography. *Progress in Human Geography* **1**, 376–86.

—— 1977b: Regional geography. *The Professional Geographer* **29**, 1–7.

—— 1978: Geography and logical positivism. In D. T. Herbert and R. J. Johnston (eds) *Geography and the urban environment: progress in research and applications, 1*. London: John Wiley, 35–61.

—— 1981a: Uncritical rhetoric: 'A classic disservice'. *The Professional Geographer* **33**, 246–7.

—— 1981b: Idealism. In M. E. Harvey and B. P. Holly (eds) *Themes in geographic thought*. London: Croom Helm, 133–47.

—— 1982: The idealist dispute in Anglo-American geography: a comment. *The Canadian Geographer* **26**, 51–7.

—— 1995: Review of D. Gregory *Geographical imaginations*. *The Canadian Geographer* **39**, 184–6.

GUTIÉRREZ, J. and LÓPEZ-NIEVA, P. 2001: Are international journals of human geography really international? *Progress in Human Geography* **25**, 55–71.

GUTTING, G. 1980: Introduction. In G. Gutting (ed.) *Paradigms and revolutions*. Notre Dame, IN: University of Notre Dame Press, 1–22.

HABERMAS, J. 1972: *Knowledge and human interests*. London: Heinemann.

HACKING, I. 1983: *Representing and intervening*. Cambridge: Cambridge University Press.

HÄGERSTRAND, T. 1967: The computer and the geographer. *Transactions, Institute of British Geographers* **42**, 1–20.

—— 1968: *Innovation diffusion as a spatial process*. Chicago: University of Chicago Press.

—— 1975: Space, time and human conditions. In A. Karlquist, L. Lundquist and F. Snickars (eds) *Dynamic allocation of urban space*. Farnborough: Saxon House, 3–12.

—— 1977: The geographers' contribution to regional policy: the case of Sweden. In D. R. Deskins *et al.* (eds) *Geographic humanism, analysis and social action: a half century of geography at Michigan*. Ann Arbor: Michigan Geographical Publications No. 17, 329–46.

—— 1982: Diorama, path and project. *Tijdschrift voor Economische en Sociale Geografie* **73**, 323–39.

—— 1984: Presence and absence: a look at conceptual choices and bodily necessities. *Regional Studies* **18**, 373–8.

HAGGETT, P. 1964: Regional and local components in the distribution of forested areas in southeast Brazil: a multivariate approach. *Geographical Journal* **130**, 365–77.

—— 1965a: Changing concepts in economic geography. In R. J. Chorley and P. Haggett (eds) *Frontiers in geographical teaching*. London: Methuen, 101–17.

—— 1965b: Scale components in geographical problems. In R. J. Chorley and P. Haggett (eds) *Frontiers in geographical teaching*. London: Methuen, 164–85.

—— 1965c: *Locational analysis in human geography*. London: Edward Arnold.

—— 1967: Network models in geography. In R. J. Chorley and P. Haggett (eds) *Models in geography*. London: Methuen, 609–70.

—— 1969: On geographical research in a computer environment. *The Geographical Journal* **135**, 497–507.

—— 1972: *Geography: a modern synthesis*. New York: Harper and Row.

—— 1973: Forecasting alternative spatial, ecological and regional futures: problems and possibilities. In R. J. Chorley (ed.) *Directions in geography*. London: Methuen, 217–36.

—— 1978: The spatial economy. *Human geography: coming of age. America Behavioral Scientist* **22**, 151–67.

—— 1990: *The geographers' art*. Oxford: Blackwell Publishers.

—— 1991: Classics in human geography revisited. *Progress in Human Geography* **15**, 300–2.

—— 1994: Prediction and predictability in geographical systems. *Transactions, Institute of British Geographers* **NS19**, 6–20.

—— 2000: *The geographical structure of epidemics*. Oxford: The Clarendon Press.

—— 2001: *Geography: a global synthesis*. Harlow: Pearson Education.

HAGGETT, P. and CHORLEY, R. J. 1965: Frontier movements and the geographical tradition. In R. J. Chorley and P. Haggett (eds) *Frontiers in geographical teaching*. London: Methuen, 358–78.

—— 1967: Models, paradigms, and the new geography. In R. J. Chorley and P. Haggett (eds), *Models in geography*. London: Methuen, 19–42.

—— 1969: *Network models in geography*. London: Edward Arnold.

—— 1989: From Madingley to Oxford. In B. Macmillan (ed.) *Remodelling geography*. Oxford: Basil Blackwell, xv–xx.

HAGGETT, P., CLIFF, A. D. and FREY, A. E. 1977: *Locational analysis in human geography* (second edition). London: Edward Arnold.

HAGOOD, M. J. 1943: Development of a 1940 rural farm level of living index for counties. *Rural Sociology* **8**, 171–80.

HAGUE, E. 2002: Intervention roundtable. Antipode, Inc? *Antipode* **34**, 655–61.

HAIGH, M. J. 1992: The crisis in American geography. *Area* **14**, 185–9.

HAINES-YOUNG, R. 1989: Modelling geographical knowledge. In B. Macmillan (ed.) *Remodelling geography*. Oxford: Basil Blackwell, 22–39.

HAINES-YOUNG, R. and PETCH, J. R. 1978: *The methodological limitations of Kuhn's model of science*. Salford: University of Salford, Department of Geography, Discussion Paper 8.

—— 1985: *Physical geography: its nature and methods*. London: Harper & Row.

HAINING, R. P. 1980: Spatial autocorrelation problems. In D. T. Herbert and R. J. Johnston (eds) *Geography and the urban environment, 3*. Chichester: John Wiley, 1–44.

—— 1981: Analysing univariate maps, *Progress in Human Geography* **5**, 58–78.

—— 1989: Geography and spatial statistics: current positions, future developments. In B. Macmillan (ed.) *Remodelling geography.* Oxford: Basil Blackwell, 191–203.

—— 1990: *Spatial data analysis in the social and environmental sciences.* Cambridge: Cambridge University Press.

HALL, P. 1974: The new political geography. *Transactions, Institute of British Geographers* **63**, 48–52.

—— 1981a: *Great planning disasters.* London: Penguin.

—— 1981b: The geographer and society. *Geographical Journal* **147**, 145–52.

—— 1982: The new political geography: seven years on. *Political Geography Quarterly* **1**, 65–76.

—— 1998: *Cities in civilisation.* London: Weidenfeld and Nicolson.

—— 2003: Geographers and the urban century. In R. J. Johnston and M. Williams (eds), *A century of British geography.* Oxford: Oxford University Press for the British Academy, 545–62.

HALL, P., JACKSON, P., MASSEY, D., ROBSON, B. T., THRIFT, N. J. and WILSON, A. G. 1987: Horizons and opportunities in research. *Area* **19**, 266–72.

HALL, P. *et al.* 1973: *The containment of urban England.* London: George Allen & Unwin.

HALVORSON, P. and STAVE, B. M. 1978: A conversation with Brian J. L. Berry. *Journal of Urban History* **4**, 209–38.

HAMILTON, F. E. J. 1974: A view of spatial behaviour, industrial organizations, and decision-making. In F. E. I. Hamilton (ed.) *Spatial perspectives on industrial organization and decision-making.* London: John Wiley, 3–46.

HAMNETT, C. 1977: Non-explanation in urban geography: throwing the baby out with the bath water. *Area* **9**, 143–5.

—— 1997: The sleep of reason? *Environment and Planning D: Society and Space* **16**, 127–8.

—— 2003: Contemporary human geography: fiddling while Rome burns? Geoforum **34**, 1–3.

HANNAH, M. and STROHMAYER, U. 1992: Postmodernism (s)trained. *Annals of the Association of American Geographers* **82**, 308–10.

HANSON, S. 1993: 'Never question the assumptions' and other scenes from the revolution. *Urban Geography* **14**, 552–6.

—— 2002: Connections. *Gender, Place and Culture* **9**, 301–3.

HANSON, S. and PRATT, G. 1995: *Gender, work and space.* London: Routledge.

HARE, F. K. 1974: Geography and public policy: a Canadian view. *Transactions, Institute of British Geographers* **63**, 25–8.

—— 1977: Man's world and geographers: a secular sermon. In D. R. Deskins *et al.* (eds) *Geographic humanism, analysis and social action: a half century of geography at Michigan.* Ann Arbor: Michigan Geographical Publication No. 17, 259–73.

HARLAND, R. 1987: *Superstructuralism: the philosophy of structuralism and post-structuralism.* London: Methuen.

HARLEY, J. B. 1989: Deconstructing the map. *Cartographica* **26**, 1–20.

—— 1990: Cartography, ethics and social theory. *Cartographica* **27**, 1–23.

—— 1992: Rereading the maps of the Columbian encounter. *Annals of the Association of American Geographers* **82**, 522–42.

HARRIES, K. D. 1974: *The geography of crime and justice.* New York: McGraw-Hill.

—— 1975: Rejoinder to Richard Peet: 'The geography of crime: a political critique'. *The Professional Geographer* **27**, 280–2.

—— 1976: Observations on radical versus liberal theories of crime causation. *The Professional Geographer* **28**, 100–13.

HARRIS, C. D. 1954a: The geography of manufacturing. In P. E. James and C. F. Jones (eds) *American geography: inventory and prospect.* Syracuse: Syracuse University Press, 292–309.

—— 1954b: The market as a factor in the localization of industry in the United States. *Annals of the Association of American Geographers* **44**, 315–48.

—— 1977: Edward Louis Ullman, 1912–1976. *Annals of the Association of American Geographers* **67**, 595–600.

—— 1978: Patterns of cities. In J. D. Eyre (ed.) *A man for all regions: the contributions of Edward L. Ullman to geography.* Chapel Hill: University of North Carolina, Department of Geography, Studies in Geography 11, 66–79.

—— 1990: Urban geography in the United States: the formative years. *Urban Geography* **11**, 403–17.

—— 1992: Areal patterns of cities through time and space: technology and culture ('The nature of cities' further considered). *Colloquium Geographicum* **22**, 41–53.

—— 1997a: 'The nature of cities' and urban geography in the last half century. *Urban Geography* **18**, 15–35.

—— 1997b: Geographers in the U. S. government in Washington, DC, during World War II. *The Professional Geographer* **49**: 245–56.

HARRIS, C. D. and ULLMAN, E. L. 1945: The nature of cities. *Annals of the American Academy of Political and Social Science* **242**, 7–17.

HARRIS, R. C. 1971: Theory and synthesis in historical geography. *The Canadian Geographer* **15**, 157–72.

—— 1977: The simplification of Europe overseas. *Annals of the Association of American Geographers* **67**, 469–83.

—— 1978: The historical mind and the practice of geography. In D. Ley and M. S. Samuels (eds) *Humanistic geography: problems and prospects.* Chicago: Maaroufa Press, 123–37.

HARRISON, P. 2002: The caesura: remarks on Wittgenstein's interruption of theory, or, why practices elude representation. *Geoforum* **32**, 487–503.

HARRISON, R. T. and LIVINGSTONE, D. N. 1982: Understanding in geography: structuring the subjective. In D. T. Herbert and R. J. Johnston (eds) *Geography and the urban environment, 5.* Chichester: John Wiley, 1–40.

HART, J. F. 1982a: The highest form of the geographer's art. *Annals of the Association of American Geographers* **72**, 1–29.

—— 1982b: Comment in reply. *Annals of the Association of American Geographers* **72**, 559.

—— 1990: Canons of good editorship. *The Professional Geographer* **42**, 354–8.

HARTSHORNE, R. 1939: *The nature of geography.* Lancaster, PA: Association of American Geographers.

—— 1948: On the mores of methodological discussion in American geography. *Annals of the Association of American Geographers* **38**, 492–504.

—— 1954a: Political geography. In P. E. James and C. F. Jones (eds) *American geography: inventory and prospect.* Syracuse: Syracuse University Press, 167–225.

—— 1954b: Comment on 'Exceptionalism in geography'. *Annals of the Association of American Geographers* **44**, 108–9.

—— 1955: 'Exceptionalism in geography' re-examined. *Annals of the Association of American Geographers* **45**, 205–44.

—— 1958: The concept of geography as a science of space from Kant and Humboldt to Hettner. *Annals of the Association of American Geographers* **48**, 97–108.

—— 1959: *Perspective on the nature of geography.* Chicago: Rand McNally.

—— 1972: Review of *Kant's concept of geography.* *The Canadian Geographer* **16**, 77–9.

—— 1979: Notes towards a bibliography of *The Nature of Geography. Annals of the Association of American Geographers* **69**, 63–76.

—— 1984: In *The Geographical Journal* **150**, 429.

HARVEY, D. 1967a: Models of the evolution of spatial patterns in geography. In R. J. Chorley and P. Haggett (eds) *Models in geography.* London: Methuen, 549–608.

—— 1967b: Editorial introduction: the problem of theory construction in geography. *Journal of Regional Science* **7**, 211–16.

—— 1969a: *Explanation in geography*. London: Edward Arnold.

—— 1969b: Review of A. Pred, *Behavior and location part I. Geographical Review* **59**, 312–14.

—— 1969c: Conceptual and measurement problems in the cognitive-behavioral approach to location theory. In K. R. Cox and R. G. Golledge (eds) *Behavioral problems in geography: a symposium*. Northwestern University Studies in Geography **17**, 35–68.

—— 1970: Behavioral postulates and the construction of theory in human geography. *Geographica Polonica* **18**, 27–46.

—— 1972: Revolutionary and counter-revolutionary theory in geography and the problem of ghetto formation. *Antipode* **4(2)**, 1–13.

—— 1973: *Social justice and the city*. London: Edward Arnold.

—— 1974a: A commentary on the comments. *Antipode* **4(2)**, 36–41.

—— 1974b: Discussion with Brian Berry. *Antipode* **6(2)**, 145–8.

—— 1974c: What kind of geography for what kind of public policy? *Transactions. Institute of British Geographers* **63**, 18–24.

—— 1974d: Population, resources and the ideology of science. *Economic Geography* **50**, 256–77.

—— 1974e: Class-monopoly rent, finance capital and the urban revolution, *Regional Studies* **8**, 239–55.

—— 1975a: Class structure in a capitalist society and the theory of residential differentiation. In R. Peel, M. Chisholm and P. Haggett (eds) *Processes in physical and human geography: Bristol essays*. London: Heinemann, 354–69.

—— 1975b: The political economy of urbanization in advanced capitalist societies: the case of the United States. In G. Gappert and H. M. Rose (eds) *The social economy of cities*. Beverly Hills: Sage Publications, 119–63.

—— 1975c: Review of B. J. L. Berry, *The human consequences of urbanization. Annals of the Association of American Geographers* **65**, 99–103.

—— 1976: The marxist theory of the state. *Antipode* **8(2)**, 80–9.

—— 1978: The urban process under capitalism: a framework for analysis. *International Journal of Urban and Regional Research* **2**, 101–32.

—— 1979: Monument and myth. *Annals of the Association of American Geographers* **69**, 362–81.

—— 1982: *The limits to capital*. Oxford: Blackwell.

—— 1984: On the history and present condition of geography: an historical materialist manifesto. *The Professional Geographer* **36**, 1–11.

—— 1985: The world-systems theory trap. *Studies in Comparative International Development* **22**, 42–7.

—— 1985a: *The urbanization of capital*. Oxford: Basil Blackwell.

—— 1985b: The geopolitics of capitalism. In D. Gregory and J. Urry (eds) *Social relations and spatial structures*. London: Macmillan, 128–63.

—— 1985c: *Consciousness and the urban experience*. Oxford: Basil Blackwell.

—— 1987: Three myths in search of a reality in urban studies. *Environment and Planning D: Society and Space* **5**, 367–76.

—— 1989a: *The condition of postmodernity*. Oxford: Basil Blackwell.

—— 1989b: From models to Marx: notes on the project to 'remodel' contemporary geography. In B. Macmillan (ed.) *Remodelling geography*. Oxford: Basil Blackwell, 211–16.

—— 1989c: From managerialism to entrepreneurialism: the transformation of urban governance in late capitalism. *Geografiska Annaler* **71B**, 3–17.

—— 1990: Between space and time: reflections on the geographical imagination. *Annals of the Association of American Geographers* **80**, 418–34.

—— 1992: Postmodern morality plays. *Antipode* **24**, 300–26.

—— 1993a: Class relations, social justice and the politics of difference. In M. Keith and S. Pile (eds) *Place and the politics of identity*. London: Routledge, 41–66.

—— 1993b: From space to place and back again: reflections on the condition of postmodernity. In J. Bird et al. (eds) *Mapping the futures: local cultures, global change*. London: Routledge, 3–29.

—— 1994: The nature of environment: the dialectics of social and environmental change. In R. Miliband and L. Panitch (eds) *Real problems, false solutions: socialist register 1993*. London: The Merlin Press, 1–51.

—— 1995: Militant particularism and global ambition: the conceptual politics of place, space, and environment in the work of Raymond Williams. *Social Text* **42**, 69–98.

—— 1996a: *Justice, nature and the geography of difference*. Baltimore: John Hopkins University Press.

—— 1996b: Cities or urbanization. *City* **1–2**, 38–61.

—— 1999: *The limits to capital*, 2nd edn. London: Verso.

—— 2000: *Spaces of hope*. Berkeley and Los Angeles: University of California Press.

—— 2002: Memories and desires. In P. Gould and F. R. Pitts, (eds), *Geographical voices: fourteen autobiographical essays*. Syracuse: Syracuse University Press, 149–88.

HARVEY, D. and SCOTT, A. J. 1989: The practice of human geography: theory and empirical specificity in the transition from Fordism to flexible accumulation. In B. Macmillan (ed.) *Remodelling geography*. Oxford: Basil Blackwell, 217–29.

HARVEY, M. E. and HOLLY, B. P. 1981: Paradigm, philosophy and geographic thought. In M. E. Harvey and B. P. Holly (eds) *Themes in geographic thought*. London: Croom Helm, 11–37.

HAY, A. M. 1978: Some problems in regional forecasting. In J. I. Clarke and J. Pelletser (eds) *Régions géographique et régions d'aménagement*. Collection les hommes et les lettres, 7. Lyon: Editions Hermes.

—— 1979a: Positivism in human geography: response to critics. In D. T. Herbert and R. J. Johnston (eds) *Geography and the urban environment: progress in research and applications*, 2. London: John Wiley, 1–26.

—— 1979b: The geographical explanation of commodity flow. *Progress in Human Geography* **3**, 1–12.

—— 1985a: Scientific method in geography. In R. J. Johnston (ed.) *The future of geography*. London: Methuen, 129–42.

—— 1985b: Statistical tests in the absence of samples: a comment. *The Professional Geographer* **37**, 334–8.

HAY, A. M. and JOHNSTON, R. J. 1983: The study of process in quantitative human geography. *L'Espace Géographique* **12**, 69–76.

HAYFORD, A. M. 1974: The geography of women: an historical introduction. *Antipode* **6**, 1–19.

HAYNES, R. M. 1975: Dimensional analysis: some applications in human geography. *Geographical Analysis* **7**, 51–68.

—— 1978: A note on dimensions and relationships in human geography. *Geographical Analysis* **10**, 288–92.

—— 1982: *An introduction to dimensional analysis for geographers*. CATMOG 33, Norwich: Geo Books.

HAYTER, R. and WATTS, H. D. 1983: The geography of enterprise. *Progress in Human Geography* **7**, 157–81.

HAYTER, T. and HARVEY, D. (eds) 1993: *The factory and the city: the story of the Cowley Automobile Workers in Oxford*. Brighton: Mansell.

HEFFERNAN, M. 2000: Balancing visions: comments on Gearoid O'Tuathail's *Critical geopolitics. Political Geography* **19**, 347–52.

—— 2001: History, geography and the French national spaces: the question of Alsace-Lorraine, 1914–1918. *Space and Polity* **5**, 27–48.

—— 2003: Histories of geography. In S,. L. Holloway, S. P. Rice and G. Valentine (eds), *Key concepts in geography*. London: Sage Publications, 3–22.

HELD, D. 1980: *Introduction to critical theory: Horkheimer to Habermas*. London: Hutchinson.

HEPPLE, L. W. 1992: Metaphor, geopolitical discourse and the military in South America. In T. J. Barnes and J. S. Duncan (eds) *Writing worlds: discourse, text and metaphor in the representation of landscape.* London: Routledge, 136–54.

HERBERT, D. T. and JOHNSTON, R. J. 1978: Geography and the urban environment. In D. T. Herbert and R. J. Johnston (eds) *Geography and the urban environment: progress in research and applications,* 1. London: John Wiley, 1–29.

HERBERT, S. 2000: For ethnography. *Progress in Human Geography* **24**, 550–68.

HERBERTSON, A. J. 1905: The major natural regions, *Geographical Journal* **25**, 300–10.

HEROD, A. 1999: Reflections on interviewing foreign elites: praxis, positionality, validity, and the cult of the insider. *Geoforum* **30**, 313–27.

——— 2001: *Labor geographies: workers and the landscapes of capitalism.* New York: Guilford.

HEROD, A. and WRIGHT, A. (eds) 2002: *Geographies of power: placing scale.* Oxford: Blackwell.

HEROD, A., Ó TUATHAIL, G. and ROBERTS, S. (eds) 1998: *An unruly world? Globalization, governance and geography.* London and New York: Routledge.

HEWITT, K. (ed.) 1983: *Interpretations of calamity.* London: George Allen & Unwin.

HILL, M. R. 1982: Positivism: a 'hidden' philosophy in geography. In M. E. Harvey and B. P. Holly (eds) *Themes in geographic thought.* London: Croom Helm, 38–60.

HINCHLIFFE, S. 1996: Technology, power, and space – the means and ends of geographies of technology. *Environment and Planning D: Society and Space* **14**, 659–82.

HODDER, I. and ORTON, C. 1976: *Spatial analysis in archaeology.* Cambridge: Cambridge University Press.

HODGART, R. L. 1978: Optimizing access to public services:. a review of problems, models, and methods of locating central facilities. *Progress in Human Geography* **2**, 17–48.

HOGGART, K., LEES, L. and DAVIES, A. (eds) 2002: *Researching human geography.* London: Arnold.

HOLLOWAY, L. and HUBBARD, P. 2001: *People and place: the extraordinary geographies of everyday life.* Harlow: Prentice Hall.

HOLLOWAY, S. L. and VALENTINE, G. (eds) 2000: *Children's geographies: playing, living, learning.* London and New York: Routledge.

HOLMES, J. H. 2002: Geography's emerging cross-disciplinary links: process, causes, outcomes and challenges. *Australian Geographical Studies* **40**, 2–20.

HOLT-JENSEN, A. 1981: *Geography: its history and concepts.* London: Harper & Row.

——— 1988: *Geography: its history and concepts,* second edition. London: Harper & Row.

HOOK, J. C. 1955: Areal differentiation of the density of the rural farm population in the northeastern United States. *Annals of the Association of American Geographers* **45**, 189–90.

HOOSON, D. J. M. 1981: Carl O. Sauer. In B. W. Blouet (ed.) *The origins of academic geography in the United States.* Hamden, CT: Archon Books, 165–74.

——— 1984: The Soviet Union. In R. J. Johnston and P. Claval (eds.) *Geography since the Second World War: An international survey.* London: Croom Helm, 79–106.

——— 2002: Geography in Russia: glories and disappointments. In G. S. Dunbar (ed.) *Geography: discipline, profession and subject since 1870.* Dordrecht: Kluwer, 225–44.

HOUSE, J. W. 1973: Geographers, decision takers and policy makers. In M. Chisholm and B. Rodgers (eds), *Studies in human geography.* London: Heinemann, 272–305.

HOWITT, R. 2002: Scale and the other: Levinas and geography. *Geoforum* **33**, 299–313.

HOYNINGEN-HUENE, P. 1993: *Reconstructing Scientific Revolutions.* Chicago: University of Chicago Press.

HUBBARD, P. 2000: Desire/disgust: moral geographies of heterosexuality. *Progress in Human Geography* **24**, 191–217.

HUBBARD, P., KITCHIN, R., BARTLEY, B. and FULLER, D. 2002: *Thinking geographically: space, theory and contemporary human geography.* London and New York: Continuum.

HUCKLE, J. 1985: Geography and schooling. In R. J. Johnston (ed.) *The future of geography.* London: Methuen, 291–306.

HUDSON, R. 1983: The question of theory in political geography: outlines for a critical theory approach. In N. Kliot and S. Waterman (eds) *Pluralism and political geography*. London: Croom Helm, 39–55.

—— 1988: Uneven development in capitalist societies. *Transactions, Institute of British Geographers* **NS13**, 484–96.

—— 2003: Geographers and the regional problem. In R. J. Johnston and M. Williams (eds), *A century of British geography*. Oxford: Oxford University Press for the British Academy, 583–602.

HUGGETT, R. J. 1980: *Systems analysis in geography*. Oxford: Oxford University Press.

—— 1994: *Geoecology: an evolutionary approach*. London: Routledge.

HUGGETT, R. J. and THOMAS, R. W. 1980: *Modelling in geography*. London: Harper & Row.

HUGHES, T. P. 2000: *Rescuing Prometheus: four monumental projects that changed the modern world*. New York: Vinlage.

HUGILL, P. J. and FOOTE, K. E. 1994: Foreword: culture and geography: thirty years of advance. In K. E. Foote, P. J. Hugill, K. Mathewson, and J. M. Smith (eds) *Re-reading cultural geography*. Austin: University of Texas Press, 9–26.

HUMBOLDT, A. von 1845–1862: *Kosmos, Entwurf einer physichien Weltbescheibung*. Stuttgart: J. C. Gotta Verlag.

HUNTINGTON, E. 1911: *Civilization and climate*. New Haven CT: Yale University Press.

—— 1945: *Mainsprings of civilization*. New York: John Wiley.

HYNDMAN, J. 2001: Towards a feminist geopolitics. *Canadian Geographer* **45**, 210–22.

IMRIE, R. F. 1996: Ableist geographies, disablist spaces: towards a reconstruction of Golledge's 'geography and the disabled'. *Transactions of the Institute of British Geographers* **NS21**, 397–403.

—— 2000: Disability and discourses of mobility and movement. *Environment and Planning A* **32**, 1641–56.

ISARD, W. 1956a: *Location and space economy*. New York: John Wiley.

—— 1956b: Regional science, the concept of region, and regional structure. *Papers and Proceedings, Regional Science Association* **2**, 13–39.

—— 1960: *Methods of regional analysis: an introduction in regional science*. New York: John Wiley.

—— 1975: *An introduction to regional science*. Englewood Cliffs, NJ: Prentice-Hall.

ISARD, W. et al. 1969: *General theory: social, political, economic and regional*. Cambridge, MA: MIT Press.

ISSERMAN, A. M. 1995: The history, status, and future of regional science: an American perspective. *International Regional Science Review* **17**, 249–96.

JACKSON, P. 1984: Social disorganization and moral order in the city. *Transactions, Institute of British Geographers* **NS9**, 168–80.

—— 1985: Urban ethnography. *Progress in Human Geography* **9**, 157–76.

—— 1988: Definitions of the situation. In J. Eyles and D. M. Smith (eds) *Qualitative methods in human geography*. Cambridge: Polity Press, 49–74.

—— 1989: *Maps of meaning*. London: Unwin Hyman.

—— 1989: *Maps of meaning: an introduction to cultural geography*. Boston: Unwin Hyman.

—— 1991: Mapping meanings – a cultural critique of locality studies. *Environment and Planning A* **23**, 215–28.

—— 1991: The cultural politics of masculinity: towards a social geography. *Transactions, Institute of British Geographers* **NS16**, 199–213.

—— 1993a: Changing ourselves: a geography of position. In R. J. Johnston (ed.) *The challenge for geography. A changing world: a changing discipline*. Oxford: Blackwell Publishers, 198–214.

—— 1993b: Berkeley and beyond: broadening the horizons of cultural geography. *Annals of the Association of American Geographers* **83**, 519–20.

—— 1999: Postmodern urbanism and the ethnographic void. *Urban Geography* **20**, 400–2.

JACKSON, P. and JACOBS, J. M. 1996: Postcolonialism and the politics of race. *Environment and Planning D: Society and Space* **14**, 1–3.

JACKSON, P. and PENROSE, J. 1993: Introduction: placing 'race' and nation. In P. Jackson and J. Penrose (eds) *Constructions of race, place and nation*. London: UCL Press, 1–26.

JACKSON, P. and SMITH, S. J. 1981: Introduction. In P. Jackson and S. J. Smith (eds) *Social interaction and ethnic segregation*. London: Academic Press, 1–18.

—— 1984: *Exploring social geography*. London: George Allen & Unwin.

JACKSON, P., SMITH, S. J. and JOHNSTON, R. J. 1988: An equal opportunities policy for the IBG. *Area* **20**, 279–80.

JACOBS, J. 1994: Negotiating the heart: heritage, development and identity in postimperial London. *Environment and Planning D: Society and Space* **12**, 751–72.

—— 1994: Earth honouring: western desires and indigenous knowledges. In A. Blunt and G. Rose (eds) *Writing women and space*. New York: Guilford, 169–96.

—— 1996: *Edge of empire: postcolonialism and the city*. London: Routledge.

JACOBS, J. and JACKSON, P. 1996: Postcolonialism and the politics of race. *Environment and Planning D: Society and Space* **14**, 1–4.

JAMES, P. E. 1942: *Latin America*. London: Cassell.

—— 1954: Introduction: the field of geography. In P. E. James and C. F. Jones (eds) *American geography: inventory and prospect*. Syracuse: Syracuse University Press, 2–18.

—— 1965: The President's session. *The Professional Geographer* **17(4)**, 35–7.

—— 1972: *All possible worlds: a history of geographical ideas*. Indianapolis: Odyssey Press.

JAMES, P. E. and JONES, C. F. (eds) 1954: *American geography: inventory and prospect*. Syracuse: Syracuse University Press.

JAMES, P. E. and MARTIN, G. J. 1978: *The Association of American Geographers: the first seventy-five years, 1904–1979*. Washington DC: The Association of American Geographers.

—— 1981: *All possible worlds: a history of geographical ideas* (2nd edition). New York: John Wiley.

JAMES, P. E. and MATHER, E. C. 1977: The role of periodic field conferences in the development of geographical ideas in the United States. *Geographical Review* **67**, 446–61.

JANELLE, D. G. 1968: Central-place development in a time-space framework. *The Professional Geographer* **20**, 5–10.

—— 1969: Spatial reorganization: a model and concept. *Annals of the Association of American Geographers* **59**, 348–64.

—— 1973: Measuring human extensibility in a shrinking world. *The Journal of Geography* **72(5)**, 8–15.

JENKINS, A. 1995: The impact of Research Assessment Exercises on teaching in selected geography departments in England and Wales. *Geography* **80**, 367–74.

JOHNSON, J. H. and POOLEY, C. G. (eds) 1982: *The structure of nineteenth-century cities*. London: Croom Helm.

JOHNSON, L. 1987: (Un)realist perspectives: patriarchy and feminist challenges in geography. *Antipode* **19**, 210–5.

—— 1989: Geography, planning and gender. *New Zealand Geographer* **45**, 85–91.

—— 1994: What future for feminist geography? *Gender, Place and Culture* **1**, 103–13.

JOHNSTON, R. J. 1969: Urban geography in New Zealand 1945–1969. *New Zealand Geographer* **25**, 121–35.

—— 1971: *Urban residential patterns: an introductory review*. London: G. Bell & Sons.

—— 1974: Continually changing human geography revisited: David Harvey: *Social Justice and the City*. *New Zealand Geographer* **30**, 180–92.

—— 1975: But some are more equal ... who gets what where, and how, in New Zealand. *Geography* **60**, 255–68.

—— 1976a: *The world trade system: some enquiries into its spatial structure* London: G. Bell & Sons.

—— 1976b: Anarchy, conspiracy and apathy: the three conditions of geography. *Area* **8**, 1–3.

—— 1976c: Observations on accounting procedures and urban-size policies. *Environment and Planning A* **8**, 327–40.

—— 1978a: *Multivariate statistical analysis in geography: a primer on the general linear model.* London: Longman.

—— 1978b: *Political, electoral and spatial systems.* London: Oxford University Press.

—— 1978c: Paradigms and revolutions or evolution: observations on human geography since the Second World War. *Progress in Human Geography* **2**, 189–206.

—— 1979a: Urban geography: city structures. *Progress in Human Geography* **3**, 133–8.

—— 1979b: *Geography and geographers: Anglo-American human geography since 1945* (1st edition), London: Edward Arnold.

—— 1980a: On the nature of explanation in human geography. *Transactions, Institute of British Geographers* **NS5**, 402–12.

—— 1980b: *City and society.* London: Penguin.

—— 1981a: Applied geography, quantitative analysis and ideology. *Applied Geography* **1**, 213–19.

—— 1981b: Paradigms, revolutions, schools of thought and anarchy: reflections on the recent history of Anglo-American human geography. In B. W. Blouet (ed.) *The origins of academic geography in the United States.* Hamden, CT: Archon Books, 303–18.

—— 1982a: *Geography and the state.* London: Macmillan.

—— 1982b: On the nature of human geography. *Transactions, Institute of British Geographers* **NS7**, 123–5.

—— 1982c: On ecological analysis and spatial autocorrelation. In L. le Rouzic (ed.), *L'autocorrelation spatiale.* Reims: Travaux de l'Institut de Géographie, 3–16.

—— 1983a: Resource analysis, resource management and the integration of human and physical geography. *Progress in Physical Geography* **7**, 127–46.

—— 1983b: *Philosophy and human geography: an introduction to contemporary approaches* (1st edition). London: Edward Arnold.

—— 1983c: Texts, actors, and higher managers: judges, bureaucrats and the political organization of space. *Political Geography Quarterly* **2**, 3–20.

—— 1983d: On geography and the history of geography. *History of Geography Newsletter* **3**, 1–7.

—— 1984a: The political geography of electoral geography. In P. J. Taylor and J. W. House (eds) *Political geography: recent advances and future directions.* London: Croom Helm, 133–48.

—— 1984b: *Residential segregation, the state and constitutional conflict in American urban areas.* London: Academic Press.

—— 1984c: The world is our oyster. *Transactions, Institute of British Geographers* **NS9**, 443–59.

—— 1984d: The region in twentieth century British geography. *History of Geography Newsletter* **4**, 26–35.

—— 1984e: A foundling floundering in World Three. In M. Billinge, D. Gregory and R. Martin (eds) *Recollections of a revolution.* London: Macmillan, 39–56.

—— 1984f: Quantitative ecological analysis in human geography: an evaluation of four problem areas. In G. Bahrenberg, M. Fischer and P. Nijkamp (eds) *Recent developments in spatial data analysis.* Aldershot: Gower, 131–44.

—— 1985a: Places matter. *Irish Geography* **18**, 58–63.

—— 1985b: *The geography of English politics: the 1983 general election.* London: Croom Helm.

—— (ed.) 1985c: *The future of geography.* London: Methuen.

—— 1985d: To the ends of the earth. In R. J. Johnston (ed.) *The future of geography.* London: Methuen, 326–38.

—— 1986a: *On human geography.* Oxford: Basil Blackwell.

—— 1986b: Four fixations and the quest for unity in geography. *Transactions, Institute of British Geographers* **NS11**, 449–53.

—— 1986c: Placing politics. *Political Geography Quarterly* **5**, s63–s78.

—— 1986d: Individual freedom and the world-economy. In R. J. Johnston and P. J. Taylor (eds) *A world in crisis? Geographical perspectives.* Oxford: Basil Blackwell, 173–95.

—— 1986e: The neighbourhood effect revisited: spatial science or political regionalism. *Environment and Planning D: Society and Space* **4**, 41–56.

—— 1986f: *Philosophy and human geography: an introduction to contemporary approaches* (second edition). London: Edward Arnold.

—— 1986g: Review of John L. Paterson: *David Harvey's Geography. Antipode* **18**, 96–108.

—— 1986h: Understanding and solving American urban problems: geographical contributions? *The Professional Geographer* **38**, 229–33.

—— 1987: Job markets and housing markets in the 'developed world'. *Tijdschrift voor Economische en Sociale Geografie* **78**, 328–35.

—— 1988: There's a place for us. *New Zealand Geographer* **44**, 8–13.

—— 1989a: Philosophy, ideology and geography. In D. Gregory and R. Walford (eds) *Horizons in human geography.* London: Macmillan, 48–66.

—— 1989b: *Environmental problems: nature, economy and state.* London: Belhaven Press.

—— 1990a: The challenge for regional geography: some proposals for research frontiers. In R. J. Johnston, J. Hauer and G. A. Hoekveld (eds) *The challenge of regional geography.* London: Routledge, 124–41.

—— 1990b: Some misconceptions about conceptual issues. *Tijdschrift voor Economische en Sociale Geografie* **81**, 14–18.

—— 1991: *A question of place: exploring the practice of human geography.* Oxford: Blackwell Publishers.

—— 1992: The rise and decline of the corporate-welfare state: a comparative analysis in global context. In P. J. Taylor (ed.) *Political geography of the twentieth century: a global analysis.* London: Belhaven Press, 115–70.

—— 1993a: The geographer's degrees of freedom: Wreford Watson, postwar progress in human geography and the future of scholarship in UK geography. *Progress in Human Geography* **17**, 319–32.

—— 1993b: Removing the blindfold after the game is over: the financial outcomes of the 1992 Research Assessment Exercise. *Journal of Geography in Higher Education* **17**, 174–80.

—— 1993c: A voice in the wilderness. *Geography* **78**, 204–7.

—— (ed.) 1993d: *The challenge for geography. A changing world: a changing discipline.* Oxford: Blackwell Publishers.

—— 1993e: Meet the challenge: make the change. In R. J. Johnston (ed.) *The challenge for geography. A changing world: a changing discipline.* Oxford: Blackwell Publishers, 151–80.

—— 1993f: Real political geography. *Political Geography* **12**, 473–80.

—— 1994: One world, millions of places: the end of History and the ascendancy of Geography. *Political Geography* **13**, 111–22.

—— 1994b: The 'quality industry' in British higher education and the AAG's publications. *The Professional Geographer* **46**, 491–7.

—— 1994c: Resources, student: staff ratios and teaching quality in British higher education: some speculations aroused by Jenkins and Smith. *Transactions, Institute of British Geographers* **NS19**, 359–65.

—— 1994d: On spatial analysis, place and realism. *Urban Geography* **15**, 290–5.

—— 1995a: Geographical research, geography and geographers in the changing British university system. *Progress in Human Geography* **19**, 355–71.

—— 1995b: The business of British geography. In A. D. Cliff, P. R. Gould, A. G. Hoare and N. J. Thrift (eds) *Diffusing geography: essays for Peter Haggett.* Oxford: Blackwell Publishers, 317–41.

—— 1995c: Territoriality and the state. In G. B. Benko and U. Strohmeyer (eds) *Territoriality and the social sciences.* Ottawa: University of Ottawa Press.

—— 1996a: The expansion and fragmentation of geography in higher education. In R. J. Huggett, M. Robinson and Douglas, I. (eds) *Companion encyclopedia of geography*. London: Routledge, 794–817.

—— 1996b: Jean Gottmann: French regional and political geographer *extraordinaire*. *Progress in Human Geography* **20**, 183–93.

—— 1996c: *Nature, state and economy: the political economy of environmental problems*. Chichester: John Wiley.

—— 1996d: Academic tribes and territories: the *realpolitik* of opening up the social sciences. *Environment and Planning A* **28**.

—— 1996e: Quality in research, quality in teaching and quality in debate: a response to Graham Gibbs. *Quality in Higher Education* **2**.

—— 1996f: And now it's all over was it worth all the effort? *Journal of Geography in Higher Education* **20**, 159–65.

—— 1997a: Where's my bit gone? Reflections on *Rediscovering Geography*. *Urban Geography* **18**, 353–9.

—— 1997b: Australian geography seen from afar: through a glass darkly. *The Australian Geographer* **28**, 29–37.

—— 1997c: *Geography and geographers: Anglo-American human geography since 1945 (fifth edition)*. London: Arnold.

—— 1998: Fragmentation around a defended core: the territoriality of geography. *The Geographical Journal* **164**, 139–47.

—— 1999a: Classics in human geography revisited. *Progress in Human Geography* **23**, 253–66.

—— 1999b: Book review. *Progress in Human Geography* **23**, 500–1.

—— 2000a: Intellectual respectability and disciplinary transformation? Radical geography and the institutionalisation of geography in the USA since 1945. *Environment and Planning A* **32**, 971–90.

—— 2000b: City-regions and a federal Europe: Robert Dickinson and post-World War II reconstruction. *Geopolitics* **5**, 153–76.

—— 2000c: On disciplinary history and textbooks: or where has spatial analysis gone. *Australian Geographical Studies* **38**, 125–37.

—— 2000d: Authors, editors and authority in the postmodern academy. *Antipode* **32**, 271–91.

—— 2001: Out of the 'moribund backwater': territory and territoriality in political geography. *Political Geography* **20**, 677–94.

—— 2002a: Robert E Dickinson and the growth of urban geography: an evaluation. *Urban Geography* **22**, 702–36.

—— 2002b: Reflections on Nigel Thrift's optimism: political strategies to implement his vision. *Geoforum* **33**, 421–5.

—— 2003a: The institutionalisation of geography as an academic discipline. In R. J. Johnston and M. Williams (eds) *A century of British geography*. Oxford: Oxford University Press for the British Academy,

—— 2003b: Order in space: geography as a discipline in distance. In R. J. Johnston and M. Williams (eds) *A century of British geography*. Oxford: Oxford University Press for the British Academy,

—— 2003c: Regionalization and classification. In K. Kempf-Leonard (ed.) *Encyclopaedia of social measurement*. New York: Academic Press.

—— 2003d: Geography: a different sort of discipline? *Transactions of the Institute of British Geographers* **NS29**, 133–41.

—— 2004a: Communications technology and the production of geographical knowledge. In S. D. Brunn, S. L. Cutter and J. W. Harrington (eds.) *Worldminds*. New York: Kluwer.

—— 2004b: Coming apart at the seams. In N. Castree, A. Rogers and D. Sherman (eds) *Questioning geography: essays on a contested discipline*. Oxford: Blackwell Publishers.

—— 2004c: Disciplinary change and career paths. In R. Lee and D. M. Smith (eds) *Geographies and moralities: international perspectives on justice, development and place*. Oxford: Blackwell Publishers.

—— 2004d: Territory and territoriality in a globalizing world. *Ekistics*.

—— 2004e: Institutions and disciplinary health: two moments in the history of UK geography in the 1960s. *Progress in Human Geography* **27**.

JOHNSTON, R. J. and BRACK, E. V. 1983: Appointment and promotion in the academic labour market: a preliminary survey of British University Departments of Geography. *Transactions, Institute of British Geographers* **NS8**, 100–11.

JOHNSTON, R. J. and CLAVAL, P. (eds) 1984: *Geography since the Second World War: an international survey*. London: Croom Helm.

JOHNSTON R. J. and DOORNKAMP, J. C. (eds) 1982: *The changing geography of the United Kingdom*. London: Methuen.

JOHNSTON, R. J. and GARDINER, V. (eds) 1990: *The changing geography of the United Kingdom* (second edition). London: Routledge.

JOHNSTON, R. J. and GREGORY, S. 1984: The United Kingdom. In R. J. Johnston and P. Claval (eds) *Geography since the Second World War: an international survey*. London: Croom Helm, 107–31.

JOHNSTON, R. J., HEPPLE, L. W., HOARE, A. G., JONES, K. and PLUMMER, P. 2003: Contemporary fiddling in human geography while Rome burns: has quantitative analysis been largely abandoned – and should it? *Geoforum* **34**, 157–61.

JOHNSTON, R. J. and HERBERT, D. T. 1978: Introduction. In D. T. Herbert and R. J. Johnston (eds) *Social areas in cities: processes, patterns and problems*. London: John Wiley, 1–33.

JOHNSTON, R. J. and PATTIE, C. J. 1990: The regional impact of Thatcherism: attitudes and votes in Great Britain in the 1980s. *Regional Studies* **24**, 479–93.

—— 2000: Ecological inference and entropy-maximizing: an alternative estimation procedure for split-ticket voting. *Political Analysis* **8**, 333–45.

—— 2001: On geographers and ecological inference *Annals of the Association of American Geographers* **91**, 281–2.

—— 2003: Evaluating an entropy-maximizing solution to the ecological inference problem: split-ticket voting in New Zealand 1999. *Geographical Analysis* **35**, 1–23.

JOHNSTON, R. J., PATTIE, C. J., DORLING, D. F. L. and ROSSITER, D. J. 2001: *From votes to seats: the operation of the UK electoral system since 1945*. Manchester: Manchester University Press.

JOHNSTON, R. J. and TAYLOR, P. J. (eds) 1986a: *A world in crisis? Geographical perspectives*. Oxford: Basil Blackwell.

—— 1986b: Political geography: a polities of places within places. *Parliamentary Affairs* **39**, 135–49.

—— (eds) 1989: *A world in crisis? Geographical perspectives* (second edition). Oxford: Basil Blackwell.

JOHNSTON, R. J. and THRIFT, N. J. 1993: Ringing the changes: the intellectual history of *Environment and Planning A*. *Environment and Planning A*, anniversary issue, 14–21.

JOHNSTON, R. J., HAUER, J. and HOEKVELD, G. A. (eds) 1990: *Regional geography: current developments and future prospects*. London: Routledge.

JOHNSTON, R. J., JONES, K. and GOULD, M. 1995: Department size and research in English Universities: inter-university variations. *Quality in Higher Education* **1**, 41–7.

JOHNSTON, R. J., TAYLOR, P. J. and O'LOUGHLIN, I. 1987: The geography of violence and premature death. In Vayrynen, R. (ed.) *The quest for peace*. London: Sage Publications.

JOHNSTON, R. J., TAYLOR, P. J. and WATTS, M. J. (eds) 1995: *Geographies of global change: remapping the world in the late twentieth century*. Oxford: Blackwell Publishers.

—— 2002: *Geographies of global change: remapping the world (second edition)*. Oxford: Blackwell Publishers.

JONAS, A. 1988: A new regional geography of localities? *Area* **20**, 101–10.

JONES, A. 1998: (Re)producing gender cultures: theorizing gender in investment banking recruitment. *Geoforum* **29**, 451–74.

—— 1999: Dialectics and difference: against Harvey's dialectical 'post-Marxism'. *Progress in Human Geography* **23**, 529–55.

JONES, E. 1956: Cause and effect in human geography. *Annals of the Association of American Geographers* **46**, 369–77.

—— 1980: Social geography. In E. H. Brown (ed.) *Geography yesterday and tomorrow*. Oxford: Oxford University Press, 251–62.

JONES III, J. P. and CASETTI, E. (eds), 1992: *Applications of the expansion method*. London: Routledge.

JONES III, J. P. and HANHAM, R. Q. 1995: Contingency, realism and the expansion method. *Geographical Analysis* **4**, 185–207.

JONES III, J. P., NAST, H. and ROBERTS, S. (eds) 1997: *Thresholds in feminist geography*. Lanham: Rowman and Littlefield.

JONES, K. 1984: Geographical methods for exploring relationships. In G. Bahrenberg, M. M. Fischer and P. Nijkamp (eds) *Recent developments in spatial data analysis*. Aldershot: Gower, 215–30.

—— 1991: Specifying and estimating multi-level models for geographical research. *Transactions, Institute of British Geographers* **NS16**, 148–60.

JONES, K. and ALMOND, S. 1992: Moving out of the linear rut: the possibilities of Generalized Additive Models. *Transactions Institute of British Geographers* **NS17**, 434–47.

JONES, K. and BULLEN, N. 1994: Contextual models of urban house prices: a comparison of fixed- and random-coefficient models developed by expansion. *Economic Geography* **70**: 252–72.

JONES, K. and DUNCAN, C. 1996: People and places: the multilevel model as a general framework for the quantitative analysis of geographical data. In P. A. Longley and M. Batty (eds), *Spatial analysis: geographical modelling in a GIS environment*. New York: John Wiley, 1–16.

—— 2002: Modelling context and heterogeneity: applying multilevel models. In E. Scarbrough and E. Tanenbaum (eds), *Research strategies in the social sciences: a guide to new approaches*. Oxford: Oxford University Press, 94–123.

JONES, K., JOHNSTON, R. J. and PATTIE, C. J. 1992: People, places and regions: exploring the use of multi-level modelling in the analysis of electoral data. *British Journal of Political Science* **22**, 343–80.

JONES, K. and WRIGLEY, N. 1995: Generalized Additive Models, graphical diagnostics and logistic regression. *Geographical Analysis* **27**, 1–21.

JONES, L.V., LINDSEY, G. and COGGLESHALL, P. E. (eds) 1982: *An assessment of research-doctorate programs in the United States: social and behavioral sciences*. Washington, DC: National Academy Press.

KAIN, R. and DELANO-SMITH, C. 2003: Geography displayed: maps and mapping. In R. J. Johnston and M. Williams (eds) *A century of British geography*. Oxford: Oxford University Press for the British Academy,

KANSKY, K. J. 1963: *Structure of transportation networks*. Chicago: University of Chicago, Department of Geography, Research Paper 84.

KARIYA, P. 1993: The Department of Indian Affairs and Northern Development: the culture-building process within an institution. In J. S. Duncan and D. Ley (eds) *Place/culture/representation*. London: Routledge, 187–204.

KASBARIAN, J. A. 1996: Mapping Edward Said: geography, identity, and the politics of location. *Environment and Planning D: Society and Space* **14**, 529–57.

KASPERSON, R. E. 1971: The post-behavioral revolution in geography. *British Columbia Geographical Series* **12**, 5–20.

KATES, R. W. 1962: *Hazard and choice perception in flood plain management*. Chicago: University of Chicago, Department of Geography, Research Paper 78.

—— 1972: Review of *Perspectives on resource management*. *Annals of the Association of American Geographers* **62**, 519–20.

—— 1987: The human environment: the road not taken, the road still beckoning. *Annals of the Association of American Geographers* **77**, 525–34.

—— 1995: Labnotes from the Jeremiad experiment: hope for a sustainable transition. *Annals of the Association of American Geographers* **85**, 623–40.

KATES, R. W. and BURTON, I. (eds) 1986a: *Geography resources and environment* (two volumes). Chicago: University of Chicago Press.

—— 1986b: Introduction. In R. W. Kates and I. Burton (eds) *Geography, resources and environment*, vol. 1: *Selected writings of Gilbert F. White*. Chicago: University of Chicago Press, xi–xiv.

KATZ, C. and MONK, J. (eds) 1993: *Full circles: geographies of women over the life course*. London and New York: Routledge.

KEARNS, G. 1984: Closed space and political practice: Frederick Jackson Turner and Halford Mackinder. *Environment and Planning D: Society and Space* **2**, 23–34.

KELTIE, J. S. 1886: *Report of the proceedings of the Royal Geographical Society in reference to the improvement of geographical education*. London: John Murray.

—— 1908: *Applied geography: a preliminary sketch*. London: G. Philip.

KENNEDY, B. A. 1979: A naughty world. *Transactions, Institute of British Geographers* **NS4**, 550–8.

KENNEDY, P. 1988: *The rise and fall of the great powers*. New York: Random House.

KEYLOCK, C. J. 2003: Mark Melton's geomorphology and geography's quantitative revolution. *Transactions of the Institute of British Geographers* **NS28**, 142–57.

KIMBLE, G. H. T. 1951: The inadequacy of the regional concept. In L. D. Stamp and S. W. Wooldridge (eds) *London essays in geography: Rodwell Jones memorial volume*. London: Longmans Green, 151–74.

KING, G. 1997: *A solution to the ecological inference problem: reconstructing individual behavior from aggregate data*. Princeton: Princeton University Press.

KING, L. J. 1960: A note on theory and reality. *The Professional Geographer* **12(3)**, 4–6.

—— 1961: A multivariate analysis of the spacing of urban settlement in the United States. *Annals of the Association of American Geographers* **51**, 222–33.

—— 1962: A quantitative expression of the pattern of urban settlement sin selected parts of the United States. *Tijdschrift voor Economische en Sociale Geografie* **53**, 1–7.

—— 1969a: The analysis of spatial form and relationship to geographic theory. *Annals of the Association of American Geographers* **59**, 573–95.

—— 1969b: *Statistical analysis in geography*. Englewood Cliffs, NJ: Prentice-Hall.

—— 1976: Alternatives to a positive economic geography. *Annals of the Association of American Geographers* **66**, 293–308.

—— 1979a: Areal associations and regressions. *Annals of the Association of American Geographers* **69**, 124–8.

—— 1979b: The seventies: disillusionment and consolidation. *Annals of the Association of American Geographers* **69**, 155–7.

—— 1993: Spatial science and the institutionalization of geography as a social science. *Urban Geography* **14**, 538–51.

KING, L. J. and CLARK, G. L. 1978: Government policy and regional development. *Progress in Human Geography* **2**, 1–16.

KING, R., CONNELL, J. and WHITE, P. (eds) 1995: *Writing across worlds: literature and migration*. London: Routledge.

KIRK, W. 1951: Historical geography and the concept of the behavioural environment. *Indian Geographical Journal* **25**, 152–60.

—— 1963: Problems of geography. *Geography* **48**, 357–71.

—— 1978: The road from Mandalay: towards a geographical philosophy. *Transactions, Institute of British Geographers* **NS3**, 381–94.

KISH, G. and WARD, R. 1981: A survival package for geography and other endangered disciplines. *Newsletter Association of American Geographers*, **16**, 8,14.

KITCHIN, R. M. 1996: Increasing the integrity of cognitive mapping research: appraising conceptual schemata of environment-behaviour interaction. *Progress in Human Geography* **20**, 56–84.

KITCHIN, R. and KNEALE, J. 2001: Science fiction or future fact? Exploring imaginative geographies of the new millennium. *Progress in Human Geography* **25**, 19–36.

KITCHIN, R. and LYSAGHT, K. 2003: Heterosexism and geographies of everyday life in Belfast, Northern Ireland. *Environment and Planning A* **35**, 489–510.

KNOPP, L. 1990: Some theoretical implications of gay involvement in an urban land market. *Political Geography Quarterly* **9**, 337–52.

—— 1992: Sexuality and the spatial dynamics of capitalism. *Environment and Planning D: Society and Space* **10**, 651–69.

KNOPP, L. and LAURIA, M. 1987: Gender relations and social relations. *Antipode* **19**, 48–53.

KNOS, D. S. 1968: The distribution of land values in Topeka, Kansas. In B. J. L. Berry and D. F. Marble (eds) *Spatial analysis*. Englewood Cliffs, NJ: Prentice-Hall, 269–89.

KNOX, P. L. 1975: *Social well-being: a spatial perspective*. London: Oxford University Press.

—— 1987: The social production of the built environment: architects. architecture and the postmodern city. *Progress in Human Geography* **11**, 354–78.

KNOX, P. L. and AGNEW, J. A. 1989: *The geography of the world-economy*. London: Edward Arnold.

KNOX, P. L., BARTELS, E. H., BOHLAND, J. R., HOLCOMB, B. and JOHNSTON, R. J. 1988: *The United States: a contemporary human geography*. London: Longman.

KNOX, P. L. and TAYLOR, P. J. (eds) 1995: *World cities in a world-economy*. Cambridge: Cambridge University Press.

KOBAYASHI, A. and MACKENZIE, S. (eds) 1989: *Remaking human geography*. Boston: Unwin Hyman.

KOELSCH, W. A. 1988: Geography at Clark: the first fifty years, 1921–1971. In J. E. Harmon and T. J. Rickard (eds), *Geography in New England*. New Britain CT: New England-St Lawrence Valley Geographical Society, 40–8.

—— 2002: Academic geography, American style: an institutional perspective. In G. S. Dunbar (ed.) *Geography: discipline, profession and subject since 1870*. Dordrecht: Kluwer, 245–80.

KOFMAN, E. 1988: Is there a cultural geography beyond the fragments? *Area* **20**, 85–7.

KOFMAN, E. and ENGLAND, K. 1997: Guest editorial. Citizenship and international migration: taking account of gender, sexuality, and 'race'. *Environment and Planning A* **29**, 191–3.

KOFMAN. E. and PEAKE, L. 1990: Into the 1990s: a gendered agenda for political geography. *Political Geography Quarterly* **9**, 313–36.

KOLLMORGEN, W. N. 1979: Kollmorgen as a bureaucrat. *Annals of the Association of American Geographers* **69**, 77–89.

KOST, K. 1989: The conception of politics in political geography and geopolitics in Germany 1920–1950. *Political Geography Quarterly* **8**, 369–86.

KROEBER, A. L. 1952: *The nature of culture*. Chicago: University of Chicago Press.

KRUMBEIN, W. C. and GRAYBILL, F. A. 1965: *An introduction to statistical models in geology*. New York: McGraw Hill.

KUHN, T. S. 1957: *The Copernican revolution: planetary astronomy in the development of western thought*. Cambridge MA: Harvard University Press.

—— 1962: *The structure of scientific revolutions*. Chicago: University of Chicago Press.

—— 1969: Comment on the relations of science and art. *Comparative Studies in Society and History* **11**, 403–12.

—— 1970a: *The structure of scientific resolutions* (2nd edn). Chicago: University of Chicago Press.

—— 1970b: Logic of discovery or psychology of research? In I. Lakatos and A. Musgrave (eds) *Criticism and the growth of knowledge*. Cambridge: Cambridge University Press, 1–23.

—— 1970c: Reflections on my critics. In I. Lakatos and A. Musgrave (eds) *Criticism and the growth of knowledge*. Cambridge: Cambridge University Press, 231–78.

—— 1977: Second thoughts on paradigms. In F. Suppe (ed.) *The structure of scientific theories*. Urbana: University of Illinois Press, 459–82, plus discussion 500–17.

—— 1991: The natural and the human sciences. In D. J. Hiley, R. Bohman, and R. Shusterman (eds.) *The interpretative turn: philosophy, science, culture*. Ithaca: Cornell University Press, 17–24.

LABEDZ, L. 1977: Anarchism. In A. Bullock and O. Stallybrass (eds) *The Fontana dictionary of modern thought*. London: William Collins, 22.

LAKATOS, I. 1978a: Falsification and the methodology of scientific research programmes. In J. Worrall and G. Currie (eds) *The methodology of scientific research programmes, philosophical papers*, vol. 1. Cambridge: Cambridge University Press, 8–101.

—— 1978b: History of science and its rational reconstructions. In J. Worrall and G. Currie (eds) *The methodology of scientific research programmes, philosophical papers*, vol. 1. Cambridge: Cambridge University Press, 102–38.

LANGTON, J. 1972: Potentialities and problems of adapting a systems approach to the study of change in human geography. In C. Board *et al.* (eds) *Progress in Geography 4*, London: Edward Arnold, 125–79.

—— 1984: The industrial revolution and the regional geography of England. *Transactions, Institute of British Geographers* **NS9**, 145–67.

LAPONCE, J. A. 1980: Political science: an import-export analysis of journals and footnotes. *Political Studies* **28**, 401–19.

LARKIN, R. P. and PETERS, G. L. 1993: *Biographical dictionary of geography*. Westport, CT: Greenwood Press.

LASH, S. and URRY, J. 1987: *The end of organized capitalism*. Cambridge: Polity Press.

LATOUR, B. 1987: *Science in action: how to follow scientists and engineers around society*. Cambridge MA: Harvard University Press.

—— 1999: *Pandora's hope: essays on the reality of science studies*. Cambridge MA: Harvard University Press.

LATOUR, B. and WOOLGAR, S. 1979: *Laboratory life: the construction of scientific facts*. Beverly Hills: Sage Publications.

LAURIA, M. and KNOPP, L. 1985: Toward an analysis of the role of gay communities in urban renaissance. *Urban Geography* **6**, 152–69.

LAURIE, N., DWYER, C., HOLLOWAY, S., and SMITH, F. 1999: *Geographies of new femininities*. Harlow: Longman.

LAVALLE, P., McCONNELL, H. and BROWN, R. G. 1967: Certain aspects of the expansion of quantitative methodology in American geography. *Annals of the Association of American Geographers* **57**, 423–36.

LAW, J. 1976: Theories and methods in the sociology of science: an interpretative approach. In G. Lemaine *et al.*, *Perspectives on the emergence of scientific disciplines*. The Hague: Mouton, 221–31.

LAW, J. and HASSARD, J. (eds) 1999: *Actor network theory and after*. Oxford and Keele: Blackwell and The Sociological Review.

LAW, R. 1999: Beyond 'women and transport': towards new geographies of gender and daily mobility. *Progress in Human Geography* **23**, 567–88.

LAWSON, V. A. and STAEHELI, L. A. 1991: On critical realism, geography, and arcane sects! *The Professional Geographer* **43**, 231–3.

LAWTON, R. and MILLER, E. W. 2001: Two economic geography texts. *Progress in Human Geography* **25**, 303–9.

LEACH, B. 1974: Race, problems and geography. *Transactions, Institute of British Geographers* **63**, 41–7.

LEACH, E. R. 1974: *Lévi-Strauss*. London: William Collins.

LEE, R. 1984; Process and region in the A-level syllabus. *Geography* **69**, 97–107.

—— 1985: The future of the region: regional geography as education for transformation. In R. King (ed.) *Geographical futures*. Sheffield: The Geographical Association, 77–91.

LEE, R. and WILLS, J. (eds) 1997: *Geographies of economies*. London: Arnold.

LEE, Y. 1975: A rejoinder to 'The geography of crime: a political critique'. *The Professional Geographer* **27**, 284–5.

LEIGHLEY, J. 1937: Some comments on contemporary geographic methods. *Annals of the Association of American Geographers* **27**, 125–41.

—— 1955: What has happened to physical geography? *Annals of the Association of American Geographers* **45**, 309–18.

LEMAINE, G., *et al.* 1976: Introduction: problems in the emergence of new disciplines. In G. Lemaine *et al.* (eds) *Perspectives on the emergence of scientific disciplines.* The Hague: Mouton, 1–73.

LEONARD, S. 1982: Urban managerialism: a period of transition. *Progress in Human Geography* **6**, 190–215.

LEWIS, G. M. 1966: Regional ideas and reality in the Cis-Rocky Mountain West. *Transactions, Institute of British Geographers* **38**, 135–50.

—— 1968: Levels of living in the Northeastern United States c. 1960: a new approach to regional geography. *Transactions, Institute of British Geographers* **45**, 11–37.

—— (ed.) 1998: *Cartographic encounters: perspectives on native American mapmaking and map use.* Chicago: University of Chicago Press.

LEWIS, J. and TOWNSEND, A. (eds) 1989: *The north-south divide: regional change in Britain in the 1980s.* London: Paul Chapman.

LEWIS, M. W. and WIGEN, K. 1997: *The myth of continents: a critique of metageography.* Berkeley: University of California Press.

LEWIS, P. W. 1965: Three related problems in the formulation of laws in geography. *The Professional Geographer* **17(5)**, 24–7.

—— 1977: *Maps and statistics.* London: Methuen.

LEWTHWAITE, G. R. 1966: Environmentalism and determinism: a search for clarification. *Annals of the Association of American Geographers* **56**, 1–23.

LEY, D. 1974: *The black inner city as frontier outpost.* Washington, DC: Association of American Geographers.

—— 1977a: The personality of a geographical fact. *The Professional Geographer* **29**, 8–13.

—— 1977b: Social geography and the taken-for-granted world. *Transactions, Institute of British Geographers* **NS2**, 498–512.

—— 1978: Social geography and social action. In D. Ley and M. S. Samuels (eds) *Humanistic geography: problems and prospects.* Chicago: Maaroufa Press, 41–57.

—— 1980: *Geography without man: a humanistic critique.* Oxford Research Paper 24, School of Geography, Oxford: University of Oxford.

—— 1981: Behavioral geography and the philosophies of meaning. In K. R. Cox and R. G. Golledge (eds) *Behavioral problems in geography revisited.* London: Methuen, 209–30.

—— 1983: *A social geography of the city.* New York: Harper & Row.

—— 1989: Fragmentation, coherence, and the limits to theory in human geography. In A. Kobayashi and S. Mackenzie (eds) *Remaking human geography.* Boston: Unwin Hyman, 227–44.

—— 1993: Postmodernism, or the cultural logic of advanced industrial capital. *Tijdschrift voor Economische en Sociale Geografie* **84**, 171–4.

LEY, D. and DUNCAN, J. S. 1993: Epilogue. In J. S. Duncan and D. Ley (eds) *Place/culture/representation.* London: Routledge, 329–36.

LEY, D. and SAMUELS, M. S. 1978: Introduction: contexts of modern humanism in geography. In D. Ley and M. S. Samuels (eds) *Humanistic geography: prospects and problems.* Chicago: Maaroufa Press, 1–18.

LEYSHON, A. 1995: Missing words: whatever happened to the geography of poverty? *Environment and Planning A* **27**, 1021–5.

LEYSHON, A., MATLESS, D. and REVILL, G. 1995: The place of music. *Transactions, Institute of British Geographers* **NS20**, 423–33.

LICHTENBERGER, E. 1984: The German-speaking countries. In R. J. Johnston and P. Claval (eds) *Geography since the Second World War: an international survey*. London: Croom Helm, 156–84.

—— 1997: Harris and Ullman's 'The nature of cities': the paper's historical context and kits impact for further research. *Urban Geography* **18**, 7–14.

LIPIETZ, A. 1993: From Althusserianism to 'regulation theory'. In E. A. Kaplan and M. Sprinker (eds) *The Althusserian legacy*. London and New York: Verso, 99–138.

LITTLE, J., PEAKE, L. and RICHARDSON, P. (eds) 1988: *Women in cities*. London: Macmillan.

LIVINGSTONE, D. N. 1984: Natural theory and neo-Lamarckism: the changing context of nineteenth century geography in the United States and Great Britain. *Annals of the Association of American Geographers* **74**, 9–28.

—— 1992: *The geographical tradition: episodes in the history of a contested enterprise*. Oxford: Blackwell Publishers.

—— 1995: Geographical traditions. *Transactions, Institute of British Geographers* **NS20**, 420–2.

—— 2000a: Making space for science. *Erdkunde* 54, 285–96.

—— 2000b: Putting geography in its place. *Australian Geographical Studies*, **39**, 1–9.

—— 2002: *Science, space and hermeneutics*. Heidelberg: Department of Geography, University of Heidelberg.

LIVINGSTONE, D. N. and HARRISON, R. T. 1981: Immanuel Kant, subjectivism, and human geography: a preliminary investigation. *Transactions, Institute of British Geographers* **NS6**, 359–74.

LONGHURST, R. 1997: (Dis)embodied geographies. *Progress in Human Geography* **21**, 486–501.

—— 2000: 'Corporeographies' of pregnancy: 'bikini babes'. *Environment and Planning D: Society and Space* **18**, 453–72.

LONGLEY, P. A. 1995: GIS and planning for businesses and services. *Environment and Planning B: Planning and Design* **22**, 127–9.

—— 1998: Foundations. In P. A. Longley, S. M. Brooks, R. MacDonnell, and B. Macmillan (eds) *Geocomputation: a primer*. Chichester: John Wiley, 3–16.

—— 2000: Spatial analysis in the new millennium. *Annals of the Association of American Geographers* **90**: 157–65.

—— 2002: Geographical Information Systems: will developments in urban remote sensing and GIS lead to 'better' urban geography? *Progress in Human Geography* **26**, 240–51.

—— 2004: Geographical Information Systems: on modelling and representation. *Progress in Human Geography* **28**.

LONGLEY, P. A. and CLARKE, G. (eds) 1995: *GIS for business and service planning*. Cambridge: GeoInformation International.

LONGLEY, P. A., GOODCHILD, M. F., MAGUIRE, D. J. and RHIND, D. W. (eds) 1999a: Introduction. In P. A. Longley, M. F. Goodchild, D. J. Maguire and D. W. Rhind (eds) *Geographical information systems* (second edition: two volumes). New York: Wiley, 1–20.

—— 2001: *Geographic information systems and science*. Chichester: John Wiley.

LONGLEY, P. A. and MESEV, V. 2000: On the measurement and generalisation of urban form. *Environment and Planning A* **32**: 473–88.

LORIMER, H. 2003: Telling small stories: spaces of knowledge and the practice of geography. *Transactions of the Institute of British Geographers* **NS28**, 197–217.

LORIMER, H. and SPEDDING, N. 2002: Excavating geography's hidden spaces. *Area* **34**: 294–302.

LÖSCH, A. 1954: *The economics of location*. New Haven, CN: Yale University Press.

LOVERING, J. 1987: Militarism, capitalism and the nation-state: towards a realist synthesis. *Environment and Planning D: Society and Space* **5**, 283–302.

LOWE, M. S. and SHORT, J. R. 1990: Progressive human geography. *Progress in Human Geography* **14**, 1–11.

LOWENTHAL, D. 1961: Geography, experience, and imagination: towards a geographical epistemology. *Annals of the Association of American Geographers* **51**, 241–60.

—— (ed.) 1965: *George Perkins Marsh: man and nature*. Cambridge, MA: Harvard University Press.

—— 1968: The American scene. *The Geographical Review* **48**, 61–88.

—— 1975: Past time, present place: landscape and memory. *The Geographical Review* **65**, 1–36.

—— 1985: *The past is a foreign country.* Cambridge: Cambridge University Press.

—— 2001: *George Perkins Marsh: prophet of conservation.* Seattle: University of Washington Press.

LOWENTHAL, D. and BOWDEN, M. J. (eds) 1975: *Geographies of the mind: essays in historical geosophy in honor of John Kirkland Wright.* New York: Oxford University Press.

LOWENTHAL, D. and PRINCE, H. C. 1965: English landscape tastes. *The Geographical Review* **55**, 186–222.

LOWENTHAL, D. et al. 1973: Report of the AAG Task Force on environmental quality. *The Professional Geographer* **25**, 39–46.

LUKE, T. W. 2000: The discipline as disciplinary normalization; networks of research. In R. Sil and E. M. Doherty (eds) *Beyond boundaries? Disciplines, paradigms, and theoretical integration in international studies.* Albany: State University of New York Press, 207–29.

LUKERMANN, F. 1958: Towards a more geographic economic geography. *The Professional Geographer* **10(1)**, 2–10.

—— 1960a: On explanation, model, and prediction. *The Professional Geographer* **12(1)**, 1–2.

—— 1960b: The geography of cement? *The Professional Geographer* **12(4)**, 1–6.

—— 1961: The role of theory in geographical inquiry. *The Professional Geographer* **13(2)**, 1–6.

—— 1964a: *Geography among the sciences.* Minneapolis: Kalamata.

—— 1964b: Geography as a formal intellectual discipline and the way in which it contributes to knowledge. *Canadian Geographer* **8**, 167–72.

—— 1965: Geography; de facto or de jure. *Journal of the Minnesota Academy of Science* **32**, 189–96.

—— 1990: *The Nature of Geography:* Post hoc, ergo propter hoc? In J. N. Entrikin and S. D. Brunn (eds) *Reflections on Richard Hartshorne's The Nature of Geography.* Washington: Association of American Geographers, 53–68.

LUTZ, C. A. and COLLINS, J. L. 1993: *Reading National Geographic.* Chicago: University of Chicago Press.

LYNCH, K. 1960: *The image of the city.* Cambridge, MA: MIT Press.

MABOGUNJE, A. K. 1977: In search of spatial order: geography and the new programme of urbanization in Nigeria. In D. R. Deskins et al. (eds) *Geographic humanism, analysis and social action: a half century of geography at Michigan.* Ann Arbor: Michigan Geography Publications No. 17, 347–76.

MacALLISTER, I., PATTIE, C. J., TUNSTALL, H., DORLING, D. F. L. and ROSSITER, D. J. 2001: Class dealignment and the neighbourhood effect: Miller revisited. *British Journal of Political Science* **31**, 41–60.

MacEACHERN, A. 1995: *How maps work.* New York: Guilford.

MACGILL, S. M. 1981: Liquefied energy gases in the UK: what price public safety? *Environment and Planning A* **13**, 339–54.

—— 1983: The Q-controversy: issues and nonissues. *Environment and Planning B: Planning and Design* **10**, 371–80.

MACKAY, J. R. 1958: The interactance hypothesis and boundaries in Canada: a preliminary study. *The Canadian Geographer* **11**, 1–8.

MACKENZIE, S. 1989: Restructuring the relations of work and life: women as environmental actors, feminism as geographic analysis. In A. Kobayashi and S. Mackenzie (eds) *Remaking human geography.* Boston: Unwin Hyman, 40–61.

MACKINDER, H. J. 1890: The physical basis of political geography. *Scottish Geographical Magazine* **6**, 78–84.

—— 1904: The geographical pivot of history. *The Geographical Journal* **23**, 421–37.

—— 1919: *Democratic ideals and reality: a study in the politics of reconstruction.* London: Constable.

MacLEOD, G. 1997: Globalizing Parisian thought-waves: recent advances in the study of social regulation, politics, discourse and space. *Progress in Human Geography* **21**, 530–3.

—— 1998: In what sense a region? Place, hybridity, symbolic shape, and institutional formation in (post-)modern Scotland. *Political Geography* **17**, 622–63.

MacLEOD, G. and GOODWIN, M. 1999: Space, scale and state strategy: towards a reinterpretation of contemporary urban and regional governance. *Progress in Human Geography* **23**, 503–28.

MacLEOD, G. and JONES, M. 2001: Renewing the geography of regions. *Environment and Planning D: Society and Space* **19**, 695–99.

MACMILLAN, B. 1989a: Quantitative theory construction in human geography. In B. Macmillan (ed.) *Remodelling geography*. Oxford: Basil Blackwell, 89–107.

—— 1989b: Modelling through: an afterword to *Remodelling geography*. In B. Macmillan (ed.) *Remodelling geography*. Oxford: Basil Blackwell, 291–313.

—— 1998: Epilogue. In P. Longley, S. M. Brooks, R. MacDonnell, and B. Macmillan (eds), *Geocomputation: a primer*. Chichester: John Wiley, 257–64.

MADGE, C. 1993: Boundary disputes: comments on Sidaway (1992). *Area*, **25**, 294–9.

—— 1997: An ode to geography. In Women and Geography Study Group (eds) *Feminist geographies: explorations in diversity and difference*. Harlow: Longman, 32–3.

MAGEE, B. 1975: *Popper*. London: William Collins.

MAGUIRE, D. J. 1989: The Domesday interactive videodisc system in geography teaching. *Journal of Geography in Higher Education* **13**, 55–68.

MAGUIRE, D. J., GOODCHILD, M. F. and RHIND, D. W. (eds) 1991: *Geographical information systems*. London: Longman.

MAHTANI, M. 2001: Racial ReMappings: the potential of paradoxical space. *Gender, Place and Culture* **8**, 299–305.

MAIR, A. 1986: Thomas Kuhn and understanding geography. *Progress in Human Geography* **10**, 345–70.

MANION, T. and WHITELEGG, J. 1979: Radical geography and Marxism. *Area* **11**, 122–4.

MANN, M. 1996: Neither nation-state nor globalism. *Environment and Planning A* **28**.

MANNERS, I. R. and MIKESELL, M. W. (eds) 1974: *Perspectives on environment*. Washington: Commission on College Geography, Association of American Geographers.

MARBLE, D. F. and PEUQUET, D. F. 1993: The computer and geography: ten years later. *The Professional Geographer* **45**, 446–8.

MARCHAND, B. 1978: A dialectical approach in geography. *Geographical Analysis* **10**, 105–19.

MARCUS, M. G. 1979: Coming full circle: physical geography in the twentieth century. *Annals of the Association of American Geographers* **69**, 521–32.

MARK, D. M., CHRISMAN, N., FRANK, A. U., McHAFFIE, P. and PICKLES, J. 1996: *The GIS History Project*. On http://www.geog.buffalo.edu/ncgia/gishist.

MARKUSEN, M. 1999: Fuzzy concepts, scanty evidence, policy distance: the case for rigour and policy relevance in critical regional studies. *Regional Studies* **33**, 868–94.

MARSH, G. P. 1864: *Man and nature, or physical geography as modified by human action*. New York: Charles Scribner.

MARSHALL, J. U. 1985: Geography as a scientific enterprise. In R. J. Johnston (ed.) *The future of geography*. London: Methuen, 113–28.

MARTIN, A. F. 1951: The necessity for determinism. *Transactions and Papers, Institute of British Geographers* **17**, 1–12.

MARTIN, D. 2002: Output areas for 2001. In P. Rees, D. Martin and P. Williamson (eds), *The census data system*. Chichester: John Wiley.

MARTIN, D., NOLAN, A. and TRANMER, M. 2001: The application of zone-design methodology in the 2001 UK census. *Environment and Planning A* **33**, 1949–62.

MARTIN, G. J. 1980: *The life and thought of Isaiah Bowman*. Hamden, CT: Archon Books.

—— 1981: Ontography and Davisian physiography. In B. W. Blouet (ed.) *The origins of academic geography in the United States*. Hamden, CT: Archon Books, 279–90.

—— 1990: *The Nature of Geography* and the Schaefer-Hartshorne debate. In J. N. Entrikin and S. D. Brunn (eds) *Reflections on Richard Hartshorne's The Nature of Geography*. Washington: Association of American Geographers, 69–88.

—— 1998: The emergence and development of geographic thought in New England. *Economic Geography* (special issue), 1–13.

MARTIN, G. J. and JAMES, P. E. 1992: *All possible worlds: a history of geographical ideas* (3rd edn). New York: John Wiley.

MARTIN, R. L. 1999: The 'new geographical turn' in economics: some critical reflections. *Cambridge Journal of Economics* **23**, 65–92.

—— 2000: In memory of maps *Transactions of the Institute of British Geographers* **NS25**, 3–6.

—— 2001a: The geographer as social critic – getting indignant about income inequality. *Transactions of the Institute of British Geographers* **NS26**, 267–72.

—— 2001b: Geography and public policy: the case of the missing agenda. *Progress in Human Geography* **25**, 189–210.

—— 2002: A geography for policy or a policy for geography? A response to Dorling and Shaw. *Progress in Human Geography* **26**, 642–4.

MARTIN, R. L. and OEPPEN, J. 1975: The identification of regional forecasting models using space-time correlation functions. *Transactions, Institute of British Geographers* **66**, 95–118.

MARTIN, R. L. and SUNLEY, P. J. 2001: Rethinking the 'economic in economic geography: broadening our vision or losing our focus? *Antipode* **33**, 148–61.

MASSAM, B. H. 1976: *Location and space in social administration*. London: Edward Arnold.

MASSEY, D. 1975: Behavioral research. *Area* **7**, 201–3.

—— 1984a: *Spatial divisions of labour: social structures and the geography of production*. London: Macmillan.

—— 1984b: Introduction: geography matters. In D. Massey and J. Allen (eds) *Geography matters! A reader*. Cambridge: Cambridge University Press, 1–11.

—— 1985: New directions in space. In D. Gregory and J. Urry (eds) *Social relations and spatial structures*. London: Macmillan, 9–19.

—— 1991: Flexible sexism. *Environment and Planning D: Society and Space* **9**, 31–58.

—— 1992: Politics and space/time. *New Left Review* **196**, 65–84.

—— 1995: *Spatial divisions of labour: social structures and the geography of production*, second edition. London: Macmillan.

—— 2000: Practising political relevance. *Transactions of the Institute of British Geographers* **NS25**, 131–3.

—— 2001: Geography on the agenda. *Progress in Human Geography* **25**, 5–17.

—— 2002: Geography, policy and politics: a response to Dorling and Shaw. *Progress in Human Geography* **26**, 645–6.

MASSEY, D. and MEEGAN, R. A. 1979: The geography of industrial reorganization. *Progress in Planning* **10**, 155–237.

—— 1982: *The anatomy of job loss*. London: Methuen.

—— 1985: Introduction: the debate. In D. Massey and R. Meegan (eds) *Politics and method: contrasting studies in industrial geography*. London: Methuen, 1–12.

MASTERMAN, M. 1970: The nature of a paradigm. In I. Lakatos and A. Musgrave (eds) *Criticism and the growth of knowledge*. London: Cambridge University Press, 59–90.

MATHER, P. M. 1999: *Computer processing of remotely-sensed images: an introduction* (2nd edn). Chichester: John Wiley.

MATHEWSON, K. (ed.) 1993: *Culture, form and place: essays in cultural and historical geography*. Baton Rouge: Louisiana State University, Department of Geography and Anthropology.

MATLESS, D. 1992: An occasion for geography: landscape, representation and Foucault's corpus. *Environment and Planning D: Society and Space* **10**, 41–56.

MATTHEWS, H. and LIVINGSTONE, I. 1996: Geography and lifelong learning. *Journal of Geography in Higher Education* **20**, 5–10.

MATTINGLY, D. and FALCONER AL-HINDI , K.1995: Should women count? A context for the debate. *The Professional Geographer* **47**, 427–35.

MAY, J. 1996a: 'A little taste of something more exotic': the imaginative geographies of everyday life. *Geography* **81**, 57–64.

—— 1996b: Globalization and the politics of place: place and identity in an Inner London neighbourhood. *Transactions, Institute of British Geographers* **NS21**, 194–215.

MAY, J. A. 1970: *Kant's concept of geography: and its relation to recent geographical thought.* Toronto: Department of Geography, University of Toronto, Research Publication 4.

—— 1972: A reply to Professor Hartshorne. *The Canadian Geographer* **16**, 79–81.

MAYER, H. M. 1954: Urban geography. In P. E. James and C. F. Jones (eds) *American geography: inventory and prospect.* Syracuse: Syracuse University Press, 142–66.

MAYER, H. M. and KOHN, C. F. (eds), 1959: *Readings in urban geography.* Chicago: University of Chicago Press.

MAYER. T. 1989: Consensus and invisibility – the representation of women in human-geography textbooks. *The Professional Geographer* **41(4)**, 397–409.

McCARTY, H. H. 1940: *The geographic basis of American economic life.* New York: Harper & Brothers.

—— 1952: *McCarty on McCarthy: the spatial distribution of the McCarthy vote, 1952.* Unpublished Paper, Department of Geography, State University of Iowa, Iowa City.

—— 1953: An approach to a theory of economic geography. *Annals of the Association of American Geographers* **43**, 183–4.

—— 1954: An approach to a theory of economic geography. *Economic Geography* **30**, 95–101.

—— 1958: Science, measurement, and area analysis. *Economic Geography* **34**, facing page 283.

—— 1979: Geography at Iowa. *Annals of the Association of American Geographers* **69**, 121–4.

McCARTY, H. H., HOOK, J. C. and KNOS, D. S. 1956: *The measurement of association in industrial geography.* Iowa City: Department of Geography, State University of Iowa.

McCARTY, H. H. and LINDBERG, J. B. 1966: *A preface to economic geography.* Englewood Cliffs, NJ: Prentice-Hall.

McDANIEL, R. and ELIOT HURST, M. E. 1968: *A systems analytic approach to economic geography.* Washington, DC: Commission on College Geography, Publication 8, Association of American Geographers.

McDOWELL, L. 1986a: Feminist geography. In R. J. Johnston, D. Gregory, and D. M. Smith (eds) *The dictionary of human geography.* Oxford: Basil Blackwell, 151–2.

—— 1986b: Beyond patriarchy: a class-based explanation of women's subordination. *Antipode* **18**, 311–21.

—— 1989: Women, gender and the organisation of space. In D. Gregory and R. Walford (eds) *Horizons in human geography.* London: Macmillan, 136–51.

—— 1990: Sex and power in academia. *Area* **22**, 323–32.

—— 1991: Life without father and Ford: the new gender order of post-fordism. *Transactions, Institute of British Geographers* **NS 16**, 400–19.

—— 1991: The baby and the bath water: diversity, deconstruction and feminist theory in geography. *Geoforum* **22**, 122–33.

—— 1992: Valid games? *The Professional Geographer* **44**, 212–5.

—— 1993a: Space, place and gender relations: Part I. Feminist empiricism and the geography of social relations. *Progress in Human Geography* **17**, 157–79.

—— 1993b: Space, place and gender relations: Part II. Identity, difference, feminist geometries and geographies. *Progress in Human Geography* **17**, 305–18.

—— 1994: Polyphony and pedagogic authority. *Area* **26**, 241–8.

—— 1995: Bodywork: heterosexual gender performances in city workplaces. In D. Bell and G. Valentine (eds) *Mapping desire: geographies of sexualities.* London and New York: Routledge, 75–98.

—— 1999: Feminist geography. In L. McDowell and J. P. Sharp (eds) *A feminist glossary of human geography*. London: Arnold, 90–3. The citation is from page 91.

—— 2000: Economy, culture, difference and justice. In I. Cook, D. Crouch, S. Naylor and J. R. Ryan (eds) *Cultural turns/geographical turns: perspectives on cultural geography*. Harlow: Prentice Hall, 182–95.

—— 2002: Masculine discourse and dissonances: strutting 'lads', protest masculinity and domestic respectability. *Environment and Planning D: Society and Space* **20**, 97–119.

McDOWELL, L. and COURT, G. 1994: Missing subjects: gender, power and sexuality in merchant banking. *Economic Geography* **70**, 229–51.

McDOWELL, L. and MASSEY, D. 1984: A woman's place? In D. Massey and J. Allen (eds) *Geography matters!* Cambridge: Cambridge University Press, 128–47.

McDOWELL, L. and SHARP, J. P. (eds) 1997: *Space, gender, knowledge: feminist readings*. London: Arnold.

—— 1999: *A feminist glossary of human geography*. London: Arnold.

McEWAN, C. 1998: Cutting power lines within the palace? Countering paternity and eurocentrism in the 'geographical tradition'. *Transactions, Institute of British Geographers* **NS 23**, 371–84.

McGUINESS, M. 1999: Geography matters? Whiteness and contemporary geography. *Area* **32**, 225–30.

McKINNEY, W. M. 1968: Carey, Spencer, and modern geography. *The Professional Geographer* **20**, 103–6.

McTAGGART, W. D. 1974: Structuralism and universalism in geography: reflections on contributions by H. C. Brookfield. *The Australian Geographer* **12**, 510–16.

MEAD, W. R. 1980: Regional geography. In E. H. Brown (ed.) *Geography yesterday and tomorrow*. Oxford: Oxford University Press, 292–302.

MEADOWS, D. H. *et al.* 1972: *The limits to growth*. New York: Universal Books.

MEINIG, D. W. 1972: American wests: preface to a geographical introduction. *Annals of the Association of American Geographers* **62**, 159–84.

—— 1978: The continuous shaping of America: a prospectus for geographers and historians. *The American Historical Review* **83**, 1186–217.

—— 1983: Geography as an art. *Transactions, Institute of British Geographers* **NS8**, 314–28.

—— 1986: *The shaping of America: a geographical perspective on 500 years of history. Volume 1: Atlantic America, 1492–1800*. New Haven: Yale University Press.

—— 1989: The historical geography imperative. *Annals of the Association of American Geographers* **79**, 79–87.

—— 1993: *The shaping of America: a geographical perspective on 500 years of history. Volume 2: Continental America 1800–1867*. New Haven: Yale University Press.

—— 2002: The life of learning. In P. Gould and F. R. Pitts (eds), *Geographical voices: fourteen autobiographical essays*. Syracuse: Syracuse University Press, 189–210.

MERCER, D. C. 1977: *Conflict and consensus in human geography*. Clayton, Victoria, Australia: Monash Publications in Geography No. 17.

—— 1984: Unmasking technocratic geography. In M. Billinge, D. Gregory and R. Martin (eds) *Recollections of a revolution*. London: Macmillan, 153–99.

MERCER, D. C. and POWELL, J. M. 1972: *Phenomenology and related non-positivistic viewpoints in the social sciences*. Clayton, Victoria, Australia: Monash Publications in Geography, No. 1.

MERRIFIELD, A. 1995: Situated knowledge through exploration: reflections on Bunge's 'geographical expeditions'. *Antipode* **27**, 49–70.

MESEV, V. 2003: *Remotely Sensed Cities*. London: Taylor & Francis.

MEYER, D. R. 1972: Geographical population data: statistical description not statistical inference. *The Professional Geographer* **24**, 26–8.

MIDDLETON, N. and THOMAS, D. S. G. 1994: *Desertification: exploding the myth*. Chichester: John Wiley.

MIKESELL, M.W. 1967: Geographical perspectives in anthropology. *Annals of the Association of American Geographers* **57**, 617–34.

—— 1969: The borderlands of geography as a social science. In M. Sherif and C.W. Sherif (eds) *Interdisciplinary relationships in the social sciences.* Chicago: Aldine Publishing Company, 227–48.

—— (ed.) 1973: *Geographers abroad: essays on the prospects of research in foreign areas.* Chicago: Department of Geography, University of Chicago, Research Paper 152.

—— 1974: Geography as the study of environment: an assessment of some old and new commitments. In I. R. Manners and M.W. Mikesell (eds), *Perspectives on environment,* Washington, DC: Commission on College Geography, Association of American Geographers, 1–23.

—— 1978: Tradition and innovation in cultural geography. *Annals of the Association of American Geographers* **68**, 1–16.

—— 1981: Continuity and change. In B.W. Blouet (ed.) *The origins of academic geography in the United States.* Hamden, CT: Archon Books, 1–15.

—— 1984: North America. In R. J. Johnston and P. Claval (eds) *Geography since the Second World War: an international survey.* London: Croom Helm, 185–213.

—— 1999: Afterword: new interests, unsolved problems and persisting tasks. In K. E. Foote, P. J. Hugill, K Mathewson and J. M. Smith (eds) *Re-reading cultural geography.* Austin: University of Texas Press, 437–44.

MILLER, D. and HASHMI, S. H. (eds), 2001: *Boundaries and justice: diverse ethical perspectives.* Princeton NJ: Princeton University Press.

MILLER, E.W. (ed.), 1993: *The American Society for Professional Geographers.* Washington DC: Association of American Geographers, Occasional Publication 3.

MILLS, C.W. 1959: *The sociological imagination.* New York: Oxford University Press.

MINCA, C. 2000: Guest editorial. Venetian geographical praxis. *Environment and Planning D: Society and Space* **18**, 285–9.

—— 2001: Acknowledgements. In C. Minca (ed.) *Postmodern geography: theory and praxis.* Oxford: Blackwell, xii–xiii.

—— 2003: Guest editorial. Critical peripheries. *Environment and Planning D: Society and Space* **21**, 160–8.

MITCHELL, B. and DRAPER, D. 1982: *Relevance and ethics in geography.* London: Longman.

MITCHELL, D. 1995: There's no such thing as culture: towards a reconceptualization of the idea of culture in geography. *Transactions, Institute of British Geographers* **NS20**, 102–16.

—— 2003: Dead labour and the political economy of landscape – California living, California dying. In K. Anderson, M. Domosh, S. Pile and N. Thrift (eds) *The handbook of cultural geography.* London, Thousand Oaks, CA and New Delhi: Sage, 233–48.

MITCHELL, R., MARTIN, D. and FOODY, G. M. 1998: Unmixing aggregate data: estimating the social composition of enumeration districts. *Environment and Planning A* **30**, 1929–42.

MIYARES, I. M. and McGLADE, M. S. 1994: Specialization in 'Jobs in geography'; 1980–1993. *The Professional Geographer* **46**, 170–7.

MOHAMMAD, R. 1999: Marginalisation, Islamism and the production of the 'Other's Other'. *Gender, Place and Culture* **6**, 221–40.

MOHAN, G. 1994: Destruction of the con: geography and the commodification of knowledge. *Area* **26**, 387–90.

MOHAN, J. 2000: Geographies of welfare and social exclusion. *Progress in Human Geography* **24**, 291–300.

—— 2003: Geography and social policy: spatial divisions of welfare. *Progress in Human Geography* **27**, 363–74.

MONK, J. 1998: The women were always welcome at Clark. *Economic Geography* (special issue) 14–30.

MONK, J. and HANSON, S. 1982: On not excluding half of the human in human geography. *The Professional Geographer* **34**, 11–23.

MONMONIER, M. S. 1993: What a friend we have in GIS. *The Professional Geographer* **45**, 448–50.
—— 1996: *How to lie within maps*, (2nd edn). Chicago: University of Chicago Press.
MONTEFIORE, A. G. and WILLIAMS, W. M. 1955: Determinism and possibilism. *Geographical Studies* **2**, 1–11.
MOODIE, D. W. and LEHR, J. C. 1976: Fact and theory in historical geography. *The Professional Geographer* **28**, 132–6.
MOOS, A. I. and DEAR, M. J. 1986: Structuration theory in urban analysis: 1. theoretical exegesis. *Environment and Planning A* **18**, 231–52.
MORGAN, M. A. 1967: Hardware models in geography. In R. J. Chorley and P. Haggett (eds) *Models in geography*. London: Methuen, 727–74.
MORGAN, W. B. and MOSS, R. P. 1965: Geography and ecology: the concept of the community and its relationship to environment. *Annals of the Association of American Geographers* **55**, 339–50.
MORRELL, J. 1990: Professionalisation. In R. Olby (ed.) *Companion to the history of modern science*. London: Routledge.
MORRILL, R. L. 1965: *Migration and the growth of urban settlement*. Lund Studies in Geography, Series B. 24, Lund: C. W. K. Gleerup.
—— 1968: Waves of spatial diffusion. *Journal of Regional Science* **8**, 1–18.
—— 1969: Geography and the transformation of society. *Antipode* **1(1)**, 6–9.
—— 1970a: *The spatial organization of society*. Belmont, California: Wadsworth, 2nd edn.
—— 1970b: Geography and the transformation of society: part II. *Antipode* **2(1)**, 4–10.
—— 1973: Ideal and reality in reapportionment. *Annals of the Association of American Geographers* **63**, 463–77.
—— 1974: Review of D. Harvey, *Social Justice and the City*. *Annals of the Association of American Geographers* **64**, 475–7.
—— 1980: Productivity of American Ph.D-granting Departments of Geography. *The Professional Geographer* **32**, 85–9.
—— 1981: *Political redistricting*. Washington, DC: Resource Publications in Geography, Association of American Geographers.
—— 1984: Recollections of the 'Quantitative Revolution's' early years: the University of Washington 1955–65. In M. Billinge, D. Gregory and R. Martin (eds) *Recollections of a revolution*. London: Macmillan, 57–72.
—— 1985: Some important geographic questions. *The Professional Geographer* **37**, 263–70.
—— 1993: Geography, spatial analysis and social science. *Urban Geography* **14**, 442–6.
—— 1994: Response to Johnston. *Urban Geography*, **15**, 296.
—— 2002: Pausing for breath. In P. R. Gould and F. R. Pitts (eds) *Geographical voices: fourteen autobiographical essays*. Syracuse: Syracuse University Press, 211–36.
MORRILL, R. L. and DORMITZER, J. 1979: *The spatial order: an introduction to modern geography*. North Scituate: Duxbury.
MORRILL, R. L. and GARRISON, W. L. 1960: Projections of interregional patterns of trade in wheat and flour. *Economic Geography* **36**, 116–26.
MORRILL, R. L. and WOHLENBERG, E. H. 1971: *The geography of poverty in the United States*. New York: McGraw-Hill.
MOSS, P. (ed.), 2001: *Placing autobiography in geography*. Syracuse: Syracuse University Press.
MOSS, R. P. 1970: Authority and charisma: criteria of validity in geographical method. *South African Geographical Journal* **52**, 13–37.
—— 1977: Deductive strategies in geographical generalization. *Progress in Physical Geography* **1**, 23–39.
MOSS, R. P. and MORGAN, W. B. 1967: The concept of the community: some applications in geographical research. *Transactions, Institute of British Geographers* **41**, 21–32.
MUIR, R. 1975: *Modern political geography*. London: Macmillan.

—— 1978: Radical geography or a new orthodoxy? *Area* **10**, 322–7.

—— 1979: Radical geography and Marxism. *Area* **11**, 126–7.

MULKAY, M. J. 1975: Three models of scientific development. *Sociological Review* **23**, 509–26.

—— 1976: Methodology in the sociology of science: some reflections on the study of radio astronomy. In G. Lemaine *et al.* (eds) *Perspectives in the emergence of scientific disciplines*. The Hague: Mouton, 207–20.

—— 1978: Consensus in science. *Social Science Information* **17**, 107–22.

MULKAY, M. J., GILBERT, G. N. and WOOLGAR, S. 1975: Problem areas and research networks in science. *Sociology* **9**, 187–203.

MULLER-WILLE, C. 1978: The forgotten heritage: Christaller's antecedents. In B. J. L. Berry (ed.) *The nature of change in geographical ideas*. de Kalb: Northern Illinois University Press, 37–64.

MUMFORD, L. 1956: Prospect. In W. L. Thomas (ed.) *Man's role in changing the face of the earth*. Chicago: University of Chicago Press, 1141–52.

MURDIE, R. A. 1969: *Factorial ecology of metropolitan Toronto 1951–1961*. Chicago: University of Chicago, Department of Geography, Research Paper 116.

MURDOCH, J. 1998: The spaces of actor-network theory. *Geoforum* **29**, 357–74.

MURPHY, A. 1991: Regions as social constructs: the gap between theory and practice. *Progress in Human Geography* **15**, 22–35.

MYRDAL, G. 1957: *Economic theory and underdeveloped regions*. London: Duckworth.

NAGAR, R., LAWSON, V., McDOWELL, L. and HANSON, S. 2002: Locating globalization: feminist (re)readings of subjects and spaces of globalization. *Economic Geography* **78**, 257–84.

NASH C. 1996: Reclaiming vision: looking at landscape and the body. *Gender, Place and Culture* **3**, 149–69.

—— 2000: Performativity in practice: some recent work in cultural geography. *Progress in Human Geography* **24**, 653–64.

NAIRN, T. 1977: *The Break-Up of Britain: Crisis and Neo-Nationalism*. London: New Left Books.

NAS-NRC 1997: *Rediscovering geography: new relevance for science and society*. Washington DC: National Research Council.

NAST, H. 1994: Opening remarks on 'Women in the field'. *The Professional Geographer* **46**, 54–66.

NATIONAL ACADEMY OF SCIENCES-NATIONAL RESEARCH COUNCIL 1965: *The science of geography*. Washington: NAS-NRC.

NATTER, W. 2003: Geopolitics in Germany, 1919–45. In J. Agnew, K. Mitchell and G. Toal (eds) *A Companion to Political Geography*. Oxford: Blackwell, 187–203.

NAYAK, A. 2003: Last of the 'Real Geordies'? White masculinities and the subcultural response to deindustrialisation. *Environment and Planning D: Society and Space* **21**, 7–25.

NEFT, D. 1966: *Statistical analysis for areal distributions*. Philadelphia: Monograph 2, Regional Science Research Institute.

NEWMAN, D. 1996: Writing together separately: critical discourse and the problems of cross-ethnic co-authorship. *Area* **28**, 1–12.

NEWMAN, D. and PORTUGALI, J. 1987: Israeli-Palestinian relations as reflected in the scientific literature. *Progress in Human Geography* **11**, 315–32.

NEWMAN, J. L. 1973: The use of the term 'hypothesis' in geography. *Annals of the Association of American Geographers* **63**, 22–7.

NICKLES, T. (ed.) 2003: *Thomas Kuhn*. Cambridge: Cambridge University Press.

NIJMAN, J. 2000: The paradigmatic city. *Annals of the Association of American Geographers* **90**, 135–45.

NYSTUEN, J. D. 1963: Identification of some fundamental spatial concepts. *Papers of the Michigan Academy of Science, Arts, and Letters,* **48**, 373–84. Reprinted in B. J. L. Berry and D. F. Marble (eds) *Spatial analysis*. Englewood Cliffs, NJ: Prentice-Hall, 35–41.

—— 1984: Comment on 'Artificial intelligence and its applicability to geographical problem solving'. *The Professional Geographer* **36**, 358–9.

OBERMEYER, N. J. 1994: GIS: a new profession? *The Professional Geographer* **46**, 498–503.

ODUM, H. W. and MOORE, H. E. 1938: *American regionalism – a cultural-historical approach to national integration.* New York: H. Holt & Company.

O'KELLY, M. 1999: Introduction to the thirtieth anniversary special issue. *Geographical Analysis* **30**, 311–17.

OLDS, K. 2001: Practices for 'process geographies': a view from within and outside the periphery. *Environment and Planning D: Society and Space* **19**, 127–36.

OLLMAN, B. 1993: *Dialectical investigations.* London and New York: Routledge.

O'LOUGHLIN, J. 2002: The electoral geography of Weimar Germany: exploratory spatial data analyses (ESDA) of Protestant support for the Nazi party. *Political Analysis* **10**, 217–43.

OLSSON, G. 1965: *Distance and human interaction: a review and bibliography.* Philadelphia: Regional Science Research Institute, Bibliography Series Number 2.

—— 1969: Inference problems in locational analysis. In K. R. Cox and R. G. Golledge (eds) *Behavioral problems in geography: a symposium.* Evanson: Northwestern University Studies in Geography 17, 14–34.

—— 1978: Of ambiguity or far cries from a memorializing mamafesta. In D. Ley and M. S. Samuels (eds) *Humanistic geography.* London: Croom Helm, 109–20.

—— 1979: Social science and human action or on hitting your head against the ceiling of language. In S. Gale and G. Olsson (eds) *Philosophy in geography.* Dordrecht: Reidel, 287–308.

—— 1980: *Birds in egg/eggs in bird.* London: Pion.

—— 1982: -/-. In P. R. Gould and G. Olsson (eds) A *search for common ground.* London: Pion, 223–31.

—— 1991: *Lines of power/limits of language.* Minneapolis, MA: University of Minnesota Press.

—— 1992: Lines of power. In T. J. Barnes and J. S. Duncan (eds) *Writing worlds: discourse, text and metaphor in the representation of landscape.* London: Routledge, 86–96.

OPENSHAW, S. 1984a: *The modifiable areal unit problem.* CATMOG 38, Norwich: Geo Books.

—— 1984b: Ecological fallacies and the analysis of areal census data. *Environment and Planning A* **16**, 17–32.

—— 1986: *Nuclear power: siting and safety.* London: Routledge & Kegan Paul.

—— 1989: Computer modelling in human geography. In B. Macmillan (ed.) *Remodelling geography.* Oxford: Basil Blackwell, 70–88.

—— 1991: A view on the GIS crisis in geography: or, using GIS to put Humpty-Dumpty back together again. *Environment and Planning A* **23**, 621–8.

—— 1992: Further thoughts on geography and GIS: a reply. *Environment and Planning A* **24**, 463–6.

—— 1994: Computational human geography: towards a research agenda. *Environment and Planning A* **26**, 499–505.

—— 1995: Human systems modelling as a new grand challenge area in science: what has happened to the science in social science? *Environment and Planning A* **27**, 159–64.

—— 1996: Fuzzy logic as a new scientific paradigm for doing geography. *Environment and Planning A* **28**, 761–8.

—— 1998: Building automated geographical analysis and explanation machines. In P. Longley, S. Brooks, R. MacDonnell and B. Macmillan (eds), *Geocomputation: a primer.* Chichester: John Wiley, 95–116.

OPENSHAW, S. and GODDARD, J. B. 1987: Some implications of the commodification of information and the emerging information economy for applied geographical analysis in the United Kingdom. *Environment and Planning A* **19**, 1423–40.

OPENSHAW, S. and OPENSHAW, C. 1997: *Artificial intelligence in geography.* Chichester: John Wiley.

OPENSHAW, S. and RAO, L. (1995) Algorithms for reengineering 1991 census geography. *Environment and Planning A* **27**, 425–46.

OPENSHAW, S. and TAYLOR, P. J. 1979: A million or so correlation coefficients: three experiments on the modifiable areal unit problem. In N. Wrigley (ed.), *Statistical Applications in the Spatial Sciences.* London: Pion.

—— 1981: The modifiable areal unit problem. In N. Wrigley and R. J. Bennett, (eds), *Quantitative geography: a British view*. London: Routledge and Kegan Paul, 60–70.

OPENSHAW, S., BLAKE, M. and WHYMER, C. 1995: Using neurocomputing methods to classify Britain's residential areas. In P. F. Fisher (ed.), *Innovations in GIS2*. London: Taylor and Francis, 97–112.

OPENSHAW, S., CARVER, S. and FERNIE, J. 1989: *Britain's nuclear waste: siting and safety*. London: Belhaven Press.

OPENSHAW, S., CHARLTON, M., CRAFT, A. W. and BIRCH, J. 1988: Investigation of leukaemia clusters by use of a geographical analysis machine. *The Lancet* 6 February, 272–3.

OPENSHAW, S., STEADMAN, P. and GREENE, O. 1983: *Doomsday: Britain after nuclear attack*. Oxford: Basil Blackwell.

OPENSHAW, S. and TURTON, I. 2001: Using a geographical explanations machine to explore spatial factors relating to primary school performance. *Geographical and Environmental Modelling* **5**, 85–101.

OPENSHAW, S., WYMER, C. and CHARLTON, M. 1986: A geographical information and mapping system for the BBC Domesday optical discs. *Transactions, Institute of British Geographers* **NS11**, 296–304.

OPENSHAW, S., WYMER, C. and CRAFT, A. W. 1988: A Mark I geographical analysis machine for the automated analysis of point data sets. *International Journal of Geographical Information Systems* **1**, 335–58.

ORD, J. K. and GETIS, A. 1995: Local spatial autocorrelation statistics: distributional issues and an application. *Geographical Analysis* **27**, 286–96.

O'RIORDAN, T. 1971a: Environmental management. In C. Board *et al.* (eds), *Progress in Geography 3*. London: Edward Arnold, 173–231.

—— 1971b: *Perspectives in resource management*. London: Pion.

—— 1976: *Environmentalism*. London: Pion.

—— 1981: *Environmentalism* (second edition). London: Pion.

ORME, A. R. 2002: Shifting paradigms in geomorphology: the fate of research ideas in an educational context. *Geomorphology* **47**, 325–42.

O'SULLIVAN, D. and UNWIN, D. J. 2003: *Geographic Information Analysis*. New York: John Wiley.

Ó TUATHAIL, G. 1992: Foreign policy and the hyperreal: the Reagan administration and the 'scripting' of South Africa'. In T. J. Barnes and J. S. Duncan (eds) *Writing worlds: discourse, text and metaphor in the representation of landscape*. London: Routledge, 155–75.

—— 1994: (Dis)placing geopolitics: writing on the maps of global politics. *Environment and Planning D: Society and Space* **12**, 525–46.

—— 1996: *Critical geopolitics*. London and New York: Routledge.

Ó TUATHAIL, G. and DALBY, S. 1994: Critical geopolitics: unfolding spaces for thought in geography and global politics. *Environment and Planning D: Society and Space* **12**, 513–14.

Ó TUATHAIL, G. and TOAL, G. 2000: Dis/placing the geo-politics which one cannot not want. *Political Geography* **19**, 385–96.

OWENS, P. L. 1984: Rural leisure and recreation research: a retrospective evaluation. *Progress in Human Geography* **8**, 157–88.

OZOUF-MARIGNIER, M.-V. and ROBIC, M.-C. 1999: The *Tableau* is alive and well ... reactions to the *Tableau de la Géographie de la France* of Paul Vidal de la Blache. In A. Buttimer, S. D. Brunn and U. Wardenga (eds) *Text and image: social construction of regional knowledges*. Leipzig: Institut für Länderkunde Leipzig, Beiträge zur regionalen Geographie **49**, 54–66.

PAASSI, A. 1991: Deconstructing regions: notes on the scales of social life. *Environment and Planning A* **23**, 239–56.

PACIONE, M. 1990a: Conceptual issues in applied urban geography. *Tijdschrift voor Economische en Sociale Geografie* **81**, 3–13.

—— 1990b: On the dangers of misinterpretation. *Tijdschrift voor Economische en Sociale Geografie* **81**, 26–8.

PACIONE, M. (ed.) 1999: *Applied geography; principle and practice. an introduction to useful research in physical, environmental and human geography.* London: Routledge.

PAHL, R. E. 1965: Trends in social geography. In R. J. Chorley and P. Haggett (eds) *Frontiers in geographical teaching.* London: Methuen, 81–100.

—— 1969: Urban social theory and research. *Environment and Planning* **1**, 143–54. (Reprinted in R. E. Pahl 1970, *Whose City?* London: Longman, 209–25.)

—— 1975: *Whose city? And other essays.* Harmondsworth: Penguin Books (2nd edn).

—— 1979: Socio-political factors in resource allocation. In D. T. Herbert and D. M. Smith (eds) *Social problems and the city: geographical perspectives.* Oxford: Oxford University Press, 33–46.

PAIN, R. 1991: Space, sexual violence and social control: integrating geographical and feminist analyses of women's fear of crime. *Progress in Human Geography* **15(4)**, 415–31.

—— 2003: Social geography: on action-orientated research. *Progress in Human Geography* 27: 677–85.

PAINTER, J. 2000: Pierre Bourdieu. In M. Crang and N. Thrift (eds) *Thinking space.* New York and London: Routledge, 239–59.

—— 2002: The rise of the workfare state. In R. J. Johnston, P. J. Taylor and M. J. Watts (eds), *Geographies of global change: remapping the world.* Oxford: Blackwell Publishers, 158–73.

PAINTER, J. M. and PHILO, C. 1995: Spaces of citizenship: an introduction. *Political Geography* **14**, 107–20.

PALM, R. 1979: Financial and real estate institutions in the housing market. In D. T. Herbert and R. J. Johnston (eds) *Geography and the urban environment,* 2. Chichester: John Wiley, 83–124.

—— 2003: Textbooks that moved generations. *Progress in human Geography* **27**, 515–18.

PALM, R. and PRED, A. R. 1978: The status of American women: a time-geographic view. In D. Lanegran and R. Palm (eds) *Invitation to geography* (second edition). New York: McGraw-Hill, 99–109.

PAPAGEORGIOU, G. J. 1969: Description of a basis necessary to the analysis of spatial systems. *Geographical Analysis* **1**, 213–15.

—— (ed.) 1976: *Mathematical land use theory.* Lexington, MA: D. C. Heath.

PARKER, G. 1985: *Western geopolitical thought in the twentieth century.* London: Croom Helm.

PARKER, W. H. 1982: *Mackinder: geography as an aid to statecraft.* Oxford: The Clarendon Press.

PARKES, D. N. and THRIFT, N. J. 1980: *Times, spaces and places.* Chichester: John Wiley.

PARRY, M. and DUNCAN, R. 1995: *The economic implications of climate change.* London: Earthscan.

PARSONS, J. J. 1977: Geography as exploration and discovery. *Annals of the Association of American Geographers* **67**, 1–16.

PATERSON, J. H. 1974: Writing regional geography. In C. Board *et al.* (eds) *Progress in geography 6.* London: Edward Arnold, 1–26.

PATERSON, J. L. 1985: *David Harvey's geography.* London: Croom Helm.

PATMORE, J. A. 1970: *Land and leisure.* Newton Abbott: David & Charles.

—— 1983: *Recreation and resources: leisure patterns and leisure places.* Oxford: Basil Blackwell.

PATTEN, R. L. 2003: From house to square to street: narrative traversals. In H. Michie and R. R. Thomas (eds) *Nineteenth century geographies: the transformation of space from the Victorian age to the American century.* New Brunswick NJ: Rutgers University Press, 191–208.

PATTERSON, T. C. 1986: The last sixty years: toward a social history of Americanist archaeology in the United States. *American Anthropologist* **88**, 7–26.

PATTIE, C. J. and JOHNSTON, R. J. 1995: 'Its not like that round here': region, economic evaluations and voting at the 1992 British general election. *European Journal of Political Research* **28**, 1–32.

—— 1995: The impact of spending on party constituency campaigns at recent British general elections. *Party Politics* **1**, 261–74.

—— 2000: 'People who talk together vote together': an exploration of contextual effects in Great Britain. *Annals of the Association of American Geographers* **90**, 41–66.

PAWSON, E. 1999: Postcolonial New Zealand? In K. Anderson and F. Gale (eds) *Cultural geographies*. Melbourne: Longman, 25–50.

PEACH, C. 2002: Social geography: new religions and ethnoburbs – contrasts with cultural geography. *Progress in Human Geography* **26**, 252–60.

—— 2003: Geography and the fragmented city. In R. J. Johnston and M. Williams (eds) *A century of British geography*. Oxford: Oxford University Press for the British Academy.

PEACH, C. and SMITH, S. J. 1981: Introduction. In C. Peach, V. Robinson and S. J. Smith (eds) *Ethnic segregation in cities*. London: Croom Helm, 9–24.

PEAKE, L. 1994: 'Proper words in proper places ...' Or, of young Turks and old turkeys. *The Canadian Geographer* **38**, 204–6.

PEAKE, L. and KOBAYASHI, A. 2002: Policies and practices for an antiracist geography at the millennium. *The Professional Geographer* **54**, 50–61.

PECK, J. 1996: *Work-place: the social regulation of labor markets*. New York: Guilford.

—— 1999; Grey geography? *Transactions of the Institute of British Geographers* **NS24**, 131–5.

—— 2000: Jumping in, joining up and getting on. *Transactions of the Institute of British Geographers* **NS25**, 255–8.

—— 2001: *Workfare states*. New York: Guilford.

PECK, J. and TICKELL, A. 1992: Local modes of social regulation? Regulation theory, Thatcherism and regional development. *Geoforum* **23**, 347–64.

—— 1995: The social regulation of uneven development: 'regulatory deficit', England's South East, and the collapse of Thatcherism. *Environment and Planning A* **27**, 15–40.

—— 1996: the return of the Manchester men: men's words and men's deeds in the remaking of the local state. *Transactions of the Institute of British Geographers* **21**, 595–616.

—— 2002: Neoliberalizing space. *Antipode* **34**, 380–404.

PEET, D. and WATTS, M. (eds) 1996: *Liberation ecologies: nature, development and social movements*. London and New York: Routledge.

PEET, J. R. 1971: Poor, hungry America. *The Professional Geographer* **23**, 99–104.

—— 1975a: Inequality and poverty: a marxist-geographic theory. *Annals of the Association of American Geographers* **65**, 564–71.

—— 1975b: The geography of crime: a political critique. *The Professional Geographer* **27**, 277–80.

—— 1976a: Further comments on the geography of crime. *The Professional Geographer* **28**, 96–100.

—— 1976b: Editorial: radical geography in 1976. *Antipode* **8(3)**, inside cover.

—— 1977: The development of radical geography in the United States. *Progress in Human Geography* **1**, 240–63.

—— (ed.) 1978: *Radical geography*. London: Methuen.

—— 1979: Societal contradiction and marxist geography. *Annals of the Association of American Geographers* **69**, 164–9.

—— 1980: The transition from feudalism to capitalism. In J. R. Peet (ed.) *An introduction to marxist theories of underdevelopment*. Canberra: Publication HG/14, Department of Human Geography, Australian National University, 51–74.

—— 1985a: The social origins of environmental determinism. *Annals of the Association of American Geographers* **75**, 309–33.

—— 1985b: Radical geography in the United States: a personal history. *Antipode* **17**, 1–7.

—— 1989: World capitalism and the destruction of regional cultures. In R. J. Johnston and P. J. Taylor (eds) *A World in Crisis?* Oxford: Basil Blackwell, 175–99.

—— 1991: *Global capitalism: theories of societal development*. London: Routledge.

—— 1993: Reading Fukuyama: politics at the end of history. *Political Geography* **12**, 64–78.

—— 1996: A sign taken for history: Daniel Shays' memorial in Peterham, Massachusetts. *Annals of the Association of American Geographers* **86**, 21–43.

PEET, R. 1998: *Modern geographical thought*. Oxford and Malden, MA: Blackwell.

PEET, R. and LYONS, J. V. 1981: Marxism: dialectical materialism, social formation and the geographic relations. In M . E. Harvey and B. P. Holly (eds) *Themes in geographic thought*. London: Croom Helm, 187–205.

PEET, R. and THRIFT, N. J. 1989: Political economy and human geography. In R. Peet and N. J. Thrift (eds) *New models in geography*, vol. 1. London: Unwin Hyman, 3–27.

PELTIER, L. C. 1954: Geomorphology. In P. E. James and C. F. Jones (eds) *American geography: inventory and prospect*. Syracuse: Syracuse University Press, 362–81.

PENNING-ROWSELL, E. C. 1981: Fluctuating fortunes in gauging landscape value. *Progress in Human Geography* **5**, 25–41.

PENROSE, J. and JACKSON, P. 1993: Identity and the politics of difference. In P. Jackson and J. Penrose (eds) *Constructions of race, place and nation*. London: UCL Press, 202–10.

PEPPER, D. 1984: *The roots of modern environmentalism*. London: Croom Helm.

—— 1987: Physical and human integration: an educational perspective. *Progress in Human Geography* **11**, 379–404.

—— 1996: *Modern environmentalism: an introduction*. London: Routledge.

PEPPER, D. and JENKINS, A. 1983: A call to arms: geography and peace studies. *Area* **15**, 202–8.

—— (eds) 1985: *The geography of peace and war*. Oxford: Basil Blackwell.

PEPPER, S. C. 1942: *World hypotheses*. Berkeley, CA: University of California Press.

PERRY, P. J. 1969: H. C. Darby and historical geography: a survey and review. *Geographische Zeitschrift* **57**, 161–77.

—— 1979: Beyond Domesday. *Progress in Human Geography* **3**, 407–16.

PETCH, J. R. and HAINES-YOUNG, R. H. 1980: The challenge of critical rationalism for methodology in physical geography. *Progress in Physical Geography* **4**, 63–78.

PETER, L. and HULL, R. 1969: *The Peter principle*. London: Bantam Books.

PHILBRICK, A. K. 1957: Principles of areal functional organization in regional human geography. *Economic Geography* **33**, 299–366.

PHILLIPS, D. R. and JOSEPH, A. E. 1984: *Accessibility and utilization: perspectives on health care delivery*. London: Harper & Row.

PHILLIPS, M. and UNWIN, T. 1985: British historical geography: places and people. *Area* **17**, 155–64.

PHILO, C. (compiler) 1991: *New words, new worlds: reconceptualising social and cultural geography*. Aberystwyth: Cambrian Printers.

—— 1992: Foucault's geography. *Environment and Planning D: Society and Space* **10**, 137–61.

—— 1994: Political geography and everything: invited notes on 'transpolitical geography'. *Geoforum* **25**, 525–32.

—— 1995: Animals, geography and the city: notes on inclusions and exclusions. *Environment and Planning D: Society and Space* **13**, 655–81.

—— 1998: Reading *Drumlin*: academic geography and a student geographical magazine. *Progress in Human Geography* **22**, 344–67.

—— 2000: More words, more worlds: reflections on the 'cultural turn' and human geography. In I. Cook, D. Crouch, S. Naylor and J. R. Ryan (eds) *Cultural turns/geographical turns: perspectives on cultural geography*. Harlow: Prentice Hall, 26–53.

PHILO, C. and WILBERT, C. (eds) 2000: *Animal spaces, beastly places: new geographies of human-animal relations*. London: Routledge.

PHIPPS, A. G. 2001: Empirical applications of structuration theory. *Geografiska Annaler* **83B**: 189–204.

PICKLES, J. 1985: *Phenomenology, science and geography: spatiality and the human sciences*. Cambridge: Cambridge University Press.

—— 1986: *Geography and humanism*. CATMOG 44, Norwich: Geo Books.

—— 1988: From fact-world to life-world: the phenomenological method and social science. In J. Eyles and D. M. Smith (eds) *Qualitative methods in human geography*. Cambridge: Polity Press, 233–54.

—— 1992: Texts, hermeneutics and propaganda. In T. J. Barnes and J. S. Duncan (eds) *Writing worlds: discourse, text and metaphor in the representation of landscape.* London: Routledge, 193–230.

—— 1993: Discourse on method and the history of discipline: reflections on Dobson's 1983 automated geography. *The Professional Geographer* **45**, 451–5.

—— (ed.) 1995a: *Ground truth: the social implications of geographical information systems.* New York: The Guilford Press.

—— 1995b: Representations in an electronic age: geography, GIS and democracy. In J. Pickles (ed.) *Ground truth: the social implications of geographical information systems.* New York: The Guilford Press, 1–30.

PICKLES, J. and SMITH, A. (eds) 1998: *Theorising transition: the political economy of post-Communist transformations.* London and New York: Routledge.

PICKVANCE, C. 1976: Housing, reproduction of capital and reproduction of labour power: some recent French work. *Antipode* **8**, 58–68.

PILE, S. 1991: Practising interpretative geography. *Transactions, Institute of British Geographers* **NS16**, 458–69.

—— 1993: Human agency and human geography revisited: a critique of 'new models' of the self. *Transactions, Institute of British Geographers* **NS18**, 122–39.

—— 1994: Masculinism, the use of dualistic epistemologies and third spaces. *Antipode* **26**, 255–77

—— 1996: *The body and the city. Psychoanalysis, space and subjectivity.* London: Routledge.

PILE, S. and KEITH, M. 1997: *Geographies of resistance.* London: Routledge.

PILE, S. and ROSE, G. 1992: All or nothing – politics and critique in the modernism-postmodernism debate. *Environment and Planning D: Society and Space* **10**, 123–36.

PILE, S. and THRIFT, N. (eds) 1995: *Mapping the subject: geographies of cultural transformation.* London and New York: Routledge.

PINCH, S. P. 1985: *Cities and services: the geography of collective consumption.* London: Routledge & Kegan Paul.

—— 1997: *Worlds of welfare.* London: Routledge.

—— 1998: *Knowledge communities, spatial theory and social policy.* Social Policy and Administration, 32: 104–9.

PIPKIN, J. S. 1981: Cognitive behavioral geography and repetitive travel. In K. R. Cox and R. G. Golledge (eds) *Behavioral problems in geography revisited.* London: Methuen, 145–80.

PIRIE, G. H. 1976: Thoughts on revealed and spatial behaviour. *Environment and Planning A* **8**, 947–55.

PITTS, F. R. 1965: A graph theoretic approach to historical geography. *The Professional Geographer* **17(5)**, 15–20.

PLATT, R. H. 1986: Floods and man: a geographer's agenda. In R. W. Kates and I. Burton (eds) *Geography, resources and environment*, vol. 2: *Themes from the work of Gilbert F. White.* Chicago: University of Chicago Press, 28–68.

PLATT, R. S. 1928: A detail of regional geography: Ellison Bay community as an industrial organism. *Annals of the Association of American Geographers* **18**, 81–126.

—— 1935: Field approach to regions. *Annals of the Association of American Geographers* **25**, 153–74.

PLOSZAJSKA, T. 1999: *Geographical education, empire and citizenship: geographical teaching and learning in English schools.* London: Historical Geography Research Group of the Royal Geographical Society.

PLUMMER, P. 2001: Vague theories, sophisticated techniques and poor data. *Environment and Planning A* **33**, 761–4.

PLUMMER, P. and SHEPPARD, E. S. 2001: Must emancipatory economic geography be qualitative? *Antipode* **33**, 194–9.

POCOCK, D. C. D. 1983: The paradox of humanistic geography. *Area* **15**, 355–8.

POCOCK, D. C. D. and HUDSON, R. 1978: *Images of the urban environment.* London: Macmillan.

PODMORE, J. 1998: (Re)reading the 'Loft Living' habits in Montreal's inner city. *International Journal of Urban and Regional Research* **22**, 283– 302.

POIKER, T. K. 1983: The shining armor of the white knight. *The Professional Geographer* **35**, 348–9.

POLLARD, J. S., HENRY, N., BRYSON, J. and DANIELS, P. 2000: Shades of grey? Geography and policy. *Transactions of the Institute of British Geographers* **NS25**, 243–8.

POOLER, J. A. 1977: The origins of the spatial tradition in geography: an interpretation. *Ontario Geography* **11**, 56–83.

POPPER, K. R. 1959: *The logic of scientific discovery.* London: Hutchinson.

—— 1967: Replies to my critics. In P. A. Schipp (ed.), *The philosophy of Karl Popper,* vol. 2. La Salle, IN: Open Court Publishing Company, 961–97.

—— 1970: Normal science and its dangers. In I. Lakatos and A. Musgrave (eds), *Criticism and the growth of knowledge.* London: Cambridge University Press, 51–8.

PORTEOUS, J. D. 1977: *Environment and behavior.* Reading, MA: Addison Wesley.

—— 1985: Literature and humanist geography. *Area* **17**, 117–22.

—— 1986: Bodyscape: the body-landscape metaphor. *The Canadian Geographer* **30**, 2–19.

—— 1988: Topocide: the annihilation of place. In J. Eyles and D. M. Smith (eds) *Qualitative methods in human geography.* Cambridge: Polity Press, 75–93.

PORTER, P. W. 1978: Geography as human ecology. *Human geography: coming of age. American Behavioral Scientist* **22**, 15–40.

PORTER, P. W. and LUKERMANN, F. 1975: The geography of utopia. In D. Lowenthal and M. J. Bowden (eds) *Geography of the mind: essays in historical geosophy.* New York: Oxford University Press, 197–224.

POWELL, J. M. 1970: *The public lands of Australia Felix: settlement and land appraisal in Victoria 1834–1891.* Melbourne: Oxford University Press.

—— 1971: Utopia, millennium and the cooperative ideal: a behavioral matrix in the settlement process. *The Australian Geographer* **11**, 606–18.

—— 1972: *Images of Australia.* Clayton, Victoria, Australia: Monash University Publications in Geography No. 3.

—— 1977: *Mirrors of the New World: images and image-makers in the settlement process.* Folkestone: Dawson.

—— 1980a: Thomas Griffith Taylor 1880–1963. In T. W. Freeman and P. Pinchemel (eds) *Geographers: biobibliographical studies,* vol. 5. London: Mansell, 141–54.

—— 1980b: The haunting of Saloman's house: geography and the limits of science. *Australian Geographer* **14**, 327–41.

—— 1981: Editorial comment: 'professional' geography into the eighties? *Australian Geographical Studies* **19**, 228–30.

POWELL, M. and BOYNE, G. 2001: The spatial strategy of equality and the spatial division of welfare. *Social Policy and Administration* **35**, 181–94.

PRATT, G. 1989: Quantitative techniques and humanistic-historical materialist perspectives. In A. Kobayashi and S. Mackenzie (eds) *Remaking human geography.* Boston: Unwin Hyman, 101–15.

—— 1992: Spatial metaphors and speaking positions. *Environment and Planning D: Society and Space* **10**, 241–4.

—— 1999: From registered nurse to registered nanny: discursive geographies of Filipina domestic workers in Vancouver, BC. *Economic Geography* **75**, 215–236.

—— 2000: Feminist geographies. In R. J. Johnston, D. Gregory, G. Pratt, and M. Watts (eds) *The dictionary of human geography* (4th edn). Oxford: Blackwell, 259–62.

PRATT, G. and HANSON, S. 1988: Gender, class and space. *Environment and Planning D: Society and Space* **6**, 15–35.

—— 1994: Geography and the construction of difference. *Gender, Place and Culture* **1**, 5–29.

PRED, A. R. 1965a: The concentration of high value-added manufacturing. *Economic Geography* **41**, 108–32.

—— 1965b: Industrialization, initial advantage, and American metropolitan growth. *Geographical Review* **55**, 158–85.

—— 1967: *Behavior and location: foundations for a geographic and dynamic location theory. Part I.* Lund: C. W. K. Gleerup.

—— 1969: *Behavior and location: foundations for a geographic and dynamic location theory. Part II.* Lund: C. W. K. Gleerup.

—— 1973: Urbanization, domestic planning problems and Swedish geographic research. In C. Board et al. (eds) *Progress in Geography 5*. London: Edward Arnold, 1–77.

—— 1977a: The choreography of existence: comments on Hägerstrand's time geography and its usefulness. *Economic Geography* **53**, 207–21.

—— 1977b: *City-systems in advanced economies*. London: Hutchinson.

—— 1979: The academic past through a time-geographic looking glass. *Annals of the Association of American Geographers* **69**, 175–80.

—— 1981a: Production, family, and free-time projects: a time-geographic perspective on the individual and societal change in nineteenth century US cities. *Journal of Historical Geography* **7**, 3–36.

—— 1981b: Of paths and projects: individual behavior and its societal context. In K. R. Cox and R. G. Golledge (eds) *Behavioral problems in geography revisited*. London: Methuen, 231–55.

—— 1984a: From here and now to there and then: some notes on diffusions, defusions, and disillusions. In M. Billinge, D. Gregory and R. Martin (eds) *Recollections of a revolution*. London: Macmillan, 86–103.

—— 1984b: Structuration, biography formation, and knowledge: observations on port growth during the late mercantile period. *Environment and Planning D: Society and Space* **2**, 251–76.

—— 1984c: Place as historically contingent process: structuration and the time geography of becoming places. *Annals of the Association of American Geographers* **74**, 279–97.

—— 1985: The social becomes the spatial and the spatial becomes the social. In D. Gregory and J. Urry (eds) *Social relations and spatial structures*. London: Macmillan, 336–75.

—— 1986: *Becoming places, practice and structure: the emergence and aftermath of enclosures in the plains villages of southwestern Skane*. Oxford: Polity Press.

—— 1988: Lost words as reflections of lost worlds. In R. G. Golledge, H. Couclelis and P. R. Gould (eds) *A ground for common search*. Santa Barbara: The Santa Barbara Geographical Press, 138–47.

—— 1989: The locally spoken word and local struggles. *Environment and Planning D: Society and Space* **7**, 211–34.

—— 1990: In other wor(l)ds: fragmented and integrated observations on gendered languages, gendered spaces and local transformation. *Antipode* **22**, 33–52.

—— 1992: Straw men build straw houses. *Annals of the Association of American Geographers* **82**, 305–8.

—— 1996: Interfusions: consumption, identity and the practices and power relations of everyday life. *Environment and Planning A* **28**, 11–24.

PRED, A. R. and KIBEL, B. M. 1970: An application of gaming simulation to a general model of economic locational processes. *Economic Geography* **46**, 136–56.

PRED, A. R. and PALM, R. 1978: The status of American women: a time-geographic view. In D. A. Lanegran and R. Palm (eds) *An invitation to geography* (second edition). New York: McGraw-Hill, 99–109.

PRETICEILLE, E. 1976: Urban planning: the contradiction of capitalist urbanization. *Antipode* **8**, 69–76.

PRICE, D. G. and BLAIR, A. M. 1989: *The changing geography of the service sector.* London: Belhaven.

PRICE, M. and LEWIS, M. 1993a: The reinvention of cultural geography. *Annals of the Association of American Geographers* **83**, 1–17.

—— 1993b: Reply: on reading cultural geography. *Annals of the Association of American Geographers* **83**, 520–2.

PRINCE, H. C. 1961–2: The geographical imagination. *Landscape* **11**, 21–5.

—— 1971a: Real, imagined and abstract worlds of the past. In C. Board *et al.* (eds) *Progress in geography 3*. London: Edward Arnold, 1–86.

—— 1971b: America! America? Views on a pot melting 1. Questions of social relevance. *Area* **3**, 150–3.

—— 1979: About half Marx for the transition from feudalism to capitalism. *Area* **11**, 47–51.

—— 2000: *Geographers engaged in historical geography in British higher education 1931–1991*. London: Historical Geography Research Series, 36.

PROCTOR, J. D. 1998a: Ethics in geography; giving moral form to the geographical imagination. *Area* **30**, 8–18.

—— 1998b: The social construction of nature: relativist accusations, pragmatist and critical realist responses. *Annals of the Association of American Geographers* **88**, 352–76.

PROCTOR, J. D. and SMITH, D. M. (eds), 1999: *Geography and ethics: journeys in a moral terrain*. London: Routledge.

PROUDFOOT, M. J. 1937: City retail structure. *Economic Geography*, **13**, 425–8.

PRUITT, E. L. 1979: The Office of Naval Research and geography. *Annals of the Association of American Geographers* **69**, 103–8.

PRUNTY, M. C. 1979: Clark in the early 1940s. *Annals of the Association of America Geographers* **69**, 42–5.

PUDUP, M. B. 1988: Arguments within regional geography. *Progress in Human Geography* **12**, 369–90.

PULIDO, L. 2002: Reflections on a white discipline. *The Professional Geographer* **54**, 42–9.

PURCELL, M. 2003: Islands of practice and the Marston/Brenner debate: toward a more synthetic critical human geography. *Progress in Human Geography* **27**, 317–32.

QUAINI, M. 1982: *Geography and marxism*. Oxford: Blackwell.

RADCLIFFE, S. 1990: Ethnicity, patriarchy and incorporation into the nation: female migrants as domestic servants in Peru. *Environment and Planning D: Society and Space* **8**, 379–93.

—— 1994: (Re)presenting post-colonial women: authority, difference and feminism. *Area* **26**, 25–32.

—— 1996: Gendered nations: nostalgia, development and territory in Ecuador. *Gender, Place and Culture* **3**, 5–21.

RADCLIFFE, S. and WESTWOOD, S. (eds) 1996: *Remaking the nation: place, identity and politics in Latin America*. London: Routledge.

RADFORD, J. P. 1981: The social geography of the nineteenth century US city. In D. T. Herbert and R. J. Johnston (eds) *Geography and the urban environment* 4. Chichester: John Wiley, 257–93.

RATZEL, F. 1882–91: *Anthropogeographie*. Stuttgart: J Engelghorn.

—— 1897: *Politische Geografie, oder die Geographie der Staaten, des Verkhers, und der Krieges*. Munich: R. Oldenbourg.

RAVENSTEIN, E. G. 1885: The laws of migration. *Journal of the Royal Statistical Society* **48**, 167–235.

RAWSTRON, E. M. 1958: Three principles of industrial location. *Transactions, Institute of British Geographers* **25**, 135–42.

—— 2002: Textbooks that moved generations. *Progress in Human Geography* **26**, 831–6.

RAY, D. M., VILLENEUVE, P. Y. and ROBERGE, R. A. 1974: Functional prerequisites, spatial diffusion, and allometric growth. *Economic Geography* **50**, 341–51.

REES, J. 1985: *Natural resources: allocation economics, and policy*. London: Methuen.

REES, P. H. 1986: Developments in the modelling of spatial populations. In R. I. Woods and P. H. Rees (eds), *Population structures and models: developments in spatial demography*. London: Allen & Unwin, 97–125.

REES, P. H. and WILSON, A. G. 1977: *Spatial population analysis*. London: Edward Arnold.

RELPH, E. 1970: An inquiry into the relations between phenomenology and geography. *The Canadian Geographer* **14**, 193–201.

—— 1976: *Place and placelessness.* London: Pion.

—— 1977: Humanism, phenomenology, and geography. *Annals of the Association of American Geographers* **67**, 177–9.

—— 1981a: Phenomenology. In M. E. Harvey and B. P. Holly (eds) *Themes in geographic thought.* London: Croom Helm, 99–114.

—— 1981b: *Rational landscapes and humanistic geography.* London: Croom Helm.

RENFREW, A. C. 1981: Space, time and man. *Transactions, Institute of British Geographers* **NS6**, 257–78.

REYNOLDS, R. B. 1956: Statistical methods in geographical research. *Geographical Review* **46**, 129–32.

RHIND, D. W. 1981: Geographical information systems in Britain. In N . Wrigley and R. J. Bennett (eds) *Quantitative geography.* London: Routledge & Kegan Paul, 17–35.

—— 1986: Remote sensing, digital mapping and GIS: the creation of government policy in the UK. *Environment and Planning C: Government and Policy* **4**, 91–100.

—— 1989: Computing, academic geography, and the world outside. In B. Macmillan (ed.) *Remodelling geography.* Oxford: Basil Blackwell, 177–90.

—— 1996: Differential research funding – a comment on Smith. *Area* **28**, 96–7.

—— 2003: The geographical underpinning of society and its radical transformation. In R. J. Johnston and M. Williams (eds), *A century of British geography.* Oxford: Oxford University Press for the British Academy, 429–62.

RHIND, D. W. and ADAMS, T. A. 1980: Recent developments in surveying and mapping. In E. H. Brown (ed.) *Geography, yesterday and tomorrow.* Oxford: Oxford University Press, 181–99.

RHIND, D. W. and HUDSON, R. 1981: *Land use.* London: Methuen.

RHIND, D. W. and MOUNSEY, H. 1989: The Chorley committee and 'Handling geographical information'. *Environment and Planning A* **21**, 571–86.

RICHARDS, K. S. and WRIGLEY, N. 1996: Geography in the United Kingdom 1992–1996. *The Geographical Journal* **162**, 41–62.

RICHARDSON, D. 2003: Federal funding for geographical education. *AAG Newsletter* **38 (6)**, 2–4.

RICHARDSON, H. W. 1973: *The economics of urban size.* Farnborough: Saxon House.

RIDDELL, J. B. 1970: *The spatial dynamics of modernization in Sierra Leone.* Evanston, IL.: Northwestern University Press.

RIESER, R. 1973: The territorial illusion and the behavioural sink: critical notes on behavioural geography. *Antipode* **5(3)**, 52–7.

RITTER, K. 1817–59. *Die Erdkunde.* Berlin: G. Reimer.

ROBERTS, S. 2000: Realizing critical geographies of the university. *Antipode* **32**, 230–44.

ROBINSON, A. H. 1956: The necessity of weighting values in correlation analysis of area data. *Annals of the Association of American Geographers* **46**, 233–6.

—— 1961: On perks and pokes. *Economic Geography* **37**, 181–3.

—— 1962: Mapping the correspondence of isarithmic maps. *Annals of the Association of American Geographers* **52**, 414–25.

ROBINSON, A. H. and BRYSON, R. A. 1957: A method for describing quantitatively the correspondence of geographical distributions. *Annals of the Association of American Geographers* **47**, 379–91.

ROBINSON, A. H., LINDBERG, J. B. and BRINKMAN, L. W. 1961: A correlation and regression analysis applied to rural farm densities in the Great Plains. *Annals of the Association of American Geographers* **51**, 211–21.

ROBINSON, G. M. 1991: An appreciation of James Wreford Watson with a bibliography of his work. In G. M. Robinson (ed.) *A social geography of Canada.* Toronto: Dundurn Press, 492–506.

—— 1998: *Methods and techniques in human geography.* New York: John Wiley.

ROBINSON, M. E. 1982: Representation, misrepresentation, and uncritical rhetoric. *The Professional Geographer* **34**, 224–6.

ROBSON, B. T. 1969: *Urban analysis.* Cambridge: Cambridge University Press.

—— 1972: The corridors of geography. *Area* **4**, 213–14.

—— 1982: Introduction. In B. T. Robson and J. Rees (eds) *Geographical agenda for a changing world.* London: Social Science Research Council, 1–6.

—— 1984: A pleasant pain. In M. Billinge, D. Gregory and R. Martin (eds) *Recollections of a revolution.* London: Macmillan, 104–6.

ROCHELEAU, D. 1995: Maps, numbers, text and context: mixing methods in feminist political ecology. *The Professional Geographer* **47**, 458–66.

RODER, W. 1961: Attitudes and knowledge on the Topeka flood plain. In G. F. White (ed.) *Papers on flood problems.* Chicago: University of Chicago, Department of Geography, Research Paper 70, 62–83.

RODGERS, A. 1955: Changing locational patterns in the Soviet pulp and paper industries. *Annals of the Association of American Geographers* **45**, 85–104.

RODRÍGUEZ-POSE, A. 2001: Killing economic geography with a 'cultural turn' overdose. *Antipode* **33**, 176–82.

—— 2004: On English as a way to preserve geographical diversity. *Progress in Human Geography* **28**.

ROONEY, J. F., ZELINSKY, W. and LOUDER, D. R. (eds) 1982: *This remarkable continent: an atlas of United States and Canadian society and cultures.* College Station: Texas A and M University Press.

ROSE, C. 1980: Human geography as text interpretation. In A. Buttimer and D. Seamon (eds) *The human experience of space and place.* London: Croom Helm, 123–34.

—— 1981: Wilhelm Dilthey's philosophy of human understanding. In D. R. Stoddart (ed.) *Geography, ideology and social concern.* Oxford: Basil Blackwell, 99–133.

—— 1987: The problem of reference and geographic structuration. *Environment and Planning D: Society and Space* **5**, 93–112.

ROSE, D. 1987: Home ownership, subsistence, and historical change: the mining district of West Cornwall in the late nineteenth century. In N. J. Thrift and P. Williams (eds) *Class and space: the making of urban society.* London: Routledge, 1, 8–53.

ROSE, D. and PEVALIN, D. J. (eds) 2003: *A researcher's guide to the National Statistics socio-economic classification.* London: Sage Publications.

ROSE, G. 1989: Locality-studies and waged labour – an historical critique. *Transactions, Institute of British Geographers* **14**, 317–28.

—— 1993a: *Feminism and geography.* Cambridge: Polity Press.

—— 1993b: Progress in geography and gender. Or something else. *Progress in Human Geography* **17**, 531–7.

—— 1994: The cultural politics of place: local representation and oppositional discourse in two films. *Transactions, Institute of British Geographers* **NS19**, 46–60.

—— 1995: Tradition and paternity: same difference? *Transactions, Institute of British Geographers* **NS20**, 414–16.

—— 1997: Situating knowledges: positionality, reflexivities and other tactics. *Progress in Human Geography* **21**, 305–20.

—— 2001: *Visual methodologies: an introduction to the interpretation of visual materials.* London: Sage Publications.

ROSE, G., GREGSON, N., FOORD, J., BOWLBY, S., DWYER, C., HOLLOWAY, S. LAURIE, N., MADDRELL, A. and SKELTON, T. 1997: Introduction. In Women and Geography Study Group (eds) *Feminist geographies: explorations in diversity and difference.* Harlow: Longman, 1–12.

ROSE, J. K. 1936: Corn yield and climate in the Corn Belt. *Geographical Review* **26**, 88–102.

ROSS, R. S. J. 1983: Facing Leviathan: public policy and global capitalism. *Economic Geography* **59**, 144–60.

ROSSITER, D. J. and JOHNSTON, R. J. 1981: Program GROUP: the identification of all possible solutions to a constituency-delimitation problem. *Environment and Planning A* **13**, 231–8.

ROTHSTEIN, J. 1958: *Communication, organization and science.* Colorado: Falcon's Wing Press.

ROWLES, G. D. 1978: Reflections on experiential field work. In D. Ley and M. S. Samuels (eds), *Humanistic geography: problems and prospects.* London: Croom Helm, 173–93.

ROWNTREE, L., FOOTE, K. E. and DOMOSH, M. 1989: Cultural geography. In G. L. Gaile and C. J. Willmott (eds) *Geography in America.* Columbus, OH: Merrill, 209–17.

RUSHTON, G. 1969: Analysis of spatial behavior by revealed space preference. *Annals of the Association of American Geographers* **59**, 391–400.

—— 1979: On behavioral and perception geography. *Annals of the Association of American Geographers* **69**, 463–4.

RUSSELL, A. T. 1997: A question of interaction: using logistic regression to examine geographic effects on British voting behaviour. In C. J. Pattie *et al.* (eds), *British elections and parties review, volume 7.* London: Frank Cass, 91–109.

RUSSELL, C. A. 1977: *Chemists by profession: the origins and rise of the Royal Institute of Chemistry.* Milton Keynes: The Open University Press.

RYCROFT, S. and COSGROVE, D. 1999: Regional knowledge for pedagogy and planning: Dudley Stamp and the Land Utilisation Survey. In A. Buttimer, S. D. Brunn and U. Wardenga (eds) *Text and image: social construction of regional knowledges.* Leipzig: Institut für Länderkunde Leipzig, Beiträge zur regionalen Geographie **49**, 122–9.

SAARINEN, T. F. 1979: Commentary: critique of Bunting-Guelke paper. *Annals of the Association of American Geographers* **69**, 464–8.

SACK, R. D. 1972: Geography, geometry and explanation. *Annals of the Association of American Geographers* **62**, 61–78.

—— 1973a: Comment in reply. *Annals of the Association of American Geographers* **63**, 568–9.

—— 1973b: A concept of physical space in geography. *Geographical Analysis* **5**, 16–34.

—— 1974a: The spatial separatist theme in geography. *Economic Geography* **50**, 1–19.

—— 1974b: Chorology and spatial analysis. *Annals of the Association of American Geographers* **64**, 439–52.

—— 1981: *Conceptions of space in social thought.* London: Macmillan.

—— 1983: Human territoriality: a theory. *Annals of the Association of American Geographers* **73**, 55–74.

—— 1986: *Human territoriality: its theory and history.* Cambridge: Cambridge University Press.

—— 1997: *Homo geographicus: a framework for action, awareness and moral concern.* Baltimore: Johns Hopkins University Press.

—— 2001: The geographic problematic: empirical issues. *Norsk Geografisk Tidsskrift* **55**, 107–16.

SAID, E. 1978: *Orientalism.* New York: Harper.

SAMERS, M. S. and SIDAWAY, J. D. 2001: Exclusions, inclusions, and occlusions in 'Anglo-American geography': reflections on Minca's 'Venetian geographical praxis'. *Environment and Planning D, Society and Space* **18**, 663–6.

SAMUELS; M. S. 1978: Existentialism and human geography. In D. Ley and M. S. Samuels (eds) *Humanistic geography: problems and prospects.* Chicago: Maaroufa Press, 22–40.

SANDBACH, F. 1980: *Environment, ideology and policy.* Oxford: Blackwell.

SANTOS, M. 1974: Geography, marxism and underdevelopment. *Antipode* **6(3)**, 1–9.

SARRE, P. 1987: Realism in practice. *Area* **19**, 3–10.

SARRE, P., PHILLIPS, D. and SKELLINGTON, R. 1989: *Ethnic minority housing: explanations and policies.* Aldershot: Avebury.

SAUER, C. O. 1918: Geography and the gerrymander. *American Political Science Review* **12**, 403–26.

—— 1925: The morphology of landscape. *University of California Publications in Geography* **2**, 19–54.

—— 1941: Foreword to historical geography. *Annals of the Association of American Geographers* **31**, 1–24.

—— 1956a: The education of a geographer. *Annals of the Association of American Geographers* **46**, 287–99.

—— 1956b: The agency of man on earth. In W. L. Thomas (ed.) *Man's role in changing the face of the earth*. Chicago: University of Chicago Press, 49–69.

—— 1956c: Retrospect. In W. L. Thomas (ed.) *Man's role in changing the face of the earth*. Chicago: University of Chicago Press, 1131–5.

SAUNDERS, P. and WILLIAMS, P. R. 1986: The new conservatism: some thoughts on recent and future developments in urban studies. *Environment and Planning D: Society and Space* **4**, 393–9.

—— 1987: For an emancipated social science. *Environment and Planning D: Society and Space* **5**, 427–30.

SAYER, A. 1979: Epistemology and conceptions of people and nature in geography. *Geoforum* **10**, 19–44.

—— 1981: Defensible values in geography. In D. T. Herbert and R. J. Johnston (eds) *Geography and the urban environment*, 4. Chichester: John Wiley, 29–56.

—— 1982: Explanation in economic geography. *Progress in Human Geography* **6**, 68–88.

—— 1983: Notes on geography and the relationship between people and nature. In The London Group of the Union of Socialist Geographers, *Society and nature*. London, 47–57.

—— 1984: *Method in social science: a realist approach*. London: Hutchinson.

—— 1985a: Realism and geography. In R. J. Johnston (ed.) *The future of geography*. London: Methuen, 159–73.

—— 1985b: The difference that space makes. In D. Gregory and J. Urry (eds) *Social relations and spatial structures*. London: Macmillan, 49–66.

—— 1987: Hard work and its alternatives. *Environment and Planning D: Society and Space* **5**, 395–9.

—— 1989a: The new regional geography and problems of narrative. *Environment and Planning D: Society and Space* **7**, 253–76.

—— 1989b: On the dialogue between humanism and historical materialism in geography. In A. Kobayashi and S. Mackenzie (eds) *Remaking human geography*. Boston: Unwin Hyman, 206–26.

—— 1992a: *Method in social science: a realist approach* (2nd edn). London: Routledge.

—— 1992b: What's left to do? A reply to Hadjimichalis and Smith. *Antipode* **24**, 214–17.

—— 1992c: Radical geography and Marxist political economy: towards a re-evaluation. *Progress in Human Geography* **16**, 343–60.

—— 1994a: Realism and space: a reply to Ron Johnston. *Political Geography* **13**, 107–9.

—— 1994b: Postmodernist thought in geography: a realist view. *Antipode* **25**, 320–44.

—— 1995: *Radical political economy: a critique*. Oxford: Blackwell Publishers.

—— 2000: Critical and uncritical turns. In I. Cook, D. Crouch, S. Naylor and J. R. Ryan (eds) *Cultural turns/geographical turns: perspectives on cultural geography*. Harlow: Prentice Hall, 166–81.

—— 2001: For a critical cultural political economy. *Antipode* **33**, 687–708.

SAYER, A. and MORGAN, K. 1985: A modern industry in a declining region: links between method, theory and policy. In D. Massey and R. Meegan (eds) *Politics and method: contrasting studies in industrial geography*. London: Methuen, 144–68.

SAYER, A. and STORPER, M. 1997: Ethics Unbound: for a normative turn in social theory. *Environment and Planning D: Society and Space* **15**, 1–17.

SAYER, A. and WALKER, R. A. 1992: *The new social economy: reworking the division of labour*. Oxford: Blackwell Publishers.

SCARGILL, D. I. 1976: The RGS and the foundations of geography at Oxford. *The Geographical Journal* **142**, 438–61.

SCHAEFER, F. K. 1953: Exceptionalism in geography: a methodological examination. *Annals of the Association of American Geographers* **43**, 226–49.

SCHELHAAS, B. and HÖNSCH, I. 2002: History of German geography: worldwide reputation and strategies of nationalisation and institutionalisation. In G. S. Dunbar (ed.) *Geography: discipline, profession and subject since 1870*. Dordrecht: Kluwer, 9–44.

SCHOENBERGER, E. 1992: Self-criticism and self awareness in research: a reply to Linda McDowell. *The Professional Geographer* **44**, 215–8.

—— 1993: On knowing what to know. *Environment and Planning A* **25**, 1225–8.

—— 1997: *The cultural crisis of the firm.* Oxford: Blackwell Publishers.

—— 2001: Interdisciplinarity and social power. *Progress in Human Geography* **25**, 365–82.

SCHULTEN, S. 2001: *The geographical imagination in America, 1880–1950.* Chicago: University of Chicago Press.

SCHUURMAN, N. 1999: An interview with Michael Goodchild, January 6, 1998, Santa Barbara, California. *Environment and Planning D: Society and Space* **17**, 3–15.

—— 2000: Trouble in the heartland: GIS and its critics in the 1990s. *Progress in Human Geography* **24**, 569–90.

SCOTT, A. J. 1982: The meaning and social origins of discourse on the spatial foundations of society. In P. R. Gould and G. Olsson (eds) *A search for common ground.* London: Pion, 141–56.

—— 1985: Location processes, urbanization, and territorial development: an exploratory essay. *Environment and Planning A* **17**, 479–501.

—— 1986: Industrialization and urbanization: a geographical agenda. *Annals of the Association of American Geographers* **76**, 25–37.

—— 1988: *Metropolis.* Los Angeles: University of California Press.

—— 2000: Economic geography: the great half-century. In G. L. Clark, M. P. Feldmann and M. S. Gertler (eds), *The Oxford handbook of economic geography.* Oxford: Oxford University Press, 19–43.

SCOTT, A. J. and COOKE, P. N. 1988: The new geography and sociology of production. *Environment and Planning D: Society and Space* **6**, 241–4.

SCOTT, A. J. and STORPER, M. (eds) 1985: *Production, work, territory.* Boston: George Allen & Unwin.

SEAGER, J. and OLSON, A. 1986: *Women in the world: an international atlas.* London: Pan.

SEAGER, J., REED, C. and STOTT, P. 1995: *The state of the environment atlas* (2nd edn). London: Pan.

SEAMON, D. 1984: Phenomenology and environment-behavior research. In G. T. Moore and E. Zube (eds) *Advances in environment, behavior and design.* New York: Plenum, 3–36.

SEMPLE, E. C. 1911: *Influences of geographical environment.* New York: Henry Holt.

SHANNON, G. W. and DEVER, G. E. A. 1974: *Health care delivery: spatial perspectives.* New York: McGraw-Hill.

SHARP, J. 1993: Publishing American identity: popular geopolitics, myth, and *The Reader's Digest. Political Geography* **12**, 491–504.

—— 2000: *Condensing the Cold War: Reader's Digest and American identity.* Minneapolis, MA: University of Minnesota Press.

—— 2000: Remasculinising geo-politics? Comments on Gearoid O'Tuathail's *Critical geopolitics. Political Geography* **19**, 361–4.

SHARP, J., ROUTLEDGE, P. PHILO, C. and PADDISON, R. (eds) 2000: *Entanglements of power: geographies of domination and resistance.* London: Routledge.

SHARROCK, W. and READ, R. 2002: *Kuhn: philosopher of scientific revolution.* Cambridge: Polity Press.

SHEPPARD, E. S. 1979: Gravity parameter estimation. *Geographical Analysis* **11**, 120–33.

—— 1993: Automated geography: what kind of geography for what kind of society? *The Professional Geographer* **45**, 457–60.

—— 1995: Dissenting from spatial analysis. *Urban Geography* **16**, 283–303.

SHEPPARD, E. and BARNES, T. 1990: *The capitalist space economy: geographical analysis after Ricardo, Marx and Straffa.* London and Boston: Unwin Hyman.

—— (eds) 2000: *A companion to economic geography.* Oxford: Blackwell.

SHORT, J. R. 1984: *The urban arena: capital, state and community in contemporary Britain.* London: Macmillan.

—— 2002: The disturbing case of the concentration of power in human geography. *Area* **34**, 323–4.

SHORT, J. R., BONICHE, A., KIM, Y. and LI LI, P. 2001: Cultural globalization, global English, and geography journals. *The Professional Geographer* **53**, 1–11.

SIBLEY, D. 1995: *Geographies of exclusion*. London and New York: Routledge.

—— 1998: Sensations and spatial science: gratification and anxiety in the production of ordered landscapes. *Environment and Planning A* **30**, 235–46.

—— 2000: Placing anxieties. In I. Cook, D. Crouch, S. Naylor and J. R. Ryan (eds) *Cultural turns/geographical turns: perspectives on cultural geography*. Harlow: Prentice Hall, 359–69.

SIDAWAY, J. D. 1992: In other worlds: on the politics of research by First World geographers in the Third World. *Area* **24**, 403–8.

—— 1997: The production of British geography. *Transactions of the Institute of British Geographers* **NS22**, 488–504.

—— 2000: Post-colonial geographies: and exploratory essay. *Progress in Human Geography* **24**, 591–612.

SIDDALL, W. R. 1961: Two kinds of geography. *Economic Geography* **36**, facing page 189.

SIMANDAN, D. 2002: On what it takes to be a good geographer. *Area* **34**, 284–93.

SIMMONS, I. G. 1993: *Interpreting nature: cultural constructions of the environment*. London: Routledge.

—— 1997: *Humanity and environment: a cultural ecology*. London: Addison, Wesley Longman.

SIMON, H. A. 1957: *Models of man: social and rational*. New York: John Wiley.

SIMONSEN, K. 2002: Global-local ambivalence. *Transactions of the Institute of British Geographers* **NS27**, 391–4.

SINCLAIR, J. C. and KISSLING, C. C. 1971: A network analysis approach to fruit distribution planning. *Proceedings, Sixth New Zealand Geography Conference*, vol. 1, Christchurch, 131–6.

SLATER, D. 1973: Geography and underdevelopment – 1. *Antipode* **5(3)**, 21–53.

—— 1975: The poverty of modern geographical enquiry. *Pacific Viewpoint* **16**, 159–76.

—— 1977: Geography and underdevelopment – 2. *Antipode* **9**, 1–31.

SLATER, T. R. 1988: Redbrick academic geography. *The Geographical Journal* **154**, 169–80.

SMAILES, A. E. 1946: The urban mesh of England and Wales. *Transactions and Papers, Institute of British Geographers* **11**, 85–101.

SMALLMAN-RAYNOR, M. and CLIFF, A. D. 1990: Aquired Immune Deficiency Syndrome (AIDS): literature, geographical origins and global patterns. *Progress in Human Geography* **14**, 157–213.

SMALLMAN-RAYNOR, M., CLIFF, A. D. and HAGGETT, P. 1992: *Atlas of AIDs*. Oxford: Blackwell Reference.

SMITH, C. T. 1965: Historical geography: current trends and prospects. In R. J. Chorley and P. Haggett (eds) *Frontiers in geographical teaching*. London: Methuen, 118–43.

SMITH, D. M. 1971: America! America? Views on a pot melting. 2. Radical geography – the next revolution? *Area* **3**, 153–7.

—— 1973a: Alternative 'relevant' professional roles. *Area* **5**, 1–4.

—— 1973b: *The geography of social well-being in the United States*. New York: McGraw-Hill.

—— 1977: *Human geography: a welfare approach*. London: Edward Arnold.

—— 1979: *Where the grass is greener: living in an unequal world*. London: Penguin.

—— 1981: *Industrial location: an economic geographical analysis* (2nd edn). New York: John Wiley.

—— 1984: Recollections of a random variable. In M. Billinge, D. Gregory and R. Martin (eds) *Recollections of a revolution*. London: Macmillan, 117–33.

—— 1985: The 'new blood' scheme and its application to geography. *Area* **17**, 237–43.

—— 1986: UGC research ratings: pass or fail? *Area* **18**, 247–9.

—— 1988a: Towards an interpretative human geography. In J. Eyles and D. M. Smith (eds) *Qualitative methods in human geography*. Cambridge: Polity Press, 255–67.

—— 1988b: On academic performance. *Area* **20**, 3–13.

—— 1994: *Geography and social justice.* Oxford: Blackwell Publishers.

—— 1994: On professional responsibility to distant others. *Area* **26**, 359–67.

—— 1995: Against differential research funding. *Area* **27**, 79–83.

—— 1996: Reply to Rhind – value for money, the continuing debate. *Area* **28**, 97–101.

—— 1997a: Geography and ethics: a moral turn? *Progress in Human Geography* **21**, 583–90.

—— 1997b: Back to the good life: towards an enlarged conception of social justice. *Environment and Planning D: Society and Space* **15**, 19–35.

—— 1998: How far should we care? On the spatial scope of beneficence. *Progress in Human Geography* **22**, 15–38.

—— 2000: *Moral geographies: ethics in a world of difference.* Edinburgh: Edinburgh University Press.

SMITH, J. M. 1996: Geographical rhetoric: modes and tropes of appeal. *Annals of the Association of American Geographers* **86**, 1–20.

—— 2001: Constructing the nation: eighteenth-century geographies for children. *Mosaic* **34**, 133–48.

SMITH, N. 1979: Geography, science and post-positivist modes of explanation. *Progress in Human Geography* **3**, 365–83.

—— 1984: *Uneven development: nature, capital and the production of space.* Oxford: Basil Blackwell.

—— 1986: On the necessity of uneven development. *International Journal of Urban and Regional Research* **10**, 87–104.

—— 1987a: Danger of the empirical turn: The CURS initiative. *Antipode* **19**, 59–68.

—— 1987b: Rascal concepts, minimalizing discourse, and the politics of geography. *Environment and Planning D: Society and Space* **5**, 377–83.

—— 1990: Geography as museum: private history and conservative idealism in *The Nature of Geography.* In J. N. Entrikin and S. D. Brunn (eds) *Reflections on Richard Hartshorne's The Nature of Geography.* Washington: Association of American Geographers, 89–120.

—— 1991: What's left? A lot's left. *Antipode* **23**, 406–18.

—— 1992: History and philosophy of geography: real wars, theory wars. *Progress in Human Geography* **16**, 257–71.

—— 1994: Shaking loose the colonies: Isaiah Bowman and the 'de-colonization' of the British Empire. In A. Godlewska and N. Smith (eds) *Geography and empire.* Oxford: Blackwell Publishers, 270–99.

—— 2001: Marxism and geography in the Anglophone world. *Geographische revue* **3**, 5–22.

—— 2003: *American Empire: Roosevelt's geographer and the prelude to globalization.* Berkeley: University of California Press.

SMITH, N. and WILLIAMS, P. (eds) 1986: *Gentrification of the city.* Boston: Allen and Unwin.

SMITH, R. G. 2003: Baudrillard's non-representational theory: burn the signs and journey without maps. *Environment and Planning D: Society and Space* **21**, 67–84.

SMITH, R. G. and DOEL, M. A. 2001: Baudrillard unwound: the duplicity of post-Marxism and deconstruction. *Environment and Planning D: Society and Space* **19**, 137–59.

SMITH, S. J. 1984: Practising humanistic geography. *Annals of the Association of American Geographers* **74**, 353–74.

—— 1986: *Crime, space and society.* Cambridge: Cambridge University Press.

—— 1988: Constructing local knowledge: the analysis of self in everyday life. In J. Eyles and D. M. Smith (eds) *Qualitative methods in human geography.* Cambridge: Polity Press, 17–38.

—— 1989: Society, space and citizenship: a human geography for the 'new times'? *Transactions, Institute of British Geographers* **NS14**, 144–56.

SMITH, T. R. 1984: Artificial intelligence and its applicability to geographical problem solving. *The Professional Geographer* **36**, 147–58.

SMITH, T. R., CLARK, W. A. V. and COTTON, J. 1984: Deriving and testing production system models of sequential decision-making behavior. *Geographical Analysis* **16**, 191–222.

SMITH, W. 1949: *An economic geography of Great Britain.* London: Methuen.

SOFFER, A. and MINGHI, J. 1986: Israel's security landscapes: the impact of military considerations on land uses. *The Professional Geographer* **38**, 28–41.

SOJA, E. W. 1968: *The geography of modernization in Kenya.* Syracuse: Syracuse University Press.

—— 1980: The socio-spatial dialectic. *Annals of the Association of American Geographers* **70**, 207–25.

—— 1985: The spatiality of social life: towards a transformative retheorization. In D. Gregory and J. Urry (eds) *Social relations and spatial structures.* London: Macmillan, 90–127.

—— 1989: *Postmodern geographies.* London: Verso.

—— 2001: Afterword. In C. Minca (ed.) *Postmodern geography: theory and praxis.* Oxford: Blackwell, 282–94.

SOJA, E. W. and HOOPER, B. 1993: The spaces that difference makes: some notes on the geographical margins of the new cultural politics. In M. Keith and S. Pile (eds) *Place and the politics of identity.* London: Routledge, 183–205.

SPARKE, M. 1994: Writing on patriarchal missiles: the chauvinism of the 'Gulf War' and the limits of critique. *Environment and Planning A* **26**, 1061–89.

—— 1996: Negotiating national action: free trade, constitutional debate and the gendered geopolitics of Canada. *Political Geography* **15**, 615–39.

SPATE, O. H. K. 1957: How determined is possibilism? *Geographical Studies* **4**, 3–12.

—— 1960a: Quantity and quality in geography. *Annals of the Association of America Geographers* **50**, 477–94.

—— 1960b: Lord Kelvin rides again. *Economic Geography* **36**, facing page 1.

—— 1963: Letter to the editor. *Geography* **48**, 206.

—— 1989: Foreword. In F. W. Boal and D. N. Livingstone (eds) *The behavioural environment.* London: Routledge, xvii–xx.

SPENCER, C. P. and BLADES, M. 1986: Pattern and process: a review essay on the relationship between geography and environmental psychology. *Progress in Human Geography* **10**, 230–48.

SPENCER, H. 1892: A *system of synthetic philosophy,* vol. 1: *First principles* (4th edn). New York: Appleton.

SPENCER, J. E. 1979: A geographer west of the Sierra Nevada. *Annals of the Association of American Geographers* **69**, 46–52.

SPENCER, J. E. and THOMAS, W. L. 1973: *Introducing cultural geography.* New York: John Wiley.

STAEHELI, L. and COPE, M. 1994: Empowering women's citizenship. *Political Geography* **13**, 443–60.

STAEHELI, L. and NAGAR, R. 2002: Feminists talking across worlds. *Gender, Place and Culture* **9**, 167–72.

STAMP, L. D. 1934: Planning the land for the future. *Science* **80**, 510–12.

—— 1946a: *The land of Britain.* London: Longman.

—— 1946b: The place of science in town and country planning. *The Advancement of Science* **3**, 337–48.

—— 1948: Applied geography. In L. D. Stamp and S. W. Wooldridge (eds) *London essays in geography: Rodwell Jones Memorial Volume.* London: Longmans, Green, 1–18.

—— 1949: The planning of land use. *The Advancement of Science* **6**, 224–32.

—— 1960: *Applied geography.* Harmondsworth: Penguin Books.

—— 1966: Ten years on. *Transactions, Institute of British Geographers* **40**, 11–20.

STAMP, L. D. and BEAVER, S. H. 1947: *The British Isles.* London: Longman.

STEEL, R. W. 1974: The Third World: geography in practice. *Geography* **59**, 189–207.

—— 1982: Regional geography in practice. *Geography* **67**, 2–8.

—— (ed.) 1987: *British geography 1918–1945.* Cambridge: Cambridge University Press.

STEGMULLER, W. 1976: *The structure and dynamics of theories.* New York: Springer-Verlag.

STEVENS, A. 1921: *Applied geography.* Glasgow: Blackie.

STEWART, J. Q. 1945: *Coasts, waves and weather.* Boston: Ginn & Co.

—— 1947: Empirical mathematical rules concerning the distribution and equilibrium of population. *Geographical Review* **37**, 461–85.

—— 1956: The development of social physics. *American Journal of Physics* **18**, 239–53.

STEWART, J. Q. and WARNTZ, W. 1958: Macrogeography and social science, *Geographical Review* **48**, 167–84.

—— 1959: Physics of population distribution. *Journal of Regional Science* **1**, 99–123.

STIELL, B. and ENGLAND, K. 1997: Domestic distinctions: constructing difference among paid domestic workers in Toronto. *Gender, Place and Culture* **4**, 339–59.

STODDART, D. R. 1965: Geography and the ecological approach: the ecosystem as a geographic principle and method. *Geography* **50**, 242–51.

—— 1966: Darwin's impact on geography. *Annals of the Association of American Geographers* **56**, 683–98.

—— 1967a: Growth and structure of geography. *Transactions, Institute of British Geographers* **41**, 1–19.

—— 1967b: Organism and ecosystem as geographic models. In R. J. Chorley and P. Haggett (eds) *Models in geography*. London: Methuen, 511–47.

—— 1975a: The RGS and the foundations of geography at Cambridge. *The Geographical Journal* **141**, 216–39.

—— 1975b: Kropotkin, Reclus and relevant geography. *Area* **7**, 188–90.

—— 1977: The paradigm concept and the history of geography. Abstract of a paper for the conference of the International Geographical Union Commission on the History of Geographic Thought, Edinburgh.

—— 1981a: The paradigm concept and the history of geography. In D. R. Stoddart (ed.) *Geography, ideology and social concern*. Oxford: Blackwell, 70–80.

—— 1981b: Ideas and interpretation in the history of geography. In D. R. Stoddart (ed.) *Geography, ideology and social concern*. Oxford: Blackwell 1–7.

—— 1986: *On geography: and its history*. Oxford: Basil Blackwell.

—— 1987: To claim the high ground: geography for the end of the century. *Transactions, Institute of British Geographers* **NS12**, 327–36.

—— 1990: Epilogue: homage to Richard Hartshorne. In J. N. Entrikin and S. D. Brunn (eds) *Reflections on Richard Hartshorne's The Nature of Geography*. Washington: Association of American Geographers, 163–6.

—— 1991: Do we need a feminist historiography of geography – and if we do, what should it be? *Transactions, Institute of British Geographers* **NS16**, 484–7.

—— 1997a: Richard J. Chorley and modern geomorphology. In D. R. Stoddart (ed.) *Process and form in geomorphology*. London: Routledge, 383–99.

—— 1997b: Carl Sauer: geomorphologist. In D. R. Stoddart (ed.) *Process and form in geomorphology*. London: Routledge, 340–79.

STONE, K. H. 1979: Geography's wartime service. *Annals of the Association of American Geographers* **69**, 89–97.

STOREY, D. W. 2001: *Territory: the claiming of space*. Harlow: Longman.

STORPER, M. 1987: The post-Enlightenment challenge to Marxist urban studies. *Environment and Planning D: Society and Space* **5**, 418–26.

—— 2001: The poverty of radical theory today: from the false promises of Marxism to the mirage of the cultural turn. *International Journal of Urban and Regional Studies* **25**, 155–79.

STOUFFER, S. A. 1940: Intervening opportunities: a theory relating mobility and distance. *American Sociological Review* **5**, 845–67.

SUI, D. 1994: GIS and urban studies: positivism, post-positivism and beyond. *Urban Geography* **15**, 258–78.

—— 1999: Postmodern urbanism disrobed: or why postmodern urbanism is a dead end for urban geography. *Urban Geography* **20**, 403–11.

SUI,. D. et al. 2000: Book review forum. *Annals of the Association of American Geographers* **90**, 579–606.

SUMMERFIELD, M. A. 1983: Population, samples and statistical inference in geography. *The Professional Geographer* **35**, 143–8.

SUPPE, F. 1977a: The search for philosophic understanding of scientific theories. In F. Suppe (ed.) *The structure of scientific theories*. Urbana: University of Illinois Press, 3–233.

—— 1977b: Exemplars, theories and disciplinary matrices. In F. Suppe (ed.) *The structure of scientific theories*. Urbana: University of Illinois Press, 473–99.

—— 1977c: Afterword – 1977. In F. Suppe (ed.), *The structure of scientific theories*. Urbana: University of Illinois Press, 617–730.

SVIATLOVSKY, E. E. and EELS, W. C. 1937: The centrographical method and regional analysis. *Geographical Review* **27**, 240–54.

SWYNGEDOUW, E. 2000: The Marxian alternative: historical-geographical materialism and the political economy of capitalism. In E. Sheppard and T. J. Barnes (eds) *A companion to economic geography*. Oxford and Malden, MA: Blackwell, 41–59.

SYMANSKI, R. 1994: Why we should fear postmodernists. *Annals of the Association of American Geographers* **84**, 301–4.

—— 2002: *Geography inside out*. Syracuse: Syracuse University Press.

SYMANSKI, R. and AGNEW, J. A. 1981: *Order and skepticism: human geography and the dialectic of science*. Washington DC: Association of American Geographers.

SYMANSKI, R. and PICKARD, J. 1996: Rules by which we are judged. *Progress in Human Geography* **20**, 175–82.

TAAFFE, E. J. 1970: *Geography*. Englewood Cliffs, NJ: Prentice-Hall.

—— 1974: The spatial view in context. *Annals of the Association of American Geographers* **64**, 1–16.

—— 1979: In the Chicago area. *Annals of the Association of American Geographers* **69**, 133–8.

—— 1993: Spatial analysis: development and outlook. *Urban Geography* **14**, 422–33.

TAAFFE, E. J., MORRILL, R. L. and GOULD, P. R. 1963: Transport expansion in underdeveloped countries: a comparative analysis. *The Geographical Review* **53**, 503–29.

TARRANT, J. R. 1968: Computers in geography. *Institute of British Geographers Newsletter* **6**, 11–25.

TATHAM, G. 1953: Environmentalism and possibilism. In G. Taylor (ed.) *Geography in the twentieth century*. London: Methuen, 128–64.

TAYLOR, E. G. R. 1937: Whither geography? a review of some recent geographical texts. *Geographical Review* **27**, 129–35.

TAYLOR, G. 1957: Introduction: the scope of the volume. In G. Taylor (ed.) *Geography in the twentieth century: a study of growth, fields, techniques, aims and trends*. London: Methuen, 1–27.

TAYLOR, P. J. 1971a: Distance decay curves and distance transformations. *Geographical Analysis* **3**, 221–38.

—— 1971b: Distances within shapes: an introduction to a new family of finite frequency distributions. *Geografiska Annaler* **53B**, 40–53.

—— 1976: An interpretation of the quantification debate in British geography. *Transactions, Institute of British Geographers* **NS1**, 129–42.

—— 1977: *Quantitative methods in geography*. New York: Harper and Row.

—— 1978: Political geography. *Progress in Human Geography* **2**, 53–62.

—— 1979: 'Difficult-to-let', 'difficult-to-live-in', and sometimes 'difficult-to-get-out-of': an essay on the provision of council housing. *Environment and Planning A* **11**, 1305–20.

—— 1981a: Factor analysis in geographical research. In R. J. Bennett (ed.) *European progress in spatial analysis*. London: Pion, 251–67.

—— 1981b: Geographical scales within the world-economy approach. *Review* **5(1)**, 3–11.

—— 1982: A materialist framework for political geography. *Transactions, Institute of British Geographers* **NS7**, 15–34.

—— 1985a: The geography of elections. In M. Pacione (ed.) *Progress in political geography*. London: Croom Helm, 243–72.

—— 1985b: *Political geography: world-economy, nation-state and community*. London: Longman.

—— 1985c: The value of a geographical perspective. In R. J. Johnston (ed.) *The future of geography*. London: Methuen, 92–110.

—— 1986: An exploration into world-systems analysis of political parties. *Political Geography Quarterly* **5**, S5–S20.

—— 1988: History's dialogue: an exemplification from political geography. *Progress in Human Geography* **12**, 1–14.

—— 1989: *Political geography: world-economy, nation-state and community* (second edition). London: Longman.

—— 1990a: Editorial comment: GKS. *Political Geography Quarterly* **9**, 211–12.

—— 1990b: *Britain and the cold war: 1945 as geopolitical transition*. London: Belhaven Press.

—— 1990c: Journeyman editor. *The Professional Geographer* **42**, 359–60.

—— 1993: Full circle, or new meaning for the global? In R. J. Johnston (ed.) *The challenge for geography. A changing world: a changing discipline*. Oxford: Blackwell Publishers, 181–97.

—— 1994: The state as container: territoriality in the modern world-system. *Progress in Human Geography* **18**, 151–62.

—— 1995: Beyond containers: internationality, interstateness, interterritoriality. *Progress in Human Geography* **19**, 1–15.

—— 1996: Embedded statism and the social sciences: opening up to new spaces. *Environment and Planning A*.

—— 1999: Spaces, places and Macy's: place-space tensions in the political geography of modernities. *Progress in Human Geography* **23**, 7–26.

—— 2003: Radical political geographies. In J. Agnew, K Mitchell, and G. Toal (eds) *A companion to political geography*. Oxford: Blackwell, 47–58.

TAYLOR, P. J. and GODDARD, J. (eds) 1974: Geography and statistics: an introduction. *The Statistician* **23**, 149–56.

TAYLOR, P. J. and GUDGIN, G. 1976: A statistical theory of electoral redistricting. *Environment and Planning A* **8**, 43–58.

TAYLOR, P. J. and JOHNSTON, R. J. 1979: *Geography of elections*. Harmondsworth: Penguin Books.

—— 1985: The geography of the British state. In J. R. Short and A. M. Kirby (eds) *The human geography of contemporary Britain*. London: Macmillan, 23–39.

TAYLOR, P. J. and OVERTON, M. 1991: Further thoughts on geography and GIS. *Environment and Planning A* **23**, 1087–94.

TESCH, R. 1990: *Qualitative research: analysis types and research tools*. Brighton: Falmer Press.

THOMAN, R. S. 1965: Some comments on *The Science of Geography*. *The Professional Geographer* **17(6)**, 8–10.

THOMAS, E. N. 1960: Areal associations between population growth and selected factors in the Chicago urbanized area. *Economic Geography* **36**, 158–70,

—— 1968: Maps of residuals from regression. In B. J. L. Berry and D. F. Marble (eds) *Spatial analysts*. Englewood Cliffs, NJ: Prentice-Hall, 326–52.

THOMAS, E. N. and ANDERSON, D. L. 1965: Additional comments on weighting values in correlation analysis of areal data. *Annals of the Association of American Geographers* **55**, 492–505.

THOMAS, R. W. 1982: *Information statistics in geography*. Norwich: Geo Books.

—— 1992: *Geomedical systems: intervention and control*. Routledge: London.

THOMAS, W. L. (ed.) 1956: *Man's role in changing the face of the earth*. Chicago: University of Chicago Press.

THOMPSON, J. H. *et al.* 1962: Toward a geography of economic health: the case of New York state. *Annals of the Association of American Geographers* **52**, 1–20.

THOMPSON, D'ARCY W. 1917: *On growth and form*. Cambridge: Cambridge University Press.

THORNE, C. R. (ed.) 1993: University Funding Council Research Selectivity Exercise, 1992: implications for higher education in geography. *Journal of Geography in Higher Education* **17**, 167–99.

THORNES, J. B. 1989a: Geomorphology and grass roots models. In B. Macmillan (ed.) *Remodelling geography.* Oxford: Basil Blackwell, 3–21.

―――― 1989b: Environmental systems. In M. J. Clark, K. J. Gregory and A. M. Gurnell (eds) *Horizons in physical geography.* London: Macmillan, 27–46.

THRALL, G. I. 1985: Scientific geography. *Area* **17**, 254.

―――― 1986: Reply to Felix Driver and Christopher Philo. *Area* **18**, 162–3.

THRIFT, N. J. 1977: *An introduction to time geography.* CATMOG 13, Norwich: Geo Books.

―――― 1979: Unemployment in the inner city: urban problem or structural imperative? A review of the British experience. In D. T. Herbert and R. J. Johnston (eds) *Geography and urban environment: progress in research and applications,* vol. 2. London: John Wiley, 125–226.

―――― 1981: Behavioural geography. In N. Wrigley and R. J. Bennett (eds) *Quantitative geography.* London: Routledge & Kegan Paul, 352–65.

―――― 1983a: On the determination of social action in space and time. *Environment and Planning D: Society and Space* **1**, 23–57.

―――― 1983b: Literature, the production of culture and the polities of place. *Antipode* **15**, 12–23.

―――― 1987: No perfect symmetry. *Environment and Planning D: Society and Space* **5**, 400–7.

―――― 1990: For a new regional geography 1. *Progress in Human Geography* **14**, 272–9.

―――― 1991: For a new regional geography 2. *Progress in Human Geography* **15**, 456–565.

―――― 1993: For a new regional geography 3. *Progress in Human Geography* **17**, 92–100.

―――― 1994: Taking aim at the heart of the region. In D. Gregory, R. Martin and G. Smith (eds) *Human geography: society, space and social science.* London: Macmillan, 200–31.

―――― 2000: Pandora's box? Cultural geographies of economies. In G. L. Clark, M. P. Feldmann and M. S. Gertler (eds), *The Oxford handbook of economic geography.* Oxford: Oxford University Press, 689–704.

―――― 2002: The future of geography. *Geoforum* **33**, 291–8.

THRIFT, N. J. and DEWSBURY, J. D. 2000: Dead geographies – and how to make them live. *Environment and Planning D: Society and Space* **18**, 411–32.

THRIFT, N. J. and OLDS, K. 1996: Refiguring the economic in economic geography. *Progress in Human Geography* **20**, 311–17.

THRIFT, N. J. and PRED, A. R. 1981: Time geography: a new beginning. *Progress in Human Geography* **5**, 277–86.

TICKELL, A. and PECK, J. 1996: The return of the Manchester Men: men's words and men's deeds in the remaking of the local state. *Transactions of the Institute of Britsih Geographers* **NS21**, 595–616.

TIEFELSDORF, M. 2003: Misspecifications in interaction model distance decay relations: a spatial structure effect. *Journal of Geographical Systems* **5**, 25–50.

TIMMERMANS, H. and GOLLEDGE, R. G. 1990: Applications of behavioural research on spatial problems: II Preference and choice. *Progress in Human Geography* **14**, 311–54.

TIMMERMANS, H. J. P., ARENZE, T. and JOH, C.-H. 2001: Analysing space-time behaviour: new approaches to old problems. *Progress in Human Geography* **26**, 175–90.

TIMMINS, N. 1995: *The five giants: a biography of the welfare state.* London: HarperCollins.

TIMMS, D. 1965: Quantitative techniques in urban social geography. In R. J. Chorley and P. Haggett (eds) *Frontiers in geographical teaching.* London: Methuen, 239–65.

―――― 1971: *The urban mosaic: towards a theory of residential differentiation.* Cambridge: Cambridge University Press.

TIVERS, J. 1978: How the other half lives: the geographical study of women. *Area* **10**, 302–6.

TOBLER, W. R. 1970: A computer movie simulating urban growth in the Detroit region. *Economic Geography* **46**, 234–40.

―――― 1995: Migration: Ravenstein, Thornthwaite and beyond. *Urban Geography* **16**, 327–43.

―――― 2002: Ma vie. In P. Gould and F. R. Pitts (eds) *Geographical voices: fourteen autobiographical essays.* Syracuse: Syracuse University Press, 293–322.

TOCALIS, T. R. 1978: Changing theoretical foundations of the gravity concept of human interaction. In B. J. L. Berry (ed.) *The nature of change in geographical ideas*. de Kalb: Northern Illinois University Press, 65–124.

TOMLINSON, R. F. 1989: Geographic information systems and geographers in the 1990s. *The Canadian Geographer* **33**, 290–8.

TOULMIN, S. E. 1970: Does the distinction between normal and revolutionary science hold water? In I. Lakatos and A. Musgrave (eds), *Criticism and the growth of knowledge*. London: Cambridge University Press, 39–48.

TREWARTHA, G. T. 1973: Comments on geography and public policy. *The Professional Geographer* **25**, 78–9.

TRUDGILL, S. T. 1990: *Barriers to a better environment*. London: Belhaven Press.

TSO, B. and MATHER, P. M. 2001: *Classification methods for remotely sensed data*. London: Taylor & Francis.

TUAN, YI-FU 1968: *The hydrological cycle and the wisdom of god: a theme in geoteleology*. Toronto: University of Toronto Press.

—— 1971: Geography, phenomenology, and the study of human nature. *The Canadian Geographer* **15**, 181–92.

—— 1974: Space and place: humanistic perspectives. In C. Board *et al.* (eds), *Progress in Geography* 6. London: Edward Arnold, 211–52.

—— 1974: *Topophilia: A study of environmental perception, attitudes and values*. Englewood Cliffs, NJ: Prentice-Hall.

—— 1975a: Images and mental maps. *Annals of the Association of American Geographers* **65**, 205–13.

—— 1975b: Place: an experiential perspective. *The Geographical Review* **65**, 151–65.

—— 1976: Humanistic geography. *Annals of the Association of American Geographers* **66**, 266–76.

—— 1977: *Space and place*. London: Edward Arnold.

—— 1978: Literature and geography: implications for geographical research. In D. Ley and M. S. Samuels (eds) *Humanistic geography: prospects and problems*. Chicago: Maaroufa Press, 194–206.

—— 1979: *Landscapes of fear*. Oxford: Basil Blackwell.

—— 1982: *Segmented worlds and self*. Minneapolis: University of Minnesota Press.

—— 1984: *Dominance and affection*. New Haven: Yale University Press.

—— 1999: *Who am I? An autobiography of emotion, mind and spirit*. Madison: The University of Wisconsin Press.

—— 2002a: *Dear colleague: common and uncommon observations*. Minneapolis: University of Minnesota Press.

—— 2002b: A life of learning. In P. Gould and F. R. Pitts (eds), *Geographical voices: fourteen autobiographical essays*. Syracuse: Syracuse University Press, 323–40.

TULLOCK, G. 1976: *The vote motive*. London: Institute of Economic Affairs.

TURNER, B. L. 1989: The specialist-synthesis approach to the revival of geography: the case of cultural ecology. *Annals of the Association of American Geographers* **79**, 88–100.

—— 2002: Contested identities: human-environment geography and disciplinary implications in a restructuring academy. *Annals of the Association of American Geographers* **92**, 52–74.

TURNER, B. L., CLARK, W. C., KATES. R. W., RICHARDS, J. F., MATTHEWS, J. T. and MEYER, W. B. (eds) 1990: *The earth as transformed by human action: global and regional changes in the biosphere over the past 300 years*. Cambridge: Cambridge University Press.

TURNER, B. L. and MEYER, W. B. 1985: The use of citation indices in comparing geography programs: an exploratory study. *The Professional Geographer* **37**, 271–8.

TURNER, B. L. and VARLYGUIN, D. 1995: Foreign-area expertise in U.S. geography: an assessment of capacity based on foreign-area dissertations, 1977–1991. *The Professional Geographer* **47**, 308–14.

TURNER, R. K. 1993: Sustainability: principles and practice. In R. K. Turner (ed.) *Sustainable environmental economics and management: principles and practice*. London: Belhaven Press, 3–36.

ULLMAN, E. L. 1941: A theory of location for cities. *American Journal of Sociology* **46**, 853–64.

—— 1953: Human geography and area research. *Annals of the Association of American Geographers* **43**, 54–66.

—— 1956: The role of transportation and the bases for interaction. In W. L. Thomas (ed.) *Man's role in changing the face of the earth*. Chicago: University of Chicago Press, 862–80.

UNSTEAD, J. F. 1933: A system of regional geography. *Geography* **18**, 175–87.

UNWIN, A. 1996: Exploratory spatial analysis and local statistics. *Computing and Statistics* **11**, 387–400.

UNWIN, A. and UNWIN, D. J. 1998: Exploratory spatial data analysis with local statistics. *The Statistician* **47**, 415–21.

UNWIN, D. J. 1981: *Introductory spatial analysis*. London: Methuen.

—— 1994: Cartography, VisC and GIS. *Progress in Human Geography* **18**, 516–22.

—— 1996: GIS, spatial analysis and spatial statistics. *Progress in Human Geography* **20**, 540–51.

UNWIN, D. J. and DAWSON, J. A. 1985: *Computer programming for geographers*. London: Longman.

UNWIN, D. J. and HEPPLE, L. W. 1974: The statistical analysis of spatial series. *The Statistician* **23**, 211–28.

UNWIN, T. 1992: *The place of geography*. Harlow: Longman.

UPTON, G. J. G. and FINGLETON, B. 1985: *Spatial data analysis by example*. vol. 1: *Point pattern and quantitative data*. Chichester: John Wiley.

—— 1989: *Spatial data analysis by example: 2 categorical and directional data*. Chichester: John Wiley.

URLICH, D. U. 1972: Migrations of the North Island Maoris 1800–1840: a systems view of migration. *New Zealand Geographer* **28**, 23–35.

URLICH CLOHER, D. 1975: A perspective on Australian urbanization. In J. M. Powell and M. Williams (eds) *Australian space, Australian time: geographical perspectives*. Melbourne: Oxford University Press, 104–59.

URRY, J. 1985: Space, time and the study of the social. In H. Newby *et al.* (eds) *Restructuring capital*. London: Macmillan, 21–40.

—— 1986: Locality research: the case of Lancaster. *Regional Studies* **20**, 233–42.

—— 1987: Society, space and locality. *Environment and Planning D: Society and Space* **5**, 435–44.

VAIOU, D. 2003: Guest editorial. Radical debate between 'local' and 'international': a view from the periphery. *Environment and Planning D: Society and Space* **21**, 133–7.

VALE, T. R. 2002: From Clements and Davis to Gould and Botkin: ideals of progress in physical geography. In R. D. Sack (ed.) *Progress: geographical essays*. Baltimore: Johns Hopkins University Press, 1–21.

VALENTINE, G. 1993: Negotiating and maintaining multiple sexual identities. *Transactions, Institute of British Geographers* **NS18**, 237–43.

—— 1993: (Hetero)sexing space: lesbian perceptions and experiences of everyday spaces. *Environment and Planning D: Society and Space* **11**, 395–413.

—— 1998: 'Sticks and stones may break my bones': a personal geography of harassment. *Antipode* **30**, 305–32.

—— 2003: Geography and ethics: in pursuit of social justice. *Progress in Human Geography* **27**, 375–80.

VAN DEN DAELE, W. and WEINGART, P. 1976: Resistance and receptivity of science to external direction: the emergence of new disciplines under the impact of science policy. In G. Lemaine *et al.* (eds) *Perspectives on the emergence of scientific disciplines*. The Hague: Mouton, 247–75.

VAN DER LAAN, L. and PIERSMA, A. 1982: The image of man: paradigmatic cornerstone in human geography. *Annals of the Association of American Geographers* **73**, 411–26.

VAN DER WUSTEN, H. and O'LOUGHLIN, J. 1986: Claiming new territory for a stable peace: how geography can contribute. *The Professional Geographer* **38**, 18–27.

VAN PAASSEN, C. 1981: The philosophy of geography: from Vidal to Hagerstrand. In A. Pred and G. Tornquist (eds) *Space and time in geography*. Lund: C. W. K. Gleerup, 17–29.

VANCE, J. E. 1970: *The merchant's world*. Englewood Cliffs, NJ: Prentice-Hall.

—— 1978: Geography and the study of cities. *Human Geography: Coming of Age. American Behavioral Scientist* **22**, 131–49.

VELKONJA, J. 1994: Geography at the University of Washington. *Yearbook of the Association of Pacific Coast Geographers*, 56.

VIDAL DE LA BLACHE, P. 1903: *Tableau de la Géographie de la France*. Paris: Hachette.

VON BERTALANFFY, L. 1950: An outline of general systems theory. *British Journal of the Philosophy of Science* **1**, 134–65.

WAGNER, P. L. 1976: Reflections on a radical geography. *Antipode* **8(3)**, 83–5.

WAKEFIELD, J., QUINN, M. and RAAB, G. (eds) 2001: Disease clusters and ecological studies. Special issue of *Journal of the Royal Statistical Society, Series A* **164**, 1–207.

WALBY, S. 1986: *Patriarchy at work*. Cambridge: Polity Press.

WALFORD, R. 2001: *Geography in British schools 1850–2000: making a world of difference*. London: Woburn Press.

WALKER, R. A. 1981a: A theory of suburbanization. In M. J. Dear and A. J. Scott (eds), *Urbanization and urban planning in capitalist societies*. London: Methuen, 383–430.

—— 1981b: Left-wing libertarianism, an academic disorder: a reply to David Sibley. *The Professional Geographer* **33**, 5–9.

—— 1989a: What's left to do? *Antipode* **21**, 133–65.

—— 1989b: Geography from the left. In G. L. Gaile and C. J. Willmott (eds) *Geography in America*. Columbus, OH: Merrill Publishing Company, 619–51.

WALKER, R. A. and STORPER, M. 1981: Capital and industrial location. *Progress in Human Geography* **5**, 473–509.

WALLACE, I. 1989: *The global economic system*. London: Unwin Hyman.

WALMSLEY, D. J. 1972: *Systems theory: a framework for human geographical enquiry*. Research School of Pacific Studies. Department of Human Geography Publication HG/7, Canberra: Australian National University.

—— 1974: Positivism and phenomenology in human geography. *The Canadian Geographer* **18**, 95–107.

WALMSLEY, D. J. and SORENSEN, A. D. 1980: What marx for the radicals? An antipodean viewpoint. *Area* **12**, 137–41.

WARD, D. 1971: *Cities and immigrants: a geography of change in nineteenth-century America*. New York: Oxford University Press.

WARF, B. 1986: Ideology, everyday life and emancipatory phenomenology. *Antipode* **18**, 268–83.

—— 1988: The resurrection of local uniqueness. In R. G. Golledge, H. Couclelis and P. R. Gould (eds) *A ground for common search*: Santa Barbara: The Santa Barbara Geographical Press, 51–62.

—— 1993: Postmodernism and the localities debate: ontological questions and epistemological implications. *Tijdschrift voor Economische en Sociale Geografie* **84**, 162–8.

—— 1995: Separated at birth? Regional science and social theory. *International Regional Science Review* **17**, 185–94.

WARD, K. G. 2001: The re-interpretation of urban politics: three authors, four papers and the 'shibboleth of regulation theory'. *Transactions, Institute of British Geographers* **NS26**, 127–33.

WARD, M. D. and GLEDITSCH, K. S. 2002: Location, location, location: an MCMC approach to modelling the spatial context of war and peace. *Political Analysis* **10**, 244–60.

WARDENGA, U. 1999: Constructing regional knowledge in German geography: the Central Commission on the Regional Geography of Germany, 1882–1941. In A. Buttimer, S. D. Brunn and U. Wardenga (eds) *Text and image: social construction of regional knowledges*. Leipzig: Institut für Länderkunde Leipzig, Beiträge zur regionalen Geographie **49**, 77–84.

WARNTZ, W. 1959a: *Toward a geography of price*. Philadelphia: University of Pennsylvania Press.

—— 1959b: Geography at mid-twentieth century. *World Politics* **11**, 442–54.

—— 1959c: Progress in economic geography. In P. E. James (ed.) *New viewpoints in geography.* Washington: National Council for the Social Studies, 54–75.

—— 1968: Letter to the editor. *The Professional Geographer* **20**, 357.

—— 1984: Trajectories and coordinates. In M. Billinge, D. Gregory, and R. Martin (eds) *Recollections of a revolution.* London: Macmillan, 134–52.

WATERMAN, S. 1985: Not just the milk and honey – now a way of life: Israeli human geography since the six-day war. *Progress in Human Geography* **9**, 194–234.

WATERMAN, S. and KLIOT, N. 1990: The political impact on writing the geography of Palestine-Israel. *Progress in Human Geography* **14**, 237–60.

WATERSTONE, M. 2002: A radical journal of geography or a journal of radical geography? *Antipode* **34**, 662–6.

WATKINS, J. W. N. 1970: Against normal science. In I. Lakatos and A. Musgrave (eds) *Criticism and the growth of knowledge.* London: Cambridge University Press, 25–38.

WATSON, J. D. 1968: *The double helix: a personal account of the discovery of the structure of DNA.* London: Weidenfeld & Nicolson.

WATSON, J. W. 1953: The sociological aspects of geography. In G. Taylor (ed.) *Geography in the twentieth century.* London: Methuen, 453–99.

—— 1955: Geography: a discipline in distance. *Scottish Geographical Magazine* **71**, 1–13.

—— 1983: The soul of geography. *Transactions, Institute of British Geographers* **NS8**, 385–99.

WATSON, M. K. 1978: The scale problem in human geography. *Geografiska Annaler* **60B**, 36–47.

WATTS, M. 1988: Deconstructing determinism. *Antipode* **20**, 142–68.

—— 1989: The agrarian crisis in Africa: debating the crisis. *Progress in Human Geography* **13**, 1–41.

—— 2000: *Struggles over geography: violence, freedom and development at the millennium.* Heidelberg: Department of Geography, University of Heidelberg

WATTS, S. J. and WATTS, S. J. 1978: The idealist alternative in geography and history. *The Professional Geographer* **30**, 123–7.

WEAVER, J. C. 1943: Climatic relations of American barley production. *Geographical Review* **33**, 569–88.

—— 1954: Crop-combination regions in the Middle West. *Geographical Review* **44**, 175–200.

WEBBER, M. J. 1972: *Impact of uncertainty on location.* Canberra: Australian National University Press.

—— 1977: Pedagogy again: what is entropy? *Annals of the Association of American Geographers* **67**, 254–66.

WEBBER, M. M. 1964: The urban place and the non-place urban realm. In M. M. Webber *et al. Explorations into urban structure.* Philadelphia: University of Pennsylvania Press, 79–153.

WEIGHTMAN, B. 1981: Gay bars as private places. *Landscape* **24**, 9–17.

WESCOAT, J. L. 1992: Common themes in the work of Gilbert White and John Dewey: a pragmatic appraisal. *Annals of the Association of American Geographers* **82**, 587–607.

WESTERN, J. S. 1978: Knowing one's place: 'the Coloured people' and the Group Areas Act in Cape Town. In D. Ley and M. S. Samuels (eds) *Humanistic geography: problems and prospects.* Chicago: Maaroufa Press, 297–318.

WHATMORE, S. 1997: Dissecting the autonomous self: hybrid cartographies for a relational ethics. *Environment and Planning D: Society and Space* **15**, 37–54.

—— 1999: Hybrid geographies: rethinking the human in human geography. In D. Massey, J. Allen and P. Sarre (eds) *Human geography today.* Cambridge: Polity Press, 281–307.

—— 2002: *Hybrid geographies: natures, cultures, spaces.* London: Sage.

WHEELER, J. O. 1998: Mappophobia in geography? 1980–1996. *Urban Geography* **19**, 1–5.

—— 2002a: Assessing the role of spatial analysis in urban geography in the 1960s. *Urban Geography* **22**, 549–58.

—— 2002b: From urban economic to social/cultural geography, 1980–2001. *Urban Geography* **22**, 97–102.

WHEELER, P. B. 1982: Revolutions, research programmes and human geography. *Area* **14**, 1–6.

WHITE, G. F. 1945: *Human adjustment to floods.* Chicago: University of Chicago, Department of Geography, Research Paper 29.

—— 1972: Geography and public policy. *The Professional Geographer* **24**, 101–4.

—— 1973: Natural hazards research. In R. J. Chorley (ed.) *Directions in geography.* London: Methuen, 193–216.

—— 1985: Geographers in a perilously changing world. *Annals of the Association of American Geographers* **75**, 10–16.

—— 2002: Autobiographical essay. In P. Gould and F. R. Pitts, (eds), *Geographical voices: fourteen autobiographical essays.* Syracuse: Syracuse University Press, 341–64.

WHITE, P. E. 1985: On the use of creative literature in migration study. *Area* **17**, 277–83.

—— 1995: Geography, literature and migration. In R. King, J. Connell, and P. White (eds) *Writing across worlds: literature and migration.* London: Routledge, 1–19.

WHITEHAND, J. W. R. 1970: Innovation diffusion in an academic discipline: the case of the 'new' geography. *Area* **2(3)**, 19–30.

—— 1984: The impact of geographical journals: a look at ISI data. *Area* **16**, 185–7.

—— 1985: Contributors to the recent development and influence of human geography: what citation analysis suggests. *Transactions, Institute of British Geographers* **NS10**, 222–3.

WHITEHAND, J. W. R. and EDMONDSON, P. M. 1977: Europe and America: the reorientation in geographical communication in the post-war period. *The Professional Geographer* **29**, 278–82.

WHITEHAND, J. W. R. and PATTEN, J. H. C. (eds) 1977: Change in the town. *Transactions, Institute of British Geographers* **NS2(3)**.

WHITTLESEY, D. 1954: The regional concept and the regional method. In P. E. James and C. F. Jones (eds) *American geography: inventory and prospect.* Syracuse: Syracuse University Press, 19–68.

WILBANKS, T. 1995: Employment trends in geography: introduction. *The Professional Geographer* **47**, 315–17.

WILBANKS, T. J. and LIBBEE, M. 1979: Avoiding the demise of geography in the United States. *The Professional Geographer* **31**, 1–7.

WILLIAMS, M. 1983: The apple of my eye: Carl Sauer and historical geography. *Journal of Historical Geography* **9**, 1–28.

—— 1989: *Americans and their forests: a historical geography.* Cambridge: Cambridge University Press.

—— 2003: *Deforesting the earth: from prehistory to global crisis.* Chicago: University of Chicago Press.

WILLIAMS, P. R. 1978: Urban managerialism: a concept of relevance? *Area* **10**, 236–40.

—— 1982: Restructuring urban managerialism: towards a political economy of urban allocation. *Environment and Planning A* **14**, 95–106.

WILLIAMS, R. 1976: *Keywords.* London: Fontana.

WILLIAMS, W. M. and HERBERT, D. T. 1962: The social geography of Newcastle-under-Lyme. *North Staffordshire Journal of Field Studies* **2**, 108–26.

WILLIAMSON, P., BIRKIN, M. and REES, P. H. 1998: The estimation of population microdata by using data from small area statistics and samples of anonymised records. *Environment and Planning A* **30**, 785–816.

WILLS, J. 2000: Political economy II: the politics and geography of capitalism. *Progress in Human Geography* **24**, 641–52.

—— 2002: Political economy III: neoliberal chickens, Seattle and geography. *Progress in Human Geography* **26**, 90–100.

WILLS, J. and PECK, J. 2002: Progress or retreat? Antipode and the radical geographical project. *Antipode* **34**, 667–71.

WILSON, A. G. 1967: A statistical theory of spatial distribution models. *Transportation Research* **1**, 253–69.

—— 1970: *Entropy in urban and regional modelling.* London: Pion.

—— 1974: *Urban and regional models in geography and planning.* London: John Wiley.

—— 1976a: Catastrophe theory and urban modelling: an application to modal choice. *Environment and Planning A* **8**, 351–46.

—— 1976b: Retailers' profits and consumers' welfare in a spatial interaction shopping model. In I. Masser (ed.) *Theory and practice in regional science.* London: Pion, 42–57.

—— 1978: Mathematical education for geographers. Department of Geography, University of Leeds, Discussion Paper 211, Leeds

—— 1981a: *Catastrophe theory and bifurcation: applications to urban and regional systems.* London: Croom Helm.

—— 1981b: *Geography and the environment: systems analytical methods.* Chichester: John Wiley.

—— 1984a: Making urban models more realistic: some strategies for future research. *Environment and Planning A* **16**, 1419–32.

—— 1984b: One man's quantitative geography: frameworks, evaluations, uses and prospects. In M. Billinge, D. Gregory and R. L Martin (eds) *Recollections of a revolution: geography as spatial science.* London: Macmillan, 200–26.

—— 1989a: Classics, modelling and critical theory: human geography as structured pluralism. In B. Macmillan (ed.) *Remodelling geography.* Oxford: Basil Blackwell, 61–9.

—— 1989b: Mathematical models and geographic theory. In D. Gregory and R. Walford (eds) *Horizons in human geography.* London: Macmillan, 29–47.

—— 2000: *Complex spatial systems: the modelling foundations of urban and regional analysis.* Chichester: John Wiley.

WILSON, A. G. and BENNETT, R. J. 1985: *Mathematical methods in human geography and planning.* Chichester: John Wiley.

WILSON , A. G. and KIRKBY, M. J. 1975: *Mathematics for Geographers and Planners.* Oxford: Oxford University Press.

WILSON, A. G., REES, P. H. and LEIGH, C. 1977: *Models of cities and regions.* London: John Wiley.

WILSON, E. O. 1998: Consilience among the great branches of learning. *Daedalus* **127**, 131–50.

WISE, M. J. 1968: Sir Dudley Stamp: his life and times. *Land use and resources: studies in applied geography.* London: Institute of British Geographers, Special Publication 1, 261–70.

—— 1975: A university teacher of geography. *Transactions, Institute of British Geographers* **66**, 1–16.

—— 1977: On progress and geography. *Progress in Human Geography* **1**, 1–11.

—— 1986: The Scott Keltie report 1885 and the teaching of geography in Great Britain. *The Geographical Journal* **152**, 367–82.

WISNER, B. 1970: Introduction: on radical methodology. *Antipode* **2**, 1–3.

WITHERS, C. W. J. 2002a: A partial biography: the formalization and institutionalization of geography in Britain since 1887. In G. S. Dunbar (ed.), *From traveller to scientist: the professionalization and institutionalization of geography in Europe and North America since 1870.* Amsterdam: Kluwer, 79–119.

—— 2002b: Constructing 'the geographical archive'. *Area* **34**, 303–11.

WITHERS, C. W. J. and MAYHEW, R. J. 2002: Rethinking 'disciplinary' history: geography in British universities, c.1580–1887. *Transactions of the Institute of British Geographers* **NS27**, 11–29.

WOLCH, J. and DEAR, M. J. (eds) 1989: *The power of geography: how territory shapes social life.* Boston: Unwin Hyman.

WOLDENBERG, M. J. and BERRY, B. J. L. 1967: Rivers and central places: analogous systems? *Journal of Regional Science* **7**, 129–40.

WOLF, A. 2002: *Does education matter? Myths about education and economic growth.* London: Penguin.

WOLF, L. C. 1976: Comments on the Harries-Peet controversy. *The Professional Geographer* **28**, 196–8.

WOLPERT, J. 1964: The decision process in spatial context. *Annals of the Association of American Geographers* **54**, 337–58.

—— 1965: Behavioral aspects of the decision to migrate. *Papers and Proceedings Regional Science Association* **15**, 159–72.

—— 1967: Distance and directional bias in inter-urban migratory streams. *Annals of the Association of American Geographers* **57**, 605–16.

—— 1970: Departures from the usual environment in locational analysis. *Annals of the Association of American Geographers* **60**, 220–9.

WOLPERT, J., DEAR, M. J. and CRAWFORD, R. 1975: Satellite mental health facilities. *Annals of the Association of American Geographers* **65**, 24–35.

WOMEN AND GEOGRAPHY STUDY GROUP, 1984: *Geography and gender: an introduction to feminist geography.* London: Hutchinson.

—— 1997: *Feminist geographers: explorations in diversity and difference.* Harlow: Longman.

WOODS, R. I. 1982: *Theoretical population geography.* London: Longman.

WOODS, R. I. and REES, P. H. (eds) 1986: *Population structures and models: developments in spatial demography.* London: Allen & Unwin.

WOOLDRIDGE, S. W. 1956: *The geographer as scientist.* London: Thomas Nelson.

WOOLDRIDGE, S. W. and EAST, W. G. 1958: *The spirit and purpose of geography.* London: Hutchinson.

WOOLF, R. D. and RESNICK, S. A. 1987: *Economics: marxian versus neoclassical.* Baltimore: Johns Hopkins University Press.

WOOLGAR, S. W. 1976: The identification and definition of scientific collectivities. In G. Lemaine *et al.* (eds) *Perspectives on the emergence of scientific disciplines.* The Hague: Mouton, 233–45.

WRIGHT, J. K. 1925: *The geographical lore of the time of the crusades: a study in the history of medieval science and tradition in western Europe.* New York: American Geographical Society.

—— 1947: *Terrae incognitae:* the place of imagination in geography. *Annals of the Association of American Geographers* **37**, 1–15.

WRIGLEY, E. A. 1965: Changes in the philosophy of geography. In R. J. Chorley and P. Haggett (eds) *Frontiers in geographical teaching.* London: Methuen, 3–24.

WRIGLEY, N. 1973: The use of percentages in geographical research. *Area* **5**, 183–6.

—— 1976: *Introduction to the use of logit models in geography.* CATMOG 10, Norwich: GeoBooks.

—— 1979: Developments in the statistical analysis of categorical data. *Progress in Human Geography* **3**, 315–55.

—— 1983: Quantitative methods: on data and diagnostics. *Progress in Human Geography* **7**, 567–77.

—— 1984: Quantitative methods: diagnostics revisited. *Progress in Human Geography* **8**, 525–35.

—— 1985: *Categorical data analysis for geographers and environmental scientists.* London: Longman.

—— 1995: Revisiting the modifiable areal unit problem and the ecological fallacy. In A. D. Cliff, P. R. Gould, A. G. Hoare and N. J. Thrift (eds) *Diffusing geography: essays for Peter Haggett.* Oxford: Blackwell Publishers, 49–71.

WRIGLEY, N. and BENNETT, R. J. (eds) 1981: *Quantitative geography: a British view.* London: Routledge & Kegan Paul.

WRIGLEY, N. and LONGLEY, P. A. 1984: Discrete choice modelling in urban analysis. In D. T. Herbert and R. J. Johnston (eds) *Geography and the urban environment: progress in research and applications,* vol. 6. Chichester: John Wiley, 45–94.

WRIGLEY, N. and LOWE, M. (eds) 1996: *Retailing, consumption and capital.* Harlow: Longman.

WRIGLEY, N. and MATTHEWS, S. 1986: Citation classics and citation levels in geography. *Area* **18**, 185–94.

YEATES, M. H. 2001: Yesterday as tomorrow's song: the contribution of the 1960s 'Chicago School' to urban geography. *Urban Geography* **22**, 514–29.

YEUNG, H. W.-C. 1997: Critical realism and realist research in human geography: a method or a philosophy in search of a method? *Progress in Human Geography* **21**, 51–74.

—— 2002: Deciphering citations. *Environment and Planning A* **34**: 2093–101.

YOUNG, I. M. 1990: *Justice and the politics of difference*. Princeton: Princeton University Press.

YULE, G. U. and KENDALL, M. G. 1950: *An Introduction to the Theory of Statistics*. London: Griffin.

ZELINSKY, W. 1970: Beyond the exponentials: the role of geography in the great transition. *Economic Geography* **46**, 499–535.

—— 1973a: Women in geography: a brief factual report. *The Professional Geographer* **25**, 151–65.

—— 1973b: *The cultural geography of the United States*. Englewood Cliffs, NJ: Prentice-Hall.

—— 1974: Selfward bound? Personal preference patterns and the changing map of American society. *Economic Geography* **50**, 144–79.

—— 1975: The demigod's dilemma. *Annals of the Association of American Geographers* **65**, 123–43.

—— 1978: Introduction. *Human Geography: Coming of Age. American Behavioral Scientist* **22**, 5–13.

ZELINSKY, W., MONK, J. and HANSON, S. 1982: Women and geography: a review and prospectus. *Progress in Human Geography* **6**, 317–66.

ZIMMERMAN, E. W. 1972: *World resources and industries*. Cambridge, MT: The Twentieth Century Fund.

ZIPF, G. K. 1949: *Human behavior and the principle of least effort*. New York: Hafner.

Subject Index

idealism, 197–201, 204, 205, 206, 397
phenomenology, 201–8, 397
practice of, 209–17
and radical geographies, 257, 258
social structure, 255
texts, 209–12
time-geography, 148, 151, 152
hypothesis development, 85, 87
see also theory development

iconoclasts, scientists as, 14
idealism, 197–201, 204, 205, 206, 397
identity, sexual, 317
identity creation, disciplines, 3, 371
identity politics, 296–7, 359
imaginative literature, 210–11
see also novels
imperialism
foundations of geography, 41, 43
postcolonialism, 292–7
women's role in, 306–7
income allocation, radical geographies, 225–6, 228
inductive (Baconian) route to scientific explanation, 83, 84
inductive statistics, 85–6
industrial development, 25
industries
location
linear programming, 78
locality studies, 233–4
relevance of geography, 334–5
postmodern geographies, 266
inequality, relevance of geography, 336, 339–41, 353, 356
information, behavioural matrix, 153–4
information technology, time-geography, 152
see also computers
information theory, entropy, 129
institutionalization of disciplines, 1–4, 371–2
intellectual revolution, 362
intensive research, 242
interactionism, 209
international relations, 347
intertextuality, 281, 284
interviews, 216
invisible colleges, 8
behavioural geography, 191–2
see also scientific communities
Iowa school, 70–2
irony, as writing device, 284, 285

islands of practice, 408
isometric maps, 73
isophletic maps, 73

journals
citation analysis, 407
English language, 389–90
feminist geographies, 301
research publication in, 30, 35–6, 323, 401
structure of geography, 389–90

knowledge
commodification, 368–9
feminist geographies, 304, 313–14
geographers' networks, 375, 376
geographers' world views, 20–3
geosophy, 190–4
models of progress of science, 16, 17–18
poststructuralism, 281–4
scientific method, 83–7
structuration theory, 244
of world and thus self, 201–2, 203

labour
division of *see* division of labour
production of 'nature', 246
labour market, geographers, 383–4, 386
land use
behavioural geography, 141–48, 153–5
relevance of geography, 334–5
social physics, 121
Land Utilization Survey (UK), 54, 334
landscapes
environmentalism, 341
existentialism, 207
feminist geographies, 313, 318
historical geography, 193–4, 210
humanistic geography, 209–10
Marxist-influenced work on, 246
modern, 272–4
political decision-making, 146
postmodern, 269–70, 272–4, 275
poststructuralism, 282
regional geography, 57, 67
scientific method, 105, 106
as text, 209–10
time-geography, 150
language
feminist geographies, 320
linguistic communities of geographers, 390–1

Author Index

Hagood, M.J. 336
Hague, E. 260
Haigh, M.J. 381, 382
Haines-Young, R.H. 87, 180, 365
Haining, R.P. 151, 165, 167, 168
Halford, S. 233
Hall, P.G. 102, 264, 330, 334, 335
Halvorson, P. 76, 91, 99, 252
Hamilton, F.E.J. 156
Hamnett, C. 297, 357, 397–8
Hanham, R.Q. 173
Hanson, S. 80, 99, 302, 310, 312, 318, 320, 378, 393
Hare, F.K. 329, 330
Harley, J.B. 193, 286–8
Harries, K.D. 250–1, 337
Harris, C.D. 63, 70, 75, 77, 80, 97, 98
Harris, R.C. 68, 194–6
Harrison, P. 292
Harrison, R.T. 255, 257, 396
Hart, J.F. 33, 36, 108–9, 238, 258
Hartshorne, R. 50–2, 64, 65–9, 79, 80, 97, 364
Harvey, D. 7, 83–5, 86, 87, 102, 104, 111, 118, 122–3, 124, 125, 154, 155, 167, 195, 219, 221, 223–4, 225–7, 228, 229, 231, 239, 243, 244, 246, 247–49, 250, 251–3, 255, 262, 274–9, 282, 323, 330–1, 332–3, 340, 352, 353, 359, 362, 365, 377, 395, 396–397, 402
Harvey, M.E. 361, 363
Hashmi, S.H. 298, 340
Hassard, J. 290
Hauer, J. 237
Haugeland, J. 7
Hay, A.M. 77, 86, 87, 121, 132, 151, 165, 168, 198, 257, 263, 396
Hayford, A.M. 302
Haynes, R.M. 118
Hayter, R. 156
Heffernan, M. 42, 43, 49, 289, 293, 372
Hepple, L.W. 164
Herbert, D.T. 100, 363
Herbert, S. 320
Herbertson, A.J. 53, 61
Herod, A. 233, 319
Hewitt, K. 143, 342
Higgs, G. (Bracken et al. 1990) 177
Hinchliffe, S. 292
Hodder, I. 104

Hodgart, R.L. 339
Hoekveld, G.A. 238
Hoggart, K. 271
Holloway, L. 308
Holloway, S.L. 300, 312, 315, 319
Holly, B.P. 361, 363
Holm, E. 130
Holmes, J.H. 344, 382
Holt-Jensen, A. 363, 365
Hönsch, I. 41
Hook, J.C. 72
    (McCarty et al. 1956) 72, 82
Hooson, D.J.M. 57
Horton, F.E. 342
Horton, J. 319
House, J.W. 326, 334
Hoyningen-Huene (1993) 18
Hubbard, D. 308
Hubbard, P. 265, 267, 274, 283–4, 298, 308, 314, 315, 317, 365, 369–70
Huckle, J. 262
Hudson, G.D. 76
Hudson, R. 147, 234, 257, 335, 382
Huggett, R.J. 127–8, 134, 143
Hughes, T.P. 122
Hugill, P.J. 190, 212–14
Hull, R. 35
Humboldt, A. von 48, 190, 212–14
Huntington, E. 47
Hyndman, J. 315, 318

Imrie, R.F. 162, 312
Isard, W. 91, 92, 123, 134, 155
Isserman, A.M. 92

Jackson, P. 120, 205, 209, 213, 214, 215, 268, 274, 292–3, 295, 296–7, 302, 309, 314, 315, 318, 320
    (Hall et al. 1987) 264
Jacobs, J. 210, 295, 304
James, P.E. 4, 41, 43, 48, 50, 51, 52, 58–9, 63, 70, 87, 94, 183, 364, 399
Janelle, D.G. 121, 152, 384
Jenkins, A. 35, 347
    (Davey et al. 1995) 407
Jessop, B. 233
Joh, C.-H. (Timmermans et al. 2001) 157, 161
Johnson, J.H. 105
Johnson, L. 302, 305, 313
Johnston, L.C. 304, 309

Lichtenberger, E. 15, 98, 380
Lipietz, A. 233
Little, J. 310
Livingstone, D.N. 4, 6, 32, 46, 50, 82, 191, 212, 213, 255, 257, 307, 364, 365, 370, 376, 396
Livingstone, I. 385
Longhurst, R. 312–13
Longley, P.A. 133, 157, 174, 175, 176, 177, 178, 183, 353
López-Nieva (2001) xi
López-Nieva, P. 389
Lorimer, H. xi, 405
Lösch, A. 78
Low, M. 297, 407
Lowe, M. 312, 360
Lowenthal, D. 58, 190–1, 194, 207, 210, 341, 3452
Luke, T.W. 31, 35, 36, 400
Lukermann, F. 50, 57, 89–90, 95, 116, 138, 194
Lutz, C.A. 3
Lynch, K. 147
Lysaght, K. 317

Mabogunje, A.K. 199
MacAllister, I. 158
MacEachren, A. 178
MacGill, S.M. 166
MacKian, S. 358–9
Mackinder, H.J. 43, 44
MacKinnon, R.D. 177
MacLeod, G. 233, 240
Macmillan, B. 159, 175, 184, 185, 354
Maddrell, A. 300
Madge, C. 300, 319
Magee, B. 14
Maguire, D.J. 177
   (Longley et al.) 174, 176, 177, 178, 183
Mair, A. 18, 235, 361, 363, 365, 367, 401
Manion, T. 253
Mann, M. 138
Manners, G. 102
Manners, I.R. 342
Marble, D.F. 78, 92, 180
Marcus, M.G. 55, 92–3, 342, 398, 399
Mark, D.M. 135, 177
   (Chrisman et al. 1989) 176
Markusen, M. 298
Marsh, G.P. 58
Marshall, J.U. 87, 263
Martin, A.F. 88

Martin, D. 171, 334
   (Bracken et al. 1990) 177
   (Mitchell et al. 1998) 170
Martin, G.J. 4, 44, 46, 48, 64, 68, 71, 183, 363, 392
Martin, R.L. 92, 150, 168, 206, 239, 285–6, 298, 356–7, 358, 365, 367, 374
Massam, B.H. 338
Massey, D. 230, 233–4, 238, 248, 262, 269, 277, 309, 355–6, 358
   (Hall et al. 1987) 264
Masterman, M. 11, 12, 16
Mather, E.C. 50
Mather, P.M. 165
Matless, D. 291
   (Leyshon et al. 1995) 282
Matthews, H. 385
Matthews, S. 407
Matthewson, K. 106
Mattingly, D. 320
May, J.A. 48, 64, 66, 137, 280, 359
Mayer, H.M. 52, 70, 80, 81
Mayer, T. 308
Mayhew, R.J. 41
McCarty, H.H. 70–2, 73, 82
McConnell, H. 86
   (LaValle et al. 1967) 86, 92
McDaniel, R. 123
McDowell, L. 234, 297, 302, 302–3, 304, 309, 310–11, 313–14, 316, 318, 319, 403
   (Bowlby et al. 1989) 305, 309
McEwan, C. 296, 306–7
McGlade, M.S. 384
McGuiness, M. 295
McHaffie, P., (Mark et al. 1996) 177
McKinney, W.M. 119
Mead, W.R. 108
Meadows, D.H. 342
Meinig, D.W. 57, 105, 108, 211, 239
Mercer, D.C. 14, 199, 203–4, 256–7
Merrifield, A. 222, 337
Mesev, V. 175
Meyer, D.R. 86
Meyer, J.T. 148
Middleton, N. 344
Mikesell, M.W. 57, 106, 108, 297, 342–4, 364, 376, 377, 382, 387, 393
Miller, D. 298, 340
Miller, E.W. 4, 46, 334
Mills, C.W. 195
Minca, C. xi, xii, 265, 280, 389–90